AVALON TRAVEL

MOON HANDBOOKS

TENNESSEE

FOURTH EDITION

JEFF BRADLEY

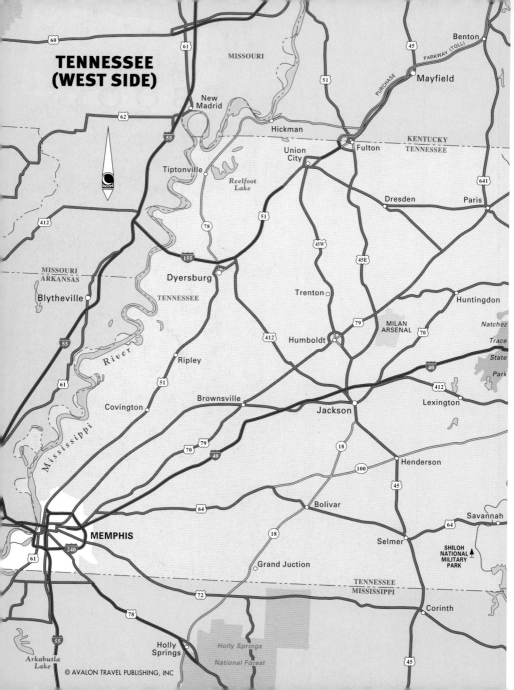

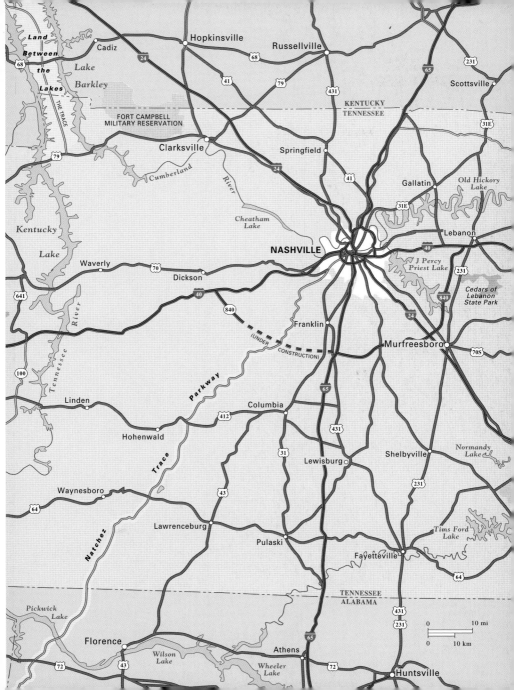

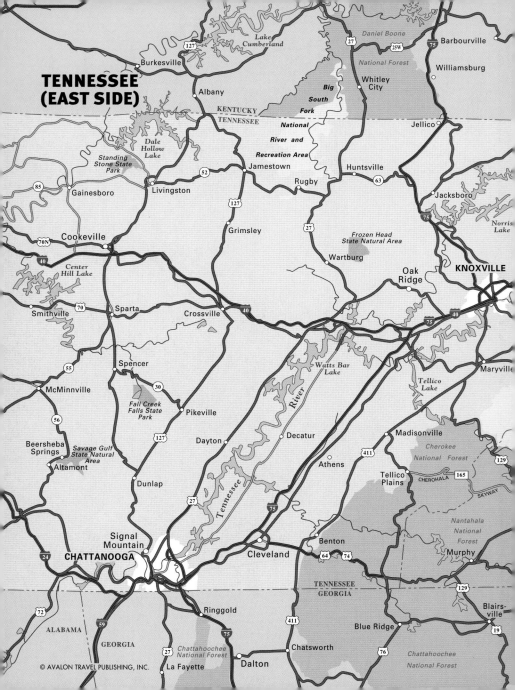

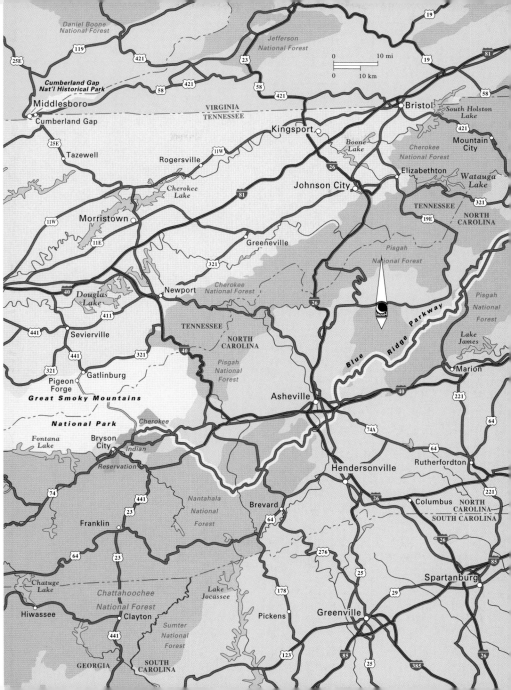

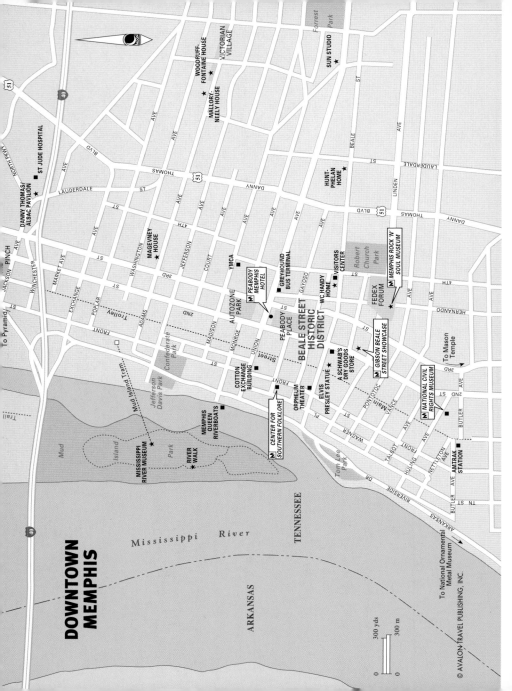

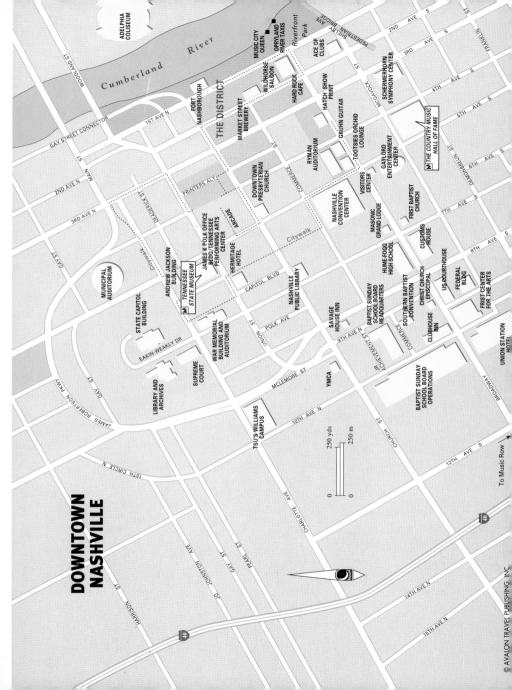

DOWNTOWN NASHVILLE

ADELPHIA COLISEUM

Cumberland River

FORT NASHBOROUGH

THE DISTRICT

MUSIC CITY QUEEN
OPRYLAND RIVER TAXIS
WILDHORSE SALOON
HARD ROCK CAFE
ACE OF CLUBS
HATCH SHOW PRINT
GRUHN GUITAR
TOOTSIES ORCHID LOUNGE
RYMAN AUDITORIUM
GAYLORD ENTERTAINMENT CENTER
VISITORS CENTER
SCHERMERHORN SYMPHONY CENTER
THE COUNTRY MUSIC HALL OF FAME

MARKET STREET BREWERY
DOWNTOWN PRESBYTERIAN CHURCH
NASHVILLE CONVENTION CENTER
MASONIC GRAND LODGE
FIRST BAPTIST CHURCH
CUSTOMS HOUSE
HUME-FOGG HIGH SCHOOL
CHRIST CHURCH EPISCOPAL
US COURTHOUSE
FEDERAL BLDG
FRIST CENTER FOR THE ARTS

PRINTERS ALY
ARCADE
HERMITAGE HOTEL
Citywalk
JAMES K POLK OFFICE BLDG/TENNESSEE PERFORMING ARTS CENTER
TENNESSEE STATE MUSEUM
ANDREW JACKSON BUILDING

MUNICIPAL AUDITORIUM
STATE CAPITOL BUILDING
WAR MEMORIAL BUILDING AND AUDITORIUM
SUPREME COURT
LIBRARY AND ARCHIVES
EAKIN-WEAKLY DR

NASHVILLE PUBLIC LIBRARY
SAVAGE HOUSE INN
BAPTIST SUNDAY SCHOOL BOARD HEADQUARTERS
SOUTHERN BAPTIST CONVENTION
CLUBHOUSE INN
UNION STATION HOTEL

YMCA
BAPTIST SUNDAY SCHOOL BOARD OPERATIONS

TSU'S WILLIAMS CAMPUS

250 yds
250 m
0
0

To Music Row

© AVALON TRAVEL PUBLISHING, INC.

CONTENTS

Discover Tennessee

Explore Tennessee

Pyramid and the Pinch · Victorian Village Historic District · Mud Island ·
Cotton Row Historic District · Peabody Place Retail and Entertainment Center ·
Beale Street Historical District · South Main Street District · Overton Square ·
Cooper-Young Entertainment District

Collierville · Rossville · Moscow · LaGrange · Grand Junction · Big Hill Pond
State Natural Area · Counce · Pickwick Landing State Resort Park · Shiloh
National Military Park · Adamsville · Selmer · Saltillo

Great Smoky Mountains National Park

The First Frontier

Know Tennessee

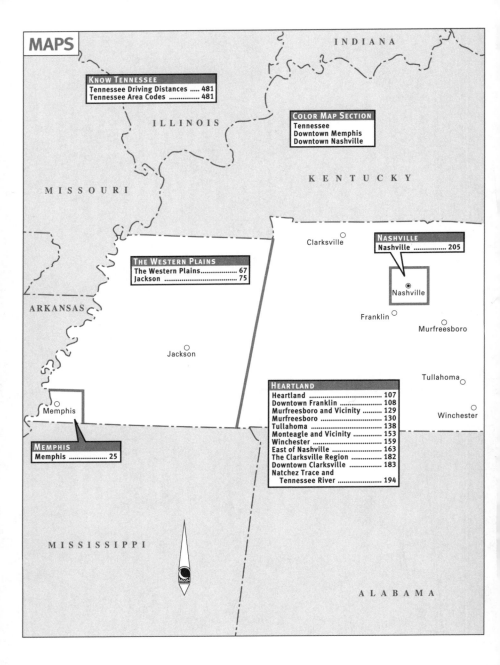

MAPS

INDIANA

ILLINOIS

COLOR MAP SECTION
Tennessee
Downtown Memphis
Downtown Nashville

KENTUCKY

MISSOURI

Clarksville

Nashville

ARKANSAS

Franklin

Murfreesboro

Jackson

Tullahoma

Winchester

Memphis

MISSISSIPPI

ALABAMA

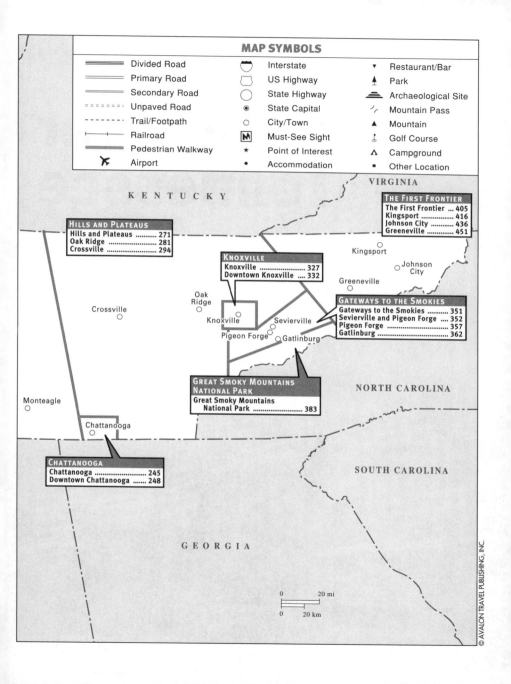

MAP SYMBOLS

Divided Road		Interstate		Restaurant/Bar	
Primary Road		US Highway		Park	
Secondary Road		State Highway		Archaeological Site	
Unpaved Road		State Capital		Mountain Pass	
Trail/Footpath		City/Town		Mountain	
Railroad		Must-See Sight		Golf Course	
Pedestrian Walkway		Point of Interest		Campground	
Airport		Accommodation		Other Location	

VIRGINIA

KENTUCKY

Kingsport

Johnson City

Greeneville

Oak Ridge

Crossville

Knoxville

Sevierville

Pigeon Forge

Gatlinburg

NORTH CAROLINA

Monteagle

Chattanooga

SOUTH CAROLINA

GEORGIA

0   20 mi

0   20 km

Discover
Tennessee

For a period of time in the 1980s, the Expository Writing Department at Harvard University contained an disproportionately large number of Tennesseans. At dinner parties and various other gatherings, New Englanders became accustomed, at least for a few years, to hearing tales of snakes, weird relatives, and blind Baptist disc jockeys blasting forth four-part gospel harmony from Alaska to Venezuela. A Massachusetts-born faculty member, perhaps in exasperation, asked one of the Tennesseans, "How come all of you guys are so good at telling stories?"

The reply, which was an utter fabrication, came quickly. "Oh, when we're in the eighth grade, everyone in Tennessee has to take storytelling—that and health class."

The questioner went away satisfied with the answer he received.

That someone from Tennessee would willingly tell such a whopper, and that someone from Massachusetts—an educated soul with a Ph.D.—would readily believe it, says a lot about the place that Tennessee holds in the national consciousness.

Why do people come to Tennessee? The first reason is the land. Stretching from the peaks of the Appalachians to the Mississippi River, Tennessee is an extraordinarily beautiful state. In some places in the mountains, people can see the same view that Native Americans beheld more than 250 years ago. The Great Smoky Mountains comprise the largest wilderness area in the eastern United States. The eroded terrain of the Cumberland Plateau reveals waterfalls and canyons to appreciate and explore. The farmland of Middle Tennessee, and the stately plantation homes and barns built on it, show the beauty of the agricultural life. The Mississippi River, which forms Tennessee's western border, recalls the days of Mark Twain.

The events that took place on that land also attract visitors. Here, British colonists, cut off from the rest of America by the wall of mountains, struggled to form their own government. More Civil War battles were fought in Tennessee than in any other state except Virginia. Important episodes of the Reconstruction and, later, the Civil Rights Movement, also occurred here.

The state's unique history influenced one of its greatest cultural contributions: music. Early British settlers brought with them ballads from the Old Country. Slaves introduced the banjo and an interpretation of music that no one in America had heard before. In the days before phonographs and radio, Tennesseans made their own music, and when new media came about, were ready to share that talent with the world. Due to its massive range of styles—from old-time music, blues, and gospel to country and rock—Tennessee is a major destination for music lovers.

The very best reason to come to this state is to meet the people. For the most part, they are friendly, colorful, and happy to share their home with visitors. And yes, they will tell you stories. Stories about themselves, about their relatives, about a 20-year-old who bought a newspaper and 11 years later owned the *New*

York Times. About a pacifist who became the most decorated soldier in World War I. About an only child, born into poverty, who became the 20th century's most influential performer.

Tennessee is full of anecdotes, like those about Adolph Ochs, Alvin York, and Elvis Presley. There's even the International Storytelling Center in Jonesborough, where you can listen to masters spin some of the best yarns in the world. Better yet, you can hear the stories Tennesseans tell about themselves, and, for a brief time, become a part of the plot.

In essence, people come to Tennessee to hear stories—and experience them. And they go home with their own stories to tell.

Tennessee is *long*—stretching 500 miles from Bristol to Graceland. To get a sense of how far that is, Bristol is closer to Canada than it is to Memphis. Many lifelong Tennesseans, particularly those living on the eastern or western ends of the state, live and die without setting foot in the parts of the state farthest from them. Tennessee has three regions so distinct that they are referred to as "the three grand divisions of Tennessee": West, Middle, and East. West Tennessee, for the purposes of this book, consists of Memphis and Western Plains. Middle Tennessee encompasses Nashville, Heartland, and the western edge of Hills and Plateaus. East Tennessee consists of Hills and Plateaus, Chattanooga, Knoxville, Gateways, Great Smoky Mountains National Park, and First Frontier.

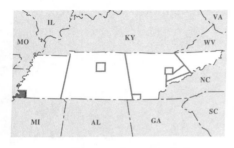

MEMPHIS

Memphis, the biggest city in Tennessee, is famous for rhythm and blues as well as rock 'n' roll. Musically speaking, Elvis Presley's Graceland used to be virtually the only game in town, but the addition of the Memphis Rock 'n' Soul Museum and Soulsville, a celebration of Stax Records, now gives more balance to the music. Beale Street has the bright lights, and lower Main Street contains the most concentrated collection of art galleries in the state. Memphis offers museums both cultural and historical, and, oddly enough, a patch of virgin forest right in the middle of town, in Overton Park. Three days will give an overview of the city, but music fans could easily stay for five or more.

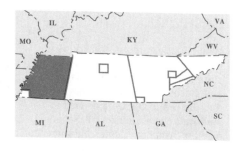

THE WESTERN PLAINS

The flat land between the Mississippi and Tennessee Rivers makes up the Western Plains, a land of cotton fields and kudzu. While few people would take a vacation in this area, there are some good back roads to drive and interesting sights to see. Four or five days will usually be enough to cover this area.

Highlights include Reelfoot Lake in the northwest corner, the Alex Haley Home in Henning, and the Shiloh and Fort Pillow Civil War sites. The most picturesque town is Brownsville, and just down the road in Mason stands the most renowned restaurant in the region, Gus's World Famous Hot and Spicy Chicken.

Western Plains's one-of-a-kind attractions include the National Bird Dog Museum in Grand Junction; Mind Field, an enormous folk art piece in Brownsville; the Buford Pusser Home and Museum in Adamsville; and the slugburgers of Selmer.

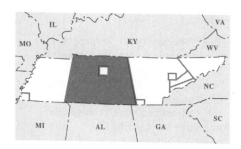

HEARTLAND

Most of Middle Tennessee is covered in the Heartland chapter. Tennessee has some wonderful small towns, and the best and most unspoiled ones are here. The closest to Nashville is Leipers Fork, just west of Franklin. Farther south lie Bell Buckle and Lynchburg, a backdrop for Jack Daniels ads. Route 64 runs from west to east from Savannah to Sewanee—the former on the banks of the Tennessee River and the latter high on the Cumberland Plateau.

As for specific places to see, the Hermitage, home to President Andrew Jackson and his wife Rachel, heads the list. Other historic sites include Murfreesboro's Stones River National Battlefield or Dover's Fort Donelson National Military Park. The Natchez Trace Parkway begins just south of Nashville and leads to the Alabama state line.

South of Nashville along Highways 31 and 43 stands a line of antebellum mansions, many of them still commanding working farms. Rippavilla, just north of Columbia, is a visitor's center and good place to begin a tour of these majestic mansions. Take a week or two to tour the Heartland.

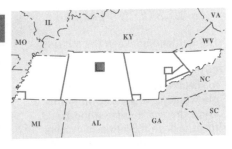

NASHVILLE

While justly famous for country music, Nashville offers visitors the state's widest range of things to do and places to go. Music lovers will find the Grand Ole Opry as well as America's newest music hall, Schermerhorn Symphony Center. Museum collections range from Civil War artifacts at the Tennessee State Museum to a collection of Alfred Stieglitz's photography at Fisk University's Van Vechten Gallery. Nashville has great buildings, most of them within a concentrated area downtown, while farther afield is the only full-size replica of the Parthenon.

If travelers want to see plantation homes, Nashville's got them. A center of African American history as well as Civil War lore, the city offers days of activities for history buffs. When the sun goes down, the club doors open, and visitors can choose from a wide range of musical entertainment.

Three days will give you a good sense of Nashville, but anyone staying a week will find something interesting to do every day.

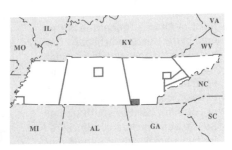

CHATTANOOGA

This is the best city in Tennessee, if not the entire South, for families. Small enough to easily get around in but packed with things to do, Chattanooga contains wonderful retro attractions such as Rock City and Ruby Falls yet has one of the finest aquariums in the world. Here is Tennessee's greatest concentration of Civil War sites, an outstanding railroad center, and easy access to day trips for hiking and white-water fun.

Three days will give a taste of Chattanooga, and families could easily spend eight days here. Chattanooga, lying at a junction of Interstate highways, is a great place to spend a day or two to break up an otherwise long trip. If families plan a trip to the Great Smoky Mountains National Park, Chattanooga is a great place to begin or end the trip. The attractions are much better than those around the national park, your money will go further here, and the crowds are nowhere near as bad as in the Gateways area.

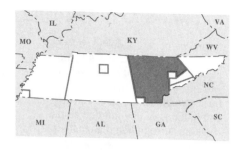

HILLS AND PLATEAUS

For outdoors lovers, this is the place to go. The Cumberland Plateau, into which rivers and streams have cut channels, provides the best hiking, white water, and rock climbing in the state. The highest waterfall in the eastern United States is here, as are wonderful rivers for float trips with families. Extending from the Big South Fork National River and Recreation Area in the north to the "Grand Canyon of the Tennessee River" west of Chattanooga, this region is one of the lesser-populated areas in the state. Perhaps for that reason, it has been the home of various experimental communities such as Rugby, and the Depression towns of Homesteads and Norris.

The home of the Scopes "monkey trial" is here, as is the wonderful Museum of Appalachia, and a host of back-road charms. Take a week here.

KNOXVILLE

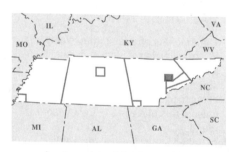

For visitors from the eastern United States who come to Tennessee, Knoxville serves as the first decent-sized city they encounter. In addition to being a great place for day trips into the countryside, Knoxville offers the oldest historic houses, museums, and best theater program in the state. A great zoo and riverboats and an old train are fun for kids. Knoxville's visitor center contains a wonderfully unsophisticated public radio station.

For visitors to the Smokies, Knoxville serves as an excellent respite from the tackiness of the Gateways towns. Here are fine restaurants and art galleries whose paintings don't always center on log cabins with an unearthly glow.

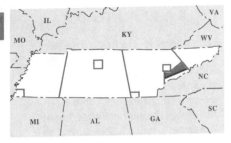

GATEWAYS TO THE SMOKIES

If you love outlet shopping, go-karts, gargantuan pancake breakfasts, a monster assortment of T-shirts that will crack up the gang down at the truck stop, this is the place for you— and millions of like-minded souls. The area surrounding the most visited national park in the country offers living proof of H. L. Mencken's dictum that "no one ever went broke underestimating the taste of the American public."

However, visitors who want to maximize their time in the Great Smoky Mountains without camping in the park will want to stay in the Gateways region.

If you take the park out of the mix, this area can be done in two days max. In the middle of the summer or on a fall weekend, however, those two days will seem like six.

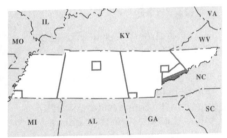

GREAT SMOKY MOUNTAINS NATIONAL PARK

The Smokies offer an unbelievably dense collection of plant and animal life. From virgin hardwood forests to mountain meadows, from black bears to lightning bugs that blink in unison, this place is a delight year-round.

The largest wilderness area in the eastern United States has two main afflictions: pollution and hordes of visitors. The first, particularly during the summer, is hard to avoid, but the latter can be dispensed with by a simple action: walk away from pavement. Visitors who get 200 yards from a road or paved trail will separate themselves from 99.9 percent of park visitors. Take 5 to 10 days here.

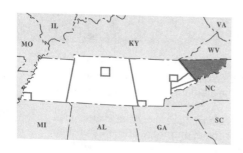

THE FIRST FRONTIER

The easternmost part of Tennessee dates to colonial times, and here are the early towns in which presidents Andrew Jackson and, later, Andrew Johnson walked. Upper East Tennessee, as locals refer to it, has a rich music heritage. Bristol was the birthplace of country music, nearby in Virginia the Carter family continues the roots music tradition, while Down Home in Johnson City plays more contemporary tunes.

The ridge of the Appalachian Mountains runs along the North Carolina border, and these mountains offer trout streams, hiking, and—at Roan Mountain—fields of flowers. Cumberland Gap is both a nature and historical treasure.

The back roads and front porches of the First Frontier's take at least a week to see.

The only state with more Civil War battlefields than Tennessee is Virginia, so if you're interested in the War Between the States, as some Southerners call it, or The War of Northern Aggression, as the die-hards like to say, you've come to the right place.

If Civil War buffs can go to only one place, that place should be Chattanooga. The battlefields there are the best preserved, and there are more of them there than anywhere else in the state. If you have the time, two trips await: the Nathan Bedford Forrest Trail in Middle and West Tennessee, and the Battles of East Tennessee Trail closer to Knoxville and Chattanooga. While there are other Civil War sites in the state, these are the chief ones—it's easy enough to fill an entire trip.

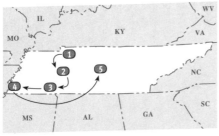

NATHAN BEDFORD FORREST TRAIL

Tennessee-born General Nathan Bedford Forrest made his biggest mark in West Tennessee. If you're interested in following his Civil War path, the best place to start is where General Ulysses S. Grant won his first major victory, at the battlefield at **(1) Fort Donelson National Military Park,** west of Clarksville. This is where Grant picked up his "Unconditional Surrender" nickname and where he let Forrest escape to torment the Union for the rest of the war.

Head upstream along the Tennessee River—from Dover take Hwy. 49 east to Erin, then south on Hwy. 13 to Waverly, then Hwy. 70 west—to **(2) Johnsonville State Historical Area,** where late in the war Forrest's cavalry attacked and defeated a naval force, the only time in history this ever happened. Here you can see what's left of Union defenses, and on the western shore you can take in **Nathan Bedford Forrest State Historical Area,** from which the Confederates fired their cannons and sank Union ships. Make a contribution to **Raise the Gunboats,** which hopes to bring one of those boats to dry land again, and hit the road. Get on Hwy. 70 west to Huntingdon, then go south on Hwy. 22.

On your way south along Hwy. 22, cross I-40 and make sure to eat at the **Cotton Patch Restaurant,** a great barbecue place with lots of Confederate memorabilia. Take one hour to take the **Parker's Crossroads** driving tour. This is where Forrest, when informed that his forces were sandwiched between Union troops, ordered his men to "Charge them both ways."

Then it's south on Hwy. 22 to **(3) Shiloh National Military Park,** the site of the first major battle of the war. Savannah is a good place to spend the night; Grant did so, staying in the Cherry Mansion. Take in the Tennessee River Museum while in town.

Drop down to Counce and head west along Hwy. 57. You'll be following the path of the railroad to Memphis. Stop in at Tennessee Pewter Company in Grand Junction and pick up a copy of the Great Seal of the Confederacy. La-Grange is a beautiful town whose antebellum homes line Hwy. 57.

Woodlawn is not open to the public, but drive by anyway to see where Union General William Sherman had his headquarters. Farther west along Hwy. 57 is where General Grant almost got captured by the Confederates. Stop by Collierville to check out its park with sidewalks in the shape of the Stars and Bars, then it's on to Memphis still along Hwy. 72.

(4) Memphis was taken by the North without a shot being fired on land, so there's no big battlefield here. Make your way to the Mississippi River Museum on Mud Island for some Civil War exhibits, then head west on Union Avenue to Forrest Park, the final resting place of Nathan Bedford Forrest. The Hunt-Phelan Home on the east end of Beale Street, although not open to the public, was where General Grant planned the siege of Vicksburg. The Elmwood Cemetery contains 18 Southern generals and two from the North.

Travel north along Hwy. 51, then turn left on Hwy. 87 to Fort Pillow State Historic Area, where Nathan Bedford Forrest's troops savagely attacked the black soldiers within. Return to Memphis.

Drive back across West Tennessee on U.S. 64, a beautiful stretch of road. Go 173 miles to Lawrenceburg, and then head north on Hwy. 43. In Mount Pleasant, stop and gaze at the privately owned Rattle & Snap, Tennessee's most beautiful plantation home; it is not open to the public. This highway is lined with antebellum homes. Just north of Rattle & Snap, pull in at St. John's Episcopal Church, one of the few surviving plantation churches.

Continue toward Columbia, and make a detour by turning east on Hwy. 50. Cross Hwy. 31 and go two miles, then turn right onto Mooresville Pike. You will pass a bowling alley on the right. Take the next right, which is Mooresville Pike, and then the first driveway on the right to Elm Springs, a plantation home and epicenter of the "Hell, no, we ain't forgettin'!" school of thinking. This antebellum home is the headquarters of the Sons of Confederate Veterans, ever vigilant for what they call "heritage violations."

Get back onto Hwy. 31 and continue north to Spring Hill and stop at Rippavilla, a plantation home turned visitors center, and walk around the corner to see the privately owned Oaklawn, where Confederate General John Bell Hood slept while an entire Union army crept past him in the dark.

Back on Hwy. 31 north to Franklin, just below Nashville, is where the hapless Confederate General Hood threw his army against dug-in Union troops late in the war in an attempt to take Nashville. Winstead Hill is the high point from which Hood watched his troops die. Historic Carnton Plantation and the Carter House still show signs of the intense fighting.

Continue north on Hwy. 31 into (5) Nashville. The ruins of Fort Negley reveal the size of the nation's largest inland fort. The Tennessee State Museum has one of the best Civil War collections in the state. A few steps away, the Tennessee State Capitol was fortified and held the offices of Andrew Johnson, Tennessee's wartime governor.

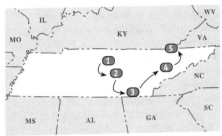

THE BATTLES OF EAST TENNESSEE

Setting off southeast from (1) Nashville, drive U.S. 70, the old blue highway, toward Murfreesboro. In Smyrna, stop to see the Sam Davis Home, where the famous Southern spy grew up. Two miles northwest of Murfreesboro is Stones River National Battlefield, and inside (2) Murfreesboro is what is left of Fortress Rosecrans, an enormous earthen fort. Oaklands is a house restored to its 1862 appearance.

Get on I-24 and head southeast toward (3) Chattanooga. This is where the nation's first national military parks were created, and consequently preservationists here don't have to fight with developers as they've had to in Franklin and other places.

To begin, go into Georgia to the headquarters of the Chickamauga and Chattanooga National Military Park. After getting the lay of the land, you can visit Point Park on Lookout Mountain. Take in the Battles for Chattanooga Museum at the bottom of Lookout Mountain, then go to the Chattanooga National Cemetery, where 12,000 Union troops rest. Missionary Ridge is not as well preserved, but worth a drive. And in Signal Mountain one can see Signal Point Reservation, from which the fledgling Signal Corps did its work.

Driving up I-75 to (4) Knoxville, one can see the mountains off to the east. East Tennesseans leaned more toward the Union than the Confederacy, and these hills and hollows saw a lot of conflict, often between neighbors.

Downtown Knoxville's East Tennessee Historical Society Museum has the best collection of Civil War items on this end of the state. The campus of the University of Tennessee holds the Frank H. McClung Museum, which contains various Civil War items. Across the Tennessee River stands the earthworks of Fort Dickerson, while west on Kingston Pike stands Confederate Memorial Hall, also known as Bleak House, which saw action during the Battle of Fort Sanders.

Northeast of Knoxville along Hwy. 33, then north on Hwy. 25 is Harrogate, home of the Abraham Lincoln Museum, then it's on to (5) Cumberland Gap National Historical Park, which changed hands several times during the war.

Most music devotees head for the axis of Memphis and Nashville, where they'll find museums and iconic sights and a lively performance scene as well. Country and blues bands are not as common outside of these larger cities. However, almost any place in Tennessee offers live music. Virtually every little festival or fair will have a bluegrass or gospel group.

© ELVIS PRESLEY ENTERPRISES, INC.;

Elvis 1968

MEMPHIS

Memphis was the home of Elvis Presley and, for all his sins, he was the most influential figure in all of 20th-century American music. Graceland, Sun Studio, and other lesser shrines keep his memory and music alive and, not insignificantly, keep those cash registers ringing. The Rock 'n' Soul Museum gives the Smithsonian treatment to music, and Soulsville celebrates the heyday of Stax Records.

The hardcore music fan cannot come to Memphis without making a trip down into the Mississippi Delta. Although outside the boundaries of this book, the people and the places there shaped the music that later found expression in Memphis.

THE WESTERN PLAINS

Leaving Memphis and heading toward Nashville, music fans should make a stop in Brownsville, the home of Sleepy John Estes and other bluesmen. Stop by the welcome center off I-40, which doubles as a small museum; from there, it's not far to drive along Hwy. 19 to Nutbush to see the rural origins of Tina Turner. Other than a store in Nutbush, there's really little to see. Back on I-40, Jackson contains the International Rock-a-Billy Hall of Fame and Museum and Suede's restaurant, which displays Carl Perkins memorabilia.

NASHVILLE

Nashville is the capital of Tennessee and the mecca of country music. Even people who never listen to country music find the Country Music Hall of Fame and Museum a fascinating place. The Grand Ole Opry mixes the old performers with the new, and if you can get a reservation to the Bluebird Cafe, you can enjoy the best possible experience—listening to songs sung by the people who wrote them.

There's more to Nashville music than country, and the club scene here offers a variety of offerings. Robert's Western World on Broadway is a good choice, as is the Family Wash in East Nashville.

A smaller center of music is up near the mountains so often sung about in country songs. Although it is just across the state line in Virginia, the Carter Family Memorial Music Center (also known as the Carter Family Fold) is a must-see for roots music fans. Here, the descendants of the first family of country music play every weekend. Nearby Bristol has the Birthplace of Country Music Alliance Museum. Johnson City's Down Home offers the best "pickin' parlor" on this end of the state.

FESTIVALS

Memphis in May is a major music event, held next to the Mississippi River. Bonaroo, put on outside Manchester in the Heartland, is one of the most talked-about festivals in the United States, with an eclectic mixture of music amid a Woodstock environment. Quite a bit more tame is the Smithville Fiddler's Jamboree (see Hills and Plateaus chapter). Festivals come and go; the best way to keep up with them is to go to websites such as www.bluegrassworld.com. Gospel music gatherings don't get the attention that other types of music do, but they exist all over the state.

Tennessee has state parks and wildlife areas from the Mississippi River to the crest of the Appalachian Mountains, but for people seeking good times in the outdoors, as a general rule, the farther east you go, the better it gets.

West Tennessee's forests are like something out of "The Bear," William Faulkner's famous story. With towering hardwoods and swampy bottoms on flat land, they have their charms, but nothing like the mountains and cliffs found in the east.

Middle Tennessee's terrain contains rolling hills and faster-moving streams, but things pick up, literally, when travelers go east of Cookeville and come to the Cumberland Plateau, which extends from the Kentucky border down to Alabama and Georgia (see the Hills and Plateaus chapter). The average elevation in this region is 2,000 feet above sea level, considerably higher than Nashville, which is about 600 feet. While the mountains to the east are beautiful and have wondrous views, for my money the best place to enjoy the Tennessee outdoors is on the Plateau. Compared to places farther east, it is relatively uncrowded.

Easternmost Tennessee, also known as the First Frontier, contains the peaks of the Appalachians, including the Great Smokies and large chunks of national forest lands.

Entire books have been written on outdoor activities in Tennessee. Here is a very general breakdown of the highlights.

HIKING

The best hikes consist of varying terrain with interesting geographical features to see. By this definition, the Cumberland Trail, now under construction from Cumberland Gap to near Chattanooga, is the best trail in the state. Segments are already open, and for day hikers or through-hikers, this walk is a delight. The Big South Fork National River and Recreation Area contains wonderful hikes to "rock houses" and along rushing streams. Fall Creek Falls State Park and Savage Gulf Natural Area, also on the Cumberland Plateau, offer superb hiking. The Cumberland Gap, significant for its place in history, also offers outstanding hiking.

In East Tennessee, the Appalachian Trail, running as it does along the crest of the eastern Continental Divide, is the premier footpath, particularly where it goes through the Great Smoky Mountains National Park. A host of other trails await the hiker in the park—short jaunts of a mile or less, all-day hikes, and multiday backpacking trips.

Other hikes can be found in the Cherokee National Forest, which extends along the western slope of the Appalachians north of the Great Smoky Mountains National Park to the Virginia border and south to the Georgia border. These hikes can be found at www.gorp.away.com or at www.southernregion.fs.fed.us/cherokee. The trails at Roan Mountain State Park beats anything in the Smokies, especially when the rhododendrons are in bloom. Beauty Spot, above Erwin on the Appalachian Trail, is another delight.

BIKING

Tennessee is great bicycling country, with a wide choice of terrain and long country roads dotted with country stores and friendly towns. West Tennessee offers 185 miles of the Mississippi River Trail (www.mississippirivertrail.org), which runs between Reelfoot Lake and Memphis. With its flat land and relatively low number of vehicles, almost anywhere in this third of the state offers an easy ride.

In the middle part of the state, the Natchez Trace Parkway attracts riders from all over the country. Running from just south of Nashville to the Alabama state line, this limited-access highway doesn't allow trucks. Land Between the Lakes, north of Dover, has extensive biking trails, and the Mountain Goat Trail from Cowan to Sewanee is fun for mountain bikers.

Riding gets more gnarly in East Tennessee, where the hills and mountains calls for the Lance Armstrong in riders. Cades Cove in the Smokies is an easy loop ride, and single-track riders will like trails in the Big South Fork National River and Recreation Area and the Old Copper Road along the Ocoee River.

Numerous books give detailed routes in the state. *Bicycling Tennessee: Road Adventures from the Mississippi Delta to the Great Smoky Mountains,* by Owen Proctor, is a good one.

PADDLING

With its abundant rainfall and many lakes and streams, Tennessee offers everything from white-water rafting to canoeing in tea-colored water amidst overhanging vines and trees.

In West Tennessee, canoeists and kayakers might like the Wolf River along the Mississippi state line, but this is relatively flat water—you'll be doing most of the work. Reelfoot Lake contains cypress "knees" sticking out of the water, a phenomenon usually seen much farther south. The Tennessee River offers a chance to get out on the water as well, but paddlers have to be mindful of barge traffic.

The canoeing gets better as you move east into Middle Tennessee with the Buffalo River near Hohenwald, Harpeth River west of Nashville, and the Elk River near Fayetteville. Rock Island State Park has fantastic kayaking as well.

East Tennessee contains the best rivers. It was on the Ocoee River in southeast Tennessee that the 1996 Olympics rolled out kayaking as a part of the summer games, and that has made all the difference. Now thousands of visitors kayak or raft that river. They can also paddle down the Hiwassee, the Nolichucky, the French Broad, the Pigeon, and the Obed-Emory River System. All of these rivers have commercial rafting available for visitors.

Tennessee is a great state for family gatherings. Many families come to Tennessee for reunions, and the state abounds in activities that delight people of any age. The secret for family fun is having a big choice of activities, so that people with varying abilities and attention spans never get bored.

An important aspect to keep in mind is the weather. It gets hot in Tennessee in the summertime, and the humidity percentage stays right up there with the Fahrenheit numbers. This can take the starch out of anyone, especially the very young and the very old. In planning family activities, leave some time to rest or spend some of the day in or near water.

If you want to pick one of the larger cities, the nod goes to Chattanooga. From the Tennessee Aquarium to Rock City, Chattanooga is the most family-friendly city in the state. Once downtown, families can walk to many of the attractions, and the city has a lot of excursions just an hour or so away, such as rafting on the Ocoee River.

PARKS

Tennessee has 54 state parks that offer a wide range of activities. To see them, visit www.state.tn.us/environment/parks. Sixteen parks have hotels, 19 parks offer cabins, and 27 offer RV camping. Depending on the park, the activities may include golf, museums, horseback riding, hiking, swimming, and boating. Many families go year after year to the same park—even the same cabin—so making reservations far ahead is a must.

Here are five great state parks, plus some fun amusement parks. All except Pickett State Park offer hotels, cabins, or camping.

Reelfoot Lake State Park, in northwest Tennessee, has a hotel that stretches out over the water, and has great fishing and bird-watching.

Pickwick Landing State Park near Counce along the Mississippi/Alabama state lines, sits beside Pickwick Dam. This park especially appeals to boaters, and is also a good place from which to visit the Shiloh battlefield.

Pickett State Park, above Jamestown, borders the Big South Fork National River and Recreation Area. This enormous park—some 17,372 acres—contains all manner of interesting rock formations, natural bridges, and caves. Kids love this place.

Fall Creek Falls State Park, on the edge of the Cumberland Plateau near Pikeville, is the best one in the state. It contains four waterfalls, including Fall Creek Falls, which, at 256 feet, is the highest in the eastern United States—higher even than Niagara Falls. Hiking, biking, and rock climbing are some of the activities offered here.

Roan Mountain State Park, way up in the eastern point of Tennessee, sits on the slopes of Roan Mountain, a 6,285-foot high peak covered with rhododendron bushes. Its main attractions are hiking, swimming, and a refreshing escape from summertime heat.

Pigeon's Forge's Dollywood is the largest amusement park in Tennessee. Memphis has the much smaller Libertyland. Across the Georgia border from Chattanooga is Lake Winnepesaukah Amusement Park.

Perhaps the place that most families go in Tennessee is the Great Smoky Mountains National Park. So, it seems, does everyone else. While the park is a delight, the towns around it, particularly Sevierville, Pigeon Forge, and Gatlinburg, constitute the worst tourist traps in the entire country. The best way to avoid the madding crowd and still enjoy the Smokies area is to stay on the Townsend side or near Cosby.

FESTIVALS

Fairs and festivals are always great for families. The website www.tnvacation.com offers a good list of events. Here are some top picks.

Mule Day in Columbia, first weekend in May, celebrates the country's most stubborn animal. Music, food, and demonstration of mule-related events make this slight goofy event a lot of fun.

The World's Biggest Fish Fry offers a chance to see Paris in April—Paris, Tennessee, that is. In addition to eating 10,000 pounds of catfish, festival-goers can hear music, go dancing, watch a rodeo, and see a parade.

Rhododendron Festival at Roan Mountain State Park takes place when these flowers are in glorious bloom—in mid June. Cloggers, music, food, and fun await.

The Tennessee State Fair, held in mid-September in Nashville, brings the agricultural community together with contests and presentations.

The National Storytelling Festival, during the first weekend in October in Jonesborough, is the largest event in the expanding universe of storytelling.

A former resident of Jackson, Tennessee now living in Cambridge, Massachusetts related the tale of going home visiting his folks. He happened to turn on the radio to a local talk show, just in time to hear one of the callers breathlessly ask, "I heard that if you catch a warsp and hold your breath it won't sting you—did you ever hear that?" The host entertained other calls on this revelation, then moved on to a female caller who proudly recited a prized recipe for potato salad.

After explaining to the uninitiated that "warsp" was Tennessee-speak for "wasp," the Cantabrigian opined that the series of eclectic calls was "the single greatest thing I have ever heard on radio."

When it comes to the offbeat in America, whether or not it happens to be broadcast on the radio, the South pegs the meter. In a region that produced writer Flannery O'Connor, folk artist Howard Finster, and wild man Jerry Lee Lewis, Tennessee more than holds its own. The weirder aspects of the state, much ignored by tourism officials, are what make Tennessee such a particular delight for visitors, who sometimes wonder why all these manifestations take place here.

The answer lies in Tennessee's combination of religion, creativity, and a joyful sort of "We Don't Care What Other People Think" attitude. You see it in barns whose owners were inspired to paint religious slogans on the roof. You see it in yards in which every tree trunk wears white paint to a height of three feet. And you see it in Confederate flag-bedecked pickup trucks whose owners consider themselves the most patriotic Americans in the country yet proudly exhibit the battle flag of the most treasonous rebellion the nation has ever known.

So as you travel through Tennessee, don't be afraid to see where the day—or the unheralded backroad—may take you. Here is just a sample of the roadside attractions that may delight you.

In West Tennessee, Memphis's Crystal Shrine Grotto is an amazing piece of folk art in an otherwise ordinary cemetery. Just up Hwy. 70, Brownsville's Billy Tripp's massive welded-steel artwork-in-progress, Mind Field, draws admirers from around the world. Farther east, the town of Selmer serves up "slugburgers," and, no, they don't have slugs in them.

In Middle Tennessee, Nashville contains an entire denomination named "The House of God Which is the Church of the Living God, the Pillar and Ground of the Truth Without Controversy, Inc.," whose most distinctive form of music is pedal steel guitars. South of the capital city, stores in Hohenwald ship in more than 1,000 bales of clothing, snip the wires, and invite pa dig for garments. In nearby Lewisburg, the Goats, Music, & More fest ebrates its signature fainting goats. The Farm, near Summertown, i America's longest-lasting hippie communities.

In East Tennessee—actually just across the line in North Carolina—**Fields of the Wood** is a Pentacostal-themed park with the world's largest concrete Ten Commandments tablets. On Hwy. 64 near Ocoee, Danny Hoskinson, also known as Bucket Man, takes five-gallon plastic buckets and transforms them into fantastic faces and other works of art. In downtown Gatlinburg, **Christus Gardens** possesses the famous Carrara Marble Face of Jesus, a sculpture that appears to stare at visitors throughout the room.

These are attractions that you just won't find anywhere else.

Explore Tennessee

Memphis

*If aerial photographs could reveal energy
the way infrared photographs reveal heat,
Memphis would be surrounded by vectors
pointing toward it: This is the place.*

Robert Gordon, It Came from Memphis

Memphis is the largest city in Tennessee. Its economic influence reaches across West Tennessee, down into Mississippi, and across the river into Arkansas; one can travel 200 miles in any direction before reaching another city its size. Some argue, convincingly, that Memphis is actually the capital of northern Mississippi.

For a long time, Memphis was the place where rural people, black and white, came when they hit the right combination of money and gumption. The itinerant bluesmen out of the Delta made the journey, as did countless sons and daughters who wanted to get off the farm and away from

little towns. Elvis Presley's parents came from Mississippi with thousands of others.

Memphis was ready for all of them. Early on, Beale Street was a place for blacks where segregation diminished, if just for an afternoon. Planters came to sell cotton. People with money came, and still come, to Memphis to buy everything from furniture to wedding gowns.

These people rubbed up against each other in a way that made the music happen. Whites heard blacks and imitated their music and clothing. Blacks played for whites, adapting the music to what would sell. Studios recorded blacks and whites, finally hitting the right formula that became rock 'n' roll, a formula that a young man named Elvis would sell to the world.

Now Memphis focuses on its music, not in the industry-sponsored vision of Nashville, but in its own peculiar fashion. Stax Records, which

began 1959, launched the careers of musicians such as Isaac Hayes, Sam and Dave, and many more.

It's been a long time since an individual or group from Memphis has made it big, but that doesn't keep local groups from trying. Memphis is still a musical town, as visits to clubs will prove. For those who come to Tennessee for the music, this is the place where each performance can become a joyful discovery.

The astute observer will note that Memphians have their big festivals in the spring and fall. Summertime is beastly hot—temperatures of 100°F combined with 95 percent humidity are not at all rare. This can take the starch out of even the most determined visitor, especially children. The best times to visit are May and October. The winters aren't very cold—Memphis seldom gets enough snow to make a snowman—but rain can come almost anytime.

Three days will give a brief overview of Memphis, but music fans could easily spend a week or more here. Travelers should base themselves downtown, ideally within a couple of stone's throws from the Mississippi River. Most of the sights and attractions are downtown within an easy walk or a ride on the trolley.

HISTORY

The site of Memphis, at the edge of the western plains of Tennessee, was occupied by people as early as 3,000 years ago. The bluffs above the Mississippi River offered protection from floods as well as from enemies. Archaeologists estimate that the first permanent village was built about A.D. 1000, and a series of villages were built there during the next 600 years.

When Hernando de Soto, the Spanish explorer of the Southeast, came through here in 1541, he described powerful rulers and populous towns on the bluffs. He and his troops spent some time here replenishing supplies and building boats with which to cross the river. Yet when Jacques Marquette and Louis Joliet arrived downstream 132 years later, they also traded with Native Americans, but reported no such large villages.

During the 1700s, trade on the river increased as Tennesseans and others drifted downstream past what was by then called the Chickasaw Bluffs. This land lay between the English colonies and Spanish territory to the southwest, and both sides had reason to claim it. James Robertson, later dubbed "The Father of Tennessee," brought troops here in 1782 and began giving goods to the Chickasaw in an effort to win their allegiance. Twelve years later John Overton set up a trading post for the same reason. The Spanish, uneasy at these approaches, sought to establish a fort in 1795 but were forced to retreat.

North Carolina, wanting to reward its Revolutionary War soldiers, began promising them land in what is now West Tennessee. North Carolina had no right to do this, but that did not dissuade it from doing so. This led the federal government to make the Chickasaw one of those "offers you can't refuse" deals for the entire area of West Tennessee. Andrew Jackson and others negotiated with the Indians, telling them that the federal government could not keep the eager North Carolina land-seekers out.

Wild West

In 1818 the Chickasaw signed away their lands, and the Jackson Purchase, as it was known, opened up the Wild West of Tennessee. Settlers poured in, and the next year a trio of land speculators—Jackson, Judge John Overton, and General James Winchester—established the town of Memphis. They took the name from the ancient capital of Egypt, a word said to mean "place of good abode."

It quickly became a place for a good time. Flatboatmen on their way downstream were happy to pull in and blow off a little steam. Landowners arrived with gangs of slaves to cut down the hardwood forests and turn the rich soil into plantations. Native Americans traded furs for liquor, and gamblers did their best to separate one and all from their money.

The 1830 federal census counted only a couple of hundred people in Memphis. By 1840, 2,000 were on hand, and 10 years later more than 8,800 people called Memphis home. By

Must-Sees

Look for **M** to find the sights and activities you can't miss and **M** for the best dining and lodging.

M Graceland: Seeing the home and final resting place of Elvis remains the number one reason to come to Memphis (page 32).

M Memphis Rock 'n' Soul Museum: Located inside the **FedEx Forum,** this is the single best place in Memphis to get a handle on the city's tremendous contribution to popular culture (page 33).

M Gibson Beale Street Showcase: This factory produced guitars for a score of music greats, including B.B. King (page 33).

M Soulsville: This affectionate look at the legacy of Stax Records gives much needed balance to Memphis's musical legacy (page 33).

M Center for Southern Folklore: Gift shop and museum combine with enthusiastic employees in a joyful interpretation of the South (page 35).

M National Civil Rights Museum: See how far Americans have come since the bad days of segregation (page 40).

M National Ornamental Metal Museum: This tribute to metalworking would be worth seeing

Peabody Memphis Hotel's famous fountain

even if it were in a concrete block building. Its setting on a high bluff above the Mississippi River is just icing on the cake (page 40).

M Peabody Memphis Hotel: Even if you can't stay at the Peabody, its lobby is worth a look. Famous as the place where the ducks march in and out to the fountain, it's also the best place in the universe to have a gin and tonic on a hot afternoon (page 45).

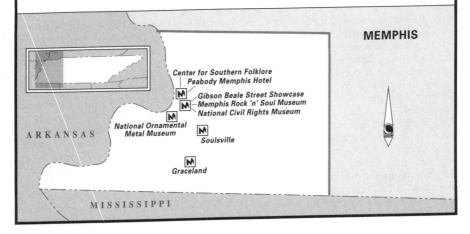

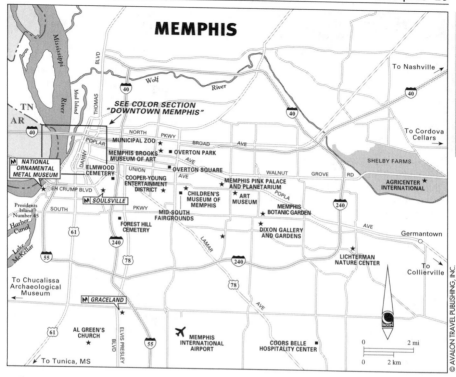

1850, according to Robert Corlew's *Tennessee, A Short History,* local plantations produced 150,000 bales of cotton valued at $7.5 million—approximately $150 million in current dollars—most of which moved through Memphis on its way to market. Ten years later traders sold three times that amount. Because of the large amount of international shipping, Memphis gained a customs office in 1850. By 1857, a railroad connected Charleston to Memphis, and by 1860, 33,000 people lived by the river.

A good number of them were slaves. Memphis had the largest slave trade in the area, and one of the traders in humans was Nathan Bedford Forrest, a man so respected by his fellow citizens that he was elected a city alderman.

Civil War

Memphis was isolated from the rest of the state

when Union troops fought their way down the Tennessee River, their struggle culminating at the battle of Shiloh. Their victory forced a Confederate retreat from Fort Pillow, which guarded the river north of the city. Memphis's last chance came when Union and Confederate gunboats fought it out on the river. Memphians watched from the bluffs above as the boats, using rams much like Roman galleys, slammed into each other. When it was all over, a Union force came ashore and erected its flag at the post office. General Ulysses S. Grant moved into an elegant mansion on Beale Steet. Memphis was in Union hands, where it would remain for the rest of the war.

This proved not entirely bad. Memphians did not undergo a siege, as did Vicksburg farther downstream, nor was Memphis shelled and burned, a fate suffered by Atlanta and other cities.

CIVIL WAR RELICS

Like Nashville a few months before, Memphis was occupied by Union troops on June 6, 1862, with hardly a shot being fired. Confederate defeats at Shiloh and other places rendered the city defenseless. People from Memphis or who had spent time there, however, fought all through the war and were commemorated afterwards in various parks and monuments.

These tributes to the Lost Cause have proved awkward in a city with such a large African American population, and tend to get omitted from official tourist publications. As one woman working at Burkle Estate/Slavehaven put it, "We can't ignore all this—it's our history—but I'm sure glad they lost."

Confederate Park

This park between North Front Street and Riverside Drive commemorates the Battle of Memphis, a sort of demolition derby of gunboats that ended when Memphis fell into Union hands. At one time this park contained Civil War cannons, but in a burst of World War II patriotism the city donated them for scrap to support the war effort. They were replaced with artillery pieces from World War I, thus providing an anachronism alongside the statue of Jefferson Davis.

Gayoso Hotel

The facade of this old hotel can still be seen at the corner of Peabody and Front Streets. Built in 1844, it was used as a headquarters by both North and South during the Civil War, but it is most remembered as one of the objectives of Nathan Bedford Forrest's 1864 raid on the city. His brother, William Forrest, rode his horse into the hotel lobby to capture a Union general who lived there. Luckily for the general, he had chosen that night to sleep somewhere else.

Jefferson Davis Park

The site of the park is believed to be the place where Hernando de Soto built boats with which to cross the Mississippi. It had no particular historical connection with the president of the Confederacy but was set off to honor him after the war. Now it is occupied by the Tennessee Welcome Center.

Site of the Jefferson Davis Home

The one and only president of the Confederacy lived in Memphis after the war, from 1867–75 while he was the president of a local insurance company. The house where he lived stood at 129 Court Avenue.

Forrest Park

This park, at Manassas and Union Avenues just east of Sun Studios, serves as the lightning rod for those who would like to downplay Memphis's Confederate history. It consists of a statue of Nathan Bedford Forrest, Memphis slave trader, alderman, famous Confederate general, and infamous early leader of the Ku Klux Klan. The statue faces south because, according to some, Forrest said he would never turn his back on the South. The general and his wife are entombed beneath the statue, which often attracts graffiti and other vandalism.

The general and his wife were originally buried in Elmwood Cemetery, but in 1905 they were moved to Forrest Park. His birthday, July 13, 1821, is regularly commemorated by the Sons of Confederate Veterans and various admirers, while others, most notably the Memphis branch of the NAACP, have mounted efforts to have his remains placed elsewhere. This would require the permission of his descendants, who have so far declined.

Indeed, merchants made a lot of money selling cotton and trading for goods that could be sold to both North and South.

The most colorful episode of Memphis's Civil War history came late in the war in August 1864, when Confederate Forrest staged a daring raid on the city where he once served as alderman. Hoping to capture three Union generals and to free Southerners held in a prison, Forrest and his men galloped into town at 4 A.M. They captured no generals—although one had to scamper in his nightgown to a nearby fort—and didn't free any prisoners, but the troops were cheered by the locals, particularly the women.

Pestilence

Memphis came through the war relatively unscathed, but disease brought it to its knees during the next 15 years. Cholera and yellow fever struck in 1867, and yellow fever returned in 1872 and far worse in 1878. In the words of the *WPA Guide to Tennessee:*

Memphis became a pest-hole. As deaths mounted, the streets were deserted except for the "dead wagons." Bodies lay rotting in the streets where they had fallen. The criminal element of the city ran wild. Looting and killing, terrific drunken brawls, gun battles, and rape were common. Not more than 20,000 people remained in the city; 14,000 were Negroes, of whom 946 died. The higher fatality was among the 6,000 whites, of whom 4,206 died.

The disparity of deaths between black and white populations came about because African Americans possessed a natural immunity. As in the Civil War, however, what brought tragedy to some brought opportunity for others. Property values plummeted, and many speculators bought land and homes from the fleeing residents.

The situation got so bad that Memphis declared bankruptcy, gave up its charter, and legally ceased to exist for 12 years. Citizens set about making sure the epidemics would never return by putting in an effective sewage system, stopping the practice of drinking river water, and draining ditches that had produced clouds of disease-carrying mosquitoes. Among the ones to buy the bonds that financed all this was former slave Robert Church.

Recovery, the Blues, and Racial Conflict

The people returned—totaling 64,589 by 1890—and with them came prosperity. A railroad bridge across the Mississippi was built in 1892, and the next year Memphis got its charter back. It remained the center of the cotton business and also became the greatest hardwood lumber center in the world.

Samuel H. Kress founded S. H. Kress & Company in Memphis, a five-and-dime store empire that at one time had more than 300 stores, mostly in the South. Kress, an art collector, believed that his stores should reflect good architecture and maintained a staff of architects to make sure they did. His first store, at 9 Main Street, is now a 46-room annex to the adjacent Marriott Springhill Suites.

The money in Memphis trickled down to the African American population. It was during this time that Beale Street became the center of life. Black professionals who had been educated in the North came to Memphis to practice their trade. Robert Church founded the Solvent Bank and Trust and became the South's first African American millionaire. In 1923 the Universal Life Insurance Company, one of the largest black-owned insurance companies, was chartered. Many rural blacks moved to Memphis, and with them they brought a new kind of music called the blues. W. C. Handy, a local bandleader and cornet player, wrote the first tune with the word "blues" in the title. His "Memphis Blues," originally written as a campaign song, was followed by the "St. Louis Blues," and popular music was changed forever.

In 1916, a grocer named Clarence Saunders opened a store with a funny name and a revolutionary modus operandi. Piggly Wiggly was the first grocery store in the country in which customers took a basket and selected items they wished to purchase—before that, clerks got goods off shelves and handed them to buyers. One year later Saunders owned 25 stores, three years later 162 stores, and by 1923 there were 1,267 Piggly

Wigglys. Saunders built a large house with pink marble, quickly dubbed "The Pink Palace" by locals, but because of various setbacks lost his stores and died penniless.

Welcome Wagon was founded in Memphis in 1928 by Thomas Briggs, whose big idea was to hire female "hostesses" to visit newly arrived families in cities and towns and give them a basket of goodies from local merchants who wanted new customers. The company built a headquarters at 145 Court Square that still stands. Welcome Wagon decamped from Memphis in the 1990s, and still exists, though in considerably diminished form.

The early 20th century saw the rise of Edward Crump, a Mississippian who was elected mayor of Memphis in 1909, 1911, and 1915. "Boss" Crump, as he became known, refused to enforce Tennessee's law prohibiting the sale of alcoholic beverages, and the state legislature passed the Ouster Law to remove him from office. Crump lost this battle but built a political machine so formidable that it ran Shelby County for years and exerted considerable influence across the state. Crump made an alliance with Republicans in East Tennessee, granting them control of patronage in their area in return for their support. Crump and his cronies thus controlled most statewide elections until Gordon Browning and Estes Kefauver beat them in the Democratic primary of 1948.

Memphis attracted its share of entrepreneurs. In 1952, Kemmons Wilson came up with the idea of a franchise motel. Naming it after a popular Bing Crosby movie, he called his creation a Holiday Inn.

The summer of the year "Boss" Crump died, a young man walked into Sun Studios and on July 5, 1954, recorded a song called "That's Alright." In a few short years, Elvis became the biggest star to come from Memphis and indeed from all of Tennessee, and he was credited with luring white audiences to what had heretofore been considered black music. Stax Records brought names such as Otis Redding, Rufus Thomas, Booker T and the MGs, Carla Thomas, and Johnnie Taylor to national attention.

Musically the races may have come closer together in the 1950s, but in other ways they were far apart, particularly in Memphis, which had the largest black population in the state. Unlike in other parts of the South, African Americans here had the right to vote, but discrimination was present in other areas. Sit-ins took place here in 1960, and a biracial Committee on Community Relations helped desegregate the city. Like other American cities, Memphis underwent great transformations after World War II, and the racial conflict accelerated white flight from downtown. Not since the days of yellow fever had white people so deserted downtown Memphis. Urban renewal efforts beginning in the 1960s leveled many of the abandoned and substandard buildings, leaving much of Beale Street off by itself amid fields of grass.

The Murder of Martin Luther King Jr.

In 1968, the city's sanitation workers went on strike. Although the usual labor issues—more money and a better working environment—were involved, this strike became in and of itself a civil rights movement, for most of the workers were black, and the city government that employed them was white. The Reverend Martin Luther King Jr. and other civil rights leaders encouraged the sanitation workers. Marchers clashed with police and the city was scarred with violence and property damage.

While King was in town getting ready for a second march, he spoke at the Mason Temple. In a final, eerily prescient sermon, he said:

I don't know what will happen now. We've got some difficult days ahead. But it doesn't matter with me now. Because I've been to the mountaintop. . . . I've seen the Promised Land. I may not get there with you. But I want you to know tonight that we as a people will get to the Promised Land. So I'm happy tonight. I'm not worried about anything. I'm not fearing any man. Mine eyes have seen the glory of the coming of the Lord.

The next day about dinnertime as King, Jesse Jackson, and others were standing outside his room on the second floor of the Lorraine Motel, James Earl Ray fired a rifle from the window of a building across the street and killed King.

This proved to be the beginning of Memphis's low point. Businesses and those who could afford to fled downtown. The iconic Peabody Memphis Hotel closed in 1975. Elvis Presley, Memphis's most celebrated resident, died in 1977.

Memphis Today

Memphis had begun its comeback in the 1970s—FedEx was founded here in 1972—but things began to happen, oddly enough, after Elvis died. A renovated Peabody reopened in 1981, Graceland began welcoming the public in 1982, and the stream of people making Elvis pilgrimages gave Memphis a renewed sense of its musical heritage.

Memphis is the locus of pilgrimages of another sorts, as it serves as the headquarters of three denominations of Protestant churches. The Church of God in Christ was founded in 1907 by Bishop Charles Harrison Mason, and claims more than five million members. The Christian Methodist Episcopal Church organized in Jackson, Tennessee, in 1870, has 850,000 members, while the Cumberland Presbyterian Church has 90,000 members.

A revival of Beale Street coincided with an upswing in interest in the blues, and with its growing number of festivals and attractions Memphis is returning as a tourist destination. The 32-story Pyramid offers a unique presence on the city's skyline, and the National Civil Rights Museum has transformed the Lorraine Motel from a place of shame and sadness to a center for education and renewal. AutoZone

MEMPHIS BY THE NUMBERS

Memphis is
- the third-largest rail center in the United States.
- the home of the largest air cargo airport.
- the hardwood lumber capital of the world.
- the fourth-largest inland port in the United States.
- the largest medical center in the South.
- the first nationally in historic listings per capita.
- the fourth most efficiently-run city according to national think tank Reason Public Policy Institute.

According to the U.S. Census Bureau, the people of Memphis
- totaled 655,656 in 2003.
- comprise the 18th-largest city in the country.
- have an estimated African-American population totaling 61.6 percent of the Memphis population in 2003.

Park, the home of the minor league baseball team, Memphis Redbirds, brings even more people downtown, as does the FedEx Center, home of the National Basketball Association's Memphis Grizzlies.

Today Memphis is the undisputed pork barbecue capital of the world, and a town that, as in the days of the flatboatmen, knows how to have a good time. More than 150 festivals and celebrations commemorate everything from Elvis to zydeco music. It is the most musical place in the most musical state.

Sights

ORIENTATION

Memphis began on the bluffs above the river, and that's where most of the interesting places remain. Much of the city's white population has moved to the east into the world of suburbia—a world that looks just like outside of Atlanta or Charlotte or any other big Southern city.

The areas described below, except for Overton Square and the Cooper-Young Entertainment District, are all along the river, running from north to south.

Pyramid and the Pinch

This area at the north of Memphis is anchored by the most stupendous structure in all of Tennessee: the 32-story Pyramid, the third-largest such edifice in the world. In the frontier days of the 1830s, the people who lived north of Market Street were derisively called "pinch guts," for they were so malnourished they had to tighten their belts so far they "pinched their guts." The place where they lived has been known ever since as "The Pinch," now Front Street and 2nd Avenue.

The Pinch became a neighborhood for German Jews; a remnant survives as the Burkle Estate/Slavehaven, a stop on the Underground Railroad. Irish fleeing the potato famine were the next influx, and their presence is remembered each March with St. Patrick's Day celebrations hereabouts. Visitors enjoy walking in the area, stopping in at Irish pubs, antique stores, and other neighborhood pleasures.

Looking east down Jackson Street from the Pinch, you can see a golden dome. This is part of St. Jude Children's Research Hospital, where there's a small museum and the tomb of Danny Thomas.

Victorian Village Historic District

The residential areas of Memphis used to begin just a few streets away from the river, but over the years the commercial district has expanded and wiped out most of the old houses. Just a few are left on Adams Street, and these make up the Vic-torian Village Historic District. Here stands Magevney House, one of the oldest homes in the city, and just down the street are the Mallory-Neely House and the Woodruff-Fontaine House, beautiful homes that reflect the taste of the wealthy families who lived in them. Several other Victorian houses hold court in the neighborhood, but these are not open to the public.

Mud Island

Mud Island contains the Mississippi River Museum, a look at Memphis and the influence of the river on it; River Walk, an enormous scale model of the Mississippi. An outdoor theater hosts many concerts. Pedestrian visitors can get to Mud Island by taking a tram that departs from the intersection of Front and Adams Streets

Cotton Row Historic District

If cotton was king in the South, Memphis was where he reigned. Seeds and supplies were sold here, bales of cotton were shipped from here, and the money that came back to the planters was very often spent here. At one time more than 200 businesses were located in this district, but now the number is declining almost by the month. Despite this trend, and although much of the cotton industry has moved farther west, Memphis still sells more cotton on the spot market than any other city in the country.

The center of the cotton trade is on Front Street, and a good place to begin walking is Confederate Park, at West Court Street on the bluff overlooking Riverside Drive. Walking south on Front Street, you'll come to a series of buildings with particular architectural features. When cotton is sold it must be graded, or classified, and before 1950 this required natural light—thus large windows. Cotton bales are big items, and the buildings needed large doors for moving cotton in and out.

Peabody Place Retail and Entertainment Center

Adding to the excitement created by AutoZone Park, this complex fills in the area between the

the liveliest section of downtown Memphis

Peabody Memphis Hotel and Beale Street. The Peabody Memphis Hotel is the grande dame of Memphis hotels, and a place once said to be the northern terminus of the Mississippi Delta. Tourists—especially children—love its twice-daily parade of ducks to and from the fountain.

Peabody Place contains a jumble of attractions: Jillian's (think Chuck E. Cheese for adults), a 22-screen movie theater, Tower Records, an Irish pub, and a variety of shops. The Peabody Place Museum has an amazing collection of Asian art, and the Center for Southern Folklore has live music, art, and the best shop in all of Memphis.

Beale Street Historical District

People who think that New Orleans is Bourbon Street tend to think that Beale Street is Memphis. It is a rollicking place, to be sure, especially on weekends. Lined with clubs and T-shirt shops and heavily policed, today's Beale Street is a sort of Disney version of the original, but it remains *the* place to go. B.B. King's Blues Club is here, as is the marvelous A. Schwab Dry Goods Store and the New Daisy Theater.

Just south of Beale is the Gibson Beale Street Showcase, which makes the hollow-bodied electric guitars loved by bluesmen and rockabilly musicians. Between Third and Fourth Streets stands the Fedex Forum, home of the Memphis Grizzlies and the Rock 'n' Soul Museum.

South Main Street District

The area of Main Street south of Beale is home to a delightful neighborhood of galleries, studios, and small restaurants. Here, too, one block east of Main, is The National Civil Rights Museum. The restored Amtrak station is two blocks off Main Street at the intersection of Poplar Avenue and 3rd Street. The trolley goes there from downtown.

Overton Square

Five miles east of Main Street, at the corner of Cooper and Madison, is Overton Square, three blocks of restaurants and shops in midtown. Playhouse on the Square, the city's only professional resident company, is here, as are more than 15 restaurants that vary from outdoor patios to formal dining. The food includes alligator chili, specialty pizzas, French crepes, and Mexican dishes. The rise of Beale Street has siphoned some of the nightlife from here, but the restaurants still hold down the fort.

Cooper-Young Entertainment District

Just north of Overton Square, at the corner of Cooper Street and Young Avenue, is the epicenter of the Cooper-Young Entertainment District, a collection of shops and restaurants. The district is marked by an overhead railroad trestle that displays art showing the area's distinctive architecture. When it is time to eat, hit the Young Avenue Deli. And if you are weary and just want to sit down in the dark and watch a movie, there's Studio on the Square, an art movie house.

MUSIC

Ⓜ Graceland

The individual associated with Memphis more than any other person is Elvis Aron Presley, who was born in Tupelo, Mississippi, and moved to Memphis as a teenager. Except for his years in the army and his numerous performances in concerts, movies, and television shows, he never left Memphis, eventually settling in a mansion called

Graceland. The legacy of The King consists of museums and exhibits from which the visitor can choose at his mansion Graceland (3734 Elvis Presley Blvd., 800/238-2000 or 901/332-3322, www.elvis.com).

To see the whole works, go for the Platinum Tour, which costs $27 for adults, $24.30 for seniors and students, and $13 for children ages 7–12. This tour takes two to three hours. The Graceland Mansion Tour goes through the fabled mansion, including the Jungle Room, the gravesite, and various outbuildings. This costs $18 for adults, $16.20 for seniors, and $7 for children ages 7–12.

The Elvis Presley Automobile Museum displays cars, motorcycles, and other vehicles owned by Elvis and costs $8 for adults, $7.20 for seniors, and $4 for children ages 7–12. The Custom Jets Tour depicts the way Elvis traveled; $7 for adults, $6.30 for seniors, and $3.50 for children ages 7–12. Then there's Sincerely Elvis, a museum offering a look at personal items: home movies, snapshots, riding tack, sports equipment, and stage outfits. This costs $6 for adults, $5.40 for seniors, and $3 for children ages 7–12. The one free item at Graceland is *Walk in My Shoes*, a 23-minute film on

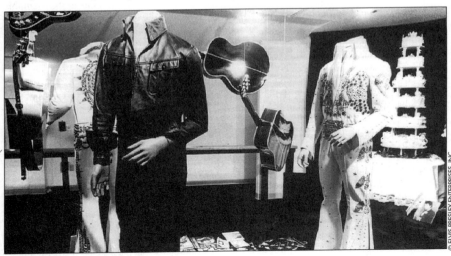

Graceland has become a shrine for millions of Elvis fans.

the life and music of Elvis presented in a theater in the middle of the plaza.

The rest of the Graceland complex includes gift shops and restaurants. Graceland is open seven days a week except November through February, when the mansion tour is closed on Tuesday. The jets and other museums, however, are open every day except New Year's Day, Thanksgiving, and Christmas. The ticket office is open Memorial Day weekend through Labor Day 7:30 A.M.–6 P.M., and the rest of the year 8:30 A.M.–5 P.M. The last mansion tour begins when the ticket office closes, and the self-paced tours stay open two hours after the ticket office closes.

Pilgrims can see the grave of Elvis for free most mornings for 90 minutes before the paying visitors start coming in. Walk-up time ends 30 minutes before that day's tours begin.

Elvis Presley's Birthday Tribute takes place January 6–8 at Graceland. The schedule of events varies from year to year, so call for specifics.

The second week in August brings Elvis Week, also known as "Death Week," built around the anniversary of his death on August 16, 1977. This is a giant reunion for his fan clubs and includes a variety of activities and Elvis movies every night. Elvis Week culminates with a candlelight vigil over his grave.

Memphis Rock 'n' Soul Museum

Between Third and Fourth Streets in the FedEx Forum, the Memphis Rock 'n' Soul Museum (145 Lt. George Lee Ave., 901/543-0800, www.memphisrocknsoul.org) includes the only exhibition that Smithsonian Institution personnel have put together for permanent display outside of Washington, D.C., and is a fitting complement for Nashville's Country Music Hall of Fame and Museum. Even if visitors are only remotely interested in music, this should be their first stop.

In addition to various artifacts—guitars, clothing, and depictions of the rural life from which blues sprang, the museum shows footage of performers from Elvis to Otis Redding. Visitors can see Ike Turner's piano, B. B. King's guitar, and clothes worn—and no doubt shaken—by Jerry Lee Lewis.

where guitars are made

Gibson Beale Street Showcase

This guitar factory (www.gibsonshowcase.com, tours at 1 P.M. Sun.–Wed., 11 A.M., noon, 1 P.M., and 2 P.M. Thur.–Sat., $10 for ages 12 and over), where hollow-bodied electric guitars are manufactured. These guitars have produced some of the most famous music to emerge from Memphis: Scottie Moore played one with Elvis, and B. B. King plays a hollow-body named Lucille. The plant offers a 25-minute tour of the factory, a 325-seat café with live music, and various interactive exhibits. No one under 12 is admitted on the tour.

Soulsville

The original Stax Records building, an old movie theater, was demolished in 1989, and "Soulsville" is the name given to two distinct entities, a museum and a music academy. In a time when too many people think that Memphis music began and ended with Elvis Presley, this museum is long overdue.

"Soulsville" was never the official name of this neighborhood, but a term coined to put Memphis on the map when music was identified with

THE FOOTSTEPS OF THE KING

COURTESY OF MEMPHIS CONVENTION AND VISITORS

During and beyond his lifetime, Elvis sold an estimated one billion records, enough to give every single person in America four Elvis albums or singles. In the United States he had 148 albums or singles that sold enough copies to be certified gold, platinum, or multiplatinum.

Perhaps no one could withstand that kind of success and the resulting adulation. To do something as simple as go to a movie, Elvis had to rent a theater and see it at night. Through it all, according to those who knew him, Elvis re-

Elvis's grave

mained a person whose greatest pleasure was sitting around a piano and harmonizing with friends. Those wanting the definitive book on Elvis—and there are scores from which to choose—should seek out Peter Guralnick's two-volume biography. The first book, *Last Train to Memphis,* was published in 1994, and the second volume *Careless Love,* came out in late 1998. The first takes Elvis from birth until he enters the army, and the second chronicles the long decline. Both are outstanding.

Elvis died on August 16, 1977, at the age of 42, a victim of his lifestyle and, some argue, a management that primarily focused on money and kept him isolated. Fans began arriving within hours of his death, and Memphis and the country marveled at the devotion and sense of loss these people displayed. He was initially entombed in a mausoleum at Forest Hill Cemetery, but the presence of fans convinced the family to move his and his mother's remains to Graceland.

The strip mall across from Graceland almost

cities: the Philly sound for Philadelphia and Motown for Detroit.

The Stax Museum of American Soul Music (926 E. McLemore Ave., 901/942-7685, www.soulsvilleusa.com, Mar.–Oct. 9 A.M.–4 P.M. Mon.–Sat., 1–4 P.M. Sun.; Nov.–Feb. 9 A.M.–4 P.M. Mon.–Sat., 1–4 P.M. Sun.; $9 adults, $8 seniors, $6 kids 6–12) offers a look at the studio from which so many Memphis musical blessings flowed. Among the 2,000 exhibits here are Isaac Hayes's 1972 "Superfly" Cadillac, Otis Redding's favorite suede jacket, Booker T. Jones's organ, a replica of the old Studio A containing the original equipment, and a 100-year-old church. The 30' by 30' church, which symbolizes the religious roots of soul music, was moved

from Duncan, Mississippi, and contains the original pews, cast-iron stove, cornerstone, and Bible.

Stax Music Academy, at the same location, offers music lessons to Memphis's children. The Performing Arts Center hosts concerts, lectures, and other events.

Soulsville is less than three miles from Beale Street. To get there from downtown, go east on Union Avenue toward South 4th Street, turn right onto South Danny Thomas Boulevard, then make a slight left onto Mississippi Boulevard, then turn left onto East McLemore.

Sun Studio

Sun Studio (706 Union Ave., 901/521-0664,

overnight became a tacky series of Elvis souvenir shops, many of them hawking bootleg Elvis paraphernalia. The fans continued to come, especially on the anniversaries of his birth and death. Vernon Presley, Elvis's father, died in 1979, and the last relative to live in Graceland, Elvis's grandmother, Minnie Mae, died a year later.

Priscilla Presley, Elvis's wife, decided to open Graceland to the public, and the first visitors came on June 7, 1982. The next year, Graceland took over the shopping center across the street and, once the tenants' leases expired, transformed it into a major part of the Graceland complex, which has become a major tourist attraction in Memphis, with some 600,000 visitors per year. The White House is the only house in America that receives more visits.

A trip to Graceland is worth taking, if for no other reason than to see one's fellow pilgrims. Guests—whether punk rockers, beehive-coiffed fundamentalists, bus tours of senior citizens, or curious teenagers—tend to speak in hushed tones as they walk through the mansion and gaze into places such as the Jungle Room, a denlike room containing heavy, hand-carved wooden furniture upholstered in fake animal fur. They reverently look up close at one of Elvis's jumpsuits or marvel at the wall full of gold records. Visitors are treated with respect and not rushed through,

and the whole experience is unlike anything else in the country.

Beyond the gates of Graceland, you'll find some more modest sites from the King's personal history. As a teenager, Elvis lived at 185 Winchester Apt. 328, Lauderdale Courts, a subsidized housing complex. Saved from demolition in the 1990s by Elvis fans, the apartment is now part of UpTown Memphis (www.uptownmemphis.org), a development of 1,000 homes and apartments. The Presley apartment has been preserved, and is open to the public during Elvis events.

Elvis attended his senior prom at the Peabody Memphis Hotel and bought records at Poplar Tunes. The owners have maintained this downtown store as it looked in the '50s—complete with photos of Elvis. Sun Studio was the site of his first recording.

The Overton Park Shell was the site of a famous 1954 Elvis performance in which with just two songs he blew away Slim Whitman, the headliner. Elvis used to rent Libertyland Amusement Park, site of his last public appearance, for all-night fun with his girlfriends and cronies. His favorite ride was the Zippin Pippin, now the oldest operating wooden roller coaster in the country. One of the cars he used to ride has been preserved, and guests are welcome to sit in it and have their photos taken.

www.sunstudio.com, $8.50 adults, free for ages 12 and under) is where it all began. In 1954, Sam Phillips recorded a song a shy truck driver by the name of Elvis Presley gave to his mother as a birthday present. The studio attracts gawkers during the day and, at night, earnest artists who fervently hope that the old luck will strike again. The Irish group U2 came here in 1988 and laid down tracks that became five songs on *Rattle and Hum.*

Visitors—an astonishing number from Europe—get a 30-minute guided studio tour, which consists of stepping into the studio, hearing a spiel, and listening to clips of songs recorded here. Vintage instruments, microphones, and photos of the stars adorn the walls.

Sam Phillips Recording Service

After selling Elvis Presley's contract, Sam Phillips opened this new recording studio (at 639 Madison, 901/523-2251) in 1959 near Sun Studio. This three-story building is where songs such as Sam the Sham and the Pharoah's "Wooly Bully," Jerry Jeff Walker's "Mr. Bojangles," The Yardbirds' "I'm a Man," and The Amazing Rhythm Aces' "Third Rate Romance" were produced. Still owned by the Phillips family, the firm offers 24-track studio time at $75 per hour. The company is not set up for tours, but it is an inevitable stop for the most fervent Elvis pilgrims.

Center for Southern Folklore

The Center for Southern Folklore (Pembroke

THE STAX STORY

Who would have thought that a white brother and sister from a tiny rural community in West Tennessee would bring into being the greatest integrated recording studio of all time?

Jim Stewart and Estelle Axton wanted to get into the record business. They formed a company from the first two letters of their last names—Stax—and set up a studio east of Memphis. They fell in with a producer named Chips Moman, and it was he who in 1960 spotted the old Capital Theater for rent on East McLemore Street in Memphis. Paying $100 a month in rent, they converted it to a studio, and Stax Records opened its doors.

the Soulsville complex

One of the first people to walk in was Rufus Thomas, WDIA-AM disc jockey and musical man about town. He got Stax to record him and his 17-year-old daughter, Carla, singing a duet, "Cause I Love You." The song became a regional hit, and Carla's second song, "Gee Whiz," this time a solo, became a national hit. Stax was on its way.

Over the next 16 years, an amazing collection of people recorded some of Memphis's most memorable music at Stax. Here is a list of just a few of the artists and songs: Isaac Hayes, "Theme from *Shaft*"; Rufus Thomas, "Walking the Dog"; Otis Redding, "(Sittin' on) the Dock of the Bay"; Staples Singers, "Respect Yourself"; Sam and Dave, "Soul Man"; Johnnie Taylor's "Who's Making Love?"; Bar-Kays, "Soul Finger"; and many more.

Over a lifetime of 15 years, artists who recorded at Stax had 167 songs in the top 100 on the pop charts and even more, 243, on the rhythm and blues charts. Even more amazing was the fact that Stax was so racially integrated, in management as well as in the studio. Stax plowed money into the Memphis community not to gain good PR, but because it was the right thing to do.

The music business is not noted for sweetness and light. Dealings and misdealings with other record companies and lawsuits and financial problems led a federal bankruptcy court judge to close the doors on Stax on January 12, 1976. In 1977, the master tapes from Stax were sold for $1.3 million. Union Planters Bank deeded the Stax building to the Southside Church of God in Christ for $1, and in 1989 the Church demolished the building. Perhaps the last look at the old Stax building can be seen in *Mystery Train*, the Jim Jarmusch movie set in Memphis.

Estelle Axton died in February 2004, having lived long enough to see Soulsville become a reality and Stax Records once more assuming a place of honor in Memphis.

Memphis

This early 1920s photo of Beale Street musicians is on display in the Maurice "Fess" Hulbert Collection at the Center for Southern Folklore.

Square inside the Peabody Place complex, 901/525-3655, www.southernfolklore.com, 11 A.M.–7 P.M. Mon.–Sat, free admission), is impossible to categorize. A combination of museum, performance space, gallery, bookstore, gift shop, and magnet for interesting people, the center exists for "documenting and presenting the people and traditions of the South through films, books, records, exhibits, and public events." Exhibits blend into the gift shop so smoothly that visitors don't realize they are getting educated on Southern music, literature, and art. The center opens into a food court complete with stage, and there is no finer place in the city to eat lunch and hear live music.

W. C. Handy Museum

The W. C. Handy Museum (Beale and 4th Sts., 901/527-3427, 10 A.M.–5 P.M. Tues.–Sat., $3 adults, $2 children) is the small home of the man who published the first piece of music with "blues" in the title: "Memphis Blues," originally written as a campaign song. Born in Alabama,

Handy made his musical name in Memphis as a composer and bandleader. Long after he died, this house was moved to Beale Street as part of the district's gentrification.

HISTORIC HOMES

Burkle Estate/Slavehaven (826 N. 2nd St., 901/527-3427, 10 A.M.–4 P.M. Mon.–Sat., $6 adults, $4 children ages 4–17, $3 students) is actually a small house built in 1849 by German immigrant Jacob Burkle. While the house is not very impressive, legend holds that it served as a station on the Underground Railroad in slavery days. A secret room in the basement has a tunnel that may have provided escaped slaves with a path to freedom. Whether this is true or not, the exhibits provide a sobering look at the South's "peculiar institution." Kids and adults alike will be intrigued by the trap door and hidden room.

Magevney House (198 Adams Ave., 901/526-4464, www.memphismuseums.org, noon–4 P.M.

THE BEALE STREET STORY

The most famous street in Memphis, if not in the entire state of Tennessee, Beale Street begins at the Mississippi River bluff and runs east for a mile or so. In the days of segregation,
Beale Street was the center of African American life and culture. Here folks could get a haircut,
get drunk, get clothes, get saved, get life insurance, get lucky, and get entertained—or do
several simultaneously.

Beale Street enjoyed its heyday from about 1880 until the Depression. Aside from serving the
large black population in Memphis, Beale Street attracted many rural African Americans who
would put on their finest clothes and come to town on weekends. Church Park, the only
public park where blacks could go, was established near Beale Street and 4th Avenue.

The street is most celebrated for the musicians who flocked here. W. C. Handy played here often;
his home is now a museum. Others who stayed or played include B. B. King—who got his "B. B."
from being called the "Beale Street Boy"—Jimmy Lunceford, Furry Lewis, Albert King, Muddy Waters, Alberta Hunter, and Memphis Minnie McCoy. In the early 1950s, a young high school student named Elvis came here to buy clothes. His statue now stands on Beale Street as well.

But by the '50s, Beale Street was a shadow of what it had been. The gradual end of segregation no longer confined blacks to specific areas, and their dollars flowed elsewhere. Thousands
had gone north, and with them went many of the musicians. The greatest threat came from
urban renewal, which in Memphis took the form of bulldozers knocking down dilapidated housing, rooming houses, and the community surrounding the once-vibrant street.

Indeed, visitors to today's Beale Street Historic District will note that the street seems off by
itself, surrounded by vast parking lots and open spaces. In *Tennessee's Historic Landscapes,* Carroll Van West notes that 530 neighborhood buildings were demolished, leaving only about
65 to carry on the legacy of Beale Street.

Beale Street began its comeback in 1983 when millions of dollars flowed into restoration projects. The city of Memphis, learning from Graceland the blessings that throngs
of music lovers can bring, saw Beale Street as a means of bringing people downtown again.
The city has relentlessly promoted the place, maintained a strong police presence here,
and converted the urban-renewal plains of destruction into parking lots.

While locals sometimes feel like Beale Street has become too much like New Orleans's
Bourbon Street, out-of-towners love it. A. Schwab Dry Goods lends a folksy look at shopping in a time long gone. Church Park is a good place to sit down. Then it's on to the
Beale Street Baptist Church, and the W. C. Handy Home. At night, Beale Street offers
several places to eat and catch some music. Blues City Cafe, B. B. King's, The New
Daisy, and Rum Boogie Cafe all feature live entertainment. A statue of W. C. Handy, the
father of it all, stands in Handy Park.

The "revitalization" of Beale Street (and parts of downtown generally) and its transfor-
mation into a tourist destination are astonishing and even disorienting to anyone who remembers it not only as a barren wasteland (deserted, boarded-up buildings, where there
were buildings) but also as literally nonexistent—the asphalt itself torn up, leaving nothing but the earth underneath, no "street" at all. It would probably be incomprehensible to
anyone who knew the city in the early part of the 20th century. Some purists insist that the
music there and elsewhere in the city today isn't "authentic," just a Disney version of the
blues. But B. B. King has his own club now, and who could be so ungenerous as not to wish
him that and any other good thing he could possibly have? These same people, a few years
back, were lamenting that nobody was paying any attention at all to the music. And
they would maintain that no outsider ever truly experiences the "real" Memphis. In the sort
of insular parochialism that is certainly not unique to Memphis, or even the South, they
would say that the real spirit can't be captured.

ELMWOOD CEMETERY

The rural cemetery movement began with the establishment of Père Lachaise Cemetery in Paris in 1804. The thinking behind this approach was that cemeteries should be pleasant places to go, with trees and landscaping, and where extravagant or simple mausoleums and markers could honor the dead.

Memphis's version of Père Lachaise is Elmwood Cemetery, which was created in 1852 with the purchase of 40 acres and later expanded to 80 acres. It is the final resting place of Civil War generals, governors, madams, jazz musicians, and all manner of people, 70,000 in all.

For the visitor, Elmwood offers a rare chance to see how famous Memphians were honored by the people who loved them and knew them best. Robert Church, the South's first African American millionaire, rests in a dignified mausoleum in the black section of the cemetery. Not far from him is the grave of big bandleader Jimmy Lunceford.

Eighteen Confederate generals sleep here, along with two of their Union counterparts. Only the Hollywood Cemetery in Richmond, Virginia, has more Confederate generals—22. A memorial to the wreck of the *Sultana* commemorates the 1,647 victims of America's worst maritime disaster.

When the yellow fever epidemics were at their worst in the 1870s, Elmwood received 50 bodies a day. There were not enough time and manpower to dig individual graves, so victims—rich, poor, whatever—were buried in trenches in what was called No Man's Land. Of the estimated 8,500 Memphians who died of yellow fever, 2,500 of them are buried here.

Other residents of Elmwood include Felicia Thornton Shover, a spy for the Confederacy; E. H. Crump, the longtime political boss of Memphis; Stephen Rice Phelan, the last resident of the Hunt-Phelan Home; Colonel Jeffrey Forrest, brother of Nathan Bedford Forrest; and Edward Pembroke, the Peabody Memphis Hotel duck master.

Elmwood welcomes visitors but reminds them that this is an operating cemetery with several services a week. Guests should conduct themselves in a manner that respects the living and the dead. Elmwood is open 8 A.M.–4:30 P.M. daily. The visitors center is on the left as you pull in, and the people there will cheerfully sell guests a $5 map of the grounds. Visitors can also rent an audiotape for $5. Guided tours are offered twice in the spring and twice in the fall. For information about these tours, call 901/774-3212, or visit www.elmwoodcemetery.org.

To get to Elmwood from downtown, go east on Union to I-240. Go south to the Lamar Avenue exit. Go west on Lamar, passing Pauline Street on the right. Turn left on Dudley Street, which leads right over the railroad tracks and into Elmwood.

For those so enchanted with Elmwood that they would like to spend eternity here, the cemetery has approximately 20,000 spaces left. They range $1,100–2,500.

Fri.–Sat., free admission but donations appreciated) was once owned by Memphis's first Irish immigrant; today it's one of the oldest buildings left in the city. No Southern mansion, it is a relatively small house that is the site of the first Mass celebrated in the city and features 1830s period furnishings.

Mallory-Neely House (652 Adams Ave., 901/523-1484, www.memphismuseums.org, 10 A.M.–4 P.M. Tues.–Sat., 1 P.M.–4 P.M. Sun., $5.50 adults, $5 seniors, $4.50 students) shows how Memphians with money spent it. This mansion was built about 1852, extensively remodeled in the 1880s and 1890s, and is decorated with original furnishings.

Woodruff-Fontaine House (680 Adams Ave., 901/526-1469, 10 A.M.–3:30P.M. Mon.–Sat.; 1–3:30P.M. Sun.,$5 adults, $4 seniors, $2 students) stands beside the Mallory-Neely House in the Victorian Village Historic District. This mansion was erected in 1870, has 16 rooms, and contains period furnishings and

THE HUNT-PHELAN HOME

East of the lights and glitter at 533 Beale Street stands the Hunt-Phelan Home, the most historic house in the city. Now a bed-and-breakfast, restaurant, and center of a condo development, it was built between 1828 and 1840, and over the years hosted presidents Andrew Jackson, Martin Van Buren, Andrew Johnson, and Jefferson Davis. When Union troops came to town during the Civil War, they commandeered the house. One of the unverifiable legends surrounding the place is that General Grant planned the campaign against Vicksburg, Mississippi, while sitting at the library table. When Grant left, a series of Union officers including William T. Sherman stayed there, and the kitchen was used as a hospital for Union soldiers. Immediately after the war the house was used as one of the first Freedmen's Bureau's schools for freed slaves.

the majestic Hunt-Phelan home

The old home stayed in the same family for a remarkable 170 years, and was opened to the public for several years. Attendance, alas, was not enough to cover costs, and the furnishings of the house were sold at auction. For more info, see www.huntphelanestate.com.

art technologies combined with artifacts and documents, the museum tells the story of the civil rights movement and presents a vivid picture of discrimination. A good example of this is a 1950s-era bus in which, when visitors sit down, they hear harsh voices commanding them to move to the back. If the would-be bus riders stay in their seats, they will feel and hear the rapping of a cane on the seats' back. The tour culminates with a re-creation of the hotel room where Dr. King was staying, and visitors can look out on the balcony where he died.

The museum has acquired the rooming house across the street from which James Earl Ray fired the shot that killed Dr. King, as well as the rifle that fired the bullet. The district attorney of Shelby County turned over 39 boxes of materials related to the trial of James Earl Ray, and these are now available to scholars. The museum is a sobering place, but one that should be on anyone's short list of things to see in Memphis.

National Ornamental Metal Museum

The National Ornamental Metal Museum (374 Metal Museum Dr., 901/774-6380, www.metalmuseum.org, 10 A.M.–5 P.M. Tues.–Sat., noon–5 P.M. Sun., $4 adults, $3 seniors, and $2 kids ages 5–18) pays tribute to metalworking. This place displays items varying in size and complexity from handmade nails to a beautiful outdoor iron gazebo. Visiting artists do their work while guests watch, and exhibits change from time to time.

The museum occupies a historic site. Across the street from the museum are the Chickasaw Heritage Mounds, which, according to local legend, is where Spanish explorer Hernando de Soto first saw the Mississippi River on May 21, 1541. During the Civil War, the Union's Fort Pickering was located here, and one of the Chicasaw mounds was excavated in order to install a coastal

changing exhibits. Occasionally special events such as mystery dinners and plays take place in the house.

MUSEUMS

National Civil Rights Museum

The National Civil Rights Museum (450 Mulberry St., 901/521-9699, www.civilrightsmuseum.org, $10 adults, $8 seniors and students, $6.50 children ages 4–17) is in the Lorraine Motel, where Dr. Martin Luther King Jr. was felled by an assassin's bullet. Using state-of-the-

Memphis

The National Civil Rights Museum preserves a lunch counter sit-in.

artillery battery. Medical research on yellow fever was conducted here in the 1870s, and a U.S. Marine Hospital was built here in the late 1800s and added to by the WPA in the 1930s.

Art

The **Art Museum of the University of Memphis** in the Communications and Fine Arts Building (3750 Norriswood, 901/678-2224, www.people.memphis.edu/~artmuseum, 9 A.M.–5 P.M. Mon.–Sat., free) displays Egyptian and West African art. The chief example of the former is the mummy Iret-Iruw. Reservations for tours should be made two weeks in advance. Other galleries exhibit contemporary works.

Dixon Gallery and Gardens (4339 Park Ave., 901/761-5250, www.dixon.org, 10A.M.–4P.M. Tues.–Fri., 10A.M.–5 P.M. Sat., 1–5 P.M. Sun., $5 adults, $4 seniors, free for students and children) features collections of French and American impressionism, 18th-century German porcelain, and European and American pewter. The gallery

hosts traveling exhibits as well. The gardens consist of 17 acres containing a formal English garden, a woodland garden, and a cuttings garden. The Dixon is in East Memphis on Park Avenue, between Getwell and Perkins, across from Audubon Park.

Memphis Brooks Museum of Art, in Overton Park, (1934 Poplar Ave., 901/544-6200, www.brooksmuseum.org, 10 A.M.–5 P.M. Mon.–Sat., 11:30 A.M.–5 P.M. Sun., $5 adults, $4 seniors, $2 students with ID and kids 7–17) is the oldest art museum in the state and one of the larger ones in the South. Given to the city by the widow of Samuel Brooks in 1915, the museum displays pieces by Pierre-Auguste Renoir, Thomas Hart Benton, and Auguste Rodin along with paintings, sculpture, prints, drawings, photographs, antiquities such as Greek vases, and African and Latin American art. The museum also offers lectures and film and performance series. The permanent collection is too large to display all at once, so exhibits are changed from time to time, and the museum also hosts traveling exhibitions.

COURTESY OF MEMPHIS CONVENTION AND VISITORS CENTER

Memphis Brooks Museum of Art

Peabody Place Museum, on the concourse level of the Peabody Place complex, (119 S. Main St., 901/523-8603, www.belz.com/museum, 10 A.M.–5:30 P.M. Tues.–Fri., noon–5 P.M. Sat.–Sun., $5 adults, $4.50 seniors, $4 children) is a collection of Asian and European art. The best reason to go there, however, is the jade carvings, which are both massive and intricate.

Science

Chucalissa Archaeological Museum (1987 Indian Village Dr., 901/785-3160, http://cas.memphis.edu/chucalissa, 9 A.M.–5 P.M. Tues.–Sat., 1 P.M. 5 P.M. Sun.–Mon., $5 adults, $3 seniors and children) is run by the anthropology department of the University of Memphis, and sheds light on the original residents of the bluff. On the site of an actual Native American village, where an estimated 800–1,000 people lived from A.D. 900–1500, buildings have been reconstructed to demonstrate life in the 1400s. At various times of the year, members of the nearby Choctaw tribe hold events at Chucalissa.

Memphis Pink Palace Museum and Planetarium (3050 Central Ave., 901/320-6320, www.memphismuseums.org, 9 A.M.–5 P.M.

Mon.–Thurs., 9 A.M.–9 P.M. Fri.–Sat., noon–6 P.M. Sun., $8 adults, $7.50 seniors, and $5 children) began in 1923 as the palatial home of Clarence Saunders, the founder of Piggly Wiggly, the nation's first self-serve grocery store. Unfortunately for him, Saunders went broke and the city took his house. The city's best natural history museum, this complex contains fossils, rocks and minerals, a planetarium, and an IMAX theater. Cultural aspects of Memphis and the surrounding area are on exhibit as well. One interesting display is the Society of Entrepreneurs, which pays tribute to local business folk such as the late Kemmons Wilson, founder of Holiday Inns, and Fred Smith, who launched FedEx.

Specialty

The Children's Museum of Memphis (2525 Central Ave., 901/458-2678 or 901/320-3170, www.cmom.com, 9 A.M.–5 P.M. Tues.–Sat., $7 adults, $5 seniors and children 12 and under) recently underwent a $6 million expansion and offers delightful hands-on fun and learning. Kids can pretend to be air-traffic controllers in a 20-foot tower, manipulate a 55-foot model of the

Mississippi River with locks and dams, and climb like rats through Skyscraper, a multistory maze. Unlike some children's museums, which delight the youngsters yet bore anyone over 14, this place is fun for adults as well. Kids must be accompanied by an adult.

The **Downtown Police Station Museum** (159 Beale St., 901/525-9800) probably has the best security system of any museum. This free museum inside a police station displays an old jail cell, police uniforms, confiscated weapons, photos of "Machine Gun" Kelly, and the extradition order for James Earl Ray, convicted assassin of Martin Luther King Jr. It's open 24 hours a day.

The **Fire Museum of Memphis** (118 Adams St., 901/320-5650, www.firemuseum.com, 9 A.M.–5 P.M. Mon.–Sat., $6 adults, $4 seniors and military, $5 children) occupies the refurbished 1910 Fire Engine House Number 1. The museum's displays include equipment, artifacts, uniforms, and photos about firefighting.

MUD ISLAND

Mud Island was a gift to Memphis from the river, which began depositing sediments early in the last century. No one in the Civil War ever saw Mud Island. According to the 1939 *WPA Guide to Tennessee,* the island formed in 1910 when a Spanish-American War gunboat headed upstream had to anchor in Memphis for six to eight months to await high water. As it sat there, an eddy deposited sand and gravel against the hull, and when the boat left town, the deposits stayed and grew to the point that the island threatened the port of Memphis. Until the Mississippi was dammed upstream, Mud Island was subject to flooding, and between floods thickets of willow trees sheltered grateful moonshiners.

The island offers a 52-acre park (800/507-6507 or 901/576-7241, www.mudisland.com, 10 A.M.–5 P.M. Tues.–Sun., $8 adults, $6 seniors, $5 children) with several attractions for visitors. It is open spring, summer, and autumn (generally April through October), with separate schedules for each season. Call ahead for specifics including all the attractions including the monorail to the

island. The park includes the Mississippi River Museum; River Walk, a five-block-long scale model of the river; gift shops, and restaurants. To get to Mud Island, catch the monorail at Front and Adams Streets.

River Walk is a five-block-long scale rendition—30 inches to one mile—of the 1,238-mile-long Mississippi River, complete with flowing water. Would-be Paul Bunyans can stroll upstream or downstream, learning about the river and its cities and points of interest along the way. The "Gulf of Mexico" in this model is a swimming pool.

The Mississippi River Museum has 18 galleries containing displays on Memphis and regional history from prehistoric times to the present. Among the offerings are 35 scale models of riverboats—flatboats, keelboats, packet steamers, ironclads, and so on. Some of these models are six to eight feet long. The museum has full-sized replicas of parts of boats such as a city-class Civil War ironclad and a packet boat, complete with grand salon, pilothouse, and foredeck, through which visitors can walk—kids love it. And music lovers will appreciate the way the museum traces the evolution of music from field hollers to blues to ragtime to rock. Exhibits include one of Elvis's performance jumpsuits and a replica of a honky-tonk.

On its north end, Mud Island is home to more than 4,000 residents, many of them in Harbor Town, a 135-acre mixture of houses, apartments, condos, and small shops that is Memphis's prime example of the New Urbanism, a growing belief that neighborhoods should be pedestrian-friendly and put less emphasis on automobiles. The houses have front porches to encourage interaction among residents. People who live here have wonderful views of the river, the Memphis skyline, and the Hernando de Soto bridge.

HOUSES OF WORSHIP

The Beale Street Baptist Church (379 Beale St., 901/522-9073) was the first church in Memphis built by blacks for a black congregation; it demonstrates the economic power generated by former slaves right after the war. People still worship here, and visitors are welcome.

St. Peter's Church (190 Adams Ave., 901/527-8282) occupies a 19th-century Gothic Revival building built in 1843 next to the Magevney Home.

Behind St. Peter's Church is the **St. Martin de Porres** (901/578-2643, www.stmartinshrine .org) just a couple of blocks off Front Street. St. Martin is the patron saint of social justice and race relations. Born of a Spanish nobleman and a black Panamanian woman, St. Martin was the first saint of mixed European, African, and Hispanic descent. He lived in Peru and died in 1639, and was canonized in 1962. This chapel has a piece of his bone encased in a cross.

The chapel contains a 1930 statue of St. Martin as well as copper and enamel icons depicting scenes from his life. Mass is celebrated at noon Tuesday–Friday.

Mason Temple Church of God in Christ (930 Mason St., 901/578-3800) is the headquarters of the Church of God in Christ, the largest African American Pentecostal denomination in the country. The temple, which was constructed in 1940, seats 7,500. Services are no longer held regularly, but people still come to see where the Reverend Martin Luther King Jr. gave his final sermon, the "I've been to the Mountaintop" speech. No tours are offered.

The **Church of the Full Gospel Tabernacle** (787 Hale Rd., 901/396-9192) is home to the

BIG-TIME BAPTISTRY

Outside of Memphis, in the suburb of Cordova, is the largest Southern Baptist church in the country—some believe the largest church of any stripe. **Bellevue Baptist Church** (2000 Appling Rd., 901/347-2000, www.bellevue.org) employs a staff of 200 people and claims more than 27,000 members. The 370-acre complex can be seen from I-40.

Adrian Rogers, the head minister at Bellevue for 32 years—he retired in 2004—was a three-time president of the 14-million member Southern Baptist Convention, the largest Protestant denomination in the country. Rogers, first elected president in 1979, pulled the Southern Baptists in a conservative direction, and was followed by an unbroken string of conservative leaders. In 2000, he led the effort to change the Baptist Faith and Message, a mission statement for the Convention, to declare the Bible free of errors.

As related in a 2003 *Memphis Commercial Appeal* interview by Tom Bailey Jr., Rogers has a progressive side as well. Early in Rogers's ministry at Bellevue, a young African American man came forward during the altar call. When members were asked to vote on accepting him to membership, an elderly woman raised her hand to object. The church was dead quiet, and Rogers invited the objecting person to come forward and stand with him and the would-be new member. "Tell me," he began, "why you don't want this man to be a member of our church?"

The parishioner said something to the effect that "they have their own churches."

Rogers told her and the congregation that if the young man was not voted into membership, "you've lost yourself a pastor." There was no more objection to minority members, and Bellevue now has black leaders and Sunday School teachers.

Sunday worship services at Bellevue take place at 8, 9:30, and 11 A.M. Approximately 5,500 people attend the 9:30 service, and 4,000 come at 11. While there is no dress code, an estimated 75 percent of the men sitting in the pews wear a tie. Services can also be seen on television at 9 and 11 A.M. on Memphis stations.

Visitors can also tour the Bellevue complex from 9 A.M. until 3:30 P.M. Monday through Saturday. Tours last from 30 minutes to one hour, and there is no charge. Groups of 15 or more should call 901/347-5444 ahead of time.

Reverend Al Green, whose talent took him to the top of the soul charts with songs such as "Take Me to the River," "Tired of Being Alone," and "Let's Stay Together." He found a higher calling, however, and gave up—well, mostly—show business for the straight and narrow. Visitors are welcome, but they should remember that this is a church and dress and act appropriately.

In an interview in the *Memphis Flyer*, Chris Herrington asked Reverend Green how he feels about tourists and curiosity-seekers coming to his church. He replied:

I don't get despondent about that. We're on the tourist map. People come to see Elvis and they come to see Reverend Al Green in the sanctuary. . . . But when they come, while they're here, our job is to be ready so that we can give them that particular religious view. With all due respect to the Elvis people and his family, our King, the one that we were told about, rose again. Memphis barbecue is good food, but you can't live off of that bread like you can this other bread.

Reverend Green's church is south of Memphis. To get there from Graceland, head south on Elvis Presley Boulevard for 1.4 miles to Hale Road. Go right and drive 0.7 mile. Visitors bound for the church should eat a good breakfast; church begins at 11 A.M., by noon this preacher is just getting warmed up, and services usually last three hours.

LANDMARKS

The Peabody Memphis Hotel

The Peabody Memphis Hotel (149 Union Ave., 901/529-4000, www.peabodymemphis.com) is the grande dame of Memphis hotels, a place once said to be the northern terminus of the Mississippi Delta. What began as a 1930s drunken afternoon prank—putting live ducks in the lobby fountain—has become a twice-daily exercise with ceremony exceeded only by Masonic rites. At 11 A.M. the ducks march in, and at 5 P.M. they march out. It's as simple as that, and

visitors can subsequently retire to one of the Peabody's watering holes for libations.

The Peabody Memorabilia Room, near the northwest corner of the mezzanine beside the Alonzo Locke Room, contains old menus, photos, tableware, and original documents donated by guests of the hotel. Together these offer a look at high society of the Old South and a grand old hotel.

The Pyramid

The Pyramid, (1 Auction Ave., 901/521-9675, www.pyramidarena.com, open non-event days for tours), is arguably the most distinctive such multipurpose building in the country. This 32-story pyramid—the third-largest in the world, behind a couple in Egypt—contains a 22,500-seat arena used for sports events, concerts, and other gatherings. Tours go through the building, through sports locker rooms, and dressing rooms for star performers. Because of demands on the building, tour hours vary and must consist of groups of 15 or more. When the Vancouver Grizzlies became the Memphis Grizzlies, they demanded a new arena. FedEx Forum was obligingly built, and now the Pyramid is somewhat at loose ends, for Memphis doesn't seem big enough to support two arenas.

Rhodes College

If you asked a Hollywood set designer to come up with an idyllic college campus, this is the one you would get. Located across the street from the north side of Overton Park, this 100-acre campus is dotted with beautiful collegiate Gothic buildings. Palmer Hall Cloister looks as if Harry Potter might stroll through at any minute. The centerpiece of the college is the 140-foot high Halliburton Tower, built in memory of Richard Halliburton, an adventurer who disappeared while attempting to cross the Pacific Ocean in a junk. The tower contains a five-ton, seven-foot wide bronze bell that bongs out the time.

Rhodes College is a liberal arts college with 1,556 students. It began in Clarksville, but moved to Memphis in 1925 as Southwestern at Memphis. The name was changed to Rhodes College in 1984.

During the school year, visitors can tour the campus, weekdays 9 A.M.–2 P.M., and 10–11:30A.M. on Saturdays. Summer tours are at 10 A.M. and 2 P.M., weekdays only. Contact Campus Services at 901/843-3000 for further information.

Delectables

Agricenter International (7777 Walnut Grove Rd., 901/757-7777, www.agricenter.org, 8 A.M.–4:30 P.M. Mon.–Fri.) consists of a demonstration farm and exhibition facilities that have frequent shows open to the public. The Red Barn operates as a farmers' market from May well into December. There is also a RV park ($18–22 daily) with more than 300 lots and electrical and water hookups, including showers.

Coors Belle Hospitality Center at Coors Memphis Brewery (5151 E. Raines Rd., 901/368-BEER [368-2337], www.coors.com, open noon–4 P.M. Thurs.–Sat., free) gives guests a look at how this Colorado-based elixir is packaged. After the tour, adults can quaff two choices of Coors products.

St. Jude Children's Research Hospital

A young entertainer with seven dollars in his pocket got down on his knees in a Detroit church before a statue of St. Jude, the patron saint of lost causes, and asked the saint to "show me my way in life." At another turning point in his life, he again prayed to the saint and pledged to someday build a shrine to St. Jude.

The young man was Danny Thomas, whom those of a certain age remember as the star of a popular television show called *Make Room For Daddy*, an episode of which was the pilot for *The Andy Griffith Show*. In the 1950s, he began to look for a way to make good on his pledge and, though he had no connection to Memphis, he decided to build a children's hospital here. Thomas, who came from a Lebanese family, joined other Arab Americans in raising money to help fund a research hospital devoted to curing catastrophic diseases in children of the world.

The hospital (332 N. Lauderdale, 901/495-3661, www.stjude.org) opened its doors in 1962 and focuses on pediatric cancer, other serious diseases, and biomedical research. St. Jude treats approximately 4,500 children each year from around the world regardless of race, religion, creed, or ability to pay. Thomas died in 1991, having lived to see his hospital—and his pledge to St. Jude—become one of the heart-warming stories in the country.

The American Lebanese Syrian Associated Charities (ALSAC) has full responsibility for all of the hospital's fundraising efforts. At the pavilion, visitors can tour a museum featuring various aspects and memorabilia of Thomas's life, and then visit his gravesite. For a tour of the hospital, call 901/578-2041.

CRYSTAL SHRINE GROTTO

The most extraordinary piece of folk art in Memphis has to be the Crystal Shrine Grotto (5668 Poplar Ave., 901/683-4003), the focal point of Memorial Park Cemetery. Concrete has been fashioned into realistic-looking logs, benches, bridges, and other shapes that depict various landscapes described in the book of Genesis.

Visitors approach the Grotto by crossing a bridge that looks for all the world to be made of logs and entwined tree branches. The thick planks appear to be held together by large nails, and the grain of the wood is clearly visible—yet there isn't a piece of wood on the entire bridge. All of it—even the nails—is concrete.

On the other side, more wonders await—ones that will challenge people who think they know the Bible or the Torah. Inside the Cave of Machpelah, or Abraham's tomb, two tombs rest under what looks like a roof of hand-hewn logs. Then there's Abraham's Oak, which looks like an enormous stump. Again, everything—even the trash cans—is concrete.

The centerpiece is the Grotto itself, a man-made cave extending about 25 feet into a hillside. Hunks of quartz line the cavern, which contains 10 niches depicting scenes from the life of Christ: the Transfiguration, Zaccheus up the tree, the Crucifixion, the Resurrection, and so on. There are literally tons of crystals here.

© JEFF BRADLEY

the bridge at the Crystal Shrine Grotto

This remarkable place came in about 1924 when E. Clovis Hinds bought 54 acres for a cemetery. He spent the rest of his life improving it. In 1935, he hired Dionicio Rodriquez, an itinerant Mexican artist, to create the Grotto and the scenes around it. Rodriquez made Hinds's visions come to life, and together they created a place unlike anywhere else in the state, if not the entire South.

To get there from downtown, go east on Poplar Avenue, or take I-240 to the Poplar Avenue west exit. Don't take the Germantown route. You can see Memorial Park from the off-ramp. It is open 8 A.M.–4:30 P.M. Admission is free.

SIGHTSEEING TOURS

The absolute best way to see Memphis and the surrounding area, or anywhere, for that matter, is with a knowledgeable local. Memphis is blessed with services that give the discerning visitor a wonderful look at the city and its music.

Sherman Willmott, who founded Shangri-La Records, and writes *Kreature Comforts' Lowlife Guide to Memphis*, a wonderfully quirky guide to Memphis and the Delta, now offers **Ultimate**

Memphis Rock 'n' Roll Tours (901/359-3102, www.memphisrocktour.com). A 10-passenger van picks up visitors at downtown hotels and whisks them on customized one-hour, three-hour, or all-day outings. The one-hour tour begins at $50 for two people, with additional participants at $10. For three hours, rates begin with $150 for two people, and add $50 for others.

For people who want to become part of the Memphis scene while receiving their schooling, **American Dream Safari** (901/527-8870, www.americandreamsafari.com) offers tours in a 1955 Cadillac with Tad Pierson. He offers tours of Memphis or, for the more adventurous, drives into the Mississippi Delta to the birthing room of the blues. The tours have wonderful names: Juke Joint Full of Blues, Drive by Shooting, Delta Day Trip, and Road Therapy. They range in cost from $75 to $225 per person, and all take place in a show-stopping set of wheels.

Heritage Tours (280 Hernando St., 901/527-3427, www.heritagetoursmemphis.com, 9 A.M.–5 P.M. Mon.–Fri.) is the first African American–owned tour company in the state of Tennessee, and it offers perhaps the best historical tour of

Memphis. The three-hour tour passes or stops at 30 or more historical sites, including Beale Street, Church Park, and many lesser-known locations. Unlike the official tourist publications, these guides do not ignore the Confederate history of Memphis. "We're glad they lost," said one guide, "but it's history nonetheless." Book reservations by calling the telephone number above or by going to the W. C. Handy House on Beale Street at 4th Street.

Germania Travel Consultant (3482 Fox Hunt Dr., 901/794-0347, www.germaniatravaltour-guide.bigstep.com) offers English, German, and French language tours of Memphis and the surrounding area. Customers can choose from walking or escorted tours.

The boats of **Memphis Queen Line Riverboats** (at 45 Riverside Dr. at Monroe Ave., 800/221-6197 or 901/527-5694, www.memphisqueen.com, $12–40) offer rides that include sightseeing cruises, dinner cruises, and daylong excursions to Helena, Arkansas.

Recreation

Tom Lee Park, on the riverfront south of Beale Street, commemorates the 1925 heroism of Tom Lee, an African American laborer who took a small boat and rescued 32 people from a sinking steamboat. Lee made repeated trips to the stricken craft, even though he could not swim.

GARDENS AND NATURE CENTERS

Memphis Botanic Garden (750 Cherry Rd., Audubon Park, 901/685-1566, www.memphis-botanicgarden.com, 9 A.M.–6 P.M. Mon.–Sat., 11 A.M.–6 P.M. Sun., $5 adults, $4 seniors, $3 children, free for ages under 6, free 12:30 P.M. until closing Tues.) is a 96-acre park of outdoor gardens featuring beautiful flowers, exotic plants and trees, and sculptures.

Lichterman Nature Center (5992 Quince Rd., 901/767-7322, www.memphismuseums.org, 9 A.M.–4 P.M. Mon.–Thurs., 9 A.M.–5 P.M. Fri.–Sat., noon–5 P.M. Sun., $6 adults, $5.50 seniors, $4.50 children ages 3–12, free Tues. afternoons) is a great place to learn about wildlife and four kinds of West Tennessee habitat: forest, field, marsh, and lake. New facilities include a visitors center, a special events pavilion, and a boardwalk. Various trails lead through the 65 acres, and guided tours take place on weekends.

MEMPHIS ZOO

The Memphis Zoo (2000 Galloway, 901/276-WILD [276-9453], www.memphiszoo.org, 9 A.M.–5 P.M. every day, $10 adults, $9 seniors, $6 children ages 2–11) has spent $30 million providing habitats such as Primate Canyon, Cat Country, Animals of the Night, and so on. These habitats are designed to reflect cultural elements of the animals' native countries. Thus North African species are shown around what looks like an abandoned temple à la Indiana Jones.

OVERTON PARK

The 355-acre Overton Park (Poplar Ave. and East Pkwy. N., www.overtonparkshell.org) is a much-beloved place, home to the zoo, the Brooks Museum of Art, and the famous band shell. That shell, now called the Raoul Wallenberg Shell in honor of the World War II hero, was built in 1936 by the WPA, and was the first place that Elvis played professionally. The 19-year-old opened for Slim Whitman and Billy Walker and played "That's Alright," and "Blue Moon of Kentucky." The crowd ate up his nervous jiggling, which he did even more energetically when he was called to the stage again and—having no other songs prepared—rocked through an uptempo version of "Blue Moon of Kentucky" all over again.

For all its urbanity, Overton Park is home to 100 acres of virgin hardwood forest. Some 475 of its trees are more than 10 feet in circumference, and some were growing there when Mem-

A MOST UNUSUAL BASEBALL OPERATION

The **Memphis Redbirds** baseball team is unique among American sports teams. Both the team and the AutoZone Park where it plays are owned by a non-profit organization, the Memphis Redbirds Baseball Foundation. This foundation puts all its earnings into two organizations: Returning Baseball to the Inner City (RBI) and Sports Teams Returning in the Public Education System (STRIPES).

RBI runs camps in Memphis during the summer at 12 sites for boys and girls ages 6 to 14, and STRIPES organizes middle school–aged children into baseball or softball teams. Both programs use sports to teach life skills to young Memphians.

AutoZone Park, downtown Memphis

Dean and Kristi Jernigan were the husband and wife who brought the Redbirds to Memphis. When the deal was announced, Dean was quoted as saying, "There's so much greed in professional sports already, and that greed stands between the fan and the team. We just said on the front end of this that we would not be taking any money out of this, forever."

phis was founded. The national champion Shumard Oak measures almost 21 feet in circumference.

When federal planners laid out I-40 across Tennessee, they intended that the road would cut Overton Park in two. They did not count on the opposition of Memphians, who brought suit and fought the government all the way to the Supreme Court. The 1971 case, *Citizens to Preserve Overton Park v. Volpe,* is still studied in environmental law classes, and I-40 does not go through the park.

SHELBY FARMS

At 4,500 acres, Shelby Farms (901/382-0235, www.shelbycountytn.gov) in the eastern part of the city is the largest urban park in the country. This place used to be a penal farm for the edification of prisoners, but now offers hiking trails that wind through hardwood forests and orchards; a 60-acre lake ideal for windsurfing, canoeing, and sailing; a herd of bison; and picnic areas. The wildlife here includes an estimated

217 species of birds. To get there, take the Walnut Grove road exit off the easternmost part I-240 and go east to the third stop light. You will see the park on both sides of the road.

SPORTS

The **Memphis Redbirds** (901/721-6000, tickets $5–118) are unusual in that they are the only professional baseball team run on a nonprofit basis. Part of the profits from the team are used to teach baseball and softball to Memphis children. The AAA team of the St. Louis Cardinals organization, the Redbirds play at AutoZone Park (3rd St. and Union Ave.); it seats only 14,320, ensuring a good seat for everyone.

The **Memphis Grizzlies,** (www.nba.com/ grizzlies,) a National Basketball Association team, opened their first season in the fall of 2001. They play at the FedEx Forum, which is between Third and Fourth Streets and Lt. George W. Lee and Linden Avenue (one-half block south of Beale Street). For tickets, call 800/462-2849 or go to www.ticketmaster.com.

The **Memphis Riverkings** (662/342-1755, www.riverkings.com) play AA level in the Central Hockey League. Games take place in the DeSoto Civic Center in Southhaven October–March.

Entertainment and Events

NIGHTLIFE

The following restaurants and nightclubs were diligently researched by Fredric Koeppel, the restaurant and book critic for *The Commercial Appeal* in Memphis. He writes nationally about wine, locally about classical music and art exhibitions, and, when it comes to the finer things in life, singlehandedly anchors the northern end of the Mississippi Delta.

At **B.B King's Blues Club,** (Beale St. at 2nd St., 901/524-5464,) the legendary namesake blues-meister himself shows up two or three times a year. Otherwise, various local or nationally known groups provide the music. The club is open daily, serves lunch and dinner, and charges a cover for big-name groups.

Blue Monkey (2012 Madison Ave., 901/272-2583) offers live music Wednesday–Friday nights, a full menu of excellent pizzas and other bar foods, and a beautiful, old wooden bar salvaged from a shed. There's another, new Blue Monkey way downtown (529 S. Front, 901/527/6665).

The theme at **Club 152** (152 Beale St., 901/544-7011) is dance, dance, dance and party till you drop. Do you need to know anything else?

Earnestine and Hazel's (531 S. Main St., 901/523-9754) across from the renovated Central Station, has served as grocery store, a restaurant, and a whorehouse, all within living memory. Now there's no getting in the place after midnight on weekends. Best to disguise oneself as someone between the ages of, oh, 22 and 23.

Glass Onion Bar & Grill (903 S. Cooper St., 901/274-5151, lunch and dinner daily), housed in an old brick bungalow, succeeds where others have failed because of great bar food, brash atmosphere, plentiful indoor and outdoor seating, and cool bands on weekends.

Hi-Tone Café (1913 Poplar Ave., 901/278-8663) drags a relentless stream of local, regional and national groups through its doors every night. **Jillian's** (150 Peabody Pl., 901/543-8800) may be in a huge, bright, downtown mall, but its huge, bright, clamorous, flashy party atmosphere demands attention from its hordes of fans.

Newby's (539 S. Highland St., 901/452-8408), near the University of Memphis, serves food and offers a bewildering variety of live music, Wednesday–Saturday. The kitchen stays open very late. There's a cover charge for bands.

P&H Café (1532 Madison Ave., 901/726-0906) offers beer, terrific cheeseburgers, a dim, smoky pool room, and the flamboyant, many-hatted Wanda Wilson, the best-known barkeeper

Beale Street by night

THE MEMPHIS MYSTIQUE

In many people's minds, Memphis is so intimately identified with music that "Memphis blues" (a phrase taken from the title of a W. C. Handy song) and "Memphis soul" are taken almost as expanded definitions. So much music has come out of the city that the first and biggest temptation facing anyone discussing Memphis music is to make grandiose and hyperbolic assertions about its importance.

You know the sort of thing—calling a style "America's Music" or "America's Gift to the World," or anointing a performer or composer as the "father" (or, much more rarely, the "mother") of something or other, all in the manner of chamber of commerce histories, tourist brochures, or liner notes. And why not? After all, you are talking about B. B. King, Elvis Presley, Johnny Cash, Otis Redding, Jerry Lee Lewis, Isaac Hayes. . . and that's only picking some of the most famous names from a list that goes on and on.

This sort of hand-waving exaggeration does have one advantage: it sidesteps any question that "Memphis music" is one particular thing. But is that true? What does the driving rockabilly of Carl Perkins's "Dixie Fried" have to do with the sweet soul of Al Green's "Call Me," the wrenching heartbreak of James Caar's "Rainbow Road," or the aching pop of the Box Tops' "The Letter"? What joins any of them to Furry Lewis or Rufus Thomas—or to Mud Boy and the Neutrons or the Grifters?

I'd Rather Be Here

In his "Beale Street Blues," a song that forever captures and mythologizes the excitement and danger of Memphis's nightlife ("business never closes 'til somebody gets killed"), Handy wrote of the blind man on the corner who sings, "I'd rather be here than any place I know."

Thousands, maybe even millions, have taken this (or something else that echoes its spirit) as a beckoning call to come to Memphis and hear, or maybe even make, that music for themselves. Memphis shares with New Orleans not just the blues but a sense that something at the heart of the city is just strange, eccentric, outside, of no

other place, and that sense permeates the music that has been made here.

But what really makes "Memphis music" is a gritty bareness of emotion, an earthbound honesty that prevails over whatever else is going on. No one would ever confuse, although each is sublime in its own way, most soul records made in Detroit or Philadelphia, or most country records made in Nashville, with recordings from Memphis.

While one cannot overestimate the desire of those involved in making music in Memphis to make it—remember Sun Studio's owner/producer Sam Phillips's famous remark (whatever he said exactly), "If I could find a white man who could sing like a black man, I would make a billion dollars"—Memphis has always been much more of a music town than a music business town, with a sense that the place has a unique spirit that can't be exactly copied or entirely suppressed or prettied up, even when someone is trying to.

They Wrote About Memphis

Fortunately, some wonderful writers have certainly tried, turning their hands to the musicians and the music associated with Memphis. Peter Guralnick's work is consistently outstanding: It exhibits the enthusiasm of a lifelong fan expressed through meticulous research and a finely honed critical sense. His *Last Train to Memphis* is the definitive biography of Elvis Presley's early years. The second volume, *Careless Love,* covering the years until Elvis's death in 1977, came out in December 1998. As the title suggests, *Sweet Soul Music* describes the development of soul in general and the explosion in the black music industry in Memphis in the 1960s and early '70s in particular, including the rise and fall of the Stax/Volt record labels. *Feel Like Going Home* and *Lost Highway* contain insightful portraits of blues and country musicians, famous and neglected alike, many of them intimately connected with Memphis.

Robert Gordon's *It Came from Memphis* provides an offbeat history of the Memphis music scene from the days when wildman disc jockey Dewey Phillips's hipster rants (on his radio show *Red Hot and Blue*) brought first rhythm and blues

continued on next page

THE MEMPHIS MYSTIQUE (cont'd)

and then rock 'n' roll to black and white audiences alike—and of what some in the audience did with the experience.

Greil Marcus has written some of the most insightful commentary on Elvis, especially in *Mystery Train*, and his *Dead Elvis* explores the posthumous neoreligious Presley subculture cult. All provide detailed guidance to particular recordings. Any one is a good place to start.

Move Out to Move Up

Despite the clubs, the crowds, and the Elvis devotees, Memphis seems, oddly, not an outstandingly good place to try to make a living as a musician. There has been no real music industry presence in Memphis since the '70s—certainly nothing on the order of that in Nashville—although there is still a lot of studio business, with everyone from internationally famous superstars such as U2 to hopeful regional favorites such as the band Joe, Mark's Brother still hoping to find someone who will catch lightning in a bottle as Sam Phillips, Jim Dickinson, Chips Moman, and other producers did for bands years ago. But in truth, their hopes are much like those of the tourists—to come and be touched by, or connected to, some bygone glory. Many local musicians resent what they see as the industry's willingness to occasionally exploit the city's sense of identity without really investing in anything that fosters it—and the city's willingness to let it happen. After a lifetime of struggling to make a career in his hometown, one (who was finally leaving town for Nashville) said that being from Memphis was "just something to put on your resume" when trying to get jobs elsewhere. Succinctly voicing his feeling that the city merely talks a good game in presenting itself as a music center, another said, "This town is so full of it."

Take Me to the River

And yet, standing next to the river, the sun going down red over the flat Arkansas horizon, it is possible to feel that there is something there, that there is, at the risk of serving up so much (barbecued) baloney, some magic in the air that the tourist promotions are only the shadows of, some music that would be playing even if no one other than the musicians themselves were there to hear it. At the end of his masterful, joyous version of Handy's song, Louis Armstrong (who knew a thing or two about playing the blues himself) sings:

I'm goin' to the river, baby by and by,

Yes I'm goin' to the river, and there's a reason why:

Because the river's wet,

And Beale Street's done gone dry.

It remains to be seen whether or not this is true. But people are still going to the river. The best thing you can do is go and listen for yourself.

(*Contributed by Franklin Jones, a writer who grew up in Jackson, Tennessee, now living in Watertown, Massachusetts.*)

in town. This haven for writers, artists, actors, and journalists sports huge caricatures of notorious local political figures on the ceiling; Michelangelo comes to mind.

At **Raiford's Hollywood Disco** (1115 Vance, 901/528-9313), one can see the spires of downtown Memphis from the front door (and the dome of the new arena), but patrons still have to check their weapons at this late-night glittery dance 'n'rap palace. Best very late Friday and Saturday nights.

The motto for the ambitious club, **Senses**

(2866 Poplar Ave., 901/454-4081), explains the attitude: "Eat. Drink. Dance. Watch." Music is provided by DJs and, on weekends, by live bands.

Wild Bill's Club (1580 Vollintine, 901/726-5473) is a discreet storefront in a quiet neighborhood. Go inside, order a quart of beer, and the blues ever take you away. Folks wear their finest to dance here. Sadly, Big bluesman Lucky Carter, a fixture at Wild Bill's, died recently; he will be missed.

Young Avenue Deli (2119 Young Ave. near Cooper, 901/278-0034) serves excellent sandwiches (try the Reuben) along with, on weekends, some of the hottest traveling and local groups available.

Gay and Lesbian

Backstreet (2018 Court Ave., 901/276-5522) holds grand drag shows Friday and Saturday at midnight and 3 A.M. and Sunday at 11 P.M. **J-Wags** (1268 Madison Ave., 901/725-1909) is a longtime local watering hole with drag shows and beauty contests Wednesday–Saturday. **Madison Flame** (1588 Madison Ave., 901/278-9839) features karaoke on Wednesday and Friday through Sunday nights. **The Metro** (1349 Autumn Ave.) does karaoke Monday and Tuesday at 10 P.M., a drag show Thursday at 11:30 P.M.

FESTIVALS AND EVENTS

Memphis has a wider range of events than any place in Tennessee. What follows are just the highlights. For complete information, call the numbers listed at the end of this chapter.

January

Elvis Birthday Week (800/238-2000 or 901/332-3322, www.elvis.com) at Graceland. The schedule of events varies from year to year. January 6–8.

Blues First Weekend (901/527-2583, www.blues.org) features a contest for blues bands featuring 90-plus entries. Last weekend in January.

April

Africa in April Cultural Awareness Festival (901/947-2133, www.africainapril.org) selects a different African country every year and organizes a festival around it. Four days of food, music, cultural, and educational events.

May

Kemet Jubilee (901/774-1118) is a wide-open event centering on African Americans. The Carnation Ball in April culminates with the crowning of the king and queen of jubilee. The largest black parade in the country steps off in early May. The Barbecue Cooking Contest is held in May, and visitors can also participate in the Las Vegas Cruise and Club Room Party on the Mississippi. Late April through mid-May.

Memphis in May International Festival (901/525-4611, www.memphisinmay.org) is the big one. This monthlong shindig salutes a different country every year. Somehow the organizers work the World Championship Barbecue Cooking Contest, the Sunset Symphony, the Sunset Symphony Rehearsal picnic, the Beale Street Music Festival, and the International Weekend into this wonderful event. Typically, the festival organizers invite a performing artist, such as the Thai Ballet, from the honored country for the international weekend. Visitors can select from a huge variety of events promoted by the festival.

W. C. Handy Blues Awards (Orpheum Theatre, 901/527-2583, www.blues.org) are the Oscars of the blues world. The event is organized by the Blues Foundation and typically. Be sure to stay for the jam session afterward. Visitors can also participate in a two-day symposium, the Keeping-the-Blues-Alive banquet, and a moonlight cruise on the Mississippi.

August

Elvis Tribute Week (901/332-3322 or 800/238-2000, www.elvis.com), also known as "Death Week," commemorates built the anniversary of the King's death on August 16, 1977. This is a giant reunion for fan clubs and includes a variety of activities and Elvis movies every night. The event culminates with a candlelight vigil over his grave. Second week in August.

September

Cooper-Young Festival (901/272-3056, www.cooperyoung.com) features live music, crafts, and various bohemian activities. This is a big neighborhood festival with quality arts and crafts celebrating the revitalization of the area. It is very well done.

International Goat Days Festival (901/872-4559, www.internationalgoatdays.com) is known for a lot of tomfoolery and a variety of goat-related competitions. This fun family event is held in USA Stadium in Millington, a northern suburb of Memphis. It includes a pancake breakfast, goat chariot races, a whistling competiti-

egg tosses, and pill (dried goat droppings) flipping. Late September.

AMUSEMENT PARK

Libertyland Amusement Park (940 Early Maxwell Blvd., 901/274-1776, www.libertyland .com, noon–8 P.M. Wed.–Fri., 10 A.M.–8 P.M. Sat., $8–18, free for ages under 3 and over 65) is a theme park with 23 rides, live music, places to eat, and things to see. This was the park that Elvis used to rent for all-night fun with his friends, riding a wooden roller coaster called the Zippin Pippin over and over. One of the roller-coaster cars on which he used to ride has been preserved, and guests can sit in it and have their photos taken. Elvis's last public appearance before he died was at Libertyland.

PERFORMING ARTS

Memphis is as far in Tennessee as one can get from the geographic origins of bluegrass music, but fanciers of that high lonesome sound can get their fill at the **Lucy Opry** (901/358-3486, 901/357-6432, or 901/357-1221, www.lucyopry.com) held monthly. While the occasional local plays, this place books name performers along the lines of the Osborne Brothers and Jim and Jesse McReynolds. This "opry" used to be held in the town of Lucy—thus the name—but now is held at the Barlett Performing Arts and Conference Center (3663 Appling Rd., Bartlett). To get there, take Interstate 40 East to Exit 15B (Appling Road North). Go North on Appling straight through two traffic lights. At the second traffic light, Appling Road changes name only to become Brother Blvd. Continue north on Brother Blvd. until you reach a four-way stop sign. Make a left at that stop sign, which will put you back onto Appling Road. The Center is located on the left a couple of hundred yards ahead.

Southern gospel is performed most Friday nights at **The "Almost Famous" Gospel Singing Jubilee** (2984 Harvester Ln., 901/299-8831, www.almostfamous.cc, $5) in Frayser (north of Memphis). The show is performed in the 250-seat old union hall; no drinking or smoking is permitted.

Visit **Blues City Cultural Center,** (205 N. Main St., 901/525-3031) for productions that explore the African American experience in the South, and performances that often celebrate the music of Beale Street.

The **Orpheum Theatre** (203 S. Main St., at Beale St., 901/525-3000, www.orpheum-memphis .com, office open 8 A.M.–5 P.M. Mon.–Fri.) was constructed in 1888 as the Grand Opera House. It has been beautifully restored with chandeliers, tapestries, and gilt architectural features, and now it hosts concerts and other productions.

Malco Studio on the Square (2105 Court St., 901/725-7151, www.malco.com), is Memphis's number-one art movie house. It's northwest of the intersection of Madison and Cooper in the Overton Square area.

Be sure to visit **Union Planter's IMAX Theater** at Memphis Pink Palace Museum (3050 Central Ave., information 901/763-4629, reservations 901/320-6362, www.memphismueums .org, $7.50 adults, $7 seniors, $6 children). IMAX movies use enormous film—one frame is the size of a playing card—projected onto a huge screen and backed with a blow-back-your-hair sound system.

The **New Daisy Theatre** (330 Beale St., 901/525-8979, www.newdaisy.com) was built in the 1940's, and hosts a variety of events today. The **Playhouse on the Square** 51 South Cooper St.,(901/726 4656 and 901/725 0776, www .playhouseonthesquare.org) is actually two theaters operated by Circuit Playhouse, Inc., a community-based organizations offering the city's only professional, resident theater company as well as many educational programs.

Accommodations

BED-AND-BREAKFAST

Quite possibly the best place to stay in Memphis is **Talbot Heirs Guesthouse** (99 S. 2nd St., 800/955-3956 or 901/527-9772, www.talbothouse.com, $125), a boutique hotel directly across from the Peabody Memphis Hotel. Here await nine guest rooms, all of which have private baths and fully functional kitchens, two phone lines with data ports, and superb concierge service. Guests have included Hal Holbrooke, David Copperfield, and Francis Ford Coppola.

HOTELS AND MOTELS

Memphis, where Holiday Inn was founded, has a host of the usual franchise places to lay your head. But if you can possibly afford it, try to spend at least one night in **The Peabody Memphis,** (149 Union Ave., 901/529-4000 or 800/732-2639, www.peabodymemphis.com, $219–319), the grande dame of Memphis hotels and home of the daily duck parade.

The Madison Hotel (79 Madison Ave., 901/333-1200, www.madisonhotelmemphis.com, $220–1,200) occupies a structure built in 1905 as a bank. Thoroughly renovated, the rooms are hip yet comfortable. The view from the roof is reason enough to stay here.

A more reasonable and conveniently located alternative is the **Sleep Inn** (Court Square, 40 N. Front St., 888/729-7705 or 901/522-9700, $90). Facing the river and with Main Street and the trolley right out the back door, this place is close enough to walk to Beale Street yet far enough away to be quiet.

It had to happen. Down at the end of Lonely Street, actually right beside the Graceland Plaza, sits the 128-room **Heartbreak Hotel** (3677 Elvis Presley Blvd., 877/777-0606, www.elvis.com, $93). By and large, the Graceland folks do a good job for the faithful, but this enterprise is a disappointment. While the '50s-themed rooms are fantastic, the public areas look as if they were decorated by Wal-Mart. Other than being able to walk to Graceland, there's not a whole lot going for this neighborhood. Rates begin at $93 but go up to more than $500 for the themed suites.

Springhill Suites Downtown Memphis (21 N. Main St., 888/287-9400, www.springhillsuites.com, $100 and up) benefits from its prime location—close enough to walk to Beale Street, yet far enough away from the revelers.

The major national chains are well represented, sometimes in duplicate or triplicate, in Memphis. Here are some choices: *Best Western Benchmark Hotel* (164 Union Ave., 800/380-3236, www.bestwestern.com, $95); Comfort Inn Downtown (100 N. Front St., 800/228-5150, www.comfortinn.com/hotel/tn235, $99); **Hampton Inn** (2700 S. Perkins Rd., 800/426-7866, www.hamptoninn.com, $50–99); **Memphis Marriott** (250 N. Main St., 888/557-8740, www.marriottse.com/memphis, $169); and **Radisson Hotel Downtown Memphis** (185 Union Ave., 800/333-3333, www.radisson.com/memphistn, $50–150).

The least expensive motels lie across the Mississippi River in Arkansas, but few people ever think of going there: **Best Western West Memphis Inn** (3401 Service Loop Rd., 870/735-7185, $50); **Budget Inn** (4361 E. Broadway St., 870/735-2350, $32); **Comfort Inn West Memphis** (1300 Ingram Blvd., 870/732-0044, $68); **Days Inn West/Pyramid** (1100 Ingram Blvd., 870/735-8600, $69); and **Quality Inn** (1009 S Service Rd., 870/702-9000, $55).

Food

The following was assembled by Fredric Koeppel, the restaurant and book critic for the *The Commercial Appeal,* Memphis's local newspaper.

BARBECUE

As far as barbecue is concerned, Memphis is heaven, mecca, and nirvana rolled into one. Before listing some of the barbecue places, a bit of explanation is in order. Most of the barbecue here is pork. A few infidels cook beef, and the more health-minded appreciate chicken, but for most people in Memphis, barbecue and pork are synonymous. Usually barbecue hereabouts comes from two cuts of meat—shoulders and ribs.

Barbecue has its own language: cognoscenti express their preferences among "white" or "brown" meat, "pulled" or "chopped," and "wet" or "dry." The first four terms refer to pork shoulders. "White" is interior meat uncolored by smoke or sauce. It tends to be more tender but not as strongly flavored as "brown" meat, which is chewier. Those who specify neither will usually get a mixture of both. "Pulled" pork is meat so tender that it can be pulled from the bone by hand and put on a plate or on a sandwich. This usually results in larger chunks. "Chopped" pork has been cleaved into submission.

Diners who order ribs will often get this question: "Dry or wet?" "Dry" ribs have no barbecue sauce on them. Often they have been cooked with a "rub" consisting of spices such as salt, pepper, cumin, and chili powder, which, if done right, seals in the juices and makes the best ribs in the world—especially for diners with handlebar mustaches. "Wet" ribs have been basted with sauce during their final hour or so on the grill. These require plenty of napkins but are worth it.

Traditional side dishes include slaw, which in Memphis goes on the barbecue sandwich; baked beans, sometimes with bits of barbecue in them; potato salad; and bread, or as they say in these parts, "laht braid." That's "light bread" to you.

Central BBQ (2249 Central Ave., 901/272-9377, dinner nightly) has found tremendous popularity in two years by serving—anathema to loyal Memphis barbecue hounds—both wet and dry-rub ribs. Each version is excellent; so are the pork shoulder and such sides as slaw, beans, and potato chips, all made at the restaurant.

Bar-B-Q Shop (1782 Madison Ave., 901/272-1277, lunch and dinner Tues.–Sat., lunch only Mon.) specializes in ribs and pulled pork shoulder.

Corky's (5259 Poplar Ave., 901/685-9744, lunch and dinner daily) may not be funky and may not be down-home, but it offers what one has to assess as one of the best pulled pork-shoulder barbecue sandwiches in the world. The ribs, well, they don't quite compete.

Cozy Corner (745 N. Parkway, 901/527-9158) *is* funky and down-home, and its barbecue

competitive barbecue

Cornish game hen is one of the unique treats that make Memphis the city it is. Pork shoulder sandwiches and pork ribs are also excellent.

The specialty at **Gridley's** (6430 Winchester Rd., 901/794-5997, and 6065 Macon Rd., 901/388-7003) is sauce-covered ribs, but they have barbecued shrimp as well.

Interstate Bar-B-Q and Restaurant, (2265 S. 3rd St., 901/775-2304, lunch and dinner daily) long had a reputation as the best of the best when it came to local barbecue, but discriminating Memphians have noticed a decline in standards since the place expanded several years ago.

M Jango's Bar-B-Que and Deli, (954 Jackson Ave., 901/578-8598, lunch and dinner daily) occupies a funny little building that has held barbecue restaurants for 50 years. James Johnson turns out extraordinarily tender pork shoulder sandwiches, meaty and chewy wet ribs, barbecue chicken, and a gloriously messy Italian sausage sandwich. If you have to count the napkins, you're in the wrong place.

Neely's Bar-B-Que (670 Jefferson Ave., 901/521-9798, and 5700 Mt. Moriah Rd., 901/795-4177, lunch and dinner daily) doesn't surprise by the excellence of its product; it's run by the nephews of Jim Neely, owner of Interstate Bar-B-Q. In addition to excellent pork shoulder sandwiches and ribs, try the barbecue spaghetti (an odd Memphis tradition) and the smoked sausage.

Payne's Bar-B-Que (1393 Elvis Presley Blvd., 901/942-7433, and 1762 Lamar Ave., 901/272-1523, lunch and dinner daily) serves shoulder and wet ribs.

Rendezvous (52 S. 2nd St., 901/523-2746, dinner nightly) inspires such loyalty that criticism of the place seems to merit fluffin' up the feathers and heatin' up the tar. Sure, Elvis had Rendezvous ribs flown to Vegas when he performed there, but he also loved banana and peanut butter sandwiches. Even the Vergos family, owners of the Rendezvous, admit that the dry ribs they produce, rubbed with a unique spice mixture, partake more of Greece than the mid-South, but that fact doesn't keep Yankee writers from proclaiming the Rendezvous ground zero of Memphis barbecue. To our minds, these ribs are interesting but not the Real Thing, but who's going to argue with 100,000 tourists? To get there, go through an alley across from the Peabody Memphis Hotel. You'll step into a place whose walls are lined with antiques and Memphis memorabilia. It seats 700 and serves dinner only.

DOWNTOWN

Aristi's (126 Monroe Ave., 901/527-6930, lunch and dinner Mon.–Sat., entrées, $8–13) offers simple, comforting, and reasonably priced Caribbean and South American cuisine in a pleasant setting.

Automatic Slim's Tonga Club, (83 S. 2nd St., 901/525-7948, lunch and dinner Mon.–Sat., entrées $15–27), has successfully maintained its Cowboy Bob–meets–Bob Marley attitude for more than a decade. The constantly evolving cuisine sometimes results in plates so busy that you don't know how to deconstruct your food (is it Southwestern, Louisianan, Caribbean, or Southeast Asian?), but what you get is always interesting and often thrilling. Various salsas, fruit sauces, and peppy accompaniments keep the spice and heat decibels high.

Cafe Samovar (83 Union Ave., 901/529-9607, lunch and dinner Mon.–Sat.) serves authentic Russian dishes, including borscht, beef stroganoff, veal *soblinka, luli kabob, kulebyaka,* and chicken and lamb kabobs. Desserts are rich and generous, and the atmosphere is festive and folksy.

M Café 61 (85 S. 2nd St., 901/523-9351, lunch and dinner daily, entrées $11–24), by the owner of Midtown's 61 On Teur, occupies a brassy, two-story rendition of a Mississippi Delta roadhouse, though those institutions never offered patrons bronzed yellowfin tuna with roasted corn and sweet pepper salsa, black Thai duck, or the crawfish macaroni and cheese. Sandwiches are of he-man proportions; desserts resort to no subtlety whatever.

M Chez Phillippe, at the Peabody Memphis Hotel (149 Union Ave., 901/529-4188, dinner nightly, entrées $25–38), is the city's most formal, most thoughtfully detailed restaurant—and its most expensive. Chef Jose Gutierrez's exquisite, artfully presented dishes reflect his French culinary background and the influence of the American South, though recently he has cast his eye back at his classical French training and sharpened up the menu. The wine list is high-toned (though not as good as it ought to be at a restaurant with this level of accomplishment), and so is the impeccable service.

Cielo (679 Adams Ave., 901/524-1886, dinner nightly, entrées $22–28) occupies an 1880s house in Victorian Village, not far from downtown. The striking decor mixes Sleeping Beauty's castle with the Jetsons rumpus room, and the food is equally unusual and as eclectic as all-get-out, lassoing influence from the Caribbean, the Southwest, and Southeast Asia. The restaurant is the creation of the energetic Karen Blockman Carrier, owner of perennial downtown favorite Automatic Slim's and the new Cooper-Young restaurants, Beauty Shop and Do. A wonderful little bar upstairs with a small separate dining room is decorated with work by legendary local artists and serves superb martinis.

Felicia Suzanne's (80 Monroe Ave. at Main St., 901/523-0872, dinner nightly, entrées $22–32), named for its New Orleans–trained chef, makes stunning use of its soaring location on the first floor of an old department store. The fare is jazzed Southern cuisine, pumped up by the chef's lively imagination and excellent ingredients. An interesting (though expensive) wine list and attentive service complete a great experience.

5 Spot (84 G. E. Patterson Blvd., 901/523-9754, entrées $15–22) feels as if it had a starring role in Jim Jarmusch's *Mystery Train,* the best movie ever made about the Bluff City's dark side. With three tables inside and a few outside, a small bar and a kitchen so close to diners that they could reach forward and wipe the sweat from the cook's brow, old jazz LPs playing on an old hi-fi set, and everything looking about a hundred years old—eating here seems about as authentic as anything about Memphis could be.

Grill 83 (83 Madison Ave., next to the Madison Hotel, 901/333-1224, breakfast, lunch, and dinner daily, entrées $20–38) is a sophisticated newcomer that offers thoughtful variations of

such upper-scale classics as an Asian-influenced "shrimp cocktail," five-spice ahi tuna, rack of lamb with a Maytag cheese glaze, and sumptuous crème brûlée and individual baked Alaska. The deep, narrow, high-ceilinged room is spare and elegant.

Harry's Detour South Main (106 G.E . Patterson Blvd., 901/523-9070, lunch and dinner daily, entrées $10–20) is an adjunct of Harry's Detour in Midtown (532 S. Cooper; 901/276-7623) and serves many of the same dishes—Chaurice Diablo, shrimp Gautier ("go-shay"), mahi "Redondo," and chicken Kingfield—but in an atmosphere much sleeker and more artful than the first, rather improvisational location. All the fare, including the inventive daily specials, tends to be full-flavored and assertive.

McEwen's on Monroe (122 Monroe Ave., 901/527-7085, lunch is Mon.–Fri., dinner Tues., entrées $18–26) is so funky and has such a great bar scene that you're surprised by the seriousness and depth of the wine list. Though no chef has stayed long, the quality of the generally rich and spicy Southern-inspired food remains consistently high. Owners Mac and Cindy Edwards—he once worked in the local wholesale wine business—look after the details of this casual but caring restaurant with devotion.

Stella (39 S. Main St. at Monroe Ave., 901/526-4950, lunch Mon.–Fri., dinner Mon.–Sat., entrées $20–32), like its neighbor Felicia Suzanne's, beautifully occupies an old retail space, in this case the first floor of the century-old Brodnax Jewelers building. A casually elegant restaurant in this restrained jewel-box setting, Stella features (like perhaps too many other spots downtown) variations and intensifications on haute Southern-style food, yet there's enough individualism to make the concept attractive and different. One feels good here.

Sawaddii (121 Union Ave., 901/529-1818, lunch and dinner Mon.–Sat., entrées $8–13) may not provide the authentic Thai food one gets on the steamy streets of Bangkok, but what they serve in this pleasant, breezy restaurant is downright delicious. Heat and spice run through everything on the menu, including a savory chicken-coconut soup, yellow curry chicken and green curry shrimp, roasted duck with a rousing red curry sauce, classic pad Thai and *nam tok* beef. Save room for a soothing, modestly creamy Thai custard.

One does not usually associate fried chicken with *GQ Magazine*; maybe the image of guys in designer clothing baring their sullen lips to bite into a piece of steaming chicken just doesn't work. Nonetheless, this publication for the hopelessly hip chose **N Gus's World Famous Hot and Spicy Chicken** of Mason, Tennessee, as one of the 10 restaurants in the world worth flying to. Gus's now has a downtown Memphis location (301 S. Front St., 11 A.M.–9 P.M. daily).

OVERTON SQUARE

Molly's La Casita (2006 Madison Ave., 901/726-1873, lunch and dinner daily) presents typical, inexpensive Mexican American fare made special by attention to detail and fresh ingredients. Particularly good are the charcoal-grilled red snapper, chicken fajita enchiladas, and any dish served with the profoundly intense ranchero sauce.

Kwik Chek Food Shop #10 (2031 Madison Ave., 901/274-9293) would differ from no other slightly seedy convenience store except for the sandwich counter at the back. There you will find on-premise-made sandwiches with agendas and attitude, such as The Turk That Was Greek and My Bleeding Heart, and sandwiches that will put hair on your chest and sweat on your forehead, like Yippee Kai Yai Yea M.IF.—don't ask—Genghis Khan, and Pecos Bill. You'll get no sympathy from the management; states the menu: "Don't come crying to us about your blistered tongue." Kwik Chek serves these cheap, unique, lethal concoctions every day.

Memphis Pizza Café (2089 Madison Ave., 901/726-5343, lunch and dinner Mon.–Sat.) provides inexpensive salads, calzones, and sandwiches, but best are the fresh and vivid pizzas, especially the vegetarian rendition and the Eclectic, with basil, garlic, and cheese.

Golden India (2097 Madison Ave., 901/728-5111, lunch and dinner daily) offers the freshest, cleanest, and most delicious Indian cuisine in Memphis. From the selection of wholesome hot breads through curries and tender tandoori dishes and fiery *vindaloos* to such comforting desserts as *kheer*, a bowl of creamy rice pudding, and suave pistachio ice cream, everything is top-notch. The service is as consistent as the food.

N Boscos Squared (2120 Madison Ave., 901/432-2222, lunch and dinner Mon.–Sat.) provides excellent wood-fired pizzas as well as standard American fare such as pork chops, steaks, and grilled fish. A nationally recognized brewpub, Boscos also serves a gratifying selection of house-made regular and seasonal beers and ale.

COOPER-YOUNG

N Bari (22 S. Cooper St., 901/722-2244, lunch Tues.–Sat., dinner daily, entrées $15 to 22) serves no red sauce, no lasagna, no pizza. Based on the cuisine of the southeast Italian coast, the fare here is simple and impeccably prepared, and features fish and seafood, fresh and grilled vegetables, and a few meat entrées. Salads and pastas are simple and delicious. The all-Italian wine list is notable for variety and reasonable prices.

La Tourelle (2146 Monroe Ave., 901/726-5771, dinner Tues.–Sat., brunch Sun., entrées $25–39) is now in *prix fixe* mode, with chef Justin Young's French-American cuisine, nicely balanced between tradition and innovation, available at reasonable prices. Young also recently instituted a "small plates" menu that offers diners reduced "tasting" portions at reduced prices. La Tourelle is one of the prettiest and most comfortable restaurants in town, with efficient and comfortable service to match.

Café 1912 (243 S. Cooper St., 901/722-2700, dinner nightly, brunch Sat.–Sun., entrées $14–20) is the informal cadet to La Tourelle and under the same ownership. Working in French bistro style, the kitchen at Café 1912 turns out hearty versions of onion soup, Lyonnaise salad, steak frites, roasted chicken, duck confit, and other classics. On the short wine list every bottle is $20; wines by the glass are $5.

N Glass Onion Bar & Grill (903 S. Cooper St., 901/274-5151, lunch and dinner daily) is an inexpensive bar with the heart and soul of a bistro. Righteously boisterous, the place serves terrific, hearty sandwiches—don't miss the grilled jerk chicken with cranberry-red onion salsa— and interesting entrées, while the sound system ferociously cranks out rock 'n' roll. The chef's mother makes the sumptuous desserts, and they're the kind that you would, well, want to take home to your own mom.

Jasmine Thai & Vegetarian Restaurant (916 S. Cooper St., 901/725-0223, lunch and dinner daily, entrées $8–15) recently moved from the suburbs to an old wood house in Cooper-Young, where it makes a fine addition to the eclectic group of restaurants. Don't neglect to order from any section of this menu; the food is exceptionally fresh and well prepared. No wimps allowed, either, because the kitchen doesn't stint on spices and chiles.

Tsunami (928 S. Cooper St., 901/274-2556, dinner dinner Mon.–Thurs., entrées $18–25) brings a distinct Asian touch to seafood in a funky artist-designed setting that has real neighborhood appeal. A terrific example is the signature roasted sea bass with soy *beurre blanc* and black Thai rice. Tsunami is a favorite place to eat outside on balmy nights and watch local residents and their dogs pass by.

Beauty Shop (966 S. Cooper St., 901/272-7111, dinner Mon.–Sat., brunch Sun., entrées $12.50–27) proves that you can open a restaurant in a former beauty salon, retain the chairs and hair dryers, pile in whole museums' worth of retro decor, and score a hit. Who else in town but Karen Carrier (Automatic Slim's, Cielo) could pull off such a stunt? Relentlessly hip from the day it opened, Beauty Shop features a witty menu dizzying in its world-beat diversity and exotic yet somehow down-home goodness.

Do (964 S. Cooper St., 901/272-0830, dinner Tues.–Sat., entrées $2–10), also a Karen Carrier creation, stands next to Beauty Shop yet could not be more different. Behind the bar of the more compact restaurant work ministers of sushi, nigiri, and sashimi, while the kitchen turns out hot and cold starters and entrées. Everything is as fresh as a slap in the kisser, as clear as a whiff of bracing sea air. All aspects of food here respect tradition but are not bound by it, and the dishes are as beautiful to look upon as they are delicious.

Asian Palace (2920 Covington Pike, 901/388-3883, lunch and dinner daily, entrées $8–20) is the best Chinese restaurant in the region. The menu is uniquely ingenious and nonrepetitive, and the fare is bright, fresh, and delicious. Don't miss the clams with black bean sauce, the duck broth, and the steamed fish, whatever it may be that day.

Ellen's Soul Food Restaurant (601 S. Parkway E., 901/942-4777, lunch and early dinner Mon.–Fri., entrées under $8.95), universally known as Miss Ellen's, serves the best meatloaf, smothered chicken, and pork chops around, bolstered with plates of fried cornbread pancakes. Friday is chitlins day, and just you try to get into the restaurant then.

Jarrett's Restaurant (5687 Quince Rd. in Winchester Square shopping center, 901/763-2264, dinner Mon.–Sat., entrées $14–26) shines with its eclectic American menu, featuring smoked trout ravioli, mixed grill of sausages, crab cakes, grilled chicken, duckling in two styles, excellent fish preparations, and a knockout cappuccino crème caramel. A recent remodeling made the restaurant more attractive; it also boasts one of the nicest outdoor eating areas in town.

M Melange (948 S. Cooper St., 901/276-0002, dinner nightly, entrées $18–24) delivers the goods in a space where three restaurants failed in a decade. Chef Scott Lenhart maintains a style of eclectic Euro-American cuisine jazzed up with a few exotic touches; the food is served by knowledgeable waiters in a comfortable, understated dining room. The ever-changing wine list, willing to take risks, is among the best in town. The bar, open until 3 P.M., offers imaginative hot and cold tapas.

Napa Café, (5101 Sanderlin, 901/683-0441, lunch Mon.–Fri., dinner Mon.–Sat., entrées $16–26) is about the sweetest, prettiest, most welcoming restaurant in Memphis. Add those qualities to thoughtfully conceived and nicely presented American cuisine, and diners are certain to remember Napa Café with pleasure. No envelope-pushing here, just comfort and care and an excellent wine list to boot.

Pete and Sam's Restaurant (3886 Park Ave., 901/458-0694, dinner nightly, entrées $15–25) is the kind of place where the great-grandchildren of the original customers still eat. Forget the forgettable southern Italian cuisine, except for the rich and sumptuous lasagna, and go straight for the best steaks in Memphis, as well as terrific thin-crust pizzas. Take your own wine.

La Playita Mexicana (6194 Macon Rd. in Shelby Crossing, 901/377-0181, lunch and dinner daily, entrées and combination dinners $7–18) does a great job with standard Mexican fare, but as a restaurant whose name means "little beach" should, it specializes in seafood. Whole red snapper is served with a variety of sauces and in combinations with steak and chicken, while what the menu calls "cocktails" brings a vat of spicy red sauce that holds a ton of boiled shrimp—or oysters or squid—with avocado and cilantro. Service is friendly and helpful.

Ronnie Grisanti & Sons (2855 Poplar Ave. in Chickasaw Crossing, 901/323-0007, dinner Mon.–Sat., entrées $15–30) balances traditional southern Italian food with racy renditions of northern Italian favorites, with emphasis on grilled meats and fresh fish, the latter recited in endless lists by waiters with seemingly perfect memories. The restaurant is comfortable and intimate, and the walls teem with artworks ranging from beautiful to bizarre.

Saigon Le (51 N. Cleveland, 901/276-5326, lunch and dinner Mon.–Sat.) features Vietnamese food so fresh, so vivid, and so good that patrons can't believe how cheap it is. A family-run restaurant with Momma in the kitchen and the kids and husbands and wives (and a few babies) in front, Saigon Le manages to move huge crowds through the dining room with never a slip in the excellence of the food, though service can get sulky. Soups are terrific, with the curry tofu soup nudging the divine.

Taqueria Guadalupana (4818 Summer Ave., 901/685-6857, lunch and dinner daily, breakfast Sun.) is one of the best of the authentic, down-home Mexican restaurants spawned by the region's burgeoning Hispanic population. In a barn-sized room, chow down on such inexpensive, simple, hearty, and delicious fare as beef tongue and barbecue goat tacos, beef fajitas done to a charred turn, a phenomenally succulent roasted chicken, and supernaturally tender short ribs. On Sunday morning, you will find a crowd imbibing menudo, the tripe soup known for hangover-dispelling qualities.

EAST MEMPHIS

M Erling Jensen: The Restaurant (1044 S. Yates Rd., 901/763-3700, dinner nightly, entrées $25–38) is patronized by expense-account darlings who dote on the sort of sumptuous, luxurious, and costly fare beloved of robber barons. Chef Erling Jensen, a quiet man steeped in European tradition but imbued with New World fervor, doesn't disappoint them. Occupying a 1950s house turned into a spare, elegant, and whimsical environment, the restaurant offers one of the best wine lists in town and excellent service.

M Wally Joe (5040 Sanderlin Ave., 901/818-0821, lunch Weds.–Fri., dinner Mon.–Sat., dinner entrées $18–35) generates excitement, from its elegant modernist setting, to its theatrical open kitchen, to its wide-ranging wine list, particularly dense with selections of French Bordeaux and Burgundy and California icon chardonnays and cabernet sauvignons, to, most importantly, the intensely witty menu, brainchild of sophisticated executive chef Wally Joe. As befits a restaurant at this level of aspiration and accomplishment, in service, ambience, and cuisine, no detail is overlooked.

Information and Services

SHOPPING

Fine Arts and Crafts

David Lusk Gallery (4540 Poplar Ave., 901/767-3800, www.davidluskgallery.com, 10 A.M.–5:30 P.M. Tues.–Fri., 11 A.M.–4 P.M. Sat.) offers the work of contemporary Southern artists.

Lisa Kurts Gallery (766 S. White Station Rd., 901/683-6200, www.lisakurts.com, 10 A.M.–5:30 P.M. Tues.–Fri., 11 A.M.–4 P.M. Sat.) carries contemporary American art with an emphasis on Southern artists, displayed in monthly exhibitions. The gallery also specializes in American paintings of the 19th and 20th centuries.

Marshall Arts, (639 Marshall Ave., 901/522-9483, www.deltaaxis.org, 1–5 P.M. Sat. or by appointment), one block west of Sun Studios, is an alternative arts space with exhibits of painting and sculpture and the occasional piece of performance art.

At **Tobey Gallery,** (1930 Poplar Ave. in Overton Park, 901/726-4085, www.mca.edu, 9A.M.–5P.M. Mon.–Fri.), hosts traveling exhibits as well as work by students and professors at the Memphis College of Art.

The Robinson Archive and Gallery (400 S. Front St., 901/576-0708, www.robinsonarchive .com, 11 A.M.–5 P.M. Tues.–Fri., 1–5 P.M. Sun.) sells of the work of Jack Robinson and other photographers.

Music

Pop Tunes (308 Poplar Ave., 901/525-6348; 4195 Summer Ave., 901/324-3855; and 2391 Lamar Ave., 901/744-0400, www.catsmusic.com) was known as Poplar Tunes in the 1950s, when a regular customer from the nearby Lauderdale Courts housing projects made purchases here. There's not much to see now—only a smattering of Elvis photos on the wall, but the Elvis faithful will want to see each and every one of them.

River Records (822 S. Highland St., 901/324-1757, 9– A.M.–5:30 P.M. daily) is for the fan who seeks rare records. There are reportedly about 500,000 records: 78s from the '20s, 45s from the '50s, and beyond. The shop offers rare Elvis records and related memorabilia and sells CDs, comic books, posters, and the like.

Shangri-La Records (1916 Madison Ave., 901/274-1916, www.shangri.com, noon–7 P.M. Mon.–Fri., 11 A.M.–6 P.M. Sat., noon–5 P.M. Sun.) is both a record store and an independent recording label. If you can go to only one music storie in Memphis, this is the one. The record store carries a lot of vinyl, and sells bricks from the old Stax studio building for $10. It also stocks a large section of Memphis music. Check their online catalog if you can't make it to the store.

Specialty Shops

Burke's Book Store (1719 Poplar Ave., 901/278-7484, www.burkesbooks.com, 10A.M.–6P.M. Mon.–Sat., 1–5P.M. Sun.) dates from 1875 and has a great selection of used and regional books as well as new volumes.

Flashback—The Vintage Department Store (2304 Central Ave., 901/272-2304, www.flashbackmemphis.com, 10:30 A.M.–5 P.M. Mon.–Fri.,

MEMPHIS RADIO

Memphis has two radio stations of note. WEVL is a volunteer-run, public station with the sort of eclectic programming one would expect in this most musical of cities. At 90.0 FM on the dial, this station dishes up bluegrass, blues, old-time country music, acoustic, and so on. Visit the station's website www.wevl.org.

At 1070 on the AM band, WDIA was the first all-black formatted radio station in the South; since 1948 generations of people have listened to its blues, gospel, and disc jockeys. This station had a profound effect on early rock 'n' roll musicians in the area, who were influenced by on-air personalities such as B. B. King and Rufus "Do the Funky Chicken" Thomas. WDIA still plays great music. Check out the station's website at www.am1070wdia.com.

1–5 P.M.) sells vintage clothing, furniture, and collectibles from the 1920s to the 1970s.

Otherlands (641 S. Cooper St., 901/278-4994, 7 A.M.–8 P.M. daily) is a coffee bar/exotic gift store. The store carries home furnishings and clothing from India, Africa, South America, and local artisans. Shoppers can find textiles, mirrors, jewelry, clothing, pottery, and more.

A. Schwab Dry Goods Store (163 Beale St., 901/523-9782, 9 A.M.–5 P.M. Mon.–Fri., 9 A.M.–midnight Sat.) seems a museum at first; merchandise for sharecroppers of another time is in abundance here, as are T-shirts, postcards, and associated frippery. Perhaps the most unusual goods are the voodoo potions and oils alleged to help one find love or luck—or both. For a bit of fun, browse in this section and listen to other customers making their decisions. Schwab's has been in business in this same location since 1876.

GETTING AROUND

The **Memphis Area Transit Authority,** also known as MATA (901/274-1757, www.matatransit.com), offers citywide bus service, van service for folks with disabilities, and the tourist-oriented Main Street Trolley. Taxis include **Yellow Cab,** 901/577-7777.

INFORMATION

Coming into town on I-40, get off at the Arlington exit 24/25 and follow the signs to for the **visitors center.** It is staffed seven days a week from 8:30 A.M. to 6 P.M. The **Tennessee Welcome Center** (119 N. Riverside Dr., 901/543-6757, www.memphistravel.com, open 24 hours a day) has information about Memphis and the rest of the state. Or visit the **Memphis Convention and Visitors Bureau** (47 Union Ave., 901/543-5300, www.memphistravel.com).

The Memphis Flyer (460 Tennessee, 901/521-9000, www.memphisflyer.com), a local weekly newspaper, lists what's happening on the local scene on its website.

The Western Plains

As Tennesseans increasingly recognize the value of their culture and heritage, they have sought to preserve historic places, memories of people who lived there, and a rural lifestyle that, in the turbulent times of the 21st Century, has renewed appeal. In the Western Plains, the least-developed and most laid-back part of Tennessee, people have not had to scramble as much as those in other places to save historic buildings and battlefields. Life is slower here, following the old rhythms of tilling the soil.

For some travelers, it is too slow; they stay on I-40 and get from Memphis to Nashville as fast as they can. For others, however, the Western Plains offer natural and historical sights that can be taken at a leisurely pace. There are few lines to stand in here.

This is a land of history. Nathan Bedford Forrest and his troops rode back and forth in this area during the Civil War, and General William T. Sherman slashed a plantation-home staircase in anger and frustration. Troops clashed at Shiloh,

© JEFF BRADLEY

the first big battle of the Civil War, and in two days more Americans died than in all previous American wars combined.

This is a land of heroic figures. It was the last Tennessee home of David Crockett and the place where a young boy named Alex Haley first heard tales of his African ancestors. A railroad engineer left Jackson and rode into legend as he tried to stop a speeding locomotive. A sheriff, walking tall in Adamsville, ran a nest of criminals out of his county.

This is a place touched by musical careers—birthplace to Tina Turner, Carl Perkins, bluesmen such as Sleepy John Estes, and to hundreds of choirs whose voices rose, and still rise, on Sunday to sing songs of faith.

It's also a land of humble pleasures. The world's largest coon hunt cuts loose here, as do the National Field Trials for bird dogs. People in McNairy County eat their slugburgers, and the smoke from barbecue pits rises over almost every town. It is a place of Doodle Soup and catfish: steaks, fillets, or "fiddlers"—whole fish minus the heads.

Two rivers serve as bookends for West Tennessee: the Tennessee flowing north and the Mississippi flowing south. Between them lies the flattest land in the state, a place of big fields of cotton that to someone hoeing or picking could seem as if they reached from horizon to horizon.

Memphis to Shiloh

COLLIERVILLE

This charming locale, like Franklin south of Nashville, is a place whose leaders have seen the encroaching suburbs of a large city and have taken steps to preserve the architecture and feeling of the past. This effort is just in time, for Collierville claims to be the fastest-growing town in the state.

Collierville was a small town along the railroad tracks east of Memphis, but it was significant enough to attract the attention of Union General William T. Sherman, who occupied the town in 1863. Confederate cavalry could not dislodge his forces from the depot, although they did manage to appropriate his horse for the Southern cause. Collierville was all but burned to the ground.

Sights

When the town was rebuilt in the 1870s, the planners laid it out in the town-square manner as if it had a courthouse in the center. No courthouse is here, so the focus of the town is a bandstand in the center of the park. In a nod to the "Hell no, we ain't forgetting" school of the Lost Cause, the sidewalks in the park are laid out to resemble the design of the Confederate

battle flag. Bluesman W. C. Handy led concerts in this park.

Rail fans will enjoy the train here. A 1912 steam engine, 1938 lounge car, diner, theater car, 1945 Pullman sleeper, and caboose sit on tracks near the old depot. These are owned by **Memphis Transportation Museum,** which opens them to the public. For further information, call 901/363-6200.

Biblical Resource Center and Museum, (140 E. Mulberry St., 901/854-9578, www .biblical-museum.org, 10 A.M.–5 P.M. Mon.– Sat., free, donations appreciated) sheds light on the people and cultures from which the Good Book came. Visitors can see a full-size replica of the Rosetta Stone as well as the Taylor Prism, a stone inscribed with an Assyrian account of the conquest of Judah. Kids and adults will enjoy an interactive exhibit titled "How We Got the Bible."

Events

For information on these and other events, contact Main Street Collierville, (151 Walnut St., 901/853-1666, www.collierville.com, 9 A.M.– 5 P.M. Mon.–Fri.).

Fair on the Square is one of the bigger and older arts and crafts gatherings hereabouts. It

Must-Sees

Look for **M** to find the sights and activities you can't miss and **N** for the best dining and lodging.

M **Shiloh National Military Park:** In the first major battle of the Civil War, more men fell here than in all previous American wars put together (page 71).

M **Pinson Mounds:** Marvel at the seven-stories-high mound that was created by soil, piled bucket by bucket more than a thousand years ago (page 79).

M **Reelfoot Lake:** In this northwest corner of the state, you'll find bald eagles, eerie cypress trees, dark water, and a violent story of creation through the country's strongest earthquake (page 92).

M **Henning:** See the roots of one of the state's most beloved writers at Henning's **Alex Haley Home** (page 96).

M **Tennessee Delta Heritage Center:** Just off I-40 at Brownsville, this museum, blues center, and gift shop should be the first stop for anyone traveling to this end of the state (page 100).

M **Mind Field:** Brownsville's folk art masterpiece is worth a detour off I-40. Its creator, Billy Tripp, who lives out back, is as interesting as the structure (page 101).

Mind Field

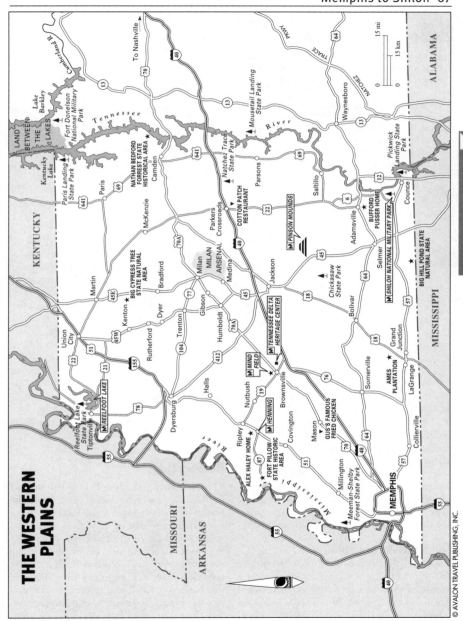

BLUE HIGHWAYS

In the days before interstate highways, mapmakers used blue ink to indicate the main roads connecting cities. Driving along these highways, known as "blue highways," gave motorists a vivid sense of the regions through which they passed. Local restaurants, not cookie-cutter franchises, dotted the roads, which often led straight down a small town's main street.

While interstate highways make it possible for the traveler to cover a lot of ground quickly, these multi-lane behemoths constitute the worst possible way to get a sense of Tennessee—or anywhere else, for that matter.

Fortunately, some of the greatest blue highways still exist in Tennessee, and, now largely free of truck traffic, they offer a wonderful look at the state, past and present. Good examples are highways 11, 70, 411, 41, 31, 64, and 51.

Along these routes, roadside fruit and vegetable stands await the traveler. Abandoned gas stations populated by the ghosts of attendants in uniforms stand guard as the tourists pass by. "See Rock City" barns shimmer in the sunlight. And retro motel signs and vintage neon rule the night.

features food, music, and kids' pastimes, and is held the first weekend in May. The **Sunset on the Square Concert Series** presents big band, country, Dixieland, and other kinds of music. Shows begin at 7 P.M. on Thursdays in June and July.

The **Fall Festival Arts and Crafts Show,** held on the last weekend in October, is a smaller version of the Fair on the Square. **Dickens on the Square Christmas Festivities** take place on the first weekend in December, and offer carriage rides, live music, an English-style marketplace, and children's games with Styrofoam "snowballs."

Food and Accommodations
Cafe Grill Steakhouse (120 Mulberry Ln., 901/853-7511), serves American dishes, and it knows its town. A sign described its certified Angus beef as "the BMW of steaks." **Captain John's Bar-B-Q** (106 U.S. 72 E., 901/853-8004)

serves three meals a day—including barbecue—every day.

The Silver Caboose (132 E. Mulberry St., 901/853-0010, 11 A.M.–2 P.M. daily) has hotplate lunches and serves fresh turnip greens year-round. Dinner items include appetizers of charbroiled shrimp followed by dishes such as filet mignon and grilled salmon. Finish off with the frozen pecan balls. **Seasons** (196 Main St., 901/854-6433, 11 A.M.–2 P.M. and 6:00 P.M. until closing, Tues.–Sat.) serves "country French cuisine," including pasta, seafood, pork loin, steak, and salad.

If you're staying over, try **Comfort Inn** (1230 W. Poplar Ave., 901/853-1235), or **Sunset Inn** (154 U.S. 72 W., 901/853-2229).

Shopping
Collierville boasts a wide variety of antique stores, some of which are noted below. A Main Street Collierville brochure lists 20 antique outlets as well as a dozen gift shops and galleries.

Hewlett and Dunn Jean and Boot Barn (on the square at 111 N. Center St., 901/853-2636, www.hewlettdunn.com, 9 A.M.–6 P.M. Mon.–Sat.) sells clothing, footwear, and tack and has a wonderful collection of old radios on the wall.

Patricia's Antiques (110 E. Mulberry St., 901/853-5470, 11 A.M.–5 P.M. Mon.–Sat.) offers some merchandise that requires a long memory indeed; the goods date from 1830 to 1940. Among its antiques are Civil War memorabilia and a special area devoted to military saddles.

ROSSVILLE
The **Wolf River,** an 86-mile-long tributary of the Mississippi which parallels Hwy. 57 on the north side, free admission, constitutes one of the few remaining tracts of floodplain forest that once covered the Mississippi Delta. For an up-close look at this fascinating ecosystem, visit The Nature Conservancy's **William B. Clark Conservation Area,** a tract of more than 500 acres that contains a 1,617-foot accessible boardwalk into the swamp. To get there, go north on Hwy. 194 from downtown Rossville, cross the river, and turn immediately to the right to a parking

area. If it is summertime, visitors should bring bug repellent, or they will experience the scriptural "present your bodies a living sacrifice."

The Civil War is full of "what if?" situations, and one of them took place hereabouts in 1862 and is recounted in Ulysses S. Grant's autobiography. It seems that Grant was riding with a small group of staff from LaGrange to Memphis. A Confederate general learned that Grant was in the vicinity and attempted to find him, but he gave up the chase early. Had he gone three-fourths of a mile farther, the man who became the Union's leading general could have been captured or killed. Grant met his pursuer years later in Colorado, and the man admitted that by that time he, too, was thankful he had not captured Grant.

Mississippi Fred McDowell, contrary to his nickname, was born here in 1904. His blues centered on bottleneck guitar and a voice that sounded as if he gargled gravel. His "You Gotta Move" appeared on the Rolling Stone's *Sticky Fingers* album.

MOSCOW

Farther up the lazy Wolf River, visitors have a chance to get into the flow. No white water here, but canoe paddlers have a chance to see ducks, beavers, and deer up close. Between here and LaGrange the river flows into a swamp and a lake, thus inspiring the name "Ghost River," for it wasn't clear just which way the Wolf went. The canoe route is now marked, however. Visit online at or www.wolfriver.org.

To get on the water, go to **Wolf River Canoe Trips** (1600 Old Stateline Dr., 901/877-3958, call ahead to make reservations, trips start at $25). This place offers canoe rentals and shuttle service for trips ranging from three to nine hours.

LAGRANGE

This lovely town, dating from 1824, was one of the first established in West Tennessee and was the first entire town in Tennessee to be placed on the National Register. Many antebellum homes lie along the highway, although at this

writing none is open to the public. One of them, **Woodlawn,** noted by a historical marker, was built in 1828. Unlike most of the houses here, which face north or south, this one looks east—seems the owner didn't want to have to stare at the railroad tracks.

The decade before the Civil War marked the peak of LaGrange, a bustling town with the La-Grange Female College and LaGrange Synodical College for Men. The latter produced only one class of graduates in 1861, and every one of them volunteered for the Confederacy. When the war came, Woodlawn was temporarily used as a headquarters by Union General William T. Sherman. General U. S. Grant and his wife also spent time in LaGrange. The men's college was destroyed, as were 40 homes.

Today LaGrange is a pleasant place to visit. Worth a stop is **Cogbill's General Store and Museum** (14840 LaGrange Rd., 901/878-1235, www.lagrangetn.com/homes-w.htm). The current proprietor, Lucy Cogbill, is the granddaughter of the original storekeeper. She carries merchandise from 104 artists and antique dealers, most of them local folks, including Armsterd Peeler, a folk artist who paints scenes on pine planks.

For more information, go to www.lagrangetn .com or call 901/878-1246.

GRAND JUNCTION

This town grew up at the crossroads of two railroads about 1854, and over the years its fortunes rose and fell with the trains. The Union army occupied the town during the Civil War, when most of the buildings were burned. A persistent local legend holds that Thomas A. Edison once operated the telegraph here.

The area's most influential visitor was Hobart C. Ames, a Yankee who came to town in the 1890s to do two things: shoot birds and spend money. The Massachusetts industrialist—his company made shovels and other tools—bought a plantation home built in 1847 and through purchases and leases amassed 25,000 acres. More than 200 families worked the fields, raising cotton and prize-winning cattle. Ames served as president of the National Field Trial Champion Association, a group that judged bird dogs, for 43 years. It was only natural that the national championships for dogs be held at Ames Plantation.

Ames and his wife usually spent only four months a year in Tennessee. When he died in 1945, his widow put the plantation in a trust to benefit the University of Tennessee, which made the 18,567-acre place the largest land research facility in the state. And it is still the epicenter of the bird-dog world.

Those who wish can tour the **Ames House** (901/878-1067, www.amesplantation.org, open on the fourth Thursdays March–Oct., and by appointment, $2). Some 19th-century homes and farm buildings have been restored and can be seen when the house is open. If a guide is available, visitors can go in the buildings. To get there, drive north of Grand Junction on Hwy. 18 toward Bolivar and turn left onto Ellington Road.

The **National Bird Dog Museum** (505 W. Hwy. 57, 731/764-2058, www.birddogfoundation.com, 9 A.M.–4 P.M. Tues.–Fri., 10 A.M.–4 P.M. Sat., 1–4 P.M. Sun., $2 adults, $1 children 18 and under) was built to honor the 36 distinct breeds of pointing dogs, spaniels, and retrievers. Displays mostly consist of paintings and photos of celebrated dogs, although saddles, videos of dogs working, and Ames memorabilia are on hand. A new Wildlife Heritage Center contains exhibits of quail, pheasant, and other game birds in their habitat.

Events

The **National Field Trials** (505 W. Hwy. 57, 731/764-2058, www.birddogfoundation.com, mid-Feb., free) is a time when dog fanciers come from all over to hobnob with each other and to watch the dogs hunt for quail and other birds. Most of this is done from "the gallery," the name for hundreds of people who follow the action while on horseback. Visitors bring their own horses, saddle up, and ride off. Those who have no horses will not see a great deal.

Shopping

Tennessee Pewter Company (133 Madison Ave., 800/764-2064 or 731/764-2064, www .tnpewter.com, 9 A.M.–4 P.M. Mon.–Thurs.) makes and sells more than 500 spun pewter products such as tabletop services, goblets, bowls, candleholders, tumblers, coffee sets, salt and pepper shakers, and steins. The company also produces cast pewter (melted and poured into molds) for jewelry, collectibles, letter openers, and key rings. More than 400 items are available, including a bust of Nathan Bedford Forrest. Visitors can see pewter being spun or cast whenever the place is open, but the best days to see the operations are Tuesday and Wednesday, when the complete staff is on site.

BIG HILL POND STATE NATURAL AREA

Eight miles south of Selmer on Hwy. 57, this 4,218-acre park (731/645-7967, www.tnstateparks .com) sits at the confluence of the Tuscumbia and Hatchie Rivers and is less developed than other state parks. Wildlife abounds here.

The park features hiking trails, a 73-foot observation tower with a 360-degree view, and 165-acre Travis McNatt Lake. The "pond" in the park's name came from a railroad embankment that restricted the drainage of the surrounding wetlands and created a 35-acre lake. The park has 30 **camping** spaces with no electrical hookups. In the winter the water is turned off and the bathhouse closed, but the campground is still open.

COUNCE

Highway 57 leading through Counce should be designated "Tennessee's Barbecue Highway," for along this road is the greatest concentration of barbecue places in the state.

Price's Bar-B-Q (off Hwy. 57, 731/689-5248, 5 A.M.–6 P.M. Mon.–Sat.) specializes in hickory-smoked barbecue, baby back ribs, and catfish. **The Red Wood Hut** (off Hwy. 57, 731/689-3260, 10 A.M.-10 P.M. daily) offers a hot buffet for lunch along with sandwiches, hot melts, and steaks. The folks here smoke their own pork barbecue. **The Ribcage** (off Hwy. 57, 731/689-3637, 10:30 A.M.–9 P.M. Mon.–Thurs., 10:30 A.M.-10 P.M. Fri.–Sun.) serves ribs and barbecue as well as smoked turkey, ham, and chicken.

Pickwick Catfish Farms Restaurant (off Hwy. 57, 731/689-3805, www.pickwickcatfishfarms.com, 5–8:30 P.M. Fri.–Sat., noon–dark Sun.) specializes in smoked catfish and offers all-you-can-eat fried catfish, ribs, and shrimp.

Counce is also home to the **Tenneco Packaging Company Arboretum** (731/689-3111, open during daylight hours, free), on the grounds of the mill just off Hwy. 57 The arboretum grows trees and shrubs native to Tennessee, Alabama, and Mississippi. Visitors can walk along a trail that leads past 73 kinds of trees, many of them labeled.

If you're staying over, try the **Hampton Inn** (Hwy. 57 and Old South Rd., 800/HAMPTON [426-7866] or 731/689-3031) or **Hardin County Tourism** (507 Main St., Savannah, 800/552-3866 or 731/925-2364, www.tourhardincounty.org, 9 A.M.–5 P.M. Mon.–Fri., 9 A.M.–1 P.M. Sat.).

PICKWICK LANDING STATE RESORT PARK

This park (731/689-3129, www.tnstateparks .com) covers 1,392 acres, but the focus here is the water. Pickwick Dam impounds the Tennessee River to create Pickwick Lake and has locks for pleasure and commercial river traffic to use.

Visitors can golf on a par-72, 18-hole course, or swimming, boat, or fish in the lake. The marina offers rental boats and slips for mariners who are passing though. The country-style **restaurant** in the inn serves breakfast, lunch, and dinner daily.

Accommodations begin with the **inn** (800/250-8615 or 731/689-3135, $73–78), with 75 single and double rooms, as well as 10 two-bedroom housekeeping cabins, each with central heat and air, TV, and a fireplace. These cost $600 year-round and can be rented only by the week in the summer. Seniors get a 10 percent discount on lodging. The inn and cabins are extremely popular, and they should be reserved as far ahead as possible.

Forty-eight **campsites** all come with electrical and water hookups and a central bathhouse. Campsites are allocated on a first-come, first-served basis. The **Bruton Branch Primitive Area,** across the lake from the main park, has a modern bathhouse and campsites with no hookups.

Jon's Pier (off Hwy. 57 S., 731/689-3575, dinner Mon.–Sat., in summer dinner also on Sun.) serves prime rib, ribs, and seafood. It's about four miles below the dam and about 1.5 miles from the Mississippi state line on the Counce side of the water.

SHILOH NATIONAL MILITARY PARK

Many Civil War parks, particularly the ones near large cities, occupy only a part of the historic ground. This one, fortunately, covers approximately 96 percent of the Shiloh battlefield. Visitors can drive a 9.5-mile auto tour route or, better yet, ride a bicycle along it.

The Battle

The battle that took place here April 6 and 7, 1862, was the first big battle of the Civil War. Forty thousand Union troops under Ulysses S. Grant had come down the Tennessee River on their way to the state of Mississippi, stopping at a little hamlet called Pittsburg Landing to await the arrival of an army under D. C. Buell. Moving toward them was a Southern army of 44,000 men commanded by Albert Sidney Johnston, who aimed to destroy the Union troops before any reinforcements arrived.

Neither force had seen much combat. Grant's troops were so green that he decided to drill them rather than fortify his positions. This was a critical mistake. The Southerners had raw troops as well, but they were eager for battle.

Grant was eating breakfast nine miles downstream in Savannah when thousands of Southerners giving the rebel yell poured through the woods and onto the Northern troops. Grant heard the cannon and ordered a steamboat to take him to Pittsburg Landing. General William

T. Sherman was in the thick of battle—one that relentlessly pushed back his troops.

The South's General Johnston thought he had the battle won. He rode up near the front, hoping to spur his troops onward. The air hummed with bullets, several of which clipped the general's clothing. One cut an artery in his leg, a wound so slight that Johnston didn't take it seriously until his loss of blood made him almost pass out. Aides lifted him from his horse to the ground, where he soon died.

Confusion reigned. Southern and Northern troops wandered around in the thick forest, getting separated from their regiments and fighting a thousand individual fights. The Union forces finally regrouped along a country lane, known as the Sunken Lane, and there repelled the repeated Confederate attacks that befell them. The fighting was so fierce that the area in front of this lane was dubbed "The Hornet's Nest." Finally, the Southerners rolled up 62 cannons—the largest concentration of artillery firepower ever seen on a North American battlefield—and forced the Union troops to retreat. Their valiant six-hour stand along the Sunken Lane had given Grant enough time to form another line, and the Confederates, now under Braxton Bragg, were too weary to pursue them.

During the night, the Union reinforcements crossed the Tennessee River to join the battle, and the next morning the Union army moved forward, recrossing ground it had given up the day before. Theirs was a gruesome march, for it took them past the dead and wounded from the day before. Some of the bodies had been partially eaten by hogs. By noon, the Southerners could see that they were losing, and they retreated toward Mississippi. The next day Grant sent Sherman in a halfhearted pursuit, but troops under Nathan Bedford Forrest dissuaded him from accomplishing anything.

As the first major battle, Shiloh it showed both sides just how terrible this conflict was going to be. Grant hoped a convincing victory would make the Confederates give up, but Shiloh changed his mind. Writing in his autobiography years later, Grant recalled, "[The Southern army] made such a gallant effort to regain what had

been lost, I gave up all idea of saving the Union except by complete conquest." The South, which had hoped that the North would lack the will to pursue the war, saw a fearsome resolve on the part of its commanders.

One of every four men in the Battle of Shiloh was killed or wounded—21,000 in all. More Americans died at Shiloh—an estimated 3,477—than in the Revolutionary War, the War of 1812, and the Mexican War put together. Ironically, "Shiloh" is a biblical word meaning "place of peace."

Information and Services

Check the park's **visitors center** (731/689-5696, www.nps.gov/shil, 8 A.M.–5 P.M. daily, $3 each for ages over 16, $10 families) for information on talks, tours, and demonstrations.

Those who would like to own a piece of the Civil War should visit **Ed Shaw's Gift Shop** (off Hwy. 22 S., 731/689-5080, 10 A.M.–4 P.M. Mon.–Fri., noon–4:00 P.M. Sat.), which sells relics of the Shiloh battle—bullets, buttons, belt buckles, and so forth. Minié balls—bullets from rifles—sell for $0.75 apiece. Other bullets go for $0.22 to $1. Native American artifacts and souvenirs are on hand as well.

Shiloh's Civil War Relics (4730 Hwy. 22, 731/689-4114, www.shilohrelics.com, 9 A.M.–5 P.M. Mon.–Sat., 1–5 P.M. Sun.) sells firearms, swords, belt buckles, and other Civil War items; there is a huge variety to choose from, and the owner was an appraiser for PBS's *Antiques Roadshow.*

ADAMSVILLE

This small town has managed to produce three men whose talents and shenanigans brought them national acclaim.

The **Buford Pusser Home and Museum** (342 Pusser St., 731/632-4080, www.talentondisplay.com/pusser.html, 11 A.M.–5 P.M. Mon.–Fri., 9 A.M.–5 P.M. Sat., 1–5 P.M. Sun., $5 adults, $2 children ages 6–18) commemorates the famed sheriff of McNairy County, whose crusade against lawless elements has become a part of popular culture.

© JEFF BRADLEY

proprietor Bobby Gibbs of Gibbs Gas-N-Oil collectibles in Adamsville

The late Ray Blanton was a member of Congress who then served as governor of Tennessee from 1975 to 1979. In general his administration ran the state well, except for the actions of a few ill-chosen cronies. Blanton's successor, Lamar Alexander, was sworn in early when it was discovered that the lame-duck Blanton staffers were taking bribes to commute the sentences of dozens of felons, many of them murderers and armed robbers. The governor was not charged with this offense, but he did serve time in prison for his involvement in illegal efforts to sell state liquor licenses. A subsequent U.S. Supreme Court ruling overturned his fraud conviction, and a Tennessee court restored his citizenship. He ran again for his old seat in Congress, telling people, "The voters know I was railroaded and falsely accused." They might have known this, but they did not vote for him in sufficient numbers.

Adamsville was also the birthplace of **Dewey Phillips,** the Memphis disc jockey who first recognized the talent of Elvis Presley.

SELMER

Several restaurants in Selmer serve a hamburger called a **"slugburger"** or "cereal burger." It originated in Corinth, Mississippi, and makes ground beef go farther by mixing it with soybean grit and other ingredients. How did it get its other-than-appetizing name? "Oh, those kids," said one restaurant worker. "They started calling them that."

Pat's Cafe (Court and 3rd Sts. 731/645-6671, 5 A.M.2 P.M. Mon.–Sat.) has full-throttle country breakfasts. Lunch consists of sandwiches and salads—slugburgers if so desired.

Wink's Diner (137 S. 2nd St., 11:30 A.M.–4 P.M. Mon.–Sat.) makes slugburgers so good that it serves an average of 400 per day, compared to only 30 or so hamburgers. "I sell a world of them," said Wink, who also offers sandwiches and other items.

Risner's Steak House (junction of U.S. 45 and Hwy. 57, in nearby Eastview, 731/645-5648, 6 A.M.–9 P.M. daily) has a special that few restaurants in Tennessee offer—all the quail one can eat.

Pusser, who was six feet, six inches tall, worked as a professional wrestler before moving back to his hometown and becoming a law officer. Elected sheriff in 1964, he took on the job of ridding the county of a group of criminals who, having been run out of Alabama, established themselves near the state line in south McNairy County. In battling the mob, Pusser was shot eight times, knifed seven times, and once fought off six men at once, sending three to jail and three to the emergency room. In 1967, a car pulled alongside Pusser's and an occupant fired shots that killed his wife and blew away much of his jaw. Eventually, he prevailed. Pusser served three terms as sheriff, and his story was made into the very successful *Walking Tall* series of movies. In August 1974, he died in the crash of his new Corvette. His home is now a museum devoted to his exploits. The **Buford Pusser Festival** remembers the legendary lawman with carnival rides, arts and crafts, and other events the weekend before Memorial Day.

This deal is offered every Thursday night, while Friday and Saturday nights feature hickory-smoked ribs.

Overnight options are the **Southland Motor Lodge** (515 E. Poplar Ave., 731/645-6155). For more information, contact **McNairy County Chamber of Commerce** (114 Cypress St., 731/645-6360, www.centuryinter.net/mccc, 8:30 A.M.–5 P.M. Mon.–Fri.).

SALTILLO

One of the last remaining ferries on the Ten-nessee River connects this little town with the eastern shore. The **ferry** runs Monday through Saturday every week. If it happens to be on the other side of the river, motorists should blow their horns for service. **Saltillo Marina Campground** (731/687-7353) in Riverview has 18 sites, but no water.

For more information, contact **Hardin County Chamber of Commerce** (507 Main St., Savannah, 800/552-3866 or 731/925-2363, www.tourhardincounty.org, 9 A.M.–5 P.M. Mon.–Fri., also during daylight saving time, 10 A.M.–4 P.M. Sat., 1–4 P.M. Sun.).

Jackson

As the largest city between Memphis and Nashville, Jackson is a good place from which to explore the Western Plains. Jackson has the largest choice of motels and restaurants, the best bookstore outside of Memphis, and a minor league baseball park that's the place to spend a summer evening.

Founded in 1821 and named after Andrew Jackson, it owes its prominence to the presence of the railroads and its location between Memphis and the Tennessee River. The tracks came to town three years before the Civil War, and by the time fighting broke out Jackson became a target for Northern armies. It was occupied by the North in 1862.

After the Civil War, the railroads worked on connecting the Deep South with the Midwest, and this directly benefited Jackson. The homes in the East Main Street Historic District reflect this prosperity, which also extended to the large numbers of freed slaves who settled in Jackson to work for the railroad. Lane College, established in 1882, was one of the first colleges established for black people by black people. It still educates students.

Musically, Jackson has been home to significant figures. Blues fans know of two "Sonny Boy" Williamsons, both of whom played harmonica—or harp, to blues folk. The first one, John Lee Williamson, was born here and played with Sleepy John Estes and other locals but did his most significant work in Chicago. Among his songs is "Good Morning Little School Girl."

Big Maybelle was a blues shouter in the '50s and '60s, while Bertha Dorsey was one of the very few black women to experience success in country music. Recorded under the name Ruby Falls, her songs appeared during the '70s, as did those of Jackson native Kenny Vernon, best known for the duet "Picking Wild Mountain Berries." The most famous Jackson musician, however, is Carl Perkins, who lived and owned a restaurant in Jackson until his death in January 1998.

Jackson was the birthplace, in 1926, of Dave Gardner, a comedian and social commentator who found national fame in 1957 on the *Tonight Show* when Jack Paar was the host. Gardner, who billed himself as "Brother Dave," was part of the vanguard of comedy albums alongside Lenny Bruce and Mort Sahl. He is credited with inventing the 100 millimeter-long cigarette; his act usually lasted as long as three of these. As the sixties progressed, his humor did not. His cracks at civil rights leaders and anti-war protestors played well in Southern nightclubs, but he all but vanished from the national scene. Brother Dave died in 1983 and is buried in Jackson.

Last but not least, Jackson is home to the branch of Procter and Gamble that makes Pringles potato chips.

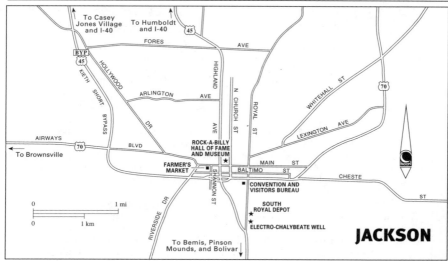

© AVALON TRAVEL PUBLISHING, INC.

SIGHTS

When Jackson was installing its first modern waterworks in the early 1880s, it tapped an artesian well and water began flowing out of the ground. Named the Electro Chalybeate Well, it became the centerpiece of a park and attracted many who believed that the waters possessed curative powers. The park is now gone, but the city has restored the old fountain and built a gazebo over it. Visitors can still drink the water, absolutely free, next to the Jackson Utility Division's water operations center on South Royal Street.

The **South Royal Depot** (Royal St., 731/425-8223, 10 A.M.–3 P.M. Mon.–Sat.) is one of two railroad museums in Jackson. Restored to its 1907 appearance, it contains exhibits of Jackson railroad history.

The most famous railroad person hereabouts was an engineer who grew up in Cayce, Kentucky. Although his given name was Jonathan Luther, his coworkers knew him as "Casey" Jones, and on a dark night in Mississippi he passed into popular history when his train rear-ended another train. The **Casey Jones Home and Railroad Museum** (off of I-40, 731/668-1222, www.caseyjones.ocm/pages/serv01.htm,

9 A.M.–8 P.M. daily, $4 adults, $3.50 seniors, $3 for children 6–12) features the engineer's home as its centerpiece. The house was moved from its original location, and now it contains a museum with various items such as the watch Casey carried on his fatal run, the hearse that carried him thereafter, and a railroad engine of the kind that he operated. The village also contains an old country store and restaurant as well as the Casey Jones Station Inn.

RECREATION

Cypress Grove Nature Park (three miles west of Jackson along U.S. 70/Hwy. 1, 731/425-8364, www.cityofjackson.net, 8 A.M.–5 P.M. daily year-round, until 7:30 P.M. during daylight saving time, free) is a 165-acre park with a 6,000-foot-long boardwalk that takes visitors through a cypress forest, an open meadow, along two lakes, and past several enclosures containing various raptors. For those who cannot make it to Reelfoot Lake place to see cypress trees, those hardwoods whose knobby "kr out of the water. Fishing is allo shore of the lakes, but most peo

THE KING OF ROCKABILLY

Carl Perkins was born in 1932 to a sharecropping family outside of Tiptonville, near Reelfoot Lake. His extended family moved to Bemis, a factory town south of Jackson, when he was 14, and he began playing with his brothers in a band called The Perkins Brothers.

Carl was signed to a contract in 1955 by legendary Sam Phillips of Sun Studio, where he met Elvis Presley and Johnny Cash. The three toured together, and back in the studio Perkins recorded his own composition, "Blue Suede Shoes," supposedly inspired when Perkins played at a dance during which a young man kept telling his partner not to step on his shoes. The song was the first record to top the pop, country, and rhythm and blues charts, and Perkins began to look like the next Elvis. Unlike Elvis, he could write his own material.

Then tragedy struck. On the way to New York City to appear on the *Ed Sullivan Show,* the band's car crashed in Delaware, breaking Carl's neck and causing injuries that later led to the death of one of his brothers. It was Elvis who wound up singing "Blue Suede Shoes" on the *Ed Sullivan Show.*

That accident stunted Perkins's career, and he was surpassed by fellow Sun artists Johnny Cash and Jerry Lee Lewis. Despite his troubles, he continued writing songs, and he always had a strong following in Europe. The Beatles recorded three of his songs—"Honey Don't," "Everybody's Trying to Be My Baby," and "Matchbox." He moved into country music, reaching a pinnacle in 1971 when Johnny Cash recorded his famous "Daddy Sang Bass." Perkins died in January 1998 after a series of strokes. He was 65 years old.

Appropriately located in the town where the late Carl Perkins made his home for years, the **International Rock-a-Billy Hall of Fame and Museum** (105 N. Church St., 731/427-6262, www.rockabillyhall.org, 10 A.M.–4 P.M. weekdays $10) serves as a great warm-up act for musical pilgrims on their way to Memphis. The museum has yet to establish its regular hours, so call ahead or see the website. To get there, take Exit 82 off I-40 and go south on U.S. 45. In the center of town, turn left onto Main Street and then left onto Church Street.

The museum contains memorabilia such as blue suede boots, a guitar, and clothing from Carl Perkins; a saxophone from Ace Cannon; drums from W. S. Holland; and oil paintings and early posters of Elvis. The most bizarre item, however, has to be the defibrillator and paddles certified to be the actual ones that medical personnel used to try to jolt Elvis back to life in Memphis's Baptist Memorial Hospital. Now there's something you won't see at Graceland.

The museum has 35 hours of videos showing conversations with early rockabilly stars; they recount tales such as loading four people, a bass fiddle, guitars, and a drum set into a car and riding—in pre-Interstate highway days—from Memphis to New York City.

to see the birds and other wildlife. Depending on the season, visitors can see hummingbirds, migratory waterfowl, and owls. Herds of deer live in the park, as do generous varieties of insects.

Jackson is home to the **West Tenn Diamond Jaxx,** who play AA baseball at Pringles Park (4 Fun Pl., 731/988-5299, www.diamondjaxx.com), re an affiliate of the Chicago Cubs organiza-Games are played April through early Sep-⁓ tickets start at $4.

ACCOMMODATIONS

Highland Place Bed and Breakfast (519 N. Highland Ave., 731/427-1472, www.bbon-line.com/tn/highlandplace, $75–95) occupies a stately 1911 three-story brick colonial built in the classic revival style. It has been remodeled from top to bottom. The three guest rooms all have private baths. Two interesting architectural features are the cherry-paneled library on the first floor, with a working fireplace—there are three in all—and the tiger-striped oak planks used throughout the house. Other meals may be served by arrangement.

Jackson offers a generous range of national chain hotels. For something different, try the **Casey Jones Station Inn** (I-40 and U.S. 45 Bypass, 731/668-3636 or 800/628-2812, $36.95–69.95). Sleep in one of the 50 rooms in a motellike place, or choose lodging in one of the four railroad cars—two cabooses or two other railroad cars. Rates include a deluxe Southern breakfast bar with country ham, sausage, Virginia ham, chocolate gravy, and redeye gravy.

Other options are the **Comfort Inn** (1936 U.S. 45, 800/4CHOICE [424-6423] or 731/668-4100, $50–55), and the **Garden Plaza Hotel** (1770 U.S. 45 Bypass S., 800/3GARDEN [342-7336] or 731/664-6900, $65–75).

FOOD

Baudo's Restaurant (559 Wiley Parker Rd., 731/668-1447, www.baudos.com, 11 A.M.–2 P.M. Mon.–Fri., 5–10 P.M. Mon.–Sat., entrées $11) serves Italian and American cuisine. For those who want to try their hands at "Blue Suede Shoes" or other songs, Baudo's features karaoke each Thursday at 9 P.M. Comedy showcases are every Friday and Saturday night at 9:30 P.M.

Brooksie's Barn (561 Oil Well Rd., 731/664-2276, lunch and dinner Tues.–Sat., lunch Sun.) was built by a gentleman who used to haul his rig and compete in barbecue contests—and win. He built this barn and has been serving barbecue, catfish, hush puppies, ribs, and fried chicken ever since.

M The Catfish Cabin (1290 S. Highland Ave., 731/422-1001, dinner Mon.–Thurs., lunch and dinner Fri.–Sun., entrées $7) has one fan who warns patrons not to fill up on "the Absolutely Magnificent God's Own Perfect hush puppies." Doing so would preclude enjoying the catfish, which is served all-you-can-eat or as a straight dinner. Catfish Cabin also serves steak, country ham, chicken, shrimp, oysters, snapper, and lobster tails. The late Carl

Perkins was one of the owne and photos and other memora on the walls.

China Cafe (31 Bowling D lunch and dinner Tues.–Sat., lu full menu as well as a buffet of Cantonese, Mandarin, and Szechuan dishes.

The Old Country Store Restaurant (Casey Jones Village, 731/668-1223, breakfast, lunch, dinner daily). Buffets of country cooking are the feature here, along with over 500 seats, although diners can order à la carte.

Pig House Barbecue (1024 Campbell St., 731/423-8566, 10 A.M.–8 P.M. daily) sells sublime barbecue sandwiches—no ribs—and a few side orders amid a bunch of University of Tennessee paraphernalia.

Suede's (2263 N. Highland Ave., 731/664-1956, www.carlperkins.com, lunch and dinner Mon.–Sat., lunch Sun.) was owned by the late rockabilly and country great Carl Perkins, featuring dishes such as A Whole Lotta Steaking Going On and Boppin' the Blues Bar B Cue. If this restaurant were in Nashville, it would be called a museum. On display are guitars, gold records, and lots of photographs—Carl Perkins with Paul McCartney, Clint Black, Elvis, George Harrison, and other admirers.

SHOPPING

Jackson boasts 14 antique stores. A brochure describing them is available at the chamber of commerce. **Brooks Shaw and Son's Old Country Store** (Casey Jones Village, 731/668-1223) displays more than 15,000 Southern antiques along with candy, collectibles, and souvenirs.

The Cheese Factory (Casey Jones Village, 800/960-3054 or 731/664-8580, 9 A.M.–6 P.M. Mon.–Sat., noon–5 P.M. Sun.) makes cheddar, Colby, flavored cheeses, and spreads. One of the more popular is a country ham-and-cheddar spread. It also sells gourmet meats, preserves, and specialty sauces.

The West Tennessee Farmer's Market (Shannon St. and Market Dr., 731/425-8308, open early mornings) has an enclosed building and open sheds. In addition to seasonal produce, the

LIFE IN A COTTON MILL COMMUNITY

In his *Tennessee's Historic Landscapes,* Carroll Van West gives considerable space to the **Bemis** community south of Jackson. In the early years of the 20th century, Northern capital flowed into Tennessee to build factories, and across the state paternalistic companies set up planned communities to house their workers.

The company here was a subsidiary of the Bemis Brothers Bag Company, which made cotton bags used to package flour, sugar, and other goods. In 1900, the company set up a mill alongside the tracks of the Illinois Central Railroad south of Jackson to manufacture cotton cloth to be sent to Bemis bag factories elsewhere. The idea was simple: locate the factory where it could buy cotton from farmers, avoiding the middlemen and shipping costs. It didn't hurt, either, that unions were hard to find in rural Tennessee. The town was named for company founder Judson Bemis and designed by his son, Albert, a graduate of M.I.T.

Albert wanted to do it right, not just to house workers but to create a model town on his 300-acre drawing board. He and his M.I.T. experts set up a village complete with homes, stores, churches, a hotel, train station, and many other features necessary for a good life. The town had everything its residents needed: doctors, dentists, law enforcement.

The younger Bemis had some good ideas. Instead of a factory town with houses that looked like they were on an Army base, he laid out neighborhoods with distinctive types of housing. When residents weren't working, they could enjoy churches, a swimming pool, parks, and a YMCA. A large theater seating 1,000 offered plays and movies.

Three thousand people lived in Bemis as late as 1940, and the company began selling the houses to workers in 1965. Jackson annexed Bemis in 1975. The Bemis company sold their mills in 1980. Other companies ran them for 11 more years, and closed them in 1991.

Efforts are underway to convert the Bemis Theater into a museum about the community. The four story Bemis Mill is now a warehouse. With its arched windows, it faintly resembles a castle. To tour Bemis, drive down Highland Avenue (U.S. 45) three miles south of the courthouse and turn right onto Bemis Lane.

market offers quilt shows, blues festivals, and the odd political rally.

Wildlife in Wood Studio (in the gazebo at Casey Jones Village, 731/668-2782, 9 A.M.–5:30 P.M.Mon.–Fri., by appointment Sat.) contains wildlife carvings in wood, original paintings, and prints. Visitors can watch the artist, Dee Moss, at work.

INFORMATION

The **Jackson/Madison County Convention and Visitors Bureau** is in the Civic Center (400 S. Highland Ave., 800/498-4748 or 731/425-8333, www.jacksontn.com, 9 A.M.–4:30 P.M. Mon.–Thurs.).

Shannon Street Blues Festival, held in June at the West Tennessee Farmer's Market, honors Sonny Boy Williamson. **Casey Jones Old Time Music Festival** (behind the Casey Jones Village, at the amphitheater, 731/686-7342), is a celebration of string music. Categories include guitar, dobro, bluegrass banjo, and buckdancing.

South of Jackson

PINSON MOUNDS

Tennessee's first three-story building wasn't built until 1823, yet this 1,162-acre state archaeological area contains a seven-story structure that has stood for at least 1,600 years. At 72 feet high, **Saul's Mound** is the second-highest Indian mound in the United States—the highest is Monk's Mound in East St. Louis.

The area's **museum** (731/988-5614, www .tnstateparks.com, 8 A.M.–4:30 P.M. Mon.–Sat., 1–5 P.M. Sun., free), which was brilliantly designed to resemble a mound itself, assembles what tantalizingly little knowledge anthropologists have about the people who worked so hard to build these structures. The mounds are piles of earth, probably carried basket by basket from surrounding land. The archaeological evidence assembled so far suggests that most of the mounds were built during the first three centuries A.D.

While a few of the mounds contain burial remains, most seem to have been used for ceremonies. When Joel Pinson, part of a group of surveyors mapping land acquired from the Chickasaw in the Treaty of 1818, found the mounds in 1820, the Native Americans in the area at that time denied building them and claimed to have no knowledge of anyone who did.

Visitors can walk up a staircase leading to a platform atop Saul's Mound, which in its heyday was no doubt higher than its current 72 feet. From the platform the visitor can see other mounds and get a sense of the immensity of this site, which consists of at least 15 mounds, an earthen geometrical enclosure, and a habitation area of more than 400 acres.

The museum contains an 80-seat theater along with video and educational displays describing the people who built Pinson Mounds. A walk-through display focuses on the various cultures that make up Tennessee's prehistoric past. Pinson Mounds is closed weekends December through February. The area contains picnic tables and hiking trails, but no camping is permitted.

HENDERSON

This town is the seat of Chester County, which in 1882 became the last county created in Tennessee. After the Civil War, a large family named Hurst moved into the western part of the county, becoming so predominant that the area was termed "Hurst Nation." Perhaps they had to stick together, for during the war they supported the Union.

The 1939 *WPA Guide* reports that this was the moonshine center for West Tennessee:

> *Under the leaves in the hollows [the moon-shiners] stashed away the fresh corn and let it charter (char) for months. When aged, the deep red liquor was clear of verdigris (fusel oil) and held a bead the size of number five shot. There were no "rabbit eyes on it to pop off" (big bubbles that foam and burst as soon as the bottle is shaken). Certain brands were known as "creeping likker," because they kicked "slow and powerful."*

The unidentified writer of the preceding sounds as if he did considerable research on that topic. Chances are he was not a graduate of **Freed Hardeman University,** which is affiliated with the Church of Christ and serves more than 1,300 students. The university maintains a museum of its memorabilia in the administration building. For more information, visit www.fhu.edu.

Six miles east of town at the intersection of Hwy. 100 and Hwy. 22, you'll find **Joyner's Bar-B-Que,** with ribs, pork, and chicken.

CHICKASAW STATE RUSTIC PARK

This state park occupies 1,280 acres of the Chickasaw State Forest, a 14,384-acre tract of timberland that stands on some of the highest ground in West Tennessee. Like many Tennessee parks, the emphasis is on recreation: swimming, picnicking, boating, fishing, tennis, basketball, archery, horseback riding, square dancing, evening movies, and campfires.

Accommodations (800/421-6683 or 731/989-5141, www.tnstateparks.com, open all year) include a group lodge, cabins, and camping. The lodge can accommodate groups of up to 40 people. Thirteen housekeeping cabins, complete with fireplaces, can sleep four or six people. These are also open all year. To make reservations, call numbers above.

The park has 110 campsites, 70 of which have hookups, and hot showers and flush toilets are available in campground bathhouses. The camping season opens in March for RVs, in May for tents; it ends in November for tents and one month later for RVs. The horse camping section is open all year, and if campers have no horse and there is still space, they can stay.

BOLIVAR AND VICINITY

Bolivar came into being as the town of Hatchie, named for the river for which the town was the head of navigation. Situated in lands bought from the Indians, it began as a trading post. Town boosters dreamed that the Mississippi and Tennessee Rivers would be joined by a canal that would go right beside the town, but it never happened. The town's name was changed in 1825 to honor Simon Bolivar, the liberator of Colombia and Venezuela—the first town in the country to be so named.

Hardeman County, of which Bolivar is the seat, produces more hardwood lumber than any other county in Tennessee. The entire area was covered with hardwood forests when planters arrived in the early 1800s, and their slaves cleared the large cotton fields that still produce today. McAnulty's Woods, a conservation site in town, is thought to be the only virgin forest remaining in West Tennessee.

After the Civil War, many of the freed slaves entered into work contracts with planters and other employers. A fascinating website, www.freedmensbureau.com, gives the exact wording and spelling of some of these documents in Hardeman County. For more information, contact **Hardeman County Chamber of Com-**

merce (500 W. Market St., 731/658-6554, www.hardemancont.org/chamber.html).

Sights

The Bills-McNeal District begins with **The Little Courthouse** (731/659-0017, open by appointment only, $3 per person) built of logs in 1824. When the county government moved into larger quarters, the logs were covered with clapboards and the erstwhile courthouse was transformed into a Federal home that's now used as the county museum. Part of its collection consists of some silver spoons commissioned by an early lawyer whose first client paid him in silver.

The Pillars (Bills and Washington Sts., 731/659-0017, open by appointment only, $3 per person) was home to John Houston Bills, who kept a private journal from 1843 to 1871. Then, as now, good help was hard to get; the builders of the town's first brick home installed the eight fluted Doric columns upside down. That didn't bother the guests, however, who included James K. Polk, David Crockett, and Sam Houston.

Also in town are two historic churches. **Bolivar Presbyterian,** at Market Street across from the post office, was organized in 1852 and is the oldest brick church in the county. During the Civil War, General Lew Wallace, later the author of *Ben Hur,* worshipped here. **St. James Episcopal Church** was built in 1870 in the Victorian Gothic style.

When most West Tennesseans think of Bolivar, they think of "being sent to Bolivar," for on the western end of the town stands **Western Mental Health Institute** (Hwy. 64, 731/228-2000). Tours of the institute can be arranged by making a reservation a week ahead, admission is free. The 1889 administration building is a great example of Victorian Gothic revival. The institute covers several hundred acres, and in past days the patients raised much of their food, had a uniformed baseball team, and participated in all manner of activities. The number of patients peaked in 1965 at 3,757 and now stands at 264. Patients come from all of West Tennessee except for Shelby County.

According to the official history of the institute, Elvis Presley spent some time here in the late

'50s, but only as a truck driver hauling away some bricks from a demolished smokestack.

Accommodations

Magnolia Manor (418 N. Main St., 731/658-6700) was built by slaves in the late 1840s from brick made on the site. Modeled on an English country home, the Georgian house was occupied during the Civil War by Union Generals Grant, Sherman, Logan, and McPherson. According to a tale still told in the house about the occupation, General Sherman mightily offended the hostess during a meal with some remark to the effect that all Southern women and children should be exterminated. She abruptly left the table and was found weeping on the back porch by General Grant. When he learned the source of her distress, he ordered Sherman to apologize. The future torcher of Atlanta did so, but he was so irked at the order that he slashed at the solid walnut stairway with his sword. The mark of that anger is still there. The house contains two suites and two other rooms, all of which share baths. Rates range $85–95.

Motel options are the **Aristocrat Motor Inn** (108 Porter St., 731/658-6451), and **The Bolivar Inn** (626 W. Market St., 731/658-3372).

Food

Joe's Restaurant (on the square on Market St., 731/658-7255, breakfast, lunch, and dinner Mon.–Sat.) offers a dinner specialty of seafood and steaks. Also in Bolivar is **Richard's Bar-B-Q** (W. Jackson St., 731/658-7652, 10:30 A.M.–8:15 P.M. Tues.–Sat.), which advertises that its barbecue is as "sweet and tender as a mother's love." Diners can choose from ribs, chicken, steaks, and even barbecued bologna.

WHITEVILLE

Heading out of Bolivar on Hwy. 100, the traveler comes to this little town, which has three wonderful sources of food. **Backermann's Bakery and Cheese Shop** (on U.S. 64, 731/254-8473, 7:30 A.M.–5 P.M. Tues.–Sat.) is a Mennonite bakery that also carries bulk foods, lunch meats,

and cheese. The bakery generally has on hand eight kinds of yeast bread and six kinds of pies and cookies.

Anderson Fruit Farms (on U.S. 64, 731/658-5524 or 731/254-9530, 8 A.M.–6 P.M. Mon.–Sat.) grows and sells a great deal of fruit and vegetables. Pears, apples, and peaches come from 12,000 trees, and other crops such as corn, peas, strawberries, cantaloupes, watermelons, and blackberries are offered for sale at the farm store. During the fall the Andersons produce more than 15,000 gallons of apple cider. Try the fried pies, which are made daily by the women of the local Pentacostal church.

Cafe 100 (at the intersection of U.S. 64/Hwy. 15 and Hwy. 100, 731/254-9409, opens at 5 A.M.) serves plate lunches Monday through Saturday.

SOMERVILLE

This town, in the center of West Tennessee's plantation area, was the scene of a little-remembered episode of the Civil Rights movement. When African Americans sought to vote in 1959, the whites who ran the county banded together to wage economic warfare in an effort to prevent this from taking place. Merchants would not sell to blacks, physicians would not treat them, and anyone who attempted to register to vote was fired from his or her job. Once that year's cotton crop was gathered, plantation owners evicted 400 families, who banded together in "Tent City" to brave the cold weather. This determination to vote won the group national attention, and the federal government brought suit against landowners and merchants. The ensuing ruling ordered them to stop standing in the way of anyone wanting to vote.

Somerville has many historic homes, and the best time to see them is in late October during the **Architectural Treasures of Fayette County Tour.** The recently restored **Hanum-Rhea House** (211 W. North St., 901/465-8690, open by appointment), circa 1832, is now being used as the Fayette County Museum and Cultural Center.

Right on the square in town stands **Farmers**

Hardware (the square, 901/465-3971, 7 A.M.–5 P.M. Mon.–Fri., 8 A.M.–3 P.M. Sat.), a wonderful old-fashioned store that occupies a building erected in 1875. The owner, while poking around in the place, once found some .28-caliber bullets last manufactured in 1862. The store has a hole in the ceiling; it seems they used to assemble carriages upstairs and then lower them to the showroom floor.

The road from Somerville to Moscow goes through **Williston,** home of **Pleasant Retreat Bed and Breakfast** (420 Hotel St., 901/465-4599, www.bbonline.com/tn/pleasantretreat, $75). This 1850 home is furnished with antiques.

A group with the delightful name of the **Jackson Area Plectral Society** holds an annual Spring Music Festival, held at the Crawford Farm outside of town. The society is dedicated to old-time string music **Hogmania Barbecue Contest** takes place in September in the square of Somerville. For more details about these events and other information, contact **Fayette County Chamber of Commerce** (901/465-8690, www.fayettecountychamber.com).

North of Jackson

Motorists on U.S. 42 in Crockett County northwest of Jackson sometimes do a double-take when they look into a field and see buffalo. This is **Hillcrest** (901/734-6005, www.picktnprod-ucts.org/tourism/farmtour.html, open by appointment, free), a farm on which the same family has lived for five generations. In addition to the American bison, owner Claude Conley stocks zebras, wildebeests, scimitar-horned oryxes, and other exotic animals. Visitors are invited to stop and look at the animals. No formal tour is given but sometimes guests can be shown around.

HUMBOLDT

In West Tennessee, this town is synonymous with strawberries and a long-running festival that commemorates the red berries. It also was the home of the late Jesse Hill Ford, author of *The Liberation of Lord Byron Jones.* The 1965 novel told the story of a black mortician who, seeking a divorce from his unfaithful wife, names a white police officer as her lover. The mortician's white lawyer tips off the policeman, who murders the mortician. The book became a best-seller and a 1970 movie and brought fame to Ford, but it infuriated the people hereabouts, who knew it was based on real people and actual events.

Ford got his comeuppance, at least in Humboldtian eyes, when he was charged with murder in the death of a black man who parked one night along Ford's long driveway. Because of a racial dispute surrounding high school football, Ford's son—the captain of the team—had received threats, and Ford feared that the driver of the car was there to ambush his son. The writer claimed that he fired his rifle just to hold the car there until police arrived, and, after a trial that received national coverage, he was acquitted. Ford died in Nashville in 1996.

Sights

The former **City Hall** (1200 Main St., 731/784-1787, 9 A.M.–4 P.M. Mon., Wed., and Fri., free) contains two museums worth a stop. The Strawberry Festival Historical Museum exhibits relate to the celebrations that have been happening since 1934, but also to the history of Humboldt and surrounding area. Exhibits include featured elements that have been donated by residents of Humboldt county, which evoke the bygone days of West Tennessee.

The **West Tennessee Regional Center for the Arts** (1200 Main St., 731/784-1787, www.wtrac.tn.org, 9 A.M.–4:30 P.M. Mon.–Fri., $2) occupies the second floor. More than 175 objects, including oil paintings, watercolors, sculptures, prints, lithographs, pastels, and silk screens, make up the collection, which was assembled by Dr. and Mrs. Benjamin Caldwell.

T. G. Sheppard, the country singer-songwriter who hit a peak during the 1980s, is remembered as Billy Browder hereabouts, where he first saw the light of day in 1944.

The **West Tennessee Strawberry Festival** (731/784-1842, free) includes fireworks, gospel singing, BBQ cook-off, a checkers tournament, parade, arts and crafts show, five- and 10-kilometer runs, and a beauty pageant in the first full week in May.

Practicalities

Armour's Barbecue (607 W. Main St., 731/784-9450, 10 A.M.–6 P.M. Tues.–Sat.) serves barbecue and ribs. **Sam's Barbeque,** across the street from Armour's (731/784-9850, 10 A.M.–5 P.M. Thurs.–Sat.), has excellent BBQ of many varieties.

Kappis Steak House (600 U.S. 45 W. Bypass, 731/784-2077, 11 A.M.–8:30 P.M. Tues.–Thurs., 11 A.M.–10 P.M. Fri., 4–10 P.M. Sat., 11 A.M.–9 P.M. Sun.) serves a lunch and dinner buffet plus full menu. Kappis's Friday night seafood buffet is a local favorite. **Wall Street Grill** (2120 N. Central Ave., 731/784-1214) features steaks, sandwiches, soups, and salads for lunch and dinner every day.

Motels options are the **Heritage Inn** (3350 East End Dr., 731/784-2278), and **Regal Inn Motel** (618 N. 22nd Ave., 731/784-9693).

For information, contact **Humboldt Chamber of Commerce** (1200 Main St., 731/784-1842, www.humboldtntchamber.org, 8 A.M.–5 P.M. Mon.–Fri.).

MILAN

During World War II Tennessee was often chosen for defense-related facilities. One that survives is the **Milan Army Ammunition Plant,** which Martin Marietta Ordnance Systems operates on 22,000 acres east of town. Here 10 production lines crank out items varying from 40 mm cartridges to 155 mm artillery shells. An ebullient publicity brochure proclaims:

The Milan Army Ammunition Plant—it's the one place you should contact for your ammunition or other explosive-related requirements when you want immediate attention and on-schedule delivery of high-quality product.

West Tennessee Agricultural Museum (off U.S. 70A/79, 731/686-8067, http://milan.tennessee.edu, 8 A.M.–4 P.M. Mon.–Fri., noon–4 P.M. Sat., free) is one of the better museums on this end of the state. Its building was designed to accommodate the museum, which presents a chronological look at agriculture in the region. Beginning with the Indians, its displays move to the era of settlers, subsistence farmers, cotton plantations, and early mechanized farming. More than 2,600 implements are on display in the museum, which measures more than 16,000 square feet.

One of the missions of agricultural colleges is to demonstrate crops and techniques that will preserve the land, enhance profits, or somehow make farming better. An example of this is "no-till" farming, in which annual plowing, which can lead to erosion, is replaced by chemical herbicides that "burn down" weeds—better living through chemistry.

The **No-Till Field Day** (http://milan.tennessee.edu, 731/686-7362) hereabouts has evolved into a festival with events that appeal to those who wouldn't know a plow from a disc. It leads into a weekend filled with the latest farm machinery, methods, and inventions. It's held on the fourth Thursday in July.

If you're sticking around, try **Ramada Limited** (U.S. 45 E./U.S. 70, 800/2RAMADA [272-6232] or 731/686-3345). For food, check out **Hig's Restaurant** (1027 Oakwood Dr., 731/686-9901, lunch and dinner Mon.–Sat.), which serves chicken, steaks, and different kinds of fish, but its specialty is catfish.

BRADFORD AND VICINITY

This little town claims to be the **"Doodle Soup Capital of the World."** Doodle Soup seems to be one of those dishes, such as Indian pudding in New England and mountain oysters in Colorado, that far more people talk about than actually eat. To make it, according to aficionados, one bakes a chicken, then mixes the drippings in the baking pan with one cup of vinegar and one cup of water. Season with red hot pepper to taste, bring to a boil, and serve over crackers or biscuits. The traditional accompanying dishes are mashed potatoes, peas, and fruit cocktail. One woman said she anoints her baked chicken with Doodle Soup, while another said with a sniff, "I never eat the stuff; it's too greasy for me." For further information, call the **Bradford City Hall** at 731/742-2271.

SKULLBONE

About three miles east of Bradford on Hwy. 105 is the community of Skullbone, which gets its name from a particularly rough sort of 19th-century prizefighting in which the combatants would face each other and trade punches to the head. Hitting anywhere below the collar wasn't considered sporting. John L. Sullivan is said to have fought here.

Skullbone was put on the map by an inspired local promoter, who got Governor Browning to issue a proclamation in 1953 recognizing "the Kingdom of Skullbonia" as "a worthy successor to the rugged frontiersmen who built its early traditions." **Skullbone Store** (the store needs no address; one cannot miss it, 731/742-3179, 6 A.M.–7 P.M. Mon.–Sat., 2–5 P.M. Sun.) is about all that is left of the kingdom, but it is a pleasant place to stop, have a cold drink, and read the clippings on the wall.

KENTON

The town of Kenton is "The Home of the White Squirrels," a group of albino gray squirrels that has been nurtured over the years into a sizable population. Protected by statute and the efforts of locals, the squirrels jump from tree to tree all over town. During the summers, a local advises, the squirrels are best viewed early in the morning or in the evening. Seems they don't like the heat.

The town has **Kenton White Squirrel Homecoming** (108 N. Poplar Ave., 731/749-5767, www.wiwt.com/Kenton), held around the Fourth of July, complete with gospel singing, grand parade, and fireworks.

RUTHERFORD

This little Gibson County town was the last Tennessee home of **Davy Crockett,** from which he departed to go off to the Alamo and glory. A replica of his cabin (open June–Labor Day 9 A.M.–5 P.M., $2 adults, $1 children), built with some of the original logs, is two blocks north of the town's sole traffic light. It contains period tools, furniture, and other items.

The town holds an annual **Davy Crockett Days Celebration** (731/665-7253), a weeklong festival that culminates on the first Saturday in October. Visitors can watch or partake of gospel music, a street dance, white bean and ham hock dinner, tall tales contest, and demonstrations of horseshoeing, spinning, and broom-making.

R&J Restaurant (455 N. Trenton, 731/665-6999, 6 A.M.–8 P.M. Mon.–Sat., 6 A.M.–3 P.M. Sun.) specializes in barbecue and ribs.

DYER

Three miles north of Dyer on U.S. 45 West stands Gibson County High School. On the school grounds, history students have built the **Pioneer Homeplace** (731/692-3616, $.50), a collection of 19th-century hewn-log structures. Eight log buildings were put together by the students, who dress in period clothing and interpret their history for visitors.

The buildings include a "dog-trot" house, smokehouse, corncrib, livestock barn, and welcome center. Students who work on the project, which dovetails with their classes, learn how to spin wool yarn and make lye soap, baskets, brooms, and quilts. Although the Pioneer Homeplace usually caters to groups, individuals are welcome to tour the buildings.

TRENTON

David Crockett helped organize Gibson County, of which Trenton is the seat. And it was to the residents of Gibson County and surrounding areas that, when they replaced Crockett as their congressman in 1835 with one

Adam Huntsman, an attorney with a wooden leg, Crockett gave one of the more memorable parting shots in American political history, "Since you have chosen to elect a man with a timber toe to succeed me, you may all go to hell and I will go to Texas."

This town is home to the world's largest collection of *veilleuses-théières,* or lighted teapots. Dr. Frederick C. Freed, a Trenton native who taught medicine in New York, fell in love with this particular kind of teapot, which came about as a way of warming tea while providing light in sickrooms or nurseries. In the early 19th century, artists took this idea and produced teapots that were works of art, some depicting people, buildings, and scenes out of literature. Dr. Freed assembled his 1750–1860 teapot collection over 40 years, buying 525 of them in antique shops from places such as Singapore, Sri Lanka, Egypt, and all over Europe.

When the teapots were given to the city, Trenton had no appropriate place for the collection, but this was rectified with the construction of a new **City Hall** (309 S. College St., 731/855-2013, usually weekdays 8 A.M.–5 P.M., free). Now the walls of the city council room are lined with glass shelves containing the collection. Visitors can view the teapots whenever the building is open and no one is using the room. The second full week in May brings the **Teapot Festival,** complete with bean dinner, crafts fair, fireworks, tractor pull, and barbecue chicken sale.

The **Nite-Light Theatre** offers three productions a year of works such as *Anything Goes* and *Hello, Dolly!,* as well as children's fare. Call 731/855-2129 to reach a tape recording listing upcoming shows, or call 731/855-2382 to reach a person who can answer questions.

Stay in the **Carrie Belle Manor** (655 N. College St., 731/855-0321). The **Majestic Steak House and Pizza** (2050 U.S. 45 W. Bypass, 731/855-4808) serves steak, pizza, spaghetti, and catfish for lunch and dinner seven days a week.

For more information, contact **Greater Gibson County Area Chamber of Commerce** (2051 U.S. 45 W. Bypass, 731/855-0973, www.gibsoncountytn.com, 8 A.M.–4:30 P.M. Mon.–Fri.).

From the Tennessee to the Mississippi

PARKERS CROSSROADS

Confederate General Nathan Bedford Forrest cut quite a swath—several of them, actually—in West Tennessee. He was successful because most of the time he was able to pick the place and the time to engage his enemies. Parkers Crossroads was a place where his luck almost ran out.

Forrest was known as the "Wizard of the Saddle," but most of the time his men fought dismounted while others held their horses to the rear of the battlefield. While attacking Union soldiers at Parkers Crossroads, Forrest received word that his horse-holders were under attack by an unexpected Union force. When asked what orders to give, he yelled, "Charge both ways!" They did, and he and his troops escaped to bedevil Union forces for the rest of the war.

At least that's the story. The most recent biographer of Forrest claims this tale is apocryphal, and anyone who wishes to argue with locals can begin at the **M Cotton Patch Restaurant,** Parkers Crossroads (off I-40 Exit 108, 731/968-5533, 6 A.M.–9 P.M. daily). This delightful place combines Civil War exhibits with a wonderful down-home restaurant, open for all three meals daily. It has a full menu but specializes in barbecued pork, catfish, and country ham.

NATCHEZ TRACE STATE RESORT PARK

Visitors familiar with the Natchez Trace Parkway in Middle Tennessee may find the name of this park puzzling. The early land route from Natchez, Mississippi, to Nashville followed a myriad of paths though the forests and canebrakes of the

Union Troops of the Volunteer Infantry fire their muskets, filling the air with black-powder smoke in a re-creation of a Civil War battle.

wilderness. When fear of robbery ran high, travelers would take this section of the route, called the Western Trace.

This 14,073-acre park (731/968-3742, www.tnstateparks.com), which sits amid the 48,000-acre Natchez Trace State Forest, provides a wide variety of wilderness and recreation experiences. Much of the land came into state hands because the farmers who lived here had more or less farmed it to death. By the 1930s the land was acquired by the U.S. Department of Agriculture, which began projects aimed at restoring the land and demonstrating soil conservation practices in hopes of preventing further devastation.

The third-largest pecan tree in North America, cleverly named the "Big Pecan Tree," grows here. Legend holds that one of Andrew Jackson's men carried a pecan from the Battle of New Orleans and gave it to a local, who planted it. The tree was measured in April 1973, and found to be 18 feet, two inches in circumference, 106 feet high, and spreading 136 feet. Locals announced that this was the largest pecan tree in the world, and soon found their tree topped by tree measurers from Virginia and Louisiana, whose claims dropped

the Natchez Trace tree to third place. Since then, no one has gotten around to measuring the tree again.

Recreational opportunities abound here. The park has four lakes full of fish, and a swimming beach is open during summer. Hiking trails—one long enough for an overnight—lead through the park, as do trails and roads for off-road vehicles. Other activities include playgrounds, sports fields, archery, and croquet.

The **Pin Oak Lodge** contains a restaurant, which is open seven days a week for all three meals April through October, and on weekends through November. Accommodations begin with the lodge, which has 20 rooms ($66–75d, $6 per night for extra guests). Housekeeping cabins sleep four (800/250-8616 or 731/968-8176, $60–68), have fireplaces and air-conditioning, and come with all linens and fully equipped kitchens. They are enormously popular. Make reservations up to one year ahead.

This park has three **campgrounds** with a total of 143 sites, each with a picnic table and hookups. Bathhouses have hot showers, and all campsites are on a first-come, first-served basis. One of the campgrounds stays open all year.

PARSONS

The Decatur County Fairgrounds south of Parsons on Hwy. 69 is the staging point for the **World's Largest Coon Hunt** (731/847-4202, www.decaturcountycoonhunt.com, free), held on the second weekend in April. Coon hunting basically consists of turning a bunch of dogs loose in the woods, whereupon they sniff around until they find the scent of a raccoon and follow it in search of the animal. Raccoons usually lead the dogs on a merry chase and then take refuge in a tree. All this takes place at night, when raccoons are most active.

Human coon hunters either build a fire and sit around it listening to the dogs or try to keep up with them through the woods. For this festival, country music is played into the wee hours and a good time is had by all. The money raised in this fashion is donated to St. Jude's Children's Research Hospital in Memphis.

CAMDEN

This Tennessee River town is home to the state's cultured pearl business and the source of seed pearls for similar operations in Japan. The Tennessee River harbors 24 species of pearl-producing mussels, and the best of these are cultivated in wire nets that hang from floating plastic pipes. Keeping them close to the surface of the water accelerates pearl production, which usually takes three years. Tennessee River pearls occur in varying colors and shapes, and all have a beautiful luster. They are sold throughout the country.

The **Birdson Resort/Marina** (731/584-7880, www.birdsongresort.com, 8 A.M.–5 P.M. daily, free), outside of Camden, cultivates freshwater pearls for export to Japan and for use in jewelry in this country. Mussel divers work April through November, but visitors can see a pearl jewelry store Rings, brooches, pins, and other jewelry as well as individual pearls are for sale, and a 350-gallon aquarium contains live mussels for close inspection.

Groups of 15 or more can take A Pearl of a Tour, which lasts at least three hours and includes, a lunch, and a diving demonstration. Call one month ahead to make arrangements. To get there, take exit 133 off I-40 and go nine miles north on Birdsong Road.

On March 5, 1963, a small plane crashed three miles north of Camden, killing country legend Patsy Cline, Cowboy Copas, and Hawkshaw Hawkins. Today a **monument** (www .patsy.nu/monument.html) stands at the site of the crash. To get there from downtown Camden, go to the intersection of U.S. 70 and U.S. 641. Head north on U.S. 641, immediately turn left onto Mt. Carmel Road, and then go approximately three miles. A green sign on the right indicates a short gravel drive that leads to the marker.

Events

Fiddler's Bluegrass Championship (731/584-3145) is held annually in the Holladay community south of Camden on the third Saturday in April. Fiddlers, mandolin players, and bands compete. A dance is held the night before.

Spring Festival (731/593-3213) takes place in Big Sandy on the Saturday before Memorial Day. The event kicks off with a parade downtown about 10 A.M. followed by local country bands and singing groups, balloon tosses, wheelbarrow races, an ice cream eating contest, and a pet show. Usually there is a special event, such as a parachute demonstration. The day ends with a street dance in the evening.

The **Waterfowl Festival** (731/593-3213) occurs in Big Sandy in late August. The big attraction is the duck-blind drawing (hunters hope to win a chance to hunt from the duck blind on the opening day of hunting season). The festival features a duck-calling championship and retriever demonstrations, and the crafts include duck carvings.

Practicalities

For accommodations, try the **Days Inn** (30 Old Rt. 1 Rd., 731/584-3111 or 800/238-6161). For campers, **Beaverdam Resort** (1280 Lodge Rd., 731/584-3963, open all year) has 11 sites. **Birdsong Resort and Marina** (Birdsong and Camden Rds., 731/584-7880, open all year) has 50 sites, a pool, boating, fishing, and hiking trails.

Country and Western Steakhouse (189 Extension St., 731/584-3026) serves lunch and dinner seven days a week, and specializes in steak and pond-raised catfish. **The Catfish Place** (U.S. 641, 731/584-3504) offers all three meals seven days a week. It runs specials all week long, with catfish served every day—fiddlers (whole fish minus the head) or fillets.

1850s Log House Restaurant (two miles north of the traffic light on U.S. 641 N., 731/584-7814, 3–9 P.M. Wed.–Sat.) serves dinners consisting of fish, shrimp, steak, or chicken dishes.

For information, contact **Benton County/Camden Chamber of Commerce** (202 W. Main St., 731/584-8395, www.bentoncountycamden.com, 8 A.M.–4 P.M. Mon.–Fri.).

NATHAN BEDFORD FORREST STATE HISTORIC AREA

This 2,587-acre park, on the west bank of the Tennessee River, complements the Johnsonville State Historical Area on the east bank of the river in commemorating one of the more amazing feats of warfare—the only known defeat of a naval force by a cavalry group.

Nathan Bedford Forrest directed his attack from Pilot's Knob, a longtime river landmark that stands at 740 feet, the highest point in West Tennessee and about 450 feet higher than the average height of the surrounding county. Now this area contains more than 20 miles of hiking trails, lots of access to Kentucky Lake, picnicking, and camping.

The **Tennessee River Folklife Center** (731/584-6356, www.tnstateparks.com, 8 A.M.–4:30 P.M. daily, free) is an interpretive center at the Nathan Bedford Forrest State Park devoted to people who made their living from the river. Exhibits include *Old Betsy*, a mussel-gathering boat built and used by T. J. Whitfield, one of the last of the old-time musselmen. Subjects covered include commercial fishing, log rafting, music, and religion, and items displayed include baskets, tools, and audio recordings of people who recall

the old days. The center's schedule changes, so call ahead to make sure it is open.

The park has two **campgrounds** with a total of 53 sites. One campground has 38 sites with hookups and hot showers, while the other offers more primitive camping. Sites are available on a first-come, first-served basis and are open all year.

Events

Summer Song Festival (731/584-6356, $3) is a gospel sing-along with live local bands at the Eva Beach area. It is held the Saturday night of the Fourth of July weekend.

Tennessee River Folklife Festival (731/584-6356, $3) and demonstrates different life skills needed in days of yore, such as quilting, making lye soap, gathering edible and medicinal plants, shooting rifles, caning chairs, making baskets, and blacksmithing. Sometimes displays cover commercial fishing and musseling. Area country, bluegrass, and gospel musicians provide the entertainment. It takes place the first Saturday in October at the Eva Beach area.

PARIS AND VICINITY

The anonymous writer of the Paris section of the *WPA Guide to Tennessee* described how Isham G. Harris, a Paris native who was governor when the Civil War broke out, reacted when asked to send troops to the Union. "He replied: 'Tennessee will not furnish a single man for coercion, but 50,000, if necessary, for the defense of our rights or those of our Southern brethren.'" Then, in a masterpiece of understatement, the writer added, "Harris was a leader in the movement for secession."

Paris also can lay claim to two country musicians. Rosan Gallimore, also known as Rattlesnake Annie, was born north of here in the Puryear community. A friend of Willie Nelson, she has achieved great success in Europe. Hank Williams Jr., who puts on one of the best shows in country music, has lived in Paris since July 4, 1986. The **Hank Williams Jr. fan club** (731/642-7455, www.hankjr.com) and Hank Williams Jr. Enterprises operate out of Paris, too.

Bocephus, as Hank Jr. was nicknamed by his father, confesses on one of his albums that "I ain't crazy 'bout nothin' but women, money, and blues." The last of the three can be found at Big Apple Cafe on U.S. 641, in the nearby community of Puryear.

Sights

Harris was one of three Tennessee governors to come from this town, the seat of Henry County. The buildings on the east, north, and west of the square constitute one of the oldest stretches of 19th-century courthouse-square buildings in the state, if not the entire South. Call the **Paris-Henry County Heritage Center** for further information, (614 Poplar St., 731/642-1030).

Paris is home to the **world's largest replica of the Eiffel Tower**. Sixty-five feet tall and built of wood and steel at Christian Brothers University in Memphis, it was erected and given to the city in 1993. The tower stands in Memorial Park and is open daily year-round. Admission is free. To get there, take Volunteer Drive, which connects U.S. 79 on the east side of town with U.S. 641.

Events

Paris is about 15 miles from the Tennessee River (Kentucky Lake), yet it has capitalized on the river in a way that towns on the banks would envy. The **World's Biggest Fish Fry** happens in the last full week in April, a time when approximately 100,000 people come to town to consume more than 13,000 pounds of fish. Between meals, they watch a parade, go to a rodeo, listen to music, shuffle over to the "Down and Dirty Dirt Dance," see crafts shows, and attend a beauty pageant. One of the more unusual events is the Catfish Race, in which selected catfish race down 15-foot-long Plexiglas troughs of water on the courthouse lawn.

For details on this event and other information, **Paris/Henry County Chamber of Commerce** (105 E. Wood St., 800/345-1103 or 731/642-3431, www.paris.tn.org, 8 A.M.–4:30 P.M. Mon.–Fri.).

Accommodations

Buchanan Resort (785 Buchanan Resort Rd., 731/642-2828, www.buchananresort.com, $68–199), 14 miles east of Paris, offers a motel, cottages, lodges, and camping open mid-March to October. Amenities include a swimming pool, a tennis courts, and superb fishing. Take U.S. 79 to Buchanan Boat Dock Road and follow signs.

Cypress Bay Resort (Rt. 2, Box 131, 731/232-8221) has eight cottages that sleep seven to 10 people. Two-bedroom cottages cost $50 per night for two people, three-bedroom cottages cost $60; each additional person costs $5. For motels, try the **Best Western Travelers Inn** (1297 Wood St., 800/528-1234 or 731/642-8881, $40–58), or the **Hampton Inn** (1510 E. Wood/U.S. 79, 800/HAMPTON [426-7866] or 731/642-2838, $41–63).

For camping, there's **Big Eagle** (no phone, open mid-Apr.–Sept.), which has 43 sites with no hookups. Take U.S. 79 east of Paris and follow signs. **KOA-Paris Landing** (731/642-6895, open Apr.–Sept.), has 75 sites. Take U.S. 79 to East Antioch Road and follow signs.

Food

Ace's Pizza (1053 Mineral Wells Ave., 731/644-0558, lunch and dinner Mon.–Sat.) has a big-screen TV and Chicago theme, and serves wonderful Chicago-type pizza. **Hong Kong Chinese Restaurant** (1021 Mineral Wells Ave., 731/644-1810) serves a daily lunch buffet and a weekend buffet in addition to menu selections).

Knott's Landing Restaurant (209 N. Poplar St., 731/642-4718, breakfast, lunch, and dinner Mon.–Sat.), serves excellent catfish, hush puppies, and white beans. **Tom's Pizza and Steak House** (2501 E. Wood St., 731/642-8842) is open Tuesday through Sunday for lunch and dinner.

Big Apple Cafe (U.S. 641 in Puryear, 731/247-5798, lunch and dinner Mon.–Sat.) serves Mexican food and deli sandwiches. It stages live blues every Saturday starting at 9:30 P.M.

At the **Old Oak Tree Restaurant** (731/642-8810) is on the Buchanan Boat Dock Road at the Buchanan Resort in Springville. It's open for three meals a day, March through October every day of the week. A 75-foot-tall red oak grows through the roof of the dining room, and diners have a beautiful view of Kentucky Lake. The restaurant is known for its catfish.

West Tennessee is not as famous for country ham as its eastern counterparts, but **Clifty Farm** (1500 U.S. 641 S., 731/642-9740, www.clifty-farm.com, 7 A.M.–3 P.M. Mon.–Fri.) holds up tradition by producing thousands of the cured delicacies a year

Sally Lane's Hand Made Candies (731/642-5801, 9 A.M.–5:30 P.M. Tues.–Sat., 2:30–5:30 P.M. Sun.), a half mile east of town on U.S. 79, sells more than 100 kinds of confections, such as peanut brittle, pink and green mints, pecan logs, pralines, and sugar-free candy.

PARIS LANDING STATE RESORT PARK

This 841-acre park (800/250-8614 or 731/642-4311, www.tnstateparks.com) lies 16 miles northeast of Paris on the shores of Kentucky Lake. The activity here focuses on the lake, the second-largest man-made lake in the United States after Lake Mead on the Arizona–Nevada border. The park also includes a swimming pool, an 18-hole golf course, and recreation and nature programs. A full-service **marina** (731/642-3048) offers 212 slips, a free boat ramp, and a full-service store with food and fuel.

With 100 rooms, the **Paris Landing Inn** (800/250-8614 or 731/642-4311, $77–83) is the largest one in the state park system. Ten new cabins sleep 10 people; each includes three bedrooms, two baths, fully equipped kitchen, great room, fireplace, central heat and air, and a balcony overlooking the lake. One cabin is wheelchair-accessible. A two-night minimum stay is required before Memorial Day ($140 per night). Between Memorial Day and Labor Day cabins are let on a weekly basis only ($850). Call for reservations.

The **campground** has 46 sites, all with hookups and access to hot showers. Sites are available on a first-come, first-served basis, open all year. Camping is available only to self-contained vehicles December through March.

MCKENZIE

The **Gordon Browning Museum** (640 N. Main St., 731/352-3510, http://gbmuseum.com, 9 A.M.–4 P.M. daily except Wed.), commemorates the Carroll County native who served as governor 1937–39 and again for two terms 1949–53, becoming the only governor in the state to return to office after a 10-year hiatus. The Republicans nominated country singer Roy Acuff to run against him in 1949, to no avail. Browning was the first governor to occupy Tennessee's governor's mansion.

The museum contains memorabilia that Browning collected in his more than 50 years of public service. One item is the first Tennessee driver's license; Browning was governor in 1938, the year the state started requiring licenses.

Practicalities

At **Hig's Restaurant** (25185 Hwy. 22, 731/352-7532, lunch and dinner Tues.–Sat., lunch Sun.), diners can order from the menu or partake of the lunch and dinner buffet. Hig's serves chicken and steaks and different kinds of fish, but its specialty is catfish. **Catfish Restaurant** (525 N. Highland Dr., 731/352-5855, 6 A.M.–10 P.M. Mon.–Sat., 9 A.M.–9 P.M. Sun.) serves catfish, grilled chicken, steaks, and sandwiches, and it offers a salad bar and lunch and weekend buffet.

For accommodations, try the **Briarwood Inn** (635 N. Highland Dr., 731/352-1083). For more information, contact **Carroll County Chamber of Commerce** (141 E. Main St., Huntingdon, 731/986-4664, www.carrollcounty-tn-chamber.com, 8 A.M.–4 P.M. Mon.–Fri.), is south of McKenzie in the county seat.

MARTIN

This town did not exist during the Civil War but was incorporated in 1874 at the behest of William Martin, a prominent local tobacco farmer who persuaded the railroad to lay tracks through his property.

In 1927 a junior college was created here, and it has grown through the years and become a branch of the University of Tennessee. Now approximately 5,600 students attend the college, which has four-year status. The **University Museum** (on University St. beside the Hall-Moody Administration Building, 731/587-7454, www.utm.edu) is open 1–4 P.M. Monday through Friday when classes are in session, and by appointment at other times. It contains items pertaining to the university as well as natural and cultural aspects of West Tennessee. Traveling exhibits are also featured.

Practicalities

Hearth Restaurant (615 N. Lindell St., 731/587-9700, breakfast, lunch, and dinner daily) offers a full menu and a buffet. It specializes in good country cooking. **K-N Rootbeer Drive-in** (241 N. Lindell St., 731/587-2551, lunch and dinner Mon.–Sat.) serves standard drive-in fare, including sandwiches, french fries, soft drinks, and ice cream cones.

Motel options include the **Econo Lodge** (853 University St., 731/587-4241), and the **University Lodge** (Hwy. 431 at U.S. 45 E. Bypass, 800/748-9480 or 731/587-9577).

For information, contact **Weakley County Chamber of Commerce** in Dresden (110 W. Maple St., 731/364-3787, www.weakleycountychamber.com, 8 A.M.–5 P.M. Mon.–Fri.).

BIG CYPRESS TREE STATE NATURAL AREA

This 330-acre natural area (731/235-2700, www.tnstateparks.com) was named for an enormous cypress tree that at one time was the largest bald cypress in the United States and the largest tree of any kind east of the Mississippi. Reaching a height of 175 feet, it had a trunk that was 40 feet in circumference and 13 feet in diameter. In 1976, alas, a bolt of lightning struck the tree, whence it fell to the ground and smoldered for two weeks. Foresters estimated that the tree had stood for 1,350 years.

It is very difficult to see the remnants of the tree, for the stump is on the far side of the Obion River, and state officials in Nashville have never seen the wisdom of paying for a bridge to reach a stump. Visitors with their own canoes are welcome to cross the river, provided they can get to it. The low-lying ground is frequently very wet nine months of the year. Those confined to the shore, however, will find evidence of a variety of wildlife that inhabits the area, including deer, turkeys, quail, rabbits, raccoons, bobcats, coyotes, ducks, squirrels, and plenty of snakes.

The Middle Fork of the Obion River, which was "channelized" by the Corps of Engineers, crosses the hardwood bottomland forest. If visitors ignore the damp ground, profusion of reptiles, clouds of insects, and disappearance of the area's namesake, this is a pleasant place to go. You will find no crowds. No camping is permitted in the area.

UNION CITY

This town was not named in honor of Northern troops; the name instead refers to the junction of two rail lines. The **Obion County Museum** (1004 Edwards St., 731/885-6774, www.ocmuseum.com, 1–4 P.M. Sat.–Sun., free) comes up with a new theme every season. Exhibits include a log cabin and a horse-drawn hearse.

Food

The Dixie Barn Restaurant (1315 Old Troy Rd., 731/885-3663) is open for all three meals Monday through Saturday and for breakfast and lunch on Sunday, and serves home-style food and fried catfish. **The Corner Barbecue** (1425 E. Reelfoot Ave., 731/885-9924) is open for all three meals seven days a week, and offers the standard barbecue and trimmings. **Catfish Galley** (1001 Marshall Ave., 731/885-0060, lunch and dinner daily) serves seafood, catfish, chicken, soups, salads, sandwiches, appetizers, and desserts, and it also offers a children's menu.

New Jade Restaurant (Reelfoot Shopping Center, 731/885-9999) offers Chinese food daily for lunch and dinner. Diners can choose from the luncheon or dinner buffet or order from the menu. **Olympia Steak and Pizza** (1705 W. Reelfoot Ave., 731/885-3611) serves lunch and dinner daily. Diners can partake of a luncheon buffet, or, for dinner, have a salad bar and order from the menu.

The Western Plains

NEED A CANNON?

U nion City is famous to firearms aficionados as the home of **Dixie Gun Works,** the center of the muzzle-loading world. Founded in 1954 by the late Turner Kirkland, who began collecting guns when he was a boy, the Gun Works puts out a 700-page catalog every year that features more than 10,000 items—-guns, parts, knives, armor, books, and camping supplies. If you've always wanted a cannon to keep annoying neighbors at bay, this is the place to get it. A two-thirds-scale Civil War replica cannon—complete with carriage—can be yours for $2,500.

Kirkland was an inveterate collector, and visitors have two areas in which to look through his acquisitions. The first is the lobby of the Gun Works. In addition to the more than 1,000 antique firearms for sale at any given time, visitors can peruse a reproduction of Shakespeare's First Folio, displays of U.S. military medals, armor, and swords. There is no charge for visiting this part of the operation.

The best part of the collection, however, is in the adjacent **Old Car Museum.** Imagine a museum put together by a grandfather eager to show children how things work and to give them a chance to switch on electric motors, blow antique car horns, and turn a hand-cranked siren. Kids love this stuff, although the cacophony can drive adults crazy. Parents need to watch small kids very carefully here.

Adults will appreciate 36 antique cars, all of which are in running condition. Highlights include a 1924 Marmon Touring Car, a 1936 Packard limousine that looks like something right out of a Mafia movie, and a 1909 Maxwell. The museum also exhibits an 1850 log cabin gun shop, 70 farm engines, three high-wheeler bikes, and an assortment of car horns and hubcaps.

The Gun Works and museum (731/885-0700, www.dixiegunworks.com) are open 7 A.M.–5 P.M. Monday–Friday and 8 A.M.–noon Saturday. Admission is $2 for adults or $5 for an entire family. From downtown Union City, go south on U.S. 51. Look for a large building on the left on Gunpowder Lane with DGW in large letters on the front.

Searcy's Cafeteria (306 S. 1st St., 731/885-0332) is open Monday to Wednesday for all three meals and Thursday and Friday for breakfast and lunch), and features home-style food and homemade pies. **Snappy Tomato Pizza Company** (509 S. 1st St., 731/885-7627), open for lunch and dinner seven days a week), serves pizza, salads, and subs. **P. V.'s Hut** (209 E. Florida Ave., 731/885-5737, lunch and dinner Tues.–Sat.), offers burgers, barbecue, great homemade potato salad, and spaghetti.

Out in the country **Flippens Hillbilly Barn** (731/538-2933, www.flippenshillbillybarn.com, 8 A.M.–3 P.M. Mon.–Thurs., 8 A.M.-8:30 P.M. Fri.–Sat.) serves wonderful fried pies made from fruit grown on the Flippen farm. The Flippens run a farm stand and restaurant that is well worth the stop. The restaurant is full-service and offers fish, country ham, and sandwiches. To get there from Union City, go west on Hwy. 22 for seven miles, then turn left on Shawtown Road and go 7.5 miles.

Information and Services

For accommodations, try the **Hampton Inn** (2201 Reelfoot Ave., 800/HAMPTON [426-7866] or 731/885-8850), or the **Super 8 Motel** (1400 Vaden Ave., 731/885-4444).

The outlet stores at **Factory Stores of America** (601 Sherwood Dr., 731/885-6465) are open daily year-round.

For more information, contact **Obion County Chamber of Commerce** (215 S. 1st St. in Union City, 731/885-0211, www.obioncountytennessee .com, 8 A.M.–4:30 P.M. Mon.–Fri.).

⊠ REELFOOT LAKE

Reelfoot Lake State Resort Park (www.tnstateparks .com, 8 A.M.–4:30 P.M. daily) is the most unusual lake in Tennessee, well worth a detour to see. The lake extends 14 miles long and five miles wide and covers 15,000 acres. Sometimes the edge of the lake merges into wetlands and is difficult to discern. A relic of the New Madrid earthquake, Reelfoot Lake averages 5.2 feet in depth, and the deepest place in the lake is only 18 feet deep. The lake contains thousands of cypress trees with knobby "knees" that stick out of the water and tangled roots that intertwine under the water.

"Reelfoot," according to Indian legend, was the name of a local chief who abducted a local Indian maiden, thus causing the earthquake, which, the legend adds, swallowed up the chief's entire tribe. It hardly seems fair.

The shallow water, the trees, and the climate have conspired to create some of the best fishing in the country. Among the 57 species of fish that live here are largemouth bass, bream, and crappie—the latter so numerous that they are commercially fished with nets. During peak fishing season, which runs April through October, the park and surrounding towns fill with anglers.

Bird-watchers are also attracted, for more than 250 species of birds visit the lake during the course of a year. Heading the list of birds to see are bald eagles, which winter in the park until mid-March. The harder the winters farther north, the more eagles show up at Reelfoot Lake, but usually at least 100 are on hand. The park has set up extensive programs to help visitors see the magnificent birds. The best place to get oriented is the visitors center, which is on the southwestern end of the lake.

Eagle tours take place December through March. Buses leave the visitors center at 10 A.M. for the two-hour tours, which cost $3 per visitor. Pontoon boat cruises begin in May and end October 1. These last one to three hours and cost $9. Reelfoot Lake is the only state park with its own airstrip.

The town of Tiptonville and various landowners got to Reelfoot Lake before the park was created, so the place is a mixture of private and public land. This can be a bit disconcerting for those accustomed to entering a park gate and leaving the commercial world behind.

Events

This park offers an extensive series of events, details of which are available at the visitors center. Here are the highlights.

Crappiethon USA (731/885-0211), usually held in April, involves the release of 1,000 tagged crappies. Lucky anglers can win prizes for catching the right fish. The **Reelfoot Waterfowl Festival** (731/885-0211) and features a duck-calling contest in mid-August. September brings the **Roundhouse Music Reunion** with '50s-style music. The **Arts and Crafts Festival** (731/885-0211) takes place in October.

Practicalities

The park's wonderful 20-unit **Airpark Inn** (800/250-8617 or 731/253-7756, $56–75) rests on pilings and extends into the lake among tall cypress trees. Walking along one of the piers late on a summer night vividly brings to mind all those *It Came from the Black Lagoon* movies. The inn has 12 rooms that sleep two, and these rent for $64 a night. The remaining eight suites accommodate up to six people, and these cost $75. The park also has a five-unit hotel at the spillway of the lake, and rooms here cost $56–75. Lodging in the park is enormously popular and should be reserved as far in advance as possible. The Airpark Inn also has a 100-seat restaurant serving country cooking and looking over the lake. It is open seven days a week for three meals from January through the first weekend in October.

Those who wish to make a living sacrifice of their bodies to the bugs—at least during summer—can camp in the park's two **campgrounds,** which between them have 120 sites. One is near the inn and the other lies at the south end of the lake. Both have bathhouses, and the one near the inn is open all year. Sites are available on a first-come, first-served basis.

TIPTONVILLE

This town, one of the closest in Tennessee to the Mississippi River, sits on the Tiptonville Dome, a ridge that, in the days before levees, kept the town above floodwaters. The proximity of Reelfoot Lake assures that the town is inundated

THE NEW MADRID EARTHQUAKE

The strongest earthquake ever to occur in North America split the land in the winter of 1811–12 along the New Madrid Fault, which was named for a village in southeast Missouri. Tremors and small earthquakes in December gave an eerie indication of what was to follow.

On February 8, 1812, the big one hit. A quake that current-day experts estimate would have hit 8.8 on the Richter scale shook the earth, causing a 14-mile stretch of land to drop 50 feet in elevation. It was so sparsely settled that there was little loss of life, and, for the same reason, few eyewitnesses. One Eliza Bryan, a resident of New Madrid, described the water: "[It] gathered up like a mountain, rising, 15 to 20 feet perpendicularly [while] fissures in the earth vomited forth sand and water, some closing immediately."

Hardwood forests were flattened as if by a giant fist. The earth itself rippled with shock waves, and the poor souls who experienced it thought they were seeing the end of the world.

At least they were on land. The passengers and crew on the maiden voyage of the steamboat *New Orleans* were making their way downstream from Pittsburgh bound for New Orleans when they steamed right into the epicenter of the quake. Edward T. Luther, writing in *Our Restless Earth*, describes what happened to the boat. The voyage was unlike any before or since: The pilot steered through tidal waves, dodging clumps of ripped-out trees and avoiding collapsing riverbanks. The boat fell over waterfalls that had never been there before and escaped from whirlpools that swirled into newly opened holes in the riverbed. Amazingly, the *New Orleans* survived its Mississippi white-water nightmare, and spectators greeted it with cries of disbelief when it pulled into Natchez, Mississippi.

Luther cites the composition of the alluvial soil as one culprit of the destruction. Carried from the Rocky Mountains and the Appalachians for eons, the sand and gravel mix was saturated with water to within 20 feet of the surface, and, when the shocks came, this soil behaved like a bowl of Jell-O in the hands of a toddler.

The Mississippi River flowed backward for 48 hours into the depression, filling it with water that became Reelfoot Lake. The world did not end, although clocks stopped in Boston. Reports later came in reporting shock waves as far away as Venezuela and Canada.

---

with anglers every year, leading one observer on a particularly intense weekend to note that it looked as if the town were having a Bubba Convention.

The late Carl Perkins, country and rockabilly artist, was born here in 1932 in a sharecropper's shack. A **museum** in a similar house next to city hall, on Carl Parkins Parkway, displays photos and a guitar as well as the sort of furnishings that a 1930s house would have had. The museum (731/253-7653, 1–5 P.M. Fri.–Sat., $2). Look for a large sign south of town on Hwy. 78 between Robertson and Church Streets. If no one is there, call city hall, and Carl's cousin Hubert will dispatch someone to open the house.

Fishing Camps and Cabins

Reelfoot Lake attracts a great number of hunters and fishing fanatics; obtain a complete listing of cabins from the **Reelfoot Lake Tourism Development** Council at 731/538-2666.

At **Blue Bank Cypress Point Resort** (near the Reelfoot Lake spillway off Hwy. 21/22, 731/253-6878, www.bluebank.com, $45 and up), 14 rooms are available at Blue Bank near the restaurant, and 32 rooms at Cypress Point down on the water. From the last week in March until the first week in June, the resort is available only for fishing packages. It also offers hunting packages and bald eagle-watching tours. The restaurant is open for lunch and dinner seven days a week. It serves fresh-cut steaks, catfish, crappie, ham, chicken, and pork chops. The resort has a marina, boats to rent, pontoon boats, game room, swimming pool, large playground, and picnic area.

Boyette's Resort about three miles east of Tiptonville on Hwy. 21, (30 Boyette Rd., 731/253-6523, www.lakereelfoot.net, $41–160), has 14 cabins. This is next to Bo's Landing.

Accommodations

The setting is the real feature at **Back Yard Bird's Lodge Bed and Breakfast** (Airpark Rd., 731/253-9064, www.bluebasin.com, $75), a two-story dwelling with a view of the lake. The lodge sits on the Mississippi flyway on the lake and a short distance from the Mississippi River. It is a good place for fishermen, bird-watchers, honeymooners, canoeists, and photographers. On one memorable day 200 pelicans and 100 cormorants rested in the yard alongside the banks of the lake. Visitors can choose from two guest suites, both with private baths and private entrances on the lake side. The suites come with fully equipped kitchens and sitting areas with color TV. The lodge also has boat slips and a bait shop. The hosts offer a bird locator service for eagles in winter (Oct.–March), songbirds, and waterfowl. A full breakfast is served on a glassed-in dining porch. To get there, go north from Tiptonville on Hwy. 78 about seven miles. Turn right on Hwy. 213/Airpark Road. The lodge is two miles on the right.

Blue Bank Resort (731/253-6878, www.bluebankresort.com) has two locations on Reelfoot Lake, both on Hwy. 21 on the south side of the lake. The Hunter's Lodge can accommodate groups up to 19, while the Marina Lodging offers individual rooms. The resort offers hunting, fishing, and eagle-watching packages.

For campers, **Bo's Landing** (about three miles east of Tiptonville on Hwy. 21, 731/253-7809, open all year, $10–14) has 25 RV sites and eight primitive tent sites. Bo's also has a boat ramp, boat rental, fishing guides, and bald eagle tours. Food is available at the deli seven days a week for all three meals.

Gooch's Resort (two miles east on Hwy. 21/22, 731/253-8955, open year-round) has 16 RV hookups and tent sites close to the lake. Eagles roost in the trees around the resort.

Food

Boyette's Dining Room (Hwy. 21, 731/253-7307, 11 A.M.–9 P.M. Mon.–Sun.) serves catfish, chicken, ham, and steak. **Blue Bank Fish House and Grill** (Hwy. 21, 731/253-6878, www.bluebankresort.com, 10 A.M.–9 P.M. daily), offers seafood, steaks, and sandwiches. You'll find it in the Blue Bank Resort on Hwy. 21.

Information

Call or visit the **Obion County Chamber of Commerce** (215 1st St. in Union City, 731/885-0211, www.obioncounty.com); or the **Reelfoot Lake Tourism Development Council** (at the junction of Hwy. 21/22 at Reelfoot Lake, 731/538-2666, www.reelfootlakeoutdoors.com).

The Western Plains

South Along the Mississippi

DYERSBURG

This is the largest Tennessee town along the Mississippi north of Memphis. It was settled as far up the North Forked Deer River as steamboats could come. This access to the Mississippi made Dyersburg a trading center, one that was enhanced when the railroad came through.

From 1942 to 1945 the Dyersburg Army Air Base trained bomber crews for service in World War II. The name of the base was misleading, for it was actually near the town of Halls.

Good accommodations choices are the **Comfort Inn** (I-155 Exit 13, 800/221-2222 or 731/285-6951, $39–47), **Days Inn** (I-155 Exit 13, 731/287-0888, $38–46), and **Dyersburg Inn** (U.S. 51 Bypass and Hwy. 78, 800/HOLIDAY [465-4329] or 731/285-8601, $49 and up).

The **Airport Restaurant** (Airport Rd. in Dyersburg, 731/286-2477, 6 A.M.–2 P.M. Mon.–Fri., 11 A.M.–2 P.M. Sun.) serves breakfast and a lunch buffet only.

For information, contact the **Dyersburg/Dyer County Chamber of Commerce** (2455 Lake Rd., 731/285-3433, www.dyerchamber.com, 8 A.M.–5 P.M. Mon.–Fri.).

RIPLEY

Ripley was for many years the home of Noah Lewis, a blues harmonica player who recorded with Gus Cannon's Jug Stompers. Today, it's known for tomatoes. The rich soil hereabouts is ideally suited for growing tomatoes, and this fact is celebrated with the **Tomato Festival** on the first weekend in July. Activities include, besides tomato tasting, gospel music, arts and crafts, barbecue contest, pistol-shooting contest, baby-crawling contest, parade, and country music.

Lauderdale Cellars (196 S. Washington St., 731/635-4321, www.lauderdalecellars.com, 11 A.M.–5 P.M. Mon.–Sat., 1–6 P.M. Sun.) is one of Tennessee's younger wineries, and it specializes in fruit wines for all tastes. It sells a particularly intriguing table wine made from locally grown tomatoes, which customers find most fun to take home and use to test the knowledge of self-appointed oenophiles. The winery also sells 12 other kinds of wine, including cabernet sauvignon and chardonnay. A gift shop stocks wine-related and agricultural items.

For accommodations, try the **Days Inn** (555 U.S. 51 Bypass, 731/635-7378). For food, the **Blue and White Cafe** (on the U.S. 51 Bypass, 731/635-1471) is open Tuesday to Sunday for breakfast and lunch, and presents a daily lunchtime buffet of country cooking.

For more information, contact **Lauderdale County Chamber of Commerce** (103 E. Jackson Ave., 731/635-9541, www.laudcc.com, 8:30 A.M.–4:30 P.M. Mon.–Fri.).

HENNING

Alex Haley, author of *Roots, The Autobiography of Malcolm X,* and other books, spent part of his boyhood with his grandparents in the railroad town of Henning. The **Alex Haley State Historical Site and Museum** (200 S. Church St., 731/738-2240, 10 A.M.–5 P.M. Tues.–Sat., 1–5 P.M. Sun., $2.50 adults, $1 children 6–18) was built by his grandfather, Will Palmer, who ran a mill and lumberyard and was prosperous enough to build a 10-room house. It was here that the young Haley heard stories about his ancestors—Chicken George, Kizzy, and Kunta Kinte—people who would become household words when *Roots* became the most popular miniseries ever shown on television.

While millions of Americans watched *Roots,* assuming it all to be true, the book never withstood the examination of historians. According to an article in the *Tennessee Encyclopedia* by Richard Marius, Haley was sued twice for plagiarism, and one of the more gripping parts of the book, the point at which Haley meets a griot in Gambia who recounts the story of Haley's very ancestor, doesn't hold up. It seems that the elderly storyteller knew in advance what the American

THE FORT PILLOW MASSACRE

Of all the Civil War sites in the state of Tennessee, this one is without a doubt the most controversial. The Confederates built this fort on a high bluff above the Mississippi to help defend Memphis from attack by gunboats, but they abandoned it in 1862 when Corinth, Mississippi, fell to Union forces. Union troops occupied the fort, which, after the North captured the Mississippi River, ceased to be of much strategic importance.

By April 1864, Nathan Bedford Forrest, who was harassing Union supply lines, turned toward the fort, which he knew contained supplies and fresh horses.

It also contained 507 of the kind of troops that Southerners hated the most—Unionists from East Tennessee and blacks. The first group, called "homemade Yankees," was beneath contempt, but the hatred of the second was more intense. Slave owners had always feared a rebellion by blacks, yet they paradoxically claimed that blacks would never prove to be good soldiers. Whenever Southerners had encountered black troops before, they refused to treat them as legitimate prisoners of war. Instead, Confederates considered them stolen property and promptly sold them back into slavery.

The occupants of Fort Pillow were accused of sending foraging expeditions into the surrounding countryside, where the soldiers allegedly robbed residents and helped themselves to livestock, furniture, and anything they wanted.

On April 12, Forrest's troops surrounded the land side of the fort and demanded an unconditional surrender. The Union troops refused—twice—so he attacked. A Union gunboat stood offshore, but its shells had little effect on the battle. When the Southerners breached the fort, the defenders made a desperate run down the bluff toward the gunboat, which pulled away, leaving them between the river and the guns of Forrest.

According to Northern reports, Forrest's men massacred at least 300 of the troops in the fort. The truth of that account of the "Fort Pillow Massacre," as Northern newspapers dubbed it, was vehemently denied by Southerners, who insisted that the Union troops died because they refused to give up.

One surviving Southern account reads as follows: "The poor, deluded Negroes would run up to our men, fall on their knees and with uplifted hands, scream for mercy, but were ordered to their feet, and then shot down."

Whatever spurred the deaths, the outcry led Congress to investigate. General Sherman was ordered to investigate the incident and, if the situation warranted, retaliate. He did nothing, leading some to argue that the whole thing was wartime propaganda.

The Fort Pillow attack diminished the reputation of Nathan Bedford Forrest, who made a chilling comment in his report of the battle. He wrote: "The river was dyed with the blood of the slaughtered for 200 yards. It is hoped that these facts will demonstrate to the northern people that Negro soldiers cannot cope with Southerners."

author wanted to hear, and conveniently told it to him. For all his literary sins, however, Haley can be credited with getting this country to think about the horrors of the slave trade and its effects on his people, fictional or real.

The museum contains copies of all his books, many of which are for sale. Personal items are on display, as is furniture that was in the house when Haley was a boy. The author, who died in 1992, is buried under the front lawn.

FORT PILLOW STATE HISTORIC AREA

This 1,650-acre tract (731/738-5581 or 731/738-5731, www.tnstateparks.com 8 A.M.–4 P.M. daily) lies on the First Chickasaw Bluff, which once overlooked the Mississippi River. Over the years the river moved its bed about a mile to the west. Fort Pillow is the only Confederate bulwark along the Mississippi in Tennessee that is open to the public.

The visitors center contains nature exhibits and information about the park. Travelers can walk a mile round-trip from the visitors center over a suspended bridge to see the battlefield. A museum, offers a video, slide presentations, and exhibits about the battle of 1864. The gift shop sells Civil War memorabilia.

The outer earthworks of Fort Pillow still exist, but the inner part of the fort has been the best-preserved. One can readily see how Nathan Bedford Forrest's troops, once they overran the outer part of the fort, could easily fire into the interior.

Hikers can take advantage of three wooded trails, one five miles long, one 10 miles long, and one a seven-mile backpacking trail. If backpacking, register at the visitors center. There is no cost, but for safety reasons the staff needs to keep track of backpackers. The fishing area is a 25-acre man-made lake with crappie, bass, bluegill, and catfish. The **campground** offers 40 camping sites and a large group tent area that holds up to 200 people and contains a pavilion with a stove and picnic tables. Fort Pillow and the campground are open year-round. To get there, go west from Henning 18 miles on Hwy. 87. Turn right on Hwy. 207, which leads into the park.

COVINGTON AND VICINITY

The seat of Tipton County is the third-largest city in Tennessee along the Mississippi. Unlike Dyersburg, Covington did not have any water access to the big river, and it owes its size to the coming of the railroad in 1873. Money flowed into the town, and the South Main Historic District, now on the National Register, shows how the townspeople of the 1880s–1900 spent it. One of the more unusual structures is the **Lowenhaupt-Simonton House,** 432 S. Main Street. It seems that a Mississippi riverboatman retired here and built a house of the kind more commonly seen in Louisiana. The house is not open to the public.

The **Tipton County Museum Veterans Memorial and Nature Center** (751 Bert Johnson Ave., 901/476-0242, 9 A.M.–5 P.M. Mon.–Sat. 9 A.M.–3 P.M. Sun., free) has the longest name of any such establishment in the state. This new museum, adjacent to Cobb-Parr Park, offers a look at military history with artifacts and uniforms as well as a look at nature both in the museum and along a nearby wooded trail.

This is cotton country, as evidenced by the presence of **Tennessee Gins** (800 Tennessee Ave., 901/476-7842, Oct.–Nov.). Call L. C. Thomas for tours.

Those beneath a certain age will light up with the knowledge that Covington is the "Blow Pop Capital of the World." Charm's Blow Pops, for candy neophytes, are lollipops with bubble gum centers. Alas, the Charms Company has neither a tour nor a company store. Another point of interest: Isaac Hayes, Memphis music man most famous for writing the theme to *Shaft,* was born here.

Recreation

Cobb-Parr Park (corner of U.S. 51 N. and Bert Johnson Ave.) is an 80-acre park and nature preserve and the site for many community festivals and activities. It includes a picnic area, playground, tennis courts, baseball fields, horse stables, and walking paths.

Glenn Springs Lake is a 310-acre fishing lake operated by the Tennessee Wildlife Resources

Agency. The lake is stocked with bluegill, large-mouth bass, sunfish, black crappie, and blue catfish. Visitors must have a fishing license and a permit, which they can buy at the full-service store right at the lake. The lake is open 30 minutes before sunrise until 30 minutes after sunset year-round. To get there take Hwy. 59 west, turn left on Glenn Springs Road, and then turn left onto Grimes Road. The lake is on the right.

A way down the road from Covington and just north of Memphis on the river lies the 13,467-acre **Meeman-Shelby Forest State Park** (800/471-5293 or 901/876-5215, www.tnstateparks.com), which gives visitors a sense of the massive hardwood forest that once covered Tennessee and that had to be cut down before the land could be farmed. The park contains hiking trails, swimming pool, six cabins, and 49 campsites.

Events

Heritage Day Festival (901/476-9727), held during the last weekend in September, consists of tours of historic homes, crafts demonstrations, music, dance, and carriage rides.

The **Tipton County Barbecue Festival** (901/476-9727, $2), begun in 1973, claims to be the oldest barbecue festival in the world. It includes a cookers' showmanship contest, arts and crafts, games and rides, and a truck pull. held annually the first week of October at the Cobb-Parr Park corner of U.S. 51 N. and Bert Johnson Avenue.

Practicalities

For accommodations, choose between the **Best Western** (873 U.S. 51 N., 800/528-1234 or 901/476-8561), and the **Comfort Inn** (901 U.S. 51 N., 800/221-2222 or 901/475-0380).

Country Kitchen (899 U.S. 51 N., 901/476-1591, www.visitcountrykitchen.com) serves breakfast all day long and offers a full menu of country cooking. **Little Porky's Pit Bar-Be-Que** (524 U.S. 51 N., 901/476-7165, 8 A.M.–10 P.M. Mon.–Sat.) serves hamburgers, shrimp, catfish, grilled chicken, and barbecue.

For more information, contact **Covington-Tipton Chamber of Commerce** (106 W. Lib-

erty Ave., 901/476-9727, www.2chambers.com/covington,_tennessee.htm, 8 A.M.–4:30 P.M. Mon.–Fri.).

MASON

This town has two culinary landmarks that make it necessary to come here for lunch and dinner, or perhaps on two consecutive evenings, to get the entire experience.

If there were such a thing as a fried-chicken juke joint, **Gus's World Famous Hot and Spicy Chicken** (south side of U.S. 70, 901/294-2028, www.gussfriedchicken.com, 11 A.M.–9 P.M. Mon.–Sat.) would be it. *GQ* magazine once listed this place as one of 10 restaurants in the world worth flying to for a great meal. Business took off. Some people, maybe those fresh from their Lear Jet will step inside, take one look, and head right back out the door. The building is long and not the most immaculate-looking place in the world. The air is heavy with frying oil. Anyone who leaves without eating, however, will miss the best fried chicken in Tennessee, if not the entire universe. And right up front is one of the best blues and soul jukeboxes in the state, with selections from Bobby Bland, John Lee Hooker, and James Brown.

Just east of Gus's is **Bozo's Hot Pit Bar-B-Q Restaurant** (342 U.S. 70, 901/294-3400, 10:30 A.M.–9 P.M. Tues.–Sat.), which is as noted in legal circles as it is in culinary ones. The restaurant was founded in 1923 by Thomas Jefferson "Bozo" Williams. Never mind how he got that nickname. Through the years, the restaurant prospered, and in 1982 the owners decided to register the name "Bozo's" as a federal trademark. Enter one Larry Harmon, also known as Bozo the Clown, who holds rights to his alter ego's name and who decided to oppose the application on the technicality that it was a local restaurant and had no interstate patrons and thus could not register a trademark. People in West Tennessee don't cotton to out-of-town clowns, legal or otherwise, and they called on friends and family from all over the country to write affidavits stating that they were out-of-state customers of the restaurant.

The Western Plains

The clown took it on the chin in court, then again on appeal, and pushed the case all the way to the Supreme Court, which in its wisdom refused to hear it. The name remains.

Now for the food: Bozo's serves barbecue plates, burgers, fried chicken, fried shrimp, and great vegetables. Locals often come to eat at Gus's and then get Bozo's barbecue to take home.

Brownsville and Vicinity

If visitors have time for just one of West Tennessee's small towns, this is one to see. Brownsville bills itself as "the Heart of the Tennessee Delta" and is working hard to promote its rich musical heritage. The town's historic district has lovely homes dating to the early 1800s, and the Tennessee Delta Heritage Center, just off I-40, is the best rest stop in the state, if not the entire South.

Heading the list of local blues players is the late Sleepy John Estes, whose country blues songs were often about his personal experiences. He lost sight in one eye as a child, and he later got his name because he liked to take naps. He recorded from 1929 through the '40s, and then returned to Brownsville when he became completely blind.

What happened later is best described by fellow West Tennessean Franklin Jones:

Sleepy John Estes lived for most of his life in Brownsville and was very important to the 1960s blues-rediscovery, white northerners, because he was to them sort of like the coelacanth was to paleontologists—a living example of a species, in this case, Delta bluesmen, considered long extinct. Many eager-eyed music writers have Sleepy John stories, and for them hunting for and actually finding him was a watershed moment in life. The line from his song, "I'm goin' to Brownsville, take that old right hand road," took on almost religious meaning.

Estes, who lived in a series of shacks and died in 1977, was largely ignored by white Brownsville and often played with the late Hammy Nixon on harmonica. Yank Rachell, one of the very few people who played blues on a mandolin, also played with Estes. In the 1960s and 1970s, it wasn't unusual for Estes

and one of his buddies to jet off to Tokyo or Berlin or Washington, D.C.

Brownsville was also the birthplace in 1900 of Richard Halliburton, a real-life Indiana Jones who combined adventuring and adroit public relations into a career that kept his name before the public in the '20s and '30s. He followed Ulysses's route through the Mediterranean, swam the Panama Canal, and ran the original marathon route at a time when almost no one did long-distance running. In 1939 he set forth from Hong Kong in a Chinese junk bound for San Franciso. He encountered a storm, and he and the boat disappeared.

Son Bonds, another bluesman, was born here, as was country musician Alex Harvey, who helped write the Kenny Rogers hit "Reuben James." He also cowrote "Delta Dawn" and "No Place But Texas."

SIGHTS

ⓜ Tennessee Delta Heritage Center

Just off I-40 at the Brownsville exit, this is a combination rest stop, museum, blues center, and gift shop (731/779-9000, www.west-tnheritage.com, 9 A.M.–5 P.M. Mon.–Sat., 1–5 P.M. Sun.). It not only provides information on regional attractions, but it also contains an excellent cotton museum and exhibits relating to local musicians: a shirt from Carl Perkins, Alex Harvey's first guitar, and information on obscure West Tennessee musicians such as Peetie Wheatstraw await the visitor. The most poignant exhibit is a ramshackle house out back that used to provide shelter to Sleepy John Estes. To find the center, take Exit 56 off I-40, turn north on Hwy. 76, and look beside McDonald's.

Ｍ Mind Field

Brownsvillian Billy Tripp, a sort of folk artist with a welding rod, has erected Mind Field, a 70-foot-high steel sculpture that is a work in progress. In a published interview, Tripp claims that he expects the work to take 20–25 more years to finish. In the meantime, there's plenty to see. It contains steel cut-outs of Tripp's hands and feet, a basketball goal, skulls and crossbones, and hearts. He charges no admission to see Mind Field, which is on U.S. 70 one block from the town square. Visitors are not allowed to walk through the work, but they are welcome to stand outside of it and gaze. Tripp lives in a welding shop behind Mind Field, and if he is not busy he is happy to discuss his work.

Tripp Country Hams

Charlie Tripp—Billy Tripp's brother—and his wife, Judy, own and operate Tripp Country Hams (207 S. Washington St., 800/471-9814 or 731/772-4883, www.countryhams.com, 7 A.M.–3 P.M. Mon.–Fri.). Their hams have won state and national awards, and they are sold whole or in slices; hams start at $2.09 per pound. Local restaurants and some convenience stores sell Tripp hams, best enjoyed with cathead biscuits. Out-of-towners can obtain this Southern delicacy by telephone or by going to the website.

Haywood County Museum

This museum (127 N. Grand Ave., 731/772-4883, www.brownsville-haywoodtn.com, 2–4 P.M. Sun., 10 A.M.–4 P.M. Mon., Wed., Thurs. and Fri., free) is one of the better small-town museums on this end of the state. It has a Confederate flag made in 1861 and military uniforms from the Civil War and the world wars. A bomber jacket that kept its owner warm on 32 missions is here, as is a small display on Richard Halliburton.

The highlight of the museum, however, is the Felsenthal Lincoln Collection, which totals 800 pieces, contains signed Lincoln documents, lithographs, books, and an 1860 campaign token. Some of the odder items are a piece of wood from the cabin in which Lincoln was born, a

© JEFF BRADLEY

Billy Tripp's Mind Field is a work in progress—it won't be finished for a quarter-century.

The Western Plains

nail from his home, and a replica of the pistol that John Wilkes Booth used to kill him. Other items include toy soldiers and a collection of three-inch statues of every president from Washington to Nixon.

The museum is housed in an 1851 brick building that was once the home of the Brownsville Baptist Female College. It later became a boys' school and then the high school for Haywood County.

Temple Adas Israel

Just off the square at the corner of College and Washington Streets, this Reform congregation, founded in 1867, occupies the oldest temple in continuous use in the state. The current building was erected in 1882.

FOOD

Backyard Bar-B-Q (703 E. Main St., 731/772-1121, lunch and dinner Mon.–Sat.) serves barbecued ribs, chicken, and pork, and sandwiches and side orders. **City Fish Market** (223 S. Washington St., 731/772-9952) sells fresh fish most of the week. On Friday and Saturday, however, the staff starts to cook and the place fills up with customers. From 9 A.M. to 6 P.M. the air is filled with the smell of fried fish and hush puppies. No pond-raised catfish are served here; the fish on this menu are the genuine article.

Curley and Lynn's (1016 N. Washington St., no phone) serves very good barbecue. Local farmers and townsfolk hold court every morning at **The Hibachi** (471 Dupree St., 731/772-3184) offers all three meals Monday through Saturday. It has a full menu, including plate lunches, sandwiches, and buffets at lunch and Friday night.

The Hickory Pit (690 Dupree St., 731/772-9926) serves ribs Monday–Saturday for lunch and dinner. **Olympic Steak House** (326 W. Main St., 731/772-5555) is open for lunch and dinner seven days a week, and features steak, Italian dishes, and seafood accompanied by a large salad bar.

United China (5 Court Sq., 731/772-3989, lunch and dinner daily) serves Chinese food. The name of **ZZ's Kream Kastle** (16 Grand Ave. S., 731/772-3132, lunch and dinner daily) suggests some kind of ice cream place, but ZZ's is more than that. It serves a wide variety of food, including salads, cheeseburgers, spaghetti, lasagna, pizza, fresh doughnuts and brownies, and jumbo stuffed baked potatoes.

INFORMATION AND SERVICES

For accommodations, try the **Comfort Inn** (2600 Anderson Ave., 800/221-2222 or 731/772-4082), **Days Inn** (I-40 Exit 56, 731/772-3297), **Motel 6** (I-40 Exit 66, 800/21-GUEST [214-8378] or 731/772-9500), or **Holiday Inn Express** (120 Sunny Hill Cove, or 800/HOLIDAY [465-4329] or 731/772-4030).

Brownsville Blues Festival, held in September, brings together performers and audiences for acoustic as well as electric blues. For details, contact **Brownsville-Haywood County Chamber of Commerce** (121 W. Main St., 731/772-2193, www.brownsville-haywoodtn.com, 8 A.M.–4:30 P.M. Mon.–Fri.) occupies a building that was a Carnegie library built in 1910.

HATCHIE NATIONAL WILDLIFE REFUGE

A staple of movies for a time was the Southern prison escape film, in which two prisoners—usually one black and one white—break out of the big house while shackled together and have to escape through the swamps. If anyone wanted to remake one of those epics, the Hatchie National Wildlife Refuge could serve as the setting.

This is the one river left in the lower Mississippi Valley that has not been "channelized"—straightened out—by a federal government with good intentions but bad ideas. The 11,556 acres here abound with wildlife: 200 species of birds, including red-shouldered hawks, barred owls, and wild turkeys; 50 species of mammals, including deer, beavers, river otters, and squirrels; and a great many reptiles, amphibians, fish, and invertebrates.

This area often floods, and sections of it are closed November 15–March 15 to provide sanctuary for waterfowl. To get information on what is open, visitors should go to the headquarters (Hwy. 76 just south of I-40 Exit 56, 731/772-0501, http://refuges.fws.gov, 7:30 A.M.–4 P.M. Mon.–Fri.).

NUTBUSH

According to local lore, Nathan Bedford Forrest named this place. Tina Turner was born here, which was commemorated in the song "Nutbush City Limits." Calling this hamlet a city was most generous, yet it has had a musical heritage far richer than many larger towns. Part of that heritage is the **Woodlawn Church,** which was the first house of worship for freed slaves in these parts. From Brownsville, the church is on the left on Hwy. 19, Nutbush's main drag.

The community here produced and listened to a variety of musicians, among them Bootsie Whitelow and Sleepy John Estes. Much of the musical heritage of Nutbush is unmarked, but can be found in *Haywood County, Tennessee* by Sharon Norris, a local writer.

The Western Plains

Heartland

In the Heartland of Tennessee, or Middle Tennessee, as locals call it, all roads seemingly lead to, or from, Nashville. This culturally and geologically diverse region spans antebellum plantations to car manufacturers.

The region from Franklin to Pulaski lies in the Central Basin, a depression in the state's Highland Rim with such rich farmland that it grows more bluegrass than all of Kentucky combined. Antebellum plantation owners become extremely prosperous, and during the Civil War suffered greatly. The other side of that coin is that much of this prosperity came about on the backs of slaves. This part of Tennessee strongly supported secession in 1860 and even today is a strong supporter of "our Southern heritage." However, this is a most welcoming part of the state with a great concentration of bed-and-breakfasts, restaurants, and places to see. General Motors, which had almost every state in the country standing on its head to land the Saturn assembly plant, chose this area.

The Monteagle area is a big resort destination. In the days before air-conditioning, Southerners who had the money and the time would escape from the heat by coming to the western edge of the Cumberland Plateau, such as Beersheba Springs.

The first settlers of Middle Tennessee came to the Carthage and Gallatin region. Lured by tales of fertile land, the "long hunters" came first, followed by Revolutionary War veterans seeking to claim land that the state of North Carolina had paid them for their wartime service. Andrew Jackson built his Hermitage here, and at one time or another visited almost all of the historic houses in the area. The Cumberland River remained an important means of transportation long after other parts of Tennessee had shifted to railroads. The Captain Ryman who found religion and then built Ryman Auditorium in Nashville ran his steamboats on this section of the river.

The Clarksville region offers some charming places and a lot of history. Its parks commemorate the state's fledgling iron industry, which produced the cannonballs that drove back the British at the Battle of New Orleans. Here Union armies began their invasion of the South. Today it contains the largest military installation in the state and the only town owned entirely by a country music diva.

Perhaps most famous in the Heartland is the Natchez Trace and surrounding areas. This section follows the historic Natchez Trace, taking in along the way the hometown of a Tennessee woman whose "Howdeeee! I'm just so proud to be here!" brightened the hearts of generations of *Grand Ole Opry* listeners.

Franklin and Vicinity

This charming town has been described as "15 miles and 100 years down the road from Nashville," a remark meant as a compliment. And it is. Franklin, unlike so many towns that let "progress" tear down their old buildings and replace them with unmitigated ugliness, took heed of the growth of Nashville and malls and interstates and then worked to protect itself. Williamson County, of which Franklin is the seat, is the wealthiest county in Tennessee and among the top 25 wealthiest counties in the country.

Franklin has done a wonderful job of preserving its 19th- and early 20th-century heritage. The entire 15-block original downtown area is listed on the National Register of Historic Places, offering the visitor a great place to shop, walk, and soak up history.

For those who like to see antebellum homes, this is the place. Franklin lies along the **Tennessee Antebellum Trail,** a 90-mile loop which runs from Nashville to Mt. Pleasant. While some homes are open to the public, others remain in private hands. A detailed guide is the excellent *Touring the Middle Tennessee Backroads,* by Nashville judge Robert Brandt.

HISTORY

Founded in 1799, the town was named for Benjamin Franklin. Many of the early settlers of Williamson County were Revolutionary War veterans who were given land for their service to their country. This patriotic spirit surfaced again during the Mexican War, when, it is said, every single, able-bodied man in this county joined the army. Such love of country—or willingness to get into a fight—caused Tennessee to be dubbed "The Volunteer State."

Ideally suited for farming, Williamson County, of which Franklin is the seat, became by the time of the Civil War one of the wealthiest counties in the state. Using slave labor, plantation owners amassed fortunes with which they built large houses that still sit in the town and along surrounding roads.

Franklin lay in the way of Confederate General John Bell Hood's ill-fated effort to attack Nashville. Going against the judgment of his officer corps, on November 30, 1864, he ordered an attack on Union troops who were dug in at Frankin. The resulting battle was one of the bloodiest of the war, though not very well known except to Civil War buffs.

Williamson County has a rich musical heritage. Brothers Sam and Kirk McGee were one of the earliest duos on the *Grand Ole Opry.* Lasting through the years, they were the first act to play in the new Opryhouse in Nashville. Franklin is the birthplace of Jack Anglin, half of the country

M ust-Sees

Look for **M** to find the sights and activities you can't miss and **M** for the best dining and lodging.

M The Carter House: This historic museum in Franklin puts a human face on the Civil War, telling how a soldier finally came home to die in his family's house (page 110).

M Bell Buckle: This arts and crafts center is a good example of how small towns can revitalize themselves (page 133).

M Jack Daniel's Distillery: Tennessee's most famous product is produced in Lynchburg, drop by drop (page 140).

M Monteagle: This delightful Victorian village, continuing site of the religious assembly begun in 1883, is proof that a good idea can last for a long time (page 152).

M University of the South: In Sewanee, you'll find the prettiest campus in the state, if not the entire South (page 155).

M The Hermitage: Just outside of Nashville, Andrew Jackson's former home offers a good look at the life of one of the state's more complex and controversial figures (page 163).

M Wynnewood: The largest log structure in the

COURTESY OF THE UNIVERSITY OF THE SOUTH

The University of the South

state offers a glimpse of Middle Tennessee before the antebellum splendor (page 174).

M Leipers Fork: If you can only get to one small town in Middle Tennessee, make it this one just south of Nashville. Surrounded by the Natchez Trace Parkway, wetlands, and farms in Land Trust, it's escaped the march of real estate development (page 195).

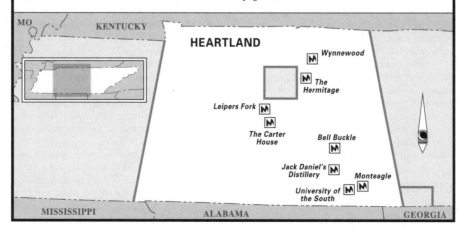

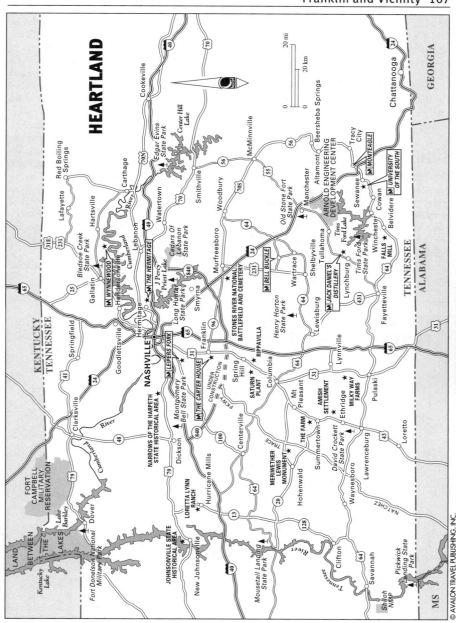

HEARTLAND

Heartland

GEORGIA

Chattanooga

24

Cookeville

40

70

20 mi

20 km

0

Red Boiling
Springs

Edgar Evins
State Park

Center Hill
Lake

McMinnville

56

Beersheba Springs

Tracy
City

MONTEAGLE

ARNOLD ENGINEERING
DEVELOPMENT CENTER

UNIVERSITY
OF THE SOUTH

Lafayette

Carthage

Hartsville

Watertown

Smithville

Woodbury

Manchester

Altamont

Sewanee

Cowan

TENNESSEE

ALABAMA

Cumberland River

70N

Edgar Evins
State Park

70

Murfreesboro

56

55

70S

64

Old Stone Fort
State Park

Shelbyville

Tullahoma

Winchester

Tims Ford Lake

Tims Ford
State Park

FALLS
MILL

Belvidere

Cowan

31E

231

Bledsoe Creek
State Park

Lebanon

Cedars Of
Lebanon
State Park

40

231

BELL BUCKLE

24

Wartrace

JACK DANIEL'S
DISTILLERY

Lynchburg

431

Fayetteville

64

KENTUCKY

TENNESSEE

25

Gallatin

Hendersonville

WYNNEWOOD

THE HERMITAGE

Hermitage

J Percy
Priest Lake

Long Hunter
State Park

Smyrna

96

Franklin

65

STONES RIVER NATIONAL
BATTLEFIELD AND CEMETERY

Henry Horton
State Park

Lewisburg

64

Lynnville

431

Pulaski

65

31

65

Springfield

Goodlettsville

NASHVILLE

LEIPERS FORK

THE CARTER HOUSE

Montgomery
Bell State Park

Spring
Hill

SATURN
PLANT

Columbia

Mt
Pleasant

RIPPAVILLA

AMISH
SETTLEMENT

MILKY WAY
FARMS

41

24

Clarksville

River

Dickson

Centerville

THE FARM

Ethridge

David Crockett
State Park

Lawrenceburg

Loretto

43

Cumberland River

48

NARROWS OF THE HARPETH
STATE HISTORICAL AREA

840

100

840

MERIWETHER
LEWIS
MONUMENT

Summertown

Hohenwald

20

NATCHEZ TRACE PKWY

UNDER CONSTRUCTION

Waynesboro

64

FORT
CAMPBELL
MILITARY
RESERVATION

79

Dover

Lake
Barkley

Fort Donelson National
Military Park

70

LORETTA LYNN
RANCH

Hurricane Mills

13

128

64

Clifton

Savannah

64

BETWEEN
THE
LAKES

LAND

Kentucky
Lake

JOHNSONVILLE STATE
HISTORICAL AREA

New Johnsonville

40

Mousetail Landing
State Park

Pickwick
Landing State
Park

Shiloh
NMP

MS

Tennessee River

© AVALON TRAVEL PUBLISHING, INC.

duo Johnnie and Jack, who reached success in the '50s and '60s. Robert Lunn, whose *Opry* specialty was the talking blues, also came from Franklin. Nowadays many country music figures live in Williamson County.

Tennessee Walking Horse fanciers revere Franklin as the home of Midnight Sun, two-time champion and legendary sire of a string of subsequent champions.

SIGHTS

Downtown

Franklin is best seen by foot. A good place to start is the **Williamson County Chamber of Commerce and Tourism** (on the square at the corner of Main St. and 2nd Ave. S., 615/794-1225). Here one can get brochures elaborating on the Battle of Franklin and local sights. Highlights of the latter include the **Courthouse,** which was built in 1859 and features four cast-iron columns.

Eaton House, an 1818 Federal townhouse down from the square on 3rd Avenue North, was home to John and Peggy Eaton, whose courtship and marriage provoked endless scandal in Washington when John served as Andrew Jackson's secretary of war. Peggy was a beautiful widow whose father owned the boardinghouse in which Eaton lived while in Washington. The two were married only four months after Peggy's first husband died, and she was reputed to be pregnant with Eaton's child when the two were wed. She wasn't, but this ugly rumor set tongues wagging in the capital, and the Eatons were shunned by polite society. Knowing the pain of false gossip about marriages, Jackson championed the Eatons, and this made things worse. Finally John Eaton resigned and returned to Franklin. Jackson was a frequent guest here. Now a law office, the house is not open to the public.

The Hiram Masonic Lodge, on 2nd Avenue South, is a Gothic structure built in 1823 for

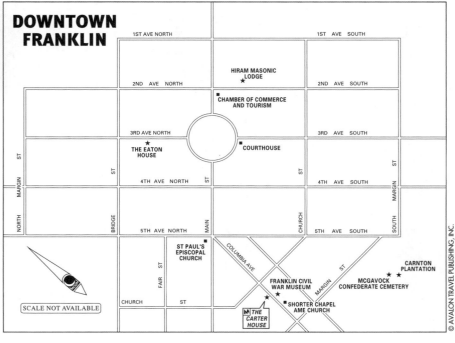

DOWNTOWN
FRANKLIN

1ST AVE NORTH   1ST AVE SOUTH

HIRAM MASONIC
LODGE

2ND AVE NORTH   2ND AVE SOUTH

CHAMBER OF COMMERCE
AND TOURISM

3RD AVE NORTH   3RD AVE SOUTH

THE EATON
HOUSE   COURTHOUSE

4TH AVE NORTH   4TH AVE SOUTH

5TH AVE NORTH   5TH AVE SOUTH

ST PAUL'S
EPISCOPAL
CHURCH

CARNTON
PLANTATION

MCGAVOCK
CONFEDERATE CEMETERY

FRANKLIN CIVIL
WAR MUSEUM

SHORTER CHAPEL
AME CHURCH

THE
CARTER
HOUSE

SCALE NOT AVAILABLE

© AVALON TRAVEL PUBLISHING, INC.

Tennessee's first Masonic organization. At that time it was the only three-story building in the entire state. In 1827 the state's first Episcopal church was organized here, and in 1830 President Andrew Jackson, his secretary of war, and others negotiated a treaty here with the Chickasaw.

The story of the Civil War experiences at **St. Paul's Episcopal Church** (at the corner of 5th Ave. N. and Main St.) could be titled "Why They Hated the Yankees for So Long." The first and oldest Episcopal church in Tennessee, this church, built in 1831, was heavily damaged during the oc-cupation by Northern troops. The pews, pulpit, and furnishings were hacked up for firewood or used as horse troughs. Organ pipes were tossed into the street, fires were built on the floor, and the tower was used as a smokestack. Luckily, the silver and church records were buried where the ma-rauders could not find them, and after the war the church was restored. The slave balcony was taken down, and in 1915 Tiffany windows were in-stalled. It is open to the public.

Another house of worship, **Shorter Chapel** (255 Natchez St., 615/790-6611) is the oldest

THE BATTLE OF FRANKLIN

The Battle of Franklin is not considered one of the important engagements of the Civil War—James McPherson's *Battle Cry of Freedom* gives it only two paragraphs—yet the toll was horrendous: Confederates alone suffered more than 6,000 ca-sualties, with 1,750 dead, six generals killed, one captured, and five more wounded.

The battle took place late in the war. By the middle of November 1864, Union General Sher-man had defeated the Confederate forces under John Bell Hood, burned Atlanta, and was sweeping toward Savannah. The situation facing the Con-federacy could be compared to the physical con-dition of Hood, whose left hand was paralyzed from a wound at Gettysburg and who had lost his right leg at Chickamauga.

Despite the debilitation of his body, however, the general envisioned sweeping north through Ten-nessee, invading Kentucky, and then heading east to rendezvous with Lee and defeat the Northern forces. Hood moved into Tennessee and headed for Nashville, where 60,000 Northern troops awaited Hood's 40,000 men.

When 30,000 of the Northerners under the command of General John Schofield came out to meet Hood, the Confederate general tried and failed to do an end run on them. Schofield's forces skirmished with Hood's at the Duck River in Columbia, then once more at Spring Hill. In preparation for the larger attack he knew would come, Schofield retreated during the night of November 29–30 and dug in at Franklin.

Franklin was a good place to do so. The Union had occupied the town for almost three years and had time to build substantial entrenchments. The Harpeth River off to the east prevented Southern troops from attacking on that side, and Schofield had plenty of artillery.

Hood made his headquarters on Winstead Hill, two miles south of town. His men faced a charge across open ground against well-dug-in defenders who were amply supported by artillery. The South-erners' own cannons were still on the road behind them. Nonetheless, shortly after 4 P.M. on the af-ternoon of November 30, Hood ordered his men to attack.

Their charge was more difficult than Pickett's fa-mous one at Gettysburg, yet these men persevered for five hours. The Southerners rushed the fortifi-cations 13 times. At one point troops under the command of Irish-born Patrick Cleburne broke through the Federal lines but were driven back. Cleburne was killed in the process.

As midnight approached, the Union troops pulled back and headed for Nashville, where even greater fortifications would protect them. They left a scene of terrible carnage. Army surgeons worked furiously at the Carnton plantation house south of town and piled up wagonloads of ampu-tated limbs.

The battle of Franklin, followed by the defeat at Nashville and the loss of Savannah to Sherman, made most people in the South realize that their struggle was almost over, and that the Confederacy was doomed.

Heartland

African Methodist Episcopal Church in the county. Slaves made the bricks before the war, soldiers used it as a hospital during the war, and freed slaves claimed it as their own after the war. **McLemore House African-American History Museum** (11th Ave. and Glass St.) was built in 1880 by an ex-slave, and now houses a five-room collection of furniture, kitchen equipment and other items from the black community.

A more secular delight is the **Franklin Cinema** (419 Main St., 615/790-7122) a restored 1936 movie house in which patrons can sit on couches or chairs and have pizza and beer while watching foreign or art films.

ⓜ The Carter House

Outlying places of interest begin with The Carter House (1140 Columbia Ave., 615/791-1861, www.carter-house.org, $8 adults, $6 seniors, $3 children under 13) which holds a particularly poignant story of the Battle of Franklin. The house was built between 1828 and 1830, and by the time of the Civil War the Carter family consisted of the father, three sons, and four daughters. After the attack on Fort Sumter, the brothers all enlisted in the Confederate army. One was captured and released to come home, and one was shot at Shiloh and discharged. Tod, second of the brothers, was captured at Missionary Ridge, yet he managed to get back in action in the army under General John Bell Hood.

Following Hood's dream of taking Nashville, Tod marched toward his home. He had seen neither his family nor his home for three and a half years. The Union army, under General John Schofield, dug in around the town of Franklin, using the Carter House as headquarters while the family took shelter in the basement.

Approaching his hometown, Tod could see Carter House behind the enemy lines. With the others, he charged the entrenched Federals, and with them he fell. When dawn rose on the horrible battle scene, word came to the family that Tod lay wounded on the Federal breastworks. Picking their way through the dead and the wounded, the family sought Tod. Finding him,

they used an overcoat to carry him home, where despite their ministrations he died two days later.

The Carter House presents a video and model of the battle, a museum, and a guided tour of the house and grounds.

Slightly South

While Carter House served as Union headquarters, **Historic Carnton Plantation** (1345 Carnton Ln., 615/794-0903, www.carnton.org, $7 adults, $6 seniors, $3 children 6–12) was a hospital for the Southerners. The house was built by a former mayor of Nashville about 1826 and was named for his father's house in Ireland, which in turn came from the Gaelic version of "cairn," a pile of stones to commemorate an event or individual. The name proved prophetic, for when John Bell Hood ordered the suicidal charges on the Union troops dug in at Franklin, the wounded and the dead were carried here. The bodies of four Confederate generals—including Irish-born Patrick Cleburne—were laid out on the back verandah.

Inside, the husband and wife of the house rolled up their carpets and tended to the wounded as best they could. Army surgeons sawed off arms and legs in the parlor, and blood stained the wooden floors.

Behind the house is the **McGavock Confederate Cemetery,** where are buried 1,481 bodies from the battle. The cemetery remains in private hands and is one of the largest Confederate resting places in the country. Carnton Plantation is being restored to its prewar appearance.

South of town along U.S. 31 is the **Winstead Hill Lookout,** from which John Bell Hood launched the Battle of Franklin and from which he watched the defeat.

ENTERTAINMENT AND EVENTS

On the Stage

Bunganut Pig Pub and Eatery (1143 Columbia Ave., 615/794-4777) offers live entertainment from blues to bluegrass every night. **Jammin' Java** (117B 5th Ave. N., 615/591-4888) is a Christian coffeehouse with live music every night. Lunchtime brings forth salads and sandwiches.

Main Street Festival (615/790-7094) brings more than 250 craftspeople, entertainment, and food to downtown the last full weekend in April.

House Tours

Heritage Foundation Town and Country Tour of Homes (615/591-8500, admission is $12 in advance and $15 the day of the tour), on the first weekend in May, gives visitors a chance to tour National Register mansions that are open at no other time.

Carter House Candlelight Tour of Homes (615/791-1861), on the first weekend of December, takes visitors to homes, churches, and other buildings, all lit by candles and decorated.

Festivals and Fairs

Franklin Jazz Festival (615/790-7094, free admission) brings traditional jazz, Dixieland, and big-band music to the town square on the first weekend in August.

Dickens of a Christmas, (615/790-7094) downtown on the second weekend of December, features carolers in Victorian costumes, horse-drawn carriage rides, and "living windows" of craftspeople.

The **Tennessee Renaissance Festival** (615/395-9950, www.tnrenfest.com), which takes place on weekends every May at Castell Gwynn, a four-tower replica of a 12th-century Welsh castle/ To get there from Franklin, go 13 miles east on Hwy. 96 to New Castle Road. Go north for three miles.

ACCOMMODATIONS

Magnolia House Bed and Breakfast (1317 Columbia Ave., 615/794-8178, or 615/828-1529, www.bbonline.com/tn/magnolia, $90–100) was built on the site of the Battle of Franklin in 1905 and was adapted to a craftsman style in the early 1920s. The four bedrooms are furnished with antiques, and a sitting area has a TV, books, magazines, and games. The host serves breakfast in the formal dining room.

Built in the mid-1800s is **A Homeplace Bed and Breakfast** (7286 Nolensville Rd., in Nolensville, 615/776-5181, $80–95). A two-

room suite on the second floor comes with washbasins, and baths in each room, canopy beds, and fireplaces in each room. The parlor suite has a fireplace, floor-to-ceiling bookcases, and a private bath. Wheelchairs are available. The separate Victorian Cottage offers a private bath and a small kitchen.

Old Marshall Inn (1030 John Williams Rd., 800/863-5808 or 615/591-4121, www.oldmarshallhouse.com, $105–150) lies east of town off Hwy. 96. The house was built in 1867 and has been restored to offer two rooms and a suite. There are three rooms and a cabin with its own bathroom.

FOOD

Herbert's Bar-B-Q (111 Royal Oaks Blvd., 615/791-0700, open daily) is famous for its corn light bread. The proprietor, who dishes up pork, ribs, and chicken barbecue, emphasizes that his place serves "inside meat"—no skin or fat.

Antonios (119 5th Ave. N., 615/790-1733, open daily) serves Italian cuisine including veal Marsala, snapper Portuguese, pasta dishes, and fresh salmon on weekends.

Bunganut Pig Pub and Eatery (1143 Columbia Ave., 615/794-4777, open daily) is a fun place to go. The complete menu includes shepherd's pie, fish and chips, and American fare such as steak, chicken, pasta, salads, and sandwiches. There's a full bar. Live entertainment from blues to bluegrass is offered every night.

Dotson's Restaurant (99 E. Main St., 615/794-2805, open daily) serves plate lunches of country cooking seven days a week. **Dumplin's Bakery** (1010 Murfreesboro Rd., 615/791-0051, open daily) in Maples Shopping Center, features freshly baked cinnamon rolls, Danish, muffins, cookies, pies, healthful desserts, specialty cakes, and cheesecakes.

Fourth and Main (Main St. and 4th Ave., 615/791-0001, open daily) offers upscale cuisine with items such as portabella mushroom sandwiches and pan-glazed salmon. A very good place for lunch. **H. R. H. Dumplin's of Franklin** (428 Main St., 615/791-4651, open daily) serves lunch-only specials such as homemade chicken 'n' dumplings, casseroles, quiches, soups, salads, sandwiches, its famous rolls, and pies and cakes.

Lille Belle's of Franklin (132 3rd Ave. S., 615/790-2300, www.lilliebelles.net, lunch Tues.–Sat., dinner Thurs.–Sat.) is in an 1880s house with 15-foot ceilings. Afternoon teas from 2:30–4 P.M. by reservation only, feature scones, Devon cream and lemon curd, finger sandwiches, and more.

Merridee's Bakery and Restaurant (110 4th Ave., 615/790-3755, open daily) is a "scratch bakery" and small restaurant. Baked goods are the specialty here, but the restaurant serves sandwiches and soups. The old wooden floors and baskets hanging overhead add a great touch.

Rebecca's English Tearoom (214 S. Margin St., 615/599-2345, lunch Wed.–Sat.) is the place for High Tea or just a cup of the beverage. Victorian finger sandwiches, scones, and other delights round out the scene.

SHOPPING

One of the more exciting developments in the Franklin area is **The Factory,** a renovation of a 46-acre industrial site that once cranked out MagicChef ranges north of Franklin along U.S. 31. It houses antique shops, shops, a coffeehouse, art galleries, and a variety of other shops.

Franklin Antique Mall (251 2nd Ave. S., 615/790-8593) occupies a building that used to house a mill and, at the turn of the century, an ice house. Now it holds something like 18,000 square feet of antiques.

Franklin Booksellers (118 4th Ave. S., 615/790-1349, 9:30 A.M.–5:30 P.M. Mon.–Fri., 9 A.M.–5 P.M. Sat.) is a good source of historical books about the area, including local interest books.

The **Harpeth Antique Mall** (529 Alexander Plaza, 615/790-7965) brings together about 80 dealers. Next door is the **Heritage Antique Gallery** (527 Alexander Plaza, 615/790-8115).

Magic Memories (345 Main St., 615/794-2848) offers a good supply of Civil War relics, such as saddles, swords, and buttons. Some smaller relics are for sale, including estate jewelry from the 1860s. The store also sells books, cards, and prints.

Rebel's Rest Civil War Museum and Artifact Shop (735 Columbia Ave., 615/790-7199) deals in high-end artifacts and other items—often in better shape than those in museums. The owner displays his personal collection of 2,796 kinds of bullets of the estimated 5,500 varieties used in the war. Also on display is a collection of tinware. Perhaps the most unusual item is a brass Parrott artillery fuse that collided with a .58 caliber minié ball. Civil War buffs can buy authentic buckles, tinware, firearms, sabers, glassware, and bullets. An authentic Confederate uniform sells for $50,000.

INFORMATION

Williamson County Visitor Information Center (just off the square at 209 E. Main St., 800/356-3445, www.williamsoncvb.org) offers various brochures, including a walking tour of the town.

SOUTH TO SPRING HILL

Now home to an enormous General Motors plant that produces Saturn automobiles, Spring Hill is more famous in Civil War circles as one of the great lost opportunities of the lost cause.

Late in the war, after Atlanta had fallen and Union General Sherman's troops were pillaging their way toward Savannah, Confederate General John Bell Hood turned his army in a last-ditch effort and headed for Nashville. Between him and the capital of Tennessee was a Union army commanded by General John Schofield, whose job it was to slow Hood down. Schofield retreated to Columbia, thinking Hood would attack him there.

In a shrewd move, Hood bypassed Schofield and got between the Union army and Nashville, then bedded his troops down for the night. He was in a good position—he could move on to Nashville or attack Schofield from the rear.

Schofield realized he had been outmaneuvered and frantically marched his troops north during the night in an effort to get back between Hood and Nashville. Fully expecting to get attacked when they approached the Southerners, the

Union soldiers quietly walked so close past the encamped Confederates that they could easily hear conversations around the fires. The Yankees passed by unmolested, and Schofield's entire army got back into position. When the sun rose, the Yankees were in Franklin, where they would later devastate the hapless Hood.

Sights

Saturn Welcome Center (100 Saturn Pkwy., 931/486-5440, www.saturn.com, free) introduces visitors to the Saturn automobile manufacturing plant, built in 1986. Saturn now employs more than 8,200 people in its approximately 2,400-acre plant and has produced more than a million cars. It was designed to preserve the rural and historical surroundings, and this huge plant is almost invisible from U.S. 31 because of the landscaping and building colors. Farming continues on the plant site, including more than 600 acres of planted corn, soybeans, barley, and shear. More than 300 acres are planted in mixed grasses and alfalfa. Saturn received the "1987 Industrial Conservationist of the Year" award for its efforts to reduce the environmental impacts of the largest private construction project in the history of Tennessee. Call the welcome center to reserve a spot on the tour.

Rippavilla (5700 Main St., 931/486-9037, Jan.–Feb. 10 A.M.–4 P.M. Tues.–Fri., Apr.–Dec. 9 A.M.–5 P.M. Tues.–Fri., 1–5 P.M. Sun., $8 adults, $6 seniors, $4 for ages 6–18) across from the Saturn plant, was built in 1852, finished in 1854 and was used as headquarters by both sides during the Civil War. The day of the Battle of Franklin, Confederate General John Bell Hood and his staff had breakfast here, and before the day was over, five of those generals were killed. The house has been restored to its 1850s appearance with 65 percent original period furniture and includes a gift shop and a museum. Special events are welcome.

Behind Rippavilla is the **Mule Museum,** (9 A.M.–5 P.M. Thurs., $3 adults, $2 seniors, $1 children) a barn containing a collection of old-time farming implements pulled by mules and horses.

While at Rippavilla, take the time to see **Oak-**lawn (3331 Denning Ln.), which is just around the corner. It was in this brick home built in 1835 that General John Bell Hood spent the night when an entire Union army sneaked past him. The house was bought in the 1970s by country crooners George Jones and the late Tammy Wynette, who inflicted shag carpeting on the floor where Civil War generals had walked. To install the carpet, the bottoms of the 140-year-old doors were sawn off and put out in the trash. A sharp-eyed local woman retrieved the strips of wood and triumphantly returned them when the house passed into the hands of a more history-minded owner. Now properly restored to the way it appeared on the fateful night while Hood slept, the view of Oaklawn offers visitors very little of anything from the 20th century. To get there from Rippavilla, go south on U.S. 31 for 0.2 mile, then turn left on Denning Lane. A 2.5-mile drive leads to the mansion. Oaklawn is privately owned, so visitors should not invade the driveway.

Events

Every September in odd-numbered years, the Sons of Confederate Veterans stages a large **reenactment.** As many as 50,000 spectators gather to watch 11,000 reenactors clash. This event is complete with authentic weapons and period costumes. Call 615/791-6533 for details.

Food and Accommodations

M Early's Honey Stand (on U.S. 31, 800/523-2015 or 931/486-2230, www.earlysgifts.com) modestly claims to be "The South's Most Famous Old-Time Eating House." Here the visitor can load up on country ham, bacon, smoked sausage, ribs, and barbecue. Other items include jams and jellies, stone-ground flour and cornmeal, soups, and cheese.

For accommodations, try the **Holiday Inn Express** (U.S. 31, 800/HOLIDAY [465-4329] or 931/486-1234).

Information

Middle Tennessee Visitors Bureau (8 Public Sq., Columbia, 800/381-1865 or 931/381-7176, www.visitplantations.com, 8 A.M.–5 P.M. Mon.–Fri.).

Columbia and Vicinity

With its rich farmland, Maury County was quickly settled in the first decade of the 1800s. Within 20 years Columbia had aspirations of becoming the state capital, and by 1850 it was the third-largest town in the state, second only to Memphis and Nashville. Not having a navigable river held Columbia back, but by 1860 the county was the wealthiest in Tennessee, as the mansions still standing here amply demonstrate. One of the wealthiest families here was the Polks. James K. Polk became the 11th president of the country, and his cousins owned enormous plantations outside of town.

William Faulkner once wrote that a mule will work patiently 10 years for the chance to kick its owner once. Many old-timers hereabouts would understand that statement, for Columbia used to be the mule capital of the world. Thousands of mules were traded each year, and it all culminated with **Mule Day,** which in 1939 boasted "1,000 girls on 1,000 mules." Although no longer celebrated with such de Millean spectacle, Mule Day is still Columbia's biggest event.

SIGHTS

James K. Polk Home

Most visitors to Columbia make a beeline to the James K. Polk Home (301 W. 7th St., 931/388-2354, www.jameskpolk.com), which was built by Polk's father in 1816 while the future president was off at college. James and Sarah Polk did not live for very long in the house, but it contains many pieces of their furniture and other items that they used. Admission is $7 for adults, $6 for seniors, $4 for ages 6–18, and $20 for a family. Open April–October 9 A.M.–5 P.M. Monday–Saturday, November–October 9 A.M.–4 P.M. Monday–Saturday, and 1–5 P.M. every Sunday.

Athenaeum

Down the street and around the corner is perhaps the oddest structure in two or three counties. The Athenaeum (808 Athenaeum St., 931/381-4822, www.athenaeumrectory.com) looks as if

it were designed as a home for one of the Shriners' Grand Potentates. Built in 1835 for one of the ubiquitous Polk family members, the surprisingly small house combines elements of Moorish, Gothic, and Italianate styles. In 1851 it became the rectory of the Columbia Athenaeum School, which educated girls until closing in 1904. The Athenaeum is open for tours during the summer and can be rented for receptions, weddings, and meetings. Admission is $5 for adults, $4 for seniors and $2 children 6–18. Children under six get in free.

Tours

Antebellum Home Tours (800/381-1865 or 931/381-7176, www.visitplantations.com) run by the Middle Tennessee Visitors Bureau, offers tours for groups of eight or more. The tours can be customized to the interests of the group but usually include the interiors of at least three homes. They are open year round and reservations must be made in advance.

Sights Nearby

Elm Springs (740 Mooresville Pike, 931/380-1844, 9 A.M.–5 P.M. Mon.–Fri., 11 A.M.–4 P.M. Sat., $5 adults, $4 seniors, $3 children 6–12) is a Greek revival home built in 1837 and which now serves as the headquarters of the Sons of Confederate Veterans (SCV), an organization dedicated to "preserving history and legacy of these heroes, so future generations can understand the motives that animated the Southern Cause." While members often dress up in Confederate uniforms and take part in ceremonies and reenactments, they also spend a lot of time on "heritage defense," such as defending the right of people to display Confederate flags and claiming that slavery was not the prime reason the Southern states fought the Civil War. These controversial stances often put the SCV in bed with some unsavory organizations such as the Ku Klux Klan, which also champions Southern symbols. The Sons "vigorously rejects any group whose actions tarnish or distort the image of the Confederate soldier or his reasons for fighting." For more information, go to www.scv.org.

Elm Springs has an unusual feature for homes of that time—a second-story smokehouse built in an ell onto the main house. Meat was hung here to cure as smoke from the downstairs kitchen wafted through it. The home survived the Civil War through the devotion of two quick-thinking slaves—referred to as "house servants" by the SCV. As Confederates approached from the South, three days before the battle of Franklin, a Union soldier placed a burning broom in a closet under the back stairs, but Ole Miss and Samson found it and put out the fire.

The home is restored to its 1864 appearance, and visitors can tour the kitchen, dining room central parlor, and two bedrooms.

To get to Elm Springs from downtown Columbia, go south on Hwy. 31, then turn east onto Hwy. 50 and travel east for approximately two miles. You will pass a bowling alley on the right. Take the next right, which is Mooresville Pike, and then the first driveway on the right to Elm Springs.

RECREATION AND ENTERTAINMENT

Canoeing and Caving

Columbia's Duck River was never suitable for steamboats, but it's dandy for canoeing. Go east of town to **River Rat Canoe Rental** (4361 U.S. 431, 931/381-2278) to get on the water. Their prices range from 5 miles for $17 per person to 29 miles for $40 per person.

Southwest of Columbia in the community of Culleoka lies **South Port Saltpeter Cave** (2171 Mack Benderman Rd., 931/379-4404 or 931/388-4846). Said to be Middle Tennessee's largest cavern, it was used during the Civil War to produce nitrate for gunpowder and is now open for guided and unguided tours. It is also open for wild flower tours in the spring and kayak and canoe rentals in the spring and summer. Call ahead before going.

Events

Mule Day (931/381-9557, www.columbiatn

.com/muleday)commemorates Columbia's most famous product. Held on the first weekend in April, it consists of a mule sale, parade, fiddler's contest, liar's contest, and checkers contest, among other things. Organizers solemnly warn potential parade participants that they can wear nothing that "would be repulsive or cause fear or anxiety to a large portion of the community and/or might incite people to violence." And they mean it. Call for more details. The office is on 1018 Maury County Park Drive.

The **Spring Garden Plantation Pilgrimage** (800/647-6724) is held in late March to early April.

Jazz in June plays on the Sunday closest to summer solstice.

Mid-South Live Steamers (www.midsouthlivesteamers.org) holds spring and falls "meets" with one-eighth size trains that operate on over 14,000 feet of tracks laid out in Maury County Park.

Majestic Middle Tennessee Fall Tour (931/381-4822) is a self-driving tour that takes visitors to homes and churches. It's usually the first week in December. This tour is run by the Athenaeum.

The **Plantation Christmas Pilgrimage** takes place on the first weekend in December.

ACCOMMODATIONS

Ridgetop Bed and Breakfast (800/377-2770 or 931/285-2777, www.bbonline.com/ridgetop, $75–95) is a contemporary house that especially welcomes bicyclists. It offers one guest room, an 1830 cottage, and another freestanding building called The Loft. Each comes with private bath. The host serves a full breakfast. Ridgetop is four miles east of the Natchez Trace Parkway on U.S. 412 in Lewis County, two miles from Maury County line. Ridgetop also has a special reservation service for all bed and breakfasts on the Natchez parkway.

Among the motel choices are **Best Value Inn** (1548 Bear Creek Pkwy., 800/424-6423 or 931/381-1410), **James K. Polk Motel** (1111 Nashville Hwy., 800/348-8309 or 931/388-4913), **Ramada Inn** (1208 Nashville Hwy., 800/2RAMADA [272-6232] or 931/388-2720), and **Richland Inn** (2407 Hwy. 315, 800/828-4832 or 931/381-4500).

Travelers RV Park (931/381-4112, open all year) has 65 sites, a pool, and a sports field. From I-65 take Exit 46 and follow the signs.

FOOD

Back Porch Barbecue (200 W. 3rd St., 931/381-3463) serves pork, beef brisket, chicken, and ribs. **J.J.'s Barbecue** (1122 Hampshire Pike, 931/380-1756) smokes it all—pork, beef, chicken, turkey, ham, and ribs.

Nolen's Barbecue (115 E. James Campbell Blvd., 931/381-4322) offers pork, beef, turkey, chicken, and ribs from the drive-in.

Bucky's Family Restaurant (1102 Carmack Blvd., 931/381-2834) looks decidedly downscale, but the food is superb. A diner can choose from four to five meats, 11 vegetables, two kinds of bread, two cobblers, and six kinds of homemade desserts Monday–Saturday. Dessert and drink are extra—if diners have room for more food.

KT's on the Square (34 Public Sq., 931/388-8543) serves continental-style breakfast and lunch. Lunches include a meat-and-three-vegetable cafeteria-style plate. Short-order items are also available.

INFORMATION AND SERVICES

Sweet 14 (808 S. High St. next to the Polk home, 931/380-2077) offers painted furniture, antiques, jewelry, vintage linens, floral arrangements, clothing, and artwork.

Call or visit **The Maury County Convention and Visitors Bureau** (931/381-7176, www.antebellum.com), behind Rippavilla, the mansion across from the Saturn Plant north of the city on U.S. 31.

Another source of information about plantation homes is the **Tennessee Antebellum Trail** (800/381-1865), which covers historic properties from Nashville to Mt. Pleasant. A gift shop and bookstore make this a good place to stop.

South on U.S. 43

THE POLK LEGACY

A 3.5-mile drive southwest of Columbia on Highway 243 brings the traveler to the territory of those members of the Polk family who left the most striking imprints on Maury County. This branch of the tribe descended from William Polk, a cousin to the president, who acquired an enormous tract of land by gambling with the governor of North Carolina. Colonial Americans apparently played a game called Rattle & Snap—the exact rules have been lost over the years—in which dried beans were shaken in the hand and then thrown forth with a snap of the fingers. However it was played, Polk won and the governor lost, and 5,648 acres changed hands. Polk divided the land among his four oldest sons by his second wife, Sarah, and all four brothers built mansions.

One of the four brothers was Leonidas Polk, who while being educated at West Point got to

know a fellow Southerner named Jefferson Davis. Polk became an Episcopal priest and persuaded his brothers to build St. John's, an Episcopal plantation church that served the Polks and their servants. When the Civil War broke out, Leonidas Polk joined his college friend in beating his plowshare into a sword and became a major general in the Confederate army. Polk's military career came to an end when he encountered a Union artillery shell in 1864.

St. John's Episcopal Church

A pull-off on the east side of the road affords a view of the Polk family church, built 1840–42. A congregation worshiped there until 1915, and now the old church holds just one service per year on Whitsunday, The Feast of the Pentecost, held the last Sunday in May. On that day, the original silver chalice used by the Polk family is used in the service, which is almost always standing room only. Most of Tennessee's Episcopal

THE DARK-HORSE CANDIDATE

Like all presidents from Tennessee so far, James K. Polk was born in North Carolina. He came to Tennessee in 1806, when he was 11 years old. He returned to North Carolina to go to the university there, then studied law with an attorney in Nashville.

In 1823 his political career began with his election to the Tennessee legislature, and it was through politics that he met his wife, Sarah Childress. She was well educated for a woman of that day and took an active role in her husband's career. The couple never had children, possibly because of a urinary tract operation that Polk underwent as a boy.

Polk was elected to a seat in Congress in 1825 for the first of seven terms, and he rose to become speaker of the house 1835–39. Polk was a strong supporter of Andrew Jackson, even to the point of backing New Yorker Martin Van Buren, Jackson's hand-picked successor, over Tennessean Hugh Lawson White for the 1836 presidential race. This struggle split the Democratic Party and led Jackson's opponents to create the Whig Party. Polk's loyalty to Jackson came back to haunt him, for in 1839 he was elected governor of Tennessee, but he lost the office in the next two elections largely because of the Whigs' efforts.

By 1844, the Democratic Party was still split, with Martin Van Buren of New York, John C. Calhoun of South Carolina, Lewis Cass of Michigan, and James Buchanan of Pennsylvania battling it out for the presidential nomination. Delegates at the convention in Baltimore agreed that if no clear winner emerged the nomination would go to New Yorker Silas Wright, with Polk as the vice presidential candidate. Wright refused the nomination, however, and on the ninth convention ballot, Polk was unanimously elected. His name did not appear on the first seven ballots, and Polk became the first "dark-horse" candidate to win a presidential nomination.

Polk defeated Henry Clay for the presidency, becoming the only former speaker of the house ever to do so, but he did not carry Tennessee. Although he lacked any sort of mandate, he came to the White House aiming to stay one term and to accomplish four goals: to acquire California for the United States, to settle the boundary of Oregon, to reduce the tariff, and to set up an independent treasury. Setting a workaholic pace, he accomplished all four. His annexation of Texas began the two-year Mexican War, and the U.S. victory led to the acquisition of even more territory. During his administration the Department of the Interior, the naval academy, and the Smithsonian were founded.

At five feet six inches, James Polk was a short man, but he was renowned as "the Napoleon of the stump," a speaker who could readily dish out ridicule and sarcasm to opponents. Because he was so short, his entry to a room during White House functions would often go unnoticed, to the great annoyance of his wife. She is said to be the person who established the custom of playing "Hail to the Chief" when the chief executive enters a room.

Polk left Washington utterly drained. Two portraits in the Polk home in Columbia show what four years in office did to his appearance. His term ended March 14, 1849, and a little more than three months later he died in Nashville. He was 53 years old. Sarah Polk returned to Nashville, where she lived until her death in 1891. During the Civil War, when so much destruction was done to local mansions, troops from both sides left the Polk house alone.

Polk is not one of the well-known presidents, but his sense of purpose and effectiveness rank him as one of the better ones. A 1996 poll of historians ranked Polk as one of the "near great" presidents, alongside Jefferson, Jackson, T. Roosevelt, and Truman. Not bad company.

bishops are buried behind the church in the cemetery.

Hamilton Place

Continuing south on Highway 243 and going 0.7 mile past Zion Road, the visitor will see Hamilton Place on the right. A brick house with double-columned porches, this relatively simple structure was the first of the Polk brothers' homes and was built in 1832 by Lucius Polk, who married a grandniece of Rachel Jackson in the White House. Most of the materials for the home came from the grounds: bricks were fired from clay there, stone was carved from the ground there, and the wood came from trees on the estate. The house is considered a classic example of Palladian architecture.

Rattle & Snap

The last and greatest of the Polk brothers' houses is across the road and farther southwest. George Washington Polk's Rattle & Snap, named for the game by which his father won the land, rests at the top of a hill; it's the most magnificent antebellum mansion in Tennessee, if not the entire South. The capitals atop the 10 Corinthian columns were cast in Pittsburgh and Cincinnati, fireplaces were fashioned from marble, and the grounds were designed by a German gardener. Rattle & Snap was finished in 1845, and the Polk family had 15 happy years there before the war.

When the Civil War struck, marauding Union soldiers took a perverse delight in torching Southern mansions, and in 1862 a group with arson in mind stepped in the front door. The officer in charge noticed a Masonic ring on the life-sized portrait of the absent owner and decided to spare the house. The Civil War ruined the Polk fortunes, however, and they lost the home in 1867. Over the decades the once-elegant Rattle & Snap became rundown to that point that in the 1930s and 1940s hay was stored in it and chickens roamed the once-elegant rooms.

The house was stabilized and renovated in the 1950s but not fully restored until Amon Carter Evans, former publisher of the Nashville Tennessean, bought the house in 1979 and assembled a team headed by Henry Judd, the retired chief restorationist for the National Park Service, and turned them loose to restore the

COURTESY OF RATTLE & SNAP

Rattle & Snap

house to its 1845 appearance. When research revealed that the downstairs doorknobs had been made from silver plate, Evans ordered silver plate replicas. To reconstruct a missing ell, an old church in Nashville that was being torn down provided 88,000 bricks of the proper vintage. Asked to comment on a report that all this work cost $6 million, Evans replied, "That is a conservative estimate." He opened the house to the public, and it delighted visitors for years.

Evans's fortunes changed, however, and Rattle & Snap was sold in late 2003 to a couple who plan to live there and open the house only on special occasions. For information, go to www .visitplantations.com.

MT. PLEASANT

Large phosphate deposits were discovered near Mt. Pleasant in 1893, and these were mined extensively for fertilizer and other uses for several decades. The **Mt. Pleasant/Maury Phosphate Museum** (108 Public Sq., 931/ 379-9511, $1 adults, free for schoolchildren) recalls those days with exhibits of ore, equipment, clothing, and Civil War relics that were found during mining operations. Tours can be arranged by appointment.

ETHRIDGE

Farther along down U.S. 43 is the town of Ethridge, home to a community of Amish, a German-speaking religious sect usually associated with Pennsylvania and Ohio. This group moved to Tennessee in 1944 and now comprise the largest community of Old Order Amish in the South. The families farm and live in the old ways, using horses and buggies for transportation and disdaining electricity, telephones, and buttons on coats. They have no churches, meeting in one another's homes.

The Amish community hereabouts extends about 20 miles east to west and five miles north to south. Visitors can stop at **Granny's Welcome Center** (4001 U.S. 43, 931/829-2433, 9 A.M.–5 P.M. daily, free) for a map, or they can

just drive through the countryside on either side of U.S. 43. Travelers who have experienced the Amish in Pennsylvania Dutch country will find Tennessee's community much less commercialized. Depending on the season, visitors might see roadside stands or signs advertising peanut brittle, baskets, bread, cedar chests, and furniture.

While the residents are happy to talk to and engage in commerce with outsiders, visitors should remember that the Amish intensely dislike having their pictures taken. This objection is based on the second commandment: "Thou shalt not make unto thee any graven image, or any likeness of anything that is in heaven above, or that is in the earth beneath, or that is in the water under the earth."

An enormous technological leap from the Amish, **Granny's Network** is the brainchild of Sarah Evetts, also known as "Granny," who runs a 10-watt television station at Granny's Welcome Center and crafts store. Here she holds forth on items of interest to her local audience and will cheerfully interview sojourners who stop by. To those who ask, she will give a videotape of the interview. (She does charge for subsequent tapes.) There is also a daily wagon tour costing $10 that leaves daily, lasting from 9 A.M.–4 P.M.

Amish Country Galleries (3931 U.S. 43, 931/829-2126) offers many objects made by local Amish craftspeople. Furniture, quilts, and baskets head the list of items available here.

Uncle Charlie's Old Amish Farm (931/829-4060, www.tennesseeamish.com, $6 adults, $5 for children 4–12), right behind Granny's Welcome Center on U.S. 43, gives visitors a chance to see an Amish farmhouse as it looked in the 1940s. This was the first farm occupied by the Amish when they came in 1944 in search of cheap land. The farm has several original buildings and farm animals.

Those with more time can take a horse-drawn wagon or buggy tour of the Amish settlement. The tours last 90 minutes and go past 12 Amish farms and include stops to buy sorghum or other goods. Tours cost $10 for adults and $5 for children 4–12.

Heartland

LAWRENCEBURG AND VICINITY

Although Tennessee sent a large number of volunteers to the Mexican War, the two-year conflict and overwhelming U.S. victory is little noted with public monuments. Lawrenceburg's town square boasts an obelisk in honor of the war. It was erected in 1849, and allegedly kept the courthouse from being burned when Union soldiers came through during the Civil War.

Nearby is a life-sized statue of David Crockett. The hero of the Alamo lived near here for about five years, and a state park marks the site. About a block and a half south of the statue is a replica of Crockett's cabin. The items inside are period pieces or replicas of items Crockett might have owned. The cabin is open every day. Admission is free.

Outside the larger cities, Catholic churches are scarce in Tennessee. This county, however, has three, all because of German immigrants who began coming here in 1870 to take advantage of inexpensive farmland. The **Sacred Heart of Jesus Church** was begun in 1887. Parishioners baked the bricks and craftsmen lovingly built the structure, which stands on Church Street.

David Crockett State Recreational Park

A half-mile west of Lawrenceburg, this 987-acre park marks the one-time home of David Crockett. He moved here in 1817 and built a mill, a black powder mill, and a distillery along Shoal Creek. Quickly winning favor with his neighbors, he was elected justice of the peace, then town commissioner, then state representative. While he was off in Nashville serving in the leg-

THE FATHER OF SOUTHERN GOSPEL MUSIC

One of the most musically influential Tennesseans was James D. Vaughan, who was born in Giles County during the last year of the Civil War. He loved music. He and his brothers formed a singing quartet and he taught music as well. In 1900, he published *Gospel Chimes,* a book of gospel songs, and two years later moved to Lawrenceburg and opened the **James D. Vaughan Music Company** on the town square.

Now known as the "Father of Southern Gospel Music," Vaughan rolled out one innovation after another. In 1910, he put the first professional gospel quarter on the road to promote his books. In 1917, he launched the Vaughan School of Music in Lawrenceburg. In 1922, he started a record company, and two years later opened radio station WOAN, the first gospel music station. By the mid-1920s he had 16 full-time quartets on the road.

People wanted new gospel music, and Vaughan provided it. He published some 105 songbooks over the years, each with about 100 songs that were taught to people in singing schools and sung by quartets. Music expert Charles Wolfe, writing in *Tennessee Strings,* says, "Vaughan was a major force in the development of gospel music throughout the country. The average songbook sold about 117,000 copies; it was paperbacked, cheap, and easily carried to the singing conventions that dotted the South until the 1960s."

According to the history section of **The Singing News** magazine's website (www.singingnews.com), "The business grew and became so good that Vaughan opened branch offices in Mansfield, Arkansas; Laurel, Mississippi; Greenville, South Carolina; and Jacksonville, Texas. He sent a man names V. O. Stamps to run the Texas office. From this event would come the famous Stamps/Baxter Music Company, currently affiliated with the Benson Company division of the Zondervan Corp, owned by Harper-Collins Publishers."

Vaughn died in 1941. The **James D. Vaughan Museum** (931/762-8991, 9:30–11 A.M., 1–3:30 P.M., free) now stands on the square in Lawrenceburg.

islature in 1821, a massive flood hit Shoal Creek and washed away most of his enterprises. Forced into bankruptcy, he moved near Rutherford farther west in the state.

The park contains an interpretive center dedicated to Crockett, with exhibits on frontier life, Crockett's industries in Lawrence County, his moves across Tennessee, and his political life. Also on exhibit are a small number of items thought to belong to the county's most famous resident.

Recreational amenities include an Olympic swimming pool ($3 per person), fishing, bicycling, hiking, boat rentals, and 107 campsites open year-round which have electricity, water, bathrooms and showers. The restaurant here seats 240 people and serves lunch Monday–Friday, Sunday breakfast, and Friday and Saturday night dinners. The David Crocket interpretive center has free classes, and on the second week in August is **David Crocket Days.** This festival has a 1700s camp with such classes as hide tanning and black

powder shooting. Call 931/762-9408 or see the website www.tnstateparks.com.

Entertainment and Events

Live local music plays every Friday night from memorial day to labor day at the Lawrenceburg City Administration Building. The **Tennessee Valley Jamboree** features bluegrass, country, and gospel music starting at 7 P.M. No alcoholic beverages are permitted, and admission is free.

Food

Big John's Barbecue (904 N. Military Ave., 931/762-9596) lays out ribs and chicken. **The Brass Lantern** (2290 U.S. 64, 931/762-0474) offers steak, seafood, pasta, barbecue, plate lunches, and sandwiches. **Rick's Barbecue** (401 N. Military St., 931/762-2030) serves pork, beef, and chicken barbecue.

Square Forty (40 Public Sq., 931/762-2868) serves steak, catfish, and riblets. The building dates to the turn of the 20th century, with the

THE FARM

Tennessee has known several deliberate communities, and The Farm (931/964-3574, www.thefarm.org) has been the most successful. Its story began in 1971, when college English professor Stephen Gaskin led a caravan of approximately 300 people from Berkeley, California, to a 1,750-acre tract northwest of Summertown where land was $70 per acre. On three square miles they set up a communal way of life in which those who joined gave everything they owned to a common treasury, built buildings themselves, and shared work. This incarnation of The Farm peaked in 1981 with 1,400 people.

As their communal forebears at Tennessee communities such as Ruskin had learned before them, it is very hard to make a living from the soil. In The Farm members' own words, "A recession, several business reverses, overcrowding, lack of experience, and mismanagement brought about severe financial crisis." In October 1983, the members reorganized their community, and now the population is about 250. They do no more large-scale farming—hay is the big crop. Several cottage industries operate at The Farm, including mushroom growing and publishing.

The Farm is perhaps best known as a center of **midwifery.** Ina May Gaskin, once married to The Farm founder, published her first book, *Spiritual Midwifery*, in 1976, and is widely credited for launching the home birthing movement. Some 2,300 babies have come into the world at The Farm, and Ms. Gaskin continues to lecture nationally and to write.

Visitors are welcome at The Farm, although residents want visitors to call ahead and make arrangements. To get there, take Hwy. 20 north out of Summertown. Turn right on Drakes Lane and follow the signs. The Farm offers **The Farm Experience Weekend** wherein visitors can sample life there as well as other events. Camping and lodging at **Youre Inn** are available beginning at $8 per night.

Heartland

original pressed tin ceiling and lots of antiques and paintings. It offers live piano music on Friday and Saturday.

Shopping

Mama J's Cabin (4716 Pulaski Hwy., 931/762-0678) halfway between Lawrenceburg and Pulaski, occupies a structure fashioned out of two log cabins, one dating from 1845. Inside are antiques, jewelry, toys, and Christmas ornaments.

Those looking for the perfect item for a recreation room should pull in at **Yesterdaze Collectibles** (2140 Pulaski Hwy., 931/762-8182). Robert Dwiggins offers perfectly restored jukeboxes, pinball machines, Coke machines, and gas pumps.

Information

Contact the **Lawrenceburg Chamber of Commerce** (1609 N. Locust Ave., 931/762-4911, www.chamberofcommerce.lawrence.tn.us, 8 A.M.–4:30 P.M. Mon.–Fri.).

LORETTO

This little town has several distinctions. First, it is home to one of the two independent telephone companies left in the state—the Loretto Telephone Company. The other is in Millington in West Tennessee. Second, the Loretto Casket Company, founded in 1950, is the oldest and largest casket company in the state. Finally, Loretto has a long tradition of dancing—an island of fun in a sea of Baptistry.

The dancing started when Loretto attracted a large number of German immigrants in the late 1800s. With them they brought their Catholic faith. The town was named for a shrine in Loretto, Italy, and the first priest in the church asked the Virgin Mary to protect Loretto from

wind. Since then, locals claim, Loretto has never suffered a tornado.

As for the dancing, one local grande dame summed it up by saying, "Those Catholics know how to have a good time." Orchestras were imported from big cities such as Sheffield, Alabama, and dances were held in the Catholic school. Square dances took place every Saturday night and attracted people for miles around.

Sights

The **Sacred Heart of Jesus Church** (Church St., 931/853-4370, free) is a Gothic brick structure built by its German congregation in the 1920s. It has beautiful stained-glass windows and stations of the cross. The **Loretto Milling Company** (2nd Ave. S.) has been run by the same family for more than 100 years. It now produces animal feed only.

The **Ralph J. Passarella Memorial Museum** (133–134 S. Main St., 931/853-4351, Tues.–Wed., free, donations appreciated) commemorates the longtime co-owner of the Loretto Telephone Company. Although its two rooms contain a good deal of old telephone equipment, they also include antiques and curiosities. Chief among the latter is a wicker body basket once used by undertakers to transport a body to the funeral home.

The **Coca Cola Palace** (corner of 2nd and Broad Sts., 931/389-9663, free admission) is a one-time general store now devoted to Coca-Cola memorabilia. Malcolm and Gail Walters, who live next door at 108 2nd Avenue South, are generally available to show visitors around.

A town with a German background has to have an **Oktoberfest** (931/762-4911) and the one hereabouts is held the first full week in October and consists of a polka band, German food, and block parties.

Pulaski

This town got its name from Casimir Pulaski, a Polish count who fought and died in the American Revolution. Settlers hacked down 18-foot-high cane stalks to build the town, which is the seat of Giles County on the Alabama border.

Pulaski never saw a major battle during the Civil War, yet it is remembered in the South as the place where Sam Davis was hanged. Davis was captured near Pulaski and executed as a spy.

Giles County, of which Pulaski is the county seat, was the crossing place of two trails on the "Trail of Tears" removal of the Cherokee to Oklahoma. Bell's Route passed east to west, while Benge's Route moved northwest.

Pulaski is most notorious as the post Civil War birthplace of the Ku Klux Klan. December 1865 was a low point in Pulaski and much of Tennessee. The economy was ruined, the state was ruled by a governor intent on punishing former Confederates, and people in Pulaski and other places were apprehensive about all the former slaves who lived around them.

On Christmas Eve of 1865, in a law office at 207 Madison Street, a group of young men dreamed up a social club to take their minds off their troubles. They named it the Ku Klux Klan and invented costumes and initiation ceremonies and weird-sounding titles. While riding around bedecked with sheets and other ghostly garb, club members noticed with delight how their appearance terrified superstitious ex-slaves. It didn't take long for this amusement to transform itself into whippings, lynchings, and all manner of violence. The Klan moved from Pulaski, but the stigma connected to the organization remains. For many years the building where the Klan was founded bore a large plaque commemorating the event. To symbolize his opposition to the Klan and what it stands for, however, the owner of the building removed the plaque, turned it around, and re-bolted it to the wall. Visitors can see it just around the corner from the Giles County Chamber of Commerce office.

Two members of the Fugitives, a group of Southern writers and poets, were born in Giles County. John Crowe Ransom, philosopher, educator, journalist, and unofficial poet laureate of the 20th-century South, was born in Pulaski in 1887. He founded the *Kenyon Review* and, while teaching at Vanderbilt University, greatly influenced two other writers, Robert Penn Warren and Allen Tate.

Donald Davidson, noted educator and poet, was born in Campbellsville, in the northeastern part of the county, in 1893. He went off to Vanderbilt as an undergraduate and stayed there to teach after getting his master's degree. He belonged to a group known as the Agrarians, who resisted industrialism and advocated small town and rural living.

SIGHTS

The **Sam Davis Museum** (931/363-3789 or 931/363-2720) stands at the site of his death, now Sam Davis Avenue, and contains the leg irons he wore as well as other Civil War artifacts.

The **Giles County Courthouse** (10 A.M.–4 P.M. daily, admission is free) in the middle of the square is the grandest such building in Middle Tennessee, if not the entire state. Built in 1909, the courthouse has a cupola supported by Corinthian columns. A balcony inside encircles the third floor.

The **Giles County Historical Museum** (122 S. 2nd St., 931/363-2720, 10 A.M.–4 P.M. Fri.–Wed., free) in the library—down the street from the Chamber of Commerce—features exhibits on the county's history containing Civil War artifacts and farming implements. World War II items include a samurai sword.

Built by a former Confederate general who became a governor of Tennessee, the **Brown-Daly-Horne House** (318 W. Madison St., 931/363-1582) began as a relatively simple structure but was transformed in the late 1890s to a Queen Anne–style house complete with a third-floor ballroom, dumbwaiter, exterior turrets, stained-glass window borders, and gabled roof. Completely restored, the building now houses

Heartland

a bank and has been placed on the National Register. Admission is free to see the interior, which is open during banking hours.

Ten minutes west of Pulaski on U.S. 64, the **Green Valley General Store** (931/363-6562) sells an estimated 5,000 fried pies a month. This and fresh lemonade, homemade ice cream, and homemade cookies, along with canned fruits and sauces—and that's just the edibles. The store also stocks quilts and Amish goods, hats, and baskets. Next door is the flea market, known for its antique farm equipment, mostly horse-drawn. A large Amish community nearby is both the biggest supplier and buyer of the equipment. The flea market varies in size from a couple of acres to 10 acres. Auctions are held the third Thursday in April and October.

THE DAY THE TOWN STOOD STILL

The **Ku Klux Klan** was founded just off the town square in Pulaski in the late 1860s, and although the organization's headquarters soon departed the seat of Giles County for other places, the town's association with the birth of the Klan continued to haunt it. Various Klan incarnations through the years came to Pulaski to march and make hate-filled speeches, confident they were among friends.

Finally, Pulaski had enough. When an Aryan Nation group announced in 1989 it was coming to town for a rally, the townsfolk took a stand. More than 5,000 people signed a resolution condemning the group. More than 200 additional petitions were circulated across the state in opposition to the white supremacists.

The townsfolk took their most dramatic step, however, on October 7, 1989, when the Aryan Nation people arrived and found the town deserted—a very unusual situation on Saturday, normally the busiest day of the week. More than 180 merchants—virtually every one in Pulaski, including Wal-Mart—closed their doors and went home. When the group made its speeches, they echoed off empty buildings and rang through deserted streets. The Aryan Nation never came back.

Buoyed by this success, Pulaski organized Giles Countians United, a group composed of blacks and whites, Jews and gentiles, who organized **Brotherhood Weekend,** an annual series of events aimed at bringing people together. In 2000, a parade and rally honored the memory of Dr. Martin Luther King Jr. Hate groups still occasionally come to town—free speech guarantees them the right to do so—but they can no longer assume they are welcome.

EVENTS

The **Brotherhood Parade,** held the Saturday before Martin Luther King Jr.'s birthday, marks Pulaski's declaration that racism and bigotry have no place here. The **Unity Service,** held in a church, is "the best church service you'll experience all year," according to a person who goes to every one. The **Chili Cook-Off** is held in October at the National Guard Armory.

The **Giles County Historical Society's Walking Tour of Historic Homes** takes place in December. The **City Sidewalks Festival** brings an old-fashioned Christmas to Pulaski with a tour of five to six houses and carriage rides.

For details about these events and other information, contact **Giles County Chamber of Commerce and Tourism** (100 S. 2nd St., 931/363-3789, www.gilescountychamber.com, 8 A.M.–5 P.M. Mon.–Fri.). The chamber specializes in setting up custom tours for groups.

FOOD AND ACCOMMODATIONS

The **Heritage House Restaurant** (219 S. 3rd St., 931/363-2313, lunch and dinner Mon.–Fri.) is in the Gladish Garner House, a 1905 structure in which a full menu is provided, including grilled salmon and shrimp scampi. It also offers a buffet of Southern-style foods, such as ribs, catfish, chicken, and a barbecue plate.

Hickory House (330 Patterson St., 931/363-0231) offers a country cooking buffet, barbecued ribs, and chicken. Head east out of town on

U.S. 64 and look for a ballpark on the right. The restaurant is beside the park. At least one local swears by the banana pudding.

Reeves Drugstore (on the square at 125 N. 1st St., 931/363-2561) may be the only place left in the state that sells nickel Cokes from an old-fashioned soda fountain. It also serves deli food, sandwiches, salads, sodas, milk shakes, and ice cream.

For accommodations, try the **Best Western Sands Motor Hotel** (U.S. 64 and I-65, 800/528-1234 or 931/363-4501), or the **Richland Inn Pulaski** (1020 W. College, 800/828-4834 or 931/363-0006). **Valley KOA** (931/363-4600) has 60 campsites, a pool, and hiking trails. From I-65 take Exit 14 and follow signs. It's open all year.

Lynnville

North of Pulaski off U.S. 31 along Hwy. 129, Lynnville is a lovely town that once had to get up and move. After the Civil War the railroad came through about one mile east of the town. Realizing that if it were to prosper, it had to be near the train, Lynnville moved to its present location beside the tracks.

Now with 59 buildings, several of them Victorian homes and churches, Lynnville is listed on the National Register of Historic Places and is

MILKY WAY FARM

While visiting a drugstore in 1922, Frank Mars and his son, Forrest, had a great idea: what if they could produce a portable version of a chocolate malted milk? The Milky Way candy bar was the result, and its success launched the famous **Mars candy company** and made Frank Mars a rich man.

Later in that decade, Mars met a woman on a train and told her of how he wanted to have a home in the countryside that he could use as a retreat and where he could raise cattle and horses. The woman and her husband happened to have a farm in Giles County that was for sale. Mars bought it in 1930 and began acquiring adjacent land until he had a total of about 2,800 acres.

By this time, the Depression gripped Giles County, and Mars became the largest employer in the county, hiring 800 men to build the farm of his dreams. Giving them rakes, he ordered that they clear his fields of stones, many of which were used to construct barns, cottages, and a large structure known as the clubhouse. Workers lined the farm with a 35-mile-long fence and painted it white. Milky Way Farm had its own railroad depot, 25 stock barns, a horse track, and more than 50 homes for employees. To further help the local economy, Mars bought his hay from area farmers and paid locals to rake his entire estate.

By 1932 the clubhouse, a Tudor-style structure, was finished. Its living room has 30-foot vaulted ceilings, but the showstopper was the dining room, which contained a 28- by 12-foot table. To place candles in the middle, someone has to take off his or her shoes and scamper to the middle while wearing socks.

Frank Mars died in 1934 and was buried in a mausoleum on the farm. The estate passed to his second wife, Ethel, whose daughter, Patricia, had married the general manager of the farm. Ethel continued to raise racehorses, and in 1940 one of them, Gallahadion, won the Kentucky Derby. Ethel may have won the race, but she lost control of the candy company to Forrest Mars. She died in 1945 and was buried alongside Frank, and Patricia sold Milky Way Farms and moved away. The bodies of Frank and Ethel were moved to Chicago.

None of the subsequent owners had the financial firepower to maintain the estate the way the Mars family did. Over the years, land was sold off, barns fell into disrepair, and the cottages were abandoned.

Now the clubhouse is operated as a corporate retreat and for weddings. House **tours** ($8 per person) are conducted by appointment only, with a four-person minimum. Call 931/363-9769.

Visitors can drive around on what is left of the estate and look at the remaining barns and other structures. This is private property, however, and people should not enter any of these buildings. To get to Milky Way Farm, take U.S. 31 eight miles north of Pulaski. Look for a massive gate on the left.

making a concerted effort to attract visitors. The chief attraction is the **Lynnville Railroad Museum** (931/527-3158, www.lynnville.org, open May–Oct.), a new depot built to resemble the original structure. The museum contains an inoperable steam engine, a passenger coach, flatcar, and caboose. An excursion train, the **Lynn Creek and Dotson's Gap Scenic Railroad** runs from here to Campbell Station, a round-trip of 10 miles.

Across the street from the museum is **Soda** **Pop Junction** (931/527-0007), a restored drugstore housed in an 1860 building. Here visitors can enjoy complete service from a 1940s vintage soda fountain while sitting in the old wire-backed chairs. For a more substantial meal, try the **Iron Horse Restaurant** on the other side of the tracks.

This a good town for a stroll, and visitors will find an art gallery and a growing number of shops to visit. For further information, call the **Giles County Chamber of Commerce** (931/363-3789, www.lynnville.org).

Nashville to Murfreesboro

SMYRNA

In 1810 Smyrna was a farming community centered around the First Presbyterian Church, a building that burned down and was replaced by the current structure.

The **Sam Davis Home** (1399 Sam Davis Rd., 615/459-2341, $8.50 adults, $6.50 seniors, $3 for kids 6–12) shows where the "Boy Hero of the Confederacy" grew up. This is not one of the ostentatious plantation homes, but it does show how a comfortable family lived in the mid-1800s. Visitors can see a museum that focuses on life during and after the civil war and farming in middle Tennessee and then tour the house and gardens. The house is decorated for Christmas, and theme exhibits are presented throughout the year.

The **Nissan manufacturing plant** (983 Nissan Dr., 615/459-1444, tours 10 A.M., and 1 P.M. Tues. and Thurs., free, reservations required), built in 1983, employs 6,300 people who build Altima sedans, Frontier pickups, and sport-utility vehicles. Locally, Nissan is considered a good neighbor, making $7 million in contributions to area programs and projects. The hour-long tours start with a film about the start-up operations of the assembly plant. Trams carry visitors throughout the plant. For safety reasons, children under 10 and visitors wearing shorts or sandals cannot go on the tour.

Events

Days on the Farm (1399 Sam Davis Rd., 615/459-2341, $5 for adults), at the Sam Davis Home, take place the first week in May over four days and present living history, including music and demonstrations of mid-1800s farm life. Between 900 and 1,000 schoolchildren take part in this event.

Heritage Days (1399 Sam Davis Rd., 615/459-2341, $5), at the Sam Davis Home, take place about the first week in October. Demonstrations deal with fall farmwork of the mid-1800s. Like Days on the Farm, this annual event attracts hordes of area students.

Practicalities

For accommodations, try **Days Inn** (1300 Plaza Dr., 800/325-2525 or 615/355-6161). **Nashville I-24 Campground** (615/459-5818, open all year) has 140 sites, a pool, cabins, and tenting. From I-24 eastbound take Exit 66B (westbound Exit 70) and follow signs.

The **Omni Hut** (615/459-4870) on U.S. 41 south, was a dream come true for Jim Wall, a World War II pilot who was stationed all over the Pacific. Between bombing runs on Japanese targets, he collected Polynesian recipes and, after retiring from the military, built this restaurant. The ambience is pure South Seas island. The decor includes a waterfall, tiki gods, and other Polynesian touches. The large menu includes traditional and uncommon South Seas dishes.

Rossi's Restaurant (114 Front St., 615/459-7992) is a family-owned Italian restaurant that

THE BATTLE OF STONES RIVER

Like the Battle of Franklin to the west, the Battle of Stones River never makes the short list of clashes that casual students of the Civil War can rattle off. The struggle was significant, however, for it proved that the South could not evict the invading Union army, thus setting the stage for the loss of Chattanooga and eventually Atlanta.

The action began in December 1862. The Union army had occupied Nashville since February of that year, and Lincoln, needing some progress on the western front, was urging General William Rosecrans and his 42,000 troops to move south. Facing him from Murfreesboro were 34,000 Southerners under the command of General Braxton Bragg.

Neither army was in a hurry to fight. The weather was miserable—cold, pouring rain that turned fields and roads to mud. Each army was reasonably well provisioned and relatively comfortable. On the day after Christmas 1862, Rosecrans at last came out for battle. By December 30, the two forces faced each other two miles northwest of Murfreesboro. The armies camped so close they could hear each other's bands. First a Union regimental band played Northern songs, which were answered by a Confederate band playing Southern favorites. Toward the end of the impromptu concert a Union band struck up "Home Sweet Home." Other bands— Northern and Southern—joined in, and a choir of thousands of men on both sides sang the sentimental verses into the night.

The two generals had come up with the same plan: attack the enemy's right. The next morning the Southerners attacked at dawn, surprising Union troops that were fixing breakfast and forcing the Union to cancel its plans and defend itself. Union forces, which had been strung out in a line, folded back on themselves like a blade into a pocketknife. This concentrated the fields of fire and reaped a harvest of death.

The din was so loud that soldiers snatched cotton still clinging to plants and stuffed it in their ears. They fought amid thick stands of cedar trees. General Rosecrans rallied his Union troops by riding up to them and shouting encouragement. On one of these rides a cannonball took off the head of an officer on horseback beside him. According to one account, the headless body stayed in the saddle for 20 paces before falling off.

New Year's Eve fell on a scene of terrible carnage. Men who had been singing the night before now cried out in agony as a chilling rain fell. Union and Confederate soldiers looked for comrades and offered help to the wounded of both sides. As the night wore on, escaped hogs ate some of the bodies, and many of the dead and wounded froze to the ground. Murfreesboro was swamped with wounded Confederates, and Union casualties had to endure a bumpy 30-mile ride back to Nashville.

Neither side attacked on the first day of 1863, but on January 2, Bragg ordered a group of Kentuckians commanded by John C. Breckinridge, a former vice president of the United States who had lost the 1860 presidential race to Lincoln, to attack a hill held by Union troops. Breckinridge protested that the charge would be suicidal, but Bragg insisted. When the Kentuckians attacked, their numbers were decimated.

On January 3, Bragg learned that the Union troops were getting reinforcements from Nashville. He decided to retreat. The Battle of Stones River had cost him 27 percent of his troops—9,239 killed or wounded. Rosecrans of the North had fared little better with 9,532 casualties, or 23 percent of his force. Neither side could claim victory, although both did so.

Bragg moved 25 miles south and set up positions along the Duck River, and Rosecrans advanced his army and occupied Murfreesboro. Both armies settled down to get over the effects of this terrible battle.

serves pizza, calzones, and other savory home-made dishes.

The **Chamber of Commerce** (315 S. Lowry St., 615/355-6565, open 9:30 A.M.–3:30 P.M. Mon.–Fri.) is inside the City Hall building.

STONES RIVER NATIONAL BATTLEFIELD

Established in 1927, this more than 600-acre national battlefield commemorates the Civil War battle of the same name. The clash at this site, which began New Year's Eve 1862, caused 23,515 casualties—one of the bloodier battles in Tennessee. While the park is open year-round—vis-itors can participate in self-guided tours of the battlefield on any day—summer is the best time to go, for during those months the Park Service offers interpretive programs and demonstrations of military life. The most exciting are cannon blasts. In July there is a Civil War encampment. The **visitors center** (3501 Old Nashville Hwy., 615/893-9501) provides additional information about this battlefield and Fortress Rosecrans, which is in downtown Murfreesboro. A three-mile walking and bicycling trail connects the national battlefield with the fortress site. It's open 8 A.M.–5 P.M. year-round, except Christmas. No charge, but donations are accepted. See the site online at www.nps.gov/stri.

Murfreesboro and Vicinity

Murfreesboro was the capital of Tennessee from 1819 to 1825. This made great sense, for the town was about one mile from the geographic center of the state. The **Geographic Center of Tennessee** is just off Old Lascassas Pike, one mile from downtown, where an obelisk stands in a place that locals call, with just a bit of tongue in cheek, the "Dimple of the Universe."

The courthouse in which the legislature met, however, burned in 1822 and, seeking a better meetinghouse, the members moved the seat of government to Nashville. Locals implored them to come back, arguing that Murfreesboro was "de-ficient in those sources of amusement which in Nashville are supposed to distract the legislators from strict attention to their duty." Apparently lik-ing the distractions, the legislators stayed put. A new **Rutherford County Courthouse** was built in 1859 and is one of the six or so antebellum courthouses still in use in the state. Murfreesboro saw action in the Battle of Stones River.

Middle Tennessee State University (615/898-2551) was founded in 1911 as a teachers' col-lege and has grown to become the second-largest (the University of Tennessee is the biggest) and fastest-growing university in the state. Enroll-ment each fall numbers about 17,500. MTSU of-fers a variety of sports and cultural activities for visitors.

As Nashville expands outward, Rutherford County is the fastest-growing county in Ten-nessee. One of the positive sides of growth has been a wave of sophistication that has swept over Murfreesboro. In the last two or three years the restaurants in town have moved three or four notches up.

SIGHTS AND RECREATION

Cannonsburgh

The casual visitor to Middle Tennessee could gain the impression that all of the historically significant structures were built right before the Civil War. Few log buildings remain, for most of them were demolished to make way for the fancier buildings. Murfreesboro was first called Cannonsburgh in honor of a local who became governor, but the name was changed to honor a Revolutionary War hero. The Pioneer Village of Cannonsburgh begins with a collection of build-ings and artifacts that show what life was like before the days of the plantations, when this area was part of the frontier, and then marches for-ward to the year 1925 with other structures and items. Included are a gristmill, one-room school-house, chappel, log cabin, 1800s doctor office, blacksmiths shop, general store, and early auto-mobile garage.

Fanciers of weird roadside attractions will love Connonsburgh's **World's Largest Cedar Bucket.** Six feet tall, and six feet in diameter at the bottom and nine feet across at its top, this bucket behemoth was created by the now defunct Tennessee Red Cedar Woodenworks Company and exhibited at the World's Columbian Exposition in Chicago in 1893.

To get to Cannonsburgh, get off I-24 onto Highway 96 and go east for two miles. Turn right onto Broad Street, stay in the right lane for a half mile, then turn right onto Front Street. Cannonsburgh will be in the first block on the right. The grounds are open year round but the season is April–December. Admission is free. Call 615/893-6565 or see them on the web at www.rutherfordchamber.org

Oaklands

Oaklands (900 N. Maney Ave., 615/893-0022, 10 A.M.–4 P.M. Tues.–Sat., 1–4 P.M. Sun., $7 adults, $6 seniors/AAA members, $5 children) is a plantation manor that traces the economic rise and fall of a doctor and his family. The oldest part of the house was built about 1815 and consisted of only two rooms and a loft. As the

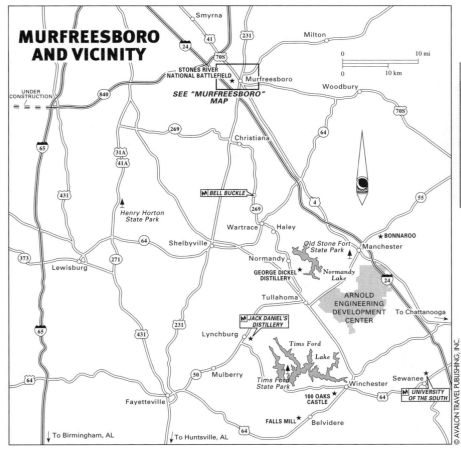

© AVALON TRAVEL PUBLISHING, INC.

Heartland

MURFREESBORO

To Milton

PATRIOT

★ THE OBELISK

OLD LASCASSAS PIKE

PITTS LN

NEW LASCASSAS RD

OLD LASCASSAS RD

96

MIDDLE TENNESSEE STATE UNIVERSITY ■

N TENNESSEE BLVD

EAST CLARK BLVD

MEMORIAL BLVD

OAKLANDS MANSION ★

N MANEY AVE

N ACADEMY ST

N CHURCH ST

N MAPLE ST

E BURTON ST

E COLLEGE ST

RUTHERFORD COUNTY COURTHOUSE ■

S MANEY AVE

S ACADEMY ST

SOUTHEAST 3RD ST

N FRONT ST

W BURTON ST

W COLLEGE ST

S FRONT ST

S CHURCH ST

CHILDREN'S DISCOVERY HOUSE ★

CANNONSBURGH PIONEER VILLAGE ■

ST

WEST MAIN

FORT PIKE

OLD FORT PIKE

NEW SALEM RD

FORTRESS ROSECRANS ★

NORTHWEST BRD ST

MANSON PIKE

STONES RIVER NATIONAL CEMETERY ■

41

70S

STONES RIVER NATIONAL BATTLEFIELD

PARK RD

To Nashville

To Franklin

To Chattanooga

24

East Main

Main St

Mercury Blvd

70S

To Woodbury

1 mi

1 km

0

0

© AVALON TRAVEL PUBLISHING, INC.

family prospered they added to the house, and by the time of the Civil War Oaklands had a long driveway with majestic oaks leading to an Italianate house containing a spectacular freestanding staircase.

As the surrounding area changed hands during the Civil War, armies from both sides occupied the plantation. The Maney family provided hospitality to the officers of both sides—albeit reluctantly in the case of Northern troops—and guests included Confederate President Jefferson Davis. By 1882 the family had to sell the home, which passed through a series of owners and reached a low point in the 1950s, when it was abandoned. The home has been restored to its appearance in 1862. About 30 percent of the furniture is original.

Children's Discovery House

For youngsters weary of old Southern mansions, the Discovery House (502 S.E. Broad St., 615/890-2300) is the place to go. This one-time house is now a hands-on museum near 20 acres of wet lands, in which kids can see 15 permanent and traveling science and nature exhibits, play in water and sand, and have a good time while learning. They can try a flight simulator or see animals such as a pot-bellied pig, iguanas, ferrets, birds, and turtles. There are even classes for adults including nature walks and bird watching. To get there take I-84 to exit 81B. After two miles take a right turn on S.E. Broad Street. Their hours are 10 A.M.–5 P.M. Monday–Saturday. Admission is $5 for adults and $4 for students. Visit online at www.discoverycenteronline.org.

Fortress Rosecrans

Fortress Rosecrans is the nation's largest earthen fort. After the Union's success at the battle of Stones River, the Union forces decided that it was strategically important to strengthen the supply line along the Nashville and Chattanooga railroad. Murfreesboro became an important depot, and Fortress Rosecrans was built in 1863 to protect that depot. Union troops and black laborers built 14,000 feet of earthworks surrounding approximately 200 acres. Approximately 30 acres of the original earth-

works have been restored. A three-mile walking and bicycling trail connects the fortress with Stones River National Battlefield. The fortress is administered by the National Park Service; its visitors center at the national battlefield can provide more complete information about the fortress. To get to the fortress, take I-24 to Exit 78B, drive about a mile to Gulf Lane, and turn left. It's open daylight hours year-round except Christmas Day.

Rock Haven Lodge

Rock Haven Lodge (462 Rock Haven Rd., 615/896-3553, www.rockhavenlodge.com) is a 25-acre naturalist (nudist) resort for whose who strongly believe the biblical passage about taking no thought about what ye shall put on. Rock Haven operates from April 1 through the first full weekend in October, offering a pool, hot tub, tennis, volleyball, shuffleboard, horseshoes, darts, Ping-Pong, and hiking.

A visit for the day costs $28 per couple, and those who would like to spend the night will pay $60–75 per night. Anyone belonging to the International Naturalist Federation receives a discount. A 100-site campground is on the grounds; the sites are available April 1–October.

EVENTS

Uncle Dave Macon Days (615/893-6565 or 800/716-7560, free) brings more than 30,000 people together for three days of old-time music, dance, and arts and crafts competitions along with a motorless parade, good food, and children's activities. It's held on the second weekend in July at Cannonsburgh Pioneer Village. For information about the festival, call the chamber of commerce.

Every year a **Civil War Encampment** (615/893-9501) takes place at Stones River National Battlefield on the second weekend in July. Demonstrations of camp life with period uniforms combine with the firing of a battery of cannons to give visitors a sense of how the soldiers who fought here lived.

Cannonsburgh Harvest Day (800/716-7560 or 615/893-6565) on the fourth Saturday in

Heartland

October, offers music, dance, food, blacksmithing, and broom-making.

Antique Tractor and Gas Engine Show, (615/274-6987, ask for Buddy Woodson) held in the little town of Eagleville in West Rutherford County, brings the South's largest exhibition of antique farm machinery on the weekend after Labor Day in September. More than 10,000 people come to this Woodstock of farm machinery.

ACCOMMODATIONS

Simply Southern Bed and Breakfast (211 N. Tennessee Blvd., 615/896-4988) sits across the street from MTSU.

Among the numerous motel choices are the **Comfort Inn** (110 N. Thompson Ln., 615/890-2811, $54–59), **Hampton Inn** (2230 Old Fort Pkwy., 800/HAMPTON [426-7866] or 615/896-1172, $49–56), **Howard Johnson Lodge** (2424 S. Church St., 800/446-7656 or 615/896-5522, $39–49), and **Shoney's Inn** (1954 S. Church St., 800/222-2222 or 615/896-6030, $45–55).

A little more expensive are the **Holiday Inn Holidome** (2227 Old Fort Pkwy., 800/HOLIDAY [465-4329] or 615/896-2420, $79–99), **Quality Inn** (118 Westgate Blvd., 615/848-9030, $39–79), and **Ramada Limited** (1855 S. Church St., 800/272-6232 or 615/896-5080, $59–65).

At the top of the heap is the **Garden Plaza Hotel** (1850 Old Fort Pkwy., 615/895-5555, where rates start at $79).

The 25-acre naturalist resort **Rock Haven Lodge** (462 Rock Haven Rd., 615/896-3553) has a 100-site campground on the grounds; the sites are available from April Fools Day until the first weekend in October.

FOOD

Bangkok Cafe (113 N. Maple St., 615/896-8399) offers pad Thai and other traditional Thai dishes.

Bunganut Pig Pub and Eatery (1602 W. Northfield Blvd., 615/893-7860) is a fun place to go. The menu includes shepherd's pie, fish

THE DIXIE DEWDROP

Warren County was the birthplace of perhaps the most colorful entertainer ever to appear on the *Grand Ole Opry*. The son of a Confederate army veteran, **Dave Macon** spent 14 years hereabouts, then moved with his family to Nashville. His family ran a hotel that was often host to traveling entertainers, and the young Macon would hang around musicians, listening to them talk and watching carefully as they rehearsed.

His father was murdered in Nashville, and the family moved to rural Cannon County, where Macon lived life like many others; he worked on a farm, got married, raised a family, and hauled freight on wagons pulled by mules.

When he was on the far side of 50, Macon began playing music professionally. He started locally, and before long "Uncle Dave Macon" was booked all over the South. His act was a combination of cornball comedy and boisterously played music with titles such as "Keep My Skillet Good and Greasy." Macon successfully combined folk music,

songs he had heard black people sing when he was a boy, and the latest from Tin Pan Alley. He would introduce his numbers with a story or a joke. Audiences loved him.

In 1924 he made his first recordings in New York City, and his records could often be found alongside those of the Carter Family on the shelves of Tennesseans and others. When the Grand Ole Opry came along, 55-year-old Uncle Dave was ready. He had played on the Opry's WSM before, and he took to the new medium with confidence.

He remained with the Opry until a few months before he died in 1952. As country music got slicker and slicker, Uncle Dave served as a connection to the simpler times, and Nashville old-timers still tell stories about him. One of them, recounted in Charles K. Wolfe's excellent *Tennessee Strings,* tells how Uncle Dave once said of Bing Crosby. "He's a nice boy, but he'll never get anywhere until he learns to sing louder so people can hear."

and chips; American fare such as steak, chicken, pasta, salads, sandwiches; and a complete bar. It offers live entertainment from blues to bluegrass every night.

The **City Cafe** (113 E. Main St., 615/893-1303) has been serving plate lunches of country cooking since 1900. **Corky's** (116 John R. Rice Blvd., 615/890-1742) is a branch of the famous Memphis barbecue eatery. It serves both wet and dry ribs, as well as great pork barbecue.

Demos' Steak and Spaghetti House (1115 N.W. Broad, 615/895-3701) has been voted "Best Restaurant" for two years in a row by The Nashville Scene. It also serves seafood and sandwiches. The **Front Porch Cafe** (114 E. College St., 615/896-6771) presents soups and sandwiches in a restored old home.

Sebastian's and Diana's Brewpub (109 N. Maple St., 615/895-8658) makes its own lager and has American dishes to eat.

At **Marina's Italian Restaurant,** (125 N. Maple St., 615/849-8885) diners have to wait 20–25 minutes for their food. People don't object, because everything here is made fresh, and you can taste it. Try the oven-baked garlic chicken or traditional Italian dishes like the chicken Marsala. Marina's has one of the better wine cellars in town as well. The **Parthenon** (1935 S. Church St., 615/895-2665) offers Greek dishes as well as American fare.

Pope Taylor's Bar-B-que (4409 E. Main St., 615/893-7191) is about four miles east of Murfreesboro on U.S. 70 S. toward Woodbury. This place has a great roadhouse atmosphere and pulled pork, ribs, and chicken halves.

Visitors will find **Lynch's Restaurant and Dairy Bar** (615/274-6427) near Eagleville City Hall at the intersection of U.S. 41A and Hwy. 99. Billy Lynch, former mayor of this tiny town, runs the restaurant himself. It is known for a meat-and-three-vegetable plate lunch, and ice cream and homemade pies.

INFORMATION AND SERVICES

Yesteryear's (3511 Old Nashville Hwy., 615/893-3470) sells Civil War relics such as swords, buckles, buttons, and guns, as well as memorabilia and letters. **Studio S. Pottery** (1426 Avon Rd., 615/896-0789) produced the china now used in the White House and has done work for almost every president since Richard Nixon. Its work is decorative yet functional.

For more details on shopping or other information, contact the **Rutherford County Chamber of Commerce** (501 Memorial Blvd., 615/893-6565 or 800/716-7560, www.rutherfordcounty.org, 8 A.M.–4:30 P.M. Mon.–Fri.),another located in an 1853 log house.

◪ BELL BUCKLE

During the Civil War, various officers from the British army came to peruse the proceedings. Colonel Arthur Freemantle witnessed a grand review of the Confederate Army of Tennessee in Bell Buckle in 1863, and he wrote the following:

Most of them were armed with Enfield rifles captured from the enemy. Many, however, had lost or thrown away their bayonets, which they don't appear to value properly, as they assert they have never met any Yankees who would wait for that weapon.

To those pulling in from the west, the tiny town of Bell Buckle seems to consist entirely of a short row of 19th-century shops facing the railroad tracks. "Is this all there is?" would be a very reasonable question at this point.

Sights

There is more to the town, as a drive down Webb Street proves. Bell Buckle was a thriving railroad town in the years after the Civil War, and in 1886 the town leaders made a very smart investment: They offered to subsidize the **Webb School's** (www.thewebbschool.com) move from Maury County to here. The school accepted the offer and through the years became one of the leading boarding schools in the South, producing 10 Rhodes Scholars, governors of three states, and a host of alumni who love to come back and spend money.

Today the school consists of about 240 students and 35 or so faculty. Visitors are invited to tour the **Junior Room Museum** on Webb Road at the edge of the campus. This museum depicts the original one-room schoolhouse. Admission is free, and the museum is open during school hours.

Despite the presence of the school, the town declined throughout the 20th century, until Railroad Square got down to one store. That's when Anne White Scruggs came to town. A profes-

THE BOY HERO OF THE CONFEDERACY

For those Southerners who make "The Lost Cause" into a religion, **Sam Davis** qualifies for sainthood. Born on a farm near Smyrna, he was only 18 years old when the war broke out. He enlisted in the Confederate army and became a member of Coleman's Scouts, a group who spied behind enemy lines.

While trying to take some information to General Braxton Bragg, Davis was stopped by Union troops near the town of Pulaski. His boot was cut open, and sewn inside were papers that held details on Union forces and locations. Although Davis was wearing a Confederate uniform, he was put on trial and charged with spying. A guilty verdict meant death by hanging.

The Union command was more concerned about who provided the information than about executing Davis, and it offered him a horse and an escort if he would reveal where he got his papers. The young man steadfastly refused to do so, and the night before he died wrote a letter to his mother saying, "I do not fear to die."

The next day he sat on his coffin in a wagon and was driven to the gallows. A Union officer told him one last time, "Speak the name of your informant, and go home in safety."

Accounts vary as to what Davis replied, but it was something akin to: "If I had a thousand lives to live, I would give them all, rather than betray a friend or my country."

This so impressed the commanding officer that he could not bring himself to give the order that would spring the trap. The condemned man finally gave the order himself, passing through the gallows floor and into history. He is buried on the grounds of the **Sam Davis Home.**

sional potter, she was looking for an inexpensive studio and bought two buildings for $4,000. "In the beginning," she recalls, "we'd have days we would only take in fifty cents. Bell Buckle is built on strong-willed people and risk-takers."

Scruggs' presence launched a renaissance for Bell Buckle, and today the town is noted for crafts, antiques, and festivals. In 1984 the National Quilt Convention was held here, bringing more than 20,000 people to this small place.

The poet laureate of Tennessee, Margaret Britton Vaughn, runs **Bell Buckle Press** (931/389-6878) on Bell Buckle's historic Railroad Square. Few people ever get to see a poet in the flesh, and this one can quote verses and sell birdhouses at the same time. Other poets and literary types have gravitated to Bell Buckle, which may be on its way to becoming a Middle Tennessee Bloomsbury.

Entertainment and Events

Bell Buckle Cafe (free admission) swings with live music Thursday–Saturday nights. The **J. Gregry Jamboree,** (931/389-9693, www.bellbucklecafe.com) a live concert and radio broadcast described as a cross between *Saturday Night Live* and Garrison Keillor's Lake Wobegon, is presented every Saturday 1–3 P.M.

Details on all of the following can be had by calling the **Bell Buckle Chamber of Commerce** at 931/389-9663. All events are on the third weekend of the month. Their website is www.bellbucklechamber.com.

Daffodil Day, a celebration of spring, kicks off the season in March with many vendors of antiques and perennial flowers. There is also live entertainment.

A **Moon Pie Festival** in June features the world's largest Moon Pie (one year it stretched four feet across and was about eight inches thick), country music, contests, games, a parade, a watermelon seed spitting contest, and a 10 mile run.

Quilt Walk in September is a tour of the town with quilts displayed in homes and churches. The **Webb School Art and Craft Festival** in October brings more than 800 exhibitors and a crowd of 70,000–80,000 to town and has been voted the best arts and crafts show in Tennessee.

The **Haunted Evening** in October brings the thrills of Halloween to Bell Buckle, and **Christmas Open House,** late in November, brings an old-fashioned Christmas to town.

Food and Accommodations

The **Bell Buckle Cafe** (Railroad Sq., 931/389-9693, www.bellbucklecafe.com) offers barbecue, steak, chicken, and other dishes. The café offers live music on Friday and Saturday nights.

The **Bell Buckle Bed and Breakfast** (17 Webb Rd., Bell Buckle 37020, 931/389-9371, $75–85) is owned by Bob and Anne Scruggs, the people responsible for the town's renaissance. They also own Bell Buckle Crafts, and, as might be expected, this house is decorated to the nth degree. The Victorian home contains three guest rooms, all of which have private baths. Rates include a heavy continental breakfast.

Shopping

Bell Buckle Antique and Craft Mall, (931/389-6174) around the corner from the row of shops on Liberty Pike, contains 50 exhibitors.

Phillips General Store (Railroad Sq., 931/389-6547) is an antique shop specializing in primitive and architectural pieces, folk art, antique dolls, and antique quilts.

Bell Buckle Crafts (Railroad Sq., 931/389-9371) is the granddaddy of all the shops hereabouts. Inside are pottery, quilts, willow furniture, and wire sculpture. Visitors can also have their photos made while dressed in antique clothing.

WARTRACE

This town's unusual name comes from "trace," an old word for road, and the fact that various Indians traveled up and down it to fight each other. Wartrace reached its peak as a railroad junction, when its one hotel was built. This hamlet is known as the "Cradle of the Tennessee Walking Horse," for the owner of the hotel trained a horse, Strolling Jim, who in 1939 became the first Tennessee Walking Horse Grand Champion. The event that eventually became the Walking Horse Celebration got its start in Wartrace, but was later moved to Shelbyville.

Eager to emulate the success of Bell Buckle, its neighboring town, Wartrace is beginning to recognize its heritage, spruce up its buildings, and attract visitors. Much of the downtown is listed on the National Register of Historic Places. A steady stream of musicians come to Wartrace to buy Gallagher guitars, which are handcrafted here.

The center of town is the **Walking Horse Hotel** (931/389-7050, $65). This is where many of the early decisions about developing the breed were made. The first grand champion, Strolling Jim, is buried behind the building, which displays Walking Horse memorabilia. The hotel, built in 1917, is on the National Register and contains 12 rooms, all with private baths, and all with access to the veranda. One room, on the first floor, is wheelchair-accessible. The building has new central heat and air-conditioning. The first floor is the **Strolling Jim Restaurant,** the second floor has shops, and guest rooms occupy the third floor. This is a town on the way back.

Shopping

If the visitor has ever had an urge to join the growing number of Civil War reenactors, the **Blockade Runner** (1027 Bell Buckle/Wartrace Rd., 931/389-6294, www.blockaderunner.com) is the place. This store carries everything needed to assume the persona of an 1860s lady or gentleman. A Confederate kepi cap starts $29.95, men's wool pants go for $74.95, and a shirt sells for $24.95. They run regular battlefield tours and have their personal museum.

Gallagher Guitars (7 Main St., 931/389-6455, www.gallagherguitar.com) every year produces just over 100 acoustic instruments, which range in price $2,200–6,000—custom models can run as high as $10,000. Customers include Doc Watson and Neil Diamond. Visitors can take a brief tour of the factory as well. **Gallagher Guitar Homecoming Festival,** held in May, offers a chance for owners of these famous guitars to get together, listen to each other pick a little, and have a good time. The high point is a concert at the Cascade School.

Heartland

Manchester

This town, the seat of Coffee County, sits at the edge of the Cumberland Plateau on the banks of the Duck River, which is the longest river completely in Tennessee. The town was named for Manchester, England, and local entrepreneurs hoped to make this place an industrial center that would live up to its namesake. They erected mills along the Duck River, and for a time Manchester enjoyed a lively business in cotton.

Music fans know Manchester as the site of Bonnaroo, a Woodstock-type music festival that began in 2002 and now attracts upwards of 150,000 fans every summer.

SIGHTS AND RECREATION

The **Manchester Walk/Drive Tour** points out historic houses, churches, and other buildings. Copies of the brochure are available at the chamber of commerce at 110 E. Main Street.

Museum Arrowheads/Aerospace Cultural Center (Exit 114 of I-24, 931/728-7159, 10 A.M.–2 P.M. Mon.–Sat., $5 adults, $4 students 7–17 and seniors, and $3 children 2–6) is a five-acre site that includes nature walks and a 7,000-square-foot museum that houses antique dolls, toys, trains, quilts, an old general store, military displays, fossils, and Indian relics. Outside is a playground. Tours and special activities, such as storytelling and Civil War demonstrations, are scheduled throughout the year.

Rutledge Falls, where Crumpton Creek has cut through the Southern Highland Rim of Tennessee, is worth seeing. Visitors should drive southwest from the town square on Hwy. 55 for 4.1 miles, then turn right onto Belmont Road (some maps show this as Wilson Road). Go 1.2 miles to Cat Creek Road, then go left for 1.5 miles to Short Springs Road. Turn right at the Rutledge Falls Baptist Church onto Rutledge Falls Road, where a parking area sits next to a large house with a gazebo. These falls are on private property, but the owners permit people to see them.

BONNAROO MUSIC FESTIVAL

In 2002, New Orleans-based Superfly Productions launched a four-day music festival on a 600-acre farm outside of Manchester. The organizers' savvy and attention to details was impressive. For example, tickets were sold on the Internet with no advertising, but with great success. Offering seven stages with performances by jam bands, bluegrass groups, jazz, and electronic music, Bonnaroo became an instant hit—and caused one of the largest traffic jams ever seen in Tennessee.

Bonnaroo continues to grow; the 2004 edition attracted 150,000 fans. In addition to performance, festival events have included artists workshops, yoga classes, and a music technology village. For details on how to attend—or when to avoid the area—go to www.bonnaroo.com.

PRACTICALITIES

My Grandmother's House (704 Hickory Grove Rd., 931/728-6293, $65) is a log home built in 1837 in Franklin County. Moved to this site, it has been meticulously restored and expanded into a bed-and-breakfast. The house has three guest rooms, all of which share baths. The rooms, one of which comes with a nursery, have period antiques and family furniture. The light fixtures—all 23 of them—were fashioned by the owner, a tinsmith. The common room contains a fireplace and hardwood floors. The host serves a full country breakfast.

North Side Clocks (2032 MacArthur/Hwy. 55, 931/728-4307, clocks@edge.net) is one of the finer timepiece shops in the state. More than 2,000 new, old, and antique clocks are for sale at any given time—so to speak—and repairs are done here as well.

Foothills Crafts (800 Woodbury Hwy./Hwy. 53, 931/728-9236) is the shop for an association of more than 600 regional artisans and craftspeople. The building is stacked floor to ceiling with finely crafted wooden furniture, textiles, stained glass, prints, pottery, jewelry, sculpture, and more. The association also offers classes and seminars in crafts.

The **Coffee County Fair** takes place in the third full week in September at the Coffee County Fairgrounds in Manchester. **Old Timer's Day** has been going for more than three decades. Held in early October, it includes clogging, music, food, a parade, and a five-kilometer race. For more information, contact **Manchester Area Chamber of Commerce** (110 E. Main St., 931/728-7635, www.manchestertn.org, 8 A.M.–4:30 P.M. daily).

OLD STONE FORT

Just northwest of Manchester on U.S. 41, this 940-acre state archaeological area along the Duck River is thought to hold the remnants of a structure built by persons unknown. The "fort" en-closes something like 50 acres with a perimeter measuring 1.25 miles. Studies by the University of Tennessee date the structure to the Indians of the Woodland period—about A.D. 12–330. The purpose of the enclosure was probably ceremonial, but there is no conclusive proof of this. The structure resembles several structures found in southern Ohio, however, it is the largest and most complex outside of Ohio.

Two forks of the Duck River cut into the Highland Rim here, resulting in a beautiful landscape. Remnants of old mills that once used the water power still stand in the park, which has excellent fishing as well. The area contains a visitors center (931/723-5073, www.tnstateparks.com, 8 A.M.–4:30 P.M. daily), a museum, 51 campsites with R.V. access, hiking trails, numerous beautiful waterfalls, picnic areas, and a nine-hole golf course. The **Old Stone Fort Arts and Crafts Festival** (931/728-9263) is held late in September.

Tullahoma and Vicinity

This town saw the Confederate army coming and going. General Braxton Bragg and his troops came back to Tullahoma after invading Perryville, Kentucky, and from here they headed north again to confront a Union army moving south from Nashville. After the disastrous Battle of Stones River in December 1862 and January 1863, the troops returned to Tullahoma, where they spent the rest of the winter. The Union army moved again, however, backing the Confederates out of Tullahoma and down into Georgia, where they clashed at the Battle of Chickamauga. A Confederate cemetery is sited in the back section of the Maplewood Cemetery.

SIGHTS

Sitting on the rail line from Nashville to Chattanooga, Tullahoma bounced back from the Civil War more quickly than surrounding towns. The town's prosperity shows in the collection of Victorian homes that make up the **Historic Depot District.** The chamber of commerce offers a brochure for a walking tour of the district.

Part of Tullahoma's 20th-century success was due to the location of Camp Forrest, an enormous, 10-square-mile center for Americans and, later, a prisoner-of-war camp for Germans. After the war, U.S. military leaders proposed studying jet propulsion, and a 40,000-acre site that included some of Camp Forrest was selected on which to build a research center. **Arnold Engineering Development Center** (931/454-3000, ext. 3396) is its name, and since 1951 jet and rocket engines have been tested here. Tours are offered Monday–Friday during business hours and last about two and a half hours. Group sizes range 12–35 people. Visitors need reservations, but there is no charge.

South Jackson Civic Center (402 S. Jackson St., 931/455-0620) in the first public school building in Tullahoma, houses the performing arts center and the Mitchell Museum. Call for a listing of the current performances.

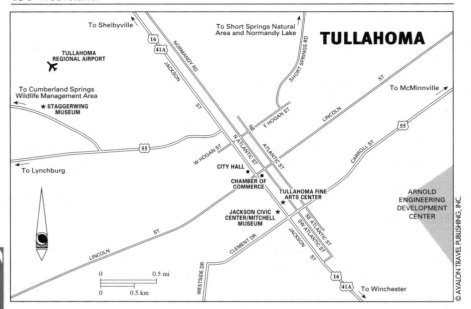

Museums

The **Walter H. Beech Staggerwing Museum** (931/455-1974, www.staggerwing.com, $4 ages 13 and over, free for 12 and under) honors a particular kind of aircraft produced by the Beech Aircraft Company 1932-46. Staggerwings were biplanes whose upper wing was set farther back than the lower wing, or "staggered." This innovative design permitted the small planes to fly at 200 miles per hour at a time when commercial airliners flew at only 175-180 mph. "These were the Lear jets of the '30s," explained a trustee of the museum.

Using a Staggerwing, Louise Thaden won a 1936 transcontinental race. Approximately 800 Staggerwings were built, about 200 survive today, and about 100 still fly. The museum occupies a complex beside the Tullahoma airport and contains an example of every model of Staggerwing Beechcraft ever built, including the very first one. The museum can be opened by special appointment, but admission then is $5 per adult. To get there, take Hwy. 130 off Hwy. 55.

The South Jackson Civic Center's **Floyd and**

Margaret Mitchell Museum (931/455-5321, 8 A.M.–4 P.M. Mon.–Fri., free) depicts Tullahoma and regional history with Indian artifacts, antique clothing, military items from the Civil War that were unearthed from Tullahoma, an exhibit of Camp Forrest items, a handcrafted Civil War diorama, items from World War I and World War II, antiques, dolls, old photographs, tools, and even the contents of the cornerstone from the old high school.

The **Tullahoma Fine Arts Center/Regional Museum of Art** (401 S. Jackson St./U.S. 41A, 931/455-1234, www.tullahomafinearts.org, free, one exhibit costs $1) occupies an 1868 house and has permanent and touring exhibits. Some items are for sale.

Short Springs Natural Area

Short Springs Natural Area (931/455-2648, ext. 109) is a 420-acre nature preserve that is noted for its wildflowers and unique botanical specimens. Hiking trails lead to two falls and Normandy Lake. Along the way are rugged rock outcroppings. This area with its underground water source was the old watershed for the community. To get there, go three miles out of Tullahoma on Short Springs Road. The chamber of commerce has further information.

Tullahoma Fine Arts and Crafts Festival

This festival (931/455-1234) takes place on the last weekend in May on the school grounds across from the Fine Arts Center. Booths and exhibits from 100 artists display artwork in a variety of disciplines: basket weaving, pottery, quilting, watercolors, and drawing. The artwork is juried and prizes are awarded to artisans in the different categories late Saturday on the festival grounds. The National Watercolors Society competition and the high school competition are simultaneously displayed in the Fine Arts Center. The festival covers about 1.5 acres and draws approximately 8,000–10,000 people.

PRACTICALITIES

Daddy Billy's Delicatessen, (931/455-6195) on North Atlantic Street north of Anderson along the railroad, is allegedly haunted by three ghosts from the Civil War who "don't like it when furniture is moved." If patrons leave the furniture alone, the sandwiches are very good. **The Stuffed Goose** (115 N. Collins St., 931/455-6673) serves chicken salad, fresh-baked bread, and light meals.

Leave Tullahoma and head northwest toward Shelbyville on U.S. 41A/Hwy. 16; Shipman Creek Road goes off to the left just past the airport. Look for the sign to **Granny Fishes** (931/857-4025). This place is famous hereabouts for fresh trout and catfish, frog legs, hush puppies, and homemade pies.

The **Coca-Cola Company Store** (1504 E. Carroll St./Hwy. 55, 931/454-1030) has all sorts of memorabilia with the famous red and white logo. **Smiling Owl Gallery and Gifts** (111 Lincoln St., 931/455-0673) carries the works of regional artists: jewelry, pottery, glassware, and woodturning.

For more information, contact **Tullahoma Chamber of Commerce** (135 W. Lincoln St.,

931/455-5497, www.tullahoma.net, 8:30 A 4:30 P.M. daily).

NORMANDY

Before Prohibition, Tennessee had more distilleries than any other state in the country. In the 1800s, one of them was the **George Dickel Distillery** (931/857-3124, www.dickel.com), which transformed spring water from Cascade Hollow into George A. Dickel's Cascade Whiskey. George died in 1894, and Prohibition put an end to the distillery. In 1956, it reopened. While not as famous as Jack Daniel's, a mere 20 miles away, George Dickel is made in pretty much the same fashion, mellowing the whiskey by dripping it through tall vats of charcoal made from sugar maple. The biggest difference from Jack Daniel's is that George Dickel is chilled before going through the charcoal. It seems that the cooler, and thus more viscous, whiskey goes through the charcoal more slowly and thus comes out purer. Free tours are offered Tues.–Sat., 9:30 A.M.–3:30 P.M.

Food and Accommodations

Parish Patch Farm and Inn (1100 Cortner Rd., Normandy, 800/876-3017 or 931/857-3017, www.parishpatch.com, $74–202) sits on a 230-acre working farm and began as a corporate retreat. It has 21 guest rooms and two cottages, all with private baths, color television, and air-conditioning. Guests can stroll along the Duck River, swim in a pool, go bird-watching, bicycle, fish, and hike. The inn also offers a playhouse for children.

Also at the farm is the **Courtner Mill Restaurant** (5:30 A.M.–9 P.M. Tues.–Sat.), which offers country dining in a scenic and historic atmosphere. The mill, built in 1848, holds 82 diners who can feast on dinners including Cornish game hens, frog legs, and rainbow trout. The specialty of the house is beefalo steaks, which are raised on the farm. Beefalos are a cross between buffalo and cattle, and the resulting meat has one-fifth the cholesterol of regular beef. To get there from Tullahoma, follow Hwy. 269 north for approximately seven miles.

Heartland

STATE
RUSTIC PARK

This 413-acre park sits on the banks of the 10,700-acre Tims Ford Reservoir between Tullahoma and Winchester. Fishing and other lake-oriented activities are the chief focus here, but visitors can also hike, bike, and enjoy a swimming pool and other recreation.

Accommodations include 20 cabins overlooking the lake. Each sleeps eight in two bedrooms and comes with a fireplace, outdoor balcony, and reasonably equipped kitchen. Cabins are available March 1–December 1 and rates begin at $100 per night. The campground offers 52 sites with tables, grills, and hookups, two of which are handicap accessible, available on a first-come, first-served basis. Bathhouses have hot showers. For information and to make reservations, visitors should call 931/962-1184 or 800/471-5295.

LYNCHBURG

If the wind is right, visitors approaching this village can detect a sweet, slightly odd smell before coming into town. This is the aroma of sour mash—fermenting corn, rye, and barley malt—which is the principal ingredient of the Jack Daniel's whiskey, Tennessee's most famous product. A long-running and highly successful ad campaign depicts Lynchburg as a place where time stands still, where various overall-wearing, hardworking good old boys crank out "sippin' whiskey, drop by drop."

It's true.

Lynchburg is a tiny town, and the distillery, the oldest registered one in the country, is the biggest game in town. The rest of Lynchburg centers on the town square, in the middle of which sits the 1885 Moore County Courthouse. Most of the businesses here are intent on separating tourists from their dollars, but an auto parts place and co-op still serve the locals.

Jack Daniel's Distillery

Jack Daniel erected his distillery (931/759-6180, www.jackdaniels.com, 8 A.M.–4 P.M. daily, closed Thanksgiving, Christmas, and New Year's Day) in 1866 below a large spring that produces superb, iron-free water. More than a quarter of a million people take a free tour here every year. They see a barrelhouse, where more than 20,000 barrels of whiskey are aged; the brickyard, where hard sugar maple is burned to produce charcoal; the bubbling, fermenting vats of sour mash; and the spring from which the water flows. The distillery serves no samples, although visitors can buy commemorative bottles for off-site consumption. Moore County is a dry county.

Lynchburg is so small and the distillery signs are so pervasive that directions are not needed. The tour is totally accessible—including the brewery from which Jack Daniel's 1866 Class Amber Lager flows. The closest place to buy the complete range of Jack Daniel's products is Tullahoma.

Museums

The **Historic Old Jail Museum,** which displays photographs of the town and the history of the jail, is open irregularly, but mostly during weekdays April–October. Admission is free, but visitors are expected to leave some sort of donation. The **Tennessee Walking Horse Museum** (931/759-5747, 9 A.M.–5 P.M. Tues.–Sat., free) uses exhibits, video displays, and interactive devices to tell the story of Tennessee's most famous equine.

Entertainment and Events

Bar-B-Que Caboose Cafe (on the square, 931/759-5180) offers country music and bluegrass jam sessions on Saturday mornings and every Saturday night, except in the wintertime.

For information on all of the following events, call the Welcome Center (931/759-4111).

Spring in the Hollow is a one-day event held in early May with antique cars, arts and crafts, food, and music.

Frontier Days late in June recalls the days when Tennessee was the wild and woolly West. People in pioneer garb take their places in a non-motorized parade amid music, food, and crafts. The **Uncle Bunt Fiddle Contest** is held the first Saturday in August each year.

Jack Daniel's Birthday Celebration on September 9 usually involves at least one country music headliner, local country music people, clogging, and crafts and food booths. About 5,000 people attend this annual event held on the square and in nearby Wiseman Park.

Jack Daniel's World Champion Invitational Bar-B-Que Cook Off is held late in September on the square and in Wiseman Park, where 20,000–25,000 barbecue fans show up to taste the offerings of 45 or so invited cooking teams. Other activities include arts and crafts, music, cloggers, and sometimes a tractor pull and greased pig contest.

Christmas in Lynchburg, on the first Saturday in December, starts with a parade and includes caroling and tours of old houses.

Accommodations

Goose Branch Farm Bed and Breakfast (Rte. 3, Box 140, 931/759-5919, $65) is exactly three miles from downtown Lynchburg. Guests can relax in a 100-year-old large farmhouse surrounded by large shady trees on about 57 acres of farmland complete with grazing cattle, a pond, two springs, and a creek. The two suites have private entrances and private baths.

Lynchburg Bed and Breakfast (931/759-7158, www.bbonline.com/tn/lynchburg, $65–75) is a big 1877 two-story house with three guest rooms, one with a queen-sized bed, one with a king, and one with two doubles. It's within walking distance of the Jack Daniel Distillery. Rates include a special continental breakfast.

Mulberry House Bed and Breakfast, (931/433-8461, www.bbonline.com/tn/mulberry, $60) midway between Lynchburg and Fayetteville on Hwy. 50, is a 115-year-old farmhouse with two guest rooms, both with private baths. It has a nice big porch to sit on.

Dream Fields Bed and Brea 8875, www.bbonline.com/tn/dre: is a Gothic revival farmhouse b more than 100 years it belonge Wiley Daniel, a brother of Jack ~~~~~~ can take walking trails over the 260 acres, stroll along creeks, or partake of the occasional hayride and music at the barn.

Food

For many years the only place to eat in Lynchburg was 🅽 **Miss Bobo's Boarding House** (931/759-7394, 11 A.M. and 1 P.M. Mon.–Sat., $14) which is just a few steps west of the square on Main Street and a short walk from the Jack Daniels distillery. First opened in 1908 in an 1867 house, it was a favorite of Jack Daniel himself. Nowadays the place serves country cooking to about 62 people at a time; they sit at large tables and introduce themselves to each other before dining. The food is served family-style, and everyone is instructed to pass the bowls and platters to the left. Meals include at least two meats, six vegetables, a drink, breads, and dessert. Reservations are absolutely necessary for weekends and weekdays—some Saturdays get booked five months in advance. Lunch is called "dinner" hereabouts in the fashion of country folks.

Countryside Restaurant (west of the square on Hwy. 55, 931/759-4430, Mon.–Sat.) serves country cooking for breakfast, lunch, and dinner. The lunch buffet offers meats, vegetables, breads, and homemade desserts.

Iron Kettle Restaurant (on the square, 931/759-4274, 10:30 A.M.–3 P.M. daily) serves country cooking three meals a day.

Information

Angels in the Holler (on the square, 931/759-6444) sells prayer and promise angles, soy candles, rock potpourri, Christian CD's, and items related to gardening.

The **Lynchburg Hardware and General Store** (on the square, 931/759-4200) offers all manner of items related to Jack Daniel: clothes, clocks, mirrors, jugs, playing cards, etc. For more information, contact the **Lynchburg Welcome**

Heartland

.er and Metro Moore County Chamber of ommerce (on the square, 931/759-4111, 10 A.M.–5 P.M. Mon.–Fri.).

FAYETTEVILLE

Visitors to Lynchburg, which can get very crowded at times, owe it to themselves to push on to Fayetteville. This lovely town is the seat of Lincoln County, a name that sounds surprising in these highly Confederate parts. The county came into being in 1809 and was named for General Benjamin Lincoln, who fought in the Revolutionary War.

In 1813 Tennesseans were mustered here under the command of Andrew Jackson to punish the Creek to the south for their involvement in the Fort Mims massacre in Alabama. One year later, 2,000 troops assembled here, this time to fight the British at Mobile, Alabama.

Just before the Civil War a beautiful stone bridge was built over the Duck River here. Its six arches spanned 450 feet, and during the war General William T. Sherman marched his troops across it to join General Grant in freeing Chattanooga. According to an old story, once his troops were across, Sherman ordered the bridge destroyed, but the Union officer sent to supervise the destruction was so impressed by the graceful structure that he refused to demolish it. A flood in 1969 finally did in the bridge, and only the abutments remain.

The center of town remains the Lincoln County Courthouse and surrounding square. The shops and restaurants around it are well worth the trip. Of particular interest are two adjoining pool halls—perhaps the only such juxtaposition in the entire state. At night the extravagant neon sign of the Lincoln Theater, an old movie theater, lights up the square.

Sights and Recreation

The Borden Company built a canned milk plant here in the 1920s, thus creating a demand for milk that sustained local dairy farms for decades. The old Borden plant, which closed in 1967, now provides a large space for the **Lincoln County Museum** (521 Main St., 931/438-0339,

free, donations accepted). To visit the museum, call the chamber of commerce for hours or to have it opened.

Fayetteville's historic district contains a great selection of old homes. One worth a detour is the steamboat Gothic **mansion** at the corner of Washington Street and North Elk Avenue. Built in 1894, this highly ornamented house contains Wyatt Antiques and is an architectural delight, with downstairs rooms paneled in maple, walnut, and cherry lumber that was cut on a local farm and finished in Nashville.

Elk River Plantation (Eldad Rd., 931/433-9767) is a working farm of about 130 acres. The owners raise emus—"the meat of the future"— llamas, water buffaloes, horses, mules, miniature donkeys, strawberries, alfalfa, and pumpkins. The plantation is open to the public for a variety of events, all listed below. The owners also run a bed-and-breakfast. To get there from Fayetteville, go east on the U.S. 64 Bypass, then go south on Eldad Road. The farm is on the right just over the hill.

Nine miles east of town on U.S. 64 in the Kelso community is **Elk Canoe Rental** (931/937-6886), where visitors can float down the placid and scenic Elk River. This place will rent the entire works—canoes, paddles, and flotation devices—and arrange for drop-off and pickup.

Entertainment and Events

The **Lincoln Theater** (north side of the square, 931/433-1943) is a 1950s movie house that hasn't changed much since the days of James Dean.

The **Lincoln County Fair,** held on the second weekend in September, is much like other Tennessee county fairs with one exception: This is the only all-weather sanctioned harness-racing track in the entire state.

During **Pumpkin Patch Days,** held every weekend in October at Elk River Plantation, sorghum is produced by mule-power. Visitors can go on hayrides, pick their own pumpkins, and visit the log museum where early pioneer family skills are demonstrated. **Haunted Hayrides** also take place on the plantation Thursday–Sunday in October.

Fayetteville: Host of Christmas Past, on the second Saturday in November, brings costumed carolers, carriage rides, live reindeer, and Santa Claus.

For more details about these events and other information, contact **Fayetteville–Lincoln County Chamber of Commerce** (208 S. Elk Ave., 931/433-1235, www.vallnet.com/chamberof commerce, 8 A.M.–4:30 P.M. Mon.–Fri.).

Accommodations

Fayetteville Bed and Breakfast (1111 W. Washington St., 931/433-9636, $65–75) is a country home, circa 1915, with a large wraparound porch. Two guest rooms are available with private baths. Rates include a full or continental breakfast.

Old Cowan Plantation (Rte. 9, Box 17, 931/433-0225, $65 and up) occupies an 1886 colonial home less than a mile from town. Three guest rooms are available, each with a private bath. A sitting room contains a fireplace and television. The host serves morning coffee on the verandah overlooking the countryside. Smoking is permitted in the common rooms and dining room. To get to Old Cowan Plantation, go west on U.S. 64 from the square, then turn right on Old Boonshill Road.

Food

Despite the admonitions of *The Music Man's* Professor Harold Hill, pool halls in Fayetteville are good places to go. **Honey's Restaurant** (109 E. Market St., 931/433-1181, breakfast, lunch, and dinner Mon.–Sat.) and **Bill's Cafe** (111 E. Market St., 931/433-5332) are adjacent to each other. Honey's claims to have invented "slawburgers"—hamburgers topped with a sweet-mustard slaw—although they are served at both places. Honey's is more of a family place and the more polished of the two.

Cahoots (114 W. Market St., 931/433-1173) occupies the town's old firehouse and jail. Diners sit in cells as they enjoy steaks, chicken, Mexican dishes, and salads.

O'Houlihan's (101 Market St., 931/433-0557) occupies an 1890s grocery store whose shelves now contain antiques. It serves muffins, nice sandwiches, salads, and soups. **Mulberry Bay** (108A Mulberry Ave., 931/433-3192) housed in an old building that was the first car wash in town, is now beautifully decorated. It serves sandwiches, salads, and desserts.

Barbecue fans should head two miles west of town on U.S. 64 to **Woodley's B.B.Q.** (931/433-3044), which serves barbecue all week and ribs on Friday and Saturday.

Heartland

Shelbyville and Vicinity

Many towns in Middle Tennessee were plotted with a courthouse in the center of a square facing various businesses. Carroll Van West, in his very good *Tennessee's Historic Landscapes,* says that Shelbyville is believed to be the first town in the nation to have such a plan. Shelbyville was a Daniel of Northern sympathizers amid the lion's den of Confederates during the Civil War. Some folks referred to it as "Little Boston," quite an insult in those days.

SIGHTS

In the 20th Century, Shelbyville became known as "Pencil City." Cedar forests nearby and water power from the Duck River made it an ideal location for pencil factories. Several existed here, but the only one left now is the Musgrove Pencil Company, which has been here since 1916 and produces up to 500,000 pencils a day.

Shelbyville's greatest claim to fame, however, rests on a horse that rose from farms and fields to become a Middle Tennessee industry. The annual **Tennessee Walking Horse National Celebration** is held here every year.

The **Old Jail** was built in 1886 using four-foot by four-foot rocks hauled to the site in a wagon by "Big Tom" Martin, who is said to have weighed 300 pounds and to have had arms eight inches longer than a normal man's. Now on the National Register, the Old Jail is behind the new jail. Visitors can see the outside only.

Tri-Star Vineyards and Winery (931/294-3062, www.tristarwinery.com, 10 A.M.–5 P.M. Fri.–Sat., noon–5 P.M. Sun., tasting and tours are free) is owned by a family who made its own wine for more than 25 years before going professional. All that expertise now produces dry, semi-sweet, and sweet reds and whites, Tennessee muscadine, and various berry wines. To get there, go seven miles north of town off U.S. 41A and turn left onto Halls Mill Road, then go a half mile and turn right onto Scales Road. Go another half mile and the winery will come into sight.

Waterfall Farms (2395 Hwy. 64 E., 931/684-7894, www.waterfallfarms.com) is a 900-plus-acre horse farm that welcomes visitors. Here Tennessee Walking Horses are bred, trained, and proudly displayed. The farm has three mare barns sheltering as many as 260 broodmares. These equine ladies receive occasional visits from one of the gentleman callers of "Stud Row," and the offspring's pedigree is intensely studied for early indications that this Walker might be a champion. The farm has an indoor riding ring, and visitors are welcome during daylight hours, and admission is free.

ENTERTAINMENT AND EVENTS

The event in Shelbyville is the **Tennessee Walking Horse National Celebration** (931/684-5915, www.twhnc.com, $7–15), which takes place on the 11 days preceding the Saturday night of Labor Day weekend. Competitions take place nightly at the 28,869-seat outdoor arena. During the day people wander around the more than 100 acres of the Celebration Grounds, stopping at some of the 1,686 stalls to look at fine horses, talk with trainers, and buy all manner of horse tack and souvenirs. Tickets are generally available for every night of the celebration.

The **Spring Fun Show** (931/684-5915) late in May is a warm-up show for the Tennessee Walking Horse National Celebration.

The **Gallagher Guitar Homecoming Festival** (931/389-6455) hosts an annual concert in Calsonic Arena in May. Call for dates and headliners.

The **Great Celebration Mule Show** (931/684-5915) in late July offers pulling contests, costume classes, four- and six-mule hitches, and a look at Tennessee Walking Mules—high-stepping mules that result from a jack's being bred to a Tennessee Walking Horse mare.

PRACTICALITIES

Bottle Hollow Lodge (931/695-5253, $95 s, $105 d) is a bed-and-breakfast inn out in the country between Shelbyville and Lynchburg on a ridgetop with a 30- to 35-mile view of the countryside. Its four guest rooms have private baths, and it is wheelchair-accessible.

Richard's Cafeteria (223 Lane Pkwy., 931/684-7288) offers breakfast from a menu and an all-you-can-eat lunch and dinner buffet seven days a week. **Pope's Cafe** (on the square, 931/684-7933) is a place with a lot of character that serves good food—meat-and-three and burgers.

Many folks say **Prime Steak House** (1057 Madison St., 931/684-0741) is the best place in town. The owner is Greek, so the Greek items on the menu are very good. **El Mexico** (713 N. Main St., 931/684-0874) is a relatively small place that offers great Mexican food.

Joe's Liquors and Wines (633 N. Main St., 931/684-0777) has one of the more extensive collections of Tennessee sour mash whiskey in Middle Tennessee. Here are collectible Jack Daniel's bottles, pints of the no-longer-made Lem Motlow whiskey, and other manifestations of the spirits world.

For information, check with the **Shelbyville**

TENNESEE WALKING HORSE

Motorists through Middle Tennessee, particularly south of Nashville, often see mailboxes or barns displaying a silhouette of a horse whose front leg is pulled up belly high and whose back legs seem to be taking enormous steps. These are Tennessee Walking Horses, a breed that means big business in these parts.

Often described as "the world's greatest show and pleasure horse," Walking Horses are a delight to ride. Unlike temperamental racehorses, Tennessee Walkers are docile animals whose natural gaits are easy on the rider. Indeed, some enthusiasts claim that the horses move so smoothly that riders can sip hot coffee—or Tennessee sippin' whiskey—from a cup while riding along.

Walking Horses were developed by breeders in Middle Tennessee to meet several needs. Plantation owners and overseers sought mounts that they could ride all day without getting saddle sore and horses that could cover a lot of ground and not get weary. Owners of small farms who could afford only one or two horses wanted ones that were strong enough to pull a plow yet easy to ride.

The Southern Plantation Walking Horse, as this breed came to be known, had a distinct gait called a "running walk." This seeming contradiction in terms is accomplished through overstriding, in which the rear foot of the horse steps over—overstrides—the imprint of the front foot by as much as 18–24 inches. The back legs of walking horses thus extend much farther forward than those of other breeds, and this produces the smooth ride that typifies the horse.

The first horse to naturally perform this running walk was born in 1837, and almost 100 years later a breeders association was founded in Lewisburg. The first Tennessee Walking Horse Grand Champion was crowned in 1939, yet it took 15 years for the U.S. Department of Agriculture to recognize Tennessee Walkers as a separate breed. In the meantime, Walking Horses found favor with trail riders, pleasure riders, and an increasing number of people whose horses competed in show rings. Producing champions brought fame to trainers, money to owners, and excitement for fans.

At the annual celebration in Shelbyville, fans began to applaud and judges began to reward horses who could do "the big lick"—picking their front feet very high off the ground and reaching forward at the same time. Putting heavy horseshoes or boots on a horse could produce the big lick, but a relentless pursuit of the crowd-pleasing tactic brought a sad chapter to the industry. Trainers began "soring" horses using chains, or in the worst cases, chemicals, to irritate the skin and thus force the horse to pick its feet up higher. After much bad publicity, legal remedies, and a lot of controversy, widespread soring has largely ended, although unscrupulous trainers still get caught abusing their horses.

Today the **Tennessee Walking Horse Breeders' and Exhibitors' Association** (www.twhbea.com) has more than 16,000 members, one-third of whom live in Tennessee. Tennessee Walking Horses bring a lot of money into the state and a lot of pleasure to their owners.

Chamber of Commerce (100 N. Cannon Blvd., 931/684-3482, www.shelbyvilletn.com. 8 A.M.–4 P.M. Mon.–Fri.).

LEWISBURG

The seat of Marshall County, Lewisburg was incorporated in 1837 and was named for Meriwether Lewis of Lewis and Clark fame. The thick cedar forests that so plagued Civil War soldiers who tried to fight among the bushy trees were put to use here by pencil factories. The **Sanford Corporation,** (1 Pencil St., 800/835-8381 or 931/359-1583) this country's largest pencil maker, has a factory here that employs more than 750 people. Visitors can tour the plant Aug.–March by appointment only.

The world headquarters of the **Tennessee Walking Horse Breeders and Exhibitors' Association** (800/359-1574, www.twhbea.com) is in Lewisburg—take Exit 37 off I-65 south, then follow the signs. Here visitors can view the Hall of Fame's pictures of all the World Grand Champions and may also see, by appointment, a 30-minute video showing the breed's aspects. Brochures with information about Walking Horses and the nearby barns that allow visitors are also available. The association provides a free copy of *Voice,* its magazine, and will arrange tours of horse barns for groups.

Marshall County is famous as well for its **fainting goats** (www.faintinggoat.com). Seems that a mysterious stranger named John Tinsley came here in the 1880s with four goats that would fall flat if startled. The stranger left town but the goats stayed, and their descendants have become celebrated in goat circles for their odd behavior. According to the website, the goats have a condition known as myotonia that causes their muscles to stiffen when the animals are scared. Though called "fainting goats," the animals never lose consciousness, getting back on their feet after ten or 15 seconds and resuming goatish pursuits. Lewisburg now offers a festival devoted to the goats. See below.

Entertainment and Events

Big Jim's (931/359-7125) is east of town on Hwy. 50. Live music plays for those who like line dancing and other forms of boot-scootin'. The barnlike structure shelters a down-home atmosphere that swings with the sounds of old and new country music, with a little hip-hop and old rock thrown in for variety. For those new to country line dancing, lessons are offered every Thursday and Sunday 7–9 P.M. These lessons are a nice place for the whole family, kids too. An open dance follows the lessons and lasts until 10:30 P.M. Friday and Saturday are livelier by far and for adults only. Dancing lasts 6 P.M.–1:30 A.M. Be prepared for a huge crowd on Saturday night.

Goats, Music, & More (931/359-1544, www.lewisburgtn.com) celebrates fainting goats in October with goat shows, a parade, music, and crafts.

Oktoberfest, held in the town square, offers crafts, local music, and food on the first weekend in October.

Practicalities

Motel options are **Walking Horse Lodge** (I-65 Exit 37, 800/528-1234 or 931/359-4005), or the **Econo Lodge** (3731 Pulaski Hwy., 800/424-4777 or 931/293-2111).

Lawler's Barbecue (1301 N. Ellington Pkwy., 931/359-5990) is a drive-through takeout establishment providing barbecued beef, pork, ham, and turkey. **Marvin's Family Restaurant** (740 N. Ellington Pkwy., 931/359-9490) offers a buffet that changes every day for lunch and supper; menu items are available too.

Marshall County Chamber of Commerce (227 2nd Ave. N., 931/359-3863, www.marshallchamber.org, 8 A.M.–4 P.M. Mon.–Fri.).

HENRY HORTON STATE RESORT PARK

This 1,135-acre park sits beside the Duck River on the former estate of Henry Horton, the governor of Tennessee 1927-33. Here visitors can choose from a variety of recreational opportunities, including golf, canoeing, horseback riding, and swimming, as well as various sports fields and courts. Perhaps the most unusual offering is a professional multifield skeet and trap range. Visitors can use their own shotguns or rent one. Instruction is available as well. The park's **restaurant** has a seating capacity of 300 and is open seasonally for breakfast, lunch, and supper. Call 931/741-1200.

Accommodations begin with the **Horton Inn** (800/421-6683 or 931/364-2222, www.tnstateparks.com, $62–67) and its 72 air-conditioned units. Four of them are suites with kitchenettes. All units have two double beds, carpeting, television, and phones. The park also has 7 cabins that each hold six people and come with air-conditioning, fireplaces, televisions, and phones. They go for $65–104 per night. There area also campsites along the banks of the river, some of which have electricity and water.

Highway 56 to Monteagle

MCMINNVILLE

Sitting on the edge of the Cumberland Plateau, McMinnville and the surrounding area are a prime location for plant nurseries. The elevation ranges from 976 feet in McMinnville to 1,892 feet on nearby Ben Lomond Mountain. Each 1,000 feet in elevation creates a climate equivalent to weather conditions 300 miles north, and thus local plants can be widely sold. Furthermore, the varying soils successfully duplicate those found both north and south of here, and nursery products can be grown on small farms. For those reasons, young trees and bushes and ornamental plants of all kinds roll out of here annually.

McMinnville is the birthplace of Dorothy Marie Marsh, the youngest of 10 children who picked cotton near here. Her mother, abandoned by her husband, opened a restaurant in the town, and by the time the little girl was 12 she had sung on the radio. She became known as Dottie West, a country star often remembered for the song "Country Sunshine." A member of the *Grand Ole Opry,* she sang many duets with Kenny Rogers and died as the result of a car crash in 1991. She is buried in McMinnville's Mountain View Cemetery.

A wonderful radio station, WCPI, gives an audio look at how small-town radio used to be—some would say ought to be. At 91.3 on the FM dial, listeners hear programming ranging from classical music to wrestling news.

Sights and Recreation

Historic Falcon Manor (2645 Faulkner Springs Rd., 931/668-4444, www.falconmanor.com, $5 adults, $3 children under 12) is a bed-and-breakfast that occupies one of the finest homes in the county. Local entrepreneur Clay Faulkner operated a cotton mill outside of town and, growing tired of commuting, told his wife he would build her "the finest home in Warren County" if she would move closer to the mill. She consented, and the house was completed in 1896. Counting porches and verandas, this Queen Anne–style Victorian mansion totals about 10,000 square feet. It later served as a hospital and is now an antique-filled bed-and-breakfast.

Cumberland Caverns (931/668-4396, www.cumberlandcaverns.com), seven miles southeast of McMinnville off Hwy. 8, is one of the larger cave systems in the United States. It was discovered in 1810 by a hapless surveyor who climbed into a hole, lost his torch, and had to wait for rescuers to find him. The cave was mined for saltpeter during the War of 1812 and the Civil War, and some of the mining equipment still sits in the cave. The cave's biggest room is called the Hall of the Mountain King.

Visitors can take tours varying from the regular 90-minute tour (season is May 1–October 31) to a 14-hour overnight "wild cave" adventure. For this, visitors spend the night in the cave, hear a ghost story, and explore their way through about a mile of totally undeveloped passageways, including a crawl through some tight spaces. The adventure is for the young at heart and youth groups, as almost all visitors get wet and muddy slogging through the infamous Bubblegum Alley—where explorers come out of 18 inches of water onto a mudbank. Daily tours cost $12.50 for adults, $7.50 for children ages 6–15, and free for 5 and under. The overnights can be taken year-round for $24–31. These tours are very popular (about 350 people spend the night each weekend), so reservations are required two weeks in advance.

McMinnville boasts an unusually large library for a town its size, and thereby hangs a tale. William Magness, a wealthy resident, donated the library to the town in 1931. He provided room for books and added an apartment for himself and showers in the basement for the benefit of any locals who wanted to take a bath. Visitors will find the **Magness Community House and Library** (118 Main St.) though they can no longer use the showers.

Halfway between McMinnville and Manchester, **The Cheese Store** (931/635-3004), along Hwy. 55 in the Morrison community, makes a variety of wines and cheeses: cheddar, hot pepper, swiss, onion, and monterey jack.

Practicalities

Historic Falcon Manor (2645 Faulkner Springs Rd., 931/668-4444, www.falconmanor.com, $95 and up) offers six guest rooms, some with private baths; all feature antiques. The inn sits on three acres of land with century-old trees that lend a country setting, but it's conveniently near town. Rates include a tour of the mansion and full breakfast.

City Drugstore (203 E. Main St., 931/473-2234) has a lunch counter for lovers of soda fountains. Chili is a favorite dish, while burgers and sandwiches round out the offerings.

Gillentines, (931/473-7757) at the Scottish Inn on the Sparta Highway, offers steaks, catfish, and plate lunches. **Peking Restaurant** (Plaza Shopping Center, 931/473-3630) is open for lunch and dinner seven days a week.

Fiesta Ranchera (202 McMinnville Plaza on Highway 56, 931/473-6423) is a great place to sample the wave of Mexican cuisine that has swept over Tennessee in recent years. Situated in a little mall, Fiesta Ranchera has a colorful, upbeat atmosphere that's just right to enjoy burritos, quesadillas, and other Mexican delights. It even serves vegetarian dishes.

For more information, contact the **Chamber of Commerce** (110 S. Court Sq., 931/473-6611, www.warrentn.com).

SAVAGE GULF STATE NATURAL AREA

The name of this area makes it sound like some sort of fearsome place. "Savage" refers to the name of Samuel Savage, an early settler, while "gulf" is a peculiar Tennessee word for canyon. The Savage Gulf Natural Area is a part of the larger South Cumberland Recreation Area, which includes seven parks spread over four counties. The **headquarters** (931/532-0001) is outside Tracy City.

This entire 11,500-acre area sits on the Cumberland Plateau, and Savage Gulf State Natural Area is made up of places where three streams have cut converging canyons into the plateau. Each of the three canyons is about five miles long, and at their deepest they extend 800 feet below the plateau. No one can drive down into any of the canyons, which means visitors will largely have the place to themselves. Here are some of the highlights.

The **Great Stone Door** is a 150-foot-long crack in a rock that suggests an enormous door that someone has barely opened. To get there, go to the town of Beersheba Springs and follow the signs to a ranger station and great views of the gulf. On some days visitors can see raptors riding thermals coming up out of the canyon. Indians used the Great Stone Door as a pathway down into the canyon, and modern-day visitors can as well. Maps available at the ranger station suggest good trails.

Greeter Falls begins the Big Creek canyon by taking a 50-foot plunge over a cliff. To get there, drive 1.1 miles from Altamont's square south on Hwy. 56 to Greeter Road. Turn left and go 0.1 mile to the trailhead. A half-mile walk leads to the falls.

Savage Gulf is on the eastern side of the area and contains more than 500 acres of virgin hardwood forest. The family who owned it resisted pressures to log this area, and thanks to them it is preserved today. To get to the **ranger station**

HIGHLANDER SCHOOL

The coalfield struggles of the southern Cumberland Plateau attracted two young Southerners, Myles Horton of Tennessee and Don West of Georgia. The two founded the Highlander School, a center for adult education, in the Summerfield community between Tracy City and Monteagle. The Highlander School soon became a center of activity for the labor movement, first in Tennessee and then all over the South. People at Highlander put out pro-union newspapers, trained activists in union organizing, and brought in textile workers and others for seminars on topics such as how to become an effective shop steward. They accomplished their mission with music as well as with more conventional forms of instruction.

Through the years, the issues have changed, but the activism has never dimmed. Highlander took an active role in the civil rights struggles. Martin Luther King Jr. and Ralph Abernathy, among others,

Celebrating the 25th anniversary of the school in 1957 are, from left, Martin Luther King Jr., Pete Seeger, Charis Horton (daughter of co-founder Myles Horton), Rosa Parks, and Ralph Abernathy.

came to Highlander for support and to plan their acts of civil disobedience. Rosa Parks, for instance, attended Highlander shortly before she refused to give up her seat on a bus in Montgomery, Alabama. "We Shall Overcome" here became the anthem of the civil rights movement. In more recent times, Earth First! activist Judi Bari participated in Highlander workshops before launching the Redwood Summer—a radical environmental series of events.

Highlander became infamous in some circles in the 1960s when a photograph of Martin Luther King Jr. taken at Highlander was splashed on billboards and captioned "a Communist training school" by the John Birch Society. The House Committee on un-American Activities also investigated Highlander.

The school ended its Grundy County existence in 1959 when local law enforcement people raided it and found that beer was being sold to those in attendance. Although the sales were more of the put-some-money-in-a-box-when-you-get-a-beer variety, this proved the tool the authorities needed to seize the buildings and try to shut down the school. Highlander then moved to Knoxville and now operates in a rural site near New Market in East Tennessee.

Today Highlander works with community groups, primarily from Appalachia and the Deep South. "We bring people together to learn from each other," says the group's mission statement. This takes the form of residential workshops, training sessions, and other methods that develop leadership in issues such as fighting corporate pollution, bringing U.S. and immigrant workers together, and combating the increasing use of part-time, temporary, and contract workers. For more information, visit www.highlandercenter.org.

Heartland

(931/779-3532, www.tnstateparks.com), go south on Hwy. 56 through Beersheba Springs and Altamont, then take Hwy. 108 to the east—left—and go through the town of Gruetli-Laager, then turn left on Hwy. 399. Follow the signs.

BEERSHEBA SPRINGS

Highway 56 from McMinnville climbs to the old resort town of Beersheba (BURR-shuh-buh) Springs. It was named for Beersheba Cain, who was traveling on horseback with her husband from McMinnville to Chattanooga when she wandered up an old Indian path and found a spring whose water contained a lot of iron. This became known as Beersheba's Spring, and in 1839 the area opened as a resort. A hotel was built at the top of the mountain, and, when stagecoaches would begin their climb up the mountain, the driver would blow his horn a number of times to indicate how many people on board would be present at dinner. By the time guests arrived, the meal would be well under way. Andrew Jackson was a frequent visitor to Beersheba Springs, as were many Nashvillians.

The hotel was expanded by John Armfield and "cottages"—rather large houses—were built. The place reached its zenith in the years just before the Civil War. Since those days the old hotel changed hands many times until its purchase in 1941 by the United Methodist Church, which still uses it for retreats. Most of the cottages are still there, including two built for Episcopal turned Civil War general Leonidas Polk.

In the last weekend of August, the hotel grounds are the scene of the **Beersheba Springs Arts and Crafts Festival** (931/692-3701), now into its third decade and involving 250 exhibitors from all over.

Beersheba Springs Porcelain (1 Dahlgreen, 30 Beersheba Ln., 931/692-2280, www.beershebaporcelain.com) offers porcelain pieces created from a process that Phil Mayhew (a former arts professor) developed. Using higher temperatures, the process increases durability and the intensity of colors. Terri Mayhew creates porcelain and handcrafted silver jewelry.

ALTAMONT

After seeing Beersheba Springs, a good place to spend the night is this little town, the seat of Grundy County, farther along on Hwy. 56. The history of the area, such as the time Nathan Bedford Forrest and 1,000 troops camped here, is displayed in the **Courthouse Museum** (931/692-3153, free), across the street from the new courthouse. This museum is housed in an 1830s log cabin that at one time served as the courthouse. Now it contains items from various periods in Grundy County history. Indian artifacts, Civil War items, and exhibits on the lumber and mining industries make up the collection. The museum is closed January–March.

The **Cumberland Craftsman** (931/692-3595), on the grounds of a mill that operated 1901–68, is the place to go for folk art, woodcarvings, walking sticks, and other items. Ron Van Dyke is the artist and proprietor.

TRACY CITY

Driving from Altamont to Tracy City, the visitor passes though an area that was extensively mined for coal after the Civil War. As in most mines here and to the east, the coal was converted to coke, a more efficient fuel. The work was hard, and this was the scene of many labor struggles. In the late 1800s owners used convict labor, thus holding down the wages of the rest of the workers. The miners finally revolted, commandeered trains, and shipped the convicts out. Labor unrest continued into the 1930s and led to the establishment of the Highlander Folk School about four miles west of Tracy City on U.S. 41.

Highway 108 leads to the community of Palmer, where the **Miner's Museum and Heritage Center** (adjacent to the library on Hwy. 108) displays a great number of artifacts from the days when this was a big coal mining area. The wide assortment of mining equipment covers pick-and-shovel days up to more modern days. On Labor Day the center always takes part in the town celebration. For information on this or any other aspect of Grundy County, visit **Sham and Shorty's,** a convenience store across from the bank on Hwy. 108 in town. Shorty has been the president of the Grundy County Chamber of Commerce and is the source of all knowledge in these parts, and can be reached at home at 931/779-3593.

Practicalities

Foster Falls, five miles east on Hwy. 150, no phone, has 26 sites with no hookups. It's open late April–mid-October.

The **Dutch Maid Bakery** (111 Main St., 931/592-3171) is the oldest family-owned bakery in the state. Among its delights are these breads: honey and nut, raisin, jalapeño, potato, six-grain, salt rising, and pumpernickel. Some of the recipes date to Swiss immigrants who came to these parts in the 1870s. The proprietors will give visitors a short tour if things in the store aren't too hectic. Look for the 1929 mixer.

SOUTH CUMBERLAND STATE RECREATION AREA

This 11,500-acre area includes seven parks with 10 different entrances spread over four counties. Though spread around, these have much to offer the visitor, beginning with flora and fauna. The areas constitute four disparate ecological zones: plateau top, bluff, gorge, and aquatic. Wildlife includes red and gray foxes, coyotes, beavers, otters, white-tailed deer, possums, squirrels, and raccoons. Migratory birds join local wild turkeys and raptors throughout the area. Wildflowers are a delight from March into October.

Hikers can choose trails that vary from strolls to grueling climbs, that pass cliffs, waterfalls, swimming holes, caves, and streams. Others will marvel at historic structures such as coke ovens. Visitors should keep in mind that hunting is permitted in several of these areas and conduct themselves accordingly during the fall hunting season.

The South Cumberland State Recreation Area has no large campsites but offers a variety of backcountry sites. A permit is required for all backcountry camping, and guests must use designated sites, all of which contain primitive toilets.

Permits are available at the headquarters or at the trailheads.

Free programs and guided hikes are offered at the **headquarters** (931/924-2956 or 931/924-2980), between Tracy City and Monteagle, which contains several natural history exhibits. One of the more interesting is a 3-D map showing all the parks; the parks detailed below are the highlights of the recreation area.

Grundy Lakes Day Use Area was donated to the state during the Depression after coal mining had ended. Here the Lone Rock Coke Ovens, run by convicts, transformed coal into coke. The area centers on Grundy Lake, and the entire park is on the National Register of Historic Places. The remains of a long row of coke ovens sit on the west side of the lake. Visitors cannot camp here, but they can hike, picnic, and swim. To get there, take Exit I-24 at Monteagle, go six miles on U.S. 41 toward Tracy City, then turn left onto Lakes Drive to the park.

Grundy Forest State Natural Area is a 212-acre tract containing the northern terminus of Fiery Gizzard Trail. The hike leads 12.7 miles to Foster Falls, but a two-mile jaunt down the northern end takes the hiker past a large rock shelter, a five-century-old hemlock tree, Blue Hole Falls and its accompanying swimming hole, the Black Canyon, and a group of house-sized boulders called The Fruit Bowl. And that's just the first two miles. To get to this area, go to Tracy City, just off U.S. 41, and follow the signs.

Foster Falls TVA Small Wild Area gets its name from a waterfall that plunges 60 feet into a large pool. It marks the southern terminus of the Fiery Gizzard Trail. To get there, take U.S. 41 east from Tracy City and look for the sign on the right.

Sewanee Natural Bridge State Natural Area used to belong to the University of the South. A short walk leads to a sandstone arch that is 27 feet high and spans 57 feet. To get there, take Hwy. 56 south from Sewanee and look for the sign on the left.

The Buggytop Trail, farther south down Highway 56 from Sewanee Natural Bridge State Natural Area, leads to **Carter State Natural Area.** The area's big feature is Lost Cove Cave, its entrance described in Thomas Barr's *Caves of Tennessee:* "[It is] one of the most impressive cave mouths in the state. It is 100 feet wide and 80 feet high and opens at the base of an overhanging bluff 150 feet high. The cave stream cascades down from the mouth and drops 40 feet in less than 100 yards."

The cave shelters rare and endangered species of bats and salamanders, which should be left alone. Occasionally rangers conduct tours of the cave.

The Buggytop Trail is only four miles round-trip but drops 620 feet in elevation. The way back from the cave is a long pull. See the recreation area online at www.tnstateparks.com.

⋈ MONTEAGLE

The Chautauqua movement began in 1874 on the shores of Lake Chautauqua in upstate New York, where Sunday-school teachers and others would spend most of a summer living in a wholesome environment, listening to lectures and con-

certs, and engaging in other uplifting activities. The trend spread across the country and came to the town of Monteagle in 1883 in the form of the Monteagle Sunday School Assembly, an annual, nondenominational gathering.

It was a great success here, for Monteagle, on the Cumberland Plateau, was cooler than most places farther south. Even better, it was far from worldly pleasures and yet accessible by railroad, the final leg of which was traveled on a small train called the Mountain Goat. Families built cottages—now numbering 163—on the 96-acre site and came there summer after summer. The adults attended classes and other events, and the children had a grand time.

One longtime veteran of the assembly recalls that not everyone who summered there always stuck to the straight and narrow. When asked if anyone ever partook of the bottled versions of spiritual comfort, he replied, "Well, you know what they say; if you find four Episcopalians, you'll always find a fifth."

Over the years the religious aspects of the gath-

moonshine still, Monteagle

ering have been emphasized less and less, but the idea of a resort for families has stayed strong. Even though few now stay the entire summer, families—some of them for the fifth generation— still come to Monteagle and take part in the educational programs. The cottages have no shortage of tenants, and some are available for rent by calling 931/924-2272. If visitors want to rent cottages, they must submit sublease applications, which include references. Other accommodations include two inns, listed below.

Monteagle attracted less religious folks as well. Mobster Al Capone, as he traveled from Chicago to and from Florida, would stop over at a beautiful stone house along the main highway. Now the **High Point** (224 E. Main St., www.highpointrestaurant.net) restaurant, the house has escape hatches in the roof and hiding places in what is now the wine cellar.

Sights

The **Monteagle Sunday School Assembly** is on the National Register, and its 19th-century buildings are a delight. Most are prime examples of carpenter Gothic and Queen Anne–style architecture. Six wooden pedestrian bridges cross

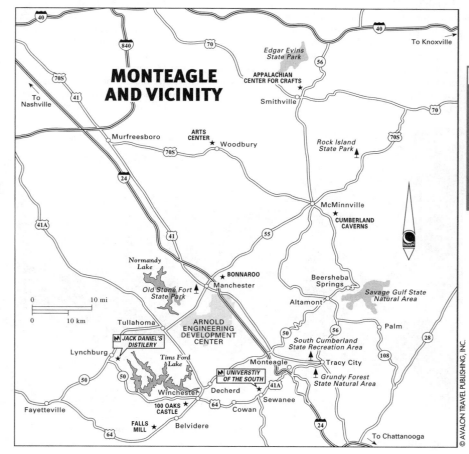

Heartland

© AVALON TRAVEL PUBLISHING, INC.

the gorges through the property, and the whole place is eminently walkable. The assembly grounds are private property, but visitors can buy one-day to entire-season admission tickets at the gate. The one-day admission is $13. For information call 931/924-2286.

Monteagle Wine Cellars (U.S. 64/41A on the west side of I-24, 800/556-WINE [556-9463] or 931/924-2120) produces wines as various as chardonnay and sweet red muscadine.

Accommodations

The **Adams Edgeworth Inn** (Monteagle Assembly, 931/924-2669, www.1896-edgeworth-mountain-inn.com, $125–200) is the grande dame of country inns in this part of Tennessee. It was built in 1896 as an inn on the assembly grounds and is richly decorated in the Chautauqua cottage style, with watercolors and yards and yards of imported fabric. The library, containing more than 2,000 volumes, is a favorite gathering place for guests.

The inn has 11 rooms plus three rooms in the carriage house. Rates include a full continental breakfast.

Jim Oliver's Smokehouse (Exit 135 off I-24, 800/489-2091 or 931/924-2268, www.thesmokehouse.com, $59.95–189) runs a lodge with 98 rooms and cabins. Amenities include a swimming pool in the shape of a country ham, 20 acres of land, and tennis, horseshoes, hot tubs, and walking trails.

Food

The **Adams Edgeworth Inn** (Monteagle Assembly, 931/924-2669) offers gourmet dinners by reservation only. Entrées include such items as grilled chicken Florentine, and Alaskan salmon steaks in dill butter. Desserts might be strawberry brûlée or Georgia pecan pie.

High Point (224 E. Main St, 931/924-4600, www.highpointrestaurant.net, dinner nightly) offers entrées such as horseradish crusted grouper, balsamic glazed ribeye, and rosemary pork.

© JEFF BRADLEY

The High Point restaurant is located in a house allegedly used by Al Capone on trips between Chicago and Miami.

Jim Oliver's Smokehouse (U.S. 64/41 west of I-24, 931/924-2268, www.thesmokehouse.com) attracts about 400,000 diners a year. They come for wonderful country ham—the place serves about 5,000 hams a year and an estimated one million biscuits—and world-class country cooking. It serves breakfast, lunch, and dinner daily.

Information

For visitor information, call the **City of Monteagle** (931/924-2265). The **Monteagle Arts and Crafts Show** takes place on the first weekend in August at the Monteagle Elementary School. Visitors will see artists, music, and good food.

SOUTH PITTSBURG

This town was founded by a group of investors in England who hoped that it would became an iron center much like its namesake. In 1896, a Pennsylvania native named Joseph Lodge established a foundry there that he named Blacklock Foundry in honor of the man who ran it. It

burned in 1909 and out of the ashes rose Lodge Manufacturing, which has been making cast-iron cookware for almost 100 years. It makes skillets, Dutch ovens, griddles, cornstick pans, muffin pans, teakettles, and more. The company website is www.lodgemfg.com.

The foundry isn't open to the public for safety reasons, but the **Lodge Discount Factory Outlet** (E. 5th St., 423/837-5919) has factory seconds at great prices. It's just off I-24 at Exit 152.

The best time to come is during the **National Cornbread Festival** (423/837-0022, www.nationalcornbread.net), held the first weekend in May. This event brings 22,000 people to town to eat cornbread, listen to music, shop at more than 60 crafts booths, and enjoy kids' events.

South Pittsburg hired a marshal named Thomas Mix in 1907 to keep law and order among the sometimes rowdy iron workers there. The young man lasted less than a year, when he headed for Hollywood and a new career in the movies. Shortening his name, he became Tom Mix, star of more than 300 cowboy films.

West of Monteagle

SEWANEE

The prettiest college campus in Tennessee, if not the entire South, highlights this town on the edge of the Cumberland Plateau.

University of the South

The university (www.sewanee.edu) was the inspiration of Leonidas Polk, Episcopal bishop of Louisiana, Confederate general, and one of the illustrious Polks of Columbia, Tennessee. Polk envisioned an Episcopal university for the South in the 1850s, and he and others decided it should be in the northern South away from the disease-plagued lowlands. The Sewanee Mining Company, hoping to stimulate traffic on its Mountain Goat rail line, donated a large tract of land atop the Cumberland Plateau for the college. Only a few buildings were on the site when the Civil War broke out, and these were destroyed.

After the war, work began again, but Southern fortunes on which university supporters had counted were largely ruined. The officials turned to England for the needed funds, and work on the university resumed, heavily influenced by the architecture of Oxford and Cambridge.

The result is a striking campus composed of buildings constructed with sandstone quarried on the 10,000-acre grounds, known as "the domain" and said to be the largest college campus in the country. **All Saints' Chapel,** completed in 1957, is anchored by Shapard Tower, from which rings the 56-bell Leonidas Polk Memorial Carillon, one of the largest such instruments in the world.

Today the University of the South is often referred to as "Sewanee" and enrolls more than 1,200 students in the College of Arts and Sciences and another 75 in the School of Theology. It is owned by 28 dioceses of the Episcopal Church spread over 12 states.

Heartland

© COURTESY OF THE UNIVERSITY OF THE SOUTH

The architecture at the University of the South resembles that of Oxford and Cambridge.

Visitors are welcome to walk on the campus and see the buildings. To find the campus, turn north on University Avenue off U.S. 64/41A. Services are held in All Saints' Chapel daily and Sunday, and visitors are welcome. The **Abbott Cotten Martin Ravine Garden,** known to the irreverent as "Abbo's Alley," lies to the west of the main campus and consists of a landscaped area containing wildflowers, a brook, stone bridges, and goldfish. A wonderful vista awaits at **Memorial View,** where a giant cross commemorates Sewanee war dead. To get there, take Tennessee Avenue off University Avenue and drive for about a mile. From here visitors can look at the Highland Rim, 1,000 feet lower in elevation.

St. Andrews-Sewanee School

This school (931/598-5651, www.sasweb.org) is the latest incarnation of boarding schools in Sewanee. Tennessee writer and Pulitzer Prize–winning novelist James Agee spent 1916 through 1924 as a student at St. Andrews School, which

was run by Episcopal monks. One of them, Father James Harold Flye, corresponded with Agee for the rest of the latter's life. These letters, which shed insight into the writer, were published after his death as *Letters of James Agee to Father Flye.*

St. Andrews is now a co-ed, Episcopal, college preparatory school for 240 boarding and day students. Visitors often come to see the red-tile-roofed chapel, which is always open. Piney Point, a 10-minute walk from the football field, offers a wonderful view from the edge of the Cumberland Plateau.

The school maintains an **Agee Room** with memorabilia connected to its most famous alumnus. The **Heritage Room** (free admission) is a small museum recalling the school's history, including photos taken by Father Flye.

Pottery

John Ray Pottery (931/598-5184, www.jrpottery.com) has to be one of the more unusual such places in the state. John Ray apprenticed in Japan for more than five years with various potters, and on returning to this country he set about building a 25-foot-long kiln in which his work is fired by wood. He produces pottery as various as four-foot-high urns and teapots and Traditional tea bowls. The pottery is eight miles from Sewanee, and visitors should call ahead for directions.

Hallelujah Pottery Gallery (U.S. 41A in Sewanee, 931/924-0141, 10 A.M.–4:30 P.M. Tues.–Thurs., 10 A.M.–5 P.M. Fri.–Sat.) produces functional stoneware such as baking dishes, pitchers, and mugs. It features wood-fired, salt-glazed pottery, all of it one-of-a-kind.

Recreation and Entertainment

The old railroad track down the mountain to Cowan, at one time the roadbed of the Mountain Goat train, is now a challenging jeep road ideal for **mountain bike** aficionados. The dirt road parallels U.S. 41A for a bit, and a good place to get on it is the historical marker for the Army of Tennessee.

Held on the campus at Manigault Park, the **Spring Craft Show** (931/598-0301) coincides with commencement at the University of the South—usually the second weekend in May—and features works by local artisans.

The **Fall Craft Show** (931/598-0301) takes place in Convocation Hall on the Saturday before Thanksgiving.

Practicalities

Sewanee Inn (University Ave., 931/598-1686) is owned by the university and open to those attending a function or in some way connected with the university.

St. Mary's Center for Spiritual Growth (931/598-5342, www.stmarysretreat.org) occupies the 200-acre grounds of a girls' school operated by the Episcopal Sisters of St. Mary 1888–1968. Now used as a retreat center, it is open to individuals from time to time and when space permits.

Four Seasons, (931/598-5544, 4 A.M.–9 P.M. Fri.–Sat., 11 A.M.–3 P.M. Sun.) midway between Sewanee and Monteagle, offers country cooking. **Pearl's Cafe** (15344 Sewanee Hwy., 931/598-9568, dinner nightly, Sunday brunch) offers a respite from country cooking. Here's the

THE KINDNESS OF STRANGERS

When the will of **Tennessee Williams** (1911–83) was probated, the University of the South learned that the playwright had left it a large sum of money. This became the seed money for the **Sewanee Writer's Conference,** an annual gathering of men and women of letters.

Tennessee Williams did not attend the University of the South, although his grandfather, the Reverend Walter E. Dakin, attended the University's School of Theology. Williams was offered an honorary degree shortly before he died, but he was sick and could not attend the ceremonies. No one knows if Williams ever laid eyes on the college.

The annual Writer's Conference is held in July. It includes workshops, readings, and lectures in fiction, poetry, and playwriting. Past participants include writers Russell Banks, Jill McCorkle, Tim O'Brien, and Maxine Kumin, as well as agents, publishers, and editors. For details call 931/598-1141 or visit www.sewaneewriters.org.

place for fried calamari, fresh Canadian mussels, and Jamaican jerk wings. One can drink imported beer while gazing at the artwork hanging on the walls—all for sale. **Quidnunc Cafe** (580 University Ave., 931/598-1595) serves pizza and sandwiches.

For more information, contact the **Franklin County Chamber of Commerce** (1927 Decherd Blvd., Winchester, 931/967-6788, www.franklincountychamber.com).

COWAN

The drive from Sewanee to Cowan, or vice versa, particularly on a snowy day, clearly demonstrates the obstacle that the Cumberland Plateau posed to travelers. This was particularly true for early Tennessee railroads, which had to climb the plateau to get from Nashville to Chattanooga. At Cowan, the railroad officials decided to dig a tunnel through the mountain. Four hundred slaves worked on the three-year effort, which

Heartland

resulted in the 2,228-foot-long Cumberland Tunnel. By 1854, trains connected Nashville with Chattanooga and points south. One of the blunders that Confederate General Braxton Bragg made as he retreated from Tennessee was neglecting to destroy this tunnel. Unscathed, it served as a vital supply line to Union troops pushing toward Atlanta.

One of the participants in Bragg's retreat was Nathan Bedford Forrest, who with his escorts brought up the rear of the sad procession. An old woman was berating the retreating troops for their cowardice. As Forrest—much taller than average—passed, the woman shouted: "A big stout man like you running away! You ought to be ashamed of yourself! If old Forrest was here, he would make you stand and fight!"

Sights and Recreation

The town's 1904 railroad depot in the middle of town is the site of the **Cowan Railroad Museum** (Front St., 931/967-7365, May–Oct. 10 A.M.–4 P.M. Thurs.–Sat., 1–4 P.M. Sun., free, donations accepted), which includes a locomotive and caboose. From here visitors can see the northern entrance of the Cumberland Tunnel. Even with the tunnel, however, the grades up the plateau are so steep that additional engines were and are still attached to trains to help them get to the top.

One of the items that no doubt came on the train in the early 1900s was a **mail-order house** from Sears Roebuck, which still stands right on the highway through town at 518 W. Cumberland Street. It is not open to the public.

Cowan is the downhill end of the old Mountain Goat railbed that leads up to Sewanee. Now a jeep trail, it is an excellent place to ride a **mountain bike**. To find the trail, park in the middle of town and ride on the right side of the railroad track toward the Cowan Tunnel. When the track enters the tunnel, the road goes over the tunnel and veers off to the left. Follow it uphill until reaching the campus of the University of the South.

Practicalities

For accommodations, try **Rolling Acres Motel** (U.S. 41A, 931/967-7428).

Buck's Market (415 W. Cumberland, 931/967-6241) has won second place in a statewide barbecue competition. Get barbecue or ribs—wet or dry. The **Corner House Tea Room** (400 E. Cumberland, 931/967-3910) is a Victorian tea house that serves such items as chicken salad, pasta, seafood, and blackberry or peach cobbler.

For more information, contact the **Cowan City Hall** (931/967-7318), or the **Franklin County Chamber of Commerce** (1927 Decherd Blvd., Winchester, 931/967-6788).

WINCHESTER

This pleasant town originated as a stop on the mail route that ran from Virginia to New Orleans. The town was laid out in 1808 and was populated in the early days by veterans of the Revolutionary War and their offspring. David Crockett came here to sign up for the militia, and later Franklin Countians pushed for secession. No Civil War battles were fought here, but armies for both sides passed through and helped themselves to livestock, burned fence rails, and made the locals miserable.

Winchester was the site of Mary Sharp College, dubbed "The Pioneer Female College of the South." Its motto was "Educate the mothers and you educate the world." Founded in 1850, it lasted for almost a half century, and it was the first women's college in the country whose graduation requirements for women were the same as those set for men.

The most famous person to come from Franklin County was Frances Rose Shore, a singer who, while attending college at Vanderbilt, sang on a WSM radio show whose theme song was "Dinah." The young woman became known as Dinah Shore, star of stage and screen, seller of cookbooks, and fan of Burt Reynolds. She is fondly remembered in Winchester, where a prominent street bears her name.

Sights

Downtown Winchester holds several attractions for the visitor. First is the town square, which is anchored by a Depression-era courthouse whose

WINCHESTER

To I-24

To Tullahoma

FRANKLIN COUNTY
CHAMBER OF COMMERCE

DECHERD BLVD

41A

BYPASS RD

Boiling Fork Creek

To Cowan

DINAH SHORE BLVD

SHARP SPRINGS RD

Wagner Creek

OLD JAIL MUSEUM

2ND AVE SE

3RD AVE SE

S PORTER ST

COLLEGE ST

S JEFFERSON ST

OLDHAM THEATER

FRANKLIN COUNTY COURTHOUSE

HAMMER'S

1ST AVE SE

3RD AVE SE

S HIGH ST

S VINE ST

2ND AVE NE

3RD AVE NE

N PORTER ST

RAINBOW ROW

BRICK CAFE

1ST AVE NE

2ND AVE NE

1ST AVE NW

To Fayetteville
and Belvidere

N JEFFERSON ST

DAVID CROCKETT HWY

64

N HIGH ST

N VINE ST

4TH AVE

N CEDAR ST

N SHEPHARD ST

3RD AVE NW

130

Boiling Fork Creek

TULLAHOMA RD

RD

50

To Lynchburg

LYNCHBURG RD

SCALE NOT AVAILABLE

© AVALON TRAVEL PUBLISHING, INC.

Heartland

WINCHESTER'S 100 OAKS CASTLE

Just west of Winchester stands an unusual edifice whose story is almost as striking as its architecture. It began as a plantation home in 1830, then passed through several families until it was bought by Albert Marks about 30 years later. Marks was governor of Tennessee 1879–81. His son, Arthur Marks, counted the trees on the plantation and came up with the name 100 Oaks.

The younger Marks accepted a diplomatic post to England, where he was influenced by the many castles and stately houses. He returned to Tennessee determined to have a castle of his own.

Beginning with the plantation house, he eventually built a castle with a great hall containing a 40-foot-high ceiling, a massive dining room, wine cellar, 12 bedrooms, and tunnels. He honored Sir Walter Scott, whose writings had long enchanted antebellum Southerners, by building a replica of Scott's study in Abbotsford, the writer's Scotland estate.

Arthur Marks died in 1882, and the house again passed through several owners. The Paulist Fathers, an order of Catholic priests, bought 100 Oaks in 1900 and operated a church, a school, and creamery on the grounds. They sold off much of the land, and they moved to greener pastures in 1953.

For the next 37 years, a variety of owners attempted to find a purpose for the castle. It became a private home, a restaurant, and an adult activity center. After a devastating fire in 1990, the old castle was boarded up. Like many other castles, it had finally become a ruin, a place frequented by the curious and by nocturnal revelers.

In 1992, a tragic car accident took the life of a young man named Kent Bramlett. His grief-stricken parents, Nashville attorney P. K. Bramlett and his artist wife, Shirley, looking for a special way to remember their son, bought the castle and began the daunting task of renovating it. As they hauled out rubble and hand-sanded blackened woodwork, they found the work therapeutic, and over the months they decided that 100 Oaks could be a place where other people could memorialize their loved ones. They began to accept donations of cash and antiques, and, through their efforts, 100 Oaks is gradually coming back to life.

Theirs is not an easy task. More than 20 rooms collapsed in the fire, and trees as thick as a man's forearm have grown up amid the ruins. The Bramletts have made great progress, however, restoring the Great Hall with flags from various countries hanging over a long table. The replica of Scott's study is lined with law textbooks, and two bedrooms have been decorated with a combination of antiques and Shirley's paintings.

The Bramletts work on 100 Oaks on the weekends, sometimes assisted by friends. They host bus tours and other groups, P. K. entertaining them by singing and playing a guitar. Their effort attracted the attention of a world-renowned gardener, the late Rosemary Verey, who visited 100 Oaks and designed a garden for it.

At this writing, 100 Oaks is open only for groups of 20 or more, and only by appointment. Weddings and receptions and special dinners take place here as well. For information about 100 Oaks, call 931/967-8583.

The fenced grounds are patrolled by one of the meaner dogs in Tennessee. Nonetheless, visitors can pull into the driveway and gaze at the old building, a special place of memory and hope. To get there from Winchester, drive west on U.S. 64. One Hundred Oaks cannot be seen from the road. Turn right on 100 Oaks Place.

design incorporates art deco elements. On one side of the square sits **Hammers,** a has-to-be-seen-to-be-believed store, and on the opposite side is the **Oldham Theater** (931/967-2516), a movie palace that has occasional plays. A few steps off the square on 2nd Avenue NW leads to **Rainbow Row,** brightly painted 19th-century storefronts containing antique shops, a restaurant, a bookstore, and a gift shop.

A walk down Dinah Shore Boulevard leads to the **Franklin County Old Jail Museum** (400 1st Ave., 931/967-0524, 10 A.M.–4 P.M. Tues.–Sat., $1 adults, $0.50 children). This town built its first jail in 1814, and the festivities surrounding the completion of the log structure reached such a euphoric state that the object of celebration burned to the ground. This version was completed in 1897 and now houses a museum containing frontier artifacts, more than 200 Civil War items as well as things from other wars, and exhibits related to Dinah Shore.

Gallery I (1319 Dinah Shore Blvd., 931/967-0646) offers limited-edition prints, local works, china, and gifts.

Those who cannot get to Memphis to see A. Schwab Dry Goods should stop at **Hammers General Store** (102 1st Ave., 931/967-3787). The store contains tons of merchandise, some of it useful and some of it junk.

The **Walls of Jericho,** said to be the prettiest place in Tennessee, can be found south of town next to the Alabama border. It consists of a 50-yard wide bowl-shaped area in a narrow gorge with a stream and luxuriant plant growth. In 2004, the Nature Conservancy bought the land, where David Crockett once lived, and has opened it to the public. Totaling 8,943 acres in Tennessee—and an adjoining 12,510 in Alabama, the land will be preserved as wilderness. To get there, take Hwy. 16 south from Winchester for 12 miles. Cross into Alabama, and look for a parking area on the right. Hiking and horse trails lead 3.5 miles one-way into the gorge, where tent-only camping awaits.

Events

Those magnificent men and their flying machines of the **Experimental Aircraft Associa-** tion (931/967-3148) gather for a monthly fly-in breakfast at the Winchester Airport on the first Saturday of each month 7:30–10 A.M.

The **"High on the Hog" Bar-B-Que Cookoff** heats up in mid-May at the Winchester City Park. Auxiliary events include 5K and 10K runs, arts and crafts, and carnival rides.

The **Arts and Crafts Fair** on the third weekend in September attracts participants from several states. For details on these events or for more information, contact the **Franklin County Chamber of Commerce** (1927 Decherd Blvd., Winchester, 931/967-6788, www.franklincountychamber.com).

Food

Brick Cafe (103 2nd Ave. NW, 931/962-2233) sits in the middle of Rainbow Row and offers hot country food for breakfast and lunch. **Hawks Steak House** (1106 Dinah Shore Blvd., 931/967-1111) makes that and much more: barbecue, chicken, soup and salad bar, and desserts. **Rafael's Italian Restaurant** (2659 Decherd Blvd., 931/962-4997) offers dishes such as veal parmesan, Grecian chicken, lasagna, and more.

U.S. 64 WEST

Hundred Oaks Castle, one mile west of town on U.S. 64 across from the Winchester Hat Company, was once a 30-room home. Built in 1891, it was for a time home to Albert S. Marks, the state's 21st governor. It burned in 1991, but the ruins are still remarkable.

Belvidere

Travelers who have passed through Pennsylvania will remember the barns built on the sides of hills or against banks so that wagons could drive right into the second story. Such barns are unusual in Tennessee, but they can be seen around this small town, which was settled by Swiss and German families after the Civil War.

Other evidence of their presence is the **Swiss Pantry** (931/962-0567, 8 A.M.–5:30 P.M. Tues.–Fri., 8 A.M.–4 P.M. Sat.), west of Belvidere on U.S. 64, which is a family run business that produces an enormous variety

FALLS MILL

" **L**ike stepping back in time" has become a cliché in travel writing, but a visit to Falls Mills is exactly that. The mill is off U.S. 64 and down a country road that leads to a shaded valley. Even on the hottest days, the trees and the stream keep it cool. The mill building has wooden floors polished over the years, and the owners are some of the most laid-back folks you will find.

Most of the mills out in the country in Tennessee are designed to grind corn or wheat into, respectively, meal and flour. This three-story brick place was built in 1873 as a cotton and wool factory; indeed, the creek on which it sits is called **Factory Creek**. After the turn of the 20th century it was transformed into a cotton gin, and after World War II the mill was changed into a woodworking shop. In the late 1960s it became a grist and flour mill.

Falls Mill has to be one of the most beautiful mills in the state. A 32-foot overshot waterwheel powers the machinery, which grinds grain between large millstones. Stone works better than steel, so say aficionados, because stones do not get as hot as steel and thus do not partially cook the grain they grind. The slightly irregular surface of stone permits a coarser grind, thus delivering more flavor. Here one can buy yellow cornmeal, white cornmeal, grits—the only difference between grits and cornmeal is the size of the cracked corn—pancake mix, rye flour, whole wheat flour, and rice flour.

Inside the mill is a **museum** of hand looms, spinning wheels, and 19th-century power looms and carding machines. The most interesting item is a dog-powered butter churn. A country store sells books, arts and crafts, and other items. Admission is $3 for adults, $2 for seniors and students, and $1 for children under 14. The museum is open 9 A.M.–4 P.M., Sunday 12:30–4 P.M., and closed on Wednesday.

And there's more. A reconstructed 1895 **log cabin** can hold up to four adults. Complete with full kitchen and bath, it has a sleeping loft, balcony, and air-conditioning. Rates start at $90. Information on all of the above can be had by calling 931/469-7161 or, after 4 P.M., 931/469-7631. Visit online at www.fallsmill.com.

To get there, go west from Belvidere on U.S. 64 to the community of Old Salem. Go right on Salem-Lexie Road, and then follow the signs to the mill.

of foodstuffs: 33 cheeses, 17 kinds of dried fruit, 22 candies, and 16 relishes. Here's where visitors can get Vidalia onion sweet barbecue sauce, Tupelo honey, smoked and peppered bacon, and horehound candy.

Belvidere Market (6334 Davy Crockett Hwy., 931/967-3872, www.belvideremarket.com) is an art gallery. The gallery features hand crafted furniture and wood turnings by Tom Church, pottery, garden merchandise, and collectibles.

David Crockett moved near here with Polly, his first wife, in 1812. She died three years later and is buried west of town along U.S. 64. A historical marker indicates the site of her grave.

Along I-40 East of Nashville

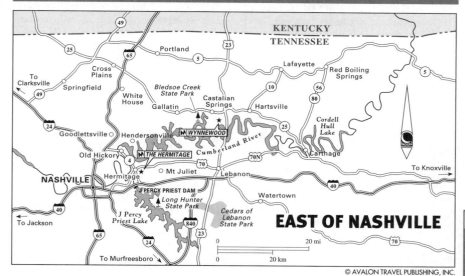

© AVALON TRAVEL PUBLISHING, INC.

HERMITAGE

Due east of Nashville, this suburb takes its name from the grand home of the nation's seventh president.

The Hermitage

Sections of Andrew Jackson's majestic house (Lebanon Rd., 615/889-2941, www.the-hermitage.com) were built 1819–21, but most of what visitors now see of The Hermitage was constructed while Jackson was living in the White House.

The Hermitage sits on 625 acres of land, and, unlike many historically significant buildings that nowadays find themselves beside fast-food outlets, this one preserves a sense of what Jackson's country setting was like when he lived here. Almost everything in the home belonged to Jackson. He and Rachel Donelson never had children, a fact that probably helped keep both The Hermitage and its contents intact.

Visitors go through a small museum displaying items owned by the Jacksons and then into The Hermitage and its grounds. The pres-

ident and his beloved Rachel are buried in the garden. Jackson was a slaveholder, and visitors can see the cabins in which his human possessions lived. Also in the tour is **Tulip Grove** ($12 adults, $11 seniors and children 13–18, $5 children 6–12), home to Old Hickory's nephew and private secretary, Andrew Jackson Donelson.

Donelson's wife, Emily, served as White House hostess during the Jackson years, and it was for her that Donelson built Tulip Grove, a brick Greek revival mansion, in 1834. On coming home to Tennessee after the years in Washington, however, 29-year-old Emily died of tuberculosis. The house now contains period antiques and also offers youth education classes.

The Grove has a cafeteria on the site, **Café Merels,** offering breakfast and lunch. To get there, take I-40 to the Old Hickory/Hermitage exit, bear left, then go about one mile to Lebanon Road. Turn right and go about a mile until the signs for the entrance, which is on the left.

Old Hickory

North of Hermitage along the Cumberland River stands the company town of Old Hickory. In 1918, in an all-out effort that foreshadowed World War II's construction of Oak Ridge, the DuPont Company built the world's largest smokeless gunpowder plant and surrounded it with a town for workers. Construction was quick: a six-room bungalow, complete with plumbing, was built in nine hours, and nearly 4,000 homes were erected. Finished just in time for the armistice, the factory was mothballed, only to open again in 1923 as a manufacturer of rayon and cellophane.

Once again workers occupied the company homes, which were sold to their occupants beginning in the late 1940s. Today the **Old Hickory Historic District** shows the visitor the company housing and other buildings built during the DuPont era.

Information

The **Spring Garden Fair,** held in mid-May at the

OLD HICKORY

Though born in South Carolina, **Andrew Jackson** is known to history as a Tennessean, and his career ran the length of the state. He began as a lawyer in Jonesborough, spent much of his life in and around Nashville, cofounded Memphis, and helped write the state constitution.

Jackson's fierce personality was evident from an early age, when as a boy he refused to shine the boots of a British officer and was struck across the face with a sword. His temper led him into arguments and duels; on one occasion he locked a man who had insulted an innkeeper in the inn's corncrib.

When he moved to Nashville, he boarded in the home of John Donelson, who had led the flotilla of boats carrying the people who originally settled the city. There the young Jackson met Rachel Donelson, living back at home to escape her abusive husband. Learning that her husband had applied to the Virginia legislature for a divorce, and thinking he had obtained one, the two were wed. In fact, Rachel's husband had only received permission from the legislature to seek a divorce, and, in a final affront to his wife, waited until she was wed and then received a divorce by claiming that Rachel had deserted him and committed adultery with Jackson. The Jacksons, learning of this to their horror, got married again, but for the rest of their lives, their enemies used this situation against them. They moved to a plantation east of Nashville called **The Hermitage.**

Jackson became one of Tennessee's first congressmen during George Washington's final term, but served only one term. Elected in 1797 as a senator, he returned to the nation's capital but resigned the next year to come home to Rachel.

Tennessee was growing, and over the years Jackson involved himself in various land transactions. At times he prospered, and other times he felt the financial pinch. He maintained close ties to Tennessee politicians and partook of horse races whenever he could. Appointed a judge, he presided in trials in various towns and became well known throughout the state.

When the War of 1812 broke out, Jackson was ready. He had long hated the British and called for 50,000 men to join him in invading Canada. The federal government sent Jackson and his army in the other direction, however, to smite the Creek, who were allied with the British. The Tennesseans utterly defeated the Creek in Alabama, and Jackson became a hero to Tennesseans and other westerners.

Operating without orders, he continued south with his army, aiming to attack the Spanish at Pensacola, Florida. Learning that the British planned an attack at New Orleans, he hastily moved to Louisiana and, in a battle that took place after the peace treaty was signed in Belgium, thrashed the British in a decisive battle. When news of this reached Washington and other eastern cities, Jackson became a national hero.

People began to talk of Jackson as presidential timber. Further military successes against the Seminoles in Florida added to his stature, and in 1823 he was again elected to the U.S. Senate. He ran for president in 1824, and when none of the four candidates received a majority of electoral votes, the election—the only time in American history—

Hermitage, brings lectures, walks, bird-watching expeditions, and all manner of events relating to gardening.

Storytelling Days take place for three days in October, when professional storytellers ply their art in large tents on the Hermitage grounds.

For more information, contact **Donelson/ Hermitage Chamber of Commerce** (5653 Frist Blvd., Ste. 703, 615/883-7896, www.dhchamber.com).

LONG HUNTER STATE RECREATIONAL PARK

Motorists on I-40 east of Nashville pass a long dam to the south of the interstate. This is J. Percy Priest Dam, which impounds Stones River to create J. Percy Priest Lake, on whose eastern shore stands this 2,315-acre park. Long Hunter is primarily a day-use park, with activities such as swimming, picnicking, and hiking.

© JEFF BRADLEY

Andrew and Rachel Jackson's tomb

Heartland

was settled in the House of Representatives. Through the efforts of Speaker of the House Henry Clay, Jackson lost to John Quincy Adams, who promptly appointed Clay secretary of state. Amid charges of a "corrupt bargain," Jackson resolved to run again and began his campaign immediately.

In 1828 it paid off. In the ugliest presidential race in the new country, Jackson ousted Adams from the White House. During the campaign, however, Adams's supporters had dragged out the old charges of adultery, and within weeks of Jackson's election, his beloved Rachel was dead—some said in part because of her intense embarrassment.

The election of Jackson marked a watershed in American politics. He was the first president from a state not bordering the ocean, and his victory marked a shift of power to those who had not had much of an opportunity to run the country. Jackson's taking the oath of office kicked off the wildest party ever held in the White House, with raw-boned Tennesseans and other westerners whooping

it up and having a grand old time. The only thing that got them back outside was an announcement that the drinks were being poured there.

Jackson's presidency was noted for his response to an 1830 move in South Carolina to leave the Union over a tax it did not like. A staunch Unionist, he threatened to invade if South Carolina seceded. Perhaps the most shameful of his actions was standing by and letting Georgia lead the Cherokees on the Trail of Tears when the Supreme Court had ruled in favor of the tribe. Nonetheless, he fares well in history. A 1996 poll of historians ranked him as "near great," a tier below only Washington, Lincoln, and F. D. Roosevelt.

Elected to a second term by more votes than his first victory, Jackson solidified the control of the Democratic Party on national politics, and he was able to virtually hand-pick his successor, Martin Van Buren.

Jackson came home to The Hermitage, where he lived the remaining eight years of his life in exceedingly bad health. He still commanded great respect in Tennessee, and his counsel was sought until his death on June 8, 1845. Jackson and his wife had never had any children, and his home and furnishings were acquired by the state, giving today's visitors a wonderful look at Tennessee's most powerful politician.

Some primitive camping is allowed, but the park has no cabins. Those wishing to camp must have a permit, which they can obtain at the visitors center.

Long Hunter contains trails and picnic areas especially accessible to visitors with disabilities, including nature trails and fishing in Couchville Lake. To get to the park, take Hwy. 171 from either I-40 east or I-24 south. Call 615/885-2422 or visit online at www.tnstateparks.com.

LEBANON

This town, the seat of Wilson County, got its name because the large cedar trees reminded early settlers of the cedars of Lebanon mentioned in the Bible. Several prominent Tennesseans lived here, including Andrew Jackson, Sam Houston, and three governors of the state, one of whom, elected when Tennessee was in the Confederacy, never took office because his capital was in the hands of the Union.

Deford Bailey, the first black entertainer on the *Grand Ole Opry* and one of its more popular performers, was born near here in 1899. An accomplished harmonica player, he was a visible symbol of country music's roots in the blues. Johnny Wright, half of country's famous Johnny and Jack duo, was born in Lebanon. Maud Woodfork, who went on to become an actress in Chicago, was born in Wilson County. She was one of several black women hired by the Quaker Oat Company to portray the character Aunt Jemima on the radio and in personal appearances.

Lebanon Woolen Mills, built in 1909 one block from the town square, was for years the town and county's largest employer. Now dubbed **Tennessee Woolen Mills** (300 N. Maple St.), the old buildings are being renovated for restaurant and shopping space.

Lebanon was home for 84 years to **Castle Heights Military Academy**, which had a 225-acre campus. Closed in 1986, it left a series of brick and stone castellated buildings, which have been recycled into offices for the town and various businesses. To see the former campus, go west from the town square on U.S. 70; the old

campus is about a mile out on the right. Look for the big gateposts.

Cumberland University (www.cumberland .edu) got its start in 1842, when most attorneys got their training by "reading the law" under the tutelage of another lawyer. The university's law school produced many prominent judges and lawmakers, but in the 20th century the institution achieved a more dubious form of fame: Georgia Tech beat it 220-0 in a 1916 football game. The law school moved to Birmingham, Alabama, during the 1960s, and the university continues today as a four-year private college with just over 1,000 students. The University is the home of the **Tillman Cavert Jr. Wildlife Museum,** a taxidermic treatment of animals dispatch by a great white hunter from the Class of '36. No admission is charged.

Today, Lebanon is known more for its antique stores, which ring the town square and extend down various side streets.

Sights

Visitors will find a dandy gathering of artifacts in the **City of Lebanon Museum and History Center** (8 A.M.–4 P.M. Mon.–Fri., by appointment Sat.), which is in the basement of City Hall on the Castle Heights Campus. One of the items is a pearl necklace presented by Confederate General John Hunt Morgan to his bride in a wartime wedding.

Wilson County Museum (236 W. Main St., one block west of the square on U.S. 70, 615/444-9127, free, donations appreciated) occupies a historic home known as Fessenden House. The museum, begun in 1870 by a doctor who served in the Civil War, is open by appointment only.

Fiddlers Grove (615/443-2626, $5) on the grounds of the Ward Agricultural Center, east of town on U.S. 70 east, consists of 20 buildings that illustrate the history of Wilson County. Structures such as a general store, doctor's office, and print shop contain items that relate to each. The season is April 15–October 31 10:00 A.M.–3:00 P.M. Tuesday–Saturday; the best time to see the grove is during the Wilson County Fair, when crafts and ac-

FRANK BUSTER AND HIS MYSTERIOUS HEAD

© JEFF BRADLEY

Frank Buster and the Head

Frank Buster's head appears on billboards all over Lebanon beckoning customers to **Cuz's,** his enormous antique emporium. For pedestrians in the town square, however, he offers a marketing technique—The Mysterious Critter—at least as old as Davy Crockett.

The attraction in his front window is a stuffed head resembling a Bigfoot kind of beast. According to a press release that Buster hands out, a couple leaving an extramarital tryst on nearby Sugar Flat Road were driving home when their truck—sounds like a country song so far—hit one of a pair of creatures. Getting out, the driver saw to his horror that he had killed one of them. Afraid he and his lover would get caught making whoopee, he dragged the hairy body into the bushes, then took his lady friend home and went home himself. Unable to sleep, he came back in the dawn's early light to bury the mysterious body.

At the last minute, according to the tale, he severed its head and took it to a taxidermist, who agreed to preserve it. The head stayed on a mantel for years before being sold to the entrepreneurial Mr. Buster.

The release ends on an ominous note:

But there continue to be spottings of the creature's mate up and down Sugar Flat Road. Residents of the area have complained that chickens, ducks, and turkeys often come up missing and the rumor is that if a dog barks at night, that dog will probably never be seen again. . . .

At least that's the tale—and not a bad one at that.

tivity demonstrators transform the old buildings into a living village.

Outside of town **Sellers Farm State Archeological Area** (615/885-2422, free) was inhabited around 1000–1300 A.D. by Native Americans who constructed a 15-foot high mound and earthen walls to protect it. Unlike similar sites from the Mississippian Period, this one is not beside a river. In 1877, archeologists from Harvard excavated the site and absconded with the remains of some of the inhabitants. Tours are available by calling Long Hunter State Park. The latest information can be found by searching on the web for the site of the Friends of the Sellars Farm State Archaeological Area.

To get there, take I-40 Exit 239A and go two miles to Poplar Hill Road. Turn left and go about one mile—Sellers Farm is on the left. A short trail with interpretive signs awaits.

Entertainment and Events

Details on all events are available from the chamber of commerce (615/444-5503). **Cedarfest,** held on the third weekend in July, brings contests—fiddling, square dancing, and buck dancing—food, and music.

The **Wilson County Fair,** held the third week in August, attracts more than 120,000 people in nine days. Featured are a carnival, rural exhibits, and live entertainment.

A **Victorian Christmas** occurs on the third weekend in November. Carriage rides, house tours, and lights make up this seasonal festival.

Nashville Superspeedway (866/722-3849, www.nashvillesuperspeedway.com) south of I-40

Heartland

in Wilson County, hosts NASCAR and other events.

Accommodations

Watermelon Moon Farm (10575 Trousdale Ferry Pike, 615/444-2356, $65) is in what used to be the summer kitchen of an old plantation house. The antebellum house is on the National Register and has verandas front and back. The cottage has its own bath and is decorated in a country style. Watermelon Moon Farm is home to Country Plus, a wholesale business that produces hand-painted crafts.

Motel options include **Best Western Executive Inn** (631 S. Cumberland, 800/528-1234 or 615/444-0505), **Knights Inn** (I-40 and U.S. 231 S., 800/BUDHOST [283-4678] or 615/449-2900), **Comfort Inn** (I-40 and U.S. 231 S., 800/221-2222 or 615/444-1001), **Days Inn** (I-40 and U.S. 231, 800/325-2525 or 615/444-5635), **Hampton Inn** (I-40 and U.S. 231 S., 800/HAMPTON [426-7866] or 615/444-7400), **Holiday Inn Express** (641 S. Cumberland, 800/HOLIDAY [465-4329] or 615/444-7020), and **Shoney's Inn** (I-40 and U.S. 231 S., 800/222-2222 or 615/449-5781).

Campers can set up at **Countryside Resort,** (615/449-5527) which has 105 sites. From I-40 take Exit 232 and follow signs. It's open all year. **Shady Acre Campground** (615/449-5400) has 125 sites and is open all year. From I-40 take Exit 238 and follow signs. **Timberline Campground** (615/449-2831) lies off I-40 on U.S. 321 S. It has 100 sites and is open all year.

Food

Allens Market (725 York St., 615/444-9415) offers deli sandwiches and beer for lunch.

Cherokee Steakhouse (450 Cherokee Dock Rd., 615/452-1515) sits next door to Reba McEntire's place. It offers all manner of steaks, seafood, chicken, and ribs for dinner only.

The **Perfect Cup Coffeehouse** (104 N. Maple St., 615/449-7939) specializes in espresso and cappuccino augmented by homemade desserts and Italian grilled sandwiches. It's only a half block from the square.

Elaine's Country Restaurant (1103-1/2 N. Cumberland, 615/443-2135) offers farm-raised catfish, frog legs, fried oysters, steak, and various interpretations of country cooking.

Shopping

Lebanon is famous among antiques fanciers for its collection of dealers. While aficionados can easily spend the better part of a day in the downtown area, other dealers have shops on U.S. 231. Of particular note are the following.

Cuz's Antique Center (140 Public Square, 615/444-8070) stocks more than 150,000 square feet of American, French, and English antiques. It also offers more than 1,000 stained-glass items. Knife fans will want to stop to see the Fightin' Rooster Cutlery Company here, which has thousands of knives.

Hidden Treasures (124A Public Square, 615/444-8280) has a great selection of maps, prints, and books.

For more information, contact the **Lebanon/Wilson County Chamber of Commerce** (149 Public Square, 615/444-5503, www.lebanonwilsontnchamber.org).

CEDARS OF LEBANON STATE RECREATIONAL PARK

This 1,000-acre park adjoins an 8,056-acre state forest and natural area, and together they constitute the largest reforested red cedar forest remaining in the country. Most of the reforesting occurred in the 1930's under WPA programs. "Red cedar" in this case is a misnomer, for the trees are actually junipers (*Juniperus virginiana*). Early settlers used this soft wood for everything from log cabins to roofing shingles. It splits easily, resists rot, and smells good. Moths will not infest woolens stored in cedar chests. Tennessee's pencil industry to the southwest of here came about because of the abundance of cedars.

In this park are cedar glades, places where the soil is too thin to support trees, even cedar trees. Prickly pear cactus and other unusual plants grow here, some of which—such as Guthrie's ground plum—are unique to this area. The **Merrit Nature Center** is open daily during summer.

Those whose interest in botany is confined to the grass on a playing field will find plenty to do in this park. Eight miles of hiking trails, 12 miles of horse trails, a large swimming pool, sports fields, and a Frisbee golf course await the visitor. Park-sponsored activities include summertime programs, evening movies, and organized games.

Nine housekeeping **cabins** that can sleep six are available for $90–100 a night. During the summer these must be rented for at least a week. A group lodge complete with kitchen can accommodate 40 people. For reservations, call 615/443-2769 or 888/867-2757. The park offers 119 **campsites**, all with picnic tables and grills; 89 have hookups. The campground is open all year, with sites available on a first-come, first-served basis. The park is six miles south of I-40 on U.S. 231. For further information, call 615/443-2769.

WATERTOWN

Due east of Cedars of Lebanon State Recreational Park lies Watertown, named for Wilson Waters, a Republican who freed his slaves before the Civil War. He founded the town on his farm, ran a store and a mill, and helped ensure that the railroad came through here.

It still does. Several times a year the **Tennessee Central Railway Museum** runs a train from Nashville to Watertown. For ticket information, call 615/244-9001. Passengers find a charming little square with period lighting, and a host of antique and art shops.

Many of the events in Watertown center occur when the excursion train from Nashville pulls into town. Among these are the following: **Mile-Long Yard Sale,** held in mid-April; **Swingin' Jazz Festival** in mid-July; **Fall Flea Market** and **Fall Foliage** in October; and **Christmas in the Country** in early December.

Practicalities

M Watertown Bed and Breakfast, just off the town square, (116 Depot Ave., 615/237-9999, www.bbonline.com/tn/watertown) occupies a railroad hotel built in 1898. Guests can relax on hammocks and swings on the upper and lower veranda. Inside, five guest rooms await, four upstairs and one down. Each bedroom has a private bath—two have whirlpools—but the ones upstairs share a shower. The downstairs room also has a private bath, but it is across the hall. Guests enjoy a library and board games, and the hosts serve a full breakfast. Rates range from $55 for the downstairs room to $125 for the whirlpool rooms.

Depot Junction Restaurant (108 Depot St., 615/237-3976) features a model train that chugs around the walls. Diners will find steak, seafood, country cooking, and homemade desserts. **Charlies** (406 Public Square, 615/237-9100) is a meat-and-three place serving lunch and dinner.

For tourist information, call 615/237-3318 or go to www.watertowntn.com.

Heartland

North of I-40

CARTHAGE

The Cumberland River downstream from Nashville isn't exactly straight, but upstream from Music City it becomes absolutely serpentine. This reflects the increasingly rugged terrain through which the river flows. These same hills made it difficult to build railroads and good roads, thus making riverboats the main form of transportation hereabouts long after railroads had vanquished them from larger rivers. Carthage was a major port on the Upper Cumberland, and one of the people who ran a fleet of packet boats, as they were called, was Thomas Ryman. Ryman fell under the influence of an evangelist and was inspired to build a building in Nashville for religious services. Originally named the Union Gospel Tabernacle, it is now known as Ryman Auditorium, the original home of the *Grand Ole Opry*.

Carthage was the home of the Albert Gores, a father and son who served as congressmen, senators, and, in the case of Al Gore Jr., vice president. The latter spent most of his time growing up in Washington, D.C., although he claims to be a Carthenagen at heart. The elder Senator Gore died December 5, 1998, at the age of 90.

Quite possibly the only place in the country still selling Gore-Lieberman campaign merchandise is on the town square here in the form of Markham's Department Store.

Tennessee has a wonderful bunch of odd community names, and two of them are northeast of here. Defeated and Difficult were used to describe a trip in which some pioneers engaged in 1786. The Indians were defeated and the trip was difficult. Thus the names.

Recreation and Events

Five miles up the Cumberland River from Carthage is **Cordell Hull Lake,** a Corps of Engineers project that was completed in 1973 and produces hydropower, extends river navigation as far as Celina, and offers an opportunity for recreation. This last benefit includes swimming, boat-

ing, picnicking, and hunting. The Cordell Hull **visitors center** at the dam (615/735-1034) features exhibits on the animals of Middle Tennessee as well as explanations of hydropower. To get there, take Hwy. 233 north from Carthage.

Smith County Fall Heritage Festival, held on the town square in October, offers a pleasant combination of arts and crafts, demonstrations of blacksmithing and other old-time activities, and good food.

Practicalities

B&B Drive-In (421 Cookeville Hwy., 615/735-9657) has, according to one regular, "the best steak and grilled chicken you have ever put your teeth into." This used to be one of the hangouts of Al Gore Jr.

La Villa (67 Dixon Springs Hwy., 615/735-1331) offers one of the bigger menus to be found in these parts. Diners can choose among hickory-smoked barbecue, catfish, oysters on the half shell, ribs, steak, burgers, and country ham.

The **Country Courtyard Restaurant** (4 E. Main St., 615/683-6441) features a country cooking buffet as well as a full menu. The **Timber Loft Restaurant** (I-40 and Hwy. 53 interchange, 615/683-8697) offers a buffet of traditional Southern cooking.

For more information, contact **Smith County Chamber of Commerce** (130 W. 3rd Ave., 615/735-2093, www.smithcountychamber.org). Another source of information is the rest area on I-40 between Exits 258 and 268.

GAINESBORO

An early account of the "long hunters" who first explored Middle Tennessee tells of a party of men from French Lick—today's Nashville—killing 105 bears, 75 buffalo, and 80 deer near here.

Gainesboro is the seat of Jackson County, and visitors can see artifacts from riverboating days at the **Jackson County Museum,** (931/268-0971) which occupies a building on Montpelier that once housed the local newspaper—just down the street from the courthouse.

"Sock a little poke sallet to me," sang Elvis. "I need me a mess of it." He could eat his fill at the **Poke Sallet Festival** (931/268-3447), held on the first weekend in May. This three-day event features all-you-can-eat poke sallet, a.k.a. poke-weed, which has leaves that, when boiled three or four times and adorned with vinegar, butter, and bits of bacon, are downright good.

EXTRATERRESTRIAL IMPACT

S outh of Gainesboro lies one of the interesting geological features of Tennessee. The **Flynn Creek Crater** is all that is left of a meteor that hit more than 360 million years ago. Unlike the round Barringer Crater in Arizona or similar un-mistakable craters on the moon, this crater has eroded, making it hard to see exactly what hap-pened here.

The Flynn Creek crater is 2.2 miles across, and 0.3 cubic miles of rock was ejected when the meteor hit. The limestone in this part of Tennessee has flat layers, and the force of the impact was such that on the edges of the crater the stone now tilts at a 30-degree angle.

No humans were around when the meteor hit, but much later the Cherokee dragged out chunks of rock and made arrowheads from them. A local amateur scientist who has studied the crater says that rocks on the rim have a high level of radiation.

To get to the crater from Gainesboro, go 8.8 miles south from the intersection of Montpelier Street and Hwy. 56. Turn right on Flynn's Creek Road, which is about 100 yards north of the Hwy. 56/290 intersection, and go west. After about one mile, a steep descent marks the edge of the crater. After going about 4.5 miles, visitors will see a marker with information about the crater. Across the creek one can easily see the stone angled down by the impact. Driving another mile takes the motorist to the center of the crater.

NASA has studied the Flynn Creek Crater, as have various geologists, but it appears to have drawn little attention from locals.

Other activities include an outhouse race, music, and crafts.

Near Gainesboro is the little community of Whitleyville, the home of **Freestone Pottery** (707 N. Fork Ln., 931/621-3456, www.free-stonepottery.com), wherein potters Tom and Sally Freestone create plates and other items adorned with Bible verses and hand-painted flower designs. To visit their studio, call ahead. Freestone pottery is also sold at Gainesboro Drugs on the square in Gainesboro.

RED BOILING SPRINGS

Of the places in Tennessee where people would come to "take the waters," this was one of the more successful. It all started, according to local lore, when a pioneer who had some sort of eye problem bathed in the waters here and over time was healed. Word spread and others came, and the first hotel was built just before the Civil War. In those days the water came out of the ground in artesian wells, but before long so many man-made wells were dug that the arte-sian pressure diminished.

Things really got rolling, so to speak, with the coming of the railroad to nearby Hartsville at the turn of the last century. By 1918 the town had four hotels, and fewer than 10 years later it had eight hotels and more than a dozen board-inghouses. Guests could partake of five kinds of water: Red, Black, and White were so named for the color they would turn a silver coin. Free-stone was said to have no minerals at all, while Double and Twist, the most memorable variety, got its name from a gastrointestinal effect so in-tense that it caused the drinker to double over and writhe on the ground.

Guests not occupied with doubling and twist-ing the night away could go dancing, bowling, roller-skating, or swimming, play tennis or shuf-fleboard, or choose from an assortment of baths, massages, and electrotherapy. Entertainer Dinah Shore came here as a girl, and the hotels catered to luminaries from Tennessee and elsewhere.

The same factors—the automobile and the Depression—that killed off other resorts did their work here. A flood in 1969 devastated the

Heartland

town, but the federal money that flowed in afterward mitigated some of the damage. Two covered bridges were built over the stream.

Luckily, two of the old hotels remain, and people still come here to take the waters, which is available from hand pumps throughout the town. Some just come to get away. One of the ways to begin is a **mineral bath and massage** (615/699-2180, $59 one-hour treatment, bath, and massage), available only at Armours, one of the old hotels. The best sources of information here are the two inns or at City Hall (166 Dale St., 615/699-2011, www.redboilingsprings.com).

In 2001, the Perrier Group of America, now doing business as Nestle Waters North America, Inc., bought the Bennett Hill Spring hereabouts and began bottling Nestle Pure Life Purified Water, which contains local water as well as some hauled in from North Georgia and Hohenwald, Tennessee.

Accommodations

Built in 1924, **Armours** (321 E. Main St., 615/699-2180, www.armourshotel.com, rooms cost $59 per person and include dinner and breakfast) was the first brick hotel in town. Now its 26 rooms have period furnishings and air-conditioning. This place is run by the founder of the Folk Medicine Festival, who makes it a point to introduce guests to each other. Another hotel owner in town said, "We are educating a whole generation of people about a slower pace of life, rocking on a front porch, taking time to talk to people, and making new friends. We see a lot of creative people from Nashville—songwriters, singers, and producers—who come here to take it easy."

The building that now houses the **Thomas House** (520 E. Main St., 615/699-3006, $95 d) was built in 1890 from bricks baked in ovens behind the building but had a devastating fire in 2002. The wood inside is chestnut that was cut on the property. Guests now have a choice of 15 rooms, instead of the old 27, all with private baths. Additional rooms display toys, Christmas decorations, and antique clothing, and an antiques store is on the premises. This inn used to have a great library, but burned as well. Outside

is a swimming pool and tennis court. Smoking is outside only. Rates include dinner and breakfast. Sunday is buffet all day.

Food

Armours (321 E. Main St., 615/699-2180) serves family-style meals of country cooking year-round. Breakfast, lunch, and dinner are by reservation only. Meals here "recall Red Boiling Springs's boardinghouse days," said the owner. "People talk about themselves and what they have been doing."

The **Thomas House** (520 E. Main St., 615/699-3006) also serves all three meals by reservation only. Country cooking is the fare, and on most nights the hotel features live entertainment. The innkeeper does a great Patsy Cline.

Shopping

Quilts and More (310 Milltown Ln., 615/699-2460) has 50–100 machine-quilted quilts on hand at any given time.

Newberry and Sons Chairs (1593 Jennings Creek Rd., 615/699-3755, www.newberryandsonschairs.com) are fifth-generation chairmakers in the community of Willette. They fashion chairs out of oak, walnut, and cherry wood, and they put woven hickory bark bottoms and backs on some of them. They make rocking chairs, dining room chairs, baby rockers, and high chairs. The Newberrys live right beside the shop, which they will open about any time.

To get there from Red Boiling Springs, head south on Hwy. 56 and go about five miles to Gibbs Crossroads, then turn east on Highway 56/262 (Willette Road). Go two miles to Highland Rim Truck Parts, a gas station. Here the road splits. Bear left on Hwy. 56 and go 1.5 miles to a gray building with a sign out front.

LAFAYETTE

This town, the seat of Macon County, contains Key Park, a dandy place for a picnic. A half block west of the town square, the four-acre park contains an 1824 log cabin housing the chamber of commerce. Those seeking an anthropological experience should head for the southeast corner of the public square, where a group of men gather on pleasant days to whittle and talk. These gentlemen are repositories of local lore, have opinions on a wide range of topics, and delight in telling lies to each other and to impressionable visitors.

Lafayette has produced two noteworthies. State Senator John Butler introduced the bill making it illegal to teach the theory of evolution in Tennessee, the passage of which led to the Scopes Trial in Dayton. In 1992, Nera White became the first woman to be inducted into the National Basketball Hall of Fame. Teams on which she played won 11 Amateur Athletic Union Championships—eight of them in a row. White played for the USA All-Star team and led it to victories. She was named Most Valuable Player at the 1957 World Games.

A first-class piano restoration establishment is about as rare in these parts as a metaphysics bookstore. The **Piano Store and More** (102 Public Square, 615/666-5706) is such a place. Step in here to see player pianos and others coming back to musical life.

Hillbilly Day (615/666-5885), held the first weekend in June, begins with a Friday night all-you-can-eat catfish fry, then rolls into Saturday with music competitions in guitar, mandolin, and other instruments; buck dancing; and singing. Crafts and food are available as well. For information, look to the **Macon County Chamber of Commerce** (208 Church St., 615/666-5885, www.maconcountytennessee.com).

HARTSVILLE

Trousdale County farmers have long grown a lot of tobacco, and the **Trousdale County Living History Museum** (White Oak St., 615/374-9243, free) shows how those 19th-century folks lived. Local buildings have been brought to Hartsville and organized to resemble a working tobacco farm.

Across the street is the restored depot, whose oldest section was completed in 1892. Inside is the **Depot Museum** (615/374-9243). which contains an antique harpsichord, Civil War pictures, and other relics from the town and surrounding area. In the days of segregation, black and white passengers bought train tickets from separate windows, examples of which visitors can see here. To visit the museum, call the chamber of commerce.

Just west of town stands a monument to one of the biggest failures of the Tennessee Valley Authority. An enormous concrete cooling tower marks the spot of the **Hartsville nuclear power plant,** which was conceived in the '60s as the agency embarked on the largest nuclear building program in the world. TVA vastly underestimated the costs of the project and vastly overestimated the demand for electricity, and the 17-reactor program had to be cut back. Billions of dollars were wasted, many of them here, where TVA had planned a four-reactor plant that would have been the world's largest. A beautiful view is spoiled daily by this example of agency hubris.

If you're staying overnight, the **Williams Motel** (782 McMurray Blvd., 615/374-2589) has rooms for $35 a night. **Dillehay's Cafe** (102 E. Main St., 615/374-2069) serves country cooking. Plate lunches are the specialty here. Find **Trousdale County Chamber of Commerce** (615/374-9243, www.hartsvilletrousdale.com) on the second floor of the Trousdale County Courthouse.

OLD HIGHWAY 25 WEST TO GALLATIN

Old State Highway 25 parallels the more modern Hwy. 25 through here, and motorists should stay on the older road as much as possible to enjoy a slower pace and a chance to look at some historic homes.

Castalian Springs

Heading from east to west, the traveler comes to the springs, an old salt lick that has been the scene of human habitation for more than 17,000 years. Evidence suggests that roving Ice Age people first came here about 15,000 B.C. Present-day visitors can see Indian mounds circa A.D. 1400 north of Hwy. 25 near the post office in this hamlet.

Castalian Springs was one of the first settlements in Middle Tennessee. When pioneers first came here, there were so many buffalo milling around that the visitors were afraid to get off their horses. Thomas Spencer arrived in 1777 and lived in a large hollow sycamore tree nine feet in diameter.

Ⓜ Wynnewood

This log structure to the south of Old Hwy. 25, 615/452-5463, is thought to be the largest log structure ever built in the state—142 feet long. Some of the logs are 32 feet long, and one can only imagine the effort it took to move and position these huge pieces of oak, walnut, and ash. Built in 1828 along with a racecourse, it served as a stagecoach inn and mineral springs resort. Among the guests was Andrew Jackson, who came to race horses. Admission is $3 for adults, $4 for seniors, $3 for kids 12–18, $0.50 for children under 12. They are closed January–March.

Bledsoe's Fort Historical Park

Across the road from Wynnewood lies this park. Most of the original settlements in Middle Tennessee became the centers of towns, and their sites have long since drowned in asphalt and concrete. Not this one. Of the 12 settlements that made up the Cumberland Compact, the agreement that originally governed Middle Tennessee, this is the only one whose original site is preserved. The land has been grazed for 200 years, and an old cabin stands here. Archaeological diggings have produced artifacts on display at the Sumner County Museum in Gallatin. Bledsoe's Fort is not open on a regular basis, but efforts were under way to offer tours. For information, call Wynnewood (615/452-5463) or simply cross the road and ask.

Just east of Bledsoe's Fort, a large Indian mound rises in the field. It is assumed this is a burial mound.

Cragfont

Cragfont, north of Hwy. 25 East, is as elegant as Wynnewood is rustic. General James Winchester, a Maryland native, brought craftsmen from Baltimore to the frontier to build him a showplace. Beginning work in 1798, the builders cut poplar, walnut, cherry, and ash lumber from trees on the property and quarried limestone for the exterior walls.

Every other structure in the area was made of logs, so Cragfont quickly became the finest house in Middle Tennessee. Among its guests were Andrew Jackson, Sam Houston, and the Marquis de Lafayette, the French hero of the American Revolution.

The house is furnished with authentic American Federal antiques, including some pieces owned by the Winchester family. The basement of the house contains displays of farm and carpentry tools and a weaving room. Cragfont is open April 15–October. Those wishing to see the house November 1–April 14 should call 615/452-7070. Admission is $5 for adults and $3 for children under 12.

Bledsoe Creek State Park

One of the smaller parks in the Tennessee system, this 164-acre area lies on a backwater of the Cumberland River. Once prime hunting ground for Indian tribes, it now offers hiking, camping, and lake access for visitors. The park has 126 campsites, all with hookups and access to hot showers, and is open all year. For further information about the park, call 615/452-3706 or visit www.tnstateparks.com.

GALLATIN

This town earned a place in Tennessee's musical history as the home of Randy's Record Shop, at one time the largest mail-order record store in the country. By advertising on Nashville's WLAC, Randy Wood cornered the market on rhythm and blues records, introducing Chuck Berry and Bo Diddley to predominantly white audiences. In 1950, Wood opened Dot Records, a label that recorded Pat Boone, Billy Vaughn, and the Fontaine Sisters. The store closed in 1991.

Sights

The **Historic Walking Tour** of the town, described in a brochure available from the chamber of commerce, shows off the town's treasures. First among them is **Trousdale Place** (185 W.

Main St., 615/452-5648, $3 adults, $2.50 seniors, $1 children 12–18, $0.50 for children
6–11). Two blocks from the Gallatin public
square, this brick home was built in 1813 by
John Bowen, a member of Congress. After his
death the property was bought by William
Trousdale, who served alongside Andrew Jackson
at Pensacola and New Orleans in the War of
1812 and later in the Seminole War of 1836.
He served in the Tennessee Senate and became
the state's governor in 1849.

Adjacent to Trousdale Place is the **Sumner
County Museum** (183 W. Main St., 615/451-
3738, Apr.–Oct. 9 A.M.–4:30 P.M. Wed.–Sat.,
$3 for adults, $1 children 6–12, $0.50 for chil-
dren under 6), whose 10,000 square feet feature
a collection that begins with Indian pots, tools,
and weapons and then moves into pioneer days
and more recent times. There extensive exhibits
from the civil war to the Vietnam conflict. Also,
there is an automotive exhibit that covers from
1900s to the 1940s. Visitors can see a black man-
tilla that belonged to Andrew Jackson's wife
Rachel, a tinsmith shop, a woodworker's shop, a
blacksmith's shop, and a few Dot records.

The **Palace Theater** (142 N. Water St.) is the
oldest movie theater in the state. Opened in
1913, its silver screen showed the best of Hollywood until 1977. Renovated and reopened, it
serves the community theater as well as cinema
lovers.

Main Street Festival, held the first Saturday in
October, offers music, food, and arts and crafts.

Practicalities

Hancock House (2144 Nashville Pike, 800/242-
6738 or 615/452-8431, www.bbonline.com/
tn/hancock, $100–200) occupies a log building
that served as a stagecoach stop and tollhouse
beginning about 1878. The inn has seven bedrooms, one of which is a cabin, and all have private baths. Each room contains period antiques,
fireplace, refrigerator, telephone, coffeemaker,
and television. Three rooms have whirlpools.
They also have a separate large house for longer-
term rental. Call ahead to arrange a special
party/engagement.

Motel options are **Comfort Inn** (354 Sumner

Hall Dr., 800/228-5150), or **Shoney's Inn** (221 W.
Main St., 800/222-2222 or 615/452-5433).

Cages Bend Campground, (615/824-4989,
Apr.–mid-Oct.) eight miles southwest on U.S. 31
East, has 49 sites but no hookups.

El Rey Mexican Restaurant (450 Cherokee
Dock Rd., 615/230-7422) offers chiles rellenos,
huevos rancheros, and the real stuff.

Gallatin has a great many antique stores. One
of the larger ones is **Antiques on Main,** a mall
containing about 200 dealers. Here are furniture, books, Civil War items, and much more.

The place to find information about the town
is the **Gallatin Chamber of Commerce** (118
W. Main St., 615/452-4000, www.gallatintn.org).

HENDERSONVILLE

This town was so small that it received no listing in the 1939 *WPA Guide to Tennessee*. This
changed when the Army Corps of Engineers
dammed the Cumberland River in the 1950s
to create Old Hickory Lake. The town's population grew, and within two decades Hendersonville became the largest town in the
county. Country music stars built some of the
bigger homes.

Historic Houses

The tradition of building big homes began in
1784, when Daniel and Sarah Smith moved here
to claim land that the state of North Carolina
had given to Daniel for his work as a surveyor. He
planned a grand home, then took off on one of
his long surveying trips and left the supervision of
the construction to Sarah, who had to cope with
two children and Indian attacks along with the
usual headaches of building a house.

The result, **Rock Castle** (615/824-0502,
www.historicrockcastle.cjb.net, $5 adults, $4 seniors, $3 children 6–12), on Rock Castle Lane off
Indian Lake Road, is a prime example of the
"glorified pioneer style," which combined Georgian and Federal architecture styles. The house
was built from limestone and wood that came
from the grounds. Inside, it has unusual floor-to-
ceiling black walnut cabinets as well as a few of
the original pieces of furniture.

Heartland

The Hendersonville Arts Council has its offices in **Monthaven** (1154 W. Main St., 615/822-0789). This Greek revival house, which contains Haven Gifts, was built around 1860.

Trinity City

Several country music stars have homes in Hendersonville, including Garth Brooks. The first country artist to open his house to the public was Conway Twitty, a rock 'n' roller turned country musician whose "Twitty City" proved a hit with fans. Twitty died in 1993, and Twitty City was sold to the Trinity Broadcasting Network, which now calls the place Trinity Music City, U.S.A. (1 Music Village Blvd., 615/826-9191).

The Trinity Network produces programs for more than 500 television stations and offers two options for visitors. The first is an overall tour of the operations beginning with the gift shop, an auditorium that looks like a transplanted European opera house, the LaVerne Tripp Ministries Recording studio, Twitty's mansion, and a memorial garden. Admission is free for this tour and any other presentation at Trinity. If a television show is being taped that day, visitors are welcome to watch. Admission is free.

The second option begins with a re-creation of the Via Dolorosa, the Jerusalem streets through which Jesus carried his cross. This leads into a theater in which a short film describes the work done at Trinity. From there it's off to a larger theater, billed as a "Virtual Reality Theater." The theater shows a movie about Jesus titled *The Revolutionary*, and during the showing the seats shake and viewers are bombarded by sound from a host of speakers. This film is shown hourly on the half-hour.

A gift shop offers Twitty items, Bibles and books, T-shirts, souvenirs from Israel, and porcelain art objects. Trinity is open every night late October–January 1 until 9 P.M., when the place is lit up with an estimated million light bulbs. Inside, *Christmas Around the World* plays daily.

As Conway Twitty views these latest developments from the great beyond, this incarnation of the former Twitty City must bring a smile to the man who went to number one with a song called "You've Never Been This Far Before."

Entertainment and Events

The Bell Cove Club (151 Sunset Dr., 615/822-7074) sits on the shore of Old Hickory Lake and is the best place to hear music in this area. Friday and Saturday are showcases for bands, which may be rock, blues, or country. Sunday brings Songwriters Grill-Outs 2–8 P.M., with tunesmiths offering their best work.

B.R.A.S.S. (615/824-2818) stands for Bike Ride across Scenic Sumner County, a series of rides that take place on the third weekend in August. The longest ride is 75 miles long.

Practicalities

Motel options are the **Hendersonville Inn** (179 W. Main St., 615/822-4240), and the **Holiday Inn** (615 E. Main St., 800/HOLIDAY [465-4329] or 615/824-0022).

Center Point Bar-B-Que (1212 W. Main St., 615/824-9330) is so named because it is close to the center point between Nashville and Gallatin. Now it's the home of pork and chicken barbecue. Try the dry ribs and homemade pecan pie. **Fortune House** (410 Main St., 615/824-2006) offers the finest in Tennessee Mandarin cooking.

Closer to Nashville, **The Shack** (2420 Gallatin Rd., Madison, 615/859-9777) is the sort of place where diners eat roasted peanuts and throw the shells on the floor while waiting on prime rib and seafood and chicken dishes.

Find information at the **Hendersonville Area Chamber of Commerce** (101 Wessington Pl., 615/824-2818, www.hendersonvillechamber.com).

EAST OF I-65

White House

White House Inn Library and Historical Museum (412 Hwy. 76, 615/672-0239, www.cityofwhitehouse.com, Mon.–Sat., free) was built as a replica of the White House Inn, a 1796 structure that provided the name for this little community. The museum contains memorabilia of the town, a spinning wheel, a still, farming implements, and old photographs. For a place to stay, try **Days Inn** (1009 Hwy. 76, 800/325-2525 or 615/672-3746).

Portland

Portland is big strawberry country and home of country artists Roy Drusky and Ronnie McDowell. The **Strawberry Festival** (615/325-9032) takes place on the third weekend in May.

Cold Springs School Museum (615/325-6029, Sunday afternoons in summer, free) is a restored school built in 1857. When the Civil War broke out, it became the main building for Camp Trousdale and later a Confederate hospital. After the war it was used as a church and then became a school once more. The museum contains community artifacts and pictures of the various schoolteachers who presided here. For more information, call **Portland Chamber of Commerce** (111 S. Broadway, 615/325-9032).

North of Nashville

CROSS PLAINS

This charming village is the home of **Thomas Drugs** (615/654-3877), which has been in business at the four-way stop since 1930. The surrounding populace still uses it as a drugstore, and visitors will delight in the old-fashioned soda fountain. Here one can sit at the fountain and order a phosphate, egg cream, or milk shake, or go whole-hog with a banana split. It also serves burgers and sandwiches. Unlike the folks at so many eateries these days, the people at Thomas Drugs will talk to customers, asking from where they have come and telling them about the area. The drugstore features the products of local artists and craftspeople.

West of Cross Plains is **Carr's Wild Horse/Burro Center** (615/654-2180), which serves as an adoption station for thousands of wild horses and burros that come from Western states for new homes in the East. Here as many as 250 animals—the overwhelming majority are horses, which cost only $125—await new owners. More than 17,000 horses and burros have come through this place, which welcomes visitors. To get to the center, go 1.1 miles north on Couts Road and follow the signs. The center is open only once a month.

Around the corner from Thomas Drugs is **G. Skippers Antiques,** (4604 E. Robinson St., 615/654-3307) which sells furniture and glassware.

SPRINGFIELD

This county seat is the home of two traditional Tennessee products—tobacco and whiskey. The former is still a mainstay of the economy, while the latter is only a memory.

Much of the tobacco grown hereabouts is cured in heated barns and called "dark-fired" to distinguish it from air-cured leaves. Plantations around here have grown the tobacco since before the Civil War, and in the early 1900s the "Black Patch Tobacco War" erupted over pricing. The larger growers banded together in an association to force a rise in prices they were offered. The American Tobacco Company, which bought most of the local product, tried to break the association's power by enticing small farmers to sell at an artificially high price.

Many of these farmers willingly accepted the higher paychecks, and this brought on nighttime visits from the "Silent Brigade," an organization that used Klanlike whippings, barn burnings, and destruction of tobacco fields. Unlike the Klan, however, black farmers belonged to the association and may have even taken part in the nocturnal activities. Several people died in the struggle, which ended when the tobacco company gave in and agreed to buy leaves only from association members.

Were it not for Prohibition, Robertson County might be as famous as Lynchburg. At one time more than 75 whiskey makers operated here, but none of them survived the passage of the 18th Amendment.

If you're hungry, **Torino's Greek and Italian Restaurant** (1701 Memorial Blvd., 615/384-6548) features dishes such as gyro platters and chicken Alfredo that reflect the two great food traditions that come together here. For more in-

Heartland

formation, contact the **Springfield-Robertson County Chamber of Commerce** (100 5th Ave. W, 615/384-3800).

GOODLETTSVILLE

This town, now a part of Nashville's sprawl, played an important role in the settling of Middle Tennessee. Kasper Mansker was one of the "long hunters"—so named because their hunting trips took them away from home for long periods of time—who first came here in 1772. The game was reportedly so thick that he killed 19 deer in one day, and he resolved to come back and settle here. He did so in 1779–80, building a fort for protection, but the pressure from the Indians was so great that he abandoned it and moved to the more secure area of Fort Nashborough. His second fort, built in 1782, was called Mansker's Station, and it provided the nucleus for the settlement that eventually became Goodlettsville.

Sights

Those interested in learning more about this should steer for **Mansker's Fort** (615/859-3678, http://manskers.historicalifestyles.com, 9 A.M.–5 P.M. Mon.–Sat., 1–5 P.M. Sun., $5 adults, $4 seniors, $3 children) in Moss-Wright Park off Caldwell Lane. This reproduction of the first settlement in Goodlettsville is about one-third the size of the original and is staffed by people who dress and act as if they were living in 1779. The tour begins at the **Bowen Plantation House,** the oldest brick house in Middle Tennessee. Now it contains period furniture, and here guests see a video that introduces Mansker's Station.

A walk down the hill brings the visitor to the reconstructed fort. Inside are a blacksmith's shop, a tannery, and a tavern. This is living history, not a museum, so guests can go up the stairs and pick up any implements they see. Usually at least three reenactors are on hand, and on special occasions as many as 300 swarm over the place. These gatherings take place in March, during the Colonial Fair in early May; on the Fourth of July; and in September, Oc-

tober, and December. Admission is $3 for adults and $2 for students.

The historic **Stone Arch Bridge** lies off U.S. 41. Go north past the place where the road goes under the railroad. Directly across the road from a KOA campground is a road leading into the Old Stone Bridge Industrial Park. Turn into the park and then go left onto a dirt road, which leads to the bridge. This structure is said to contain no mortar.

Entertainment and Events

The **Long Hollow Jamboree** (3600 Long Hollow Pike, 615/824-4445) presents live music on Tuesday, Friday, and Saturday nights. Usually it's country on Saturday, bluegrass on Friday, and open-mike on Tuesday.

Rook is a Southern card game in which "getting the bird" is not an affront. A **Rook Tournament** takes place in Goodlettsville during the first weekend in May.

The **18th-Century Colonial Fair** is a trip back in time to the 1750–90 days. Every event is juried, attracting the best in crafts, merchants, and reenactors. This is the place to buy colonial furniture, weapons, and leather goods, or to watch blacksmiths, hear music of that time, and enjoy the beggars, trollops, long hunters, and Indians. It's held for two days in May at Mansker's Station.

The **Fall Fiddlin' Jamboree** is a three-day event that takes place the third weekend in October and features competitions, food, and crafts.

For more information, contact the **Goodlettsville Chamber of Commerce** (100 S. Main St., 615/859-7979, www.goodlettsvillechamber.com, 8 A.M.–4:30 P.M., Mon.–Fri.).

Shopping

Antique-lovers can spend a long time on North Main Street in Goodlettsville. Among the antique stores are the Main Street Antique Mall, Antique Corner Mall, Goodlettsville Antique Mall, Sweet Memories, and others.

Quilter's Attic (126 N. Main St., 615/859-5603) usually has 10–20 quilts, 1,500 bolts of cloth, and 300–400 books on hand at any given time. It also carries quilting notions and rug-hooking supplies.

Northwest of Nashville

ASHLAND CITY

Many towns in these parts came into being because the Cumberland River eased the transportation of people and goods. Ashland City, by contrast, was founded in a place where the river refused to cooperate. Steamboats on the Cumberland ran aground at a shallow place called the Harpeth Shoals and were obliged to unload their cargo, steam past the shoals, then load everything up again. A community grew up there, was ambitiously dubbed a city, and remains a pleasant place to visit. A dam and set of locks solved the shoals headache in 1907, and these were replaced by a newer dam in 1950. The locks lie 12 miles northwest of town.

Bridge fanciers should drive northeast of town about three or four miles on Highway 49. Just as the road crosses Sycamore Creek, a gaze to the right will reveal the last remaining 1800s cable-stayed bridge in the country. The bridge led to a gunpowder works that for a time served the Confederacy.

Pat Head Summitt, who coaches the Lady Vols basketball team at the University of Tennessee, grew up in Montgomery County and should have gone to Clarksville High School. That school, however, had no girls' basketball team, so her family moved across the line into neighboring Cheatham County, in the little community of Henrietta on Hwy. 12, so she could play on the girls' basketball team at Cheatham County High School in Ashland City. The future coach graduated from UT-Martin and played on the 1976 U.S. Olympic team, which won a silver medal. She then became the first and only head coach of the Lady Vols and has led them to a record number of women's NCAA championships.

Ashland City is the birthplace of Redd Stewart, country music vocalist and cowriter of "The Tennessee Waltz," perhaps the most famous song with Tennessee in the title. Cheatham County is also the birthplace of Amos and Gale Binkley, prominent members of an early *Grand Ole Opry* band called the Dixie Clodhoppers.

The **Cumberland River Bicentennial Trail,** once a railway, is now a 6.5 mile trail ideal for hiking, biking, or horseback riding. To get there from downtown Ashland City, take Hwy. 12 South through Main Street. Turn left after the bridge by Deerfield Inn.

Practicalities

El Rey Restaurante Mexicano (104 S. Main St., 615/792-1330) offers authentic Mexican food. **Bill's Catfish** (1.5 miles south of town on Hwy. 12, 615/792-9193) features catfish, its own barbecue, steaks, seafood, and chicken. **Stratton's Restaurant and Soda Shop** (201 S. Main St., 615/792-9177) has great burgers and fries and other fast food, all offered in a 1950s atmosphere. **River View Restaurant and Marina** (across the river from town on Hwy. 49, 615/792-7358) offers diners a view of the passing river traffic while they enjoy steak, chicken, and seafood dishes.

Ashland City boasts a string of antique shops along Main Street. Among them is **B. J.s Attic,** (108 N. Main St., 615/792-7208) offering primarily furniture. For more information, contact the **Cheatham County Chamber of Commerce** (605A N. Main St., 615/792-6722, www.cheathamchamber.org).

ADAMS AND VICINITY

The Bell Witch is this town's claim to fame, and visitors in search of this phantom should head immediately for The **Bell Witch Cave** (615/696-3055, www.bellwitchcave.com, May–Oct. 10 A.M.–5 P.M. daily, $7, free for children 5 and under), which can be reached by driving 0.7 mile south of town on Keysburg Road, then turning right at the sign and going 0.3 mile.

The cave has the usual unusual formations, but the operators note that curious events take place here as well. Weird noises are allegedly heard in the cave—a screen door creaking open or mysterious voices. Sometimes cameras refuse to function. They also have the John Bell log

Heartland

THE BELL WITCH

Tennessee's most famous supernatural figure is the Bell Witch, an apparition who is never seen but whose presence is keenly felt. According to a long account in *WPA Guide to Tennessee*, the Bell family moved near Adams from North Carolina in 1804. They bought some property from a cantankerous neighbor, one Kate Batts, who later claimed she had been cheated in the transaction, and who on her dying day swore she would come back and "hant John Bell and all his kith and kin to their graves."

That's when things got lively in the Bell household. No one ever saw the witch or ghost or whatever she was, but she made her presence felt in constant mischief. She threw furniture and dishes, pulled the Bell family's noses and hair, poked them with needles, and yelled all night to keep them from sleeping.

As if that weren't enough, the witch attended local revivals, where she sang loudly and out-shouted the other participants. Not overly pious, she would sometimes raid moonshiners' stills and come back to the Bell household to create more of an uproar than usual.

Andrew Jackson, he who had fought duels and the British, came up from Nashville with some friends to dispatch this terror. As the story is told, the Jacksonian ghostbusters rolled up to the Bell farm in a wagon whose wheel suddenly stopped and refused to turn. Jackson's cursing and mules straining produced nothing. Then a voice called out, "All right, General, the wagon can move on." And it did.

That night the witch further entertained the party by singing, swearing, throwing dishes, over-turning furniture, and yanking the covers off everyone. After a sleepless night, Jackson left early for home, telling John Bell, "I'd rather fight the British again than have any more dealings with that torment."

The Bell Witch was heard from no more when John Bell died. His farmhouse was eventually razed, and since then, to the intense frustration of local boosters, the witch has yet to put in an appearance.

cabin and tours can be had for $5. Canoes can be rented on the weekend. They are open on the weekends of May, September, and October and in Wednesday–Monday through June–April.

Northwest of Adams on U.S. 41 lies **Red River Valley Canoeing** (615/696-2768), an enterprise offering canoes, camping, and the occasional country music concert.

Entertainment and Events

The nightlife in town centers on the **Bell Witch Opry** (no phone, www.bellwitchfansite.com), a gathering of local talent that performs every Saturday night in the local school. The music is mostly bluegrass and country and the stage is open, as one regular put it, "to anyone who wants to pick and grin and sing." Occasionally someone gets up and belts out a classical piece, but not too often. Shows take place Saturday 7:30–10:30 P.M.

The threshing of wheat and other grains—separating the grains from the rest of the plant—was a special time on Tennessee farms. Aside from railroad locomotives, threshing machines were the most impressive pieces of machinery that most country people ever saw. Most farmers did not own threshing machines, so someone who owned one of these behemoths would come to process their grain. A threshing crew, often made up of neighboring farmers, would arrive in the fields to do the work. Older threshing machines were powered by steam and rolled from farm to farm on massive steel wheels, belching smoke all the way. Women cooked huge meals to serve the crews, and the whole time was one of great excitement.

A sense of those days pervades the annual **Tennessee-Kentucky Threshermen's Show,** (615/696-2721) held in Adams in mid-July, when antique threshers, steam engines, and tractors are brought together. A tractor pull and a mule pull, arts and crafts, dancing, music, and storytelling are also included.

The **Bell Witch Bluegrass Festival and Arts and Crafts Show** (615/696-2593) is held in August. The name says it all.

Port Royal State Historical Area

Port Royal was once a thriving little town on the Red River, upstream from Clarksville. From here goods were shipped as far away as New Orleans. At one time local entrepreneurs tried to launch a silk business, planting thousands of mulberry trees to fuel the silkworms, but one of the organizers who was sent to England to buy machinery absconded with the money.

The covered bridge washed out, and now sits on the bank amid 34 acres. The result is a beautiful little park for walking and picnicking. A museum keeps the memory of Port Royal alive. Admission is free, and the park (931/358-9696, www .tnstateparks.com) is open 8 A.M. until sundown.

Clarksville and Vicinity

Downstream from and northwest of Nashville, Clarksville long benefited from its location at the confluence of the Red and Cumberland Rivers, and today long barges still stop at the "Queen City" to do business. Tennessee's fifth-largest city, like Rome, is built on seven hills, and those out for a stroll can readily get their hearts pumping. One of the areas in town bears the name Dog Hill Architectural District. It seems that the local canines would howl whenever a steamboat or train blew its whistle.

In the downtown area lies the River District. Adjacent to the River District is the Riverwalk, a symbol of Clarksville's rediscovery of its riverfront. On the north end are a playground and parking lot, which were to be joined by a river master's house, an amphitheater, and floating courtesy docks where boats can tie up. Plans for the southern end of the park called for a bell tower and pedestrian overpass above Riverside Drive. The Clarksville Area Chamber of Commerce offers a brochure giving routes for walking and driving tours of the city.

Tennessee grows a lot of tobacco, and the variety hereabouts, cured in heated barns, is called "dark-fired" to distinguish it from the air-cured version produced farther east. Used in smokeless tobacco products and cigars, this crop is so economically important that the local newspaper is named the *Leaf Chronicle,* and Clarksville tobacco warehouses sell more than five million dollars' worth of the plant per year.

The city is more famous as the home of the late Wilma Rudolph, the first female runner to win three gold medals in an Olympics. As recounted in her autobiography, *Wilma,* her story is impressive. Childhood illnesses left her with a paralyzed leg, and at age six she could only hop. The little girl persevered, and she eventually competed in the 1956 and 1960 Olympics, winning her three medals in the latter. Rudolph died in 1993. Frank Sutton, a local boy who played Sergeant Carter on television's *Gomer Pyle, USMC,* was also from Clarksville and is buried there.

Clarksville is home to **Austin Peay State University** (931/648-7876, www.apsu.edu), which educates more than 7,000 students and brings a variety of cultural events to town.

SIGHTS

Historic Buildings

The flamboyant building containing the **Customs House Museum and Cultural Center** (200 S. 2nd St., 931/648-5780, www .customshousemuseum.org, 10 A.M.–5 P.M. Tues.–Sat., 1–5 P.M. Sun., $4 adults, $3 seniors, $2 college students, $1 for ages 6–18, free on Sunday) was built as a post office and customs house in 1898. Exhibits feature quilts and coverlets, military matters, and a Victorian small-town avenue. They also have local art, math and science, model train, bohem porcelain, and a sports gallery.

The **Smith/Trahern Mansion** (1st and McClure Sts., 931/648-9998, $1 adults, free for children and students) was built in 1858 for a wealthy tobacco merchant and features a widow's

Heartland

Heartland

walk, a lovely curved staircase, and period furniture. The house is often rented for weddings and parties on weekends.

The New Providence community of Clarksville contains **Sevier Station** (Walker St., 931/648-5780), the oldest structure in Montgomery County. Built in 1792 by Valentine Sevier, the stone structure was designed to survive attacks, but late in 1794, Indians killed several members of Sevier's family who had ventured outside. Nearby on B Street stands the earthworks of **Fort Defiance** (931/648-5780), which Southerners built along the Cumberland River during the Civil War to repel the Yankees. After Fort Donelson upstream surrendered, however, the fort's occupants got much less defiant and retreated to Nashville. Sevier Station and Fort Defiance have no visitors center and can be seen virtually anytime. There's not a great deal to see here, however.

Beachaven Vineyards and Winery

Beachaven (1100 Dunlap Ln., 931/645-8867, www.beachavenwinery.com) produces wine of such quality that one of its entries bested 990 others in a 1993 contest. The offerings vary from chardonnay to muscadine to blackberry and wines. Tours and tastings are available daily year-round, and several free jazz concerts take place on the grounds every year.

Historic Collinsville

This restored 19th-century settlement (931/648-9141, www.historiccollinsville.com) lies 10 miles south of Clarksville along the Cumberland River. Ten structures give a glimpse of the life of a family from those times. One cabin dates to 1842 and contains period furnishings. An 1870 house and its contents show how a family living there would have increased their standard of living 30 years later. It's open May 15–October 8 A.M.–4 P.M. Monday, Tuesday, Thursday, and

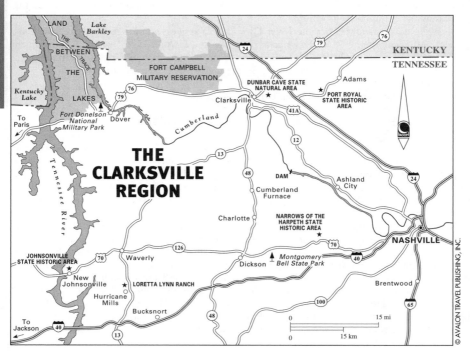

THE CLARKSVILLE REGION

Friday. Admission is $4 for adults. Children under 5 get in free.

Fort Campbell

Sitting astride the Tennessee-Kentucky state line, this is the largest military base in Tennessee. Established in 1942 and covering 105,068 acres—about one-fifth the size of the Great Smoky Mountains National Park—the army base holds approximately 23,000 military personnel and about 5,000 civilian employees. Ten thousand family members live at the base, while another 28,000 family members live around it. Fort Campbell (www.campbell.army.mil) encompasses 48 ranges, five major drop zones, one assault landing strip, two demonstration areas, 48 maneuver areas, and 304 artillery firing points. Visitors to the base can hear troops singing cadence during physical training, helicopters overhead, and sometimes the distant firing of guns.

Fort Campbell is the home of the 101st "Screaming Eagles" Airborne Division, the world's only air assault division. Its paratroopers were the first Americans to set foot in France during the D-Day invasion, and the 101st has participated in every American war since and many other military operations. Other combat groups, such as the Green Berets, operate out of Fort Campbell; also based here are the infamous black helicopters so beloved by conspiracy fans.

Civilians, especially those with kids, should make a beeline for the **Don F. Pratt Memorial Museum** (Screaming Eagle Blvd. and Tennessee, 270/798-3215, 9:30 A.M.–6:30 P.M. Mon.–Sat., free), which houses more than 50 years of Screaming Eagles history including the 101st airborne division. The museum displays a World War II tank, German weapons, personal articles that belonged to Adolf Hitler, a glider, various weapons, and other artifacts.

Heartland

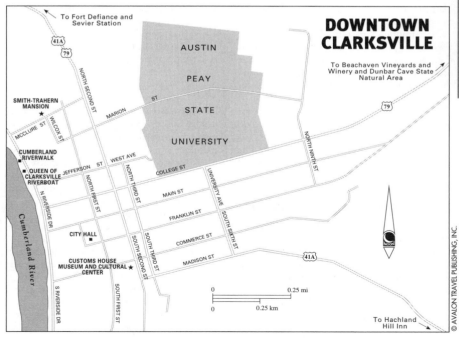

To Fort Defiance and
Sevier Station

41A
79

AUSTIN

PEAY

**DOWNTOWN
CLARKSVILLE**

To Beachaven Vineyards and
Winery and Dunbar Cave State
Natural Area

SMITH-TRAHERN
MANSION

ST

STATE

MARION

79

UNIVERSITY

MCCLURE ST
WILCOX ST

NORTH SECOND ST

NORTH NINTH ST

CUMBERLAND
RIVERWALK

WEST AVE

QUEEN OF
CLARKSVILLE
RIVERBOAT

JEFFERSON ST

COLLEGE ST

NORTH THIRD ST

NORTH FIRST ST

UNIVERSITY AVE

MAIN ST

N RIVERSIDE DR

FRANKLIN ST

SOUTH SIXTH ST

CITY HALL

COMMERCE ST

41A

CUSTOMS HOUSE
MUSEUM AND CULTURAL
CENTER

SOUTH THIRD ST

SOUTH SECOND ST

MADISON ST

Cumberland River

S RIVERSIDE DR

SOUTH FIRST ST

0   0.25 mi

0   0.25 km

To Hachland
Hill Inn

© AVALON TRAVEL PUBLISHING, INC.

Outside and across from the museum are aircraft such as a C-47; a C-19, the so-called "Flying Boxcar"; an A-10 "Warthog"; and various helicopters. To get there, go to Gate 4 and ask for a pass.

Plans are underway for a new museum, slated to open in 2007. The **Wings of Liberty** museum will offer six times the exhibit space of the Donald Pratt Memorial Museum. For information, visit www.fortcampbell.com.

Dunbar Cave State Natural Area

Caves riddle this part of Tennessee, and one of the larger ones lies under the 110 acres making up this natural area within the Clarksville city limits. Indians first used the eight-mile-long cave, but it became most famous as a concert venue during the big-band era, when acts such as the Tommy Dorsey Band and Count Basie played to large audiences. Country singer Roy Acuff bought the property and resumed the concerts, this time with big-name country music stars. The state of Tennessee bought the cave in 1973 and opened it as a public park.

No camping is permitted in this park, but visitors can picnic, fish on a 15-acre lake, tour the cave, and see a small museum in the **visitors center.** The staff offers guided cave hikes during the summer every day. Call 931/648-5526 for information, to secure reservations, and for times of tours the rest of the year. Hikes cost $4 per person. The tours cover culture, history, and geologic features such as stalactites and stalagmites. The cave is chilly; wear a jacket. The passageways are not paved, so shoes with good traction are recommended.

ENTERTAINMENT AND EVENTS

The **Roxy Theatre** (100 Franklin St., 931/645-7699), built in 1911 as a movie hall, now serves as home to the Roxy Community Theater. The season, which consists of 10 productions, includes musicals, classic plays, and comedies.

The **Old Time Fiddler's Contest** (931/648-0001), held in March at the Clarksville High School on Warfield Boulevard (Hwy. 374), offers competitions in 14 categories.

The **Clarksville Rodeo** (931/648-0001) is held in early August. Bareback riders, bull riders, calf ropers, and others compete for prizes.

Riverfest (931/645-7476), held all over town early in September, includes art exhibits, a 5K run, country dancing, arts and crafts, concerts, drag racing, and food.

For more information, contact **Clarksville Tourist Commission Visitors Center** (180 Holiday Rd., just off I-24 Exit 4, 931/551-3572 or 931/648-0001, www.clarksville.tn.us).

ACCOMMODATIONS

The **Hachland Hill Inn** (1601 Madison St., 931/647-4084) sits on a wooded hill in downtown Clarksville alongside three cedar cabins built in the late 1700s. The inn is decorated with primitive antiques and has eight rooms with private baths. The three cabins respectively sleep 14, 10, or four people. There is a banquet hall that can fit 300 people and a picnic ground outside. Smoking is not permitted in the cabins. Rate at the inn is $95 per night for two, and the cabins cost $95 for the first two people and $10 for each additional person. The rate for two couples in the four-person cabin is $95 per couple.

FOOD

Blackhorse Brewery and Pizza Kitchen (134 Franklin St., 931/552-3726) brews four beers, which run from the house light ale to the dark Coalminer stout. It serves 18 gourmet pizzas, such as shrimp and scallops or bleu cheese and spinach. Or diners can build their own pizzas, choosing from more than 60 toppings. The Blackhorse also has a strong salad menu.

Brunie's Bar and Grill (101 Legion St., 931/645-8414) is a friendly little place featuring German and American food. Diners can sit down to a dish of jaeger schnitzel or hamburger steak, and before the night is over Brunie herself will wander over and ask how things are going.

The **Franklin Street Pub** (132 Franklin St., 931/552-3726) offers Irish greetings on its menus and serves barbecue. A long list of appetizers, including stuffed jalapeños, precedes dinners of steak, chicken, and pork chops. Billiards and darts are available to patrons, as are 60 kinds of beer.

The **Hachland Hill Inn** (1601 Madison St., 931/647-4084) is a bed-and-breakfast that offers gourmet meals to nonguests as well—up to 300 at one time. Owner Phila Hach has written eight cookbooks, and her kitchen cranks out delights such as Moroccan leg of lamb, coquilles St. Jacques, and garden-fresh vegetables.

The aroma in **Red's Bakery** (101 Riverside Dr., 931/647-5646) will make visitors hungry before they even get in the door. This is a great place for a country breakfast.

The **Sportsman's Restaurant and Lounge** (on Sportsman's Lane, 931/431-4140) offers German and American food, including a sort of in-between item called Cow Poke Schnitzel. Lunch features a range of sandwiches.

Wilson's Catfish House (2560 Wilma Rudolph Blvd., 931/552-2342) has been turning out fried fish and hush puppies for more than 50 years.

DOVER

This little town west of Clarksville gives no clue today to the important role it played during the heyday of river traffic. Steamboats called here to deliver goods and to transport iron products made by the Cumberland Iron Works, which operated 14 furnaces hereabouts. Things went rapidly downhill during the Civil War, when the town came under attack by the Union army as it pounded Fort Donelson.

Sights

Civil War fans should go to the **Dover Hotel** (at the end of Petty Street, 931/232-5348, Memorial Day–Labor Day 8 A.M.–4 P.M.), the place where General Simon Bolivar Buckner met General U. S. Grant and surrendered 13,000 Confederate troops. The hotel, also known as "Surrender House," was one of the few buildings left standing after the war. The hotel's exterior has been restored to its Civil War appearance.

Reaching upstream from Dover to Cumberland City, **Cross Creeks National Wildlife Refuge** provides 8,862 square miles of habitat for migrating birds. About one-third of the refuge

is hardwood forest, with the remainder of it wetlands and farmland. Visitors here can see all manner of waterfowl as well as hawks, ospreys, and bald eagles.

A **visitors center** with exhibits and a slide show stands three miles east of Dover off Hwy. 49, 931/232-7477. Admission is free, and no camping or fires are permitted.

Practicalities

Cindy's Catfish House (2148 Donelson Pkwy., 931/232-4817) features a lunch and dinner buffet.

Get information from the **Stewart County Chamber of Commerce** (323 Watson Building, Spring St., 931/232-8290, www.stewart-countytn.org).

FORT DONELSON NATIONAL MILITARY PARK

Lying one mile west of the town of Dover on U.S. 79, Fort Donelson National Military Park (931/232-5706, www.nps.gov/fodo) marks the Union's first significant victory in the Civil War. A driving tour takes visitors to batteries that overlook the Cumberland River, which has been dammed to create Lake Barkley. An interpretive trail leads through the park as well. The National Cemetery contains 655 Union dead, 504 of whom are unknown. Admission is free. The **visitors center** is open 8 A.M.–4:30 P.M.

LAND BETWEEN THE LAKES

The thin strip of land between the Tennessee and Cumberland Rivers used to be home to about 800 families, whose farms surrounded four Tennessee and five Kentucky villages. Along came the Tennessee Valley Authority, which in 1961 proposed making the land into a national recreation area that would stimulate the local economy.

Land Between the Lakes (270/924-2000, www.lbl.org) as it was named, is a 170,000-acre park offering recreation, education, and lots of sanctuary for wildlife. Now administered by the Forest Service, admission to the park is free, although there are fees for camping and various attractions.

UNCONDITIONAL SURRENDER

The Tennessee and Cumberland Rivers, flowing northward out of Tennessee, provided a perfect means by which to invade the Confederacy. The South, realizing this, built two forts that stood back to back across a 12-mile neck of land that separated the two rivers. They didn't have long to wait.

An obscure general, Ulysses S. Grant, proposed a combination land and river attack on the forts. Fort Henry, a stockade lying on low land along the Tennessee River, fell in short order on February 6, 1862, and its defenders retreated to the Cumberland River's Fort Donelson near Dover.

Opening the Tennessee River was important, to be sure, but the Cumberland River led straight to Nashville, a real prize. Fort Donelson had its pluses and minuses. It was more of a stockade than a fort, yet it stood atop a 100-foot bluff in which the Confederates had dug trenches and prepared for a fight. When Union gunboats approached, the Confederate gunners blasted them with cannon fire and forced them to retreat.

Nonetheless, the Southerners were surrounded. They tried to break through the Union lines, but their commander decided in the confusion to pull them back, and Grant quickly took up the slack. The three Confederate generals decided that Simon B. Buckner, an old friend of Grant's who had once lent him some money, should offer to surrender. The other two generals slipped away with about 2,000 men.

Nathan Bedford Forrest, who commanded a cavalry battalion that he had raised and equipped with his own funds, refused to give up the fight, leading his 700 troops through the icy waters of Lick Creek to safety.

Buckner sent a message to Grant asking about terms of surrender. Grant's reply was succinct: "No terms except an unconditional and immediate surrender can be accepted." Buckner was in no position to negotiate and handed over his 13,000 troops, who spent the rest of the war in prison camps. Despite this, Buckner remained Grant's friend and was one of the former president's pallbearers in 1885.

After the Southern triumph at Bull Run, the North badly needed this victory. Abraham Lincoln appointed Grant to the post of major general, and newspapers hailed the new hero. The path to the South's heartland lay open.

The best reason for going to Land Between the Lakes is the **Elk & Bison Prairie** ($3 per carload), where visitors can see animals that last roamed here 150 years ago. Elk were imported from Canada as well as the Great Smoky Mountains. Bison, which were once so populous in this region that a visitor to what is now Nashville was afraid to get off his horse, herds here, too.

As for recreation, visitors have a lot to choose from—fishing, hiking, off-road biking and driving, camping, picnicking, backcountry camping, shooting, hunting, archery, swimming, canoeing, and paddleboating.

The educational sites, approached from the Tennessee side, begin with **The Homeplace** (9 A.M.–5 P.M. Mon.–Sat., 10 A.M.–5P.M. Sun., Apr.–Oct.; closed Mon.–Tues., Mar. –Nov., $3.50 adults, $2 children 6–17). Here are 16 log structures from the region to give visitors a sense of life back in the days when family farms weren't flooded out by government agencies. Staff members dress in 1850 clothing and do chores relating to those times—cutting wood with old tools, tending livestock, cooking on a woodstove, spinning thread, or quilting. Even the vegetables in the garden are of the old-time variety.

Crossing into Kentucky, the motorist soon comes to the **Golden Pond Visitors Center** (270/924-2020, daily year-round). Admission is free, although seeing the Golden Pond Planetarium, costs $2.75 for adults and $1.75 for children 5–12.

The **Woodlands Nature Station** (Apr.–Oct., daily; Nov.–March Wed.–Sun., $3.50 adults, $2 children 6–17) farther north on the shores of Lake Barkley (the Cumberland River), offers live animals—eagles, coyotes, deer, snakes, and raptors. Exhibits focus on the flora and fauna of the region.

West of Nashville

HARPETH NARROWS

This 200-acre park (615/797-6096, www .tnstateparks.com) is home to two interesting sights—one natural and one man-made. As it flows toward the Cumberland River, the Harpeth River swoops back and forth across the land west of Nashville. At one place in Cheatham County, the river comes back and almost meets itself; the loops are separated by a bluff that narrows to 180 feet. Thus the name—the Harpeth Narrows.

Montgomery Bell was an early iron magnate in Tennessee who built up a healthy enterprise out of iron forges in the region. Despite all the iron he produced, he lacked the ability to manufacture it into a wide range of products. For that he needed huge hammers that could pound red-hot iron into sheets or flat pieces that could be more easily transformed into tools and other goods.

Bell noticed that the Harpeth on one side of the narrows is 16 feet lower than on the other side of the bluff, and he reasoned that if he could cut a tunnel from one side to the other he would have an enormous source of water power. Using crude tools and black powder, sometime about 1818 Bell's slaves cut a large tunnel—16 feet wide, eight feet tall, and 100 yards long—through the bluff. It may have been the first tunnel in the country, diverting enough water to spin eight large water wheels, which provided power for the hammers and bellows of the Patterson Forge.

In its heyday this forge ran day and night, four huge hammers ringing as they rose and fell and pounded out the iron. Bell's goods were carried by steamboat to Vicksburg and even to New Orleans. Indeed, it was cannonballs from here that Andrew Jackson fired at the British in the Battle of New Orleans. Bell died in 1858 and was buried within sight of his tunnel, and the Civil War brought an end to his enterprise.

Today the **tunnel** is virtually the only remnant of Bell's industry. When the waters of the Harpeth are low, visitors can wade into the tunnel and inspect it closely. Other activities at the area include swimming in the river, three hiking trails, canoeing, and picnicking. Call 615/797-9052 for further information.

Between the historic area and Nashville lies the community of Pegram; the **Pegram fish fry** (615/792-6722) attracts thousands of people every March. This event is a bit out of the way.

MONTGOMERY BELL STATE RESORT PARK

The 3,782-acre Montgomery Bell State Resort Park (615/797-9052) lies between Nashville and Dickson on U.S. 70. Like Tennessee's other state parks, this one benefited from the attentions of the Civilian Conservation Corps during the Depression, and its work endures in the beautiful stone dams. The story of Montgomery Bell is recounted above under Narrows of the Harpeth State Historic Area, and this park contains the remains of his 1815 Laurel iron furnace and the pits from which iron ore was dug.

A schism of the Presbyterian denomination took place here in 1810 amid the "Great Revival" that swept through American Protestantism at the turn of the last century. Three ministers came to Samuel McAdow's cabin and, after an all-night session of prayer, decided to form the Cumberland Presbyterian Church, a group whose ministers, unlike those of the Presbytery from which it sprang, did not have to be formally educated. The park contains a replica of the cabin and an early 1800s chapel in which many weddings take place.

Montgomery Bell State Resort Park offers a host of leisure activities: golf, swimming, boating, fishing, hiking, tennis, and archery, as well as various athletic courts. There are also three backcountry sites and a dumping station. The only places to eat in the park are the golf course snack bar, or the restaurant at the inn, which is open year-round offering three meals a day every day except two weeks around the Christmas and New Year's holidays. See it online at www.tnstateparks.com.

Heartland

THE RUSKIN COLONY

It all began with Julius Augustus Wayland, an Indianan with a noble-sounding name and even nobler visions of how society should be run. His principles took shape in the Ruskin Colony, an experiment in socialism eagerly followed by thousands of people around the country.

As described in John Egerton's excellent *Visions of Utopia,* Wayland lived in a time of great economic uncertainty in the United States. The stock market crashed in 1893, and populists such as William Jennings Bryan found many people willing to listen to new ideas of government and economics. A well-to-do man, Wayland in 1893 began publishing his own newspaper, *The Coming Nation,* in which he took socialism as defined by English thinkers, particularly John Ruskin, put it in easy-to-understand language, and printed weekly editions.

The Coming Nation boomed; within six months 13,000 people paid $.50 for a year's subscription, and by the spring of 1894 circulation topped 50,000. Wayland had long wanted to set up a community based on cooperation and socialism, and in 1894 his representatives bought 1,000 acres in Dickson County near a hamlet called Tennessee City. He called it the Ruskin Colony. As in Rugby, a colony founded on idealistic principles in East Tennessee, the founders' philosophical vision was clearer than their agricultural one; the land they bought had very poor soil.

Nonetheless, about three dozen people from all over the country came to the colony. They bound themselves legally into a corporation, built a building in which to print *The Coming Nation,* built homes for themselves, and set out to live the cooperative life. All work, whether hoeing corn or setting type, was valued at the same rate. Members paid for various goods with scrip issued by the corporation, and prices were expressed in hours. A pound of coffee cost seven hours of work, a quart of peanuts cost one hour, and a pair of men's pants cost 37 hours.

In the beginning, the colony boomed. The eager Ruskinites set up a kiln and planing mill, and they manufactured and sold items such as suspenders, wool pants, chewing gum, cereal, and a patent medicine. Almost 100 people lived in the colony by fall 1894.

Having that many idealists together, however, proved a challenge. The hard workers began to notice that slackers got paid the same as those who strove industriously. And people complained that Wayland, despite all his talk of socialism, retained ownership and control of his newspaper. He donated the ownership of *The Coming Nation* to the colony, yet tried to retain editorial control. Wayland quarreled with his one-time followers until he had had enough. In the summer of 1895 he left the colony, moved to Kansas, and started another newspaper.

In the meantime, the colonists decided to move to literally greener pastures. They bought 800 acres north of Tennessee City, property that contained two enormous caves. By 1897 they had built **Commonwealth House,** an enormous, three-story structure holding the printing operation and topped by a 700-seat auditorium. Here things hit a peak. The colony owned 75 buildings, telephones, a gristmill, machine shop, café, laundry, bakery, commissary, school, and a variety of cottage industries. The colonists used the large cave on their property for a cannery.

Two hundred fifty residents from 32 states and several foreign countries came to Ruskin, and the place hummed with activity. Increasingly, however, it also hummed with controversy. Some of the newcomers proved more radical than the founders and complained about the way things were run. A few disdained marriage and advocated "free love," and accounts of this school of thought did nothing to enhance Ruskin among the locals.

The colony ended amid a ton of bickering. The fact that the colony was incorporated led various shareholders to attack other shareholders in the courts. After a series of court proceedings, a judge declared that the litigants had irreconcilable differences and ordered that the assets be sold at auction and distributed to the shareholders.

Accommodations

The **Montgomery Bell Inn** (800/250-8613 or 615/797-3101, www.tnstateparks.com, $60–78) contains 120 rooms and is open year-round. Overlooking 35-acre Acorn Lake, the inn is a popular place, and reservations can be made up to a year in advance.

Nine two-bedroom cabins lie across a cove from the inn and connect to it via a rustic bridge. They are fully equipped for housekeeping and are open year-round. During the summer, cabins rent by the week, but during the off-season visitors have only a two-night minimum. Cabins cost $60–70.

The park **campground** offers 120 sites, 92 of which have water and electrical hookups. Hot showers are available for all, and the campground is open year-round.

DICKSON

Although the county with which it shares its name was chartered in 1803, Dickson is a relatively new town, one that came into being because of a railroad built by Union soldiers. After the turn of the 20th century, it became a manufacturing center.

Dickson is the birthplace of Frank Clement, who was the youngest governor of Tennessee and who holds second place in number of years in that office. He burst on the national scene by making the keynote address at the 1956 Democratic Convention but rendered the speech in a histrionic, pre-TV style more suited to revival tents. One acerbic newspaper reporter wrote that Frank Clement "last night slew the Republican party with the jawbone of an ass."

Individuals who use "small-town" as a pejorative should make it a point to see Dickson's extraordinary **Renaissance Center** (two miles north of I-40 Exit 272, 615/740-5600, www.recenter.org). There's nothing small-town about this multi-million operation. Home to an art gallery, concerts, and theater, all in a stunning building, the center offers locals classes in a variety of conventional and high-tech fields, including 3-D animation. Dickson received this boon from the Jackson Foundation, established from the pro-

ceeds of the sale of a local hospital. **Old Timer's Day**, with arts and crafts, a flea market, and contests, is held in downtown Dickson on the first Saturday in May. The festivities begin with a two-hour parade that steps off at 10 A.M.

Practicalities

The **Catfish Kitchen** (615/446-4480), 2.5 miles east of town on U.S. 70, offers Tennessee's favorite fish as well as other seafood, frog legs, and steaks. **Fossie's BBQ** (603 E. Walnut, 615/446-8674) serves homemade barbecue with all the usual sides.

Wang's China (107 W. Christi Rd., 615/446-3388) offers Chinese dishes, including a lunch and supper buffet.

And in nearby White Bluff, **Hog Heaven Barbeque** (4142 U.S. 70 E., 615/797-4923) serves great barbecue, full breakfasts, plate lunches, and homemade desserts.

For more information, contact **Dickson County Chamber of Commerce** (119 U.S. 70 E., 615/446-2349, www.dicksoncountychamber.com).

VICINITY OF DICKSON

Charlotte

North of Dickson lies a small town once prominent in the state. Established in 1804 as the county seat, Charlotte sat on an important stagecoach route, and Andrew Jackson and Thomas Hart Benton practiced law here. Such was the town's stature that it was proposed as the state capital, losing to Nashville in 1843 by only one vote.

To this town in the winter of 1862 came Nathan Bedford Forrest and his troops after escaping capture at Fort Donelson. According to the tale, Forrest's men happily filled the taverns and availed themselves of the products therein. Forrest, a teetotaler who was eager to move on, kept riding his horse up to the saloons, sticking his head in the door while still on horseback, and ordering that no more whiskey be served to his troops. In a final effort to rally his men, Forrest and a few of his more sober troopers rode to a hill east of town, where they fired guns and

Heartland

gave the Rebel yell. The revelers, fearing the Yankees had followed them, leapt on their horses and rode off to what they assumed was another battle. In a couple of minutes, not one of them was left in Charlotte.

The Civil War and getting bypassed by the railroad greatly impeded the town, but it held onto its position as county seat, despite numerous efforts to move it to Dickson. The courthouse here, built in 1833, is the oldest one in use in the state. Among the buildings to see is the **Charlotte Cumberland Presbyterian Church,** built in 1850 and still containing many of its original furnishings.

Cumberland Furnace

This town, farther north on Hwy. 48, is where the iron industry in this part of the state began. Montgomery Bell, of park fame, built the fledgling industry hereabouts before selling out. The Civil War halted production, but it resumed after the war and continued as recently as World War II—a remarkable run. The town is listed on the National Register as a Historic District.

A brochure put together by Cumberland Furnace Historic Village gives the visitor a **walking tour** of the town. Highlights include a former furnace owner's mansion on the hill, the old train depot, and some buildings present when Nathan Bedford Forrest's troops camped here in 1862.

Jewel Cave

To get to the following take Hwy. 46 (Exit 172 from I-40) and go about 10 miles northwest out of Dickson. This cave offers formations in abundance. The many colors of the stalactites and stalagmites and other features led to the cave's name. Admission to the Jewel Cave is by appointment only. It costs $4 per person for a groups must be no smaller than ten people, year round. To schedule a visit to the cave, call 615/740-5600 or visit www.rcenter.org.

Bon Aqua

This former resort community south of Dickson is home to an interesting clothing company as well as a good place to eat. **Diamond Gusset Jeans** (10296 Hwy. 46, 888/8-GUSSET [848-

7738] or 931/670-3589, www.gusset.com, 10 A.M.–6 P.M. daily) is out to reform the world of jeans, one crotch at a time. David Hall and his cousin Jeff took conventional jeans and added a triangular or diamond-shaped piece of cloth in the crotch. This piece of cloth, called a gusset, relieves the strain that causes normal jeans to rip or wear out. The jeans are attracting a wide following and can be ordered by mail or in stores. Call for a list of outlets.

The **Beacon Light Tea Room** (6343 Hwy. 100, 931/670-3880) was named for an aviation beacon erected in the 1930s across the road from the restaurant. The light is no more, but the food here has not changed since those days. People come here for country ham, fried chicken, hot biscuits, and homemade preserves. Breakfast is served anytime.

JOHNSONVILLE STATE HISTORICAL AREA

By November 1864, the South was headed for defeat. General Sherman had just burned Atlanta and was marching for the sea. His supply lines, which began in Louisville, Kentucky, stretched longer and longer as he moved toward Savannah. Johnsonville—named for Andrew Johnson, then military governor of Tennessee—was the crucial link in the chain. Here supplies were transferred from steamboats to railroad cars and then shipped south following Sherman's army. It was this weak link that Confederate Cavalry General Nathan Bedford Forrest resolved to smash.

Commanding a force of 3,000 men and 10 cannons, he sneaked up along the west side of the Tennessee River, set up a gauntlet of artillery, and captured a Union gunboat, the *Undine*. After firing on the warehouses, the *Undine* set off with three other Union boats in hot pursuit. The *Undine* led them within range of Forrest's artillery, which sank them. Then Forrest turned his guns on the warehouses and fired at will.

When the bombardment was over, the damage was impressive: four gunboats, 14 steamboats, 17 barges, and quartermaster stores worth an estimated $6.7 million. Forrest lost only two men, with nine wounded, and made military history in becoming the only cavalry to engage and defeat a naval force.

The attack, costly as it was to the Union, had little effect on Sherman, who had resolved to live off the land as he scourged the South. Nonetheless, on hearing of this tremendous loss, Sherman said, "That devil Forrest must be hunted down if it costs 10,000 lives and bankrupts the Federal treasury!"

A group called **Raise the Gunboats, Inc.** is hoping to raise the Undine and other gunboats. Using professional divers, they have recovered various artifacts from the wrecks, which sit in 38 feet of water. One of the more remarkable finds were pieces of hardtack, a flour and salt delicacy eaten by Civil War soldiers-still intact after 136 years under water. For the latest news on the project, go to www.gunboats.com.

The creation of Kentucky Lake in the 1940s flooded the battle site, leaving only the higher elevations. The Johnsonville State Historical Area occupies this high ground. Here visitors can tour a small museum and walk among what is left of the Union rifle pits and other defensive works. Admission is free, and the area is open daily 8 A.M. until sunset. Call 931/535-2789 or find out more online at www.tnstateparks.com.

HURRICANE MILLS

This is a one-woman town. Country music icon Loretta Lynn and her husband bought a large farm here in 1967, and with it came a mill and the tiny town of Hurricane Mills. In 1975 the couple opened a campground on the property, and since then Hurricane Mills has attracted a steady stream of her fans.

The "ranch" covers 6,500 acres, and admission to the grounds and various shops in Hurricane Mills is free. However, those wishing to tour the Lynn home—the **original farmhouse, Coal Miner's Daughter Museum,** and reconstructed **Butcher Holler cabin**—must pay $12.50. Children under 6 are admitted at no charge.

Lynn no longer lives in the house—she lives in a home not visible from any roads—but her furniture and decorations look as if she has just

stepped out. Visitors are led and other rooms on the firs and can see for themselves tastes of Lynn and her "Mooney," who died in 19

The museum, expanded in 2000, contains items such as the dress she wore when she first sang on the *Grand Ole Opry*, every award she's won in country music, scripts from movies and television shows, letters from presidents and other famous people, and lots of photos.

Across the road and on the side of a hill sits a house that is a reminder of how far Lynn has come. As her most famous song and biographical movie declare, she was a "Coal Miner's Daughter." Newspaper is used for wallpaper, the woodstove in the kitchen is the one used in the movie, and the exterior of the house has no paint. Down the hill is a walk-through depiction of a coal mine, complete with authentic tools.

After recording the *White Blood Cells* CD in Memphis, Jack and Meg White, members of the White Stripes, stopped off at Hurricane Mills and, after taking the tour, decided to dedicate the album to Loretta Lynn. The singer sent them a note of thanks and invited them to return. All this led to Jack White producing Loretta Lynn's comeback CD of 2004, *Van Lear Rose.*

The ranch hosts diverse events though the year, among them motocross motorcycle competitions, trail rides, and an Indian powwow. Loretta Lynn performs two to three times a year, always during the summer. Other concerts present gospel and country music. Get further information about the events by calling 931/296-7700.

BUCKSNORT

The **Bucksnort Budget Inn** and a service station mark the Bucksnort exit on I-40, a rural spot in Hickman County. Originally, this area was known as Old Furnace, named for the nearby old iron furnace. When I-40 was built, Bucksnort was the unforgettable name selected to identify the exit. The original Bucksnort was a store and mill run by the Spence family in the 1830s about a mile west of Old Furnace. It got

THE WIZARD OF THE SADDLE

Historian Shelby Foote has said that the Civil War produced two authentic geniuses—Abraham Lincoln and Confederate Cavalryman **Nathan Bedford Forrest**. Of all the Civil War generals, Forrest remains the most controversial, one whose deeds and misdeeds are still argued today.

Born in 1821 on a farm in Bedford County, he grew up with little schooling but with a good head for business. He moved farther west, living for a time in Mississippi, then achieved prosperity as a slave trader in Memphis. When the war broke out, Forrest signed on as a private. He was 40 years old.

As the Southern armies took shape, Forrest raised his own cavalry battalion, paying for it out of his own pocket. Although he had never been in a battle before, he quickly became one of the most feared Southern commanders, eventually rising to the rank of lieutenant general—the only man on either side to rise so far from the rank of private. Forrest used his mounted force to cover ground quickly and to strike when unexpected, usually dismounting before battle. He refused to surrender at Fort Donelson, fought at Shiloh, and saw action in Tennessee, Mississippi, Alabama, and Georgia.

Forrest used some simple axioms to guide his actions. "Fighting means killing" was one of these that he took to heart. During the war he personally killed 31 men and had 29 horses shot out from under him. He captured 31,000 prisoners and thought nothing of shooting his own men if they tried to run from battle. "Keep up the skeer" (scare) was another slogan. He relentlessly pursued Union forces, chasing and attacking one force for hundreds of miles.

When General William T. Sherman was storming through Georgia toward the sea, Forrest hit the Union supply lines, leading his cavalry against gunboats on the Tennessee River and utterly destroying the Federal warehouses at New Johnsonville. These attacks led Sherman to write that his adversary was "the very devil" and "There will never be peace in Tennessee until Forrest is dead."

Late in the war, Forrest overran Fort Pillow, a Mississippi River stronghold of Union troops, many of whom were black. According to Northern reports, Forrest's men needlessly killed at least 300 of the troops in the fort. Southerners vehemently denied that version of the "Fort Pillow Massacre," as Northern newspapers dubbed it. They insisted that the Union troops died because they refused to give up.

When the war ended, Forrest entertained the notion of refusing to surrender and riding off to Mexico, but he finally laid down his arms and gave all his men a printed copy of his final orders. The final paragraph contained the following:

I have never, on the field of battle, sent you where I was unwilling to go myself; nor would I now advise you to a course which I felt myself unwilling to pursue. You have been good soldiers; you can be good citizens. Obey the laws, preserve your honor, and the government to which you have surrendered can afford to be, and will be, magnanimous.

This lofty-sounding advice, no doubt crafted in part by one of his staff, was not followed by Forrest himself, for late in 1866 he became the Grand Wizard of the fledgling Ku Klux Klan. In 1871 he was summoned to Washington to testify in Congressional hearings on the organization. During the hearings he claimed no Klan affiliation whatsoever. By then, this may have been true, for he and others thought that the Klan's increasing violence might bring a return to martial law in Tennessee and elsewhere. He had apparently resigned his post and urged that the Klan disband.

Forrest never prospered after the Civil War, and biographer Jack Hurst groups the final years of the general's life into a section called "Penitent." While living in Memphis, Forrest participated in the decoration of Union graves and accepted an invitation to attend a barbecue hosted by local blacks. In 1875, after a lifetime of indifference to religion, he became a Christian. Two years later at the age of 56, he died in his home on October 29, 1877. One of the last people to see him alive was Jefferson Davis.

Forrest is buried in downtown Memphis under a statue of him mounted on a horse. Vandals regularly deface his grave.

its unusual name because it sold whiskey; its motto was "For a buck you can get a snort." The store remained in business until the 1920s. To get to the site of the original Bucksnort, get off I-40 and turn onto the dirt road that runs alongside Sugar Creek and the interstate. Proceed for about a mile. All that remain are the rocks that formed the foundation of the store.

Along the Natchez Trace

THE NATCHEZ TRACE PARKWAY

The Natchez Trace might be called one of the country's first interstate highways. Following game trails, Indians tramped back and forth along it to trade or wage war on each other. Europeans, beginning with Hernando de Soto, traveled it as well.

The Trace reached its heyday in the early 1800s, and most of the travel on it was one-way. In the days before steamboats, virtually all traffic on rivers was downstream. Tennesseans and others would build flatboats, crude crafts that drifted with the current, and use them to ship hides, corn, whiskey, or whatever. When the boatmen got to Natchez or New Orleans, they found buyers for their goods, sold their boats for lumber, and set out to walk the 600 miles home.

It was a perilous trek, for robbers knew that the northbound travelers were carrying money. For this and other reasons, the Trace shifted paths from time to time and followed a myriad of routes. In 1800 the federal government designated the Trace a mail route and later improved it as a military road. Andrew Jackson and his troops marched down the Trace to whip the British in New Orleans, then marched up it in triumph. Steamboats, which

Heartland

COURTESY OF NATCHEZ TRACE PARKWAY

The bridge that carries the Parkway over Highway 96 is the first of its kind in the United States.

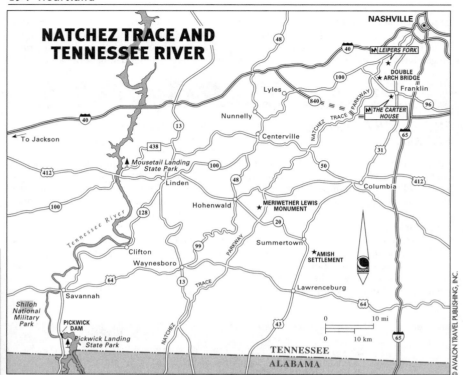

NATCHEZ TRACE AND TENNESSEE RIVER

could easily go upstream, finished off the Trace about 1815.

Efforts to commemorate the old Trace began about 1900, but it took the Depression and the need to put people to work that led to today's parkway. Much like its Blue Ridge counterpart along the crest of the Appalachians, the Natchez Trace Parkway provides a limited-access road that offers a pleasant drive for motorists and a great ride for bicyclists.

Sights

Only one-fifth or so of the Trace is in Tennessee, but it offers some interesting sights. The first is a bridge that carries the parkway over Hwy. 96—well worth getting off the parkway to take a good look. The first post-tensioned, segmental concrete arch **bridge** in the United States is 1,648 feet long and is supported by three pier columns

and two soaring arches. One arch spans 582 feet, while the second stretches 460 feet. On conventional arched bridges, the section containing the road is connected to the arches by vertical columns. The designers of the parkway bridge, to escape the cluttered appearance characteristic of a row of columns, came up with a bridge that omitted these columns entirely. The weight of the bridge rests on the very top of the arch, resulting in a striking bridge that cost $12 million.

The Old Trace at milepost 403.7, is a 2,000-foot section of the original Trace on which visitors can walk.

Devil's Backbone State Natural Area, just south of The Old Trace, offers a three-mile loop trail through a steeply sloped valley.

The **Grave of Meriwether Lewis** is at milepost 385.9, and thereby hangs a tale. Meriwether Lewis of Lewis and Clark came to spend the night of October 10, 1809, at a "stand"—one of the rude inns that offered shelter to travelers on the Trace. The innkeeper heard a shot in the night, and a wounded Lewis tried to come in her cabin. She refused to open the door, and the next morning Lewis died in his room. His death was ruled a suicide, and he was buried on the grounds. The grave of one of the greatest explorers in the history of the country is marked with a simple monument.

Information

Meriwether Lewis Arts and Crafts Fair, held the second week in October on Main Street, brings together local and regional craftspeople at the Meriwether Lewis monument on the Natchez Trace Parkway.

The **Natchez Trace Parkway headquarters** (800/305-7417 or 601/680-4025) is in Mississippi. The **Natchez Trace Bed and Breakfast Reservation Service** (800/377-2770, www.nps .gov/natr) can help plan auto or bicycling trips.

✱ LEIPERS FORK

Thomas Hart Benton, a friend and later rival of Andrew Jackson, lived near here for many years, before moving to Missouri and becoming the first man to serve in the U.S. Senate for 30 years. The community that is now Leiper's Fork was named Bentontown in his honor, then Hillsboro after a town in North Carolina from which several residents had come. When residents wanted a post office, the Postal Service told them that another Tennessee town was named Hillsboro, so they chose Leiper's Fork.

In the 20th century, this was the poor end of Williamson County. Here locals scratched out a living legally and, at least for some, illegally, by distilling moonshine whiskey. Indeed, the fabled Rocky Top immortalized in the Boudleaux and Felice Bryant bluegrass song by the same name, is said to be northwest of town.

Leiper's Fork was one of the last places in Williamson County to be discovered by people with money, and, having seen the excesses of other towns, they were determined to retain the village-like feel of the place. They've done it right, and

In downtown Leipers Fork, this grocery store serves a seafood buffet every weekend.

Leiper's Fork is one of the most delightful places to visit in the entire state. The town is surrounded by the Natchez Trace Parkway, wetlands, and farms that have been put into Land Trust, which means they cannot be developed. Old buildings here have been preserved and renovated, and new ones look like the old ones. A drive in almost any direction from this hamlet takes the visitor past beautiful farms and houses—several of them owned by people in the music business.

While anyone with enough money can make a place look like a community, it takes something special for a place to feel like one. Whatever that illusive element is, Leiper's Fork has it. Visitors are greeted by townsfolk, and made to feel welcome at concerts and other events. During the summers, movies are projected onto an outside screen, and residents and visitors alike sprawl on blankets to watch the show.

Practicalities

A good place to begin is **Leiper's Fork Flintlocks** (4144 Old Hillsboro Pike, 615/791-1747, www.leipersforkflintlocks.com) where proprietor Greg Murry crafts working, black powder, flintlock rifles that are works of art.

© JEFF BRADLEY

Heartland

Concerts and weekly movies take place at this gathering place for the town.

Using exotic woods, gold and silver inlay—he even makes the screws—these firearms take part every year in the Leiper's Fork Computer Shoot, an event to which locals bring obstreperous computers. Murry supplies the flintlocks, and participants take delight in taking aim at monitors and other hardware. "This is where Old World Technology meets New World Technology," comments Murry. "Old Technology wins."

Just down the street is **Backyard Cafe** (4150 Old Hillsboro Pike, 615/790-4003) with homemade soup, sandwiches, and live music on Sunday from 2 to 4 P.M.

The place to eat, however, on the weekends is **Puckett's Grocery** (4142 Old Hillsboro Rd., 615/794-1308) a regular-looking grocery store that sets up tables on Friday and Saturday nights and puts on what has to be the biggest seafood spread in the state.: shrimp, crab legs, oysters on the half shell and fried, salmon, monkfish, scallops, fried catfish. And then a man came around offering lobster tails!

Namaste Acres Country Ranch Inn (5436 Leipers Creek Rd., 615/791-0333, www.namasteacres.com) is a Dutch colonial country home. A pool beside a large, outdoor deck overlooks grazing horses and a scenic mountain view. Rates are $75 (no breakfast) to $85 with a full country breakfast. Children over 12 welcome. You can board your horses here.

PRIMM SPRINGS

Like Red Boiling Springs to the northeast, this little community was one of those places that people went to "take the cure" or just have a good time in the 1800s and the early part of the 1900s. Five kinds of water were available—black sulfur, white sulfur, lime, calomel, and arsenic.

The old hotels are gone, but **Heartland Manor Bed and Breakfast** (7621 S. Harpeth Rd., 800/484-1326 [pin #9367] or 615/799-1326, $85–125) offers three bedrooms, two of which have private baths. Guests can also enjoy a pool, exercise room, full gourmet breakfasts, a recreation room with a pool table, and more.

CENTERVILLE

This is the seat of one of the more rural counties in the state. Even now, the county has just one caution light. Hickman County is the birthplace of Beth Slater Whitson, a prolific songwriter best known for her 1908 "Let Me Call You Sweetheart."

Centerville is more famous for producing another sweetheart, the late Sarah Colley, who became Minnie Pearl, one of the most famous characters on the *Grand Ole Opry.* Colley based her modest "I'm so proud to be here!" routine on the behavior of girls she had observed all over the South while working with a theatrical company. Much of her humor revolved around her attempts to "land a feller," and she often set her stories in the local Grinders Switch community. Although she affected an unsophisticated routine, she was the product of a Nashville finishing school and in her off-stage life was a distinguished lady. She died in 1996.

Hickman County produced three prominent country music sidemen: Ernest Ferguson, a mandolin player who played in several bands; Howdy Forrester, a fiddler who backed Bill Monroe and Roy Acuff; and Paul Warren, another fiddler who played alongside Kitty Wells, Flatt and Scruggs, and Johnnie and Jack.

Details on these and other facets of local life can be seen at the **Hickman County Museum** (117 N. Central Ave., free) in the Chamber of Commerce building.

Practicalities

McEwen Farm Log Cabin Bed and Breakfast (931/583-0714, $95) is out in the country between Centerville and the Natchez Trace Parkway. Lodging is available in two log cabins built with logs used in the 1820s construction of the original buildings on this working farm. Guests can also stay in a restored Victorian train depot of the North Carolina and St. Louis line. The host provides a continental breakfast. Guests can cook in the cabins and the depot.

Breece's Cafe (111 S. Public Sq., 931/729-3481) has been in the same location since 1939. Diners can get a meat and four vegetables for $3, then add on homemade pies or blackberry cobbler.

Fish Camp Restaurant (406 Hwy. 100, 931/729-4401) specializes in two Tennessee favorites: catfish and barbecue. The catfish is served as fillets or fiddlers—the whole fish minus the head—and diners can also choose from hickory-smoked barbecue, steaks, chicken, and seafood. It's one mile north of the town square.

Manley's (139 N. Central Ave., 931/729-2948) features country cooking—plate lunches, a buffet, and steaks, catfish, barbecue, and chicken.

Remember When (108 S. Public Sq., 931/729-0052) sells antique furniture and lamps.

Get information at **Hickman County Chamber of Commerce** (117 N. Central Ave., 931/729-5774, www.hickmanco.com).

HOHENWALD

This pleasant little town was settled in 1878 by German immigrants, who gave it a name that means "high forest." A group of Swiss settlers who had found slim pickings in Nebraska arrived 16 years later, and the town maintains a European feel to this day.

Hohenwald is the birthplace of **Tootsie Bess,** the late owner of Tootsie's Orchid Lounge, a famous watering hole next to the Ryman Auditorium in Nashville. The area also spawned William Gay, whose literary novels, *The Long Home* (1999) and *Provinces of Night* (2000), take rural Lewis County settings and elevate them to art.

Sights

A good place to begin is the **Hohenwald Depot** (112 E. Main St.), built in 1885 and now home to the Lewis County Chamber of Commerce.

Compared to many small-town museums that consist of unlabeled relics and dusty junk, the professionalism of the **Lewis County Museum of Natural and Local History** (108 E. Main St., 931/796-1550, 10 A.M.–4 P.M. Tues.–Sat., $4 adults, $2 for ages 13–17, $0.50 for children under 13) is a delight. Visitors here can see one of the largest single hunter's collections of exotic game mounts in the country. Cape buffalo, Persian ibex, and African dik-diks are some of the animals bagged by Dan Maddox, whose collection forms the centerpiece of this museum. While "great white hunters" may not be in vogue anymore, this museum offers a chance to examine well-mounted specimens seldom seen outside of much larger institutions. Other exhibits include Lewis County artifacts.

Willis Furniture Company, (995 Centerville Hwy., 931/796-4517) two miles north of town on Hwy. 48, offers a huge collection of ornamental concrete items for one's yard. The best-sellers hereabouts are fountains, frogs, and alligators.

Entertainment and Events

Maifest in early May reflects Hohenwald's Germanic heritage with a parade, German music and food, and events such as a tractor pull.

Oktoberfest Heritage Festival on the second weekend of October offers German music and food and a variety of events.

Buffalo River Canoeing (18 W. Linden, 800/339-5596 or 931/796-3622) rents canoes for the nearby Buffalo River.

Shopping

Hohenwald's Main Street junk stores are famous for **Dig Days**—occasions when large bundles of clothing arrive from distant cities. The compacted bundles, which weigh as much as 1,000 pounds, are placed on the floor, the wires are snipped, and customers literally dig in. Sharp-eyed diggers, who arm themselves with pillowcases to stash their finds, sometimes emerge with brand-new designer clothes, cashmere coats, and men's suits. Once the diggers are done, the proprietors separate the clothing, hang it up, and offer it for sale.

A&W Salvage (336 E. Main St., 931/796-3026) has digs on Saturday and Sunday. The wires are snipped on Wednesday and Saturday at 8 A.M. and on Sunday at 1 P.M. Dig in.

Dig Days at **Lawson's Stores** (100 E. Main St., 931/796-4380) start at 8 A.M. on Saturday.

Practicalities

Try **Shadow Acres Motel** (931/796-2201) on Highway 48 north.

Buffalo River Canoeing (18 W. Linden, 931/796-3622 or 800/339-5596) offers primitive camping all year along the Buffalo River. **Natchez Trace Parkway** (seven miles east on Hwy. 20, 800/305-7417, open all year) has 32 campsites with no hookups.

For information, contact **Lewis County Chamber of Commerce** (995 Centerville Hwy., 931/796-4517); also visit one of the best websites for a small town at www.visitlewis.com.

WAYNESBORO

The county seat of the second-largest county in the state, Waynesboro is the hometown of country singer Mark Collie, whose debut album was *Hardin County Line.*

Visitors who have had too much driving and country cooking should stay for a week at **Tennessee Fitness Spa** (between Waynesboro and Hohenwald off Hwy. 99, 800/235-8365 or 931/722-5589, www.tfspa.com). Healthy meals, lots of exercise, and classes get people in a fit frame of mind and body. Facilities include a 10-person hot tub, aerobics gym, weight room, covered pool, and hiking trails. Rates run $625–1,495 per week, and the program runs daily.

The grounds of the spa contain a geologic wonder—a double-span natural bridge. A stream carved out one bridge and then turned and cut out another one. These bridges are on private property, so visitors should call ahead. Sunday afternoon, when spa guests come and go, is the worst time to try to see it.

Crazy Horse Canoes (12 miles north of town on Highway 13, 931/722-5213) offers float trips on the Buffalo River April–September.

Buffalo River Trail Rides (931/722-9170) offers trail rides for those who have their own horses. No rental steeds are available. Rides last for one week and include live entertainment and meals.

Practicalities

Buffalo River Trail Rides (P.O. Box 591, Waynesboro 38485-0591, 931/722-9170) has camping spaces along the Buffalo River. **Crazy Horse Park** (on Hwy. 13 N., 931/722-5213) offers shaded campsites, swimming, fishing, a store, and a restaurant.

Emerald's Restaurant (on the square, 931/722-5611) serves lunch and dinner every day. Country cooking is the fare, and the walls are lined with old photos of the town. This is a surprisingly nice place, one that attracts diners from far-flung towns.

For more information, contact **Wayne County Chamber of Commerce** (Wayne County Courthouse, 931/722-9022, 8:30 A.M.– 4 P.M. daily except Wed.).

North along the Tennessee

SAVANNAH

Originally a group of cabins on a bluff, Savannah is the largest town on the Tennessee River as it makes its second pass across the state. Main Street leads right down to the river, where a ferry used to take travelers to the west bank. The Cherokee came through here during their Trail of Tears march on the way to Oklahoma. Savannah is the largest town near the Shiloh National Military Park, across the river and described in the Western Plains chapter.

Sights

The **Savannah Historic District** stretches for two miles and includes 16 impressive homes, most built 1860–1930. A map available at the chamber of commerce can show the route; the chamber also offers a brochure for the **Historic Savannah Walking Trail.**

On April 6, 1862, word came to a man eating breakfast in the **Cherry Mansion** (800/552-FUNN [552-3866] or 901/925-2363) that the Battle of Shiloh had begun. He stood up and said, "Gentlemen, the ball is in motion. Let's be off." And with that, General U. S. Grant climbed aboard a steamer in Savannah and headed up the Tennessee River. Visitors can walk the grounds of the mansion and make arrangements with the chamber of commerce office to tour the house.

The best place to get oriented here is the **Tennessee River Museum** (507 Main St., 800/552-FUNN [552-3866] or 901/925-2363, $2 for adults, free for children), which has five exhibit areas pertaining to the river and the area. More than 200 fossils are displayed along with Indian artifacts and weapons from the Civil War. The museum shares space with the

Hardin County Chamber of Commerce, which has the same hours.

Queen and Alex Haley Sr., the grandparents of *Roots* author Alex Haley, lived on a small farm outside of Savannah. He ran a ferry across the river while she worked as a maid in the Cherry Mansion. Queen was dramatically featured in a television miniseries of the same name; the couple is buried on the hill behind the courthouse.

The **Saltillo Ferry,** north of town on the Pitts Bend of the river, crosses the Tennessee to Saltillo. The ferry runs on demand during daylight. To get there, take Hwy. 128 north of town and turn left on the Saltillo Ferry Road.

Events

Information on all of these is available from the **Hardin County Tourism Office** (800/552-FUNN [552-3866] or 901/925-2364).

The **Tennessee River City Bluegrass Festival,** on the first weekend in July, brings forth local pickers and regional favorites.

The **National Catfish Derby Festival** runs for most of the summer, with various events held on different weekends. Events include arts and crafts; gospel, country, and bluegrass music; and a catfish-skinning contest. The Catfish Cook-off and the World's Best Hush Puppy Competition are the highlights.

The **Hardin County Fair** is the first weekend in September at the Hardin County Fairgrounds.

Accommodations

N White Elephant Bed and Breakfast Inn (304 Church St., 800/458-2421 or 901/331-5244, $100–120) is a two-story Queen Anne–style Victorian home built in 1901. On 1.5 grassy acres, it is five blocks from the Tennessee

Heartland

THE DESERT FOX

Lawrence Wells wrote a novel called *Rommel and the Rebel* that puts into fiction the recurring tales that Erwin Rommel, the German "Desert Fox" of World War II, came to the United States to study the Civil War and came to Tennessee to examine the cavalry tactics of Confederate General Nathan Bedford Forrest.

Forrest and his troopers rode into Clifton in November of 1862 and built flatboats to cross the Tennessee River. Reaching the other side, they sank the boats and rode off to harass Union troops and supply depots in West Tennessee. Headed back, they refloated the flatboats and crossed the river again, this time to the cheers of Cliftonians.

That much is fact. The rest is a collection of memories from old people, missing hotel registers, and perhaps fanciful thinking. In a 1995 article in *The Oxford American* magazine, Wells wrote of interviewing an 82-year-old Clifton woman who recalled that Rommel was riding the first motorcycle she had ever seen. Rommel was reported to have visited novelist Thomas Stribling, who along with his wife spoke fluent German, and who recounted in his autobiography that one day Rommel appeared out of the blue, introduced himself, and chatted on the porch about Forrest.

Much like Forrest and his cavalry against the Union, Rommel bedeviled the British in North Africa with his tanks. In 1944 he took part in an attempt to assassinate Adolf Hitler and was forced to swallow a lethal dose of poison as a result.

Wells traveled to Germany and talked to Manfred Rommel, son of Erwin, who flatly denied that his father was ever in America. He admitted that his father rode a motorcycle and traveled to Italy to study tactics, but insisted he was never in America, much less Clifton.

Wells ended his article with the following:

Indeed, to anyone with a reverence, not to say, a vulnerability, for the past, Clifton's ghostly motorcyclist, whoever he was—anonymous wanderer or future war hero—lives on in their imaginations. They can still hear the rumble of his motorcycle, the click of polished knee boots as he bows to the Striblings, the rhythmic creak of the porch swing, questions asked in Prussian-accented English, answers given in West Tennessee English.

River and downtown Savannah. Inside are two parlors, fireplaces, and antique furnishings. The two guest rooms are furnished with antiques and each has a private bath. The host serves a full country breakfast.

The Botel (901/925-4787, $36 and up), south of Savannah below Pickwick Dam, is one of the more unusual lodgings in the state. The "Botel" is a lodging boat built in 1900 and used by the Corps of Engineers to house people working on dams, levees, and so on, up and down the river. The 140-foot-long boat now holds 12 rooms plus a restaurant. Four "cooking units" are on the shore.

Information

The **Savannah Art Guild** (112 Williams St., 901/925-7529, open Monday–Saturday 9 A.M.–4 P.M.) operates a gallery featuring the work of members.

Hardin County Chamber of Commerce (507 Main St., 800/552-FUNN [552-3866] or 901/925-2363, www.hardincountytn.com) is open Monday–Friday 9 A.M.–5 P.M. and (during daylight saving time) Saturday 10 A.M.–4 P.M. and Sunday 1–4 P.M.).

CLIFTON

Until a new bridge crossed the Tennessee River, Clifton was home to one of the last ferries in the state. One of the more famous river crossings without a ferry was made on New Year's Day of 1863 by Confederate General Nathan Bedford Forrest, who, pursued by Union troops, moved approximately 2,000 men, their horses, six artillery pieces, and an entire wagon train over the river to Clifton. The river at that time was about three-quarters of a mile in width; most of the horses made the crossing by swimming, and the entire force came across the cold water in about 10 hours.

Sights

The town's most famous resident was novelist Thomas S. Stribling, who was born here in 1881 and who wrote many novels while living here. Stribling's books about the South were closer to those of Erskine Caldwell than to any sort about mansions and magnolias. He won the Pulitzer Prize in 1933 for *The Store*. The **Stribling Museum**, in his Water Street house overlooking the river, contains original furniture, clothing, and books.

A great many out-of-towners come to Clifton to live, some of them for years. Clifton is home to the South Central Correctional Center, a privately owned prison housing approximately 1,000 inmates. No tours are given.

The **Horseshoe Bend Festival** (931/676-3311), held in September, features boat races, a carnival, music, barbecue, and dancing.

Mousetail Landing State Rustic Park

Downstream from Clifton lies this 1,249-acre park. It supposedly got its name when a local tannery caught fire during the Civil War. Mice in great numbers poured from the conflagration, giving rise to the name.

The mice are long gone, and today's visitor will find hiking trails, a swimming pool, 26 campsites, and backcountry camping. Call 901/847-0841, or go online at www.tnstateparks.com.

Practicalities

Pillow Street Bed and Breakfast (305 W. Pillow St., 888/305-0305, $55–85) occupies a restored 1870 house overlooking the river. Guests can take it easy on the balcony. The five rooms all have private baths, and a full country breakfast is served daily.

Riverside Restaurant (410 Water St., 931/676-3944) specializes in fish—catfish, shrimp, and grilled salmon. It also serves frog legs, six kinds of steak, chicken, and wonderful hush puppies. It overlooks the river.

In the sea of fried catfish and the flow of cholesterol that characterize country cooking, **River View Restaurant** (Water and Main Sts., 931/676-3770) offers a healthy alternative. Here diners will find a daily buffet of homemade breads, vegetables, and salads, all low in fat and salt, and totally free of preservatives. This place is famous for its Tennessee River mud balls, a concoction of carob, toasted almonds, and toasted coconut.

City Hall (130 Main St., 931/676-3370) is the best source of information about Clifton.

Nashville

For better or worse, many people think Nashville is Tennessee. The image of country music and the city with which it is most associated has spread around the world. Tourists from Japan and Europe unload at Nashville's airport and join the throngs riding buses, clapping at the *Grand Ole Opry,* riding buses, dancing at the Wildhorse Saloon, and riding buses. This is a city that is imminently ready to accommodate one and all.

From the beginning, Nashville has attracted people who like to make money. The first settlers here carved out a place on the river and traded upstream and down. They quickly adapted to steamboats, the railroad, and the electronic waves of radio. Printing and other businesses thrived here because of Nashville's location between North and South. So did music.

The city that spawned it all, however, retains a laid-back approach that travelers will appreciate. The courtesy extended by people who have the toughest jobs—those who deal with thousands of tourists a day—makes Tennessee's capital seem like a much smaller place. Even the celebrities, unlike most other famous people, keep in touch with their supporters through events such as CMA Music Festival. Nashville, more than any city in Tennessee, is geared for visitors. The welcome extended, whether a helping hand off the *General Jackson* riverboat, or the smile of a server who submerges turkey and dressing in gravy, makes this a most pleasant place to visit.

HISTORY

It all began with salt. Deer and other grazing animals crave sodium in their diets and will return again and again to places where naturally occurring salts appear on the surface of the ground. For thousands of years, buffalo, deer, bears, and other animals came in great numbers to the salt licks at what is now Nashville. Their presence attracted Indians, who hunted them and built mounds, but these first Americans never established as firm a presence in this part of Tennessee as they did in other places. Although the Cherokee did not live in Middle Tennessee in great numbers, they regarded the land as their hunting grounds and did not take kindly to interlopers.

During the time of the long hunters—so named because they would leave home and be gone a long time killing game and collecting furs—the French established a trading post known as French Lick about 1710. The 1763 Treaty of Paris put the land under English control, but a French-Canadian long hunter, one Timothy Demonbreun, established residence in a cave and stayed long enough to be considered the first resident of Middle Tennessee.

As settlers pushed into what is now East Tennessee, they heard tantalizing tales of rich land to the west, a place where buffalo were so thick that travelers were afraid to get off their horses and where a hunter could kill 19 deer in one day. The land was rich and much flatter than that in the East, and every long hunter who came back from the land around the Cumberland River found ready listeners for his tales.

Fort Nashborough

Richard Henderson, a land speculator, gained control of this desirable acreage, and in the spring of 1779 dispatched James Robertson and a crew of men to investigate the land about which everyone had heard so much. To get around the barrier of the Cumberland Plateau, which separates East and Middle Tennessee, Robertson and his party traveled through the Cumberland Gap into what is now Kentucky and then descended into Tennessee's Central Basin.

There they built a few cabins, planted corn, and came back to ready a group of settlers. By the fall of 1779 they were ready to move to their new home. Robertson split his party into two groups. About 200 men and boys would walk with Robertson to the banks of the Cumberland River, driving their livestock with them. John Donelson, a few men, and all the women and children would float downstream in flatboats and canoes—down the Holston, down the Tennessee—and then laboriously pole the fleet up the Ohio and up the Cumberland.

The parties had the misfortune to pick a brutal winter in which to travel. The men and boys made the long walk to French Lick by December, suffering no Indian attacks and losing none of their party. The Cumberland River was frozen so thick that the livestock could walk across. They settled in to await the others, who arrived in April after a harrowing, 1,000-mile trip by water.

The settlers built a stockade, which they named Fort Nashborough in honor of a Revolutionary War general. Far from any kind of established government, the residents drew up the Cumberland Compact, which outlined the duties of judges and other points of law.

The fort was soon put to use, as the Indians quickly attacked the settlements in the area. Indeed, residents abandoned several smaller settlements and moved closer to the protection of Fort Nashborough. The Chickamauga Indians who had fired on John Donelson's flotilla attacked the fort in the spring of 1781, cutting off James Robertson and about 20 men from safety. His quick-thinking wife opened the gates and released a pack of dogs, which fell upon the surprised Indians with much barking and biting. Between avoiding the dogs and trying to catch the settlers' horses, the attackers were distracted and their would-be victims escaped.

Growth in Trade

Through treaties and retaliatory raids the settlers gradually lessened the Indian problem, and Fort Nashborough began attracting more residents. The area came under the control of the state of North Carolina, whose legislature in 1784 named the town Nashville—Nashborough

Must-Sees

Look for **M** to find the sights and activities you can't miss and **N** for the best dining and lodging.

M The Parthenon: This monument to the "Athens of the South" continues to inspire its beholders (page 214).

M The Country Music Hall of Fame: This top tourist sight redefines the roots and the impact of country music (page 214).

M Fisk University: This campus remains a monument to African-American education (page 218).

M Tennessee State Museum: It truly is the best look at Tennessee's remarkable history in the state (page 220).

M *Grand Ole Opry:* This worthwhile diversion— even for people who don't think they like country music—offers a glimpse into a good idea hatched in 1925 (page 227).

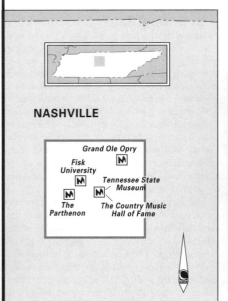

NASHVILLE

Grand Ole Opry **M**

Fisk University **M**

Tennessee State Museum **M**

The Parthenon **M**

The Country Music Hall of Fame **M**

Country Music Hall of Fame

COURTESY OF TIMOTHY HURSLEY, NASHVILLE CONVENTION AND VISITORS BUREAU

Nashville

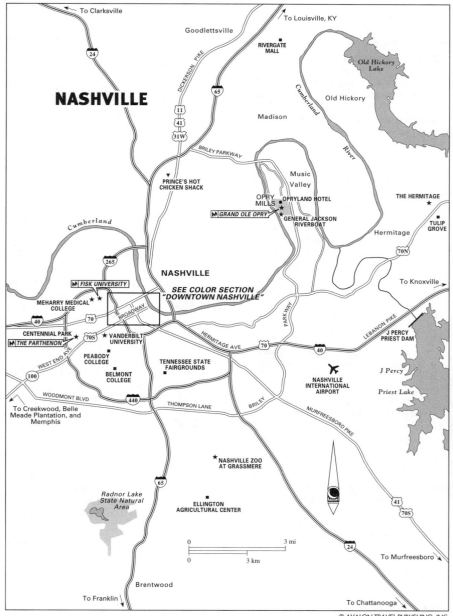

BY BOAT TO FORT NASHBOROUGH

The river voyage of Captain John Donelson and the rest of his party would make a great adventure movie. A flotilla of 30 boats shoved off from the Long Island of the Holston—present-day Kingsport—on December 22, 1779. The largest flatboat measured 100 feet long by 20 feet wide. The weather was so cold that the would-be settlers had to stop after going only a few miles, and they resumed their journey in mid-February. Other settlers farther downstream learned of the journey and joined the group along the way.

Almost everything that could go wrong did so on this trip. The dreaded smallpox broke out during the voyage, forcing the travelers to quarantine diseased people in separate vessels. Boats ran aground and got stuck. The food supply ran low. Then there were the Indians and the river itself.

As the boats descended the Tennessee, they floated past the Chickamauga, a breakaway group of Cherokee who had vowed to kill off settlers. One of the boats ran aground at the worst possible time—while Indians were firing on it—and men and women dodged bullets to get the boat moving again. One of these women had borne a child the night before, and during the battle the baby was killed.

Two sections of Tennessee River white water terrified the travelers. "The Suck" was a formidable whirlpool below what is now Chattanooga, and farther along in Alabama lay Muscle Shoals, where the currents ran the boats aground. Some of the party, weary of this journey, bailed out here. Others, when it came time to push the boats upstream along the Ohio and Cumberland Rivers, decided to drift down the Mississippi to Natchez.

Donelson and his party were reunited with James Robertson and the others on April 24, 1780. Their journey had covered more than 1,000 miles, taken four months, and suffered 33 casualties. One of the survivors of this epic trip was Rachel Donelson, the 15-year-old daughter of the captain. Rachel later married Andrew Jackson.

sounded too English, and the colonies wanted nothing that recalled their colonial oppressors. By 1787 the town had a newspaper, and the next year a young attorney came to town and hung up his shingle. His name was Andrew Jackson.

Jackson came to a town that was booming. The Cumberland River location was ideal for trade, and Nashville produced iron, guns, cloth, and other goods and sold them upstream and downstream. Tennessee became a state in 1796, and in 1806 Nashville was granted a city charter.

Andrew Jackson's fortunes rose with Nashville's, and he came to national attention with his Battle of New Orleans victory over the British in 1815. In 1829, Jackson was elected president, the first from west of the Appalachians.

The first steamboat came to town in 1818, and this new form of shipping enhanced the city's growing commerce, as did a series of roads and turnpikes that radiated outward like spokes from the city.

The Tennessee legislature first met in Nashville in 1812 for one year and returned for good in 1826. Work was begun on a capitol building in 1845.

Along with the rest of Middle Tennessee, Nashville achieved great prosperity in the 1850s, which witnessed the construction of the Belmont and Belle Meade plantation houses. The railroad came to town in 1854, which further cemented Nashville's commercial success.

The Civil War Years

When the Civil War broke out, Nashville became a prime target. Its role as a transportation center was critical to help the North invade the Confederacy, and for the South it was an important manufacturing center—one of the few it had. The city's fate was sealed in February 1862, when Union General U. S. Grant captured Fort Donelson, which guarded the downstream approach to the city. The Confederates burned the bridges across the Cumberland River but did not have the manpower to defend Nashville, and they were forced to surrender it to Northern troops.

Abraham Lincoln appointed Andrew Johnson, the Tennessee senator who had kept his seat despite Tennessee's secession, military governor of the state. Johnson had twice been elected governor in the 1850s. The new state capitol building was surrounded with enough artillery to make it look like a fort. Johnson infuriated Nashvillians by arresting preachers who delivered pro-South sermons, closing hostile newspapers, and summarily dismissing the mayor and city council and appointing Northern sympathizers in their places.

One of the few groups who welcomed the influx of northerners were Nashville's prostitutes, whose entrepreneurship so annoyed military leaders that in 1863 some 150 of them were rounded up and packed onto a steamboat meant to take them away. Downstream cities such as Louisville and Cincinnati would have no part of this shipment, and sent the boat and its passengers back to Nashville.

The South tried twice to get Nashville back. In January of 1863 Union General William Rosecrans defeated Confederate General Braxton Bragg at Murfreesboro's Battle of Stones River,

forcing the Southerners to retreat. Late in the war, when Union General William T. Sherman was marching toward the sea, John Bell Hood moved his Confederates toward Nashville in a desperate move. He was crushed at the Battle of Franklin in 1864 by General John Schofield, but he persisted in following the Union troops as they retreated into Nashville. On December 15 and 16, Union forces marched out of the city and further devastated Hood's army, and Nashville stayed in Union hands until the war was over.

Return to Prosperity

Tennessee was the first state to return to the Union, and once again Nashville's location in the middle of the nation provided it a means to regain its prosperity. A cholera epidemic in 1866 was followed by another in 1873. City officials traced the disease to contaminated springs and wells and moved to improve the city's infrastructure.

COURTESY OF VANDO ROGERS, NASHVILLE CONVENTION AND VISITORS BUREAU

Nashville

The Fisk Jubilee Singers sang across the United States and in England to raise money for Fisk University.

Nashville had enjoyed a university since 1828, but in the post–Civil War years education flowered. The Fisk School, later called Fisk University, was founded in 1866 to provide higher education for recently freed blacks. To raise money for the fledgling college, a group of students called the Fisk Jubilee Singers toured the nation and Europe. The same year another black college, Central Tennessee College, was chartered. In 1876 it gained a medical school, which was named Meharry Medical College, which became a separate institution in 1915.

Vanderbilt College got its charter in 1873, and, in an effort to improve the education of schoolteachers, the Peabody State Normal School of the University of Nashville was founded in 1875.

The presence of these and other colleges led Nashville to adopt the name "the Athens of the South," and in 1897 the city was host to the Centennial Exposition. This fair featured a life-size, plaster replica of the Parthenon, and residents so admired it that they would not let it be torn down after the event was over. It was eventually replaced with a more permanent concrete replica, which still stands.

The Rise of Country Music

Nashville is best known to the world, however, as the mecca of country music. The city had a long musical tradition, and as a Southern crossroads it was visited by musicians of every stripe. Radio came to Nashville in 1922, and three years later the National Life and Accident Insurance Company built a station it called WSM, an acronym of the company's motto, "We Shield Millions." WSM hired George D. Hay, a young announcer from WLS, a big Chicago station, but a man with Tennessee roots. A one-time writer for the Memphis Commercial Appeal, he achieved success with a column called "Howdy, Judge" that consisted of conversations between a white judge and assorted black defendants. Hay picked up the nickname "the solemn old judge" although he was neither old nor particularly solemn and had nothing to do with the judiciary.

Looking to duplicate the success of Chicago's National Barn Dance radio show, Hay first called Nashville's version the Barn Dance. The first band

to play country music on the radio in Nashville was led by Dr. Humphrey Bate, a Vanderbilt-educated physician whose string band wore business suits while on stage. Hay pushed things in a cornball direction, however, and Bate's band became "The Possum Hunters." Other groups were given similar names such as "The Fruit Jar Drinkers" and "The Dixie Clodhoppers," and the die was cast: country equaled corny. Another much-loved entertainer was Uncle Dave Macon, whose renditions of songs such as "Keep My Skillet Good and Greasy" delighted rural listeners.

THE OTHER NASHVILLE MUSIC

The shorthand musical descriptions that attach themselves to Tennessee's two musical cities go like this. Memphis, with the exception of four white guys who passed through Sun Studios, is the center of black music. Nashville, with the exception of DeFord Bailey and Charley Pride, is the center of white music.

It ain't necessarily so.

From 1945 through 1970, Nashville record companies released an astonishing array of **rhythm and blues** music. B. B. King, whose very initials derived from his nickname of "Beale Street Blues Boy," cut his first record in Nashville. The most influential Southern radio station playing rhythm and blues music was in Nashville. Artists such as Etta James, Joe Tex, the Fairfield Four, Big Joe Williams, and Willie Dixon recorded here, and far more other R & B greats regularly performed in Nashville.

This hidden side of Nashville's musical heritage is finally getting some attention. In 2000, Bear Family Records issued an eight-CD set called *A Shot in the Dark: Nashville Jumps: Rhythm and Blues on Nashville Independent Labels.* The Country Music Hall of Fame and Museum featured an 18-month exhibit on R&B, and a 2004 two-CD release entitled *Night Train to Nashville* gives listeners a delightful sampling of African American music associated with Nashville. The Country Music Foundation Press issued *You Can Make It If You Try: The Ted Jarrett Story of R&B in Nashville.*

The audiences loved it, although proper Nashvillians were appalled at the image of their city that was broadcast by one of the more powerful radio signals in the country. In 1927, Hay started calling his show the *Grand Ole Opry,* a not-so-sly dig at the Grand Opera that was a favorite of the Athens of the South set.

As the *Opry* grew in popularity, the management allowed its musicians to tour but insisted that they be available every Saturday night for the show. This meant they couldn't go far, and thus would return to town almost every week to pick up new songs, work out deals, and form new bands. A growing group of songwriters and publishers took up residence in Nashville, and the industry slowly but surely grew.

World War II helped country music, dispersing Southerners all over the country and the world, where they demanded the music they loved and exposed others to it as well. The *Opry* moved into Nashville's Ryman Auditorium in the middle of the war, and more and more people clamored to see the country stars. As a measure of country music's growing audience, mainstream entertainers such as Bing Crosby and Tony Bennett began recording songs that were first heard in Tennessee.

It wasn't all country music. After World War II, independent Nashville record producers recorded all manner of musicians, people such as rhythm and blues great Rufus Thomas, gospel singers the Fairfield Four, and bluesmen Willie Dixon and B. B. King. Although Memphis likes to be known as Tennessee's center of the blues, between 1945 and 1970, Nashville held its own.

Country music began to predominate, however, although it still wasn't accepted in Nashville. Hank Williams's biographer Colin Escott tells how Roy Acuff threw a party at the Ryman Auditorium in 1943 to celebrate his radio show's being carried coast-to-coast on 129 stations. He invited Governor Prentice Cooper to attend the festivities. The governor declined, in Escott's words, "saying he would have no part of a "circus," adding that Acuff was bringing disgrace to the state by making Tennessee the hillbilly capital of the United States."

All this time country music was called "folk music." *Billboard* magazine finally replaced its "American folk tunes" with a new name: "country and western." Whatever it was, Nashville was the place from which it came. Entertainers such as Elvis Presley and Buddy Holly recorded in Nashville, although neither made it as a country star. Nashville lost ground as rock 'n' roll ascended and young people began asserting their musical tastes.

In an effort to make country music more mainstream, producers such as the late Chet Atkins created the "Nashville sound." Singers were backed with soft choruses or even violins— not fiddles anymore. Uncle Dave Macon probably spun in his grave, but country music was heading uptown. The *Grand Ole Opry* moved to Opryland in 1974, and television shows began to feature country music. One of the more successful of these was CBS's *Hee Haw,* whose cornball comedy and down-home music were direct descendants of the vision of George Hay.

The recording expertise of Nashville did not go unnoticed by other musicians. Ex-Beatle Paul McCartney and other musicians came to record in Nashville to take advantage of the supply of excellent sidemen and the relaxed recording atmosphere. In 1975 Robert Altman filmed *Nashville,* a complex film that puzzled residents of the city; they were honored to be noticed by Hollywood but somewhat suspicious that they were being mocked. Some of Altman's allegedly fictional characters seemed very similar to icons of country music.

Nashville remains the center of the country music empire. Busloads of fans come to the Opry, spend money at the various "museums" of the stars, and prowl Music Row for a glimpse of someone famous. Would-be stars come here as well, playing in the parking lot at Shoney's or hoping for a slot at the Bluebird, with the ghosts of Johnny Cash and Hank Williams walking the streets, welcoming them all.

Big City?

Nashville now has a professional hockey team and the Tennessee Titans, a National Football League franchise. Does this make it a city big enough to rub shoulders with the Chicagos and Bostons of the country? While in some areas—music is the obvious choice—Nashville is right up there, the town is full of people from small towns who are incapable of shedding the inherent politeness and religion with which they grew up. This leads to unexpected juxtapositions sometimes—a Mercedes with a bumper sticker that says, "I am an organ donor. I gave my [heart symbol] to Jesus." It also leads to a city by and large full of nice folks—far more pleasant people than any big city you can mention.

Sights

ORIENTATION

Nashville is a city on a hill, the state capitol at the top and the rest of the downtown area flowing down to the Cumberland River. Visitors to Downtown and The District should park their cars and get out. All those in decent shape should be able to walk to wherever they want to go. A particularly good route to follow is **Citywalk,** a two-mile walking tour that follows a blue line painted through Downtown and The District. It begins and ends at Fort Nashborough, although walkers can pick up brochures at various places along the route. For more information, call 615/862-7970 Monday–Friday.

The rest of town requires some wheels. Music Row is on one of the many spokes heading out of town, and the West End is farther out. Music Valley, beside the Opryland Hotel and the Grand Ole Opry, is upstream on the Cumberland River.

City buses are run by the **Metropolitan Transit Authority.** Fare is $1.45 for adults; call 615/862-5950 for information about routes and schedules, or go to www.nashvillemta.org.

And then there are taxis. Call **Allied Taxi** (615/244-7433) or **Music City Taxi** (615/262-0451).

Downtown

Bob Dylan once recorded an album here called *Nashville Skyline,* and, viewed from afar, the city has a good collection of modern skyscrapers, including the corporate offices of BellSouth, which locals call "the bat building." The Tennessee State Capitol sits at the top of a cluster of state buildings, among them the Tennessee State Museum and the Performing Arts Center.

Downtown Nashville—the area near the state capitol—feels almost like an archaeological site because of the different historical layers that exist, if not vertically, then side by side. As in a lot of inner cities elsewhere, a lot of the businesses are still of the Woolworth's/Dollar Store/Discount Furniture type. This is the world that the shrines of country music—Ryman Auditorium, Tootsie's Orchid Lounge, Ernest Tubb Record Shop—inhabit; tourist sites from a different era, most of them still look like it. Then there's the Country Music Museum and Hall of Fame, luring tourists south of Broadway.

Downtown contains a delightful array of architectural wonders, which are described in greater detail below.

The District

Like Knoxville's Old City and Memphis's Beale Street, The District is the old made new. In this case it's a bunch of 19th-century warehouses that once serviced steamboats on the Cumberland River. A very downsized replica of Fort Nashborough sits in a park along the river, but the real action begins across the street to the west. Here is a collection of shops, restaurants, and clubs. The biggest is the Wildhorse Saloon, which is just a side-slide away from the Market Street Brewery. Printer's Alley, a collection of nightclubs, beckons visitors with a wink and a hint of naughtiness.

The western boundary of The District is more vaguely defined, but it includes several icons of country music. West on Broadway, as if to herald the wonders ahead, are Hatch Show Print, then Gruhn Guitars, then Tootsie's Orchid Lounge. Just up 5th Avenue, like a wide-hipped matron at a concert, sits Ryman Auditorium, the longtime home of the *Grand Ole Opry*.

On Broadway

Broadway runs through The District, but there are so many places to see along it that it deserves a section of its own.

To the southwest lies the Union Station, once the flagship station of the Louisville and Nashville Railroad and elegant in ways that airports can never be.

Right beside Union Station is the High Victorian Gothic Christ Church Episcopal on the left. Across from the church stands the 1876 Customs House, and one block east is Hume-Fogg High School, built in 1912. The next block to the left is the massive Nashville Convention Center and Nashville Arena. By now foot traffic has increased, and the visitor has come to The District.

One block south of Broadway, the Shelby Avenue Bridge, which opened to traffic in 1909, now carries pedestrians and human-powered vehicles only. While offering a pleasant stroll over the Cumberland River, the east end of the bridge deposits the visitor into the vast wasteland of parking lots for Adelphi Stadium. The west end leads down to Nashville's new Schermerhorn Symphony Center.

East Nashville

The construction of the Coliseum for the Tennessee Titans football team on the East side of the Cumberland River brought new attention to a long-neglected neighborhood. A small but vibrant group of clubs and restaurants have spring up here. The main access route from Downtown is Woodland Avenue.

North Nashville

Many of the landmarks in Nashville's black history can be found in North Nashville, northwest of downtown. The area is bounded by Charlotte Avenue to the south and Jefferson Street to the north. Jefferson Street, in the days before integration, was Nashville's equivalent to Beale Street in Memphis.

The neighborhood's musical heyday lasted from 1940 through 1960, when clubs hosted

© JEFF BRADLEY

a pedestrian bridge over the Cumberland River

rhythm and blues, jazz, and blues performers. When I-40 was built through here, it cut the neighborhood in two and marked the beginning of a decline.

Hereabouts are the campuses of Fisk University and Meharry Medical College, two of the most historically significant colleges in the country. The largest college is nearby Tennessee State University. Jefferson Street contains a variety of African American shops. An excellent website with a black perspective on Nashville is www.soulofamerica.com.

Music Row

This highly publicized place is neither a row nor a place of much music for visitors. Record companies have their offices here, and limousines glide in and out, but there is little reason for music fans to come here at all unless they like to look at office buildings.

Sited on land once owned by the inhabitants of Belmont Mansion, 16th and 17th Avenues between Demonbreun Street and Grand Avenue mark the center of the entertainment business in Nashville, a collection of studios and offices for the music companies and assorted hangers-on. One place unrelated to music is The Upper Room Chapel and Museum, a religious museum whose centerpiece is a carved version of Leonardo da Vinci's *The Last Supper.*

Hillsboro Village

For those who weary of country music and anything to do with it, the sophistication of Hillsboro Village awaits. This is the closest thing in Tennessee to Harvard Square. Following 21st Street from Music Row leads into an enclave of book and coffee shops, The Belcourt Theatre and Provence Breads and Café, the home of the best bread in the state. You can buy a *New York Times* here and not feel self-conscious carrying it around.

West End

If there's anything left of the Athens of the South, it hides out here in the shadow of Vanderbilt University and occasionally receives company in Centennial Park. Here are the Parthenon and a host of record stores and boutiques whose clerks couldn't name a Hank Snow song if a customer held a gun on them. Elliston Place, a collection of bars, restaurants, and shops in a strip a couple of blocks long, includes several where actual musicians, who are spending their own money, and music industry types, who are spending somebody else's, hang out. These places tend to be funkier and not as gussied up as those closer to Music Row/Division Street, in many cases because they've been here much longer.

Belle Meade

"Belle Meade" sometimes confuses visitors, for it is at once a plantation, a town, and, some would argue, a state of mind. The plantation from which it sprang is still considered one of the finest in Tennessee. The town, which the 2000 census listed as the fifth-richest per capita town in the country, consists of a mere 3,000 souls and is almost completely surrounded by Nashville. Al Gore lives here.

The people who live here permit no commercial establishments to sully their world. The Belle Meade Country Club is perhaps the most exclusive in Nashville. The riff-raff come in to see Belle Meade Plantation and Cheekwood art museum, or to ride bikes, jog, or glide along on in-line skates.

Music Valley

The centerpiece of this part of Nashville should be called the Grand New Opry. Here are the *Grand Ole Opry,* the Opryland Hotel, and the home wharf of the General Jackson Riverboat. It is also the home of Opry Mills, a shopping mall.

ARCHITECTURE

Nashville is home to the widest variety of architectural jewels of any major city in Tennessee. The following are celebrated for their buildings per se. The first group of buildings is downtown—most of them along Broadway or close to it, and anyone in reasonable shape can reach them all by walking. An excellent website for architecture fans is www.midtennhistory.com. Or visitors can obtain a copy of the Citywalk brochure from a visitors center and follow it.

Downtown

The Hermitage Hotel (231 6th Ave. N., 615/244-3121, www.westinhermitage.com) is the last of the old grand hotels in Nashville. Although not "renovated" to the grandeur of, say, the Peabody in Memphis, it's a relatively small matron surrounded by huge moderns. Delicate bas-reliefs decorate the outside walls; inside are a two- or three-story lobby, stained glass and marble, and a brass "cashier" window.

One of the more humble architectural delights is the **Arcade,** an ancestor of today's shopping mall. Between Union and Church Streets and connecting 4th and 5th Avenues, the Arcade opened in 1903 and is said to be one of only four such structures left in the country; its two floors of shops are sheltered by metal-girdered glass skylights. Some of the shops have seemingly been here forever and couldn't care less about tourists—shoe repair, tobacco, and so forth.

Half a street down from the Arcade is Church Street, where 104-foot-high twin brick towers mark the **Downtown Presbyterian Church** (427 Church St.). While the exterior is appropriately somber, the interior looks like it ought to be in Cairo. From 1849 to 1851, architect William Strickland, who also designed the state capitol, created a house of worship in the Egyptian revival style. Most of the interior work, however, was done in the 1880s. The result is perhaps the most striking sanctuary in the entire state, all the more impressive because of a $1.2 million renovation finished in 2001. The six massive interior columns, stained glass with Egyptian themes, and massive pipe organ will impress even heathens.

Tours of the church can be arranged for groups of five or more by calling 615/254-7584, or one can walk down a sidewalk on the left of the church and get buzzed in. Visit www.dpchurch.com.

Just down the street from the Presbyterian Church is the **Nashville Public Library** (615 Church St., 615/862-5800, www.library.nashville .org). This $50 million temple of knowledge contains a reading room that looks toward the

state capitol. Overhead, a painted blue sky presides over beautiful wooden tables. Hand-hammered copper panels relate Tennessee history, and the children's section contains a theater with tree trunks on each side of the stage. Even if you have no plans to check out a book, this wonderful building is worth a walk-through.

A walk downhill to Broadway, crossing the street, and strolling to the right brings the visitor to the Victorian Gothic **Customs House** (701 Broadway). Now in private hands and used for offices, the Customs House was Nashville's post office and the center of federal government activity in the city for decades. President Rutherford B. Hayes laid the cornerstone in 1877 in the first visit by a president below the Mason-Dixon line since the Civil War.

The Frist Center (919 Broadway) occupies a lovingly restored building that served as Nashville's post office 1934–86. Erected in the depths of the Depression, the post office has a stripped classic or "classic moderne" style often used in federal buildings at that time. As with the Presbyterian Church, a rather somber exterior conceals a lively inside, where stainless-steel railings and shiny marble combine in a wonderful example of art deco. The restoration project cost $45 million, and it shows.

Union Station is worth a detour. Built in 1900 for the Louisville and Nashville Railroad, this transportation palace sports a tower that is 237 feet high. Although now a hotel, visitors can still come in and admire the building. The vaulted ceilings are 67 feet high in what was once the main terminal room; the room is illuminated by Tiffany-style windows. Behind the check-in desk hangs an old schedule board with names of trains—Pan American, Azalean, and Dixieland.

Jubilee Hall

In North Nashville on the campus of Fisk University, this is the architectural legacy of the Fisk Singers, nine men and women who in 1871 sang the college out of debt and raised money for this Victorian Gothic edifice. This is believed to be the oldest surviving building erected for the purpose of educating African Americans.

The Parthenon

The Parthenon (Centennial Park, 615/862-8431, www.parthenon.org, $4 adults, $2.50 seniors and kids 4–17) is a legacy of the days when American cities hosted large exhibitions and built extravagant structures meant to last only for those celebrations. This duplicate of the quintessential Greek building in Athens is actually the second such replica. The first, hastily constructed of wood and plaster for the 1896 exposition, was so popular that citizens didn't want it torn down. The "temporary" building stood for 24 years, then was demolished in preparation for a permanent Parthenon, which opened in 1931.

The new and improved Parthenon—the only full-size replica in the world—was built of concrete, with floors of Tennessee marble and a ceiling of Florida cypress. The building is impressive: 46 Doric columns encircle it, and the largest bronze doors in the world, 7.5 tons each, stand at the east and west entrances. The sculptures and friezes are modeled on the Elgin Mar-bles in London, which the British stole from Greece. Spruced up after a 10-year, $12 million renovation, the Parthenon is now more beautiful than ever.

Inside stands a statue of Athena, the Greek goddess from whom came the name of Greece's capital city. The 42-foot-high goddess stands here in her concrete Parthenon, billed as "the largest indoor sculpture in the Western World," solemnly reflecting on the days when Nashville strove to be known as the Athens of the South.

The Parthenon's basement contains an art museum with four galleries. One holds the Cowan Collection, 63 works by 19th- and 20th-century American painters. Another exhibit is plaster casts of the Elgin Marbles.

MUSIC
The Country Music Hall of Fame

This second iteration of the Country Music Hall of Fame and Museum (222 5th Ave. S., 615/416-2001, www.countrymusichalloffame.com,

The Country Music Hall of Fame is possibly the best music museum in the country

10 A.M.–6 P.M. daily, $15.95 adults, $7.95 children 6–15) occupies an entire block downtown and is something every visitor to Nashville should see.

The experience begins with a movie about country music in a 214-seat theater. When this is over, visitors make their way to exhibits of one-of-a-kind items that belonged to the greats—Jimmie Rodger's guitar, Tex Ritter's saddle, Minnie Pearl's hat—complete with its famous price tag. Some exhibits are testaments to people of uncertain taste who had ready access to lots of money. You can see a suit and cowboy boots worn by Hank Williams, flashy rhinestone garments from "Nudie" Cohn, and a Webb Piece Cadillac with silver dollars embedded in the interior.

It's interesting to see how this place handles Elvis Presley, who was posthumously inducted into the Hall of Fame in 1998. Although the King recorded some numbers that could be considered country, he—more than anyone else—came the closest to killing off country music when he burst on the scene in the 1950s.

Elvis gets a lot of attention here. One of his Cadillacs gleams under the lights, and his *Live in Las Vegas* gold record (a country album?) is right up there on the wall with albums by Loretta Lynn. Amid the video screens featuring past and present performers, the one with Elvis is bigger than the others and often attracts more visitors than anything else.

Exhibits in the museum feature essential parts of country music such as the role of songwriters and interesting, although more tangential ones, such as the rise of Southern Rock. Other exhibits include a look at country music television shows such as *Hee Haw, The Porter Wagoner Show,* and *The Johnny Cash Show.*

The final stop is the Hall of Fame itself, a series of plaques in a circular room whose centerpiece is a replica of the WSM radio antenna that has for so many years broadcast the *Grand Ole Opry.* The famous musicians and singers, such as Chet Atkins and Patsy Cline, are there with lesser-known figures such as Paul Cohen and Jo Walker-Meador, whose names cause visitors to step up and read the plaques closely. All in all, this is a very good way to spend two or three hours.

Studio B, near Music Row, is the legendary studio where Elvis Presley, with Chet Atkins in the control room, laid down the tracks at 4 A.M. for "Are You Lonesome Tonight" on April 4, 1960. Other artists who recorded here include Dolly Parton, Roy Orbison, Waylon Jennings, and the Everly Brothers.

As an add-on to the Country Music Hall of Fame and Museum, visitors can take a shuttle to the studio. The entire trip takes one hour, and, counting HOF admission, costs $22.95 for adults and $13.95 for kids 6–17. These tours begin at 10:30 A.M. and run hourly through 2:30 P.M. Reservations are available by calling 800/852-6437.

Ryman Auditorium and Museum

The Ryman (116 5th Ave. N., 615/254-1445, www.ryman.com, $8 adults, $4 children 4–11) was built because a steamboat captain got religion, and now it is the mother church of country music. Tom Ryman was a rough-and-tumble operator of a fleet of packet boats on the Cumberland River. He converted to Christianity in 1881 and provided much of the money that built what was originally called—and still bears the name—the Union Gospel Tabernacle. Its wooden interior proved to be a dandy concert hall, and it began to host traveling shows starring Enrico Caruso, Charlie Chaplin, Mae West, W. C. Fields, and the Ziegfield Follies. People in Nashville called it the Ryman Auditorium, and in 1943 it got its most famous tenant, the *Grand Ole Opry* radio show. Virtually everyone who was anyone in country music trod the boards there until the Opry moved to newer quarters in 1974.

Visitors here can sit in the pews, walk up on the stage, and imagine how a packed house must have looked to Hank Williams, Patsy Cline, and the many others who sang here. A small museum displays memorabilia of performers, and there is a gift shop. Performances still take place in the hall; visitors can find out what is on tap by calling 615/889-3060.

Nashville

www.nashvillesymphony.org or call the box office at 615/783-1212.

Show Business

Hatch Show Print (316 Broadway, 615/256-2805, www.hatchshowprint.com, free) uses over 10,000 hardwood, single-letter pieces of type to produce posters that look very much like their 1905 counterparts. Visitors can watch the staff print posters and can purchase some of the famous ones of Elvis, Bill Monroe, and other subjects. Price range is from $3 to $500.

Country Music DJ Hall of Fame is a series of plaques commemorating famous country radio hosts. These can be seen in the walkway between the Nashville Convention Center and the Radisson Hotel, or at www.crb.org.

Music Valley

Grand Ole Opry Museum, Roy Acuff's Museum, and **Minnie Pearl's Museum** are all at the **Opryland** complex (2802 Opryland Dr., 615/889-6611, www.opry.com, free to Minnie Pearl's and Roy Acuff's museums). Exhibits at the Grand Ole Opry Museum honor legendary performers such as Patsy Cline, George Jones, and Little Jimmy Dickens, as well as more current stars along the lines of Reba and Garth. This place offers artifacts, interactive devices, and many opportunities to hear music. The Roy Acuff and Minnie Pearl museums center on the late "King of Country Music" and the *Opry's* longtime comedienne, who died in 1996.

Of all the museums devoted to country music figures, here's one that stands out—its subject can be found in there almost every week. **The Louvin Brothers Museum** (2416 Music Valley Dr., www.charlielouvinbros.com), located next to the Ernest Tubb Theater, features Charlie Louvin, half of the most influential brother acts in country music. The museum's hours are irregular—septuagenarians get that privilege—but a good bet is to arrive there on Saturday afternoon. Charlie often performs on the *Opry,* and likes to greet fans before the show.

Across from the Opryland Hotel, **Willie Nelson and Friends Showcase Museum** (2613A McGavock Pike, 615/885-1515, $3.50 adults,

The renovated Ryman was once the home of the Grand Ole Opry.

Printer's Alley

The alley between 3rd and 4th Avenues and Union and Commerce Streets got its name from various printing operations that used to be located nearby. When presses weren't running, their operators would gather in the alley to talk and smoke. And drink. Speakeasies flourished here during Prohibition, and even though the printing shops moved away, the name stuck. Nightclubs offered burlesque shows, drinks, and entertainers such as Chet Atkins, Roger Miller, and Connie Francis. Boots Randolph, he of "Yakety Sax," owned a nightclub here. Things are pretty tame there now, although the garish signs work hard to bring a little bit of Bourbon Street to Nashville.

Schermerhorn Symphony Center

Slated to open in the fall of 2006, the new hall for the Nashville Symphony occupies a block between 3rd and 4th Avenues South, north of Demonbreun. Seating 1,900, the hall is the only major concert hall in North America using natural light. For information on concerts, go to

$1.50 children 6–12, free for children under 6) in the Music Valley Gift Emporium pays tribute to Willie Nelson, Elvis, J. D. Sumner, Patsy Cline, and others. It includes Nelson's gold and platinum albums and guitars and has a gift shop.

HISTORIC

Tennessee State Capitol

The state capitol (Charlotte Ave. between 6th and 7th Aves,. 615/741-1621, free) was finished just in time for the Civil War. Architect William Strickland considered it his crowning achievement and went so far as to work into the plans a tomb for himself. He died in 1854, while the building was still under construction, and he rests today above the cornerstone in the northeast corner.

Nashville fell quickly and relatively painlessly to Union troops, and the new capitol building, high on a hill overlooking the city, was barricaded and surrounded by cannons and was used as a fortress. Abraham Lincoln installed Andrew Johnson as military governor, and from here he ruled the captive state until he was nominated as vice president in 1864.

The capitol was built of local limestone, which was largely replaced in the 1950s. The interior

THE RUINS OF FORT NEGLEY

The Union Army occupied Nashville on February 25, 1862, and the next month President Lincoln appointed Senator and future running mate Andrew Johnson as Tennessee's military governor. Johnson, fearing that the Confederates would try to retake Nashville, sought to fortify the city, and commanding general James S. Negley was ordered to prepare the defenses.

To do this, the Army needed workers, so they simultaneously recruited and forced much of Nashville's black population and put them to work on the fort. An estimated 2,000 workers dug foundations, laid stone walls, put down heavy wooden flooring to support cannons, and finished Fort Negley by December 7, 1862.

The largest fort west of Washington, D.C., Fort Negley never actually saw combat; the Confederates attempted to retake Nashville in 1864, but were stopped in Franklin. The Union Army pulled out of the fort in 1867.

The Ku Klux Klan met clandestinely in the fort, and it was there in 1869 that Grand Wizard Nathan Bedford Forrest called a final meeting at which he hoped to disband the organization. Klan robes were burned in the fort.

The ensuing years saw stones from Fort Negley removed for various building projects. Beginning in 1936, the Works Progress Administration set out to restore the fort, but this effort never accomplished much and, historically speaking, did considerable damage to the ruins. Over the years a forest encircled the fort, and visitors to the Adventure Science Center on its periphery had no idea that they were close to a Civil War site.

At long last Nashville decided to reopen the fort, but to preserve it as a ruin and not attempt to restore it. Visitors can find the fort, logically enough, on a hill south of Broadway. You can get there from I-40 take Exit 210C or, from downtown, Take 8th Avenue South to Chestnut. Turn left onto Chestnut and proceed about 300 yards crossing over the interstate overpass bridge. Turn left onto Ft. Negley Boulevard.

© JEFF BRADLEY

The largest inland fort built during the Civil War, Fort Negley was constructed by freed blacks and the Union Army.

Nashville

walls consist of East Tennessee marble. In the late 1980s several sections of the capitol were restored to their 19th-century appearance, and visitors are invited to take a brochure and walk the old halls.

The capitol grounds contain statues of famous Tennesseans. The one of Andrew Jackson riding a horse is said to be the first equestrian statue in America. President and Mrs. James K. Polk are buried on the capitol grounds, and statues of Sergeant Alvin York and Sam Davis and other luminaries surround the building. There is no charge to visit the Tennessee State Capitol, which is uphill from virtually anywhere in downtown Nashville.

Fisk University

Nashville also became known as the "Black Athens of the South" because of the presence of four colleges for black people: Fisk University, Tennessee State University, Meharry Medical College, and Roger Williams University. Of those four, the first three are still going strong.

Fisk University (1000 17th Ave. N., for escorted tours call 615/329-8666, ext. 225, www.fisk.edu) was established in 1866 as Fisk Free Colored School, and since then it has educated thousands of young men and women. The University was named after Clinton Fisk, a general in the Union Army when it occupied Nashville. Famous graduates include W. E. B. DuBois and poet Nikki Giovanni. Faculty member James Weldon Johnson wrote "Lift Every Voice and Sing," for years known as the "Negro National Anthem." Today, in proportion to their enrollment, more Fisk graduates receive Ph.D.s than African American graduates of any other college or university. Graduate and undergraduate enrollment totals approximately 950.

The 40-acre Fisk campus is on the National Register, and many people come to see Jubilee Hall, a building paid for by a triumphal tour of Europe by the Fisk Singers. The building contains a floor-to-ceiling portrait of the original Jubilee Singers painted by Queen Victoria's artist. The hall also is home to the famed "Golden Staircase," on which young men would propose marriage to their sweethearts. Now the staircase can

be used only by alumni who graduated more than 50 years ago. The Van Vechten Gallery contains 101 pieces of art that make up the Alfred Stieglitz Collection of modern art.

Cravath Hall, which houses administrative offices, contains some newly restored Aaron Douglas murals.

Meharry Medical College

Right beside Fisk is Meharry Medical College (www.mmc.edu). Indeed, many Fisk graduates crossed the street to begin their medical education. From its beginnings in 1876 as the first medical school in this country for African Americans, Meharry has produced many of the African American doctors and dentists in this country. Enrollment is just over 800 students. The college got its name from Samuel Meharry, a young man whose wagon got stuck while he was traveling through Nashville. He was so impressed with an impoverished black family who helped him that he vowed to "do something for your race." Meharry and his brothers gave a $30,000 gift, and the college now bears their name.

Tennessee State University

The largest historically black college in Nashville is Tennessee State University. Created as the Agricultural and Industrial State Normal School in 1909, it opened to students in 1912, was raised to the status of a four-year teachers' college in 1922, and elevated to full-fledged land-grant university status in 1958. Graduate and undergraduate enrollment totals 8,750. Oprah Winfrey attended TSU.

Other Sights

City Cemetery (1001 4th Ave. at Oak St., 615/862-7970) opened in 1822 and was Nashville's first public cemetery. Among the notables laid to rest here is James Robertson, the "Father of Middle Tennessee." The cemetery has about 23,000 graves and accepts burials only of anyone whose family plot has room.

Fort Nashborough (in Riverfront Park, 170 1st Ave. N., 615/862-8400, free) is a reconstructed miniature version of the settlement that started it all.

Leaving Nashville and heading south on I-

65, the motorist soon comes upon what has to be the most hideous Civil War statue ever erected. Using what appears to be singularly cheap plastic, the **Nathan Bedford Forrest Statue** depicts the famed Confederate general and infamous first Grand Wizard of the Ku Klux Klan, astride an anatomically incorrect horse. The pained expression on the Wizard of the Saddle's face looks as if he has been in the saddle too long or has just eaten a big plate of undercooked chitlins.

With 13 Confederate flags flying behind it, the statue has caused all manner of fulmination in Nashville, which is probably the reason it was put up in the first place. It is on private land, and gives mute witness to America's cherished and oft-exercised right to exhibit bad taste.

PLANTATION HOUSES

Belle Meade Plantation

Belle Meade Plantation (5025 Harding Rd., 615/356-0501, www.bellemeadeplantation.com, $10 adults, $8.50 seniors, $4 children 6–12) is a tribute to the kind of lifestyle possible when one doesn't have to pay one's workers. Belle Meade, known as "The Queen of Tennessee Plantations," focuses on an 1853 Greek Revival mansion, which once commanded a 5,300-acre plantation staffed by 130 slaves. The stone columns still bear scars from Civil War bullets. Now down to a more manageable 30 acres, the plantation includes the mansion, the log house that preceded the mansion, a carriage house, and various outbuildings. While Belle Meade is an antebellum mansion, the house has been restored to its appearance in the 1880s. Thirty-eight percent of the furniture is original to the house.

This plantation figures prominently in the annals of thoroughbred horse racing. John Harding, the patriarch of the family that owned Belle Meade, began breeding horses here in 1816 and boarded horses for Andrew Jackson. The oldest racing silks in America are from here, and when the first Kentucky Derby was run, six of the 15 horses had ties to Belle Meade. In 1881, Iroquois, the first American-bred and owned horse to win the English Derby, came from this plantation.

One of the plantation's odder claims to fame is

that it was the place where President William Taft, a portly soul, got stuck in one of the mansion's bathtubs. His hosts were so mortified that they installed a "stand-up tub" in which the water came out of "a multitude of tubes." This was Nashville's first shower, and Taft—who came back to Belle Meade—liked it so much he had one put into the White House.

Tour guides dress in period outfits. To get there, head out of Nashville on West End Avenue (U.S. 70) and follow the signs.

Belmont Mansion

Belmont Mansion (1900 Belmont Blvd., 615/460-5459, www.belmontmansion.com, $8 adults, $7 seniors, $3 kids 6–12), now the centerpiece of Belmont College, is an Italianate mansion built in 1850 as a summer home by Adelicia Acklen, a woman who charmed Confederate and Union troops into letting her sell close to a million dollars' worth of cotton during the Civil War. Her grand salon was considered the most elaborate room in Tennessee, if not the entire South.

Some 45 percent of the furniture here is original to the house. The Grand Salon is considered by architectural historians to be the most elaborate domestic interior built in antebellum Tennessee. This is the closest antebellum mansion to downtown and well worth the time.

Travellers Rest Plantation

Travellers Rest (636 Farrell Pkwy., 615/832-2962, www.travellersrestplantation.org, 9 A.M.–4 P.M. Mon.–Sat., 1–4 P.M. Sun., $8 adults, $7 seniors, $3 children 6–12) has a name expressing the hospitality often extended by homeowners in a time before bed-and-breakfasts. John Overton established a plantation here in 1796 and built the house in stages. Closely aligned with Andrew Jackson, Overton was Old Hickory's law partner, presidential campaign manager, and fellow land speculator—these two were and one other person founded Memphis. The house has been restored and contains a variety of exhibits, some of them pertaining to the Civil War, when Confederate forces occupied the house during the ill-fated Battle of Nashville.

COURTESY OF MICHAEL MICHOLS, BELMONT MANSION

This grand salon of Belmont Mansion was considered the most elaborate room in Tennessee, if not the entire South.

Travellers Rest Plantation is just south of Harding Place off Franklin Road. Traveling on I-65 South, take the Harding Place west exit, and continue to the Franklin Road/Harding Place intersection. Turn left on Franklin Road and go to Farrell, which is the first left beyond the signal at Tyne Boulevard. Follow the brown signs.

RELIGIOUS

The focal point of **The Upper Room Chapel and Museum** (1908 Grand Ave., 615/340-7207, www.upperroom.org/chapel, free, donations encouraged) is an eight- by 17-foot wooden carving of da Vinci's *The Last Supper.* The chapel also contains an eight- by 20-foot stained-glass window. The museum exhibits religious paintings, books by John Wesley, and English porcelains. At Christmas the museum brings out 100 nativity scenes, and at Easter it displays 73 Ukrainian

eggs. To get there from downtown, go west on Broadway until it becomes 21st Avenue. Turn left onto Grand Avenue.

An increasing number of people have begun praying or meditating while walking a labyrinth, and several Episcopal churches have labyrinths open to the public. The closest one to Nashville is in Antioch, a little town out on U.S. 41 (Murfreesboro Pike). The outdoor **St. Mark's Episcopal Church Labyrinth** (3100 Murfreesboro Pike, 615/361-4100) is patterned after the one in Chartres Cathedral; it is 45 feet across and made of grass outlined by brick.

MUSEUMS AND GALLERIES

Tennessee State Museum

The Tennessee State Museum (5th Ave. between Union and Deaderick Sts., 615/741-2692, www.tnmuseum.org, free) offers an excellent look at the state's history. Combining

THE PROTESTANT VATICAN

Nashville provides a home so many religious organizations that one of the city's nicknames is the Protestant Vatican. The Southern Baptist Convention (www.sbc.net), the largest Protestant denomination in the country, has its headquarters here. Their Sunday School Board produces more Sunday school literature here than is published anywhere else in the world.

The United Methodists have five of their 14 general agencies offices here, including the Methodist Publishing House, which prints hymnals and other religious material. The National Baptist Convention USA (www.nationalbaptist.com) is the largest black denomination in the country, and the largest Bible publisher in the country, Thomas Nelson Publishers, operates here as well.

The House of God (www.hogc.org) is perhaps the most interesting denomination headquartered in Nashville. Founded in 1903 by a woman, Mary Magdalena L. Tate, the church's full name is The House of God Which is the Church of the Living God, the Pillar and Ground of the Truth Without Controversy, Inc. It is the home of "sacred steel," a joyous music played with electric pedal-steel guitars.

Despite the emphasis on Protestantism, Nashville has a very diverse religious population, with synagogues, mosques, and houses of worship to fit the needs of almost any visitor.

Art

The **Aaron Douglas Gallery of African Art** (3rd floor of Main Library, Fisk University, 615/329-8720, www.fisk.edu, free, donations requested) houses the university's collection of African ceremonial items, masks, musical instruments, games, and other items.

Frist Center for the Visual Arts (919 Broadway, 615/244-3340, www.fristcenter.org, 10 A.M.–5:30 P.M. Mon.–Sat., until 8 P.M. on Thurs., 1–5 P.M. Sun., $8.50 adults, $7.50 seniors, free for ages 18 and under) hosts traveling exhibits as well as some from its own growing collections. One attraction for children is the Artquest for Kids section in which youngsters can try everything from watercoloring to "Be a Curator."

The Georgian mansion of **Cheekwood** (1200 Forrest Park Dr., 615/356-8000, www.cheekwood.org) houses the **Museum of Art** and sits amid the 55-acre **Tennessee Botanical Gardens.** This estate owes its existence to coffee. Joel Cheek, a wholesale grocer who specialized in coffee, created a blend that became known as Maxwell House, named for the Nashville hotel where it became famous. With exquisite timing, Cheek sold his formula for millions of dollars in 1928, just before the Depression, and used some of the money to buy 100 acres of land overlooking Nashville. Construction of Cheekwood during 1929-32 provided paychecks to many Nashville workers. The Cheek family moved into the mansion in 1933, and Joel died two years later. His daughter, Huldah, and her husband transformed the home into the museum and botanic gardens in 1957, and it has been open ever since. The three-story mansion now houses a collection of 18th- and 19th-century American art, antique silver, snuff bottles, and period furniture.

While Cheekwood's art is impressive, the best reason for going there is the gardens. Outside, the grounds contain a boxwood garden, flowering trees, perennial borders, and display gardens.

To get there, take Broadway/West End Avenue/Harding Road to Belle Meade Boulevard (a half-mile beyond White Bridge Road). Turn left from Harding Road onto Belle Meade Boulevard; travel to the end of Belle Meade

permanent exhibitions with changing ones, it covers individuals such as Andrew Jackson, David Crockett, and Sam Houston as well as specific periods such as the Civil War and Reconstruction.

Walk one block west on Union Street to the **Military History Branch** (same website, also free) in the War Memorial Building. The collection here focuses on the willingness of Tennesseans to involve themselves in wars, both foreign and domestic. Here are old uniforms—American as well as enemy—weapons, and other combat-related items.

Boulevard (approximately 2.5 miles). Turn right from Belle Meade Boulevard onto Page Road. Turn left from Page Road onto Forrest Park Drive (the first street). Cheekwood is at the top of Forrest Park Drive on the right.

Leu Gallery (Belmont University, 1900 Belmont Blvd., 615/460-6770 or 615/460-6771, free) hosts traveling exhibits, with occasional student and faculty shows.

The Parthenon Gallery (Centennial Park, 615/862-8431) presents several permanent collections, such as The Cowan Collection of late 19th- and early 20th-century American paintings. Two rotating galleries change exhibits about every six weeks; these generally display contemporary local or regional work in all media, including photographs, sculpture, paintings, mixed media, graphics, textiles, and ceramics. Some of these works are available for purchase. Every other year in the even-numbered years (in May), this gallery hosts the TACA Biennial Crafts Exhibition.

Sankofa-African Heritage Cultural Museum (Winston-Derek Center at MetroCenter, 615/321-0535, $2 adults, free for seniors and children under 17) offers artifacts and artworks from Africa.

The **Sarratt Gallery** (on the fourth floor of the Sarratt Student Center at Vanderbilt Place, 615/322-2471, www.vanderbilt.edu/sarratt/gallery, free) is run by students—they select the shows and present an annual student art show every year.

Although primarily a history museum, **Tennessee State Museum** (505 Deaderick St., 615/741-2692, www.tnmuseum.org, free) also displays antique portraits of Tennesseans, work by local artists, and traveling exhibits.

Van Vechten Gallery (Jackson St. and D. B. Todd Blvd., 615/329-8720, www.fisk.edu, free, donations encouraged) is a treat. Carl Van Vechten, critic, writer, and photographer, was a supporter of the Harlem Renaissance, and he talked artist Georgia O'Keeffe into donating the 101-item art collection of her late husband, photographer Alfred Stieglitz, to Fisk University. When O'Keeffe did so, Fisk found itself in possession of the best collection of modern art in the state, if not the entire South. The paintings include works by Picasso, Cézanne, O'Keeffe, and Renoir. (Visitors to the Van Vechten Gallery should also consider seeing the nearby Aaron Douglas Gallery of African Art.)

Vanderbilt University Fine Arts Gallery (23rd and West End Aves., 615/322-0605, www.vanderbilt.edu, free) features about five exhibitions per year, some of which are traveling shows. The other exhibitions are pulled together from the university's 7,000-piece collection, which represents more than 40 countries and cultures.

Specialty

The part of Nashville's that kids will like most is the **Adventure Science Center** (800 Fort Negley Blvd., 615/862-5160, www.adventuresci.com, $8.75 adults, $6.75 kids 4–12). A 75-foot-tall Adventure Tower gets their attention before they step in the door, and, once they get there, some amazing exhibits will keep them busy. "The Amazing Aging Machine," for instance, shows kids what they will look like in 30 years if they smoke and if they don't. The Sudekum Planetarium ($2 more with admission to the museum) rounds out the offerings.

Hartzler-Towner Multicultural Museum (inside the Scarritt-Bennet Center, 1008 19th Ave. S., 615/340-7481, www.scarrittbennett.org/museum, daily) has as its goal to enhance understanding and appreciation of diverse ethnic and cultural heritages. The collection contains some 14,000 items from various cultures around the world as well as 700 dolls.

Lane Motor Museum (702 Murfreesboro Pike, 615/742-7445, www.lanemotormuseum.org, 10 A.M. to 5 P.M. Thurs.–Sun., $5 adults, $3 seniors, free for ages under 18) contains a collection of more than 130 cars, trucks, and motorcycles. Most are from Europe, and include a two-seater Messerschmidt that looks like an aircraft fuselage, the largest Tatra collection outside Europe, military vehicles, microcars, and more.

Music Valley Car Museum (2611 McGavock Pike, 615/885-7400, $3.50 adults, $3 seniors, $1.50 kids 6–12) sits across from the Opryland Hotel and contains about 50 cars, about half of which belonged to stars. The obligatory Elvis model is the limousine in which his family rode to his funeral. Visitors can buy a combination ticket that admits them to Shotgun Red's Collections, right next door.

At **Nashville Toy Museum** (2613 McGavock Pike, 615/883-8870, $3.50 adults, $2.50 kids), kids may be bored with the items, but adults will find these antique and not-so-old toys fascinating. One thousand tin soldiers stand steadfast, and old trains run tiny routes. Best of all, none of the miniature cars in this place were owned by Elvis. Displays include antique dolls, bears, model ships, and comic figures.

The **Tennessee Agricultural Museum** (Ellington Agricultural Center, 615/837-5197, www.pickingproducts.org/agmuseum, free) is located about six miles below Nashville off I-65 at the Harding Place exit. A large barn here houses a collection of household and farm implements that date from the 1800s up to the 1940s, when electricity came to Tennessee farms. Among the items are a massive steam engine by which threshing machines or sawmills could be powered, a rural mail buggy used into the 1940s, and a very early wooden plow. The Tennessee Agriculture Hall of Fame is here as well.

At the **Tennessee Central Railway Museum** (220 Willow St., 615/244-9001, 9 A.M.–3 P.M. Tues., Thurs., and Sat., $5 adults, $3 senior, free for children under 18), visitors can do more than just look at old trains—they can ride them. The collection of cars includes entertainer Jackie Gleason's sleeper car as well as passenger cars, cabooses, work/camp cars, boxcars, motorcars, baggage cars, locomotives, and a passenger business car.

The **Tennessee Sports Hall of Fame and Museum** (615/242-4750, www.tshf.net, $3 adults, $2 children) sits on the first floor of the Gaylord Entertainment Center and consists of interactive games, college football and basketball exhibits, and two theaters with videos.

OPRY MILLS AND THE OPRYLAND HOTEL

Opryland, the beloved theme park beside the Opryland Hotel, closed years ago, to the great unhappiness of families and tourism officials. In its place, the owners have built **Opry Mills** (www.oprymills.com), a much-hyped shopping mall that will disappoint anyone accustomed to upscale malls.

The usual anchor stores for malls are nowhere to be found here. In their place is the gargantuan **Bass Pro Shop,** just the place for folks who crave a mailbox that looks like an enormous fish. Discerning shoppers can emerge with a new handgun, shotgun, compound bow, and enough camouflage to outfit their own militia. Passing from the Bass Pro Shop to the rest of the mall, the visitor sees a sign that sounds like a line from comedian Jeff Foxworthy: your mall may be a redneck if it has a sign that says Firearms Not Permitted Past this Point.

Assuming that one is unarmed, the best part of Opry Mills is the **Gibson Bluegrass Showcase** (615/514-2233, www.gibson.com), where visitors can watch workers create guitars, mandolins, and banjos. A shop offers Gibson instruments—$1,869 for a beautiful dobro—as well as Gibson-themed clothing and gimcrack. Performances and jams take place on Monday and Wednesday evenings.

The **Opryland Hotel** (www.gaylordhotels .com) is the seventh-largest hotel in the country and the largest one outside of the state of Nevada. This Las Vegas–scale extravaganza consists of a series of jaw-dropping lobbies fronting 2,881 rooms and suites. One of the lobbies is the Cascades, a 2.5-acre greenhouse containing tropical plants and a four-story-high waterfall.

The Opryland Hotel hosts all manner of meetings and conferences, which fill the place with nametag-bedecked individuals who thread their way through lobbies filled with nonguests who walk slowly while gaping at the wonders. When they are tired of walking, they can make their way to the dome-topped Delta, more than four acres of tropical plants, a river, and a 560-foot-long moving sidewalk.

Nashville

CRUISES AND TOURS

Many Tennessee cities and towns have riverboats, usually small, boxlike affairs that seem rather puny. The *General Jackson* **Riverboat** (2802 Opryland Dr., 615/458-3900, www.gaylordhotels.com, $25–60), however, is enormous—300 feet long and four stories high—and looks appropriately majestic as it steams up and down the Cumberland River. A variety of cruises are offered morning, noon, and night, all with live entertainment and all departing from the dock near the Opryland Hotel.

The **Tennessee Central Railway** (220 Willow St. east of downtown, 615/244-9001, www.tcry .org) offers excursion as far as Monterey, a 92-mile round-trip, beginning in April and going through December.

The ability to laugh at itself has never been one of Nashville's strengths, but two sisters who call themselves **"The Juggs"** are finding plenty of people willing to pay for a wildly funny "Nash Trash Tour" on a lurid pink bus through Music City.

Sheri Lynn and Brenda Kay—perfect Nashville names—pick up passengers at the Farmer's Market (900 8th Ave. N.) in their pink bus, and the show begins. There's singing, make-up tips, tacky hors d'oeuvres, and "celebrity" sightings. Any man wearing a cowboy hat and walking down the street is likely to hear a "There's Garth Brooks!" booming from the bus. It's all in great fun. Tours run year-round, but can fill up weeks ahead. For info, call 800/342-2132 or 615/226-7300 or visit www.nashtrash.com. Tours cost $25 for adults, $22 for anyone over 55, and $18 for kids 6–12.

Bill Daniel of **Nashville Black Heritage Tours** (5188 Almaville Rd., Smyrna, 615/890-8173) gives a 2.5–3-hour escorted tour of significant sites pertaining to black heritage. He can make arrangements for any size group and prefers a three-day notice.

The Jugg Sisters take visitors on an unforgettable tour of Music City.

Recreation

BICENTENNIAL MALL STATE PARK

With statewide events and much hoopla, Tennessee celebrated its 200th birthday in 1996. One legacy of that year is the Bicentennial Mall State Park (600 James Robertson Pkwy., 615/741-5800, www.state.tn.us, free), which stretches forth from the back side of the state capitol. This was the site of French Lick, the salt deposit that attracted the deer and other game, which in turn attracted the people who founded Nashville. This 19-acre site features a 250-foot granite map of the state, a Walk of Counties containing information about all 95 of them, a Walk of History, and a 31-fountain extravaganza called the Rivers of Tennessee. The 2,000-seat amphitheater is a good place for concerts.

One of the more imaginative aspects of the mall is the World War II Memorial, a nine-ton granite globe that depicts the world as it was from 1939–45. The huge ball rests on a constantly flowing stream of water, and visitors can rotate it to view various parts of the world.

Farmer's Market (900 8th Ave., 615/880-2001, www.nashvillefarmersmarket.org) is located right beside the Bicentennial Mall State Park, open year-round, It has about 200 vendor stalls spread over an 11-acre site. The market features two restaurants, fresh fruits and vegetables in season, a meat market, a seafood market, and—every weekend—a flea market.

At the north end of the Bicentennial Mall is the delightful Germantown neighborhood, which was Nashville's first suburb. The houses date from the mid-1800s, and Monell's restaurant is located here as well.

NASHVILLE ZOO AT GRASSMERE

The zoo (377 Nolensville Rd., 615/833-1534, www.nashvillezoo.org., $8 adults, $6 children 3–12, free for seniors) occupies the grounds of Grassmere, an 1880s farm. Highlights include

Gibbon Island, a habitat for the lesser apes. For a chance to see another group of primates, go to the Jungle Gym, a maze of wooden climbing structures said to be the largest community-built playground in the world. This 66,000-square-foot playground can accommodate more than 1,000 children at one time. Good luck keeping up with yours.

Visitors can get to the zoo from either I-65 or I-24. From I-24, take Harding Place Exit 56 to Nolensville Road. From I-65, take Harding Place Exit 78A to Nolensville Road.

RADNOR LAKE STATE NATURAL AREA

Radnor Lake (615/373-3467, www.tnstateparks .com, sunrise–sunset daily, free), in southern Nashville, calls to those who have had too much

© JEFF BRADLEY

Gaylord Entertainment Center

Nashville

© JEFF BRADLEY

view from the Shelby Avenue Bridge

of the city. The 85-acre lake was created by the L&N Railroad as a source of water for steam engines. Bought by the state in 1973, the lake's 1,000 acres offer wildlife refuge and nature trails. Here one can see deer, foxes, beavers, and all manner of birds. Wildflowers flourish in spring and fall.

To get there, take I-65 South's Harding Place exit, go west on Granny White Pike, and then go south on Otter Creek Road. Follow signs to the area.

SPORTS

The professional football team the **Tennessee Titans** (www.titansonline.com) came to town and delighted supporters by making it all the way to the 1999 Super Bowl. They play in 67,000-seat Adelphia Coliseum across the Cumberland River from downtown. Games are almost always sold out.

The **Nashville Sounds**, (615/242-4371, www.nashvillesounds.com, usual game times are 7 P.M. for night games and 6 P.M. on Sunday) part of the Pittsburgh Pirates baseball organization, play 72 home games at Herschel Greer Stadium. To get there, take the Wedgewood exit off I-65 and follow the signs.

The **Nashville Predators** (Gaylord Entertainment Center, 615/770- 7825, www.nashville predators.com, tickets are $12 to $90), is a National Hockey League team.

The **Nashville Metros** (5135 Harding Place, 615/832-5678, www.nashvillemetrossoccer.com, tickets cost $15–45) play professional soccer in Ezell Park. The season goes April–October.

Entertainment and Events

the legendary Grand Ole Opry stage, of the famed stage and radio show

LIVE MUSIC

N Grand Ole Opry

The *Opry* (2804 Opryland Dr., 615/889-6611, www.opry.com, tickets $16–45), the legendary country music show, is a must-see in Nashville. Old-timers such as Porter Wagoner share the stage with newer performers such as Alison Krauss and Alan Jackson. Shows take place on Friday and Saturday nights, usually at 6:30 and 9:30 P.M. During the winter the 9:30 P.M. Friday show is omitted, and during the summer matinees take place on Tuesday and Thursday at 3 P.M.

Ernest Tubb Record Shop's Midnight Jamboree

If it just happens to be Saturday night about midnight, check out the jamboree. This free live radio show, much like the *Grand Ole Opry,* features *Opry* stars as well as some new faces. It all takes place after the Saturday night *Opry* at the **Texas Troubadour Theatre** (2416 Music Val-

ley Dr. near the Opryland Hotel, 615/889-2474, www.etrecordshop.com, 11:30 P.M., free). For those who can't stay up that late but who can buy tickets, there's "A Closer Walk with Patsy Cline" show at 7 P.M.

NIGHTLIFE

The following reviews were compiled by Paul Griffith, a Nashville freelance writer and drummer.

East Nashville

When it opened in 2003, the **Family Wash** (2038 Greenwood Ave., 615/226-6070, www.familywash.com) was a much-needed addition to East Nashville's nightlife. An up-and-coming neighborhood, East Nashville is home to many of the area's musicians and artists who needed a hip, casual place to hang out. The Family Wash still retains the exterior look of its previous occupant, a laundromat, but its tidy, well laid-out interior is comfortable and inviting. Its small stage has played host to some of Nashville's best rootsy and alternative songwriters, such as Jennifer Nicely, Paul Burch, and Tim Carroll. The club opens at 6 P.M. and things tend to go late; beer and wine are served, as is gourmet pub food.

In East Nashville, they tend to convert old buildings rather than demolish them. The **5 Spot** (1006 Forest Ave., 615/650-9333, www.the5spot.net, open at 7 P.M. daily, happy hour until 9 P.M.) is a former branch bank that now brings in a wide variety of local and touring bands, from country to alternative rock and blues. The 5 Spot has a funky, retro feel and is located in the Five-Points section of East Nashville, an area known for its casual bars, restaurants and vintage stores. Sandwiches and bar food are served.

Downtown

Downtown Nashville is the focal point for most visitors, who usually wind up on 2nd Avenue, the home to country music's famous **Wildhorse Saloon** (120 2nd Ave. N., 615/902-8200,

Nashville

BLUEBIRD OF MUSICAL HAPPINESS

A remarkable woman named Amy Kurland had the idea: bring together songwriters and people who want to hear them perform their songs in a setting with good food. That's the concept of the **Bluebird Cafe** (4104 Hillsboro Rd., 615/383-1461, www.bluebirdcafe.com, open every night).

For a typical Bluebird evening, three or four songwriters sit on a small stage surrounded on three sides by the audience. The performers each take turns singing, and the others sometimes accompany them or just wait their turn. The magic of the Bluebird is that you never know whose career will take off. In 1988, a songwriter from Oklahoma played the Bluebird and was offered a contract that night. He was Garth Brooks. The Bluebird was the setting for *The Thing Called Love*, a 1993 movie directed by Peter Bogdanovich. *The Bluebird Café Scrapbook*, a collection of memories by and about Bluebird performers, was published in 2002.

The Bluebird is a small place with only 21 tables, plus seats at the bar and on benches. Getting reservations can be challenging. They are only taken by phone, and no more than one week ahead. The admission price varies from $7 to $30, usually on the lower end. If you can't get in, the club offers live and archived shows on the Web.

To see who is playing when, check the schedule on the website. Most of the names will mean nothing to people who do not follow country music—you just have to take it on faith that if they are playing the Bluebird, they are good.

To get to the Bluebird, take Exit 3 off I-440, and take the Hillsboro Pike side of the exit. Drive 1.5 miles and look for the Bluebird on the left side of the road in a strip mall just after a Shell station and this side of a McDonald's.

COURTESY OF ROBIN HOOD, NASHVILLE CONVENTION AND VISITORS BUREAU

where songwriters come to live their dreams

www.wildhorsesaloon.com) and **B.B. King's Blues Club** (152 2nd Ave. N. 615/256-2727, www.bbkingsclubs.com). Those searching for a more authentic honky-tonk experience, however, need only walk three blocks down Broadway to "Lower Broad," where a row of vintage Nashville bars await.

Tootsie's Orchid Lounge (422 Broadway, 615/726-0463, www.tootsies.net, 10–2 A.M. Mon.–Sat., noon–2 A.M. Sun.) is a legendary Lower Broad nightspot. Back when the *Grand Ole Opry* was held at the Ryman Auditorium, country stars such as Webb Pierce and Patsy Cline used to slip across the alley to Tootsie's, which served as the *Opry's* unofficial backstage.

These days, stars like Lorrie Morgan and Elvis Costello still head to Tootsie's to relax after a show and hobnob with fans.

Also located on Lower Broad is **Robert's Western World** (416 Broadway, 615/244-9552, www.robertswesternworld.com, 9–3 A.M. Mon.–Sat., noon–3 A.M. Sun.). Robert's sells boots and hats, but during the afternoons and evenings they also serve up cold beer, ham steak sandwiches, and nonstop, honky-tonk music from bands such as Brazilbilly, who play an eclectic mix of Latin music and traditional country.

On the southwestern fringe of downtown, in an entertainment and development area known as "the Gulch," lies a well-worn nightclub that's a regular stop for touring bands and popular local acts. **12th & Porter's Playroom** (114 12th Ave. N., 615/254-7236, shows usually start around 9:30 P.M.) is a purple and black converted garage that, over the years, has hosted shows by artists such as Emmylou Harris and King Crimson (who played a four-night stand there several years ago). The Playroom's sound is impeccable—for its size, the club has one of the finest P.A. systems in the South—and there's a restaurant attached that provides continental dining with a southern twist late into the evening.

The Gulch, an active railroad yard, is also home to the **Station Inn** (402 12th Ave. S., 615/255-3307, www.stationinn.com, shows usually start at 9 P.M.), the best place on the planet for bluegrass music. A small cinderblock roadhouse, the Station Inn has been around for 30 years; regular performers include bluegrass royalty such as Ralph Stanley, Del McCoury, Vassar Clements, and Ricky Skaggs.

West End and Music Row

West End Avenue, 21st Avenue, and Music Row (16th & 17th Avenues) are adjoining thoroughfares running southwest from downtown. This area is home to Nashville's established music community, as well as Vanderbilt University and a giddy array of businesses. Among the many entertainment options in this part of town are three long-standing bars that typify Nashville's diverse nightlife. Located just off West End Avenue, the **Exit-In** (2208 Elliston Pl., 615/331-3240, www.exitin.com) is perhaps Nashville's best-known live music venue. The club has undergone several renovations since opening in 1971 and is best known for its appearance in Robert Altman's classic 1975 movie *Nashville*. Over the years the Exit-In has featured shows by everyone from Jimmy Buffett to R.E.M. The club has live music seven days a week, and start times vary.

From the Exit-In, if you cross through Centennial Park (home to the Parthenon, which was also featured in Altman's movie), you'll find yourself at the **Springwater Supper Club & Lounge** (115 27th Ave. N., 615/320-0345, www.springwatersupperclub.com, noon–3 A.M. Mon.–Sun.).

Don't let the name fool you—the Springwater is a divey roadhouse pure and simple. Though no one's eaten food there in recent memory, the roadhouse does serve the coldest, cheapest beer in town—a banner at the bar reads "A Dollar A Swaller." Other than a pool table, a jukebox, and a mid-'70s nudie poster above the bar, the Springwater is pretty Spartan, but if you're looking for the hottest in hardcore, indie, and underground music, this is the place.

Music Row's oldest continuously operating bar is a little, NASCAR-friendly beer bunker known as **Bobby's Idle Hour** (1010 16th Ave. S., 615/726-0446, 10–3 A.M. daily). Though it's open late, Bobby's isn't really a nightclub. Most of the regulars drop by in the late afternoon, when the Row's many recording studios, publishing companies and record labels shut down for the day. In fact, it's not unusual to see songwriters passing around the old guitar that serves as Bobby's primary source of entertainment. If you're new to the place, don't be surprised if they hand the guitar to you—around these parts it's taken for granted that you've got a song or two up your sleeve.

Eighth Avenue South

Eighth Avenue South is a useful artery that takes you out of downtown Nashville towards the charming town of Franklin, which is about 15 miles south. There are several establishments here that cater to a variety of entertainment needs.

The Basement (1604 8th Ave. S., 615/254-1604, www.thebasement.bargeek.com) is a little tricky to find but worth the effort if you're looking for an intimate bar that features cutting-edge live music. Former Slow Bar owner Mike Grimes serves as booking agent for the Basement, and his ultra-hip musical sensibilities are reflected in the club's schedule, which features local and national indie and alternative bands. In fact, Grimes's popular, eclectic record store, Grimey's, is located upstairs. Hours of operation vary; shows tend to start early.

If Nashville's hyperkinetic music scene has you worn-out, **Melrose Billiards** (2600 Franklin Rd., 615/383-9201, 10–1 A.M. Mon.–Sat., noon–1 A.M. Sun.) provides an interesting change of pace. The old-school billiard parlor is a trip back in time. A terrazzo staircase takes you down into its dark confines, which house 11 regulation size pool tables, a snooker table, Ping-Pong, shuffleboard, and an exquisite art-deco bar. Melrose Billiards also serves a limited menu from the Sportsman's Grill, a Vanderbilt-area restaurant.

The Melrose Lanes (2600 Franklin Rd., 615/297-7142, 7A.M.–midnight Mon.–Thurs., 7–1 A.M. Fri.–Sun.) is a vintage, two-level bowling alley that's located in the same World War II–era entertainment mall as the billiard parlor. It's a cheap date with a great bar and a short-order menu that includes one of the best burgers in town.

Zanies (2025 8th Ave. S., 615/269-0221, www.zaniesnash.com, showtimes 8 P.M. Wed., Thurs., and Sun., 8 and 10:15 P.M. Fri., 7, 9, and 11:15 P.M. Sat.) is another nonmusical 8th Avenue option. As Nashville's only full-time comedy club, Zanies has been booking comedy's brightest stars for 20 years.

Green Hills

Located in the Green Hills neighborhood, **F. Scott's** (2210 Crestmoor Rd., 615/269-5861, www.fscotts.com) is primarily known as an upscale restaurant, but it's also the best jazz venue in town. The bar is small but sophisticated, recalling Manhattan's Upper Eastside at the height of the jazz era. Items from F. Scott's AAA Three Diamond–rated menu are available to bar patrons. Live jazz is featured at 6:45 P.M. Sunday–Thursday, 7 P.M. on Friday, and 8 P.M. on Saturday.

Gay and Lesbian

The Church Street corridor, southwest of downtown Nashville, is home to a developing commercial district that caters to gays and lesbians. As of now, a bookstore and two bars anchor the area. **Tabu** (1713 Church St., 615/320-3808, 4 P.M.–2 A.M. Mon.–Fri., 4 P.M.–3 A.M. Sat., 2 P.M.–midnight Sun.) is casual, with New Orleans–themed murals on the wall, a mirrored dance floor, and comfy lounge areas.

On the other hand, **Tribe** (1517 Church St., 616/329-2912, www.tribenashville.com, 4 P.M.–midnight Sun.–Thurs., 4 P.M.–2 A.M. Fri.–Sat.) is quieter and more posh. There's a dance floor, but it's separate from both the lounge area, which is upstairs, and the club's upscale restaurant.

The Connection (901 Cowen St., 615/742-1166, 8 P.M.–3 A.M. Wed.–Mon.) is an enormous dance complex with rooms dedicated to techno and country music as well as a theatre for the club's extremely popular drag shows. Located in East Nashville at the end of a desolate industrial road, the Connection may cater to a predominantly gay and lesbian crowd, but it's straight-friendly and arguably the best dance club in town.

Regardless of one's sexual orientation, East Nashville's **Lipstick Lounge** (1400 Woodland St., 615/226-6343, www.thelipsticklounge.com, 11 A.M.–2 P.M., 4–11 P.M. Tues.–Fri., 7–11 P.M. Sat., 11 A.M.–11 P.M. Sun.) is one of the friendliest bars around. Established in 2002 by twin sisters Ronda Landers and Jonda Valentine, the club blends urban sophistication with the eclectic funkiness for which the Eastside is famous. Martinis and jazz are the order of the evening in the main bar, with the upstairs reserved for lounging and shooting pool. The Lipstick Lounge also features entertainment of a campier nature; local burlesque troupe, Panty Raid, is a fave.

The Gas Lite Lounge (167 1/2 8th Ave S., 615/254-1278) hasn't changed much since its days as a speakeasy during the Prohibition era. With its antique chandeliers and dark wood fixtures, it's an intimate throwback to the days before pounding dance beats and mind-numbing lightshows. Located downtown, next door to the Towne House Tea Room, you'll find the Gas Lite at the end of a long, lamplit walkway. Inside, the mature gay crowd is friendly but respectful of their fellow patron's privacy. Be sure to check out the jukebox, which contains a mixed bag of tunes from techno and dance to traditional country.

EVENTS

February

Americana Spring Sampler Craft, Folk Art, and Antique Show (615/227-2080) takes place at the Tennessee State Fairgrounds and brings more than 200 artists and antique dealers from a 30-state area.

April

The **Dove Awards,** (615/242-0303, www.gospel music.org) gospel music's version of the Academy Awards, are given out during the third week in April.

Tin Pan South (615/251-3472, www.tinpan south.com) brings more than 300 songwriters to town as an event of the Nashville Songwriters Association. Tunesmiths play various clubs around town, and the whole thing culminates with a wonderful acoustic concert at the Ryman Auditorium.

Nashville Film Festival (615/322-4234, www.nashvillefilmfestival.org) has a 30-plus-year history of bringing offbeat films as well as the people who make them to town.

Southern Festival of Books (War Memorial Plaza, 615/320-7001, www.tn-humanities.org) brings together Southern and national writers for panel discussions, readings, and book-signings. Ninety to 100 exhibitors take part, and two stages provide storytelling and music.

May

The **Annual Running of the Iroquois Steeplechase** (615/322-7284, www.iroquoissteeplechase.org) brings Nashville's horsey set to Percy Warner Park to watch a steeplechase that benefits Vanderbilt's Children's Hospital. The big hats and fancy duds and tailgating make this a delight.

Tennessee Crafts Fair (615/665-0502, www.tennesseecrafts.org), held at Centennial Park, claims to be the largest market of Tennessee-made crafts. More than 165 artists take part, and the event includes live music and food.

The **Tennessee Jazz and Blues Society Concert Series** (615/386-7500, www.jazzblues.org) takes place at Belle Meade, Cheekwood, and The Hermitage, offering music under the stars.

June

The **American Artisan Festival** (615/298-4691, www.americanartisan.citysearch.com) invites craftspeople from more than 35 states to Centennial Park.

The **CMA Music Festival** (Adelphia Coliseum, 615/889-7503, www.cmafest.com), usually just called Fan Fair by Nashvillians, brings more than 100,000 country music fans to town to rub shoulders, get autographs, take photos of their favorite stars, and listen to hours of concerts. Unlike stars in any other entertainment genre, country music kings and queens are expected to make themselves available during these sweltering days. Why do they do it? One fan explained it like this: "These guys are smart. They know that if they take care of their fans while on top, those fans will stick with them later on when that performer may no longer be a headliner."

Makes sense.

This weeklong event features concerts and a variety of events. For those not particularly interested in country music, this week might be a good time to avoid Nashville. Tickets usually sell out in advance.

Dancin' in the District (Riverfront Park, Broadway and 1st Ave., www.dancininthedistrict.com) features live music and good times every Thursday night June–August.

July

Nashville's **Independence Day Celebration** (615/862-8400) takes place along the Cumberland River at Riverfront Park. Music kicks off the event at 5 P.M., with a massive fireworks show after it gets dark. This is a no-alcohol event.

August

Also held in February, **Americana Summer Sampler Craft, Folk Art, and Antique Show** takes place at the Tennessee State Fairgrounds.

The Athens of the South holds the **Nashville Shakespeare Festival** (Centennial Park band shell, 615/862-8400, www.nashvilleshakes.org), where each year a free play by the bard is presented on Thursday–Sunday evenings in mid-August.

September

The **Tennessee State Fair** (615/862-8980, www.tennesseestatefair.org) takes place at the state fairgrounds and includes all manner of agricultural displays, rides, livestock, and the usual offerings of corn dogs and other health food.

The **African American Street Festival** 615/251-0007, www.africanamericanculturalalliance.com), held on Tennessee State University's campus, celebrates black culture with music, food, storytelling, fashion show, and lectures.

Belle Meade Plantation Fall Fest (615/356-0501, www.bellemeadeplantation.com) takes place over two days at the plantation and includes food, antiques, crafts, and other items for sale.

Tennessee Association of Craft Artists Fall Crafts Fair (Centennial Park, 615/665-0502) is a juried crafts fair at. Crafts demonstrations highlight the event.

October

NAIA Pow Wow Fall Festival (615/726-0806, www.chattanooga.net/membersites/naia), sponsored by the Native American Indian Association, brings Indian dance contests, demonstrations, traditional foods, and storytelling from a variety of tribes. Held outside of town at Four Corners Marina and Recreation Area. This is largest powwow east of the Mississippi.

November

Still another Americana Sampler, this one the **Americana Christmas Sampler Craft, Folk**

Art, and Antique Show, occurs this month—see February for details.

Opryland Hotel stages **A Country Christmas** (615/872-0600) November 1–Christmas. Imagine if Joseph and Mary had gone to Las Vegas instead of Bethlehem. Tennessee's largest hotel is decorated for the season, and a variety of events, musical and otherwise, take place there.

December

The **Tribute to African Americans in the Battle of Nashville** (615/963-5561) commemorates the Civil War defenders of Nashville with tours and lectures.

CINEMAS

In addition to the usual multiplexes, Nashville has two movie theaters that show classics, art films, and imports. Both of them are close to Vanderbilt:

Surratt Cinema (24th Avenue South and Vanderbilt Place, 615/322-2425 or 615/343-6666.)

Belcourt Theatre (2102 Belcourt Ave., 615/383-9140, www.belcourt.org) opened as a silent movie theater in 1925 and still occasionally shows silent films with live musical accompaniment along with live theater and concerts. This is one of the very few movie theaters in Tennessee where patrons can enjoy alcoholic beverages without sneaking them in.

Nashville

Accommodations

BED-AND-BREAKFASTS AND INNS

 **End O' the Bend Lodge and Landing** (2517 Miami Ave., Nashville 37214, 615/883-0997, www.bbonline.com/tn/bend, $185–245) is a five-room rustic log cabin on a bluff overlooking the Cumberland River about one mile from the Opryland Hotel.

The *General Jackson* **Showboat** steams majestically by twice a day. Guests rent the entire cabin, which comes with fully equipped kitchen, an outdoor grill, and a great room with a fireplace. No host is on site, and no breakfast is served, but the privacy is hard to beat.

The **Hillsboro House** (1933 20th Ave. S., 800/ 228-7851 or 615/292-5501, www.bbonline .com/tn/hillsboro, $100–130) is a gingerbread cottage built in 1904; it's between Music Row and Vanderbilt. Its three guest rooms have feather beds and private baths.

Savage House Inn (167 8th Ave. N., 615/ 244-2229, $65–75) occupies one of the very few townhouses left in the central part of Nashville.

This one, built in 1852 and home to a physician whose last name was Savage, is two blocks from the Convention Center and a short walk to many downtown attractions. The six guest rooms are all decorated with antiques, some with fireplaces, and some with private baths.

HOTELS AND MOTELS

Nashville, offers dozens of motel and hotel rooms, most of them belonging to the major national chains.

Opryland Hotel

If visitors don't mind squeezing in between conventions, this is the place to stay in Music City. Guests can get married, view exhibits, eat, drink, and collapse. Doubles go for $209–249, plus tax.

Downtown

Some of the good options include  **Best Western Downtown Convention Center** (711 Union St., 800/627-3297, www.bestwestern.com/downtownconventioncenter, $109), **Comfort Inn**

COURTESY OF GAYLORD ENTERTAINMENT

Nashville

The gigantic Opryland Hotel

Downtown (1501 Demonbreun St., 615/ 255-9977, $70 and up), **Days Inn-Downtown Convention Center** (711 Union St., 615/242-4311), **M Doubletree Hotel Nashville** (315 Fourth Ave. N., 800/ 222/TREE, www.nashville.doubletree.com, $75–150), **M Hilton Suites Nashville Downtown** (121 4th Ave. S., 800/445-8667, www.nashvillehilton.com, $159), **Holiday Inn Express Nashville Downtown** (920 Broadway, 800/465-4329, www.hotel-nashville .com, $60 and up).

West End

Options in the West End include **M Courtyard By Marriott—Vanderbilt/West End** (1901 West End Ave., 800/321/2211, www.courtyard.com/ bnawe, $89 includes breakfast), **Daisy Hill Bed & Breakfast** (2816 Blair Blvd., 800/239-1135, www.daisyhillbedandbreakfast.com, $110–150), **M Hampton Inn Vanderbilt** (1919 West End Ave., 888/880-5394, www.hamptoninnnashville .com, $79), **Holiday Inn Select Vanderbilt** (2613 West End Ave., 800/633-4427, www .holiday-inn.com/bna-vanderbilt, $60 and up).

Food

The following restaurants were reviewed Thayer Wine, who was the restaurant critic for *The Tennessean,* for 14 years, one of the best jobs in town.

Once Nashville was known for "meat-and-three's," dinners featuring old-fashioned Southern-style foods with one meat and three sides for one price. Barbecue is another favorite food of the area, with many barbecue places that emphasize slowly cooked pork over hickory wood. There's turkey and chicken, too, and now even Texas-style beef brisket.

Lately, though independent Nashville restaurants have come into their own, with chefs who plant their styles on our taste buds in most delectable ways.

GOO GOO CLUSTERS

Hershey supposedly produced the first candy bar in 1894, and just two years later Howell H. Campbell of Nashville rolled out the first combination bar—chocolate, marshmallow, caramel, and peanuts. Allegedly dubbed the Goo Goo Cluster after the only words that Campbell's baby boy could say, the concoction has sold ever since.

Those who can't wait to get to Tennessee can order Goo Goos by calling 800/231-3402. They cannot be shipped during the summer. Go Goo Goo on the Internet at www.googoo.com.

The following sampling of Nashville restaurants describes mostly the places unique to this town. Although most of them have been around awhile, their hours could have changed or they could have morphed into something else, so it's always a good idea to call before you go.

DOWNTOWN

Jack's Bar-B-Que (416-A Broadway, 615/254-5715, lunch and dinner daily, closes at 6 P.M. Sun.) is down on lower Broadway, among the honky-tonks, a good place to grab a bite of 'que and slaw so you can go dance it off at one of the spots on the block. There is a sister restaurant at 334 Trinity Lane (615/228-9888).

Rippy's Smokin' Bar & Grill (429 Broadway, 615/244-7477, lunch and dinner daily, $10–12) is almost across the street from Jack's downtown place. Both places are very close to the Gaylord Entertainment Center where you can catch all sorts of shows and watch the Predators play. It's a casual place where the barbecue (including the pulled pork, ribs, and chicken) is served in paper baskets. Good place for a beer, too.

Ichiban Japanese Restaurant (109 Second Ave. S., downtown 615/244-7900, under $10) has a sushi bar, lots of typical Japanese soups and noodle dishes, as well as the teriyaki chicken for the less adventurous diners.

GERMANTOWN

Swett's (2725 Clifton Ave., 615/329-4418, lunch and dinner daily), one of the oldest family-owned restaurants in Nashville. Politicians, downtown lawyers, blue-collar workers, and all sorts of people go to this cafeteria-style restaurant to get fine traditional Southern dishes. Be sure to save room for peach, blackberry or whichever cobbler is there the day you visit. Swett's also has a satellite (900 8th Ave. N., inside the main pavilion at the Farmer's Market, lunch daily).

Another place to find good Southern-style foods in a unique setting is **M Monell's** (1235 6th Ave. N., 615/248-4747, lunch Sun.–Fri., dinner Thurs.–Sat.). The main sit-down restaurant is located in a restored Victorian home in the old Germantown section not far from the Bicentennial Mall. Guests dine at big communal tables and pass platters of mashed potatoes, fried chicken and other Southern favorites. Usually there are two meats and several vegetables, dessert, and beverages (nonalcoholic) for less than $15 per person. There's also a big country breakfast served Saturday and Sunday mornings, with heaps of pancakes, fried potatoes, mounds of bacon, ham and sausage, eggs, corn pudding, cheese grits and, of course, biscuits. You can't beat it if you're hungry, and you'll probably meet someone interesting in the bargain. It's sometimes closed for dinner during winter. There are Monell's Express carry-out places with limited choices of these popular Southern foods in several locations around town, too.

WEST OF DOWNTOWN

For Vietnamese food, try **Kien Giang** (5825 Charlotte Pike, 615/353-1250, $12–15). It's located in a cluster of Asian markets and restaurants up and down a section of Charlotte Pike just west of White Bridge Road. The chicken soup with lemongrass and the fresh, not fried, spring rolls are memorable.

EAST NASHVILLE

M Margot Cafe and Bar (1017 Woodland St.,

BONGO JAVA AND THE NUN BUN

The Bongo Java coffeehouse had its 15 minutes of fame when a cinnamon bun came out of the oven bearing a remarkable resemblance to the late Mother Teresa. The "Nun Bun," as it was dubbed, made television appearances and was widely covered by newspapers. The Bongo Java folks, knowing a marketing miracle when they saw one, began selling Nun Bun T-shirts and other goods.

Word eventually reached Calcutta, where the real Mother Teresa was not amused. Her organization asked Bongo Java to knock it off, and the coffeehouse respectfully obeyed. The Nun Bun is still there, however, where it still draws the faithful. See it for yourself on www.bongojava.com or in person at 2007 Belmont Boulevard.

615/227-4668, dinner Tues.–Sat., entrées $14–20) is a cozy neighborhood eatery in East Nashville owned by Chef Margot McCormack. Eat inside or outside on the patio bordered by flower boxes in the summer. Her menus change almost daily. Generally, the fish, beef, and duck dishes shine.

MIDTOWN

This area is west of Downtown but not quite in the West End.

Go to the **M Bound'ry** (911 20th Ave. S., 615/321-3043, dinner nightly, entrées $10–22) for innovative foods that seem to have no boundaries. Their gorgeous presentations on unusual plates feast the eyes. There are plenty of familiar items such as pork chops and salmon fillet among the "large plates," but you might want to explore the "tastings" which are large appetizer portions—the barbecue egg roll, pizzas from the wood-burning oven are among them. The Bound'ry salad is a favorite. This place has a list of more than 200 beers and a fine wine list of more than 300 wines.

M Virago (1811 Division St., 615/320-5149, dinner nightly)has the feel of the big city, with its

HOT CHICKEN

One of the foods unique to Nashville is "hot chicken." By hot, we mean skillet or deep-fried chicken that has been seasoned with lots of spicy seasonings, mostly cayenne pepper. **Prince's Hot Chicken Shack** (123 Ewing Dr., 615/226-9442, lunch and supper Tues.–Sat., until the wee hours Fri.–Sat.) is the oldest and best known because of secret recipes passed down through the Prince family.

© JEFF BRADLEY

You can order the chicken

Prince's Famous Hot Chicken, a Nashville delicacy

mild or medium, and they will probably have a good hit of spice, but if you get the hot chicken—be prepared. Have your coins handy. The cold drink machine is in the corner. It's one of the mayor's favorite places for lunch, so you might see him there.

To get to Prince's from downtown, take I-65 North and get off at the Ewing Street exit. Head east. Prince's is in a nondescript little strip mall on the left. If you want the scenic route from downtown, cross the Cumberland River on the Jefferson Street bridge or Woodland Avenue bridge, then turn left onto North First Street. This street becomes Dickerson Pike. Go a little over four miles north on Dickerson Pike, and turn left past a Kroger's onto Ewing Drive. Prince's is on the right.

dark lounge area and "ambient sound" that increases as the evening goes on. The emphasis here is on seafood, with lots of unusual versions of sushi. Other dishes are influenced by Asian, Spanish, Latin and French flavors. There are a few entrées at $17–29, but most other dishes are portioned smaller so you can explore more of them, $6–15. Also, it has a good selection of wines, exotic sake, and champagne drinks, among others.

Big splurge: Go to the M **Wild Boar** (2014 Broadway, 615/329-1313, www.wildboarrestaurant.com, dinner Mon.–Sat., entrées $25–145) when you're in the mood to be spoiled by tuxedoed waiters, impeccable service, and contemporary food with flavors and ingredients from all over the world. This place has earned four stars from the *Mobile Travel Guide* and four diamonds from AAA. The wine list has been recognized with the Grand Award from the *Wine Spectator,*

too. The salads are always interesting, both in taste and display. You'll be able to choose among the fish, game, beef or fowl ranging in price from $23–35, or you can have the tasting menu of four courses without wines for $65–75 a person or $110–145 with wine. Reservations recommended.

WEST END

For three generations, people have feasted on the popular corn cake appetizers and steak at **Jimmy Kelly's** (217 Louise Ave., 615/329-4349, dinner Mon.–Sat.). Chicken and fish are on the menu for the non-steak lover. Count on a celebration with plenty of beer and music on St. Patrick's Day at this place, too.

Debra Paquette, chef/owner of M **Zola** (3001 West End Ave., 615/320-7778, www.restaurant-zola.com, dinner Mon.–Sat.) is one of the most creative chefs in town. She has well-honed skills to deliver on her passion for Mediterranean flavors from Morocco to Catalan and from Greece to Italy and France. Her menus change with the season, but always promise a lovely exchange of flavors. The well-planned wine list particularly complements the foods. Reservations recommended.

Stop at the **N Tin Angel** (3201 West End Ave., 615/298-3444, brunch Sun., lunch Mon.–Fri., dinner Mon.–Sat.) for an upscale meal in comfortably casual surroundings. The steak salad is a lunch favorite; pastas are attention-getters at night.

When you're in town and have a taste for barbecue, head for **N Hog Heaven** (115 27th Ave. N., 615/329-1234, lunch and early supper Mon.–Sat., $10–15), a humble barbecue shack with a walk-up window and a couple of picnic tables out front. It's perfectly situated next to Centennial Park, where you can take your barbecue sandwiches or platefuls of barbecued pork, brisket or smoked chicken or turkey with beans and slaw.

Go to **Calypso Café** (2424 Elliston Pl., 615/321-3878), a locally owned series of small restaurants with a simple but excellent menu of rotisserie chicken, slightly sweet turnip greens, big salads with black beans and chicken or beef, or chicken salad with mandarin oranges, among others. The fruit tea is a favorite, too. Two can eat here for $15. Open for lunch and dinner daily. Other locations are at 700 Thompson Lane (615/297-3888); 600-A Frazier Drive, Franklin, near the CoolSprings Galleria (615/771-5665); and 5101 Harding Road (615/356-1678).

Sitar (116 21st Ave. N., 615/321-8889, lunch and dinner daily), located in the Vanderbilt area, serves a lunch buffet of typical Indian dishes, including tandoori chicken, vegetable curry and delightful, fresh *naan,* Indian bread made in the tandoor oven. The lunch buffet is $5.95 and dinner entrées are $7–15.

HILLSBORO VILLAGE

N Sunset Grill (2001 Belcourt Ave., 615/386-3663, www.sunsetgrill.com, lunch Tues.–Fri.,

dinner nightly, entrées $12–32)is the place to see and be seen, as lots of people from nearby Music Row are likely to drop in. Dinner entrées cover everything from pasta to steak and venison. For dessert lovers, the dessert trio is fun to share. This place has late night menus and wine classes. Reservations recommended.

Tennessee is famous for biscuits and cornbread and variations such as hush puppies. Nashvillians, however, now have access to "artisan" bread—a stylized form of baking that originated in France. The founder of **Provence Breads and Café** (1705 21st Ave. S., 615/386-9990, www.provencebreads.com) apprenticed himself to French bread bakers and then came to Nashville with French ovens to see if he could make it in the land of Martha White Flour.

This bakery produces breads that are a treat for the eye as well as the palate. Choices include classic French baguettes, rustic sourdough, challah, fougasse brushed with olive oil, and more. Then there are the desserts: cookies, cakes, and the best pastries in town.

If you just need some coffee, try **Fido** (1812 21st Ave. S., 615/777-3436, open daily).

GREEN HILLS

F. Scott's (2210 Crestmoor, 615/269-5861, dinner at 5:30 P.M. nightly) has always been known for its fish, though they have lovely chicken and beef dishes, too. Salads shine and the extensive wine list ought to please the wine-lovers in the crowd. The bonus here is the daily live jazz in the bar area. Reservations recommended.

Shintomi Japanese Restaurant (2184 Bandywood Dr., 615/386-3022, under $10) offers a sushi bar, Japanese soups and noodle dishes.

SYLVAN PARK

Due west of the Vanderbilt campus is Sylvan Park.

N Park Café (4403 Murphy Rd., 615/383-4409, dinner Mon.–Sat., entrées $16–22) is a romantic spot with lots of cozy corners. Chef Guillermo "Willie" Thomas, who owns this place, likes to collect china, and often displays his lovely plates under the food. His salads are always noteworthy, as is the beef tenderloin, however he prepares it. The menu changes frequently, but look for something chocolatey for dessert.

For Italian beyond pasta, go to **Caffe Nonna** (4427 Murphy Rd., 615/463-0133, www.caffenonna.com, lunch Tues.–Fri., dinner Mon.–Sat., $11–22). This cozy chef-owned place offers a fine minestrone, hearty lamb shanks in winter, lighter pastas in summer, and desserts like ricotta cheesecake you come to crave. Reservations recommended.

The bagels at **Star Bagel** (4502 Murphy Ave., 615/292-7993, breakfast and lunch daily) were once voted top bagels in town. It's a good stop for a dandy sandwich and cup of coffee.

NEAR BELMONT UNIVERSITY

Coffeehouse **Bongo Java** (2007 Belmont Ave., 615/385-5282, open 24 hours daily) across the street from Belmont University, are the places to hang out, read the paper, and nibble on sandwiches, omelets, or pastries.

Nearby is **Portland Brew** (2605 12th Ave. S., 615/292-9004, open 24 hours Mon.–Sat.) is another good stop for specialty coffees and pastries and bagels.

The **Frothy Monkey** (2509 12th Ave. S., 615/ 292-1808, open Mon. - Fri. 6:30 A.M. to 11 P.M. and 7:30 A.M. to 11 P.M. Sat. and Sun.) is another coffeehouse only a block up the street from Portland Brew. It has a nice selection of coffees roasted in New Orleans, and a modest menu of interesting deli sandwiches and pastries. It's located in a remodeled old home with a clean, open floor plan. The large outdoor deck is appealing on nice days.

ELSEWHERE

For Southern foods prepared in more contemporary ways, go to **Martha's at the Plantation** (5025 Harding Rd., 615/353-2828, lunch Mon.–Sat., brunch Sun.). This upscale restaurant is above a gift shop on the grounds of the historic Belle Meade Plantation. You'll find lush salads, crab cakes, pork, chicken, and other entrées prepared with homemade preserves, rel-

ishes, and other special touches by Martha Stamps, local restaurateur and cookbook author. Reservations are recommended, especially for brunch Sunday.

Some folks come to Nashville to eat black-eyed peas, cornbread, fried chicken, and chicken-fried steak, as well as barbecue. One good place to find these delicious foods is **Arnold's Country Kitchen** (605 8th Ave. S., 615/256-4455, lunch Mon.–Fri.) is a typical Nashville "meat and three" cafeteria-style diner—been there forever and looks it. This is the place to look for comfort foods: mashed potatoes, meat loaf, chicken 'n' dumplings, and the like.

If you're in the mood for Japanese food, head for **Benkay Japanese Restaurant** (Lions Head shopping center, 40 White Bridge Rd., 615/356-6600, under $10) with sushi, great soups, and a variety of great Japanese dishes.

The following restaurants can be found (roughly) along the I-65 corridor south of Nashville.

Expect the menu to change with the seasons, with bright tastes that suggest Mexico and Mediterranean influences at **The Yellow Porch** (734 Thompson Ln. near 100 Oaks Mall, 615/386-0260, lunch and dinner Mon.–Fri. and dinner Sat., dinner entrées are $12–22). Eat inside or outside on nice days at this casual, neighborhood restaurant.

Next door to the Yellow Porch is locally owned **Baja Burrito** (722 Thompson Ln., 615/383-2252, lunch and dinner Mon.–Sat.) is another place to eat cheap. It was here long before the other "fresh Mex" places were. Order your burrito the way you like it with fresh grilled meats, beans, rice, and condiments loaded into it as you watch. If you don't feel like a big burrito, they'll pile the goodies on fresh salad greens for you. If you're looking for something sweet, look for brownies. Sometimes they are at the end of the line where you check out.

Although **Judge Bean's Bar-B-Que** (611 Wedgwood, 615/244-8884, lunch Mon.–Fri., early supper Wed.–Fri., $11.99 or less) hasn't been there all that long, it's been crowded with people gobbling up the Texas-style barbecued beef brisket, pork, ribs, and diablo shrimp, or jalapeño peppers stuffed with shrimp, cheese, and bacon. You'll see the big smokers as you approach. Their foods are flavored with mesquite instead of hickory wood, which is more common in Tennessee. Inside, you'll order from the counter to the rear and take your food to red-and-white-checked oilcloth-covered picnic tables. A roll of paper towels will be your napkin and a loaf of cottony store-bought white bread, still in its wrapper, will be next to it. You might need the bread if you order the hot sauce. Bean's often has music on Thursday and Friday.

When you're in the mood for some fine ribs, take a drive out to **Carl's Perfect Pig** (4991 Hwy. 70, White Bluff, 615/797-4020, lunch Wed.–Sun., early supper Wed.–Sat., $10 and under). It may be a little way out of town, but worth the trip. The ribs and pulled pork are slowly cooked over hickory wood fires, and served with lots of Southern-style vegetables.

For over 50 years, Nashvillians and savvy visitors have made their way southwest of the city to the **N Loveless Motel and Café** (8400 Hwy. 100, 615/646-9700, www.lovelesscafe.com, 6 A.M.–9 P.M. Mon.–Fri., and 7 A.M.–5 P.M. Sat.–Sun., dinner entrees $10–19), which has become internationally famous for Southern cooking. The Loveless hasn't been a motel since 1985, but they still serve breakfast every morning bright and early—try the country ham and biscuits. Dinner patrons can choose from fried chicken, catfish, steaks, and barbecue. There are two ways to get to the Loveless from Nashville. Country-music figures often stop by as well. First, take I-40 west towards Memphis, and take Exit 192, McCrory Lane. Turn left and go four miles until you dead end into Highway 100. Turn left on Highway 100 and the Loveless Cafe is located directly ahead on the left. Second, from West Nashville, take West End Avenue to the Hwy. 100/70 split and stay in the left lane as it becomes Hwy. 100. Travel approximately 7.5 miles to the Loveless. It is on the right before the Natchez Trace bridge.

Shopping

FINE ARTS AND CRAFTS

The American Artisan (4231 Harding Rd., 615/298-4691) offers contemporary and traditional handmade crafts in a variety of media, including pottery, wood, glass, leather, metal, and small furniture.

Auld Alliance Gallery (Westgate Center, 6019 Hwy. 100, 615/352-5522) carries contemporary landscapes and still lifes from 25 to 30 local Tennessee artists along with more far-flung folks, as well as prints and antique prints.

Collector's Gallery (6602 Hwy. 100, 615/356-0699), in business for about 30 years, is one of the oldest in Nashville. It features 19th- and 20th-century American art in all media, but the focus is oils on canvas and watercolors. It also carries sculpture (some bronze) and features nationally known Tennessee artists, the most popular being Carl Sublett.

Cumberland Gallery (4107 Hillsboro Circle, 615/297-0296) features contemporary art in a variety of media, including paintings, works on paper, sculpture, photography, and limited-edition prints. It specializes in emerging artists, approximately 50 percent of whom are from the southeastern United States.

In the Gallery (624A Jefferson St., 615/255-0705), across from the Bicentennial Mall, features contemporary pieces, African American art photography, special collections, and African antiquities.

Local Color Gallery (1912 Broadway near Music Row, 615/321-3141) represents Tennessee artists with contemporary painting, sculpture, pottery, jewelry, and furniture. **Midtown Gallery and Framers** (1912 Broadway near Music Row, 615/322-9966) carries a variety of works from local, national, and international artists in the form of ceramics, mixed media, oil paintings, acrylics, and others.

Tennessee Art League (3011 Poston Ave. near Centennial Park, 615/298-4072) has three galleries and features original art by Tennesseans.

A small gallery presents small works, such as eight- by 10-inch pieces on canvas, various media, and sculpture.

Woodcuts (1613 Jefferson St., 615/321-5357) offers fine art prints, figurines, cards, and other items by African-American artists.

The **Zeitgeist Gallery** (21st Ave., Hillsboro Village, 615/256-4805) features paintings, sculpture, and photos from emerging artists. Most are regional, with the occasional interloper from St. Louis or New York.

MUSIC

The **Ernest Tubb Record Shops** (original location at 417 Broadway across from Ryman Auditorium, 615/255-7503, www.etrecordshop.com) are the places to find the newest hits and those golden oldies. The original spot used to host a radio show that took to the airwaves as soon as the *Grand Ole Opry* ended. Newer ones are at 1516 Demonbreun (615/244-2845) and at 2416 Music Valley Driver (615/889-2474).

Gruhn Guitars (400 Broadway, 615/256-2033, www.gruhn.com) is perhaps the best source of vintage guitars in the world. This store, within yodeling distance of the Ryman Auditorium, carries all manner of guitars, mandolins, banjos, fiddles, National Steel guitars, dobros, and you name it. One can spend $10,000 here on one instrument—and have several to choose from.

Lawrence Brothers (409 Broadway, 615/256-9240) is much more of a collector's place, with lots of old stuff, vinyl, thousands of 45s, and old junky music souvenirs—none of it cheap. These people are the record equivalent of an antique store as opposed to a used furniture store. The store looks as if the decoration, or lack thereof, hasn't changed in ages.

The Great Escape (1925 Broadway, 615/327-0646, www.greatescape.citysearch.com) sells used and new recorded objects of all kinds, all the way back to 78s. On sale one day were a 78 of T. Texas Tyler's "You Turned a Good Man Down" ($2) and an LP of "Kitty Wells Country Hit Parade" ($5). This place also sells all kinds of comic books, music magazines, collector cards, Star

the best guitar store in Tennessee, if not the entire country

Trek stuff, used paperbacks, and so forth. It's great for browsing but not for something music fans want to be certain to find.

BOOKSTORES

The bibliophile should head for Hillsboro Village, where most of these bookstores hold court. Farther south on Hillsboro Road is **Davis-Kidd,** one of the biggest bookstores in the state.

Bookman Bookwoman Books (1713 21st Ave., 615/383-6555, www.bookmanbookwoman.com) is the place for first editions and signed books from the famous and the obscure. **Dad's Old Book Store** (4004 Hillsboro Rd., 615/298-5880) sells autographs as well as the odd volume.

COURTESY OF ROBIN HOOD, NASHVILLE CONVENTION AND VISITORS BUREAU

Nashville

Elder's Book Store (2115 Elliston Pl., 615/327-1867, www.eldersbookstore.com) specializes in rare books on the Civil War, Tennessee history, and first editions. It also carries Tiffany-style lamps and fine children's books.

Davis-Kidd Booksellers (4007 Hillsboro Rd., 615/385-2645 or 615/292-1404) is the largest independent bookstore in Middle Tennessee and home to a great many literary events. It has an in-store café and some sort of event for kids almost every Saturday morning.

Outloud! Books and Gifts (1805C Church St., 615/340-0034) offers gay and lesbian titles, fiction and nonfiction, as well as music and gift items.

SPECIALTY

A. J. Martin (2817 West End Ave., 615/321-4600) offers some of the finest estate jewelry in Middle Tennessee. It also carries African art, modern glassware, pottery, and pillowcases. Jewelry customers appreciate the fact that this place can fix antique pieces as well as sell them.

Alkebu-Lan Images (corner of 28th and Jefferson, 615/321-4111, www.alkebulan.com) has African American books, art, and gifts. It carries figurines, masks, tapestries, statues, and music boxes.

Manuel Exclusive Clothier (1922 Broadway, 615/321-5444) is the source of many of the fancy clothes worn by country music stars. Manuel, the owner, has designed custom clothing for Dolly Parton, John Lennon, Johnny Cash, Dwight Yoakum, and Bob Dylan. He offers a ready to wear line for mere mortals.

The Southern Historical Showcase (1907 Division St., 615/321-0639, www.southernhistorical.com) offers paper items from the Civil War and antebellum times—autographs, prints, and books.

The Phillips Toy Mart (5207 Harding Rd. in Belle Meade, 615/352-5363) was founded in 1946 and has supplied toys to generations of Nashvillians. This family-owned place is crammed with toys, hobby items—four gauges of model trains—and all kinds of dolls.

Venus and Mars (2839 Bransford Ave., 615/269-8357) has men's and women's vintage clothing from the '50s, '60s, and '70s.

Information and Services

TOURIST INFORMATION

The Nashville Convention and Visitors Bureau (in the Arena, 541 Broadway across from the Convention Center, 615/259-4700, www.nashvillecvb.com, open daily) has two drop-in centers, but the one inside the convention center surpasses. Another source of brochures is the rest area off I-40 east of the city.

At the airport, the **Welcome Center** in the terminal is staffed during business hours.

Disabled visitors to Nashville need only call the **Disability Information Office** (615/862-6492) to get information on transportation and accessible attractions, restaurants, and clubs, as well as other issues. Furthermore, the Convention and Visitors Bureau puts out a publication describing the accessibility of various Nashville locations.

LOCAL PUBLICATIONS

Nashville's daily newspaper, the **Tennessean,** (www.tennessean.com) has weekly entertainment sections that list events and activities. The **Nashville Scene** (www.nashscene.com), a weekly newspaper, also covers Nashville happenings.

GETTING AROUND

The Metropolitan Transit Authority (615/862-5950, www.nashvillemta.org, $1.45 for adults) runs city buses. Call for information about routes and schedules.

Nashville

Chattanooga

More than any other city in Tennessee, Chattanooga has transformed its downtown—at least the portion close to the Tennessee River—into a place attractive to visitors as well as residents. Chattanooga now regularly lands a high position on various lists that rate good places to live, best places for people interested in the outdoors, and so on. The city is also the home of some classic Southern junk food: Moon Pies and, in nearby Collegedale, Little Debbie snack cakes.

Chattanooga got its name from a Creek Indian word for Lookout Mountain, which dominates the city's skyline. The mountain was the scene of a bloody Civil War battle, and in the 20th century it became the site of legendary tourist stops.

Rock City and Ruby Falls and the newer Chattanooga attractions still manage to compete with modern-day theme parks and the frenetic activity around the Smoky Mountains. Downtown Chattanooga has a variety of worthwhile attractions, most within walking distance of each other, and especially for kids.

Note to visitors: the name of this city has four syllables—not "CHAT-nooga," as pronounced by persons from points north.

HISTORY

The fourth-largest city in Tennessee sits just upstream from what used to be the wildest section of

the Tennessee River. After flowing peacefully down the Great Valley, the river turns west, confronting two prongs of the Cumberland Plateau that point to the south, and cuts through them in gorges so deep that they are called "The Grand Canyon of the Tennessee River." Though the nickname is an exaggeration, the terror that flatboaters faced in these waters was not. The worst of the obstacles to navigation was a whirlpool called "The Suck."

Dragging Canoe

Flatboaters faced other hazards. Dragging Canoe, the Cherokee who was so opposed to the Sycamore Shoals sale of his people's land, in 1777 led more than 1,000 renegade followers to this part of Tennessee, where they called themselves the Chickamauga and continued to wage war on settlers. They allied themselves with British forces and did whatever they could to make life difficult for the colonists.

When the women and children of the Donelson Party came floating down from Long Island in 1779 on their way to the site of Nashville, the wild waters caused a boat in their flotilla to wreck. While trying to rescue the passengers, the group came under fire from the Chickamauga. One of the survivors was 15-year-old Rachel Donelson, the future wife of Andrew Jackson.

John Sevier's militia led a raid in 1782 on Dragging Canoe's villages and destroyed them. Since Dragging Canoe was allied with the British, local boosters have seized upon this attack as "The Last Battle of the Revolutionary War," occurring as it did after Yorktown and before the United States and England signed a peace treaty. Knowing that they were a part of this larger effort would no doubt have been of little interest to Dragging Canoe and John Sevier, whose mutual detestation would probably have led to the battle, war or no war. Dragging Canoe, after more raids, died in 1792 after an all-night party. He was 60 years old, a ripe old age for someone in his line of work.

Steam and Rail

Once the Chickamauga were defeated, relations between the settlers and Native Americans improved. The Cherokee owned the south side of the Tennessee River, and about 1815 Chief John Ross built Ross's Landing on the south side of the river, a place to which white traders came by ferry. After the Cherokee were rounded up and removed to Oklahoma, whites poured across the river and named the town Chattanooga. Increasing steamboat traffic helped the town grow, but it took the railroad to put Chattanooga on the map. Tracks from Atlanta, Nashville, and Knoxville converged here, and when the Civil War broke out, the city became an immediate prize.

The war was bad enough, but in 1867 a severe flood, followed by another eight years later, crippled the city. The 1870s marked a turnaround in Chattanooga, however, as money from the North flowed in to exploit the area's coal and iron resources. Soon iron and steel mills rose to such an extent that Chattanooga was called "The Pittsburgh of the South." These mills brought a lot of money and good jobs to the town, but they also belched forth clouds of smoke, which, because of the surrounding mountains, tended to pool in Chattanooga. Anyone with any money built a house on the surrounding ridges—Lookout Mountain, Signal Mountain, and Missionary Ridge. From their lofty perches, the citizens of Chattanooga took great pride in their city. The Chickamauga and Chattanooga battlefields became the first national military parks.

Adolph Ochs, who later made the *New York Times* into the nation's best newspaper, bought the *Chattanooga Times* in 1888, when he was just 20 years old. Bessie Smith, a blues singer who became famous around the world, was born here in 1894. And in 1899, two Chattanoogans gambled that people might like to drink a new concoction from Atlanta, and paid $2 for the rights to bottle Coca-Cola—the first bottlers to do so.

Arrival of the TVA

The Depression brought the Tennessee Valley Authority to town and an increasing number of tourists who took the advice painted on scores of barns to "See Rock City." One reason for the founding of the Tennessee Valley Authority was flood control, and Chattanooga was perhaps the chief beneficiary of this aspect of the agency. TVA took over an existing utility, established a

Must-Sees

Look for **M** to find the sights and activities you can't miss and ⚄ for the best dining and lodging.

M Tennessee Aquarium: With its new expansion, the aquarium is a continuing testimony to how a city can revitalize its downtown with a flagship attraction (page 248).

M Walnut Street Bridge: Walk across to **Coolidge Park** and the funky neighborhood surrounding it (page 249).

M Chattanooga Choo-Choo: Glimpse the railroad's importance in this town, still celebrated wherever big bands play (page 249).

M Chattanooga African-American Museum: The exhibits on Bessie Smith make it a must for music lovers (page 250).

M Rock City Gardens: Heralded for decades by barns and birdhouses, Rock City remains much the same as in the days when people traveled on blue highways to see its wonders (page 258).

CHATTANOOGA

Walnut Street Bridge — **M** — Tennessee Aquarium

M Chattanooga African-American Museum

Chattanooga **M** Choo-Choo

M Rock City Gardens

ALABAMA

GEORGIA

Needle's Eye at Rock City

© JEFF BRADLEY

Chattanooga

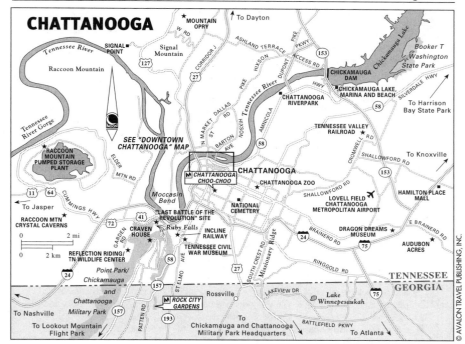

presence in the city, and controls its immense power-producing plants from here.

Like the other main Tennessee cities, Chattanooga saw its downtown deteriorate after World War II and the decline of the railroads. The Interstate highway system came through, following the paths of the railroads, and funneled lots of traffic through the city. But most of that traffic was not going downtown. And no wonder—in 1969 the federal government pronounced Chattanooga "the dirtiest city in America." This galvanized the city, which put teeth in pollution controls, and by 1989 Chattanooga was one of the few cities in the East that fully complied with air-quality standards. But this came with a price. For a variety of reasons, downtown lost 18,000 manufacturing jobs between 1973 and 1984. The city looked to its two strong points—the river and the stream of people passing through—and decided to do something that would get those people to stop and spend money.

Chattanooga Today

The 1980s and 1990s brought a dramatic revitalization of downtown Chattanooga. The Tennessee Aquarium and Ross's Landing Park and Plaza have breathed new life into this interesting city. Chattanooga believes in constant innovation. The city is completing a Tennessee Riverpark that will put a greenway from downtown to Nickajack Dam, 22 miles downstream through the "Grand Canyon of the Tennessee." The National Park Service has acquired 638 acres of historic Moccasin Bend, an area of significance to Native-Americans and Civil War buffs.

With new hotels and attractions, Chattanooga has become the most family-friendly downtown of Tennessee's major cities. It's a place where you can check into a motel, walk to take in a museum or the aquarium, have a nice lunch, and then come back to the hotel for a nap or a swim, go to a professional baseball game, and eat a fine dinner—all without getting in a car.

Chattanooga

THE BATTLE FOR CHATTANOOGA

By 1863, things were not looking good for the South. In July, Ulysses S. Grant took Vicksburg on the Mississippi River, and the Battle of Gettysburg marked an end to any chance of the Confederacy's attacking the North. The Union turned its attention toward Georgia, and to get there it had to come through the rail center of Chattanooga.

Braxton Bragg was commander of Southern forces numbering 43,000 in Chattanooga when a Union army of 60,000 commanded by William Rosecrans approached. Chattanooga, beside the looping Tennessee River and next to high mountain ridges, was a very good place to get penned, so the Confederates retreated into Georgia. Sensing the chance to catch and defeat Bragg, Rosecrans pursued him into the heavily wooded plains near Chickamauga Creek. He did not know that Confederate troops from Gettysburg and other places had come by train to reinforce Bragg, bringing his forces to 66,000. The armies skirmished on the night of September 18, and at dawn the next day clashed in one of the bloodiest battles of the war.

Unlike Gettysburg or other places where battles were fought out in the open, the land here was covered with trees and thick underbrush. Much of the fighting was hand-to-hand, and officers had no clear idea of what was happening. This situation—and a huge piece of luck—determined the outcome of the battle.

One of the Union officers erroneously reported to General Rosecrans that there was a gap in the lines, and the general ordered a division to shift over and fill it. It did so, thus creating a real gap at the exact place where General James Longstreet—who had roomed with Rosecrans at West Point—poured 11,000 soldiers, who broke through the Union lines.

Rosecrans took the advice of his chief of staff, future president James A. Garfield, and retreated toward Chattanooga. One Union commander was not so willing to go. George Thomas took a stand on Snodgrass Hill and held off the Southerners long enough for the Union to make an effective retreat. For this he became known as "The Rock of Chickamauga," while Rosecrans in his retreat was labeled a coward.

Despite the victory, Bragg didn't fare well either. He refused to pursue the fleeing Northerners, to the disgust of Nathan Bedford Forrest and other Confederates. The cost of the battle was appalling. Bragg lost an estimated 30 percent of his men, and Union and Confederate losses totaled 4,000 men dead—among them 10 Southern generals—and 35,000 wounded.

The Union forces stumbled into Chattanooga, and Bragg, following them at last, took up positions high above the city on Lookout Mountain and Missionary Ridge. His guns commanded the rail and river approaches, and other troops were so placed that no one could supply the vanquished troops. Bragg meant to starve them into submission, and the situation for the Union got so bad that a newly promoted general was summoned to help. His name was Ulysses S. Grant, and his arrival set the scene for the battle of Lookout Mountain and Missionary Ridge.

Sights

ORIENTATION

Downtown

More than any of the other main cities in Tennessee, Chattanooga's downtown seems custom-made for visitors. There's plenty of parking, not a great deal of traffic, and many of the attractions are clustered close together. Here are the Chattanooga Aquarium, Ross's Landing Park, the IMAX Theater, BellSouth baseball park, the Creative Discovery Museum, and the Chattanooga Regional History Museum. The Chattanooga Visitors Center at 2 Broad Street is a great place to get oriented.

There may be plenty of parking in Chattanooga, but you will pay for it. Owners of every vacant lot, it seems, have their hands out, so don't waste time driving around looking for something free. Pay it and get over it.

Bluff View Art District

For a totally different experience, take a three-block hike from the visitors center to the Bluff View Art District, a small community on a cliff overlooking the Tennessee River with galleries, restaurants, and a European feel. Here is the Hunter Museum, the Houston Museum, and the River Gallery Sculpture Garden.

North Chattanooga

If things seem a little hectic around the Tennessee Aquarium and downtown, walk across the pedestrian/bicycle/in-line skate–only Walnut Street Bridge to this delightful neighborhood. As you approach the north side, you can look down into Coolidge Park, the nicest city park in the entire state. Check out the wonderful carousel, and enjoy the restaurants and shops. Keep in mind before heading across the span that it is 2,370 feet long—almost a half-mile—and the trek can be tough on small children.

Lookout Mountain

Coming from downtown and heading south, Broad Street becomes Hwy. 58, which leads to Lookout Mountain, home of the retro tourism attractions of the Incline Railway, Rock City, Ruby Falls, and the site of the Civil War "Battle above the Clouds." Cooler than downtown Chattanooga, it's also home to beautiful, shade-filled neighborhoods as well.

Signal Mountain

This community occupies the southern end of Walden Ridge, a piece of the Cumberland Plateau that extends like a finger toward Georgia. To get there, take Hwy. 127. Signal Mountain is home to the Mountain Opry; Signal Point Reservation, a Civil War site; and wonderful old homes. Don't miss the house on the left that looks like a flying saucer as you ascend Hwy. 127.

ROSS'S LANDING PARK AND PLAZA

Visitors sometimes think that Ross's Landing is part of the Tennessee Aquarium, which is the focal point of what is sometimes called "Chattanooga's Front Porch." Ross's Landing at once provides open space and pays homage to Chattanooga's history. It accomplishes this with landscaped bands that use public art and native plantings to tell Chattanooga's story. With surfaces that are alternately paved, grassed, or covered with running water, the bands begin with the year 1992, the dedication date, and work back in time as they move toward the river. Commemorated subjects include Sequoyah and his Cherokee language syllabary, Chattanooga's railroad heritage, and Bessie Smith.

The **Chattanooga Visitors Center** (2 Broad St., 800/322-3344 or 423/756-8687), just off Ross's Landing, is a great place for visitors to orient themselves and plan their sightseeing. In addition to a huge collection of brochures, the center offers a slide show about the city, a reservation service for local hostelries, and information about events soon to take place. The slide show costs $2 for adults and $1 for children 6–12.

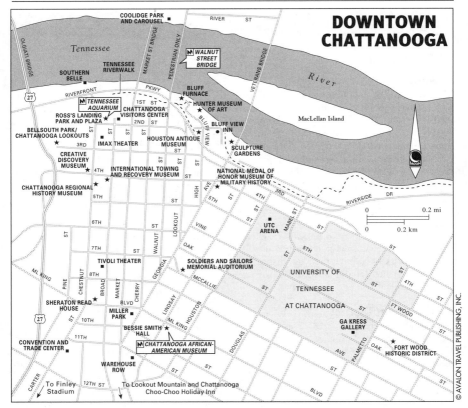

DOWNTOWN CHATTANOOGA

© AVALON TRAVEL PUBLISHING, INC.

◪ TENNESSEE AQUARIUM

This dazzling aquarium (800/262-0695, www .tennesseeaquarium.com, 10 A.M. to 6 P.M. daily, $14 adults, $7.50 children) sits smack in the middle of Ross's Landing Park and Plaza, and was the first of its kind devoted to freshwater aquatic life. The displays replicate the habitats that water falling in an Appalachian mountain forest would go through as it made its way to the sea. Visitors can see plant life and animals—7,000 species of mammals, fish, reptiles, and amphibians—as different in distance and evolution as mountain salamanders and Gulf Coast sharks. Life from rivers around the world is included—South America's Amazon, Africa's Zaire, Japan's Shimanto, and

Siberia's Yenisey. It takes about two hours to see all this.

The aquarium is enormously popular and at times gets very crowded. Ordering tickets ahead of time by phone or on line is an excellent idea. A combination ticket to the IMAX and the aquarium costs $18 for adults and $10.50 for kids. The gift shop is free and open to the public.

To get there, take I-24 to downtown Chattanooga to Exit 1C, U.S. 27 North. Take a right onto 4th Street, then turn left at the second stoplight onto Broad Street. Go two blocks and the aquarium will be in sight.

IMAX Theater (Chestnut St., 800/262-0695, www.tnaqua.org/IMAX, daily, $7.75 adults, $5.25 for kids 3–12) is advertised as a part of

PARK IT AND RIDE

Chattanooga is a user-friendly city, and accordingly many of Chattanooga's attractions can best be reached by foot or free shuttle. The Shuttle Park South, adjacent to the Chattanooga Choo-Choo on Market Street. A 500-space parking garage offers a safe place to leave the vehicle before setting out to explore downtown. The electric shuttle buses—free to all—run from here to the Tennessee Aquarium and all points in between. The schedule is as follows: 6 A.M.–10 P.M. Monday–Friday, 9 A.M.–10 P.M. Saturday, and 9 A.M.–8:30 P.M. Sunday.

the Tennessee Aquarium, but as far as visitors are concerned, is a separate operation. Movies are projected on a six-story-high screen backed with a blow-your-hair-back sound system. Most films last about 45 minutes.

ALONG THE RIVER

Bluff Furnace Historical Park

Bluff Furnace Historical Park, on the Riverwalk between the Walnut Street Bridge and the Hunter Museum, marks the site of the city's first heavy industrial plant. Completed in 1854, Bluff Furnace produced bars of pig iron. In 1859, the plant was leased by Northern industrialists and began burning coke, a fuel used nowhere else in the South. Today the park features a stainless steel outline of the original furnace stack, a scale model of the complex, explanatory signs, and a multimedia, interactive computer program highlighting the history of the riverfront. Admission is free.

ⓜ Walnut Street Bridge

The 2,370-foot-long Walnut Street Bridge was built over the Tennessee River in 1891 and carried pedestrians, trolley cars, and motor traffic. It served the locals for 87 years before it was closed. Unlike similar situations, in which such bridges are demolished or left to decay in public, Chattanoogans had the vision to renovate the bridge and dedicate it to human-

powered traffic. Thus the visitor will see walkers, runners, bicyclists, and in-line skaters crossing what is billed as the longest pedestrian walkway bridge in the world. No fee is charged to use it.

Coolidge Park

Across the Tennessee River from the aquarium, eight-acre Coolidge Park contains open space, an open-air stage, an fountain through which kids of all ages can run, and—best of all—a delightful **carousel.** Rides cost $0.50 for children and $1 for adults. In the spring, summer, and fall, the carousel is open daily from noon (1 P.M. on Sundays) until 6 P.M. All of the figures on the ride were carved by students at the Horsin' Around school for carvers. This park was named for Charles Coolidge, a World War II soldier who won the Congressional Medal of Honor. The park is a part of the 22-mile Riverwalk along the Tennessee River.

ⓜ CHATTANOOGA CHOO-CHOO

The Chattanooga Choo-Choo (1400 Market St., 423/266-5000 or 800/872-2529, www .choochoo.com) is the latest incarnation of Chattanooga's 1909 Southern Railway Terminal, where in its heyday 68 trains arrived and departed daily on 14 tracks. The 85-foot dome is the highest freestanding such structure in the world. The last regularly scheduled train pulled out of Chattanooga in 1971, and the terminal was boarded up and all but abandoned. Twenty-four investors had other ideas, however, and after a year of renovation the station opened once more. It's been going strong ever since.

The 30-acre complex includes four restaurants, a Holiday Inn, and shops. Guests can stay in railroad coaches that each contain two complete rooms. Visitors can ride around the grounds in a 1930s New Orleans trolley, shop in a variety stores, and view an enormous 174- by 33-foot H. O. gauge model train display that contains more than 3,000 feet of track, 1,000 freight cars, and model cities.

A BRIDGE'S LEGAL LEGACY

The **Walnut Street Bridge,** justly celebrated as a renovation and pedestrian delight, was also the scene of a shameful event that precipitated a change in American jurisprudence. In 1906, a black man named Ed Johnson was arrested for raping a white woman, tried in a sham court, convicted, and sentenced to death a mere 17 days after the alleged offense took place. Two black attorneys appealed to the U.S. Supreme Court for a stay of execution, and it was granted.

On hearing that Johnson would not be executed on schedule, people began to talk of lynching him. Sheriff Joseph Shipp, who was up for reelection in just over a week, gave his deputies the night off and posted no extra guards at the jail where Johnson was held. That night, a mob stormed the jail and seized Johnson, walking him to the second steel span of the Walnut Street Bridge. The rope around his neck, he was asked if he had anything to say. He made a short speech proclaiming his innocence that ended with these words: "God bless you all. I am innocent." He was then hanged.

The Supreme Court justices were furious, and brought contempt charges against 27 people: the sheriff, various deputies, and men in the mob. They were tried in the U.S. Capitol. This case marked the first time that the Supreme Court had ever brought contempt charges and enforced them itself. The sheriff and others were sentenced to 90 days in a federal prison in Washington, D.C., but their sentences were reduced for good behavior. When the sheriff returned to Chattanooga, stepping off a train at the station that is now the Chattanooga Choo-Choo, he was greeted by a crowd estimated at more than 10,000 and given a hero's welcome.

In 1999, a book called *Contempt of Court,* by Mark Curriden and LeRoy Phillips Jr., recounted the story of the Johnson case. On February 25, 2000, the authors filed papers seeking to have Johnson's name cleared, and five days later a judge did so. In the book, the authors say that the case "marks the first glimpse of the federal-court system's exercising its power to protect an individual's rights from wayward state authorities."

Johnson's tombstone, which reads "God bless you all. I am an innocent man." can be seen in the Chattanooga African-American Museum.

MUSEUMS

ⓜ Chattanooga African-American Museum

The Chattanooga African-American Museum (200 E. Martin Luther King Blvd., 423/267-1076, www.caamhistory.com, 10 A.M.–5 P.M. Mon.–Fri., $3 adults, $2 students K–12) houses cultural and historical documents and artifacts pertaining to the city's black community. The museum is in Bessie Smith Hall, which also contains a 264-seat performance hall and exhibits relating to the blues singer. Blues and jazz concerts of national, regional, and local artists are presented here, and visitors can use a listening room to hear tapes of Bessie Smith and others.

Chattanooga Regional History Museum

Two blocks from the Tennessee Aquarium, the Chattanooga Regional History Museum (400 Chestnut St., 423/265-3247, www.chattanoogahistory.com, 10 A.M.–4:30 P.M. Mon.–Fri., 11 A.M.–4:30 P.M. Sat.–Sun., $4 adults, $3.50 seniors, $3 children 5–18) interprets the various strands of local history—Native American, music, the Civil War, sports, and business—for all ages. *Chattanooga Country: Its Lands, Rivers, and Peoples* is the museum's permanent exhibit, which includes hands-on activities for kids.

Art and Antiques

The **Houston Museum of Decorative Arts** (201 High St., 423/267-7176,, www.chattanooga.net/houston, 9:30 A.M.–4 P.M., $7 adults, $3.50 children 4–12) is the legacy of one Anna Safely Houston, who had 10 siblings and who managed to get married nine times. She opened an antiques shop in 1920 and built up a collection that consisted of more than 10,000 pieces of art glass, pressed glass, and furniture. She was partial

THE EMPRESS OF THE BLUES

Bessie Smith was born on April 15, 1894. As a little girl, she sang and danced as a street per-former on Chattanooga street corners. As a teenager, she joined the Moses Stokes group of performers and was heavily influenced by Gertrude "Ma" Rainey, a great blues singer.

Smith stayed less than a year with the group before setting out on her own to tour Southern theaters. Though renowned as a blues singer, she branched into jazz, and during the 1920s she was the highest-paid black performer in the country. In 1923, Columbia Records released her "Down Hearted Blues," which sold 750,000 copies in one month—an unprecedented number of sales. She was billed as the "Greatest and Highest Paid Race Star in the World" and the "190-Pound Favorite of Negroes Everywhere."

Smith succeeded because she was a brilliant lyricist, a captivating performer, and one of the wildest women of her era. She penned such classics as "Black Water Blues," "Preachin' the Blues," and "Wasted Life Blues," which singers still perform today. Critics regard her as the first important jazz singer. She recorded "St. Louis Blues" and "Careless Love" with a young trumpet player named Louis Armstrong, who recalled:

Bessie used to thrill me at all times. It's the way she could phrase a note in her blues, a certain something in her voice that no other singer could get. She had real music in her soul and felt everything she did.

En route to a concert in Mississippi in 1937, she was injured in a car accident and bled to death. A famous myth contends that she died after being turned away from a whites-only hospital. This is not true. Bessie Smith was only 43 years old when she died.

to pitchers, and the collection contains several thousand of them. Hard times in the Depression caused her to close the shop, sell her house, and move into an old barn that had glassware from floor to ceiling, with pitchers hanging on ropes. For years she would let no one see this collection, but willed it to the city of Chattanooga in 1951. In 1957, a group of citizens established a museum to house it. However eccentric its founder, the collection is world-class, containing Peachblow, Tiffany, and Steuben pieces as well as cruets and miniature lamps. Now the collection is at home in a turn-of-the-20th-century house.

The **Hunter Museum of Art** (10 Bluff View, 423/267-0968, www.huntermuseum.org, $5 adults, $4 seniors, $3 students, $2.50 children) sits on a 90-foot-high limestone cliff overlooking the city and the Tennessee River. Newly renovated and expanded, the museum houses a collection of 1,500 works, only a small part of which can be displayed at any one time. Here, the visitor will find works by Mary Cassatt, Thomas Hart Benton, Ansel Adams, Albert Bierstadt,

Willem de Kooning, and Alexander Calder, to name a few. The pieces are rotated every two to four years, although some favorites remain on display all the time. The museum hosts touring shows as well.

Religious

The **Messianic Museum** (off Hwy. 153 at 1928 Hamill Rd., Hixson, 423/876-8150, www.ibjm.org, 9 A.M.–4:30 P.M. Mon.–Fri., free), just north of Chattanooga, is housed in the headquarters of the International Board of Jewish Missions (IBJM), whose purpose is to convert Jews to Christianity—very controversial in Jewish circles. The two-story museum focuses on Jews and Israel and the founder of the IBJM. Exhibits include dioramas depicting events such as Moses on Mt. Sinai, large photos of Israel, 250-year-old Torahs, lamps, scrolls, and works of art.

The **Siskin Museum of Religious Artifacts** (Siskin Children's Institute, 1101 Carter St., 423/634-1700, www.siskinfoundation.org, free) resulted from a promise to God. In 1942, Garrison

Siskin was badly injured in a train accident and promised to God that if his life and injured leg were saved, he would spend the rest of his life helping others. His brother, Mose, joined him in that promise. Siskin lived, and he and his family became prominent philanthropists in Chattanooga. The family dispatched its rabbi to Europe in the 1950s to find and buy significant Jewish religious artifacts. Over time the family acquired items from other faiths, and now visitors can see the collection at this museum.

Specialty

The Creative Discovery Museum (321 Chestnut St., 423/756-2738, www.cdmfun.org, 10 A.M.–5 P.M. Mon.–Sat., noon–6 P.M. Sun., $7.95 adults, $5.95 kids 2–12) is a wonderful $16.5 million hands-on place for kids. With structures to climb, a watercourse to control, and bones to dig, children can learn and play at the same time.

Dragon Dreams Museum (6724A E. Brainerd Rd., 423/892-2384, www.dragonvet.com, 10 A.M.–6 P.M. Wed.–Sat., 1–6 P.M. Sun., $6 adults, $3 children 14 and under) occupies a house with eight rooms containing more than 2,000 dragons. The curator says the museum sprang from a personal collection "that was making the house a little strange." Each room of the museum has a theme—Fun Room, Fantasy Room, Japanese Room, and so on.

The International Towing and Recovery Hall of Fame and Museum (3315 S. Broad St., 423/267-3132, www.internationaltowingmuseum.org, 9 A.M.–5:30 P.M. open Mon.–Sat., 11 A.M.–5 P.M. Sun., $8 adults, $7 seniors, $4 children ages 6–18) sounds like a joke—especially if you've ever had your car towed—but this museum has the noble goal improve the towing industry's negative image. Exhibits include antique wreckers and other vehicles and a 1930s filling station.

ARCHITECTURAL SITES

The **Dome Building** (8th St. and Georgia Ave.) was built in 1891 to house the offices of the *Chattanooga Times,* which was owned at that time by Adolph Ochs, who five years later bought the *New York Times* and made it into the world's most influential newspaper.

Across the street stands Chattanooga's **Flat Iron Building,** a four-story version of the famous 1902 New York City landmark by the same name. This one was built in 1911.

A few steps south along Georgia Avenue stands Chattanooga's **Carnegie Library,** built in 1905 and used as a library until 1940.

Built in 1921, the **Tivoli Theatre** (709 Broad St., 423/757-5042) was known as "The Jewel of the South," and no wonder. With a high domed ceiling, crystal chandeliers, and grand lobby, it was a wonderful movie palace wherein the likes of Buster Keaton and Mary Pickford appeared on the silver screen. It was the first theater in the South to have air-conditioning, but over the decades the theater almost slipped into oblivion. In the 1980s, fortunately, it underwent a $7 million renovation and expansion to its current 1,762 seats, plus the construction of the hydraulic orchestra pit, dressing rooms for 70 performers, and state-of-the-art theatrical equipment. Here, one can enjoy an eclectic mixture of blues, classical, country, opera, theatrical productions, and dance. Any show is worth the price of admission just to see the building.

Recreation

Of late, Chattanooga is showing up in *Outside* magazine and is sometimes called "the Boulder of the East." When it comes to outdoor activities, Chattanooga has got a lot going for it: the Tennessee River, its proximity to white-water rafting and kayaking on the Ocoee River, and hiking and rock climbing and biking in surrounding areas.

For all the talk, however, most of the Boulderesque activities take place out of town. To facilitate people coming to town, the city has set up a website meant to be a clearinghouse for outdoor info www.outdoorchattanooga.com, which lists various outdoor doing and where to do them.

PARKS, ZOOS, AND SANCTUARIES

Chattanooga's Riverpark stretches for 20 miles from Chickamauga Dam downstream past the city to Moccasin Bend. This greenbelt includes walkways, playgrounds, a rowing center, fishing piers, and boat docks.

In the middle of the river near downtown lies **MacLellan Island,** an 18.8-acre wooded area owned by the Audubon Society and operated as a wildlife sanctuary. To explore the island, get permission from the Audubon Society by calling 423/892-1499—there's no charge—then get a ride from the Chattanooga Ducks (423/756-3825, www.chattanoogaducks.com)—for which there is a charge. Take a cell phone so as to call the Ducks to pick you up.

Chattanooga Zoo (1101 McCallie Ave., 423/697-1322, http://zoo.chattanooga.org, daily Apr.–Oct.9 A.M.–5 P.M., Nov.–Mar. 10 A.M.–5 P.M., $4 adults, $2 children 3–15) is a small zoo—3.5 acres—with exhibits of spider monkeys, an aviary, and jaguars.

Booker T. Washington State Park (5801 Champion Rd., 423/894-4955), comprising 353 acres on Chickamauga Lake created from TVA land, offers a swimming pool, boating and fishing, and a group camp for 40 people, but no individual campsites.

GARDENS

Audubon Acres (423/892-1499, www.audubon-chattanooga.org, 9 A.M.–5 P.M. Mon.–Sat., $4 adults, $2 children 5–12) is a 130-acre wildlife sanctuary east of Chattanooga where visitors can see a cabin built by the Cherokee, cross a swinging bridge, and take hikes on 10 miles of trails. To get there from I-75, take Exit 3A to East Brainerd Road east. At the second traffic light, turn right onto Gunbarrel Road. Follow Gunbarrel Road as it becomes North Sanctuary Road until it reaches the dead end at Audubon Acres, a distance of about two miles from East Brainerd Road.

Reflection Riding Arboretum and Botanical Garden (423/821-9582, www.chattanooga.net/rriding, 9 A.M.–5 P.M. Mon.–Sat., 1– 5 P.M. Sun.) is a great place with a confusing name. Joint admission for Reflection Riding and the Chattanooga Nature Center, below, is $6 for adults, $3 for kids 4–12 and seniors. This 375-acre preserve, which snugs up against the west side of Lookout Mountain, does not offer horseback rides. The "riding" in the name is an affectation involving an English usage of the word to mean "path of pleasure." A three-mile drive goes through the park and connects to more than 12 miles of trails. Here one can see more than 1,000 species of plants, Civil War skirmish sites, and more than 300 kinds of wildflowers. The Great Indian Warpath goes through here and is maintained in its original condition. Hernando de Soto is alleged to have come this way. Those who wish to see just the Riding can pay $6 per car, but this does not include access to the center's restrooms.

To get there from downtown, go south on Broad Street, towards Lookout Mountain. When you get to signs for Ruby Falls and Rock City, follow the signs to Ruby Falls. Go under the railroad underpass and follow Cummings Hwy., the road you are now on around the base of the mountain. You will pass the sign to go up the mountain to Ruby Falls; continue around. After the Lookout Valley apartments and Mountain View apartments you will take a left turn Onto Old Wauhatchie. Take the next right from Old Wauhatchie—this is Garden Road—follow to end to the parking lot.

Next door to Reflection Riding is the **Chattanooga Nature Center** (400 Garden Rd., 423/821-1160, www.chattanature.org, 9 A.M.–5 P.M. Mon.–Sat., 1–5 P.M. Sun.) is a great place to see native Tennessee animals. The educational center has exhibits as well as the 1,400-foot Blue Heron Boardwalk. Children will love the 750-square-foot treehouse, built in the branches of an oak tree that's more than 100 years old. This delightful structure includes antique windows from Scotland.

The 1,199-acre **Harrison Bay State Park** (423/344-6214, www.state.tn.us/environment/parks/harrison) sits off Hwy. 58 on the Chickamauga Reservoir (the Tennessee River), just northeast of Chattanooga. With 39 miles of shoreline, the water is the chief focus here, and the park has one of the most complete marinas on any of the TVA lakes. It also has a restaurant (open March–Oct.), camping, hiking trails, and stables.

HORSIN' AROUND

Outside of Chattanooga in the Soddy-Daisy community is the only carousel-carving school in America. Horsin' Around (423/332-1111, www.carouselcarvingschool.com) attracts people from all over the country who come to learn the art of carving figures for merry-go-rounds. They come for different reasons—to try something new, to get beyond problems, or because of a fascination with carousels—and they produce all manner of realistic and fantastic wooden figures: horses, dragons, frogs, elephants, and fish, to name a few.

Visitors are welcome to tour the studios. To get there, go north of Chattanooga on U.S. 27. Take the Soddy-Daisy exit. Horsin' Around is behind the Wal-Mart, which is visible from the exit. Admission is free, and the studios are open 9 A.M.–6 P.M. Monday–Saturday.

Be careful. More than one individual has

Chattanooga's Horsin' Around school for carvers

toured this place, gone home, pulled up stakes, and moved to join the studio. It is that appealing.

LOOKOUT MOUNTAIN

Lookout Mountain rises just outside of Chattanooga's city limits and extends southwest more than 50 miles into Georgia and Alabama. If the National Register had a category for "Historic Tourism Destinations," then surely Lookout Mountain would be on this list. Ruby Falls and Rock City have survived the days of tourist homes and blue highways, and the Incline Railway still goes up and down what's called the steepest track in the world. Because of the fancy neighborhoods at the top, however, there are not many places to eat, particularly of the fast-food persuasion. Visitors are advised to pack a picnic lunch or order takeout from restaurants in Chattanooga.

To save money, look into package deals for the Incline Railway, Ruby Falls, and Rock City.

© JEFF BRADLEY

Lookout Mountain Incline Railway

The railway (827 E. Brow Rd., 423/821-4224, www.carta-bus.org, summer 8:30 A.M.–9:30 P.M., hours reduced at other times, $10 round-trip for adults, $5 kids 3–12) was built in the 1890s, when Lookout Mountain had large hotels where people came and stayed for weeks at a time. The cars operate like San Francisco's cable cars by grasping a moving cable that stretches from top to bottom between the tracks. At their steepest, the cars climb a 72.7 percent grade, perhaps the steepest tracks in the world.

Once at the top, visitors who wish to see Ruby Falls or Rock City can take a shuttle bus during summer and can walk the three blocks to Point Park. The Incline Railway is open every day but Christmas, and cars leave three or four times per hour. A round-trip ride takes 30 minutes. Tickets are available at either end of the railway or at the visitors center downtown.

Lookout Mountain Natural Bridge

This natural phenomenon is a rock arch that is 85 feet long and, at its highest, 15 feet off the ground. Utterly publicized, the arch rises in a

Since 1895, the Incline Railway has been climbing some of the steepest tracks in the world.

ravine between Bragg Avenue, which turns off Hwy. 148, and Good Shepherd Episcopal Church, located at 211 Franklin Road. A sign indicates the presence of the arch, but visitors must park several hundred feet south.

Lively times used to take place here. The Southern Association of Spiritualists bought this property and an adjacent hotel in 1883 and conducted séances and pseudo-Indian ceremonies on the arch, some of them lasting well into the night and complete with Indian chants. This is a good place for a picnic. Don't forget the Ouija board.

Ruby Falls

Ruby Falls (423/821-2544, www.rubyfalls.com, 8 a.m.–8 P.M. daily, $12.95 adults, $5.95 kids 3–12), on the Lookout Mountain Scenic Highway, is the latest incarnation of a cave with a long history. Local Native Americans long knew of a cavern extending under the north end of Lookout Mountain. During the Civil War it was

Chattanooga

CIVIL WAR TOUR

Chattanooga is perhaps the best place in Tennessee to take in the Civil War. Significant battles were fought here and, because of the lay of the land, what happened here is relatively easy to follow.

In the decades after the war, Union and Confederate veterans held reunions at the battlefields and saw a need to protect them from encroaching development. *Chattanooga Times* publisher Adolph Ochs lent his support, and in 1890 Congress passed a bill creating Chickamauga and Chattanooga as the nation's first national military parks. The **Chickamauga and Chattanooga National Military Park** was dedicated September 18–20, 1895. Veterans carefully placed about 1,400 monuments and historical markers indicating which brigade fought where. Ochs, even after he moved to New York to run the *New York Times,* was instrumental in buying land on Lookout Mountain and donating it to the public.

The best place to begin is the **headquarters** of the park, across the state line in Georgia. To get there, take U.S. 27 South or get off I-75 on Battlefield Parkway and follow the signs west. The visitors center holds various artifacts, a collection of 355 weapons, and an excellent bookstore. A multimedia production gives an overview of the battle. During warm weather, the museum often demonstrates activities related to the Civil War. Visitors can drive a seven-mile tour of the battlefield. If the weather is nice, bicycles are the best way to get around.

The Chickamauga battle was fought in a forested area with visibility of about 100–150 yards, one of the reasons that commanders were confused and the casualties were so high. The present-day forest, which has much more underbrush, may prove frustrating to those expecting a wide vista where one can clearly see who fought where. If visitors are pressed for time, they should see the visitors center and depart for Lookout Mountain.

The **visitors center** (706/866-9241) is open 8 A.M.–5 P.M. daily, although the battlefield stays open from dawn to dusk. The *Battle of Chickamauga* slide show costs $3 for adults, $1.50 for children 6–16, and $1 for seniors. Admission is free to the visitors center or the park.

The **Gordon-Lee Mansion** (706/375-4728), south of the Chickamauga Battlefield site, served as headquarters for Union General Rosecrans before the battle and as a hospital afterward. The mansion is now a bed-and-breakfast. To get there, drive south of the battlefield on U.S. 27. Turn right on Lee/Gordon Mill Road and go 2.5 miles to the town of Chickamauga. The mansion is on the right. Visitors can tour it in the afternoon in groups of 15 or more for $5 per person if they call ahead.

Known for years as "Confederama," the **Battles for Chattanooga Museum** (3742 Tennessee Ave., 423/821-2812), another private enterprise, now has a name likely to appeal to Yankees as well. The museum's centerpiece is a three-dimensional, 480-square-foot layout consisting of 5,000 miniature soldiers, 650 lights, and sound effects that illustrate the battles of Lookout Mountain and Missionary Ridge. The museum also features dioramas and Civil War artifacts. During the summer, Sergeant "Fox Jim" McKinney holds forth and answers questions about the war. At other times he can be summoned by advance phone call at no additional cost. Admission is $7 for adults, $5 for children 3–12, with discounts for seniors. The museum is open 10 A.M.–5 P.M. daily except Christmas.

Closer in, **Point Park** occupies the end of Lookout Mountain. The Park Service maintains a small visitors center here. During summer rangers offer walks, talks, and demonstrations of Civil War–related activities. Parking is limited here, so if there's no room in the Park Service parking lot, visitors should keep an eye on the meters.

The entrance gate to the park is the world's largest replica of the Corps of Engineers insignia. It was erected in 1905, not surprisingly, by the Corps. Various batteries contain different kinds of cannons used in the battle, and the Ochs Museum and Overlook offers a very good view of Chattanooga. The hike down to it descends 500 feet and may tax those not up to a good climb back.

Craven House, the Confederate headquarters during the early parts of the battle, lies off Hwy. 148, the Scenic Highway. The original house was pretty much shot up during the battle and demolished for firewood afterward, so what visitors see is rebuilt and furnished to reflect the life of the Craven family. Admission is $2 for those ages 16–62, or $4 for an entire family. Hours vary, according to the park budget, but usually Craven House is open April–May on weekends, June–August daily, and September–October on weekends.

The **National Cemetery** (1200 Bailey Ave., 423/855-6590) was established in December 1883 by Union General George Thomas, the famous "Rock of Chickamauga." Soldiers tended to be buried haphazardly after battles, and this was an effort to give them a final resting place with honor and dignity. More than 12,000 Union soldiers—half of them unknown—from various battles, as well as veterans from all of this country's wars, including the Revolution, make up the largest national cemetery in the state. No Confederates are buried here.

Oddly enough, Germans are buried here as well, 186 prisoners of war from World Wars I and II. Chattanooga is the only national cemetery containing prisoners of war from both world wars.

The most famous marker is that of James Andrews's Raiders, a group of Union spies who slipped into Georgia, stole a locomotive named The General, and headed north. The daring Raiders were eventually caught by the Confederates and hanged for their activities. Eight of them rest beneath a marker topped by a replica of The General. Four of them were the first recipients of the newly created Medal of Honor. Andrews himself is not buried here, for he was not in the military.

Keep in mind that this cemetery still has funerals and behave accordingly. Admission is free.

The **Orchard Knob Reservation,** in downtown Chattanooga, marks the hill from which Grant directed the assault on Missionary Ridge. It contains a tall marker but little else to see.

For the Civil War buff, **Missionary Ridge** did not fare so well as Lookout Mountain. During the various real estate booms in the late 1800s, homeowners snapped up property along the ridge, and now most of it is in private hands. When the veterans came back in the 1890s, they found houses on many of the places they had fought. Several significant sites lie along Crest Road, among them the Bragg Reservation, Ohio Reservation, De Long Reservation, and Sherman Reservation. From the south, you can get to Crest Road from U.S. 27 in Rossville, Georgia. Several streets in Chattanooga, such as Shallowford Road, run up to the ridge.

Signal Mountain faces Lookout Mountain and was, as its name implies, a place for Union communications after the Confederates had cut telegraph lines. **Signal Point Reservation** commemorates the efforts of the U.S. Signal Corps and offers an imposing view of the "Grand Canyon of the Tennessee River."

Note: visitors may note a lively trade in Civil War artifacts—bullets, buttons, and the like—in local shops. These are supposed to have come from private lands. It is strictly against the law to dig for artifacts, remove them from national park property, or damage them in any way. Visitors who observe any suspicious activity should notify park officials.

used as a hospital; later, a railroad tunnel cut off the original entrance. In 1928, a man named Leo Lambert hired a crew to drill a shaft down to the cave so he could commercialize it. On the way down, the crew hit a hitherto unknown cave, and when Leo and his wife, Ruby, explored it, they discovered a 145-foot-high waterfall. Leo named it after his wife.

Visitors descend to the cave in an elevator, then stroll approximately 2,200 feet back to the waterfall. The walk is very flat, almost like walking along a mine. At the falls visitors are greeted with a light show and music only slightly less portentous than that planned for the Second Coming. Back on top kids can enjoy a "Fun Forest" consisting of various climbing structures.

Ⓜ Rock City Gardens

Those who choose to see Rock City (706/820-2531, www.seerockcity.com, summer 8:30 A.M.–8 P.M., reduced hours at other times, $12.95 adults, $6.95 children 3–12) find a delightful retro tourism site whose "See Rock City" barns and birdhouses have become American icons. The actual "city" is a series of paths winding among large and unusually shaped rocks. Steps lead over rocks, bridges span chasms, and visitors walk through tight places with names such as Fat Man's Squeeze. The culmination is the highly promoted view of seven states. Given today's pollution, this probably is not possible anymore, but it's an impressive view nonetheless.

To get there, get on Hwy. 58 heading south up Lookout Mountain and follow the signs into Georgia. Food and, needless to say, plenty of souvenirs are available here.

Fairyland

If you cannot abide the crowds or gnomes at Rock City, the same neighborhood on Lookout Mountain offers a chance to explore very interesting neighborhood. In the mid-1920s, Garnet Carter, the same man who created Rock City, developed a 700-acre residential neighborhood here called Fairyland, where the streets had names such as Red Riding Hood Lane, Robin Hood,

peering through the Needle's Eye at Rock City

and so on. The neighborhood filled with beautiful stone houses, and most are still there.

The community contained the Fairyland Country Club, where Carter made a mighty contribution to popular culture by inventing miniature golf. The story goes that a guest at Carter's Fairyland Inn, wishing that the golf course was open, jokingly suggested putting a putting green in front of the inn. Using the odd piece of pipe and other materials, Carter built the first miniature golf course. This archetype was such a hit that Carter franchised the idea all over the country.

To explore Fairyland from Rock City, simply walk or drive in any direction away from the edge of the mountain. You'll soon find yourself coming to Alladin Road, Peter Pan Road, Cinderella Road, and so on.

Lookout Mountain Flight Park

For those not content to just look off the mountain, the Flight Park (800/688-5637 or 706/398-

3541, www.hanglide.com), below Covenant College on Hwy. 189 in Georgia, offers the opportunity to fly off it. Claiming to be the number one hang-gliding school in the United States, it provides a variety of training/flight packages. The simplest is a tandem flight, in which visitors are buckled into a two-person hang glider with an experienced pilot, towed by an airplane to a height of 2,000 feet, and released. The flight down is about 20 minutes long and costs $129. For $60 more the airplane will cut riders loose at 4,000 feet. If wind conditions are right, the school offers flights off the side of the mountain. Visitors can watch free of charge.

SIGNAL MOUNTAIN

Downstream from the city of Chattanooga the Tennessee River cuts through the Cumberland Plateau, and the mountains that face each other across the gorge are Signal Mountain on the north bank and Raccoon Mountain on the south side.

If you want a driving thrill, start up Hwy. 127 and turn right onto Mountain Creek Rd. Go to a rotary and then go straight up the hill. This is the famous old "W" road, an amazingly curving Tennessee version of San Francisco's Lombard Street.

Signal Mountain got its name from the belief that Indians used it for signal fires, but it truly lived up to its name when the Union army was under siege in Chattanooga. The Confederates had cut the telegraph wires, forcing the brand new U.S. Signal Corps to send coded "wig-wag" messages using flags by day and torches by night. This location has been preserved as **Signal Point Reservation.** To get there, take Hwy. 127 up to the town of Signal Mountain and follow the signs. There is no charge to visit this place, which is an excellent place from which to gaze at the "Grand Canyon of the Tennessee River."

Signal Point Reservation is the southern terminus of **The Cumberland Trail,** an ambitious project underway to create a trail from here to Cumberland Gap. For more info, see www.cumberlandtrail.org.

To get to Signal Point Reservation, you drive through the town of Signal Mountain. People began moving here in number when Chattanooga suffered cholera and yellow fever epidemics in the 1870s, but what really sparked development was a trolley line from downtown Chattanooga that first came up Walden Ridge in 1913. The Signal Mountain Inn was soon built, and with 200-plus rooms, a casino, and dancing, the good times rolled. The Great Depression and changes in travel brought an end to the hotel, which was purchased in 1936 by the Alexian Order, who built a monastery and turned the hotel into a rest home for men. Now it is large retirement home where some 500 men and women live. Visit it at www.alexianvillage.com.

SEE ROCK CITY

Those of a certain age who traveled through the South can recall the "See Rock City" barns and birdhouses. Though long associated with Chattanooga, **Rock City Gardens** is actually on the part of Lookout Mountain that extends into Georgia. No matter where it is, this is perhaps the South's most famous attraction.

Rock City began with Garnet and Frieda Carter, who owned 10 acres on the top of Lookout Mountain. The property was filled with enormous pieces of rock in odd shapes. In the depths of the Depression, the couple got the notion to charge admission to their "rock city." The problem was that it lay quite off the beaten path—not the kind of place that people would see while driving along.

The Carters had the inspiration to hire a paint crew and put it on the road painting enormous signs on barn roofs. The farmers got a few dollars and a new paint job, and Rock City gained invaluable publicity. As if this weren't enough, the Carters designed birdhouses whose roofs read "See Rock City" and scattered them far and wide. At one time approximately 900 barns as far as Michigan, Texas, and Florida lured tourists and unforgettably brightened America's blue highways.

Chattanooga

Visitors to Signal Point Reservation will drive through a neighborhood of lovely homes, and can see the old trolley tracks running along some of the streets. Signal Mountain does not receive many tourists, and has several restaurants and shops to comfort the visitor who is weary of the heat and humidity of Chattanooga.

RACCOON MOUNTAIN

Across the Tennessee River from Signal Mountain, Raccoon Mountain from the air looks like a left thumb sticking up where Chattanooga is the palm of a giant hand. The old blue highways 41 and 64 cut across a gap on Raccoon Mountain.

Raccoon Mountain is home to TVA's most unusual source of electric power: the **Raccoon Mountain Pumped-Storage Project** (423/825-3100, www.tva.gov/sites/raccoonmt.htm, 9 A.M.– 5 P.M. daily, free). Since it is impossible to store large amounts of electricity, utilities have to have the capability to produce or buy enough power to meet peak needs. Power plants that run flat out from 6 A.M.–11 P.M., however, sit largely idle during the hours when most power users are asleep—the "off-peak" time.

The Pumped-Storage Project uses off-peak power to pump water from the Tennessee River 1,204 feet up tunnels to a 528-acre reservoir.

When TVA needs power, the water flows down a passageway to the same pumps, only this time turning them to generate electricity. It takes 27 hours to fill the reservoir and 20 hours to release the amount used to generate power. This is a good place for picnics and other recreation. Because of the ups and downs of the reservoir, however, no boating or fishing is allowed.

Raccoon Mountain Caverns (one mile off I-24 Exit 174, 800/823-CAMP or 423/821-9403, www.raccoonmountain.com, summer 9 A.M.–9 P.M., $9.95 adults, $5.50 kids 5–12) offers a 45-minute tour through a cave full of formations. Visitors can choose from a 45-minute walk in the cave—or various "wild cave" tours, which go off the beaten path. These can run from two hours to overnight, costing $26–50 per person.

SPORTS

The **Chattanooga Lookouts** (423/267-4849, www.lookouts.com) play AA minor league baseball every summer in the Southern League. A part of the Cincinnati Reds organization, the Lookouts play at the new BellSouth Park— an easy walk from downtown on Chestnut Street. Tickets cost between $2 and $8 per game.

Entertainment and Events

Chattanooga boasts more than 60 art, cultural, and historic groups that put on a wide variety of events. **Allied Arts** (423/756-2787, www .alliedartschattanooga.org.) supplies information on what is happening.

NIGHTLIFE

Chattanoogans will always love the country sound. But in recent years, they've developed quite a taste for just about every other kind of music, too. The result is a bigger and better club scene, catering to many tastes and all age groups. Check the Friday edition of the *Chattanooga Times Free Press* for current listings. The following were reviewed by Suzanne Hall, a local freelance writer.

Ari's Lakeshore (5600 Lake Resort Terrace, 423/877-7068) offers rock 'n' roll dance music Fridays and Saturdays and sometimes on Thursday evening.

Since 1985, **Comedy Catch** (3224 Brainerd Rd., 423/622-2233 info line, 423/629-2233 reservations) has presented nationally known comedians Wednesday–Sunday. Occasionally, amateurs get a chance at open mike night.

Dancers can do the two-step, the 10-step, or any step they want to live music Thursday, Friday, and Saturday, at **Governor's Lounge & Restaurant** (4251 Bonny Oaks Dr., 423/624-2239). The dance floor is usually crowded. Some big names often headline or stop in to do a late set.

North of Signal Mountain, the **Mountain Opry** (2501 Fairmont Pike, 423/855-4346)is a bit out of town but well worth the trip. Every Friday night from 8–11 P.M., local musicians gather to play traditional bluegrass music.

To get there, take I-124 across the Tennessee River. Exit onto Signal Mountain Boulevard, which becomes Taft Highway (Hwy. 127). Go to the top of Signal Mountain and through town past the shopping center. Go 1.6 miles from the shopping center to Fairmont Pike and turn right at the Fairmont Orchard sign. The Civic Center that houses the Opry is 0.4 miles ahead on the left.

Rhythm and Brews (221 Market St., 423/267-4644) offers a wide variety of rock, country, and other sounds, Wednesday–Saturday. The talent is national and regional. Reservations are suggested.

Boot scooters wanting to rockabilly their babies around the floor should head for the **Rock and Country Club** (6175 Airways Blvd., 423/855-4346). The music is live Wednesday–Sunday.

The Tropicana Room (at Chattanooga Billiard Club East, 110 Jordan Dr., 423/499-3883) serves up a mix of live music several nights a week.

EVENTS

The **Chattanooga Conference on Southern Literature** (www.artsedcouncil.org/literature), held in odd-numbered years April, brings big-name Southern writers to town for lectures, panel discussions, and a chance to meet their readers.

In May, barbecue lovers should come to the **River Roast** (423/265-4397), a barbecue cooking competition, volleyball tournament, and rowing regatta. Held at Ross's Landing.

The **Nightfall** series of concerts (423/756-2787)plays on summer Fridays at Miller Place, at the corner of Market Street and Martin Luther King Boulevard. Lasting 7–10 P.M., Nightfall consists of blues, jazz, zydeco, country, or bluegrass music, along with various concession stands.

Mid-June brings the **Riverbend Festival** (423/756-2211, www.riverbendfestival.com), a nine-day, six-stage salute to music. Each day a different kind of music takes center stage—classical, country, blues, rock, etc. Local, regional, and up-and-coming national performers hit the stages along with a daily headliner—always a big-name star. One of the events is the Bessie Smith Strut.

The **Fall Color Cruise and Folk Festival** (800/766-CRUISE or 423/892-0223, www .marioncountychamber.com/colorcruise2) takes

Chattanooga

place at the height of the fall foliage season and is held downstream from Chattanooga at the Shellmound Recreation Area. Participants can travel by riverboat, bus, or car. Music, dance, other entertainment, and food await.

Christmas on the River (423/265-0771), held on the fourth Saturday in November, centers on a fleet of lit-up boats that cruise past Ross's Landing and also includes a parade of lighted floats. Local groups sing carols, and the event ends with a fireworks display.

AMUSEMENT PARK

The **Lake Winnepesaukah Amusement Park** (1730 Lakeview Dr. in Rossville, Georgia, 877/525-3946 or 706/866-5681, www.lakewinnie.com) is six miles from downtown Chattanooga but the kids won't mind crossing the state line for the more than 30 rides and attractions. During the season, this place offers concerts by big-name country and oldies entertainers. Open in summer noon–10 P.M. Thursday–Sunday, admission to the park is $3 for adults and children—rides cost extra.

EXCURSIONS AND CRUISES

Rail

Chattanooga has long been associated with railroads, and visitors can still on board. The largest operating historic railroad in the South, the **Tennessee Valley Railroad** (4119 Cromwell Rd. and North Chamberlain St., 423/894-8028, www.tvrail.com) operates steam- and diesel-powered trains. The 1911 steam locomotive No. 4501 is the gem of the collection, which among other rolling stock includes a 1917 office car, a 1926 dining car, and a 1929 caboose. The railroad owns 40 acres that includes four bridges and the 986-foot Missionary Ridge Tunnel. Grand Junction Depot is a 1900-vintage station containing an orientation center, a deli, and a large gift shop. On the other end of the line is a replica of a small-town station.

The Missionary Ridge Local ride lasts about a half-hour between stations. On weekends during the summer, the trains go to the Chattanooga Choo-Choo. Rides cost about $12.50 for adults and $6.50 for kids 3–12. Other, longer rides take place during the year; check the website for current information.

On the Water

The 500-passenger *Southern Belle* (800/766-2784 or 423/266-4488, www.chattanoogariverboat.com) offers visitors a variety of cruises departing from Ross's Landing at the foot of Chestnut Street. Trips include rides through the "Grand Canyon of the Tennessee River" and dinner cruises. Call for schedule information. The *Belle* cruises from Valentine's Day through New Year's Eve.

Chattanooga Ducks (corner of Broad and 5th Sts., 423/756-3825, www.chattanoogaducks.com, daily Mar. 1–Oct. 31, $14 adults, $8 children 3–12) are amphibious vehicles formerly used by the military. They drive along the streets and then plunge into the river and keep going. Excursions usually last one hour.

Accommodations

BED-AND-BREAKFASTS AND INNS

The **Mayor's Mansion Inn** (801 Vine St., 423/265-5000, www.mayorsmansioninn.com, $150–275) occupies an 1886 home designed for a man who was mayor of Chattanooga. The stone house is adorned with porches, balconies, gables, and balustrades built in a Victorian Romanesque style. Inside are hand-carved coffer ceilings, arched doorways, and Tiffany glass. Guests in any of the seven rooms, or four suites, can lie in bed and gaze at 16-foot ceilings surrounded by fine antiques and original artwork. All rooms have private baths, televisions, and telephones; some have fireplaces.

Alford House (5515 Alford Hill Dr., 423/821-7625, $75–155) sits on the lower side of Lookout Mountain between I-24 and Ruby Falls. Adjacent to National Park land, the house was built in the 1940s and features two decks and a hot tub. The three rooms, and suite all have private baths, and the breakfast here is "light and healthy."

Charlet House Bed and Breakfast (111 River Point Rd., 423/886-4880, $120–210) sits in the Olde Towne section of Signal Mountain. A quiet place where the property backs up to woods, the house was built in the 1930s and has a heated pool. The large rooms inside are decorated with antiques. All three suites have private baths, and one has a whirlpool bath. "The Retreat" comes with a full-size kitchen, fireplace, and screened porch. Smokers are welcome.

Chanticleer Inn (1300 Mockingbird Ln., 706/820-2002, www.stayatchanticleer.com, $110–180) is close to Rock City on Lookout Mountain, and offers 17 guest rooms in the lodge and five cottages. Built in the 1930s of native stone, the inn was renovated in 2002 and offers a retro feel with all the modern conveniences. This is an excellent place to retreat to after a long day in Chattanooga.

HOTELS AND MOTELS

Chattanooga is loaded with accommodations of the franchise persuasion. To look at several of them, go to www.chattanoogafun.com.

The Sheraton Read House (827 Broad St., 888/625-5144 or 423/266-4121, www.starwood.com/sheraton, $79–149) is to Chattanooga as the Peabody is to Memphis, serving as Chattanooga's grande dame since 1872. Five U.S. presidents and Winston Churchill have stayed here. The hotel fell on hard times as Chattanooga's downtown declined, but new owners poured $10 million into the hotel and have brought the old girl back with a complete renovation.

If you want a place where you can park the car and walk to most of Chattanooga's attractions, go to the **Hilton Garden Inn** (311 Chestnut St., 423/308-9000, www.hiltongardeninn.com, $143).

Another close-in place is **Chattanooga Clarion Hotel** (407 Chestnut St., 800/252-7466 or 423/756-5150, www.chattanoogaclarion.com, $79), which is two blocks from the aquarium.

The **Chattanooga Choo Choo** (1400 Market St., 800/872-2529 or 423/266-5000, www.choochoo.com, $125–225) offers some of the more unusual accommodations in the state. Guests can stay in 48 suites on board sleeping cars-these cost $159 or stay in a Holiday Inn on the premises.

The **Chattanoogan Hotel** (1201 S. Broad St., 877/756-1684, www.chattanooganhotel.com, $60 and up) and **Courtyard by Marriott Downtown** (200 Chestnut St., 800/321-2211, www.marriott.com, $100 and up) are other choices.

CAMPING

Best Holiday Trav-L-Park of Chattanooga (706/891-9766, www.chattacamp.com) has 170 sites with full amenities. It's open year-round. Take East Ridge Exit 1 and follow signs.

Chester Frost Park at Hamilton County Park (423/842-0177, www.hamiltontn.gov/parks/camping) has 188 sites. It's open all year, offering lake swimming, boating, and fishing. From I-75 take Hwy. 153, exit at Hixson Park, and follow signs.

Harrison Bay State Park (423/344-6214, www.state.tn.us), 11 miles northeast on Hwy. 58, has 164 sites. It's open all year and offers a pool, canoeing, and hiking trails.

Raccoon Mountain Campground (423/821-9403, www.raccoonmountain.com), one mile north of I-24 at Exit 174, has 140 sites. It's open all year and features lots of amenities, including the Raccoon Mountain Caverns' Crystal Palace Tour.

Shipp's RV Center and Campground (423/892-8275, www.shippsrv.com), 100 yards east off I-75 Exit 1, offers more than 100 shady sites for RV's and numerous more for tent camping, with full amenities. It's open all year, but reservations are recommended.

Food

Food, wine, and travel writer Suzanne Hall has monitored the restaurant scene in Chattanooga for 25 years. According to her, the restaurant scene in Chattanooga keeps getting better and better. In the past 15 years, one success story has bred another. Today, while the city can't compete in variety to bigger sisters Nashville and Memphis, when it comes to high quality, locally owned, and operated restaurants, Chattanooga holds its own very nicely.

DOWNTOWN

Long a favorite with Chattanoogans, **M** **212 Market Restaurant** (212 Market St., 423/265-1212, lunch and dinner daily, entrées $15–27) never disappoints. A consistently imaginative kitchen staff led by a chef/owner turns out a menu featuring pork, poultry, beef, fish, and lamb served with a flare. The appetizers, pasta dishes, and desserts are excellent. There's live music on Friday night and a great Sunday brunch, enhanced once a month by live jazz. Across from the Tennessee Aquarium.

M **Southside Grill** (1400 Cowart St., 423/266-651, lunch and dinner Mon.–Sat., entrées $16–26) is another restaurant frequented by locals in the know. The talented kitchen staff specializes in dishes of the New South, giving traditional ingredients like pork, chicken, fish, and vegetables an upscale, contemporary flair. The restaurant's wine bar offers

wine flights as well as wine by the glass and bottle from an award-winning list. In a restored historic building near the Chattanooga Choo-Choo. The restaurant is totally nonsmoking except for the patios.

M **St. John's Restaurant** (1278 Market St., 423/266-4400, dinner Mon.–Sat., entrées $18–30) housed in the restored 1915 hotel, is a place to see and be seen. Seating is in the bar with its soaring ceiling, in a small room adjacent to it or on the balcony above. It's noisier in the bar and quiet and romantic in the other dining areas. The extremely creative menu changes regularly and can include dishes like veal cheeks, monkfish, Peking duck, or even antelope. This is another Chattanooga restaurant with an excellent wine list. The **St. John's Meeting Place,** located in the same building, is a more casual and less expensive dining spot.

Big River Grille & Brewing Works (22 Broad St., 423/267-2739, lunch and dinner daily, entrées $7–19) has good food, a casual atmosphere, and beer and soft drinks made on the premises. The menu includes sandwiches, salads, and full meals, including pasta, seafood, steaks, chicken, and other dishes. The blue crab–stuffed chicken is excellent. Near the Tennessee Aquarium.

The **Broad Street Grille** (1201 S. Broad St., 423/424-3700, daily, entrées $19–29) is the elegantly appointed, upscale restaurant in the Chattanoogan Hotel. Steaks are a specialty here and

LITTLE DEBBIE

<small>COURTESY OF MCKEE FOODS CORPORATION</small>

Thousands of American children remember traipsing off to school carrying a lunch containing a Little Debbie oatmeal crème pie. The Little Debbie image, which looks like a girl from the 1930s, was actually patterned on the granddaughter of company founder O. D. McKee. The real Little Debbie was four years old in 1960.

the image made famous from cakes and other delights baked in Tennessee

Little Debbie cakes became a huge hit—they sold 21.5 million in their first 10 months on the market—and now Little Debbie's face graces 75 varieties of cakes and cookies. Her fudge brownies were reportedly a favorite of Elvis.

The headquarters for **McKee Foods** is outside of Chattanooga in Collegedale, where the company operates a gift shop. For a closer look, go to www.mckeefoods.com or www.littledebbie.com.

BLUFF VIEW ART DISTRICT

Back Inn Café is an upscale bistro featuring dishes from around the world. Ravioli and an interesting assortment of pizzas are specialties. The view from the dining room and outdoor terrace is spectacular. The recently expanded **Tony's Pasta Shop and Trattoria** offers a good selection of handmade pastas and freshly made sauces. **Rembrandt's Coffee House** specializes in European breads and pastries, sandwiches, and fine coffee. All are open for lunch and dinner. Entrées at the Café and Trattoria are $10–20. Rembrandt's is less expensive. Sunday brunch is served in the district at **Renaissance Commons.**

NEAR DOWNTOWN

The **Chattanooga Choo-Choo** complex (1400 Market St., 423/266-5000) has been a popular location for tourists and conventioneers for years. It offers a selection of decent dining spots, including the **Station House,** where servers also take to the stage to sing and dance. The dinner-only menu (Mon.–Sat.) includes chicken, steak, and ribs, and a salad bar. The **Gardens** restaurant offers Southern specialties like fried chicken, catfish, and rainbow trout. Saturday night usually brings a prime rib buffet. Bread pudding is a highlight on the dessert menu. Open seven days a week for breakfast, lunch, and dinner, the Gardens is a great place for families. An authentic Victorian railway car is the setting for **Dinner in the Diner,** the Choo-Choo's upscale restaurant. Entrée choices include steak au poivre, jerk chicken pasta, and a fish and chicken dish.

Upstream from the Bluff View Art District, at the **Boathouse Rotisserie & Raw Bar** (1011 Riverside Dr., 423/622-0122, lunch and dinner daily, entrées $8–25), oysters are a specialty and they're shucked by the hundreds at the bustling bar. The dining room is noisy but fun. The best seats in the house, though, are on the deck overlooking the Tennessee River. The daylong menu is eclectic, offering everything from beef brisket to grilled salmon and fried catfish, shrimp, and oysters. There's also a nice selection of salads and sandwiches.

they come in a cut and size to please any palate. Shrimp, chicken, and other dishes round out the dinner menu. The family-friendly Grille also serves breakfast, lunch, and an exceptional Sunday brunch. The adjacent Foundry bar makes some mean martinis.

Chef Nathan Winowich established himself as one of the city's best chefs at Southside Grill. Now he runs the kitchen at **Nathan's** at the Stone Fort Inn (120 E. 10th St., 423/267-7866, dinner Tues.–Sat., entrées $18–30). This fine dining room features modern American cuisine with a European flair. Entrées might include rabbit, quail, steak, diver scallops, and other delicacies, all accompanied by imaginative side dishes produced from organically grown, regional ingredients.

<small>Chattanooga</small>

MOON PIES

The scene: Two Southerners and someone else in Cambridge, Massachusetts, are planning where to eat lunch. Amid the various options, one Southerner suggests "a Moon Pie and an R.C. Cola." The second Southerner bursts out laughing, but the third person doesn't get it, not recognizing a longtime favorite lunch for working-class Southerners.

Moon Pies were invented at the Chattanooga Bakery in 1919. The originals consisted of a marshmallow-type filling between two four-inch-diameter cookies. The whole thing—at least the classic version—is covered with a chocolate coating. These "pies" became enormously popular throughout the South, and for some people a Moon Pie and a Royal Crown Cola was as good a snack as one could get.

Because of vending machine requirements, today's Moon Pies are smaller and thicker than the original, but now they have three cookies separated by filling. Nowadays they also come in a low-fat version and, seasonally, with vanilla, banana, strawberry, and other flavored icings and fillings.

The **Chattanooga Bakery** (www.moonpie .com) turns out about 300,000 Moon Pies a day and sells them as far away as Japan, where they are known as Massi Pie. The epicenter of Moon Piedom, however, is the annual **Moon Pie Festival** in the middle Tennessee (Heartland) village of Bell Buckle in June.

Northshore Grille (16 Frazier Ave., 423/757-2000, lunch and dinner daily, entrées $6–30) is a center of activity in the shopping district just across the Tennessee River from the Tennessee Aquarium. In warm weather, the front windows slide open to produce a sidewalk café atmosphere. The bar is noisy and crowded. The dining room is quieter and family-friendly. The menu is extensive and includes salads, sandwiches, baskets of fried shrimp, fried oysters or ribs, and steak, chicken, fish, and vegetarian dishes.

At **Terra Nostra Tapas & Wine Bar** (105 Frazier Ave., 423/634-0238, dinner nightly), just across the river from the Tennessee Aquarium, chef Efren Ormaza (formerly of 212 Market) offers an international menu of "small plates," ranging in price from $3 to about $14. The idea is to order several and share them while enjoying a selection from the restaurant's extensive by the glass or bottle wine list.

N Canyon Grill (Lookout Mountain at Hwy. 189 and Hwy. 136, 706/398-9510, dinner Wed.–Sun., entrées $14–29) is in Signal Mountain, about a 35-minute drive from downtown Chattanooga. The scenic drive and the food are worth it. The wood-fired grill puts out such specialties like slash and burn catfish, pork tenderloin and whole local trout. All go beautifully with Canyon Grill's signature grilled cabbage and spicy squash. Fish, chicken, and pasta dishes round out the menu. Bring your own beer or wine (no spirits).

Top of the Mountain Restaurant and Grill (411 Wood St., Signal Mountain, 423/886-6531, lunch and dinner Tues.–Sat., lunch Sun., entrées $11.50–14) is about 15 minutes from downtown Chattanooga and well worth a visit for traditional Southern foods served in a cozy atmosphere. The Sunday buffet is especially appealing and always offers two carving stations with numerous side dishes. At dinner, the signature crab cakes are a stand-out. Entrées might include fried chicken, catfish, pasta, or steak.

In an area inundated with chain restaurants adjacent to Hamilton Place Mall, **Acropolis** (2213 Hamilton Place Blvd., 423/899-534, lunch and dinner daily, entrées $8–20) stands out as a longtime, family-owned restaurant. The reasonably priced menu features well-prepared Greek, Italian, and American dishes.

Information and Services

SHOPPING

Across the street from the Hunter Museum, the **River Gallery** (400 E. 2nd St., 423/267-7353) offers original fine arts and high-end crafts. Visitors can peruse woodcarvings, jewelry, sculpture, basketry, studio art glass, handmade books, art furniture, and textiles. The gallery has a sculpture garden outside.

Eight of Chattanooga's old railroad warehouses make up **Warehouse Row** (110 Market St., 423/267-1111) outlet shopping in downtown Chattanooga. More than 40 shops of high-end merchandise are open daily.

North of Town

The area north of the Tennessee River via the Walnut Street Bridge, offers a collection of interesting shops.

Hundreds of contemporary crafts workers sell their goods at **Plum Nelly** (1101 Hixson Pike, 423/266-0585). Shoppers can find functional pottery made by more than 150 potters and jewelry from more than 100 artists.

Mole Hill Pottery (1210 Taft Hwy. on Signal Mountain, 423/886-5636) sells all kinds of pottery, glass, jewelry, dishes, objets d'art, and kitchen items.

Rock Creek Outfitters (www.rockcreek.com) has three locations where one can buy the gear necessary for all the opportunities in this region. Backpacking and camping gear is at a store near the Hamilton Place Mall (423/485-8775) as well as a store at 100 Tremont Street (423/265-5969), near Coolidge Park across the river from downtown. For those who want to get on the water, a third location at 191 River Street (423/265-1836 or 888/707-6709), also near Coolidge Park, can sell you a kayak as well as tell you where to use it.

South of Town

Reenacting aspects of the Civil War is a growing hobby, and **Mountain City Mercantile** (126 Gordon St. in Chickamauga, 706/375-3800, www.mountaincitymercantile.com, 10 A.M.–6 P.M. Thur.–Sat.) can outfit visitors to the army of their choice. This place has uniforms, women's clothing, insignia, boots, and items such as period pocketknives as well.

INFORMATION

For information, contact **Chattanooga Area Convention and Visitor's Bureau** (2 Broad St., 800/322-3344 or 423/756-8687, www.chattanoogafun.net, 8:30 A.M.–5:30 P.M.).

Chattanooga

Hills and Plateaus

The area northwest of Knoxville is the most remote in Tennessee, so remote that when the late James Earl Ray, the convicted killer of Martin Luther King Jr., escaped from Brushy Mountain Prison in 1977, he had nowhere to go. Though the terrain is not as rugged as in places farther east, the thin soil never did support farming on a level that attracted a great many people. Most of the value lay under the ground in the form of coal or on top in the form of timber.

Nonetheless, the land attracted visionaries. England's Thomas Hughes came here in 1880 to establish Rugby, a colony of "second sons" who sought to earn a living in a place not bound by Victorian notions of what constituted acceptable work. He was followed by a group of industrialists who set up the town of Harriman, which they hoped would become the "Utopia of Temperance." The Tennessee Valley Authority built its first dam in these parts, constructing beside it a town to serve as an example of a very livable place. And mil-

itary leaders and scientists came here in the 1940s in a desperate effort to defeat the forces of Germany and Japan with uranium processed in the secret city of Oak Ridge.

This area might not be known for great crops, but it produced some remarkable individuals. Samuel Clemens was conceived here. Alvin York was a Fentress County conscientious objector who became World War I's greatest hero, a man who renounced fame to come home and run a mill. Cordell Hull, born not too many miles from York, won the 1945 Nobel Peace

© JEFF BRADLEY

Prize. And John Rice Irwin single-handedly cre-ated the greatest collection of Appalachian items and artifacts in the world.

As Tennesseans and tourists explore the state, this area will delight them. Here stand enormous state parks filled with clear lakes and steep canyons. The Big South Fork National River and Recreation Area, with its rock formations and thrilling white water, stacks up well against the Great Smoky Mountains National Park, with only a tiny fraction of the larger park's visitors. The oldest winery in the state, historic Rugby, and a place where grown men play a unique kind of marbles are just three of the things that await the traveler.

The Cumberland Plateau

Sojourners heading west from Knoxville find themselves climbing the Cumberland Plateau, an obstacle once so formidable to Nashville-bound travelers that they would go through Ken-tucky to get around it. The plateau is 1,000 feet higher than the Knoxville area, and its soil is thin and not much given to raising crops.

Heading the sightseeing list is Fall Creek Falls State Park, home to the highest waterfall in the eastern United States. Crossville's Homesteads Tower Museum recalls a Depression-era attempt at an ideal community.

The route south down the Sequatchie Valley certainly marks one of the more pleasing drives or bike rides in the state. The river offers canoeists a gentle drift ideally suited for families or those who like to take their rivers easy.

Knoxville to Chattanooga

Most of this part of the state, stretching between Knoxville and Chattanooga, lies in Tennessee's Great Valley. The land is much flatter than in upper East Tennessee and is ideally suited for farming. Held back by TVA's dams, the Tennessee River follows the valley to the southwest, slowly flowing and gathering the waters of the fast-rush-ing streams that pour out of the mountains to the east. The white-water rafting in one of these rivers, the Ocoee, is unsurpassed in the state.

This area was the center of activity for the Cherokee. Their principal towns were here, and it was from this area that the infamous Trail of Tears began. Towns in the southeast part of Ten-nessee have banded together to promote them-selves as "the Tennessee Overhill," the old name given to the Cherokee strongholds.

The coming of the railroad created many towns in this section, bringing industry and jobs. Towns dreamed of businesses or schemes that would "put them on the map," and one of them—Dayton—did so with a "monkey trial" that is still argued about and discussed today.

The area east of the Tennessee River poses problems for books such as this one that adhere to the "lay out a route and they will follow" school of travel writing. Two main highways roughly parallel this side of the Tennessee River, each with a string of interesting towns and villages along the way, so it behooves the visitor to read the entire section before choosing which route to take. The resulting itinerary may turn out to re-semble "Drunkard's Path," a classic Appalachian quilt pattern, but the side trips will be well worth the effort.

The first tour from Knoxville to Chattanooga heads down U.S. 11, a road that runs alongside I-75. The second tour begins where U.S. 411 crosses the Little Tennessee River, a route that runs alongside the railroad tracks. And the final section abandons both highways, turns east, and heads for the hills.

Must-Sees

Look for **M** to find the sights and activities you can't miss and **M** for the best dining and lodging.

M Museum of Appalachia: This collection, just outside of Norris, offers a wonderful look at the ingenious people who populated the mountains (page 272).

M American Museum of Science and Energy: Look back to the Manhattan Project and ahead to future energy problems—and solutions (page 280).

M Rugby: Sometimes called "the last colony," this village was founded by Victorians who had high hopes of providing a new way of life for aristocratic young men (page 285).

M Fall Creek Falls State Resort Park: This park, near Pikeville, is centered around the highest waterfall in the eastern United States (page 298).

M Fort Loudoun: This State Historical Area and the nearby **Sequoyah Birthplace Museum** reflect the interaction of two sets of people, one who prevailed and the other who were exiled from their ancestral home (page 315).

COURTESY OF THE MUSEUM OF APPALACHIA

Sherman Wooten, chairmaker

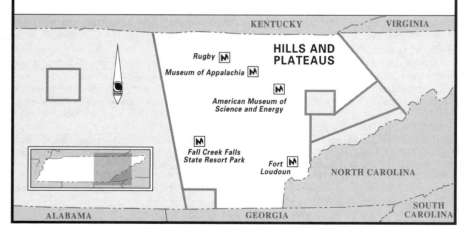

© AVALON TRAVEL PUBLISHING, INC.

North of Knoxville

NORRIS AND VICINITY

For students of urban design, Norris is a great stop. The town, named after Senator George Norris of Nebraska, began as housing for the workers who built TVA's first dam. In those vision-filled early days of the agency, however, the town took on greater import. This was to be a model community, a place to try out ideas and to set up an example from which others could learn.

These innovations took several forms: all-electric houses, because TVA wanted to demonstrate the uses of its chief product; roads that were adapted to the existing contours instead of forcing the land to conform to a plan; and houses clustered around common areas of land. The road leading to Norris was designated the "Norris Parkway," and billboards were banned, a radical concept in the 1930s. The people in the various houses—there were 12 designs from which to choose—loved their town, but there was one big catch: TVA owned everything.

In 1947, TVA announced it would sell the entire town to any buyer who could come up with $1.8 million. A Philadelphia company bought the town, and then began selling the houses to their owners. By 1953, the parks and town buildings had been sold as well, and Norris could govern itself much as any other town. Today the town stands as an example of good planning and the willingness of the residents to adhere to high standards.

Museum of Appalachia

Norris is renowned for two museums of Appalachian culture. The Museum of Appalachia (865/494-0514, www.museumofappalachia.com) is a nationally known collection of 250,000 items brought together by John Rice Irwin, a remarkable individual who was awarded a "genius" grant by the MacArthur Foundation. The items are

COURTESY OF THE MUSEUM OF APPALACHIA

making music at the Museum of Appalachia

displayed in 20 buildings on a 65-acre farm just off I-75 at Exit 122.

Irwin started out collecting odd items as a boy, and as he grew up he realized that the tools and other objects that marked Tennessee mountain life were slowly slipping away, as was the knowledge of what they were and how to use them. Using his own money, he assembled his collection of musical instruments, traps, bits, hand tools, and axes. He has millstones, stagecoach horns, blacksmith tools, sheep shears, and on and on and on. The visitor is simultaneously impressed with how hard life was in "the old days" as well as with the ingenuity and imagination of the people who lived in those times and confronted basic problems without the benefits of hardware stores. Irwin believes that museum objects "should be tied in some way to the people who used them." This philosophy has produced a museum with a warm personality—not a sterile place where visitors walk around with their hands clasped behind them.

An important part of the museum is the **Appalachian Hall of Fame,** which recognizes, among others, Sergeant Alvin York, the Carter Family, and Cordell Hull, with artifacts from each person. A relatively new exhibit is a Jamestown cabin that once belonged to the parents of Samuel Clemens. His parents moved down to Hannibal, Missouri, before Samuel was born, but the calendar suggests America's foremost humorist was conceived while they lived in Jamestown. The museum periodically sponsors demonstrations of crafts, tool use, music, quilting, and a once-a-year "shooting of the anvil." This earth-shaking event involves two anvils, black powder, and a long fuse.

Admission to the museum is $12.95 for adults, $5 for children ages 6–13. Families get in for $30, and seniors receive a discount. It is open during daylight hours year-round.

Norris Dam State Park

Although TVA took over several dams when the agency came into existence, this was the first one it built. Work began in 1933, during the Great Depression, and ended three years later. The dam gave over 3,000 men badly needed jobs, and their

AN APPALACHIAN HOMECOMING

I f a visitor to Tennessee can go to only one event in the state, this is the one.

Held every October, the Homecoming (865/494-0514, www.museumofappalachia.com) brings together musicians, craftspeople, writers, and plain old folks for a lively celebration of Appalachia. College presidents rub shoulders with retired farmers, all tapping their feet to bluegrass music that pours forth from two stages.

Musically, it doesn't get much better than this. Here is a partial list of the participants who have appeared in recent years: Mac Wiseman, Ralph Stanley, Joe and Janette Carter, Doyle Lawson, and Quicksilver.

Visitors can watch demonstrations of many old-time crafts and activities, such as apple butter– and molasses-making, pottery, quilting, woodcarving, spinning and dyeing, rifle firing, and white-oak basketmaking. Country cooking is dished up from wood-burning stoves and open pots and washed down with fresh-squeezed cider and sassafras tea.

Admission for this four-day event is $75 for adults and $15 for children. Daily admission begins on Wednesday at $20 for adults and $5 for children. For subsequent days, rates go to $25 for adults and $8 for children. Advance tickets are a very good idea.

work resulted in a 265-foot-high dam that stretches across the valley for 1,860 feet, holding back two rivers that form a lake covering 34,000 acres of land and having 800 miles of shoreline. Before the waters rose, 2,899 families had to move, and over 5,000 graves had to be relocated to higher ground. The dam was closed by an electric signal coming from Franklin Roosevelt in the White House on March 4, 1936. Like the town, the dam was named for Senator George Norris, a strong supporter of the TVA and rural electrification. The dam's website is www.state.tn.us/environment/parks/parks/NorrisDam.

The park that commemorates Norris Dam covers 4,038 acres and also contains the **Rice Gristmill,** a 1798 mill that was once operated by the kinfolks of John Rice Irwin. During the summers this mill still grinds corn, and the meal is available in a gift shop.

The **Hill Cave Tour** (865/426-7461, $2, call for reservations) offered twice a week during the summer, enables the intrepid to walk and crawl through this local cavern.

The **Lenoir Museum** (865/494-9688, open daily in summer, reduced days the rest of the year, free) in the park is the work of the late Will Lenoir, another of those individuals who was driven to collect odd items—Appalachian and otherwise. Among the latter is a German barrel organ dating from 1826 with 44 moveable figures. Another is a Ming dynasty vase. Every Sunday afternoon features live traditional music.

The park maintains 29 cabins and 85 campsites for use by visitors. Amenities include boat rentals, swimming pool, and hiking trails. The **campground** is open all year. For information or reservations, call 800/543-9335 or 865/426-7461.

Big Ridge State Rustic Park

Norris was TVA's demonstration town, and Big Ridge was the agency's demonstration park. The heavily wooded 3,642 acres overlook Norris Lake and feature 52 campsites, cabins, hiking trails, swimming, boat rentals, and a visitors center with nature exhibits. To get there, take Hwy. 61 northwest from I-75. For information, call 865/992-5523.

Practicalities

The **Fox Inn Campground** (865/494-9386) is in Norris, right off I-75's Exit 122 on Hwy. 61. Ninety-three sites are open all year, with a swimming pool and other amenities.

The Museum of Appalachia has a **restaurant** that is open daily. Diners do not have to pay admission to the museum to eat cornbread, soup, beans, and chicken pot pie, as well as burgers and hot dogs.

NORTH TO KENTUCKY

Cove Lake State Recreational Park

Right outside the town of Caryville on Hwy. 25

West sits Cove Lake State Recreational Park, a 673-acre park with nature trails and bike paths from which visitors can see Cumberland Mountain. The lake is home to hundreds of Canada geese in the winter, and other visitors will find tennis courts, 97 camping sites open all year, swimming, fishing, and boat rentals. For more information about the park, call 423/566-9701 or visit www.state.tn.us/environment/parks/parks/CoveLake.

Elk were released near here in the Royal Blue Wildlife Management Area in 2000, and they have begun having calves and reestablishing themselves in the Tennessee mountains. The last native elk in Tennessee was killed in 1865 in Obion County in West Tennessee.

Jellico

This little town on the Kentucky border was the scene of a terrible explosion on September 21, 1906, when a railroad car full of 10 tons of dynamite blew up. Nine people died, 200 were injured, and almost one-fourth of the town was left homeless. The explosion broke every pane of glass in a one-mile radius and could be heard 20 miles away. The crater left by the blast was 20 feet in diameter and 20 feet deep.

That same year, a little girl named Grace Moore and her family moved to Jellico from Del Rio, Tennessee. She sang in the local Baptist choir and went on to become Tennessee's most famous opera singer, making her debut at the New York Metropolitan Grand Opera Company in 1927 and appearing in *La Bohème, Tosca,* and *Romeo and Juliet,* to name a few. She went on to star in a series of movies, of which *One Night of Love* is the most famous. "The Tennessee Nightingale" died in a plane crash outside Copenhagen in 1947.

Motels include the **Best Western Holiday Plaza Motel** (Exit 160 off I-75, 423/784-7241), **Billy's Motel** (Exit 160, 423/784-4362), **Days Inn** (Exit 160, 423/784-7281), and **The Jellico Motel** (Exit 160, 800/251-9498 or 423/784-7211).

The small **Indian Mountain State Camping Park** (423/784-7958, open all year)—only 213 acres—was developed on land that had been strip-mined for coal. It offers 49 campsites, walking trails, fishing, and boating.

ONEIDA

As the biggest town on the eastern end of the Big South Fork National River and Recreation Area, this is the place to rest one's head, get something to eat, and find other necessities of life.

It is also the birthplace of the Smith Brothers, not the cough lozenge duo, but two brothers whose career ran from the '30s to the '60s. "Tennessee" and "Smitty" played country, Western swing, and other varieties of music, eventually winding up with gospel.

The **Sorghum Festival** (800/645-6905 or 423/569-6900) marks the annual arrival of members of the Muddy Pond Mennonite Community, who set up a horse-powered mill that grinds cane to extract the sap, which is then boiled down to produce sorghum (molasses). The festival, usually held on the second weekend in September, includes live music, arts and crafts sales, and lots of food.

for sale at the Muddy Pond Mennonite Community: a brand-new Mennonite Buggy for a mere $3,500

© JEFF BRADLEY

Practicalities

For accommodations, try the **Williams Creek Wilderness Resort** (423/569-9847), **Galloway Inn** (south U.S. 27, 423/569-8835), or **Holiday Inn Big South Fork** (U.S. 27, 800/HOLIDAY [465-4329] or 423/663-4100).

Flonnie's Drive-In (423/663-2851, open for lunch and dinner every day), south of town at the intersection of U.S. 27 and Hwy. 63, is a good example of the kind of restaurant that preceded McDonald's, Hardee's, and others of the franchise ilk. Patrons can sit in their cars or inside. The food includes the popular "Flonnieburger" as well as other dishes such as chicken and chili. Milkshakes are made one at a time.

For more information, contact the **Scott County Chamber of Commerce** (410 N. Alberta St., 800/645-6905 or 423/569-6900, www.scottcounty.com/Chamber, 8 A.M.–4 P.M. Mon.–Fri.).

Big South Fork National River and Recreation Area

If the millions of people who speed south on I-75 or east on I-40 heading for the Great Smoky Mountains National Park knew what they could see and do in the Big South Fork National River and Recreation Area, the people in the outlet stores of Pigeon Forge and parking lots of Gatlinburg might have a little more room. The Smokies can't be beat for sheer size and grandeur, but when it comes to hikes with fascinating natural features, the Big South Fork wins hands down. And it's just 65 miles from Knoxville and less than 30 miles from I-75. As one Big South Fork ranger admitted, "This is where people who work in the Smokies come for their vacations."

The name comes from the south fork of the Cumberland River, and the park looks like a gerrymandered political district as it snakes upstream from Tennessee into Kentucky. Like the Smokies, the land that makes up this park was once exploited for timber. Coal was mined in some areas. Underlying it all is a geology that, combined with running water, created some of the most interesting landscapes in the entire state, but this is not apparent on first entering the area. In this part of Tennessee, visitors initially look down to see the scenery, not up.

The Cumberland Plateau on which this area lies is covered with a hard layer of sandstone. Underneath this surface layer, however, sits much softer sandstone. When a stream breaks through the hard capstone, it readily cuts through the underlying material. Thus Big South Fork has 500-foot-deep gorges, dramatic cliffs, arches, and shelters under bluffs where present-day visitors can see the same stones that sheltered Native American hunters and settlers. White-water aficionados will find water varying from family float trips all the way to Class V expert-only runs. Unlike the Smokies, Big South Fork permits mountain biking on several designated trails.

All this is relatively new. The Army Corps of Engineers long had its eye on damming the river, at one time proposing what would have been

the highest dam in the East, but, luckily, it could never get funding from Congress. Local conservationists began making noises about preserving the land and rivers in the 1960s, but it took the political push of then-Senator Howard Baker to bring the efforts to fruition. The area has an unwieldy name, but nothing a handy acronym—BSFNRRA—can't solve. The park, which extends into Kentucky as well as Tennessee, totals more than 113,000 acres, not counting the adjacent Pickett State Rustic Park and Forest, which adds 11,700 acres, or the Daniel Boone National Forest, with 500,000 acres.

RECREATION

Hiking

Almost 150 miles of hiking trails range through Big South Fork. They vary from less-than-one-mile jaunts to trips lasting for days. Here are a couple of examples, one on the east side and one from the west.

From the east, the **O&W Bridge Trail** goes 4.6 miles round-trip to an old railroad trestle for trains on the Oneida and Western Line that once connected Oneida and Jamestown. To get to the trailhead, go 2.2 miles from the park's east entrance on Hwy. 297 to the Leatherwood Ford River Access and Leatherwood Ford Trailhead.

Begin walking south under the Leatherwood Ford Bridge to a trail junction sign. Don't climb the steps leading to the bridge. Instead, follow the John Muir Trail straight into the woods. Hike along the river on the right until you see another junction with a trail going to the left up the bluff. Don't take the trail to the left, but follow the John Muir Trail about 1,200 feet, where it begins to climb the bluff.

At the top, the trail joins an old roadbed that descends to cross a creek. The trail then goes downstream, and soon the bridge comes into sight. According to Russ Manning and Sondra Jamieson, authors of *Tennessee's South Cumberland,* the bridge is of Whipple Truss design, used from 1847 to 1900. This particular bridge was moved here from another site in 1915, and it was used until 1954. The park has built a pedestrian walkway across the bridge.

From the west, **Twin Arches Trail** leads 1.4 miles round-trip to one of the more amazing geological wonders in these parts, two big sequential arches in which one begins where the other ends. One reaches a length of 135 feet and a height of 70 feet, while the other extends 93 feet with an opening 51 feet high. To get to the trailhead, turn right out of the Bandy Creek Visitors Center onto the Bandy Creek Road and follow it for two miles to the intersection with Hwy. 297. Go right and continue to Hwy. 154. Turn right and continue on Hwy. 154 for 1.8 miles. Turn right onto Divide Road. In 1.3 miles the road will fork, but drivers should remain to the left on Divide Road for another 2.7 miles. Turn right onto the Twin Arches Road, and the trailhead is 2.4 miles ahead.

The trail begins at the parking area. Hike out a narrow ridge and go to the left, where two steep sets of stairs lead to the base of the bluff. Turning right, walk along the bluff line to North Arch. An exhibit here explains how the arches were formed, and then the trail leads up and over South Arch. While exploring South Arch, look for the "fat man's squeeze," a narrow tunnel leading out to the end of the ridge where one can go left or right to come back to the arch. The stairway between the two arches leads up to the top of the bluff and back across the top of North Arch to form a small loop. Hikers will return to the trailhead by the same route they came down.

Hikers should keep in mind that hunting is permitted in Big South Fork. The prudent hiker will either wear blaze orange or avoid the woods entirely during deer and boar hunting season, which generally runs for two weeks beginning in the middle of November. Rangers can explain when and where hunters might be lurking.

Bicycling

Bikers can ride on any road within the park. Mountain bikes can go on any trail designated by Bike signs and on any horse trails, which are

---

THE CUMBERLAND TRAIL

The most unusual state park in Tennessee is 303 miles long and just a few yards wide. Cumberland Trail State Park will eventually extend from Cumberland Gap to the Tennessee River just below Chattanooga.

The trail crosses the Cumberland Plateau, the most geologically interesting place in the state, connecting steep cliffs, gorges, waterfalls, and passing through beautiful forests.

When finished, this trail will rival the Appalachian Trail, its famed counterpart to the east. Construction of the trail, done by volunteers, will be completed in 2008. As this book went to press, 146 miles of trail was ready. To see which sections are open, visit www.cumberlandtrail.org.

---

marked with yellow horse heads on trees along the trail. Bikers must yield the right of way to horses and, given the skittishness of some equines, it's not a bad idea to dismount the bike and move to the side of the trail.

The 5.3-mile **Duncan Hollow Loop** bicycle trail leaves from and returns to the Bandy Creek Visitors Center. The trail crosses a creek and includes several sections of single track riding.

Fishing

Everyone fishing in Big South Fork must have either a Tennessee or Kentucky fishing license—depending on where they are fishing—which are available at stores in surrounding towns. The area is noted for smallmouth bass, rock bass, and bream. Any rafters or kayakers hooked come under catch-and-release rules.

Horseback Riding

With more than 130 miles of trails on which to ride, Big South Fork is a horse fancier's dream. Visitors with their own horses can board them at stables at Bandy Creek and take advantage of two horse camps in the park. The **Station Camp Horse Camp** is on the east side of the park, with 25 sites, each of which has four tie stalls. In Kentucky, the **Bear Creek Horse Camp** also has 25 sites.

Hills and Plateaus

One place in the park rents horses. **Bandy Creek Stables** (931/879-4013, www.bandy creekstables.com, May–Oct, guided one-hour rides cost $17.50 per person, overnight rides are $185) offers rides varying from a few hours to several days. The overnight rides include food and lodging at the Charit Creek Lodge; riders need only bring personal items, but these rides require a six-person minimum group.

Riders can also choose from other stables that are listed at visitors centers.

Hunting

Hunting is permitted in sections of Big South Fork, and hunters are governed by the laws and rules of the state in which they hunt. For information, contact the Tennessee Wildlife Resources Agency at 800/262-6704 or 931/484-9571 in Tennessee, or Fish and Wildlife Information in Kentucky at 502/564-4336.

White Water

Big South Fork has water varying from stretches that are ideal for beginners to sections that will challenge experts. As with all white-water areas, a key piece of information is the flow rate. Rivers that are easy to raft at 2,500 cubic feet per second (CFS) will become monsters at 10,000 or 20,000 CFS. Boaters should also understand that once they head down certain areas of Big South Fork, they cannot come back. A free paddler's guide is available at visitors centers, and rangers are always willing to advise those who would head downstream.

Although based in Kentucky, **Sheltowee Trace Outfitters** (800/541-RAFT [541-7238] or 606/376-5567, www.ky-rafting.com, $45–80) in Whitley City, offers raft trips and canoe rentals in Tennessee. From mid-March through fall, it offers full-day raft trips that last approximately five to six hours and vary from gentle to white-knuckle. Different trips have a different minimum age.

The outfitters also rent canoes for specific sections of the river, for trips varying from several hours to several days. Its practice is to meet parties at the anticipated take-out point and then shuttle canoes and canoeists to the put-in point.

ACCOMMODATIONS

Oneida, the largest town on the eastern end of the park, offers various accommodations for travelers. Within the park, visitors have the choice of staying in a lodge or camping.

Charit Creek Lodge

Sitting at the confluence of Charit Creek and Station Camp Creek on the west side of the park, **Charit Creek Lodge** (865/429-5704, www.charitcreek.com) is accessible only by foot or horseback. The shortest trail is 0.8 miles long, yet the ambitious visitor can use a network of connecting trails to take all day to get to the lodge, if desired.

Once there, by horse or foot, the weary traveler finds a big log building, a bathhouse, and outlying cabins. Accommodations consist of a lodge with two rooms each sleeping up to 12 people, and two freestanding cabins, each of which can hold up to 12. Guests sleep in bunk beds—most of them double bunk beds—that come with linens. On weekend nights the cabins have a six-person minimum, and unless guests arrive in a large group, they will share their bedroom with strangers—not recommended for honeymooners.

A cabin that makes up part of the lodge was built here in 1817. There is no electricity, but cabins come with kerosene lamps and wood-stoves and access to a solar-heated shower and flush toilets. The lodge maintains libraries of books and board games inside as well as horseshoe pitching and volleyball outside. A hearty dinner and country breakfast are included in the price, which is $53.50 for adults and $43.50 for children ages 4–10.

Reservations for weekdays are relatively easy to get. Weekends are another matter. The lodge begins accepting phone reservations in August for the next calendar year.

Wildwood Lodge

Just 12 miles west of the Bandy Creek section of Big South Fork is one of the better places to stay on the entire Cumberland Plateau, the Wildwood Lodge (931/879-9454, www.wildwood

lodge.ws, $75–85). The lodge's 10 rooms have private baths, televisions, private entrances from the parking lot, and comfortable furniture. A big country breakfast is served, and if they make reservations, guests can have a dinner prepared by the proprietor, a European-trained chef. Reg and Julie Johnson are from England and have a wonderful attitude toward hospitality. Says Reg, "We cater to activity people. We don't do dainty things for breakfast—we give them a bloody country breakfast—cause they're going to be out burning energy all day."

Camping

Big South Fork has two developed campgrounds. **Bandy Creek** has 150 sites—100 with hookups— all available year-round on a first-come, first-served basis. **Blue Heron,** in Kentucky, has 20 sites open April–October. **Alum Ford,** farther north in Kentucky, has primitive camping with 10 sites. There is no charge for using it.

Backcountry campers can generally stay wherever they want in Big South Fork, with the following exceptions: No one should camp within 25 feet of a cave, cemetery, grave site, historic site or structure, rock shelter, rim of the gorge (that makes sense!), trail, road, or any area designated with a No Camping sign. Camping is not permitted within 100 feet of the center line of the major roads running through the park.

Big South Fork shows some evidence of overuse. Campers should work to minimize their impact on the land; for example, pitch tents on existing sites rather than create new ones. Fires are allowed, except under arches, rock shelters, or near historic structures. Only trees that are both dead and down can be used for wood.

Permits are not required for backcountry camping, but they are a good idea. If campers should have an emergency, the permits give the park personnel a place to start looking. Permits cost nothing and are available from visitors centers or by calling 931/879-3625.

INFORMATION

Big South Fork offers a large number of pamphlets covering various aspects of the park. These are available at the **Bandy Creek Visitors Center** (931/879-3625). The visitors center is on the west side of the river to the north of Hwy. 297.

A good book covers this area in great detail. *Hiking the Big South Fork,* by Brenda D. Coleman and Jo Anna Smith, contains topographical maps of the trails and is available at visitors centers.

Although the Park Service provides free maps, a much better map of the area is available from **Trails Illustrated.** These excellent topographical maps are available at the visitors center or by calling 800/962-1643. Or visit online at www.nps.gov/biso.

Hills and Plateaus

Oak Ridge and Vicinity

John Hendrix had it all figured out. This 19th-century prophet predicted this about the area around Black Oak Ridge:

[It will be] filled with great buildings and factories. . . . Thousands of people will be running to and fro. They will be building things and there will be a great noise and confusion and the world will shake.

People at the time thought he was a crackpot, but his visions came to pass when Oak Ridge played its role in the race to build an atomic weapon.

Oak Ridge is no longer a secret city, giving visitors, whatever their thoughts on the A-bomb, a look at wartime city planning and logistical accomplishment in a town that has turned out to be a very pleasant place to spend some time. This is one place where the predominance of cuisine is not "country cooking," and where museums and culture play a prominent role in the lives of the residents.

The Atomic City is not exactly a hotbed of country music, and at this writing has yet to produce any famed figures. The nearby hamlet of Oliver Springs, however, is the birthplace of Hugh Cross, an early country musician best known for his 1928 recording of "You're As Welcome As the Flowers in May."

For more information, contact the **Oak Ridge Welcome Center** (302 S. Tulane Ave., 865/482-7821, www.oakridgevisitor.com).

SIGHTS

M American Museum of Science and Energy

The American Museum of Science and Energy (300 S. Tulane Ave., 865/576-3200, www.amse .org, $3 adults, $2 children) is one of the better science museums in the state. Taking visitors first back to the days of World War II, it gives a vivid sense of "life behind the fences" with rationing, government housing, and the intensity of the war effort. Visitors can see models of eight nu-clear weapons, among them Hiroshima's "Little Boy." Live demonstrations of scientific principles take place from time to time, among them a static electricity device that makes volunteers' hair stand straight out. The museum isn't entirely about atomic energy. Exhibits also cover "Earth's Natural Resources," "The Age of the Automobile," and "The American Experience."

Oak Ridge National Laboratory

This laboratory once focused solely on producing plutonium from uranium. Visitors to Oak Ridge can tour present-day Oak Ridge National Laboratory or the landmarks of the past. Tours are offered for all three DOE Oak Ridge facilities—Oak Ridge National Laboratory, the Y-12 National Security Complex and the East Tennessee Technology Park—and include a stop at ORNL's Graphite Reactor Museum. Tours begin outside the American Museum of Science and Energy (AMSE), and are offered April–Sept., Tues.–Fri. U.S. citizens ages 10 and up can sign up on a first-come, first-served basis at AMSE beginning at 9 A.M. on the days the tour is offered. The tour officially begins at noon, with an introductory AMSE historical exhibit, and the bus leaves promptly at 12:20 P.M. and returns at 2:30 P.M. The charge is a group rate of $2 per person The most interesting sight is the graphite reactor, world's first operational reactor. Graphite is the material used to regulate the rate of fission of the reactor's fuel. The K-25 overlook displays the enormous—and at one time top-secret—facility used to produce fissionable uranium.

Oak Ridge Art Center

The Oak Ridge Art Center (201 Badger Ave., 865/482-1441, www.korrnet.org/art, 9 A.M.–5 P.M. Tues.–Fri., 1–4 P.M. Sat.–Mon., free) displays permanent collections of modern and contemporary art, as well as changing exhibitions.

Specialty Museums

It's no surprise that a town this devoted to science would have a first-rate **Children's Museum** (461

© AVALON TRAVEL PUBLISHING, INC.

W. Outer Dr., 865/482-1074, www.childrens museumofoakridge.org, open 9 A.M.–5 P.M. Mon.–Fri. year-round, 1:30–4:30 P.M. Sat.–Sun., closed Sun. during summer, $6 adults, $5 seniors, $4 children). This hands-on place enables kids to learn in 12 exhibit areas, among them "Pioneer Living," "Coal in Appalachia," and "Waterworks."

Most railroad museums occupy an old depot that has been restored. The **Southern Appalachian Railroad Museum** (865/241-2140, www.techscribes.com/sarm), however, occupies a new building containing a visitors center, display area, and a station for excursion trains. It's on Hwy. 58 between I-40 and Oak Ridge.

The University of Tennessee Arboretum

The arboretum (865/483-3571) consists of 260 acres of former farmland whose timber was harvested before World War II. The land was acquired by the Manhattan Project and in 1961 given to the University of Tennessee, which uses it to study the effectiveness of plants in reclaiming strip mines, to test-breed late-blooming and

frost-resistant magnolias, and to determine which plants can attract wildlife to urban settings.

For visitors, however, the arboretum is a great place to walk in the woods. Admission is free, and trails of less than a mile take visitors through various habitats. The arboretum visitors center is open 8 A.M.–4:30 P.M. Monday–Friday; the grounds stay open until sunset. Visitors cannot take pets, have picnics, jog, ride bikes, cross-country ski, or collect any plants.

Outside Town

TVA's **Bull Run Fossil Plant** (865/632-8800, 7 A.M.–3:30 P.M. Mon.–Fri., free) sits right outside of town, one very visible example of how electricity in the region is produced. Powered by coal, the steam turbines turn generators that send electricity into TVA's power grid. Unfortunately, the combustion process also sends pollutants into the atmosphere—pollutants that contribute to the reduction of visibility in the Smokies and elsewhere. TVA has installed "scrubbers" on the smokestacks to remove some of the pollution, and how that is accomplished is explained here. Visitors can see exhibits on power production in the lobby.

THE OAK RIDGE STORY

In a very real sense, Oak Ridge is the most extraordinary city in all of Tennessee. Other towns have been built from scratch by industry or government—Alcoa, Norris, Homesteads—but nothing on the level of Oak Ridge.

It all began with the 1939 realization that a weapon of hitherto unimaginable power could be made from splitting the atom. The Manhattan Project, a top-secret effort, swung into action to bring this bomb into existence as fast as possible. Planners needed a place that was out of reach of enemy bombers, had plenty of available electricity, a good workforce, and rail and highway connections. They also needed, it must be said, a remote site far from population centers in case something went dreadfully wrong.

Government officials came in and bought up approximately 60,000 acres—about 10 miles by two miles—forcing 3,000 people living in 1,000 homes to move. Fences went up around the compound, which was dubbed Oak Ridge after the nearby Black Oak Ridge.

Scientists determined that three methods showed the most promise of producing fissionable material from natural uranium; the government decided to go with all three. The electromagnetic process emerged as the Y-12 plant, about 170 buildings spread over a factory covering 500 acres. The gaseous diffusion method was given its chance in a 44-acre building called K-25. The final method, thermal diffusion, was tested in the S-50 complex of 160 buildings occupying 150 acres. A graphite reactor, code-named X-10, served as a pilot plant for a larger plutonium-producing plant in Hanford, Washington.

In each of these buildings, men and women worked round the clock at labor whose goal was a mystery to them. They could see trains full of ore go into the buildings, but nothing seemed to come out. A worker might spend an entire shift watching one gauge and using knobs to control some unknown force to keep the needle in the appropriate zone.

The various uranium plants represented only one aspect of the enormous logistical operations going on in the city. People and materials poured into the town, making it within three years the fifth-largest city in the state—75,000 people in all. Planners had to lay out an entire city in a matter of weeks and months. Architects furiously designed buildings that could be raised in a hurry. None of them were designed to last a long time—one kind of housing had canvas roofs. As things got a little less frantic, single-family homes called "cemestos" appeared in a variety of plans, schools were built, and shopping centers sprang up.

The dropping of the first atomic bomb on Hiroshima meant that the curtain of secrecy at Oak Ridge could be partially lifted. At last, the workers and their families found out what they had been doing, and a surge of pride roared through the town. Oak Ridgers called and wrote to relatives all over the country, telling what they had been doing for all those months.

The end of World War II, however, did not mean that Oak Ridge was entirely open. Production of fissionable material increased as the Cold War set in, as did efforts to prevent loss of atomic secrets. Children who repeated at school something their parents said over the dinner table about work could expect a visit from security personnel and a lecture on the need to keep quiet. The town was opened to the public in 1949, and six years later the government permitted residents to buy their homes and land. The city was incorporated in 1959.

In 2000, Oak Ridge had a population of 27,387. While production of fissionable material has largely halted, the focus of the town is Oak Ridge National Laboratory, which works on deciphering the human genetic code and coming up with ways to deal with nuclear and other toxic waste. Some of the nuclear waste is in Oak Ridge itself; weapons producers during World War II and the subsequent Cold War did not always properly dispose of their hazardous materials.

The high education level of Oak Ridge residents expresses itself in many ways. The town supports the oldest performing symphony orchestra in the state, a ballet association, contemporary dance, an art center, and the Oak Ridge Playhouse, whose productions began during the war. A final benefit of all those Ph.D.s is a lively craving for Chinese food, which fuels a hearty competition among the restaurants hereabouts.

The **Eagle Bend Fish Hatchery** (865/457-5135, 8 A.M.–4:30 P.M. Mon.–Fri.) provides lake fish for Tennessee: striped bass, walleyes, bluegills, and largemouth bass. The fish are raised in ponds, and if employees have time they will give brief tours to visitors. To get to the hatchery, take Hwy. 61 northeast from Oak Ridge through Clinton. The hatchery lies along the Clinch River just outside of town. Sometimes no one is there; they are all out stocking fish.

FOOD

For those whose palates and arteries are weary of country cooking, Oak Ridge provides a culinary oasis, and it probably has more Asian restaurants per capita than any place in Tennessee.

Big Ed's Pizza (101 Broadway in Jackson Square, 865/482-4885) is a nonfranchise pizza place of the type not often seen in Tennessee. A local institution for years, its dark interior has great pizza and a series of displays organized by the late Big Ed himself.

Bleu Hound (80 E. Tennessee Ave., 865/481-6101, lunch Mon.–Fri., dinner Mon.–Sat.) features dishes such as grilled quail, roast duckling, and fresh fish every evening.

Buddy's Bar-be-que (328 S. Illinois Ave., 865/481-8102, lunch and dinner daily) is a local franchise offering very good pork barbecue and ribs.

The **Daily Grind** (Jackson Square, 865/483-9200, 7 A.M.–4 P.M. Mon.–Sat.) makes the best muffins in town. Diners also enjoy deli sandwiches, pastries, and salads.

Kim Son Restaurant (171 Robertson St., 865/482-4958, lunch and dinner Mon.–Sat.) serves Vietnamese and Chinese dishes. **Magic Wok Restaurant** (202 Tyler Rd., 865/482-6628, lunch and dinner Mon.–Fri.).

New China Palace (695 Melton Lake Dr., 865/482-3323, lunch and dinner daily) is perhaps the fanciest Chinese of the restaurants in these parts. It overlooks the lake. **Wok 'N' Roll** (1169 Oak Ridge Turnpike, 865/481-8300) dishes up lunch and dinner Monday–Saturday.

HARRIMAN

This seems to be the part of Tennessee that favors planned cities. Lying to the west of Oak Ridge, Harriman was founded as an offshoot of the Prohibition movement of the late 1800s. A group of investors—among them Clinton B. Fisk, the founder of Nashville's Fisk College—set out to build a model city of culture, sobriety, and industry. They also hoped to make money in the process.

The East Tennessee Land Company was chartered in 1889, bought 10,000 acres of countryside, and began selling lots. Three years later, 3,672 people lived and worked in 29 manufacturing companies in Harriman, which was named for Walter C. Harriman, former governor of New Hampshire. During the Civil War, Colonel Harriman had camped with his troops at the site and remarked that this would be a good place for a town. After the war, he never came to Tennessee again, but his son, Walter C. Harriman moved here as a member of the East Tennessee Land Company.

Every deed contained a provision "forbidding the use of the property, or any building thereon, for the purposes of manufacturing, storing, or selling intoxicating liquors or beverages as such." This was to be a "Utopia of Temperance," complete with American Temperance University, a somewhat ambitiously named prep school. Prohibition was very much a women's issue, and the Prohibition Party strongly supported women's suffrage. Women voted in Harriman's first election in 1891, possibly the first time in Tennessee they did so.

The town prospered until the Panic of 1893, which bankrupted the East Tennessee Land Company. Harriman continued to grow, however, until hit later on with a double whammy—a 1929 flood and the Great Depression. The flood took out the entire industrial area, and hard times did the rest. Not until nearby Oak Ridge came into existence did Harriman make a comeback. The Utopia of Temperance now has four liquor stores.

Today's visitor should head for the **Harriman**

Heritage Museum (330 Roane St., 865/882-0335, free). This 1891 building served as the offices of the East Tennessee Land Company, then American Temperance University, and later on as City Hall. The restored building, known to locals as the Temperance Building, contains beautiful woodwork, the original vault, and the usual small-town collection of memorabilia—Masonic items, photos, and a communion set from a Universalist church.

Victorian houses can be found in the **Corn Stalk Heights Historic District** on the hill above town. Coming out of the museum, turn right on Walden Street and left on Trenton Street. The district covers 10 blocks and includes 135 buildings.

Harriman celebrates itself on Labor Day weekend with **Hooray for Harriman** (865/882-8570), a street fair complete with music, food, crafts, and so on.

Accommodations

Bushrod Hall (422 Cumberland St., 865/882-8406, www.bushrodhall.com, $75–125 d, $10 less for single, $20 more per additional guest) has a massive oak staircase from Sweden, and guests can use it to climb to three rooms, all with private baths.

THE ROAD TO RUGBY

Leaving Oak Ridge, the traveler goes to Oliver Springs and ascends Walden Ridge, the eastern edge of the Cumberland Plateau. The rich farmland and wide rivers of the Ridge and Valley are gone, replaced by mountains of sandstone. Here is Tennessee's only wild and scenic river, along with more waterfalls than anywhere else in the state. It's an area of exceptional beauty.

This is also a place with a lot of what are termed "extractive industries," mostly coal and timber. Strip mines slice off the tops of mountains, and clear-cuts remove hundreds of acres of trees seemingly at once. Although most of the coal hereabouts is now extracted by strip mining, a great many people here can testify from experience that Merle Travis was right when he sang, "It's dark as a dungeon way down in the mines." Oliver Springs hosts an annual **Coal Miners**

Convention (865/435-2307) on the first Saturday in October. The "convention" features bluegrass or country music, food booths, and a 100-foot-long board of mining memorabilia. To get there, turn east just before Oliver Springs's sole traffic light and follow the signs to the Union Valley Baptist Church.

Farther up Hwy. 62, the visitor can take Hwy. 116 to see a place where people do not have fond memories of mining. **Brushy Mountain Prison** (www.state.tn.us/correction/institutions/bmcx) lies off Hwy. 62 along Hwy. 116 in the town of Petros. Tennessee used to believe that prison inmates should earn their keep, and in the 1890s the state bought coal lands and erected the prison, using convict labor to build it. Prisoner/miners worked two 12-hour shifts, while others labored on the farm or worked at various other duties. Mining by prisoners continued until 1966.

In 1977, the late James Earl Ray, convicted killer of Martin Luther King Jr., escaped from here into the surrounding forest. The prison is so remote that the warden, on hearing that certain roads had been closed, said, "We've got him. It's just a matter of time." The guards released bloodhounds, and in 54 hours the escapee was back in custody.

Frozen Head State Natural Area

This is wonderful place to take children. To get to it, visitors must drive though the Morgan County site of the Brushy Mountain Prison complex, and kids can press their noses to the glass for a look at a place where bad things happen to bad people. The Natural Area is named for Frozen Head Mountain, elevation 3,324 feet, a peak that stays frozen longer than anything else in these parts. Comprising almost 12,000 acres, the area offers great hiking—more than 50 miles of trails—and little crowding. Activities include camping, fishing, mountain biking, and horseback riding. The **campground** has 20 spaces, flush toilets, and hot showers and is open March 16–November 1. Backcountry camping is also available. The **visitors center** (423/346-3318, www.state.tn.us/environment/parks/frzhead) is open every day 8 A.M.–4:30 P.M.

Obed Wild and Scenic River

Over the millennia this river has cut through the sandstone of the Cumberland Plateau to a depth of 400 feet—sometimes straight down. Virgin forests exist in some places along the river and its tributaries. The Obed was added to the national park system in 1976 as a wild and scenic river—the only one with this designation in the state. The federal government owns only the land right along the river, yet much of it flows through Tennessee's Catoosa Wildlife Management Area. The federal government has yet to acquire land necessary to fully protect the streams from pollution and the surrounding land from development.

For these reasons, not much has been done to date to develop hiking trails and campgrounds—the one campground there has only five spaces. This ensures that the visitor will find the river uncrowded, but it also limits access to the area. **Camping** is permitted along the river all year, and no permits are required. To get a good look at the river, go to the Lilly Overlook, which lies off Hwy. 62 on Ridge Road about 12 miles from Wartburg.

The white water on the Obed, during late winter and early spring, is superb. The rapids range from Class II to Class IV. The **visitors center** (423/346-6294, www.nps.gov/obed) for the Obed is in Wartburg on Hwy. 62 just west of its intersection with U.S. 27. For information on paddling the Obed, visit **Tennessee Paddle** at www.tennesseepaddle.com.

◪ RUGBY

In this most backwoods part of Tennessee, it seems astonishing to come upon a town full of anglophiles drinking tea and paying homage to a place often called "the last English colony in America." Yet it is this remote land that caused Rugby to be established here, contributed to its demise, and yet preserved it. Today, Rugby pulls in a lot of visitors and is well worth the trip.

The best place to get one's bearings, as the British might put it, is the **Schoolhouse Visitor Center** ($4.50 adults, $4 seniors, $2.25 children, $15 families), where exhibits tell the story

of Rugby with photos, artifacts, and displays. After collecting admission, a guide takes visitors to the first stop, **Kingstone,** Rugby founder Thomas Hughes's home when he visited in Rugby. The **Thomas Hughes Free Public Library** attests to the literate colonists who founded Rugby. Inside is a wonderful collection of Victorian books. On the other side of the road is the Gothic **Christ Church, Episcopal,** which was built in 1887. The little church contains a rosewood organ made in London in 1849.

Farther west on Central Avenue—Hwy. 52—is the Harrow Road Cafe, and beside it is the Rugby Commissary, both described below. Visitors can walk or drive the old streets of Rugby, whose names—Donnington Road, Farringdon Road—sound very British indeed. Many of the original houses are private homes, and visitors should not intrude.

The visitors center has maps showing trails that lead down to the "Gentlemen's Swimming Hole" and the "Meeting of the Waters." Go west on Hwy. 52 and turn right onto Donnington Road. This leads to the **Rugby cemetery,** where Margaret Hughes and other colonists are buried. Nearby are a parking lot and trailhead for a 0.4-mile jaunt to the **swimming hole** on the Clear Fork River. Continuing for 1.7 miles brings the hiker to the "Meeting of the Waters"—where White Oak Creek and the Clear Fork River meet.

Some people have become so enthralled with Rugby that the old street plans have been dusted off and used to create Beacon Hill, a residential neighborhood in Rugby comprised of houses that replicate Victorian cottages. A growing number of new Rugbeians are moving into "The New Jerusalem."

Entertainment and Events

The **Spring Music and Crafts Festival,** held in May, brings British Isles and Appalachian music and dancing, and more than 80 craftspeople demonstrating and selling their work. Tours of buildings and horse and buggy rides round out the offerings; there's an admission fee.

Crafts workshops (423/628-5166), held throughout the year, allow participants to make something under the instruction of an expert.

THE NEW JERUSALEM

One of the more frustrating notions in Victorian England was primogeniture—the practice whereby aristocratic parents would leave all their worldly goods to their oldest son. Daughters, if they were lucky, married into other wealthy families, but the younger sons were out of luck. Social pressures of the day permitted them to enter only the professions of law, medicine, clergy, or the military. If these did not work out, they were expected to "starve like gentlemen." Any sort of manual labor was considered scandalous.

Thomas Hughes thought this situation was outrageous and determined to do something for these "younger sons." Having written *Tom Brown's School Days*, a best-seller, he funded a group that bought 75,000 acres in the Cumberland Mountains of Tennessee and set about founding a place where these unfortunate lads could toil with dignity, far from a disapproving society. **Rugby** was often called the "New Jerusalem," an allusion to William Blake's poem by the same name.

Thomas Hughes, founder of Rugby

© COURTESY OF HISTORIC RUGBY, INC.

In 1880, the colony opened, and approximately 200 people moved there and began putting Hughes's ideas into action. The colonists erected buildings, planted crops, and built a cannery. They also built a library, a church, and an inn. Hughes's 83-year-old mother, Margaret Hughes, settled in Rugby in 1881 and became the center of a burgeoning social life.

The younger sons might have been short on cash, but they all knew how to have a good time, and in short order they also built cricket fields, a tennis court, rugby fields, and croquet grounds. They organized themselves into literary societies, music and drama clubs, and a cornet band. The proverbial good time was had by all.

Especially visitors. Rugby's experiment was followed with great interest by the British and American press, and a good many people, British and American, came calling on Rugby. The **Tabard Inn** was built to accommodate these guests. When it burned in 1884, another was built to take its place.

Although everyone had a marvelous time, Rugby was doomed. Its agricultural production never came close to meeting the costs of the place. A typhoid epidemic hit in 1881, thus preventing Rugby from cashing in on the health-resort boom of the time. Hughes poured as much money as he could into the effort, but even he had to say "enough" at last, and the colony began to dwindle.

Rugby slumbered through most of the 20th century. Too remote to be threatened with development, its Victorian architecture bore silent witness to the dreams of Thomas Hughes and the others. In the 1970s, however, a young man named Brian Stagg took on the task of restoring Rugby and spreading the word of its glory days.

Now the town is on the National Register, and more than 20 of the original buildings remain and four are open to the public. Rugby's various festivals draw increasing crowds, and bed-and-breakfasts and the like are opening in the area. Several of the original streets have been opened for new housing construction, with all of the houses to be built in the Rugby style. While it's not exactly the New Jerusalem that Hughes envisioned, his efforts to make a better life have been given new life themselves.

Typical subjects from the past include honeysuckle basketry, Nantucket basketry, bark basketry, and dulcimer playing.

Every other year during the **Rugby Pilgrimage,** private homes built in the colony's heyday are open to the public—the only time of year that this happens. The pilgrimage takes place the first weekend in August, and a small admission fee is charged. The pilgrimage also includes music, food, dancing, and crafts.

The **Halloween Ghostly Gathering** begins with a fireside buffet dinner, then ghost stories with area tellers, a "calling of the spirits of Rugby past" in the library, and a candlelight walk to the cemetery for more stories. Reservations are required for this event and there's a small admission fee.

Thanksgiving Marketplace consists of a regional art show and sale, an early look at Christmas decorations, hot cider, and tours of historic buildings. It's usually held the Friday after Thanksgiving.

Christmas at Rugby, held the first two Saturdays in December, brings classical musicians, carolers, and Rugbeians of the past portrayed by professional actors. A sumptuous Victorian dinner is available at the Harrow Road Cafe, and buildings are decorated and lit with candles. There's a small admission fee.

Accommodations

Visitors can capture a bit of Rugby experience with a stay at **Newbury House Bed and Breakfast** (888/214-3400, $66–90), a restored house that contains some of the original Rugby furniture. The house has a two-bedroom suite and six single bedrooms, three of which have private baths. After a day of seeing the local sights, guests can relax in the Victorian parlor and enjoy coffee or tea. Included in the price is a full breakfast at the Harrow Road Cafe.

Guests can rent two Rugby houses in their entirety as housekeeping cottages. **Pioneer Cottage** (423/628-2441, $75 d; $10 per additional guest) was the first house built in Rugby in 1879. Thomas Hughes stayed there on his first visit to the colony. **Percy Cottage** (423/628-2430, $66)

is a reconstructed Victorian Gothic cottage offering a two-room suite and it is rented under the same policies as Pioneer House.

Not a part of historic Rugby, but very much in the spirit of the town, **Grey Gables Bed 'n Breakfast Inn** (800/347-5252 or 423/628-5252, www.bbonline.com/tn/greygables, $115 and up) was built to be an inn. Each of the eight bedrooms is decorated with country and Victorian antiques. Four rooms have private baths. Rates include lodging, a gourmet evening meal, and breakfast. Breakfasts at Grey Gables are full country ones, and reasonably priced lunches and dinners are available as well for guests and others. A typical dinner might include grilled pork tenderloin with hickory nuts, bananas Foster, and homemade rolls. Madame Hughes' Afternoon Tea, served 2–4 P.M. during the annual Rugby Pilgrimage, includes fresh-baked scones and crumpets and assorted tea sandwiches. Reservations are required for all meals.

Grey Gables also sponsors events throughout the year, such as an Herb Luncheon and Workshop, Valentine High Tea Dinner, and other holiday events. To get to Grey Gables, go west of Rugby on Hwy. 52.

The **Central Avenue Motor Lodge** (423/628-2038, $35), just west of downtown Rugby, is the least expensive place to stay hereabouts.

Food

In the town of Rugby, the **Harrow Road Cafe** (423/628-2350, breakfast, lunch, dinner daily March–Dec., 9 A.M.–4 P.M. Jan.–Feb.) is the only non-lodging place to eat. Among the items on the menu are Welsh rarebit, grilled leg of lamb, and bangers and mash.

The **Grey Gables Bed 'n Breakfast Inn** serves lunch and dinner.

Information

At **Rugby's Schoolhouse Visitor Center** (423/628-2430, www.historicrugby.org, Mar.–Dec., 9 A.M.–5 P.M. daily, Jan.–Feb. 10 A.M.–4:30 P.M. daily), tours take place 9 A.M.–5 P.M. Monday–Saturday, noon–5 P.M. Sunday.

The **Rugby Commissary** offers a selection of fine crafts by more than 100 area artists as well as English goods. The **Board of Aid Book Store** stocks *Tom Brown's School Days* and books about Rugby and the region.

Between Rugby and Jamestown

Just west of Rugby on Hwy. 52, the **R. M. Brooks General Store** (423/628-2533) gives a look at a time before Wal-Marts and shopping malls. Filled with antiques, the store still sells staples and serves simple lunches. Ask for a bologna and hook cheese sandwich.

Crossing into Fentress County, travelers move from eastern to central time. About 10 miles from Rugby is a sign for **Colditz Cove State Natural Area.** Erosion combined with the geology of this area has led to the creation of many "rock houses," or cavelike overhangs. These were used by Native Americans and whites alike as shelters and still provide comfort to hikers caught in a storm. Colditz Cove, between Allardt and Rugby, contains both a rock house and a 60-foot waterfall. Depending on the local rainfall, the falls can be a roaring torrent or a much smaller stream of falling water. The natural area totals 75 acres, which include some large hemlock trees. To get there, look for the sign on Hwy. 52 at Crooked Creek Lodge Road. It's a 1.5-mile hike to see the falls and a rock house.

ALLARDT

A group of Germans settled this area about the same time the English came to Rugby. Unclouded by any particular mission other than making money—and taking no time off for afternoon tea—they prospered, making a living from timber, coal, and farming. Their architecture was never as distinctive as that in Rugby, which in part explains why people usually blitz through here en route to the better-known colony to the east.

The first weekend in October brings the **Allardt Pumpkin Weigh-Off and Festival,** which includes a parade, food, music, and costume contests.

Visitors will find some good places to stay here. The **Old Allardt Schoolhouse** (800/771-8940 or 931/879-8056, www.bboline.com/tn/schoolhouse, $75 and up) at the junction of Hwy. 52 and Hwy. 296, is just that—a small schoolhouse that has been transformed into two rooms furnished with antiques, private baths, and fully equipped kitchens.

Bruno Gernt House (Baseline Rd., 800/978-7245 or 931/879-1176, $75–85) is a farmhouse built in 1845 and restored to its original appearance. It has four bedrooms. **Scott House,** at $85 per night, and various log cabins scattered throughout the woods, $60–75, are available from the owners of the Gernt House. These properties come with linens and fully-furnished kitchens.

Jamestown and Vicinity

This town can boast one incontrovertible fact: Samuel Clemens was conceived here. He was born in Hannibal, Missouri, but that in no way diminishes his Tennessee roots. Clemens's father owned 75,000 acres of land here, and to his dying day he believed it would make his family's fortune, telling his wife to hold onto it at all costs. The land never did pay off, but it provided material from which the younger Clemens spun *The Gilded Age,* whose "Obedstown" closely resembles Jamestown. The **Mark Twain Spring** in a downtown park commemorates the town's embryonic connection to the author; fortunately, his output was greater than the spring's is today.

About the time the Clemens family headed for points west, a Jamestown resident, one Joseph Stout, was hauled in on charges of witchcraft. A suspicious character, he frequently sat up late reading, had little to say, and few friends to whom to speak. Locals whispered that he could enter houses through keyholes, and a posse armed with silver bullets was dispatched to bring him to court. Wiser heads prevailed, however, and the man's persecutors were themselves arrested.

Jamestown is home to one of the best high schools in the state. While Sergeant Alvin York steadfastly refused to cash in on his worldwide reputation, he was instrumental in helping Fentress County by establishing the **York Institute,** a school for local children. He personally ran the school from 1926 until 1937, when it was taken over by the state. Now it remains the only high school administered directly by the state of Tennessee, and it occupies a campus of 400 acres.

JAMESTOWN

Despite a long and honorable tradition of drinking, it took Tennessee decades to get over the thinking that led to Prohibition, but finally the state legislature saw the light. **Highland Manor Winery** (931/879-9519) on U.S. 127 south, sprang into being in 1980 and thus became the oldest winery in the state. Housed in an Eng-

lish Tudor building, the vintner produces a variety of wine—and not all of it the sweet varieties so favored in this state. Visitors can choose from, among others, chardonnay, cabernet sauvignon, white riesling, and rosé. The best-sellers, however, are rosé and muscadine, the latter so popular that the winery maintains a two-year waiting list for bottles. It also makes a muscadine champagne that flies off the shelves. It offers free tours and tastings.

East Fork Stables (800/978-7245 or 931/879-1176) lies on 12,000 acres five miles south of Jamestown on U.S. 127. It offers more than 100 miles of marked trails and two rustic cabins for riders. It's open all year.

Accommodations

The **Big South Fork Lodge** (931/879-7511, $50–325), 13 miles west of Jamestown on East Port Road off Hwy. 52, has 20 cabins. It also rents houseboats, with daily rates of $130–535.

Northwest of town and close to Pickett State Rustic Park is **Wildwood Lodge** (931/879-9454). **East Port Marina and Resort** (931/879-7511) lies halfway between Jamestown and Livingston; to get there, drive north on East Port Road.

Laurel Creek Travel Park (931/879-7696, open May–Nov.) lies northeast of Jamestown and contains 48 sites. The park has a swimming pool, fishing, and recreation facilities. Take Hwy. 154 north out of town for nine miles.

PICKETT STATE RUSTIC PARK

If this park weren't in such a remote area on the Tennessee-Kentucky border, it would no doubt be one of the most-visited places in the state. Created from 12,000 acres donated to the state in 1933 by the Stearns Coal and Lumber Company, the park contains 15-acre Pickett Lake, rock houses, caves, and natural bridges.

Activities include more than 58 miles of hiking trails, fishing, swimming at a cliff-lined beach, rowing, and canoeing. During the summer,

TIME ZONES

Travelers in this part of Tennessee should be mindful of the time. To the east, the state runs on eastern time, while parts northwest of Knoxville operate on central time. Scott and Morgan Counties are in eastern time, while Pickett and Fentress Counties are in central. The "time line" runs right through the Big South Fork National River and Recreation Area.

naturalists lead walks, demonstrate various activities, and conduct campfire talks.

The **accommodations** at the park include five chalets, five stone cabins, five wooden cabins, and five new "villas" with three bedrooms each; all come with fully equipped kitchens and linens. Open year-round, they cost $65–115.

The park has 35 campsites, 31 of which have hookups. The **campground** has a bathhouse with hot showers. It accepts no reservations; campers are accommodated on a first-come, first-served basis and can stay for two weeks maximum.

The park is open in the summer 8 A.M.–6 P.M., and in the winter 8 A.M.–4:30 P.M. For further information, or to make reservations, 888/ TNPARKS (867-2757), 931/879-5821, or visit www.tnstateparks.com.

SERGEANT ALVIN YORK GRISTMILL AND PARK

The steep descent from Jamestown to Pall Mall reminds motorists that they are leaving the Cumberland Plateau. The park contains Alvin York's home, a country store, a Bible school founded by York, and his family's gristmill.

The house has been restored and contains original furniture, a telephone, and household items owned by the York family. Best of all is the park ranger, Andrew Jackson York, who is the son of Sergeant York and a wonderful source of information and stories about his famous father. The mill is open daily 8 A.M.–5 P.M., and the house is open daily 9 A.M.–5 P.M. Admission is free. For informa-

tion about the park, call 931/879-6456 or visit www.tnstateparks.com.

BYRDSTOWN

What Alvin York was to war, another native of these parts was to peace. Byrdstown, west of Pall Mall, is the birthplace of Cordell Hull, congressman, senator, secretary of state under Franklin Roosevelt, winner of the 1945 Nobel Prize for Peace, and widely regarded as the "father of the United Nations." Hull was not always peaceably inclined. He is said to have delivered "a thorough Tennessee tongue-lashing" to the Japanese diplomats who were in his office in 1941 when word came that Pearl Harbor had been attacked.

A reconstruction of the log cabin in which Hull was born is the centerpiece of the **Cordell Hull Birthplace and Museum** (931/864-3247, 7 A.M.–3:30 P.M. Mon.–Fri., 8 A.M.–4 P.M. Sat., free). The museum contains his Nobel Peace Prize, library, chair and desk, photos of Hull with world leaders, and other items and documents from his long and productive life in politics.

The **Cordell Hull Folk Festival** (931/864-3247), usually held on the Saturday closest to his October 2 birthday, brings together local music-makers, craftspeople, and townsfolk for a friendly festival in honor of their native son.

LIVINGSTON

This little town became the seat of Overton County through some inspired chicanery. The original county seat was in Monroe, and by the 1830s residents clamored to have it moved to Livingston, which was closer to the center of the county and much more convenient. The matter was put to a vote in 1833, and a group of six to eight men, among them one "Ranter" Eldridge, set forth to cast their votes. The journey required the men to spend the night in an inn. When Eldridge learned that his companions intended to vote to keep the county seat in Monroe—which he opposed—he rose earlier than his neighbors and turned their horses loose. The proponents of Livingston won the referendum by four votes.

Holly Ridge Winery and Vineyard (931/823-8375), in business since 1998, is the newest one in the state, although the vintners here have been coaxing wine out of grapes for longer than that. Twenty-three kinds of wine are bottled here, including the sweet wines that Tennesseans love

so well, along with drier wines such as a good vidal blanc and a merlot. To find the winery, take Hwy. 85 three miles out of Livingston toward Hilham and follow the signs.

Court Square Emporium (East Court Square, 931/823-6741) sells quilts, baskets, pottery, books, and many more items from 40 area and regional craftspeople.

ALVIN YORK

In a time when anyone with an iota of fame immediately wrings every drop of value from it, a man such as Alvin York seems absolutely unreal. Born in 1887, he lived an unimpressive early life, working as a laborer on a farm that belonged to a minister. Under his employer's influence, York became a Christian and gave up his drinking and card-playing, but he continued squirrel hunting, becoming known as a crack shot.

So devout was young York that when he was drafted for World War I, he tried to obtain conscientious objector status. Draft officials in the Volunteer State turned him down flat, so he entered the army and was sent to the European front. On October 8, 1918, his platoon came under withering fire from the Germans.

© JEFF BRADLEY

The famous hero of World War I operated this century-old gristmill when he returned to Tennessee.

When his commanding officers were killed, Corporal York took charge, leading seven men in a charge on the machine-gun nest responsible for the deaths of so many of his comrades.

The machine guns were silenced, and York and his men captured four German officers and 128 men and marched them back across the lines. York himself marched into instant fame and was awarded more than 40 decorations. He came home to a media blitz hitherto unseen for a common soldier. He was offered almost everything: movie roles, advertisements, and all manner of product endorsements.

Turning it all down, he returned to Pall Mall, married his childhood sweetheart, and operated a gristmill north of town. He did accept a farm paid for by admirers' donations and lived there the rest of his life. He also headed the **York Institute,** a Jamestown school he established to benefit the mountain children of the area.

Right before World War II, York was persuaded to allow Hollywood to tell his story. He hoped it would encourage patriotism and wanted the money to build an interdenominational Bible school. Gary Cooper won an Oscar for his starring role, and *Sergeant York* introduced a new generation to the story of the brave mountain soldier.

Not used to large sums of money, York ran into tax troubles. A 1954 stroke left him bedridden and owing $172,723 to the government. The IRS settled for much less, and U.S. Speaker of the House Sam Rayburn led a drive to collect the money. An industrialist set up a trust fund enabling York to live comfortably for the rest of his life. Alvin York died on September 2, 1964, and is buried in Pall Mall.

STANDING STONE STATE RUSTIC PARK

This 2,555-acre park was named for a stone that is no longer standing and that was never in the park. According to a Cherokee legend related in Russ Manning's *The Historic Cumberland Plateau,* a god told a man to build a raft, for a flood would soon come and destroy everything. The man finished the raft as the water was rising, and just as he was about to shove off, a dog spoke to him from the bank and asked to go with him, telling the man, "When you are in danger of losing your life, let me be the sacrifice." The man agreed, and the two drifted for 40 days. The man began dying of hunger, and the dog reminded him of its earlier pledge. The man threw the dog into the water, and seven days later it came back with mud—evidence that land lay nearby. This land was North America. In appreciation to the dog, the Native Americans carved a statue of him out of sandstone as a reminder of the god who had helped them find their home.

That's the story. Settlers came upon the stone, which stood outside the town of Monterey, and over the years chipped away at it. Blasting for a railroad line demolished what was left of the stone, and later its largest piece was put at the top of a park monument in Monterey. The second Thursday in October is always **Standing Stone Day,** and Cherokee groups come to the park to commemorate their ancestors.

The park, no matter how it got its name, offers a lot to do. It adjoins the 8,445-acre Standing Stone State Forest. An X-shaped lake surrounded by forested cliffs marks the center of the park. In addition to fishing and boating, the park offers hiking trails, nature trails, a playground, a swimming pool, tennis courts, and a recreation building. Overnight **accommodations** include 24 cabins, which cost $55–100. Thirty-six **campsites** are available on a first-come, first-served basis, and a group camp and lodge is available by reservation. Call 931/823-6347.

Standing Stone State Park is the site of the annual **Rolley Hole National Championship,** a game involving two-person teams who endeavor to shoot stone marbles into a hole. Competitors using marbles made of flint—mere glass marbles cannot withstand the impact—have played for decades in these parts. The championship usually takes place two weeks after Labor Day weekend (mid-September) and features pancake breakfasts, demonstrations of marble-making, and other amusements. For information on activities, accommodations, and event, call 931/823-6347 or visit www.state.tn.us.

CELINA

This little Cumberland River town used to be a center for rafting, but not the white-water variety. Beginning about 1870, lumberjacks would cut down trees and drag the logs to the river, then send them downstream to Nashville's lumberyards in huge rafts—sometimes as long as 300 feet and three logs thick. This practice continued through the 1930s.

In recent years, recreation on the water has become important around Celina. The **Dale Hollow Dam** (931/243-3136), which was finished in 1943, backs up the Obey River into a lake with 620 miles of shoreline. Unlike most Tennessee lakes, the water here is very clear, making it popular with scuba divers as well as with the usual boaters and anglers. The fishing here is very good; the record-holding smallmouth bass—11 pounds, 15 ounces—came from these waters. Fifteen marinas are scattered around the lake. Many have boats, including houseboats, available for rent. Interested parties can obtain a complete list of marinas by calling the Army Corps of Engineers, which administers the lake.

The **Dale Hollow National Fish Trout Hatchery** (931/243-2443, 7:30 A.M.–3:30 P.M. daily, free), two miles north of town on Hwy. 53, raises thousands of rainbow, brown, and lake trout for federal waters in several states.

In the years before the Civil War, a North Carolina slaveholder named Virginia Hill bought 2,000 acres here and gave them to her slaves along with their freedom to create the community of **Free Hills,** just north of Celina. After the war, former slaves also moved here, and the community continues today.

The **Clay County Museum** (805 Brown St., 931/243-4220) contains artifacts from the county's old days, photographs, and information about the town.

On the square you'll find **Gone Country Cafe** (931/243-9302). **Crow's Nest Restaurant** (820 E. Lake Ave., 931/243-3333) offers breakfast, a buffet lunch, and menu service for lunch and dinner every day.

The **Clay County Chamber of Commerce** (427 S. Brown St., 931/243-3338) stocks brochures and other information about the surrounding area.

West on U.S. 70

Before I-40 was built, U.S. 70 was one of the great "blue highways" across America. Now, with most of the traffic roaring by on I-40, it is a delightful road on which to motor along. Visitors go right through the middle of towns, and between them see the remains of gas stations built in the '30s. The resulting look at residents, past as well as present, provides a portrait of Tennessee that a Natchez Trace Parkway or other roads of that ilk can never deliver. If you're coming from Knoxville, a good place to get on U.S. 70 is at Rockwood, Exit 347.

CRAB ORCHARD

This little hamlet is surrounded by a distinctive kind of stone. This is Crab Orchard stone, a sandstone with a lot of silica that is common on the Cumberland Plateau. Early settlers used the stone in their fireplaces, the first commercial use was in 1903, and locals built houses with the tan, buff, gray, or blue-gray stone.

Crab Orchard stone got a big boost when Scaritt College in Nashville chose the stone for a chapel and other buildings. Most of the New Deal's Homesteads Houses were built with the stone, which can also be seen in Rockefeller Center, the headquarters of the United Auto Workers Union in Detroit, at Graceland, the Nintendo office building in Honolulu, and at the vice presidential residence in Washington, D.C.

Local companies find Crab Orchard stone by strip-mining—digging down until they hit a layer of acceptable stone. These layers might be 18 to 36 inches or as thick as four feet.

BLACK MOUNTAIN

Black Mountain, besides being the namesake of a fiddle rag, is a stupendous place to hike. The mountaintop looks like Chattanooga's Rock City on steroids, with enormous boulders that form tunnels and pathways.

To get there, take the Crab Orchard exit off I-40 and go south for two miles to a crossroads. Turn left onto Ow's Roost Road and follow it to the top. The Cumberland Trail crosses this mountain, and hikers can see all the way to the Smokies. For more info, visit www.cumberlandtrail.org.

CROSSVILLE

For 19th-century travelers, this town on the Cumberland Plateau was an important crossroads. It still is, serving as a jumping-off point from which to explore the area.

Many of the buildings here are constructed of Crab Orchard stone. The Palace Theatre on Main Street is a good example of this. Newly restored, the theater hosts talent shows, beauty pageants, and other local events.

During World War II, Crossville was the site of one of the 11 prisoner-of-war camps established in Tennessee.

Sights

The **Homesteads Tower Museum** (931/456-9663, Mar.–Dec., 10 A.M.–5 P.M. Mon.–Sat., noon–5 P.M. Sun., $2) sits south of town at the junction of U.S. 127/Hwy. 28 and Hwy. 68. Here, one can see documents and photographs of the Depression-era Homesteads Project as well as furniture made by the residents.

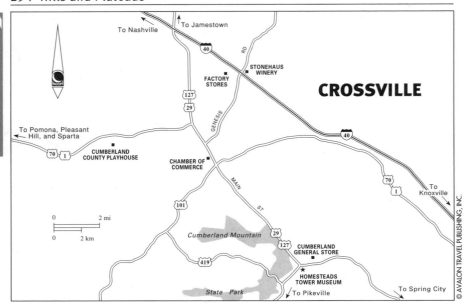

The 1,562-acre **Cumberland Mountain State Rustic Park** (931/484-6138, www .state.tn.us), originally part of the Cumberland Homesteads, was built for the pleasure of the inhabitants. The seven-arch dam was built of Crab Orchard stone by Civilian Conservation Corps workers and is said to be the largest steel-free structure built by that agency. The road goes right over the dam.

The park has 37 **cabins,** some of them open year-round. Prices range $57–130. In the summer they must be rented for one week and can be reserved up to one year ahead. The group lodge is a lovely stone building originally intended to serve as a mill below the dam. The park has 145 **campsites,** 28 of which are open through the winter.

The park has a **restaurant** (931/484-7186) overlooking the lake, where iron skillet–fried chicken is the most popular dish in the buffet. It's open for lunch and dinner every day March to mid-December. It closes mid-December to mid-January and is open only on weekends until March.

Grassy Cove

Motorists who leave the Homesteads community and follow Hwy. 68 will find themselves descending into a lovely valley called Grassy Cove. This 3,000-acre valley is full of caves, into which most of the water here flows only to emerge in the Sequatchie River to the south. All of the caves are on private property, and none have been commercially developed. Visitors can see one, the **Old Mill Cave,** behind the **J. A. Kemmer and Sons Store** (6 A.M.–6 P.M. Mon.–Sat.) on Hwy. 68. Ask permission at the store.

The store, one of two in the cove, is owned by the descendants of one Conrad Kemmer, who came to these parts from Pennsylvania in the early 1800s. The **J. C. Kemmer General Store** (931/484-4075, 7:00 A.M.–6 P.M. Mon.–Sat.), on the southern end of the valley, has been in operation since 1886. Visitors will find a selection of hardware, boots, work clothes, and staples such as Vienna sausage and Moon Pies.

Entertainment

The **Cumberland County Playhouse**

THE SHOWPLACE OF THE NEW DEAL

Among the social experiments generated as the United States endeavored to escape the Depression, the **Cumberland Homesteads** project stands as an interesting chapter. The idea was simple: Take people of good character who would work hard, put them in good housing with enough land to raise a garden, and then lure industry that would gainfully employ them. That's what the federal government set out to do.

It bought 10,000 acres of land south of Crossville from a timber company and in 1934 began work on the community. More than 4,000 people applied for the 250 homesteads, each of which consisted of approximately 20 acres. Cottages of Crab Orchard sandstone and wood interiors were built, and people moved in. By and large, the inhabitants were delighted to do so; the houses were wired for electricity and had indoor plumbing—luxuries that were new to many locals.

Cooperatives were set up so that women could make their family's mattresses, can their own food, and make cloth on looms. Men were taught construction trades and put to work building more houses and administrative buildings. A cooperative store, a sorghum mill, and a coal mine were among the enterprises that sprang up under the guidance of social planners. The most striking presence of the

Homesteads was an 80-foot-high tower erected over an administrative building. Eleanor Roosevelt visited the Homesteads twice and pronounced it good.

Like many things in the New Deal, the idea was a decent one, but problems arose in keeping it on track. The community was shifted from agency to agency, and residents grew frustrated as their goals were repeatedly changed. Furthermore, the independent-minded people of the Cumberland Plateau did not mesh well with the socialist dreams of the planners and the ineptitude frequently displayed by the managers.

In 1939, the government offered the residents an opportunity to buy their land and houses. Virtually all of them did so, and the social experiment came to an end. While it lasted, however, it drastically improved the standard of living for the fortunate people who became residents, pumped a lot of needed funds into the economy, and left the area with houses of a type found nowhere else in the state.

Visitors can pick out the distinctive cottages by looking for stone houses with chimneys on each end. Some have additions, but others look just as they did when Eleanor Roosevelt came to call. All of the houses are privately owned, so a close inspection is not a good idea.

(931/484-5000, www.ccplayhouse.com) came about when Paul and Mary Crabtree drew on their New York theatrical experience to create one of the best regional theaters in the South. Operating since 1965, the playhouse has delighted audiences with Shakespeare, musicals, and original plays with Tennessee themes. The season runs year-round, and more than 100,000 people per year attend. The playhouse lies six miles off I-40 Exit 317. Follow the signs.

Food
The Bean Pot (on Peavine Rd. at Exit 322, 931/484-4633) is open 24 hours a day and serves country cooking. **China One** (1601 West Ave. N., 931/484-3178) is open for lunch and dinner seven days a week.

The Donut Shop (777 West End Ave., 931/484-4312, open only in the mornings and afternoons) makes the best omelets in town—so large they almost cover the plate.

Lefty's Bar-B-Que (Peavine Rd., 931/484-4205, lunch and dinner daily) dishes up pork barbecue, chicken, and ribs.

Halcyon Days (931/456-3663) in the same building as Stonehaus Winery, serves continental cuisine Tuesday–Saturday for dinner. Typical entrées include stuffed quail, chicken Wellington, and lobster.

Shopping
South of town on U.S. 127/Hwy. 28, the **Cumberland General Store** (931/484-8481, www.cumberlandgeneral.com) offers an eclectic mixture of books, cast-iron cookware, veterinary

CUMBERLAND NATURALIST RESORTS

Timberline Lodge (I-40 Exit 311, south one mile to a stop sign, then left for a half-mile, 800/TAN-NUDE [826-6833] or 931/277-3522, www.tannude.com) has been in operation for more than 30 years. This family-oriented resort features a swimming pool, private lake and beach, dancing, and indoor and outdoor hot tubs. When it's time to turn in, guests have a choice of a lodge with 12 rooms, a campground, cabins, or mobile homes. The season begins on Valentine's Day and rolls on until December's Christmas Party. During the summer, the house band plays beach music on Friday night, and dancers take to the floor in the 4,000-square-foot clubhouse.

Approximately 25 percent of the clientele comes from Tennessee and Kentucky, and most of the rest hail from the Midwest. Timberline also gets a lot of European visitors, according to a spokesperson. Timberline has a relaxed policy toward clothes. If shy visitors want to wear them, that's perfectly fine.

Another nudist option is the 350-acre **Cherokee Lodge** (I-40 Exit 311, 931/277-5140, www.cherokee-lodge.com). It is a private club that has room for travelers on a space-available basis March–November only. Accommodations include rooms in a lodge, cabins, and a campground. Guests can enjoy a swimming pool, hot tub, volleyball, tennis court, game room, and clubhouse. Dances are held on Saturday nights.

supplies, crocks, honey, and quirky items that appeal to travelers.

Made By Hand (931/484-8827) carries local and regional weavings, pottery, toys, and woodwork. Travelers will find it at Betty's Bed and Breakfast across from Fairfield Glade's entrance on Peavine Road, four miles north of I-40.

Fine-food fanciers should stop at **Stonehaus Winery** (931/484-WINE, www.stonehauswinery.com, wine tasting and tour are free), north of I-40 at Exit 320, which offers red, white, rosé, and blush wines, plus a gift shop featuring 40 kinds of cheeses. The winery also has a deli and kitchenware shop.

The next stop for picnic assemblers is **Simonton's Cheese House** (1226 Industrial Blvd., 931/484-5193). This place makes some of its own cheese and ships it all over the country.

The **Merrimack Canoe Company** (170 Harper Ave., 931/484-4556, www.merrimackcanoes.com) cranks out fiberglass and Kevlar canoes with wooden ribs. Visitors can see samples of its work at the Stonehaus Winery by the Interstate, and visitors who call ahead can get a tour of the manufacturing operations.

Information

For more information, contact the **Greater Cumberland County Chamber of Commerce** (34 S. Main St., 931/484-8444, 8 A.M.–4:30 P.M. Mon.–Fri., www.crossville.com).

POMONA

Homesteads and Rugby are two examples of idealistic communities on the Cumberland Plateau. Another was Pomona, west of Crossville on U.S. 70. John M. Dodge, a portrait painter whose subjects included Andrew Jackson and Daniel Webster, bought 5,000 acres, moved here in the mid-1800s, and planted 82,000 apple trees. Others in his artistic circle joined him, and the resulting community was named Pomona for the Roman goddess of fruit. A poet named Margaret Bloodgood Peake hit town and founded a philosophical cult whose young female devotees began their summer days by rolling without any clothing in dew-drenched fields of clover. This came to an end when members looked up from their gamboling to see the woods full of local boys, all grinning, as the expression goes, like a mule eating briars.

The spirit of Pomona lives on at Timberline Lodge and Cherokee Lodge, where visitors can roll in the dew-drenched clover with like-minded enthusiasts in "naturalist," that is, nude, resort settings.

PLEASANT HILL

Farther west on U.S. 70/Hwy. 1 in the Pleasant Hill community is the 10-room **Pioneer Hall Museum** (on Main St., 931/277-3872, May–Oct. 10 A.M.–4 P.M. Wed., 2–5 P.M. Sun, or by appointment, free). It was the first dormitory of the Pleasant Hill Academy, a school operated 1884–1947 by the American Missionary Society of the Congregational Church when the public schools in these parts were almost nonexistent. Later it became a boarding school with students from a much wider area.

Through the efforts of the principal's wife, a physician named May Wharton, Pleasant Hill gained a hospital that was later transformed into a sanitarium for tuberculosis patients. When new drugs eliminated the need for this sort of treatment, the hospital became a retirement center. Dr. Wharton also founded the Crossville Medical Center.

Visitors can see exhibits pertaining to the academy—a girl's room and a boy's room—as well as medical artifacts from Dr. Wharton's time. Other exhibits include an early kitchen, a country store, and antique tools.

Just down the street from the museum is **Polly Page's Mountain Crafts** (Main St., 931/277-3402), which is worth a stop just to talk to the gregarious Ms. Page. She carves dolls from red cedar and has been doing so since 1922, when a crafts teacher came to her school.

BRIDGESTONE/FIRESTONE CENTENNIAL WILDERNESS

The Bridgestone/Firestone company, makers of tires, have done wilderness lovers a good deed by donating 10,000 acres of land that includes Scott's Gulf and 12 miles of the Caney Fork River Gorge. This "Grand Canyon of the Cum-berlands" offers superb day hikes as well as multiday treks, camping, fishing, caving, mountain biking, and more. Here are hardwood forests, overlooks, deep gorges, and flowing water. An effort to restore the American chestnut tree is under way here, and the wilderness is home to rare and endangered wildflowers.

Camping is permitted at designated areas, and no fees are charged. Fall visitors should stay out of the wilderness during hunting season. These dates are posted at trailheads or can be obtained by calling the regional office of the Tennessee Wildlife Resources Agency at 931/484-9581. What does all this have to do with a tire company? Seems that the firm bought this land in the early '70s with plans to develop it as a resort for employees.

To get there from I-40, go west on U.S. 70 approximately 14 miles from the Crossville exits to the community of De Rossett. Turn left (south) onto Eastland Road at the Bondecroft Headstart Village. Go about 5.7 miles on East-land Road to the junction of Eastland Road and the Scott's Gulf Road (entering from the right). Go right on Scott's Gulf Road.

SPARTA

Coming to Sparta from the east, motorists descend approximately 1,000 feet from the Cumberland Plateau to Tennessee's Highland Rim. **Sunset Rock** on U.S. 70 offers a great view to the west. Nineteenth-century travelers passing this way were on a toll road and would have no doubt stopped at the **Rock House Shrine** (931/836-3552, 2–4 P.M. Sat.; call to arrange visits at other times), 3.7 miles east of town on U.S. 70. Built of sandstone sometime between 1835 and 1839, it served as a tollhouse and stagecoach inn.

Nearby Overton County is the birthplace of Lester Flatt, the country flat-picker whose 21-year partnership with banjo player Earl Scruggs constituted the most famous bluegrass duo ever. Flatt sang "The Ballad of Jed Clampett," the theme song for TV's *Beverly Hillbillies*. Flatt died in 1979 and is buried in Sparta.

One of the many people to play with Flatt and Scruggs was the late Benny Martin, a Sparta native who for a time was managed by Colonel Tom Parker and opened for the young Elvis Presley.

Recreation

Golden Mountain Park (931/526-5253, open daily Mar.–Oct.), east of O'Connor Crossroads off Hwy. 111, is a 300-acre private park offering bumper boats, sports fields, arcade games, and pavilions for picnics and gatherings.

Bowater, Inc., has extensive timber holdings in the South and has opened certain areas to the public. These "Pocket Wildernesses," as they are called, contain scenic trails, waterfalls, and occasional places to camp. Brochures with topographic maps are available at chambers of commerce or by calling 931/336-7424. One of these is close to Sparta.

Virgin Falls Pocket Wilderness centers on a waterfall that emerges from a cave, drops 110 feet, and enters another cave. The round-trip hike is eight miles. To get to the trailhead, drive 11 miles east of Sparta on U.S. 70 to the community of De Rossett. Turn right and go 5.9 miles on Mourberry Road to a sign for Chestnut Mountain Wilderness. Go right on the Scott Gulf Road for two miles to the parking area for the trail.

Information

For more information, contact the **Sparta/White County Chamber of Commerce** (16 W. Bockman Way, 931/836-3552, 9 A.M.–5 P.M. Mon.–Fri., www.sparta-chamber.net).

Country Treasures and Gifts (447 W. Bockman Way, 931/836-3572) occupies a two-story log house with a 14-foot wooden Indian out front. Inside are folk art, quilts, and antiques.

FALL CREEK FALLS STATE RESORT PARK

If visitors can go to only one Tennessee state park, this should be the one. Its almost 20,000 acres make it one of the largest state parks, but its waterfalls are the main attraction. The highest, Fall Creek Falls, drops 256 feet, the highest waterfall east of the Rocky Mountains—90 feet higher than Niagara Falls. The amount of water varies with the season, but it's an impressive drop anytime. Scenes from Disney's live-action version of *The Jungle Book* were filmed here.

Cane Creek Cascades has a swinging bridge that crosses the creek, and just downstream is Cane Creek Falls, an 85-foot drop. Nearby is 110-foot Rockhouse Falls, and the park also houses 85-foot Piney Creek Falls.

The state of Tennessee has extensively developed this park, building an 18-hole golf course and a **lodge** with 144 rooms. Thirty cabins sit by the 345-acre lake, which offers fishing and boat rentals. These lodgings are enormously popular and should be booked as far ahead as possible. Rates begin at $119. For information, call 423/881-5241.

Campers will find 227 developed sites as well as backcountry sites, and all visitors can avail themselves of a swimming pool, an archery range, bike rentals, tennis courts, a Frisbee golf course, and a restaurant.

To get there, go south on Highway 111 from Sparta or I-40 in Cookeville and turn left on Highway 284. For further information about the park, call 423/881-3297. To make reservations at the inn, call 800/250-8610. For **campground** reservations, call 800/250-8611 or visit www.state.tn.us.

ROCK ISLAND STATE PARK

Many people who want to see waterfalls head for Fall Creek Falls State Park. While the falls there are the highest in the state, the water in them comes from creeks. At Rock Island State Park, on the other hand, the water for the falls comes from three rivers, and the resulting falls absolutely roar. In this 883-acre park, the Rocky, the Collins, and the Caney Fork Rivers merge and pour into a gorge that drops 100 feet in the space of two miles. A dam holds back the Great Falls Reservoir and releases water that goes over the **Great Falls**—a cascade that is a photographer's delight.

Asa Faulkner, an early capitalist, designed a three-story brick cotton mill here, and his son

RUMBLING FALLS CAVE

W ith all its limestone and lots of water, Tennessee has more caves than any other state, many of which are open to the public. The most stupendous one, however, sits under Fall Creek Falls State Park and will probably never be open to the public—people who know won't even tell visitors where it is.

For good reason. The opening to Rumbling Falls Cave was has an 80-foot drop—straight down. That didn't deter John Hutchison, who discovered the cave in 1997 and, with the help of others, set out to explore it. Walking, crawling, and sometimes climbing up chilling waterfalls—all in pitch blackness illuminated only by the lights they carried—the explorers camped and mapped 15.5 miles. Their biggest find was the **Rumble Room,** a 200-foot-high room covering some five acres, the second-largest room ever found in an American cave. (For some amazing photos of this room and the rest of the cave, visit www.darklightimagery.net.)

Cavers are by nature a secretive bunch; they don't want delicate natural areas ruined by idiots, but when they learned that the upstream town of Spencer was going to release treated sewage water into the stream that goes through the cave, they had to go public to protect the delicate cave creatures in Rumbling Falls.

The cave remains a secret, studied by biological and geological scientists and explored by expert cavers. John Hutchison, now in his 50s, continues to seek new caves in Tennessee.

Clay and others completed it in 1892. The water powered the mill, which at one time produced 4,000 yards of cotton sheeting a day. It ran until 1902, when a bad flood stripped it of its water wheel. The building still sits in the park.

Across the road from the cotton mill is a stone structure known as the Spring Castle. Built about the time the dam was built, it was originally a springhouse. This was a resort area for Middle Tennesseans wishing to escape the heat of the summer, and modern-day visitors will see why they found this place so appealing.

One fun thing to do is take a drive across a dam on what feels like a rickety bridge. The park also has a **visitors center,** boating and fishing on the lake, ball fields, tennis courts, and a natural sand beach. Four picnic areas are available, as are tours of nearby **Big Bone Cave,** a dry cave from which saltpeter was mined. Admission is free for the tours, which should be arranged as far in advance as possible.

The park has 10 modern **cabins,** all built in a Victorian style with front and back porches and capable of sleeping 10 people. The cabins are very popular; from Memorial Day to Labor Day they must be rented by the week and cost $430 plus tax. At other times they cost $65 for week-nights and $85 on weekends.

The park also has 50 year-round **campsites** and, unlike those in most Tennessee parks, these can be reserved ahead of time by calling 800/421-6683 or 931/686-2471; visit www.state.tn.us.

SMITHVILLE

This town might better be named Evinsville in honor of the prominent Evins family. Edgar Evins was a local businessman who had a hand in many operations in the town. He served as mayor and represented the town in the state Senate. His son, Joe Evins, continued the tradition of public service and extended it to a 30-year career in the U.S. Congress. While there, he looked out for his district and made sure that federal money flowed its way. Al Gore won this congressional seat in his first election.

Back in town on the square is **F. Z. Webb and Son** (931/597-4185), an old-fashioned drugstore that has been in the same family since 1881. The soda fountain is gone, but the store still sells coffee for a nickel a cup as well as locally made pottery, and visitors can gaze on pharmaceutical antiques such as a wooden label dispenser.

The **Smithville Fiddler's Jamboree and Crafts Festival** (615/597-8500, www.smithvilletn.com/jamboree) is one of the larger such events in the state. Held on the weekend closest to the Fourth of July, it features competitions in a wide variety of events—flat-pick guitar, dobro, junior buckdancing, and country harmonica, to name a few. Craftspeople from more than 35 states usually show up.

Practicalities

Sundance (107 E. Main St., 615/597-1910) has something different every day of the week. This place, inside a former 19th-century stable, sells vitamins as well as meals, and the food here is healthy but good.

Griffin's Fruit Market (W. Broadway St., 615/597-5030) sells local homegrown tomatoes and other fruit and vegetables in season. It also has cider, honey, and other good things.

For more information, contact the **Smithville/ DeKalb County Chamber of Commerce** (in the courthouse on the square, 615/597-4163, open weekdays 9 A.M.–3 P.M., closed Wed., www.smithvilletn.com/chamber).

EDGAR EVINS STATE RUSTIC PARK

This 6,280-acre park sits on the edge of Ten-

nessee's Eastern Highland Rim, an area with steep bluffs and narrow ridges. In 1948 the Army Corps of Engineers built the Center Hill Dam, damming the Caney Fork River to create Center Hill Reservoir. The park was created in 1975 and named to honor the former mayor of nearby Smithville. Like many Tennessee state parks, this one emphasizes recreation. Fishing and boating are popular here, as are picnicking and playgrounds.

At the marina visitors can rent boats or buy fishing licenses, food, fuel, and gifts at the store. The **restaurant** here serves three meals a day and is open year-round, except for Christmas and New Year's Day.

Accommodations include 34 cabins, each of which sleeps six people and comes with a housekeeping kitchen. A swimming pool serves cabin guests only. The cabins stay open year-round, except mid-December to mid-January, and cost $69.88. For reservations, call 931/858-2114. The park also has 60 **campsites,** open year-round and available on a first-come, first-served basis. Each comes with electrical and water hookups, and bathhouses offer hot showers. To get further information, call 800/250-8619 or 931/858-2446.

Cookeville and Vicinity

Cookeville is unusual in that it has two downtowns—one where the town was founded and another surrounding the train station. It is the home of Tennessee Technological University, ostensibly an engineering college, but one that wields a considerable liberal arts influence in the area. This is the place where rural McGovernites come in to town and go on a spree consisting of the Sunday *New York Times,* espresso, and a week's supply of organic tofu.

The best place to start here is the old train station, which has been transformed into a museum. Across the street a cultural district—the West Side—has sprung up containing good places to eat and shop.

COOKEVILLE

The **Depot Museum** (116 W. Broad St., 931/528-8570, 10 A.M.–4 P.M. Tues.–Sat., free) is in the old Tennessee Central Railroad Station, which was built in 1909. Permanent exhibits include railroad artifacts, photographs, and two cabooses—both of which have been restored. Temporary exhibits focus on topics such as World War II.

Existing as they do so close to the countryside, most towns hereabouts do not have extensive parks. Cookeville, however, boasts 260-acre **Cane Creek Park,** which has bike and hiking trails, fishing, paddleboats, and plenty of places to picnic. To get there, go three miles off I-40 Exit 286.

City Lake Natural Area at Bridgeway Road is a 40-acre park with hiking, a waterfall, and a boat-launching ramp. It's open all year.

And east of town, **Hidden Hollow** (off U.S. 70 at I-40 Exit 290, 931/526-4038, $1) offers outdoor activities for the whole family. A mill, covered bridges, and waterfalls sit among a petting zoo and places to swim and fish. Spread over 86 acres, this park is the vision of Arda Lee, a retired tool design engineer.

Food

Bobby Q's Barbeque and Catfish (1070 N. Washington, 931/526-1024, lunch and dinner Tues.–Fri., dinner Sat.) has barbecue so good that this place ought to be in Memphis. The Sampler Plate has pulled pork, beef, and pork ribs. The catfish is great as well.

Mamma Rosa's Restaurant (200 S. Lowe St., 931/372-8694, lunch and dinner Mon.–Sat.) offers good Italian food. It serves pizza, pasta dishes, lasagna, and manicotti.

Poets, beside Bookworks on the square at East Broad Street, has a good selection of coffees, bagels in the morning, and desserts after lunch.

Spankies (203 E. 9th St., 931/528-1050) has good food and drinks that seem that much better when served on an outdoor patio. The food here includes salads, sandwiches, chicken, steak, and shrimp.

World Foods (22 N. Cedar St., 931/525-6539) can serve an Italian sandwich on peasant bread, put stuffed grape leaves as a side dish, and finish the meal with baklava. It's in the West Side neighborhood.

Shopping

The West Side neighborhood across from the depot contains several interesting shops.

The **Potter's Wheel** (119 W. Broad St., 931/528-2555) has works of art as well as beautiful everyday items. Classes are offered for locals, and sometimes the visitor can find Larry Patton of the Flying Burrito Brothers in there. His wife, Pamela Patton, runs the place.

New Century Books and Goods (101 W. Broad St., 931/528-6780) occupies a bank build-ing erected in 1919. It contains new and used books, crystals, local crafts, and all your New Age needs.

An excellent bookstore is **Bookworks** (on the square at 230 E. Broad St., 931/372-8026). One room leads to another here, with chairs for sitting and browsing.

Chocolate lovers should pull over at the **Russell-Stover Candy** factory's outlet store (1976 Chocolate Dr., 931/526-8424) for great prices on seconds and bulk candy. To get there, take I-40 Exit 288.

For more information, contact the **Cookeville Chamber of Commerce** (302 S. Jefferson Ave., 800/264-5541 or 931/526-2211, www.cookeville chamber.com, Mon.–Fri.).

WOODBURY

The land on the Highland Rim here is not very fertile, and to make a living the residents got very good at making baskets and chairs, which were traded for goods that the farmers could not raise or grow. The basket patterns have come down through the years to the point that no one can name their origins. Some people speculate that when the Cherokees were marched through here on the infamous Trail of Tears, some of the women stayed behind to marry local men and brought the basketmaking with them. Wherever it came from, the tradition of high-quality craftwork continues in Cannon County in a greater concentration than about anywhere in the state. Woodbury has been named one of the 100 best arts towns in America.

Just east of town is the highest mountain between the Appalachians and the Ozarks. Oddly enough, it is named **Short Mountain.**

Arts and Crafts

The first stop should be **The Arts Center of Cannon County** (1424 John Bragg Hwy., 615/563-ARTS, www.artscenterofcc.com). Here are exhibits of local crafts, some of which are for sale. Better yet, the center gives directions to makers of baskets, chairs, and quilts. (The **Robert Mason Historical Museum,** 615/563-ARTS, free, shares the building with the Arts Center. Permanent exhibits include the Confederate uniform of a member of Forrest's cavalry and a samurai sword.)

Thelma Hibdon (615/563-5445) is a fifth-generation white-oak basket maker, the daughter of Ida Pearl Davis, who has made baskets for the Smithsonian.

There are many other people who do excellent craftwork in Cannon County, and invite visitors into their homes to look over their wares. The Arts Center is the best place to get information on who makes what.

Events

The **Arts Center** features wonderful cultural events varying from classical guitar concerts to theatrical productions.

White Oak Country Crafts Fair, held the second weekend in August, is a juried event bringing together the best local craftspeople. It includes demonstrations and food.

Food and Accommodations

Main Street Deli (108 West Main St., 615/563-6118) offers subs made with its own tuna, chicken, and seafood salads served on freshly baked bread. Pizzas, soup, and a salad bar are available as well, and diners can round off the meal with cheesecake and fresh pies.

Joe's Place (108 Tatum St., 615/563-4140) features country cooking—plate lunches, sandwiches, and steaks. **D.J. Pizza and Steak** (805 West Main St., 615/563-2821) serves Italian dishes in addition to the items for which it's named.

BURGESS FALLS STATE NATURAL AREA

Water from the Cumberland Plateau flows to its western edge and falls 130 feet over three falls in this delightful park south of Cookeville. Early settlers, appropriately enough, named this the Falling Water River and used it to power grist- and sawmills. In the days before TVA, the city of Cookeville built a dam and used the water power to generate electricity. TVA's power made the dam obsolete, but Cookeville held onto the dam and land around it nonetheless.

a store in the Muddy Pond Mennonite Community

This wise decision resulted in this beautiful 155-acre park, which is great for hiking and picnicking. It has no restaurants, lodging, or camping, and the park is closed December to February. For information, call 931/432-5312 or visit www.tnstparks.com.

MONTEREY

This little town holds the only existing remnant of the "standing stone" for which Standing Stone State Park was named. The stone allegedly resembled a gray dog and had significance to the Cherokee Indians. Chunks of the stone were chipped away, however, and all that is left sits atop a monument on East Commercial Avenue.

Hwy. 164 leads east out of Monterey toward the **Muddy Pond Mennonite Community.** After driving about seven miles, turn right on Union B Road and follow the signs. These folks sell a variety of homegrown and homemade products at a local store. They raise cane all summer and make sorghum (molasses) on October weekends.

Garden Inn (1400 Bee Rock Rd., 888/293-1444 or 931/839-1400, www.thegardeninnbb .com, $135–145) is for people who like to live on the edge. The inn sits on 15 acres that lead to the edge of a 100-foot cliff with a great view into Stamps Hollow. The 10 rooms in this new structure all have private baths.

The Sequatchie Valley

PIKEVILLE

This friendly town lies in the Sequatchie Valley, a 70-mile valley in the Cumberland Plateau. Unlike the thin-soiled plateau, the valley is great for farming, and the visitor will see beautiful farms here. Downtown, there are still residences on the square surrounding the 1909 courthouse. Many Middle Tennessee towns used to be this way, but in most the houses have been supplanted by shops or businesses.

Just north of the Bledsoe County Courthouse stands the **John Bridgman House** (423/447-2931, free), a Federal-style home built between 1810 and 1830, constructed of handmade brick. Its walls are one foot thick and in some places are brick on the inside as well. Owned by the First National Bank of Pikeville, the house is furnished in period antiques and shown by appointment during banking hours.

Theron Hale and his daughters, an early group on the *Grand Ole Opry,* hailed from Pikeville. Their most popular song was "Listen to the Mockingbird."

Pikeville is home to a sort of radio station that has all but vanished from the American scene. **WUAT**—1110 on the AM dial—can be seen through the window of the Mini Outlet on U.S.

127. Owner Joyce Bownds plays country music, delivers local news, and opines on whatever she wants—a refreshing change from the world of automated playlists. The commentary may be old-fashioned, but Ms. Bownds is no technological slouch; her station can be heard on the Web at www.wuatradio.com.

Food and Accommodations

The **Vaughn House** (233 Main St., 423/447-2678, open Monday–Friday) serves elegant lunches and dinners in a 100-year-old house—by reservation only. Typical lunch entrées include quiche or baked chicken, while dinner brings forth stuffed flounder or prime rib.

Colonial Bed and Breakfast (303 S. Main St., 423/447-7183, $45–50) occupies a two-story, 100-year-old house. It has four rooms, all with private baths. Handmade quilts cover each bed, and guests can enjoy two sitting rooms. Alcoholic beverages are not permitted.

Fall Creek Falls Bed and Breakfast (423/881-5494, www.bbonline.com/tn/fallcreek, $75–140) is a manor home on 40 acres one mile from Fall Creek Falls State Park. The eight rooms are air-conditioned, and each has a private bath and is decorated in country or Victorian style. To get there from the Fall Creek Falls State

THE CHILDREN'S HOLOCAUST MEMORIAL

The town of Whitwell is home to a re-markable middle school where, in 1998, Linda Hooper, the principal, and David Smith, teacher and assistant principal, offered an after-school, eighth grade course on the Holocaust. The students, struggling to grasp the enormity of the death of six million Jews, decided to collect that many paperclips. They got this idea upon learning that many Nor-wegians, after seeing Jews forced to wear yel-low Stars of David, wore paperclips in solidarity with them.

Students sent letters requesting paperclips, word got out about the project, and paper-clips poured in from around the world, along with letters from Jewish families telling stories about their experiences in World War II. As the paperclip collection and a pile of what

on display at the Children's Holocaust Memorial: a rail car used in Germany to transport Jews to death camps

would become 30,000-plus documents grew, the students decided to construct a Holocaust me-morial on their school grounds.

The effort attracted the attention of two journalists in Washington, D.C., Peter Schroeder and his wife, Dagmar Schroeder-Hildebrand, who became intrigued that a school in a small Southern town had taken on such a project. The two wrote about it for German and Austrian newspapers, and more paperclips poured in. The couple drove to Whitwell, where the entire school welcomed them, and the writers were so impressed that they decided to obtain an actual German railroad car used to transport Jewish prisoners to the camps, ship it to America, and pre-sent it to the school.

The surprisingly small railcar, built in 1917, looks like an antique cattle car, and was used by the Nazis to transport 80 to 150 people. One of only four such cars in the United States, it now sits in a small park beside the school, along with six million paperclips and other materials the children have assembled. The Holocaust course is still taught there, and remains one of the most popular curricular offerings. The school is raising money for a building to house their collection of documents, and the paperclip collection now totals more than 30 million. For more details, see www.marionschools.org/holocaust.

There is no charge to see the memorial, although during school hours visitors should call 423/658-5635 first. To get there, go to Whitwell on Hwy. 28. Turn west on East Spring Street for 500 feet, then right on Hwy. 108, which is Main Street. Go north on Main Street—stay on it when Hwy. 108 veers to the left—and the school is on the right less than a mile ahead.

Park entrance, visitors should go one mile up Hwy. 284 until they see the sign.

Shopping

The **Fabric House** (100 Main St., 423/447-6195) in a 100-plus-year-old building, offers one of the largest collections of quilts that visitors will find in this part of the state—hundreds at any given time. Pillows, crocheted items, and 2,000–3,000 bolts of cloth are available as well.

The **Vaughn House** (233 Main St., 423/447-2678) features antique furniture, Depression glass, and collectibles. Run by the same people and just up the street is **Yesterday and Today,** selling similar goods.

For more information, contact the **Bledsoe County Chamber of Commerce** (203 Cumberland Ave., 423/447-2791, 8 A.M.–4:30 P.M. Mon.–Fri., www.pikeville-bledsoe.com).

DUNLAP

An old Tennessee joke centers on the definition of Dunlaps Disease: a man so portly that his stomach done laps over his belt. The affliction has nothing to do with this town, although a few individuals hereabouts appear to suffer from it.

The Cumberland Plateau above the Sequatchie Valley contains coal, and at the **Dunlap Coke Ovens Historic Site** (423/949-3483, free), visitors can see how coal was converted to coke, a concentrated form of fuel used in iron foundries and steel mills in Chattanooga. The operation ran from 1902 until 1927, and at one time employed 350 men who ran 268 stone ovens. Now in a leafy forest, the site has a **visitors center** that is open on weekends between Memorial Day and Labor Day, and perhaps other times. To get there, go west on Cherry Street in the middle of town off U.S. 127 and follow the signs.

Scott's Choo Choos (423/949-4400), across from Canoe the Sequatchie, is a display of Lionel "O" and "O-27" gauge railroad trains, open to the public on summer mornings and around the second Sunday in December. Admission is free.

Between Whitwell and Dunlap in **Sequatchie Valley Institute** (423/949-5922, www.svionline.org), whose mission is "to offer society an opportunity to experience and learn about living in harmony with nature." This group welcomes visitors to various workshops and programs that they put on, all described on their website.

Canoe the Sequatchie, (423/949-4400, www.sequatchie.com/canoe), south of town on U.S. 127 at the river, enables visitors to do just that. The Sequatchie River is a gentle stream ideally suited for families or for those who wish to take it easy. It's open weekends only from April until Memorial Day, daily during the summer, and weekends after Labor Day until the first snow. Trips vary from the three- to four-mile variety to overnight excursions.

The **Dunlap Restaurant** (U.S. 127 N., 423/949-2595) offers great country breakfasts, lunches, and dinners seven days a week. The **Hickory Pit** (108 New Hwy. 8, 423/949-4222) serves pork, beef, ribs, and chicken daily for lunch and dinner.

WHITWELL

Farther down the Sequatchie Valley is the town of Whitwell, which seems the last place in the world that would contain a Holocaust memorial, but has become world-renowned for doing so.

At one time the Sequatchie River had over 20 mills on its banks. Now the only one left is **Ketner's Mill,** downstream from Whitwell on Ketner Mill Road. The oldest part of the Mill dates from 1824, and the brick building was added in 1882. The **Ketner's Mill Country Arts Festival** takes place in mid October here, when the old mill comes alive again to grind corn.

Down the Tennessee

KINGSTON

By 1800 the seat of Roane County, built on an easily defensible hill above the Clinch River, lay on the eastern end of the first road to Nashville and was an important trading town. The state legislature met here once in 1807, making Kingston the state capital for a day. The **Roane County Museum of History and Art** (865/376-9211, www.roanetnheritage.com, 9 A.M.–noon and 1–4 P.M. Mon.–Fri., free) occupies one of the seven antebellum courthouses left in the state and contains displays on each town in the county as well as prehistoric artifacts from Indian mounds.

In 1979, **Fort Southwest Point** (www.southwestpoint.com, Apr.–Dec., donation is requested) was built where the Clinch River joins the Tennessee River. This was the frontier between United States and Indian lands, and the structure was built there to help keep the peace between the settlers and the Cherokee. It served as the headquarters for Jonathan Meigs, the Indian Agent for these parts. The town of Kingston owns the site and has erected structures and walls in the same locations as the original. There are a good many reconstructed forts in the state, but this claims to be the only one reconstructed on its original foundations. To get there, take Exit 352 off I-40 and go south.

Practicalities

Whitestone Inn (1200 Paint Rock Rd., 865/376-0113, $125–250) occupies 360 acres on Watts Bar Lake. The 20 rooms all have a fireplace and whirlpool tub. This place is much in demand for corporate retreats and weddings.

Mama Mia's (705 W. Race St., 865/376-5050, lunch and dinner Tues.–Sat.) offers homemade pizza, ravioli, and other Italian dishes as well as sandwiches made with homemade bread.

For more information about Kingston, contact the **Roane County Visitors Bureau** (1226 S. Kentucky St., 865/376-4201, www.roanealliance.org).

SPRING CITY

Travelers who follow Walden Ridge to the southwest come to Spring City, named for the many sources of water here. One of them, Rhea Springs, was said by the Native Americans to possess healing properties. Slave traders apparently believed in the power of the waters, for they would bring work-wearied slaves here before selling them so they would become rejuvenated and thus worth more money.

Spring City is the only place to examine all three sources of TVA electricity. **Watts Bar Dam,** southeast of town, was built in 1939–42 and supplies hydropower. As demand grew, a steam plant (now mothballed) was added during World War II, and in the '70s the agency began building the Watts Bar nuclear power plant, which loaded fuel for the first time in 1995. Visitors can view the dam from an overlook on its west end and see the locks from an east end overlook. Hwy. 68 passes right over the top of the dam.

Spring City is also the birthplace of Hargus "Pig" Robbins, whose piano playing graced many Nashville recording sessions.

For more information, contact the **Spring City Chamber of Commerce** (384 Front St., 423/365-5210), which sits in a caboose.

Recreation

A waterfall that drops 30 feet highlights the 104-acre **Stinging Fork Pocket Wilderness.** The round-trip hike to it is three miles. To get to the trailhead, go out of Spring City on the Shut-In Gap Road for five miles.

Twin Rocks Nature Trail, 2.5 miles round-trip, leads to a Walden Ridge overlook. To get there, go out of Spring City on the Shut-In Gap Road for one mile.

The **Piney River Trail** follows the Piney River and connects a picnic area and the Newby Branch Forest Camp near Dayton. The trailhead is the same as the Twin Rocks Nature Trail.

TENNESSEE VALLEY AUTHORITY

During the depths of the Great Depression, the administration of Franklin D. Roosevelt took a look at the area surrounding the Tennessee River—all of Tennessee and parts of Alabama, Georgia, Kentucky, Mississippi, North Carolina, and Virginia. It saw that a large number of people lived in abject poverty, only one of 30 farms had electricity, and that there were few industries, even in the cities. The Tennessee River was a capricious stream that periodically caused massive flooding, yet at other times ran so shallow that using it for shipping was all but impossible.

The solution to a lot of these problems was the Tennessee Valley Authority (TVA), which came about through the efforts of George Norris, a progressive senator from Nebraska. TVA was set up as an independent corporate agency of the federal government, run by three directors appointed by the president and confirmed by the Senate. Relatively free of governmental meddling, TVA was able to move decisively and, backed with federal dollars, effectively. It was charged with a list of tasks, among them to improve the region's "general social and economic welfare."

In the early years, it took over **Wilson Dam** and other properties from other federal agencies, but TVA soon began building its own dams. **Norris Dam** was the first, and now the agency operates 51 dams on the Tennessee River and its tributaries. This has all but eliminated the flooding, and a system of locks provides a channel for year-round navigation all the way to Knoxville from the Gulf of Mexico.

Other benefits of the agency included efforts to curb malaria, education about soil conservation techniques, and examples of city planning such as the town of Norris. TVA built roads, constructed water purification and sewage treatment plants, and helped develop fertilizers.

It took thousands of people to accomplish all this, and the jobs provided to Tennesseans and others boosted economies, local and statewide. The downside of TVA's aggressive flood control and dam building was that thousands of families were forced to move from places where, in some cases, their families had lived for generations. Whole towns were flooded, and residents had to remove their dead to higher cemeteries.

One of TVA's missions was to provide electricity to the valley, and in doing so it literally brightened the lives of thousands of people. The relatively cheap electricity lured industries, thus providing jobs. At first, the electricity was produced by falling water at the dams, but later the demand became so great that other sources were needed. Gradually, the production of electricity became the prime focus of TVA, and today the agency operates 38 hydroelectric sites, 12 coal-fired generators, and two nuclear power plants.

The abundance of electricity was one of the reasons that the Manhattan Project leaders chose to build their complex at Oak Ridge, yet it was the emphasis on power production that got TVA in trouble later on in the 1970s. By then the agency, the largest utility in the Western Hemisphere, had embarked on the most ambitious nuclear power plant–building effort in the world. At the same time, coal-fired plants were belching out pollutants and creating a demand for strip-mined coal, playing unprecedented environmental havoc in mountain communities in Tennessee and Kentucky. Electricity that had once been some of the cheapest in the nation soared in price, leading to complaints from the very people TVA had been designed to serve.

It must be said that TVA has worked hard on its pollution problems and tried to help consumers save electricity through special programs, such as one aimed at better insulating houses. And it scrapped most of its nuclear power plants.

In recent years, TVA has downsized, and, feeling pressure from Congress, has cut back on many programs. Its legacy for Tennessee, however, remains in the form of lakes on which millions of people play, a strong industrial base, and a better life for its people. TVA was perhaps the best thing ever to come from the federal government to this state.

DAYTON

Most people who come to Dayton head for the **Rhea County Courthouse** (pronounced RAY, 1475 Market St., 423/775-7801), where the famous Scopes Trial of 1925 took place amid great hoopla. During court recesses or when court is not in session, visitors can tour the third-floor courtroom, which has been restored to its 1925 appearance. Downstairs is the **Scopes Museum** (free), where documents and memorabilia tell the story of the most famous trial in Tennessee.

Just outside of town lies Bryan College, founded to honor the proponent of the biblical version of creation.

Recreation

Laurel-Snow Pocket Wilderness totals 710 acres and includes two waterfalls. Laurel Falls drops 50 feet and Snow Falls drops 30 feet. The round-trip hikes to each are, respectively, five and six miles. One can reach the trailhead for both by going north on U.S. 27, left for 1.5 miles on Walnut Grove Road, left on Black Valley Road, then right on Richland Creek Road.

Events

Dayton's **Strawberry Festival** (423/775-0361, www.tnstrawberryfestival.com) takes place in early May when the berries get ripe. Along with fresh strawberries, visitors can partake of carnival rides, crafts shows, a country music concert, a parade, and a beauty pageant.

The **Scopes Trial Play and Festival** (423/775-0361), held the third weekend in July, is a reenactment of the famous trial in the historic courtroom using dialogue from 1925 court transcripts. Unlike *Inherit The Wind*, the play and film that left local hero William Jennings Bryan looking rather bad, this theatrical production leaves it to the audience to interpret the result of Tennessee's most famous trial. Other events include a crafts festival, traditional Appalachian and gospel music, an antique car show, and an occasional academic colloquium on the events of 1925.

Practicalities

The best breakfast in town is at the **Dayton Coffeeshop** (280 Main St., 423/775-6156, open Sun.–Fri. at 5 A.M.).

Diners at **Rafaels** (7835 U.S. 27 N. in the Best Western, 423/775-0707, Mon.–Sat.) can enjoy Italian cuisine amid memorabilia of the Scopes Trial.

Smiths Crossroads (1356 Market St., 423/775-8007) offers a coffee bar and Italian sodas in the middle of a large space selling antiques, collectibles, and art.

For more information, contact the **Dayton Chamber of Commerce** (107 Main St., 423/775-0361, www.rheacountyetc.com 8:30 A.M.–5 P.M. Mon.–Fri.).

SOUTH OF DAYTON

The confluence of the Hiwassee River and the Tennessee River, the **Blythe Ferry Unit of Hiwassee Refuge,** just off Hwy. 60 south of Dayton, offers birders a chance to see the only sizeable gathering of cranes—sandhill and whooping—between Florida and Canada. From November through late March, more than 7,000 of these majestic birds transform this area into a rest stop. The best time to come is March. An observation tower is here, and crane lovers can walk gravel roads and pastures to see them up close—but not too close.

Although beautiful now, this was a place of great sadness for the Cherokee Indians, for it was here that many of them last saw their ancestral lands. Nine of the 17 detachments of men, women, and children were ferried across the water here to begin their Trail of Tears to Oklahoma. A small **Cherokee Memorial Park** commemorates their passage.

The **Cherokee Indian Heritage & Sandhill Crane Viewing Days** (423/334-5850, www.southeasttennessee.com) takes place at the refuge and the nearby Birchwood School on one weekend February.

Hills and Plateaus

THE SCOPES "MONKEY TRIAL"

If there were a hall of fame for public relations stunts that backfired, the Scopes trial would be one of the first entries. It all began in 1925 with a group of Daytonians sitting in Robinson's Drug Store, discussing, as people in small towns did and still do, what it would take to "put them on the map." The newspaper had recently carried an article on a new Tennessee law that forbade the teaching of evolution.

In walked John Scopes, an amiable young man who had recently substituted for the high school biology teacher, and he admitted that he had taught the illegal subject. The drugstore publicists convinced him to take part in a test case of the law, and he agreed. A call was placed to the Chattanooga newspaper that a teacher had been arrested and would be tried for breaking the anti-evolution law. The news went out on the telegraph to the nation and the world, and the show got under way.

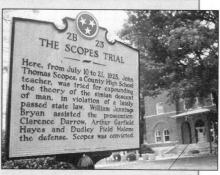

Rhea County Courthouse, site of the trial

More than 200 newspaper writers flooded the town, a Chicago radio station set up the first nationwide radio hookup, and newsreel photographers hand-cranked their movie cameras. An estimated 10,000 people showed up in town, which quickly took on a carnival atmosphere. There was even talk of moving the trial to a local ballpark to accommodate the masses.

William Jennings Bryan, three-time Democratic nominee for president, was invited to lead the prosecution team. This inspired Clarence Darrow, a famed trial lawyer and noted agnostic, to defend young Scopes. The trial culminated when Bryan agreed to take the stand as an expert witness, and Darrow baited "The Great Commoner" into testifying, among other things, that humans were not mammals.

The Dayton boosters succeeded beyond their wildest dreams in publicizing the town, but the stories that flowed through the fingers of the 22 Western Union telegraph operators weren't quite what the drugstore planners had in mind. Perhaps the most acerbic commentary came from H. L. Mencken of the Baltimore Sun, who wrote this about Bryan: "His one yearning was to keep his yokels heated up—to lead his forlorn mob of imbeciles against the foe."

The locals responded as best they could. A still-quoted line has a Dayton waitress denying food service to Mencken and then saying, "And furthermore, I have mistletoe tied to my apron strings!"

Both sides claimed victory. Scopes was duly convicted, but the conviction was overturned on appeal because of a mistake by the judge. Bryan died in Dayton five days after the trial, and in his honor Bryan College was established nearby. The law stayed on the books, an embarrassment that was largely ignored until an enlightened legislature repealed it in 1967. As for Scopes, Tennessee's most famous high school teacher, he accepted a scholarship to the University of Chicago and became a geologist for oil and gas companies.

Knoxville to Chattanooga — U.S. 11

This highway follows the Tennessee River Valley, an area of rich farmland. The mountains to the right are the edge of the Cumberland Plateau, while the ones to the left are the Appalachians. Getting away from the thundering trucks on nearby I-75, it is hard to believe that this road, still two-lane in some stretches, once carried most of the motor traffic from the northeastern United States to Alabama, Mississippi, and points west.

LENOIR CITY

Ambitiously named a city by a man who built the area's first cotton mill, this town benefited from its location at the confluence of the Tennessee and the Little Tennessee Rivers, and from the railroads that passed through. About the turn of the century, Northern capital established industries in Lenoir City, among them factories making chairs and hosiery. Chief among these was the Lenoir Car Works, which built railroad cars.

The famed Lee Highway, connecting Virginia to points south, rolls through Lenoir City. For years most of the traffic across Tennessee came to Dixie Lee Junction east of town, where U.S. 11 heading southeast split off from U.S. 70 headed west.

Dixie Lee Junction is the birthplace of the late Richard Marius, an educator, scholar, and perhaps the best writer to come from East Tennessee. His 1969 novel, *The Coming of Rain*, was set in East Tennessee after the Civil War. In his 1994 *After the War,* he transformed the story of his father, a Greek immigrant who rose to head the Southern Railroad's Lenoir City Car Works, into a powerful work of the imagination. *An Affair of Honor,* released posthumously in 2001, continues this story.

Gerald's Smokehouse (501 U.S. Hwy. 321 N, 865/986-6159) offers barbecue—pork, beef, chicken, and ribs—along with other American entrées.

For more information, contact the **Loudon County Tourist Information Center** (near I-75 Exit 81 at 1075 U.S. 321, 865/986-6822,

www.loudoncountychamber.com, 9 A.M.–5 P.M. Mon.–Sat.).

LOUDON

Loudon was settled in 1790 and grew up around a ferry across the Tennessee River. Farmers in the area got accustomed to trading in the town, and steamboats did a lively trade out of this port. At particularly busy times, the docks were so full that boats had to wait several days to unload. Until a bridge over the river was built, trains coming from the south were turned around on a turntable here. The 1855 opening of a railroad bridge over the river ended the heyday of the town. It became the seat of Loudon County in 1872 and remains a pleasant place to visit.

Sights

The **Historic Loudon Walking Tour** offers a chance to see Loudon's historic buildings up close. Among them are Victorian houses, a home that was lost in a bet on a presidential election, and the Mason Place, where after the Civil War an unrepentant Southerner built the balusters of his upper porch to resemble the Confederate battle flag. The 1883 Cumberland Presbyterian Church is a fine example of the carpenter Gothic style, and the 1810 Carmichael Coach House serves as the **Loudon County Museum** (865/458-1442, 10 A.M.–4:30 P.M. Mon.–Fri.). For a map, go to the museum, which houses local artifacts, furniture, and documents, and is staffed by enthusiastic locals who sometimes wear period dress.

Loudon is blessed with two wineries. The first, **Loudon Valley Winery** (865/986-8736), on the banks of the Tennessee River, produces dry, semi-dry, and sweet wines from 15 kinds of grapes. The tasting room overlooks the river. To get there, take Exit 76 off I-75, go east on Sugar Limb Road, and follow the signs.

The **Tennessee Valley Winery** (Exit 76 off I-75, 865/986-5147, 10 A.M.–6 P.M. Mon.–Sat., 1–5 P.M. Sun.) offers tastings and gives tours dur-

A TALE OF TWO DAMS

Lenoir City offers the visitor a chance to compare two dams, one built in TVA's heyday, the other erected when many in the valley reviled the agency. **Fort Loudoun Dam** spans the Tennessee River east of town on U.S. 321. The dam has the highest set of locks in TVA's system, and its completion in 1943 created Fort Loudoun Lake and played an important role in flood control and navigation. Visitors can go to a deck and watch the locks, which raise or lower boats and barges 70 feet.

By contrast, many people opposed construction of the **Tellico Dam.** It wasn't necessary, they argued, and would flood the Little Tennessee River, a wonderful trout-filled river that flowed past significant archaeological sites. TVA countered that the dam would send more water through Fort Loudoun's Dam generators, would aid in flood control, and would create more recreation opportunities.

Construction on the dam proceeded until a University of Tennessee researcher identified a new species of fish—the snail darter—that seemed to exist only in the Little Tennessee River. Under the provisions of the Endangered Species Act, work on the dam had to stop. Eventually the snail darter was found to inhabit other streams, the dam was finished, the floodgates closed, and Tellico Dam became TVA's 51st dam. It has no visitors center.

ing the winemaking season. This place produces a variety of wines, including classic red, muscadine, and a Lambrusco-like Cherokee Red.

Musicians gather in a big tent for the **Smoky Mountain Fiddler's Convention** (865/986-6822) late in August in Loudon. The competition features bluegrass bands, banjo, mandolin, and other instruments, as well as gospel music, clogging, and antique cars. Vendors sell crafts, antiques, and food.

Practicalities

The **Mason Place** (600 Commerce St., 865/458-3921, $108–120) is a bed-and-breakfast occupying an 1865 Greek revival home on

the Tennessee River and is listed on the National Register. Both sides in the Civil War camped here, and when General Longstreet advanced on Knoxville, he and 30,000 troops crossed the Tennessee River at this point. A swimming pool, gazebo, and wisteria-covered arbor await visitors outside amid the three-acre grounds, from which Civil War artifacts are still unearthed. The five guest rooms have private baths, period antiques, fireplaces, and feather beds. A gourmet breakfast of items such as stuffed french toast is served daily.

Loudon boasts a good number of antique stores. Among them is the **General Store** (411 Mulberry St., 865/458-6433 or 865/458-5989), which has antiques, contemporary folk art, textiles, and advertising spread over three floors.

For more information, contact the **Loudon County Tourist Information Center** (near I-75 Exit 81 at 1075 U.S. 321, 865/986-6822).

SWEETWATER

As scores of billboards will remind the traveler, Sweetwater is the home of the **Lost Sea** (423/337-6616, www.thelostsea.com, 9 A.M.–6:30 P.M. daily, $11 adults, $5.50 children 6–12), an underground lake approximately 800 by 200 feet in size, which the management claims is the largest such underwater pool on the planet. It occupies a section of the Craighead Cavern System, in which divers have found 13 acres of flooded rooms so far.

The drier parts of the cave have been put to various uses. Cherokee artifacts have been found here, and during the Civil War the South mined saltpeter, an ingredient of gunpowder, from the cave. Moonshiners and cockfighters drank and gambled in the large rooms, and when the cave was commercially opened in 1915 it was used for a dance hall.

Visitors cruise the sea in glass-bottom boats and walk though other areas. To get there, take Exit 60 off I-75 and follow Hwy. 68 southeast to the cave.

Usually hotel food is to be avoided like the plague, but the **Sweetwater Motel and Convention Center** (I-75 Exit 60, 800/523-5727 or 423/337-3511) does a good job. The rolls, said to be made by a little old lady back in the kitchen, are divine.

NIOTA

Niota, south of Sweetwater on U.S. 11, boasts the **Niota Depot,** an 1853 structure said to be the oldest train station in the state. One of the passengers who caught the train here was Henry Thomas Burn, who in 1920 at age 23 was the youngest state legislator in Tennessee. On August 18 of that year, he cast the most significant vote of his life: His "Aye" gave American women the right to vote. He put Tennessee's ratification of the 19th Amendment over the top, with Tennessee as the 36th state to ratify. Burn had previously voted against the amendment but got a letter from his mother encouraging him to support it. "Hurray and vote for suffrage," his mother penned. An excellent book on the fight for women's suffrage in Tennessee is *The Perfect 36— Tennessee Delivers Woman Suffrage,* published by Serviceberry Press.

ATHENS

Like many towns between Knoxville and Chattanooga, Athens saw its fortunes rise with the coming of the railroad. Billing itself as "The Friendly City," it is home to **Tennessee Wesleyan College** (423/745-9522, www.tnwc.edu), a four-year, 600-student institution owned by the United Methodist Church. The college occupies 40 acres in downtown Athens and provides concerts and cultural and sports events for the edification of local residents.

Sights

Housed in a former high school building, the **McMinn County Living Heritage Museum** (522 W. Madison, 423/745-0329, 10 A.M.–5 P.M. Mon.–Fri., 10 A.M.–4 P.M. Sat., $5 adults, $3 seniors and students) offers more than 7,000 items arranged into 30 exhibit areas covering Cherokee times through 1940. Visitors can see displays on rural doctors, a print shop, and military uniforms, to name a few.

Mayfield Dairy Farms Visitor Center (4 Mayfield Ln., 423/745-2151, 9 A.M.–4 P.M. Mon.–Fri., 9 A.M.–4 P.M. Sat., free) is a great place to take kids. A film history of the dairy precedes a plant tour that shows milk bottling and ice cream production.

Strikers' Premium Winery (480 County Rd. 172, 423/507-8816, 9 A.M.–7 P.M. Mon.–Fri., noon–7 P.M. Sun.) is one of the newer sources of wine in the state. Twelve of the 17 wines offered are sweet or semi-sweet. To get there, take Exit 49 off I-75, go east on Hwy. 30, then left on Lee Irwin Road. Follow the signs.

Outside of town at the McMinn County Airport is the **Swift Museum** (423/745-9547, www.napanet.net/~arbeau/swift, 9 A.M.–5 P.M. Mon.–Fri., free), which is devoted to Globe and Temco Swift airplanes—aluminum-bodied, two-seat aircraft made from 1946 through 1951. These aircraft, with their all-metal bodies, retractable landing gear, and 135-miles-per-hour top speed, were state-of-the art in their day, and now about 800 still take to the air all over the country. The museum displays fully restored planes and other related items, and sponsors several annual events, among them the Annual Swift National Fly-In on the week preceding Memorial Day, to which as many as 100 planes arrive.

Practicalities

Majestic Mansion Bed and Breakfast (201 E. Washington St., 423/746-9041, rates are $85, $125 with children's room) occupies a 1909 home that now has three guest rooms and a children's room, the three main rooms have private baths.

A bit farther afield is **Cross Creek Farm,** (Hwy. 30 E., 423/334-9172, $85), which has a restored early 1800s two-bedroom cabin for guests. From the porch visitors can watch alpacas and Shetland sheep safely graze. Guests can participate in farm chores if so inclined.

Riddle and Wallace Drugstore, on the square, has what can only be called "drugstore food"— chicken salad, cherry cokes, and grilled cheese sandwiches. It's open Monday–Saturday for breakfast and lunch.

Artist's Alcove (6 S. White St., 423/745-7312), on the square, features handmade pottery, jewelry, wood items, glass, and weavings. Some are locally produced, but most items come from different places all over the country.

For more information, contact the **Athens Area Chamber of Commerce** (13 N. Jackson St., 423/745-0334, www.athenschamber.org).

RICEVILLE

Sunshine Hollow (County Rd. 52, 423/745-4289) has such extensive daylily plantings that busloads of perennial fanciers come to visit. It also offers hosta perennials—shade-loving plants said to be the most favored herbaceous perennial in the United States. The bakery specializes in pecan fruitcakes and other delights.

CLEVELAND

Of the towns along the railroad between Chattanooga and Knoxville, Cleveland prospered the most. Relatively untouched by Civil War hostilities, the town was poised to take advantage of the industrial boom that came to the South in the 1870s and '80s. Locals are justifiably proud of the Victorian homes built during that period and around the turn of the century.

Cleveland is also the headquarters of the Church of God denominations—at least two of them—and therein lies a tale. As explained by Charles A. Sherrill in the *Tennessee Encyclopedia,* the Church of God sect came into existence in 1906, a group whose services contained "fervent prayer, weeping, shouting, and speaking in tongues." The next year Cleveland minister Ambrose Tomlinson was appointed to head the organization.

Tomlinson helped increase church membership by 20-fold, but in 1922 he was accused of mismanaging the money and forced out. Refusing to go gentle into that charismatic night, he stayed in Cleveland, formed his own church, and called it the Tomlinson Church of God. This prompted the original Church of God to take the splinter group to court to resolve who could use the name they shared. A court ruling held

that the newer sect had to append the words "of Prophecy" to its "Church of God."

Tomlinson died in 1943, and his two sons, Milton and Homer, each sought the leadership role. Milton won out, leaving Homer to move to New York City, where he abandoned the church, pronounced himself "King of the World," traveled with a throne, and ran for president four times on the Theocratic ticket.

Approximately 75 percent of the Church of God of Prophecy members live outside the United States, although the church reports 2,000 congregations in this country, and 133 in Tennessee.

Meanwhile, the original Church of God managed to thrive without the Tomlinsons. It founded Lee University and the adjoining Church of God Theological Seminary, which enroll, respectively, 2,850 and 262 students. The denomination claims more than 51,000 members in Tennessee, 792,000 in North America, and 3.2 million in the world.

Now that the feuding factions have largely gone on to their respective heavens, the two denominations with their shared heritage have come much closer together. In the meantime, they both have to sometimes deal with confusion caused by the existence of another denomination, the Church of God in Christ, the second-largest black denomination in the country, headquartered in Memphis.

As if this weren't enough religion for one town, from 1933 through 1947 Cleveland also contained the campus of Bob Jones University, perhaps the most theologically fundamentalist educational institution in this hemisphere. BJU moved to Greenville, South Carolina, where it remains today.

Sights

Apple Valley Orchards (351 Weese Rd. S.E., 423/472-3044, Aug.–Dec. 9 A.M.–6 P.M. Mon.–Sat., noon–6 P.M. Sun.) has 50 acres growing 23 kinds of apples. People can buy apples, watch cider being pressed, and go through the gift shop and bakery, from which all manner of apple-related goods flow forth.

The **Morris Vineyard** offers visitors an opportunity to pick scuppernong, muscadine, and other grapes as well as blueberries—it's the largest such enterprise in the state.

Reconstructed log cabins, furnished with authentic farm and household items, make up **Primitive Village,** (423/476-5096, open daily Apr.–Sept., $5 adults, $2 children 6–12), which lies six miles east of Cleveland. To get there from I-75, take the U.S. 64 Bypass east toward Polk County. Turn into Kinser Road; the village is about a mile on the left. Each cabin is full of antiques, some of them dating to the age of their structure.

The **Tennessee Mountain View Winery** (352 Union Grove Rd., 423/479-7311, July 4–Sept., 8 A.M.–8 P.M. Tues.–Sun.; Nov.–July 3, noon–6 P.M. Tues.–Sat. and 1–5 P.M. Sun.) in Charleston, a community eight miles north of Cleveland on U.S. 11, sells muscadine, Concord, Niagara, Catawba, and white riesling wines.

Practicalities

The **Gondolier** (3300 Keith St. N.W., 423/472-4998, lunch and dinner daily) serves homemade lasagna, spaghetti, and manicotti as well as American dishes.

Jordan's BBQ (910 Stuart Rd. N.E., 423/478-2171, lunch and dinner Mon.–Sat.) serves pork, beef, and ribs, and is famous for stuffed potatoes—potatoes filled with barbecue and topped with cheese or various sauces. Follow this with homemade desserts, including Key lime pie.

For more information, contact the **Cleveland/Bradley Chamber of Commerce, Convention and Visitors Bureau** (2145 Keith St. N.W., 423/472-6587, www.clevelandchamber.com).

RED CLAY STATE HISTORIC AREA

The 260 acres that make up this historical area served as the last seat of the Cherokee Nation's government before the Trail of Tears. The visitors center shows a film about the Cherokee and displays artifacts and documents from the 1832-38 period. Outside are replicas of a council house, a farm, and the sleeping quarters that tribe members would use when they gathered for a council. The Great Council Spring, also known as the Blue Hole, is about a half million deep and still produces more than a half million gallons of water daily. The Eternal Flame of the Cherokee burns here.

Cherokee Days of Recognition take place on the first weekend in August, when 18,000 people come for authentic Cherokee food and crafts, storytelling, dancing, and a blowgun competition.

The **visitors center** is open Monday–Saturday 8 A.M.–4:30 P.M. and Sunday 1–4:30 P.M. The park is open daily 8 A.M.–sunset. In the winter, December–February, the visitors center is open Monday–Friday 8 A.M.–4:15 P.M., weekends 1–4:15 P.M. The park is open daily 8 A.M.–4:30 P.M. Admission is free. To get here from Cleveland take either Blue Springs Road or Dalton Pike south from U.S. 64/40 Bypass. Follow the signs for 12 miles to the park. For more information, call 423/478-0339 or visit www.state.tn.us.

Knoxville to Chattanooga—The Railroad Route

The highway U.S. 411 roughly follows the path of the railroad from Knoxville to Chattanooga. The rails were first laid in 1855 and had a profound effect on the towns along the way. Etowah first came into being as a railroad town, and the others benefited from their proximity to the rails.

FORT LOUDOUN

The land along the Little Tennessee River was the stronghold of the Cherokee. Here were their chief towns, and from here came the leaders of their people. Three sites just off U.S. 411 shed light on the troubled relations between the Cherokee and the whites.

This reconstructed fort commemorates the first British fort built west of the mountains; it served as the empire's southwesternmost outpost. Unlike most forts in Tennessee, this one was built at the request of the Cherokee, who had allied themselves with the British during the French and Indian War and wanted protection for their families while their warriors were fighting French-allied Indians to the north.

Fort Loudoun was built in 1756, just as relations between the colonists and the Cherokee entered uncertain times. Various outrages and misinterpretations led to bloodshed, and the Cherokee laid siege to the fort. An agreement permitted the besieged colonists to leave in August of 1760, but the Cherokee attacked the departing group one day later and then burned the fort to the ground. This provoked retaliatory attacks on the Cherokee towns in the area and led to further bloodshed.

Today the reconstructed Fort Loudoun gives a good look at the old enclosure, although the visitor must keep in mind that nearby Tellico Lake was just the Little Tennessee River in the 1700s. The walls are made of upright logs sharpened to a point at the top. Inside are several buildings and gun platforms. The **visitors center,** a separate building, contains a good museum. Children will like this place, which is open daily 8 A.M.–sunset. The visitors center is open daily 8 A.M.–4:30 P.M.

Admission is free. For more information, call 423/884-6217, or see www.state.tn.us.

Blockhouse and Birthplace

In three decades after the 1760 fall of Fort Loudoun, several things changed. The British were gone, the United States government was in place, and the Cherokee knew they could no longer dream of pushing back the whites. The old Fort Loudoun site marked the boundary between the Cherokee lands and those of the United States. Once again, Native Americans requested that the Americans build an outpost in which to regulate trade, conduct negotiations, and prevent the more rapacious settlers from violating tribal lands. William Blount, governor of the Southwest Territory, was happy to do this, for it gave him an excuse to station troops there who could readily and quickly deal with any uprisings.

In 1794, Blount had the **Tellico Blockhouse** erected within sight of the Fort Loudoun site. People traveling downstream to New Orleans often made a side trip up the Little Tennessee River to see the blockhouse. The most prominent of these early tourists was the Duke of Orleans, who later became King Louis Philippe of France. Carolyn Sakowski, in her book *Touring the East Tennessee Backroads,* tells how the duke fell ill and, following the medical practices of the day, bled himself. This mightily impressed the Cherokee, who asked him to do the same to an elderly chief. The duke obliged, and the old gentleman improved so quickly that his tribe members were astonished. For his services, the duke was thanked by getting to sleep in the chief's house on the family mat in the place of honor—between the grandmother and the great-aunt. It is not recorded whether or not the duke was inspired to continue his medical practice.

The Tellico Blockhouse site has not been restored, and there isn't a great deal to see there. Visitors can drive off the island, go right on U.S. 411, then turn right onto Old Hwy. 72 and follow signs to the blockhouse site.

SEQUOYAH

In 1771, a Cherokee woman and a colonial soldier produced a boy named **George Gist,** or, to his Cherokee relatives, Sequoyah. He grew up in Tennessee and Alabama, never attended school, and fought for General Andrew Jackson at the War of 1812 Battle of Horseshoe Bend against the Creek.

One of Sequoyah's legs was disabled during the war, and about that time he and many other Cherokee willingly moved to the Arkansas Territory. It was there that he began to work on an alphabet for the Cherokee language. The story goes that Sequoyah came up with the idea when a relative came home from an American school and Sequoyah saw him writing letters.

Withdrawing to a cabin outside his house, he labored on the alphabet, suffering ridicule from his neighbors in the process. By 1821, he had devised a syllabary—so named because its letters stand for syllables—of 86 letters, some of them English ones, that captured the language of the Cherokee. He taught it to his daughter, Atoya, and together they demonstrated it to a council of tribal leaders. First Sequoyah wrote down a message from the elders. Then Atoya came in, picked up the paper, and, to the astonishment of the council, read their words back to them. Sequoyah's creation was an immediate success; it was so simple that people could teach it to each other and could then send letters back to their relatives in the East.

Sequoyah achieved renown among his own people and the nation at large; Congress passed a bill to give him $500 for his accomplishment. The Cherokee people gained access to a printing press and by 1828 were publishing their own newspaper in New Echota, Georgia. Ten years later came the Trail of Tears, when the Cherokee were forced to move to Oklahoma. Those in Arkansas moved there first, and the county in which Sequoyah lived was named in his honor, as were the enormous redwood trees in California. He lived until 1843, a leader who helped his people in Oklahoma and elsewhere. He died while on a trip to New Mexico.

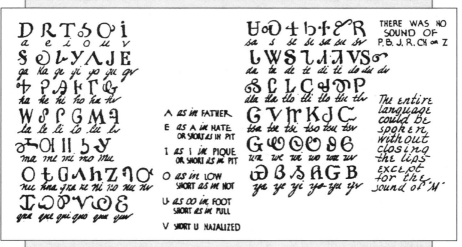

Cherokee alphabet

A mere half-mile away is the **Sequoyah Birthplace Museum** (423/884-6246), which is owned and operated by the Eastern band of the Cherokee, who live in a reservation on the North Carolina side of the Great Smoky Mountains National Park. The museum commemorates the inventor of the Cherokee alphabet and includes artifacts from villages, Cherokee crafts, and explanations of various myths and legends. Outside the museum is a memorial to 191 Cherokee whose remains were unearthed during the frantic archaeological efforts that preceded the damming of the river and the creation of Tellico Lake. The museum is open 9 A.M.–5 P.M. Monday–Saturday, and noon–5 P.M. Sunday. Admission is $3 for adults and $1.50 for children 6–12.

Events

The **Memorial Day Encampment** brings forth a re-creation of the South Carolina Independent Company, the British soldiers who were garrisoned at Fort Loudoun. As many as 170 actors in period dress take part, some of them as British soldiers, some of them "provincials," and some Cherokee. Admission is free for this event.

During the year 10–20 people in period dress participate in **Garrison Weekends.** These are held approximately once a month, February to December. Call the fort for exact dates.

September brings the **18th-Century Trade Fair to Fort Loudoun,** with craftspeople selling replicas of period textiles, pewter, jewelry, blown glass, and other products. All are for sale, as are food and drink. Call the fort for dates and details.

Christmas at Fort Loudoun brings period decoration, a candle-lined trail, carols and games germane to the 18th century, and often a buffet of traditional foods. For information and dates, call the fort.

MADISONVILLE

Madisonville is the birthplace of Estes Kefauver (1903–63), who served in the House and the Senate and was the Democratic vice-presidential nominee on the Democratic ticket in 1956 with Adlai Stevenson. He achieved national fame when in the early '50s he conducted nationally televised hearings into organized crime. He and Senator Albert Gore Sr. were the only Southern senators who refused to sign the 1956 Southern Manifesto, a document opposing school integration.

Country crooner Eddy Arnold was born near here in 1918. Early in his career he was dubbed "The Tennessee Plowboy," but his singing reached a level of smooth sophistication far beyond any rural nickname. His country hits were played from the 1940s through the '80s, and he survived rock 'n' roll with songs such as "Cattle Call" and "Welcome to My World."

Madisonville is now home to **Orr Mountain Winery** (423/442-5340, 10 A.M.–6 P.M. Wed.–Sat., 2–6 P.M. Sun.; daily July–Aug., irregular Jan.–Feb.), which offers tours and tastings of its six wines—blush, sweet red, and white, and dry red, rosé, and white. To get there, go west on Hwy. 68 from Madisonville toward Sweetwater. Turn left onto Hwy. 117 at the sign between Mileposts 8 and 9. Go one mile and turn right onto Hwy. 121, then 0.3 miles and turn right again.

For more information, contact the **Monroe County Chamber of Commerce** (intersection of Hwy. 68 and U.S. 411, 800/245-5428 or 423/442-9147, www.monroecountychamber.org, 8:30 A.M.–5 P.M. Mon.–Fri.).

ENGLEWOOD

This town was built on textile manufacturing and at one time had 25 mills. Women and children as young as 10 years old worked here. The **Englewood Textile Museum** (423/887-5455, 10 A.M.–5 P.M. Tues.–Sat.,free), on the square in Englewood, commemorates this time with exhibits on mill workers, mill life, and the history of Englewood. Exhibits include pre-industrial items—a flax wheel and a hand loom—and actual mill machinery. Hard times are depicted by a feed sack dress. The saddest exhibit is a complete trousseau sewn by a bride whose parents would not allow her to marry her chosen. Miss Ellie, as she was known for the rest of her life, lived to be 81 years old. Next door is a little white house that was the birthplace of an early textile mill owner. Newly restored, Now it contains an art gallery.

ETOWAH

This is a town where almost everyone could sing, "I've been workin' on the railroad. . . ."

COUNTRY HAM

In the days before refrigerators, Tennesseans preserved hams by rubbing them with a mixture of salt and sugar and hanging them in smokehouses for months to cure. The result is country ham, a down-home version of prosciutto that can be served as hors d'oeuvres, as a main dish, or as flavoring for beans and other foods. Perhaps the favorite way of serving country ham is frying it for breakfast, then pouring water and a little bit of coffee into the frying pan to whip up what is called "red eye gravy," best served over biscuits or grits. Country ham is very salty and is an acquired taste. Novices should cut off a little piece and eat it with a big biscuit.

When it comes to hams, Allan Benton, the proprietor of **Benton's Smoky Mountain Country Hams** (2603 U.S. 411 N., 423/442-5003, www.bentonscountryhams.com), makes the best country ham in the state. "I am the product of a mixed marriage," he explains. "My father's family sugar-cured hams, and my mother's people salt-cured them." He uses a mixture of brown sugar and salt, which he and his crew apply to approximately 14,000 hams per year. They begin with a 20- to 26-pound ham, then apply the sugar and salt and store it for 75–80 days. "Hams lose a lot of their moisture during this part of the process." Then the hams are hung for 60–80 days in a room kept at 50°F. "At the end of that time, they've lost 16–18 percent of their weight." Finally, some of the hams are smoked for three and a half days and all of them are hung to cure for 90 or 100 days.

One can get Benton hams plain or smoked— whole or by the slice—and country bacon, all available by mail order as well. Benton's is open 8:30 A.M.–5 P.M. Monday–Saturday.

The L&N Railroad picked this site in 1902 as its Atlanta division administrative headquarters and also set up a facility to manufacture wooden boxcars. The town was built in 1906 virtually from scratch—a two-story station was built first—and by 1927 the people working for the railroad numbered more than 2,250. This was a young man's town; a newly established funeral home almost went broke during its first 10 years, and a music store in Knoxville claimed that it sold more instruments and sheet music in Etowah than anywhere else in East Tennessee. All this changed in 1928, however, when the railroad switched to steel boxcars and moved its offices to Knoxville, a two-punch combination that reduced the number of employees here to 80.

The centerpiece of town today is the wonderfully restored 1906 **L&N Depot and Railroad Museum** (423/263-7840, 8:30 A.M.– 4 P.M. Mon.–Fri., free). Inside, amid wonderful wooden floors and wainscoting, is the museum and art gallery; outside sits a caboose. The museum gives an excellent picture of Etowah's railroad days.

The depot is also the home of the **Tennessee Overhill Heritage Association** (www.tennesseeoverhill.com), a source of excellent information about the sites and events in McMinn, Monroe, and Polk Counties. Etowah is still a rail town and a magnet for rail buffs; the CSX Railroad's main line from Cincinnati to Atlanta passes right by the station, and just across the tracks the railroad maintains a yard office where crew changes are made.

Events

Across and a little way up the street is the 540-seat **Gem Theater,** (www.gemplayers.com) a 1927 moviehouse that now features live events such as the **Gospel Explosion** (423/263-7232) and the **Cousin Jake Tullock Bluegrass Convention** (423/263-7608), which take place, respectively, in the middle of March and the third Saturday in February. The gospel music is of the exuberant black variety, and Cousin Jake was the bass player for the Flatt and Scruggs bluegrass band for 20 years.

Other local events of note include the **Starr Mountain Street Rodders Annual Rod Run** (423/263-7909), which takes place on the first weekend in June, and the **Delano Bluegrass Festival** (423/263-7498), south of Etowah on the second weekend in September.

DELANO

Flower fanciers know this little town as the home of **Delano Daylilies** (153 County Rd. 854, 423/263-9323, www.delanodaylilies.com), where visitors can roam over four acres planted with 1,200 varieties of daylilies. It's open 10 A.M.– 5 P.M. Tuesday–Saturday during flowering season, usually late May through mid July—other times by appointment only. It's located 0.3 miles off U.S. 411.

On Hwy. 163 between Delano and Calhoun is **Trew's Store** (open until midafternoon every weekday but Tues.), a country store that's more than 100 years old. Here visitors can get a sandwich made with hoop cheese and fresh-sliced bologna.

For information, go to the **Tennessee Overhill Heritage Association** (L&N Depot, 423/263-7232, www.tennesseeoverhill.com).

BENTON

Deep in Cherokee country, the grave of **Nancy Ward,** perhaps the most famous Cherokee woman, lies west of the Ocoee River on U.S. 411/Hwy. 33 between Benton and Ocoee. She held the position of "Honored Woman," which entitled her to sit on the tribal council. She could decide the fate of captives and vote on whether or not to wage war. Ward befriended the settlers many times, once sending word that an attack was imminent. She readily introduced practices of the whites, such as raising cattle, to her people, yet adopted bad practices as well; later in life she owned slaves.

The **Old Fort Marr Blockhouse** sits east of the Ocoee. This "fort" is actually one blockhouse from a larger stockade that was first used to supply Andrew Jackson in his war against the Creek. Later it served to protect the Cherokee whose warriors were off fighting the Creek. Its final and most shameful use was that of holding the Cherokee before the Trail of Tears march to Oklahoma.

For more information, contact the **Polk County Chamber of Commerce** (on U.S. 411, 423/338-5040, www.ocoeetn.org, 8:30 A.M.–5:30 P.M. Mon.–Fri., 9 A.M.–2 P.M. Sat.).

White Water and Green Mountains

At Ocoee, U.S. 64 crosses U.S. 411 and follows the Ocoee River upstream. The first body of water is Lake Ocoee, home to personal watercraft and bass boats. Farther upstream the river emerges once more, and the craft become decidedly less motorized—canoes, kayaks, and rafts predominate. The highway follows "The Old Copper Road," the road by which copper was brought from the mines at Ducktown and Copperhill.

This is a beautiful drive, but motorists should be mindful that there are very few gas stations or eateries along the way until getting to the Ducktown/Copperhill area.

OCOEE

Head east on U.S. 64 to the **Ocoee White-** water Center, a log structure built for the white-water events at the 1996 Olympics and host of various competitions ever since. This is a good place to have a picnic, pick up some information about the area, and see the manmade kayaking course. About 2.4 miles of the original Copper Road awaits the hiker or mountain biker, and a 44-mile trail system is under development.

Five miles past Ocoee beside Wildwater Deli and Steakhouse on Hwy. 64 is the **Bucket Man,** also known as Danny Hoskinson, who takes five-gallon plastic buckets and, using a blowtorch and other artistic tools, transforms them into fantastic faces. His art van turns heads wherever he goes. This one-of-a-kind folk artist travels to many shows, but when he's at his shop during warm months he is well worth a stop.

RELIANCE

The center of everything in the village of Reliance is **Webb Brothers Store,** along the Hiwassee River at the intersection of Hwy. 30 and Hwy. 315. This is a good place to, as locals might put it, "come in and sit a spell."

Harold Webb serves as proprietor, ardent preservationist, and provider of "Duckies"—inflatable canoes with kayak paddles that are just perfect for descending the Hiwassee River, a gentle stream very suitable for families. He hauls people up the river and they drift back down to the store. When things are slow, get him to talk about the historic structures hereabouts.

DUCKTOWN

This town got its name from Cherokee chief Cowanneh, whose name translated into "Duck." The town, which sits almost in the middle of the Copper Basin, was dominated for decades by the copper mines whose ore processing denuded the landscape. The National Register of Historic Places lists more than 200 area buildings as part of the Copper Basin Historic District. Smog afflicting the Great Smoky Mountains National Park is Tennessee's most obvious form of air pollution, but for decades that dubious honor was held by an area called the **Copper Basin.**

The **Ducktown Basin Museum** (Burra Burra St./Hwy. 68, one mile from U.S. 64, 423/496-

RAFTING ON THE OCOEE AND HIWASSEE

White-water enthusiasts have long known of the Ocoee River, but the 1996 Olympics vividly showed the whole world the thrills available on this Class III and IV Tennessee stream. Gentler, Class I and II rafting is available on the Hiwassee River.

The Ocoee water is controlled by the Tennessee Valley Authority (TVA), and rafting can only take place when the TVA releases water. A schedule for releases can be found at www.tva.com/river/recreation/ocoeesched. The Hiwassee has no such limitations.

Outfitters offer guided raft trips on weekends April–October and on weekdays June–August. As a general rule, rafters have to be at least 12 years old (6 years old on the Hiwassee) and should plan to get wet; wear sneakers and shorts or a bathing suit. On cold days, put on wool clothing and raingear. Some rafting companies make wetsuits available to customers. In any case, an extra set of dry clothes is a good idea.

Reservations, especially on summer weekends, are a good idea. If you haven't made reservations, however, drive east of Cleveland on Hwy. 64 and you'll see all manner of roadside operations offering to get you into the white water.

An up-to-date list of rafting companies resides at www.tennesseeoverhill.com. Here are some of them:

COURTESY OF THE CHATTANOOGA AREA CONVENTION AND VISITORS BUREAU

On the Hiwassee River:
Hiwassee Outfitters, www.hiwasseeoutfitters.com
Ocoee Outdoors, 800/533-7767 or 423/338-2438, ocoee-outdoors.com
Webb Brothers Float Service, 888/368-7468 or 423/338-2373

On the Ocoee:
Nantahala Outdoor Center, 800/232-7238 or 423/338-5901, www.noc.com
Ocoee Outdoors, 800/533-7767 or 423/338-2438, ocoee-outdoors.com
Ocoee Rafting, 800/251-4800 or 423/496-3388, www.ocoeerafting.com
Quest Expeditions, 800/277-4537 or 423/338-2979, www.questexpeditions.com

5778, Apr.–Sept., 10 A.M.–4:30 P.M. Mon.–Sat.; Oct.–Mar., 9:30 A.M.–4 P.M. Mon.–Sat., $3 adults, $2 seniors and students 12–18, $0.50 for children) recounts the fascinating story of the Copper Basin and those who lived in it. The museum occupies a building on the site of the Burra Burra mine, one of the larger copper mines.

One of the southernmost native cranberry bogs sits amid the **Ducktown Green-Gold Conservancy,** 100 acres with trails and a garden of plants used by the Cherokee.

Fields of the Wood

Visitors to the Ocoee River/Ducktown area are a mere nine miles from Fields of the Wood, possibly the largest piece of religious folk art in the country. The Church of God of Prophecy (COGOP), erected a collection of religious monuments in 1941 that they billed as one of the "Biblical Wonders of the 20th Century."

It certainly is that. Here on 216 acres stands the world's largest cross—150 feet tall and 115 feet wide; the world's largest representation of the **Ten Commandments** on tablets 300 feet square, with letters five feet high and four feet wide; and a replica of the tomb in which Jesus was laid to rest. **Prayer Mountain** has a series of concrete monuments relating church history. Capping it all is a 24-foot-high, 32-foot-wide version of an open **New Testament,** complete with a platform on top, to which visitors are invited to climb. According to COGOP's website, the purpose for all this is to "provide a powerful Gospel witness to multitudes who are unsaved and/or unchurched and who are not being reached by conventional evangelistic methods."

Admission is free to this unconventional place, which is open every day of the year from sunrise to sunset. To get there from Hwy. 64, go north on Hwy. 68 toward Turtletown. Turn right onto Hwy. 123, which, upon crossing the North Carolina state line, becomes Hwy. 294. Fields of the Wood is 1.2 miles ahead on the left. Call 828/494-7855 for more information or take a peek online at www.fieldsofthewood-biblepark.com.

Accommodations

The **White House Bed and Breakfast** (104 Main St., 800/775-4166 or 423/496-4166, www.bbonline.com/tn/whitehouse, $75–85) occupies a two-story Victorian house, circa 1900, listed on the National Register. It features a wraparound porch with rocking chairs. Inside three bedrooms await, all have private baths. The host serves a full country breakfast daily.

The **Company House** (125 Main St., 800/343-2909 or 423/496-5634, www.companyhousebandb.com, $79–89) is an 1850 house with a rocking-chair porch. The six rooms all have private baths and are filled with antiques or reproductions. A fully country breakfast is served.

Also try the **Best Western Copper Inn** (U.S. 64, 800/528-1234 or 423/496-5541).

COPPERHILL

In 1843, when a prospector found a rich vein of what at first looked like gold. Eight years later three mines opened, and soon the town of Copperhill was born. The mines were the source of 90 percent of the copper used by the Confederacy to manufacture bronze cannons in Richmond, Virginia.

To separate the copper from the ore, huge fires built to "roast" out the copper burned 24 hours a day. This created devastation in three stages: Loggers seeking timber to fuel the roasters denuded 30,000 acres of surrounding hillsides; sulfur dioxide fumes from the roasting process killed off any remaining vegetation; and the 50-plus-inch annual rainfall did the rest, carrying the soil into streams and rivers and turning the land into a 56-square-mile moonscape called the **Copper Basin.**

Old-timers claimed it wasn't all bad. The pollution that eliminated the vegetation also drove off flies, mosquitoes, ticks, rats, and snakes. Residents took stubborn pride in where they lived and in the way it shocked outsiders. Locals referred to their blighted area as the "Beloved Scar."

Technological improvements around 1900 led to the end of the open roasting. By 1907, the

COURTESY OF THE TENNESSEE DEPARTMENT OF TOURISM DEVELOPMENT

Copper mining created a moonscape in the mountains.

sulfur dioxide was captured and processed into sulfuric acid, a valuable by-product, and by the 1930s, the company made more money from sulfuric acid than it did from copper. But the damage was done, and it existed for most of the 20th century. Reforestation efforts have ended the blight, which now exists only in the memory of the oldest residents.

Many houses were built on the sides of steep hills in this longtime mining town. Residents would park their cars at the bottom of the hills and climb long staircases, some of which survive. Just north of town is a huge pile of slag, the impurities removed in processing copper. Just one mine produced an estimated 15.6 million tons of ore. Mineshafts, ruins of mining structures, and piles of slag still mark the area.

The **Lodge at Copperhill** (12 Grande Ave., 423/496-9020), once the home of Copperhill's famous Dr. Hicks, bills itself as "the only European-style inn in Appalachia." This means that it charges by the person—$25 per head—not the room. Unlike the inns of old, it does not put guests in with strangers.

New York Restaurant (95 Ocoee St.,

423/496-3855) has country cooking seven days a week, for all three meals.

COKER CREEK

According to an old tale, one day a settler asked a Cherokee lass where she got the gold nugget she wore on a necklace. She told him Coqua Creek, and, for the Native Americans, things went downhill from there. This was the second gold strike in the United States—the first was south of here in Dahlonega, Georgia—and fortune seekers poured into the area, even though it was on Cherokee land. Operations reached a peak before the Civil War but slowed because the gold was too difficult to separate from the surrounding material.

Coker Creek Gallery (Hot Water Rd. off Hwy. 68, 423/261-2157, 10 A.M.–5 P.M. Tues.–Sat.) offers the works of more than 30 area and regional artists in pottery, candles, dolls, metal, woodcarving, weavings, watercolors, and oak baskets.

At **H&W Frontier Willowcraft** (9 A.M.–7 P.M. Mon.–Sat., 9 A.M.–6 P.M. Sun.), 4.9 miles up the mountain from Tellico Plains and 1.5 miles north

THE CURIOUS LEGACY OF DR. HICKS

In the 1950s and '60s, a quiet stream of upper-class women with unwanted pregnancies came from Chattanooga and Atlanta to Copperhill or across the river to McCaysville, Georgia, where a discreet country doctor either performed their abortions or delivered their children. At the same time, couples seeking babies to adopt drove south from the Midwest, returned home with a newborn infant and, a few weeks later by mail, received a false birth certificate attesting they were the child's real parents. For this they were charged anywhere from $250–1,000.

The man at the center of this enterprise was Dr. Thomas Hicks, who practiced medicine in Copperhill for decades and who died in 1972 at the age of 83. His medical sideline was revealed in 1997 when an adopted Ohio woman, curious to learn about her birth parents, found out that she was "a Hicks baby." Her research revealed the existence of as many as 200 children who came into the world in the hands of Dr. Hicks. In 1997, his picture was featured in the *New York Times*, *USA Today*, and on network television. Although the stories were datelined McCaysville, Dr. Hicks, the great-uncle of the author of this book, lived in Copperhill in what is now the Lodge bed-and-breakfast.

Dr. Hicks leaves a curious legacy. He lost his Tennessee medical license in the 1940s after being convicted of illegally selling narcotics. He served time in prison, and upon his release he moved his clinic a few blocks across the state line into Georgia and resumed business as usual. Some of the residents, however, recall him as a generous man who provided free medical care to more poor people than any other local doctor.

---

of Coker Creek, craftspeople make furniture from willow wood. Operators couldn't agree on who would pay for the phone, so they took it out. Nonetheless, visitors can watch the production of chairs, loveseats, tables, and baskets. No furniture is made on Sundays.

TELLICO PLAINS

It was from the site of one of the Cherokee's main towns, Talequah, that a group of Native Americans departed in 1730 to spend four months in England. They toured Canterbury Cathedral, met the king, and were feted all over London. One of this party was Chief Attakullakulla, whose friendship with the British proved invaluable in keeping the Cherokee from joining the French in the French and Indian War and in subsequent dealings with settlers.

Bald River Falls drops 100 feet to the Tellico River, and visitors can see it by driving 4.2 miles out of town on Hwy. 165 and turning right on Forest Service Road 210 and following it for another six miles. The waterfall is easy to see from the car, and a foot trail leads to the top.

To get to the **Tellico Trout Hatchery**

(423/253-2661, usually open 8 A.M.–4 P.M. daily), continue up Forest Service Road 210. Follow it to Sycamore Road, where one can see the hatchery. Someone is almost always there, but call ahead.

CHEROHALA SKYWAY

"Cherohala" sounds like one of the many Native American words that mark Tennessee's landscape and provided the name of the state itself. However, this road owes more to what might be called the Delmar school of nomenclature, also frequently seen in the state, in which two names—Delbert and Margaret, for instance—are joined together to create the name of a trailer park or restaurant. This 52-mile road crosses from the Cherokee National Forest into the Nantahala National Forest, so there you have it—Cherohala.

However it got named, this new road is one beautiful drive. It begins at Tellico Plains—look for Hwy. 165—and crosses the Appalachians into North Carolina, where it inexplicably becomes Hwy. 143, and it ends in Robbinsville. The 40-plus-mile road partially follows an old

Cherokee trading route. The drive features scenic overlooks, picnic areas, **campgrounds,** a swimming beach, hiking and biking trails, but no gas stations or restaurants. Motorists reach an elevation of 5,390 feet at the Santeetlah Overlook, where it will be considerably cooler than at the beginning of the route.

Those who want to make a day of it can drive over the Skyway to Robbinsville, a lovely little burg, turn left on U.S. 129, and come back to Tennessee along Lake Santeetlah. This is a long and winding road, but one with a lot of scenery.

Another option is staying on Hwy. 143 and turning left on Hwy. 28, which will take the motorist along Fontana Lake, with a possible stop at the 480-foot-high **Fontana Dam,** the highest such structure east of the Mississippi. This route should be avoided by those who dislike curvy roads. Either route will eventually put the traveler back on U.S. 129. Still another option is to cross the mountains and turn right on U.S. 129, then right again on U.S. 74 and again on U.S. 64 into Copperhill.

Or one can simply drive over and then come back. As poet David McCord once wrote, "Sometimes it's nice to do things twice."

Knoxville

"We are now talking of summer evenings in Knoxville, Tennessee, in the time that I lived there so successfully disguised to myself as a child." Those words begin James Agee's novel *A Death in the Family*, a wonderful evocation of 1915 life in the Fort Sanders neighborhood.

Agee is part of a long line of creative people to emerge from or do significant work in Knoxville. Clarence Brown, the Metro-Goldwyn-Mayer stalwart who directed more Greta Garbo movies than anyone else, grew up in Knoxville. Actors Patricia Neal, Polly Bergen, and John Cullum also came from Knoxville; Quentin Tarantino spent his early years here.

Radio stations WROL and WNOX were incubators of country music, with Roy Acuff, Chet

Atkins, Archie Campbell, Homer and Jethro, and other luminaries making their marks there before moving on to Nashville. Hank Williams stopped at the Andrew Johnson Hotel before taking his last ride in a Cadillac up Hwy. 11. Don Everly of the Everly Brothers wrote "Cathy's Clown" about his West High School girlfriend, and a shy Sevier County girl first faced television cameras in Knoxville, where early morning viewers caught their first glimpse of Dolly Parton. Eva Barber, the country singer for Lawrence Welk, was born here, as was country singer Carl Butler.

Blues brothers Brownie and Sticks McGhee came from Knoxville; Ida Cox, who penned "Wild Women Don't Have the Blues," lived and died here; and blues violinist Howard

Must-Sees

Look for **M** to find the sights and activities you can't miss and **N** for the best dining and lodging.

M Women's Basketball Hall of Fame: Experience this hotbed of women's collegiate basketball here—or, better yet, go see a University of Tennessee Lady Vols game in person (page 333).

M Classic Theatres: With its mighty Wurlitzer organ console rising through the floor, the **Tennessee Theatre** and its sisters keep the glories of the movie palace alive (page 333).

M Knoxville Museum of Art: Exhibits stir the imagination, perched above the site of the 1982 World's Fair (page 334).

M Blount Mansion: Knoxville's most significant historical site is this first frame house in a town of log cabins (page 335).

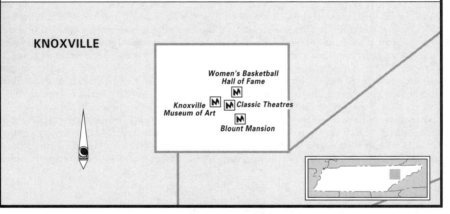

KNOXVILLE

Armstrong lived in Knoxville and wrote songs about it.

Novelist and National Book Award winner Cormac McCarthy grew up in Knoxville and used it as the setting for some of his work. And the city is home to the Reverend J. Bazzel Mull, a gospel-music disc jockey whose gravelly voice has pushed Chuck Wagon Gang records and tapes on clear channel stations from Alaska to Venezuela.

From its earliest days, East Tennessee's largest city has served as the pipeline from the north to the south, and vice versa, with people passing through and headed for greatness.

HISTORY

Like so many of the early towns in Tennessee, Knoxville's location was determined by how eas-

ily it could be defended from the Native Americans. In 1786, James White built a fort on a hill a few miles downstream from where the Holston and French Broad Rivers combine to form the Tennessee River. When William Blount, a signer of the U.S. Constitution whom George Washington appointed governor of the Southwest Territory, came from Rocky Mount to look for a permanent capital for the territory, White's Fort seemed just right. It just happened that Blount owned land nearby.

William Blount was the kind of man who insisted on wearing powdered wigs and silver buckles even on the frontier. Ever the politician, he renamed White's Fort Knoxville in 1791 in honor of Henry Knox, Washington's secretary of war, who doled out money to the Native Americans in hopes of keeping them in line. In short order

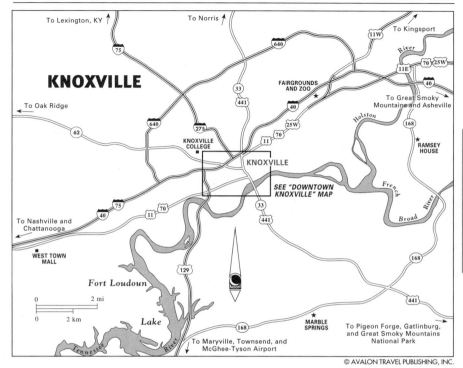

To Lexington, KY
To Norris
To Kingsport

KNOXVILLE

FAIRGROUNDS
AND ZOO

To Oak Ridge

To Great Smoky
Mountains and Asheville

KNOXVILLE
COLLEGE

RAMSEY
HOUSE

KNOXVILLE

*SEE "DOWNTOWN
KNOXVILLE" MAP*

To Nashville and
Chattanooga

WEST TOWN
MALL

Fort Loudoun

0   2 mi
0   2 km   Lake

MARBLE
SPRINGS

To Pigeon Forge, Gatlinburg,
and Great Smoky Mountains
National Park

To Maryville, Townsend, and
McGhee-Tyson Airport

© AVALON TRAVEL PUBLISHING, INC.

Knoxville

Knoxville grew into a booming place with its own newspaper and a college, and it became a center for trade, most of it aimed downstream. Adventuresome merchants cut down trees, built flatboats, loaded them with goods such as flour, lime, and cotton, and shoved off. They drifted down the Tennessee, down the Ohio, and down the Mississippi to New Orleans, where they would sell everything, including their boats.

As Tennesseans moved toward statehood, they wrangled and wrote their state constitution in Knoxville. On June 1, 1796, Tennessee became the 16th state, with Knoxville as its capital. Although it was the state capital, Knoxville never had a capitol. The legislature met in taverns and other convivial buildings to work through its business. As the population in more western parts of the state grew, the pressure to move the seat of government closer to the center of the state led to Nashville's designation as the state

capital in 1826. Fortunately for Knoxville, the college—by 1840 called East Tennessee University—stayed; it was later renamed the University of Tennessee.

Civil War Siege

When the Civil War broke out, Knoxville was a Confederate lion in a den of Daniels; the city had many Southern sympathizers, but they were surrounded by staunch Unionists (some say the city was also full of Unionist sympathizers). In any case, both sides recognized that East Tennessee's largest city was a strategic prize, and accordingly, a Confederate army under General Felix Zollicoffer occupied the city for the first two years of the war.

In 1863, Union General Ambrose Burnside, the popularizer of sideburns, occupied the town. The Southerners had abandoned it to attend to matters near Chattanooga. When they returned in the form of General James Longstreet, they found a well-fortified city awaiting them. Longstreet set up his headquarters west of the city in "Bleak House," built and named by an admirer of the Charles Dickens novel. Longstreet began a siege, planning to bombard and starve the city into submission. The loyal Unionist farmers, however, flummoxed these plans by floating rafts full of food down the river at night.

Longstreet finally attacked Fort Sanders, an earthen fort at the western edge of Knoxville, and was repulsed in a brief but bloody battle. When Union General William Tecumseh Sherman's impending arrival forced Longstreet to give up the siege, the future torcher of Atlanta rode into town expecting to find a starving populace. Instead, he and his staff were served a turkey dinner with all the trimmings, delicious proof that Knoxville was able to withstand a prolonged Civil War siege.

Prosperity

In the years after the Civil War, railroads boomed and so did Knoxville. Its location as a gateway to the South led to a flow of people, goods, and money through the city. Tennessee State University received designation as a land-grant college, rebuilt its bombarded buildings, and became the University of Tennessee. The United Presbyterian Church founded Knoxville College in 1875 to train young black teachers.

Rebuilt railroads and increased steamboat traffic made Knoxville's cash registers jangle. By 1900, the city was the fourth-largest center for wholesale trade in the South, most of this business taking place in what is now the Old City.

With all of this prosperity, the city felt a need to show off. This took the form of the 1910 Knoxville Appalachian Exposition, and the populace had such a good time that three years later the city did it again with a federally financed National Conservation Exposition. One of the ideas that came from this exposition was the notion that a national park should be established in the East. The ideal place would be the Great Smoky Mountains.

Arrival of the TVA

Knoxville suffered along with the rest of the nation in the Great Depression, but because of that economic calamity the city landed the headquarters of the Tennessee Valley Authority (TVA), a federal agency born of the New Deal. It was charged with reducing floods, producing abundant electrical power, and, in a grandiose mission statement, assisting in "the development of the natural resources of the Tennessee River drainage basin and its adjoining territory for the general social and economic welfare of the Nation."

How successfully TVA did all that is still debated, but the impact on Knoxville was overwhelmingly positive. By the time TVA was finished damming Tennessee rivers, the lakes had almost as much shoreline as Florida has coastline. The once-wild Tennessee River that had subjected so many of the old boatmen to harrowing rides became a safe waterway plied by stately barges and a host of pleasure craft.

Sights

ORIENTATION

Knoxville is a city on a hill, or a series of hills, and for visitors can be divided into five areas: Volunteer Landing, Downtown, Old City, the World's Fair Site, and the University of Tennessee (UT). Many of the city's restaurants line Kingston Pike, a four-lane street that heads west from the UT area and extends for miles in parallel with I-40/75. For decades, this was the main east/west route of U.S. 11/70, and now it is the clogged artery serving most of Knoxville's sprawl.

The best place to begin exploring Knoxville is the Knoxville Visitor Center at 301 South Gay Street. Unlike most places of this kind, this one contains a radio station, WDVX, a gourmet coffee bar, and gift shop. To get there from I-40 Eastbound, take Exit 388 to Western Avenue. Turn left onto Western, which becomes Summit Hill Avenue at the intersections with Henley street. Turn right at the third light onto Gay Street and take an immediate right into One Vision Parking lot. Visitor parking is on the left. From I-40 Westbound, take Exit 388A, James White Parkway, to Summit Hill Avenue. Turn right and proceed on Summit Hill to the second light—Gay Street. Turn left onto Gay Street, and take immediate right into One Vision Plaza parking lot.

Volunteer Landing

Tucked down along the Tennessee River and under a bridge, is Volunteer Landing, a great place to catch an excursion boat or train or hoist a microbrew. Exit the interstate at either the Henley Street exit, Exit 388, or the James White Parkway. Once off the Interstate, just follow the signs.

Up the hill from the visitors center is a replica of James White's Fort, the beginnings of Knoxville. The nearby Women's Basketball Hall of Fame, in the building with the big basketball on top, gives visitors a look at this burgeoning sport.

Tennessee Riverboat Company boards passengers for cruises. The Three Rivers Rambler, an excursion train, departs from here, and the Riverside Tavern or Calhoun's will happily quench the thirst of anyone passing through.

Downtown

The hill that constitutes downtown Knoxville is bookended by the twin towers of the TVA's headquarters to the north and the Volunteer Landing on the Tennessee River to the south. Like Chattanooga, Nashville, and Memphis, Knoxville has rediscovered its waterfront, and this, plus a renewal of interest in downtown, has made it a good place to visit.

Blount Mansion, which was the seat of government for America's first territory, sits above the river on a bluff. This is a good place to begin. History fans will also like the East Tennessee History Society Museum on Market Street, which also contains several restaurants and spots to sit down.

Right beside the museum is Krutch Park, an inspired blend of greenery and water that offers respite to the footsore tourist. Farther down Market Street is Market Square, an open-air gathering place for Knoxvillians and site of many events.

Parallel to Market Street is Gay Street, Knoxville's historic main drag. The principal hotel for a long time was the Andrew Johnson Hotel, and it was here that Hank Williams spent his last day on earth. Two wonderful old theaters hold court here, and both are worth a visit. The Lamar House–Bijou Theatre is a former hotel with a theater behind it, while the Tennessee Theatre is a restored 1928 movie palace. A stroll north on Gay Street leads to the edge of the Old City. On the way is Yee-Haw Industries, perhaps the most remarkable print shop in the entire state.

For a downright medieval experience, go to St. Johns Episcopal Cathedral on the north side of the federal courthouse on Main Street and walk the labyrinth. It's just inside the gates.

A CITY WITH MANY IDENTITIES

I t's easy to skip Knoxville, which can seem like only a clot of congestion on the Interstate between various higher-profile tourist destinations. But those who enjoy a good riddle might find something peculiarly satisfying about a few days in Knoxville.

For more than two centuries, Knoxville has struggled with the question of what sort of place it is. It began in 1791 as a federal and later state capital; by the mid-19th century, it had lost that distinction and was becoming a city of factories, one of the most industrialized cities in the South. Many of its textile mills, iron foundries, lumberyards, marble mills, and railroad shops were stumbling in the first half of the 20th century as the city was becoming something else, headquarters for the Tennessee Valley Authority, the nation's largest utility, and a booming university. Although it was here all along, University of Tennessee grew to become a major part of Knoxville's economy and culture in the 20th century.

Though often called an "Appalachian" city, Knoxville is in fact at the bottom of a broad river valley. Knoxville long touted itself as the "Gateway to the Smokies"—but before roads were built into the Smoky Mountains in the early 20th century, the mountains were considered rugged and remote, and few Knoxvillians had even visited them. For those with money, it was easier and faster to get to New York.

Considered a "western" city for much of the 19th century, Knoxville once seemed like one, with 100 saloons and pool halls and deadly gunfights in the streets, a rough-edged, unfinished frontier town even a century after its founding. But most of its trade was with cities of the Atlantic seaboard; today it's in the eastern time zone.

On a map, Knoxville looks like a "Southern" city. During the Civil War it did serve a strange position as the seat of Confederate sympathy in predominantly Unionist East Tennessee. But Knoxville was also one of the most Unionist cities in the South. Soldiers for both sides were recruited on the same downtown street, within sight of each other. Here, as in few other American cities, abolitionists lived next door to slaveholders, who lived next door to free blacks. Some Civil War historians have called it the most evenly divided city in America. In 1861, partisans on both sides fled the city, fearing for their lives.

Old City

A walk north on Gay Street, and right on Jackson Avenue, leads into Old City, a collection of turn-of-the-20th-century brick buildings whose offices and warehouses made Knoxville the center of commerce for East Tennessee. It was also called the Bowery for various debaucheries that reminded people of the New York City area of the same name. Left to slumber for years, the old buildings became home in the '80s to an eclectic mixture of eateries, drinkeries, boutiques, antique shops, galleries, and nightclubs. Here, you'll also find the greatest collection of live music in East Tennessee—dance music, jazz, rock, and blues. On Sunday and other mornings, the Old City offers several places to drink very good coffee while leisurely reading the paper. Don't miss the mural of famous Knoxville musicians; it is on

the side of Sullivan Street Market on Jackson Avenue. During busy weekends, parking can be tight in these parts, so if at all possible try to hoof it.

World's Fair Park

Knoxville was the scene of the 1982 World's Fair, which the world little noted nor long remembered. Now the site is home to a new convention center, which helps tie downtown to the city to the west.

Perhaps the oddest legacy of the World's Fair is one of the weirder-looking buildings in the entire state. The 26-story Sunsphere looks like an architectural paean to a golf ball or a water tower fresh off the set of *The Jetsons*.

The fair site contains several places to stop. The restored L&N Station anchors the upper

Perhaps it was Knoxville's inherent tendency toward interior conflict that bred a unique literary heritage in the city that began with seminal American humorist George Washington Harris and English-born novelist Frances Hodgson Burnett. It has carried on through well-known postwar writers such as journalist and Pulitzer Prize–winning novelist James Agee, National Book Award–winning novelist Cormac McCarthy, and radical poet Nikki Giovanni, all of whom used their peculiar hometown in vivid detail as a setting for some of their best-known work.

That conflict may also have done something to propel a great number of local musicians—Roy Acuff, Brownie McGhee, the Everly Brothers, many others—to national influence.

Today, partly through its connections to the university and Oak Ridge National Laboratories, Knoxville supports clusters of high-tech firms, and it is headquarters to the world's largest theater chain and several national cable-TV shows and channels, including HGTV. UT's now one of the largest universities east of the Mississippi. Knoxville touts an art museum, an opera company, ballet companies, and the South's oldest symphony orchestra. But somehow, beneath its concrete tangle of interstates, much of Knoxville still has the feel of an old working-class industrial railroad city, rusty, overgrown, a little past its prime, but still changing, mutating into something else as yet unknown. Knoxville's story is a complicated one and is, at its core, the history of America.

It's also been called the nation's "Thunderstorm Capital." With a rainfall considerably greater than that of most American cities (including Seattle) in the warmer months, few cities north of Guatemala are as green as Knoxville. The honeysuckle and kudzu have their way, hiding each part of the city from the others. It's a city that people can visit or live in for many years and still not feel that they know it very well. For the curious, that's its charm.

(*Contributed by Jack Neely, a writer for* Metro Pulse *in Knoxville. His latest book is* From the Shadow Side: Stories of Knoxville, Tennessee.*)*

Knoxville

end of the park. Built in 1905, the station now contains a restaurant and shops.

The Candy Factory will further please kids of all ages. This 1919 building was built to house a candy factory, and now it is home to an unabashed firm named The South's Finest Chocolate Factory, which does all of its production here. Visitors can peer through windows to see machines and people busily cranking out the calories, and the shop sells more than 100 kinds of candy.

The University of Tennessee

Cumberland Avenue dips from downtown to a creek and then climbs a hill to the University of Tennessee. The Knoxville campus of UT is the largest in the statewide system; approximately 19,000 undergraduates and 7,000 graduate students study here. The campus contains 229 buildings spread over 532 acres, and a driving tour is the best way to take in the sights.

On the left at the corner of Stadium Drive and Cumberland Avenue is the University Center, which houses an art gallery, two restaurants, and the university's enormous bookstore. Here you can buy books as well as every imaginable item colored orange and white and bearing the UT logo. The center is a good place to find out what's happening on campus—speakers, plays, movies, and so on.

The oldest and most architecturally unified part of the campus lies up a hill adjacent to the University Center. This "hallowed hill," as UT's alma mater puts it, has brick buildings in the collegiate Gothic style. Of these the most impressive is the 1919 Ayres Hall, which crowns the hill.

Knoxville

DOWNTOWN KNOXVILLE

To Mabry-Hazen House

To Knoxville College

SUMMIT HILL DR

E CHURCH

HILL AVE

RIVERSIDE DR

CIVIC AUDITORIUM AND COLISEUM

WOMEN'S BASKETBALL HALL OF FAME

VOLUNTEER LANDING

JAMES WHITE FORT

CRAIGHEAD-JACKSON HOUSE

BLOUNT MANSION

LAMAR HOUSE / BIJOU THEATRE

CLASSIC THEATERS

TENNESSEE THEATRE

FEDERAL COURTHOUSE

EAST TENNESSEE HISTORICAL SOCIETY MUSEUM

CITY/COUNTY BUILDING

KNOXVILLE VISITORS CENTER

KRUTCH PARK

TVA TOWERS

MARKET SQUARE

SUN-SPHERE

KNOXVILLE CONVENTION CENTER

CANDY FACTORY

L&N STATION

KNOXVILLE MUSEUM OF ART

LAUREL THEATRE

UNIVERSITY CENTER

CLARENCE BROWN THEATRE

NEYLAND STADIUM

McCLUNG MUSEUM

THOMPSON-BOLING ARENA

PHILLIP FULMER DR

UNIVERSITY OF TENNESSEE

CRESCENT BEND

FORT DICKERSON

Tennessee River

GAY STREET BRIDGE

HALL OF FAME DR

JAMES WHITE PKWY

S CENTRAL

STATE ST

GAY ST

MARKET ST

WALNUT ST

LOCUST ST

WALL AVE

UNION AVE

CLINCH AVE

CUMBERLAND AVE

W CHURCH AVE

W HILL AVE

MAIN ST

POPLAR ST

ESTABROOK RD

MIDDLE WAY DR

CLARENCE CIRCLE

MELROSE PL

CUMBERLAND AVE

CALEDONIA AVE

TERRACE AVE

LAKE AVE

VOLUNTEER

FRANCIS ST

20TH ST

ANDY HOLT

HOLT BLVD

VOLUNTEER BLVD

PAT HEAD SUMMIT DR

LAKE LOUDON BLVD

PARK DR

UT DR

STADIUM DR

LOWER DR

MELROSE AVE

JAMES AGEE ST

LAUREL AVE

CLINCH AVE

WHITE AVE

GRAND AVE

FOREST AVE

HIGHLAND AVE

16TH ST

17TH ST

14TH ST

13TH ST

12TH ST

11TH ST

10TH ST

BRIDGE ST

CHAPMAN HWY

FORT AVE

CHAPMAN

KINGSTON PIKE

0   0.25 mi

0   0.25 km

© AVALON TRAVEL PUBLISHING, INC.

Red Heads, a barnstorming women's team; and a place to shoot hoops.

Perhaps the most obvious question to out-of-towners is "Why is this museum in Knoxville?" Thanks Pat Head Summitt, head coach of the University of Tennessee Lady Vols, UT became the leading women's program in the country, regularly selling out its 24,535-seat arena.

To get there from I-40, take the James White Parkway exit (Exit 388A). Take the Summit Hill Drive exit off James White Parkway. Turn left onto Summit Hill Drive. At the light, make a right onto Hall of Fame Drive. Proceed through three lights. At the fourth light, turn left onto Hill Avenue. The Hall of Fame will be on the left with parking available next to the building.

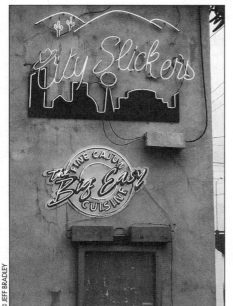

© JEFF BRADLEY

bright lights, Old City

UT has a wonderful theater program with the Clarence Brown Theatre and Carousel Theater. Museum-goers should check out the Frank H. McClung Museum, East Tennessee's main natural history collection, while art lovers should wander over to Ewing Gallery of Art and Architecture.

WOMEN'S BASKETBALL HALL OF FAME

The Women's Basketball Hall of Fame (700 Hall of Fame Dr., 865/633-9000, www.wbhof .com, 10 A.M.–7 P.M. Mon.–Sat., 1–6 P.M. Sun., $7.95 adults, $5.95 seniors, and $5.95 children 6–15) offers a state-of-the-art look at this ascending sport. While most of the inductees, alas, are not as famous as they should be, this story of the female version of basketball takes place in a striking building. Highlights include the old "bloomer" uniforms; a stretch limousine once used to transport the All American

CLASSIC THEATRES

Two wonderful old theaters hold court on Gay Street, and both are worth a visit. **Bijou Theatre** (803 Gay St., 865/522-0832, www.bijouthe-atre.com) began in 1816 as a tavern, then saw service as a hotel. In 1909 the two-balconied Bijou Theatre was built onto the back of the hotel, and vaudeville and other live performances of all kinds entertained generations of Knoxvillians.

Farther north sits the **Tennessee Theatre** (604 Gay St., 865/525-1840, www.tennesseetheatre .com), a movie palace opened in 1928 in the waning days of silent films. Seating over 1,500 people in a massive Moorish-themed hall, this extravagant theatre still has its "mighty Wurl-itzer," an organ console that rises impressively from the floor and whose thunderous notes resonate in the chests of theatergoers.

Although built as a moviehouse, in the past 20 years the theater has increasingly hosted stage shows and concerts, with performers and stagehands bumping into each other in crowded spaces.

Responding to the need for more space, the Tennessee Theatre underwent a $20 million expansion/restoration in 2004, deepening the stage, expanding the orchestra pit, and providing more dressing rooms. Most of this is invisible to theater patrons.

Knoxville

What they can see is the jaw-dropping opulence, with Czech crystals in French chandeliers, Italian marble floors in the lobby, along with painted and gilded sculptures in the main hall. Sitting there as the organ console rises from the floor, hearing and feeling the music, is a treat.

KNOXVILLE MUSEUM OF ART

The Knoxville Museum of Art (1050 Worlds Fair Park Dr., 865/525-6101, www.knoxart.org, noon–8 P.M. Tues.–Wed., noon–9 P.M. Thurs.–Fri., 11 A.M.–5 P.M. Sat.–Sun., $5 adults, free for those under 17) occupies a beautiful building. Pink Tennessee marble graces the outside, while inside visitors will find traveling exhibits as well as exhibits from the museum's collection. Items include folk art, sculpture, paintings, and works on paper. The museum also has a café and a shop.

OTHER MUSEUMS AND GALLERIES

The **Ewing Gallery of Art and Architecture,** in the Art and Architecture Building at on the UT campus (1715 Volunteer Blvd., 865/974-3200, www.sunsite.utk.edu/ewing_gallery), features traveling exhibits as well as those generated from within the university. Admission is free. It's open during weekday work hours and, during the academic year, on Sunday afternoon.

The **East Tennessee Discovery Center** (865/594-1494, www.etdiscovery.org, 9 A.M.–5 P.M. Mon.–Fri., and on varying hours on Sat., $4 adults, $3 seniors and children ages 5 and over, $2 ages 3–4) is one of those children's museums where there are no Don't Touch! signs. Exhibits include, to list a few, "Rocks, Minerals, and Fossils," an insect zoo, and a planetarium. To get there, take Exit 392 off I-40 east of downtown. Take Rutledge Pike southeast until it hits Magnolia Avenue. Go right, then turn right again onto Beaman Road. Follow the signs.

The **Beck Cultural Exchange Center** (Gateway Center at Volunters Landing, 865/524-

8461, www.korrnet.org/beckcec, 10 A.M.–6 P.M. Tues.–Sat., free) houses collections relating to Knoxville's black citizens. Old photographs depicting community events and church life are the bulk of the exhibits.

East Tennessee Historical Society Museum (601 S. Gay St., 865/215-8824, www.east-tennessee-history.org/museum, 10 A.M.–4 P.M. Mon.–Sat., 1–5 P.M. Sun., free) focuses on regional history beginning in the mid-18th century. Exhibits include the surveying equipment used by James White to lay out the original town; "Old Betsy," one of David Crockett's rifles; and early furniture made in East Tennessee. The Civil War section displays uniforms, rifles, pistols, and a regimental flag.

UT's **Frank H. McClung Museum** (1327 Circle Park Dr., 865/974-2144, http://mcclung museum.utk.edu, 9 A.M.–5 P.M. Mon.–Sat., 1–5 P.M. Sun., free) has the best depiction of Tennessee's Indians in the state. Exhibits include life-size murals depicting scenes from five cultural periods beginning in 10,000 B.C. Children will like the pullout drawers containing hands-on items they can examine. One of the more remarkable items is a 32-foot-long canoe carved from a single tulip poplar tree. The museum also has an ancient Egypt collection, minerals and fossils from Tennessee, and Civil War items from Knoxville.

The **Volunteer State Veterans Hall of Fame** (4000 Chapman Hwy., 865/577-0757, 10 A.M.–4 P.M. Thurs.–Sat., 1–4 P.M. Sun., free) contains more than 2,000 war-related artifacts from the Revolutionary War up to and including Operation Desert Storm.

HISTORIC SITES
Andrew Johnson Hotel

This tall, thin brick building at the intersection of Cumberland and Gay Street (912 S. Gay St.) is no longer a hotel, but at one time it was the place to stay in Knoxville. Local historian and author Jack Neely claims that it is the only building that housed Jean-Paul Sartre, Hank Williams, Amelia Earhart, Duke Ellington, Tony Perkins, Liberace, and Sergey Rachmaninoff, who gave the last performance of his life in Knoxville. The

THE WORLD'S MOST GHOULISH RESEARCH FACILITY

In a fenced-off, wooded area behind a parking lot at the UT Medical Center—on the east side of U.S. 129 after it crosses the Tennessee River—lies a three-acre tract innocuously called the Anthropological Research Facility. Those who know its purpose, however, refer to it as "**The Body Farm.**"

Begun in 1977 by Bill Bass, a UT professor and pioneer in the field of forensic anthropology, the Body Farm got its macabre moniker from a 1994 Patricia Cornwell novel by the same name. Here, more than 235 human bodies have been allowed to decay in various situations—in the ground, on the ground, in plastic bags, in vehicles, and in water—so that researchers can learn more about the process of decomposition.

This work is of keen interest to law enforcement people and coroners, who follow research at the Body Farm very closely. Most are interested in finding more accurate means of detecting the time of death of a murder victim. Clues such as the presence of empty pupal cases of maggots, the acids that decaying flesh leaks into the ground, and the smells of putrefaction can help determine the time of death—a crucial part of finding the killer.

The cadavers at the Body Farm come from people who donate their bodies to science, or from unclaimed corpses from crime investigations.

No tours are offered to visitors. For more information, go to www.utk.edu and search for "forensic anthropology."

Knoxville

top floor was once the home of radio station WNOX's *Midday Merry-Go-Round,* a live show famous for launching the careers of country music stars.

Market Square

One block off Gay Street in downtown Knoxville, this open area has been a gathering place for Knoxvillians for over 150 years. Adolph Ochs, who made the *New York Times* into the newspaper we know today, learned his craft in a building facing the Square. James Agee mentions it in *A Death in the Family,* and it was here in 1954 that a local record store began playing a new version of "That's Alright" over loudspeakers in the Square. Hundreds of people flocked in to buy the 45-record, including an RCA talent scout who happened to be in Knoxville. It was just a few months later that RCA bought Elvis Presley's contract from Sun Studios in Memphis.

James White's Fort

Kids love this replica of James White's Fort (205 E. Hill Ave., 865/525-6514, Jan.–Mar. 10 A.M.– 5 P.M. Mon.–Fri.; Apr. 1–Dec. 15, 9:30 A.M.– 5 P.M. Mon.–Sat., $5 adults, $3.50 seniors, $2 children under 12, free for those under 6), not far from the Gateway Regional Visitor Center. Had James White been more assertive, Knoxville might be Whitesville, for he was here first. White built a fort in 1786, and thus provided a place for William Blount to move the capital of the Southwest Territory. James White's fort no longer stands at its original location, but his house and the buildings that surround it give a vivid picture of Knoxville in its earliest days.

Blount Mansion

Blount Mansion, possibly the most significant historic building on this end of the state, introduces the visitor to downtown Knoxville. People who have seen grand houses in Middle and West Tennessee sometimes find Blount Mansion a bit disappointing. It's a nice house, to be sure, but a mansion?

To understand the importance of this house, one has to put it in context. George Washington appointed William Blount governor of the Southwest Territory, and for the first two years Blount operated out of someone else's house at Rocky Mount, near Johnson City. When it was time to move his capital to Knoxville, he wanted to do it in style. With this aim, he ordered one of the first frame—that is, not log—houses west of the mountains, a house with so many glass windows that the Native Americans who saw it called it the

THE DEATH OF HANK WILLIAMS

Hank Williams, who wrote so many great country songs, and who lived his life as if it were a country song, spent his last day in Knoxville. As recounted in Colin Escott's *Hank Williams, The Biography*, Williams had left Montgomery, Alabama, headed for a New Year's Eve show in Charleston, West Virginia. On December 31, 1951, he rode into Knoxville in a Cadillac driven by an 18-year-old Auburn University freshman, Charles Carr. Bad weather had delayed the two, and in an attempt to get to the show on time, they caught a plane at Knoxville's airport, but a snowstorm forced the plane to turn back.

Realizing they couldn't make the Charleston show, Williams and his young driver checked into the Andrew Johnson Hotel on Gay Street. Williams had to be carried to his room. Long plagued by back pain that was exacerbated by long car trips, Williams found relief in morphine shots, and that night, allegedly suffering from violent hiccups, he found a doctor who was willing to administer two shots of the opiate and pronounce him fit to travel.

Porters carried an inanimate Williams back out to his Cadillac, and he and Carr set off at 10:45 P.M. up U.S. 11 West. Carr drove quickly and was pulled over for speeding near the town of Blaine. The arresting officer expressed concern about the comatose figure in the back of the car but was assured that Williams had been sedated.

Carr discovered that Williams was dead after pulling off the road in Oak Hill, West Virginia. Biographer Escott suggests that Williams died either in Knoxville or shortly after leaving town. His most recent single, "I'll Never Get out of This World Alive," reached number one on the country charts. Williams was 29 years old when he died.

"house with many eyes." Knoxville was so raw at this time that it didn't even have a sawmill capable of producing the lumber; it all had to be shipped from points east.

In this house walked Andrew Jackson, and in an office behind the house Blount and others wrote the state constitution. The office served as the territorial capitol from 1792 through 1796, when Tennessee became a state, with Blount as one of its first two senators.

Today's guests can see original Blount family furnishings, a period garden, and occasional demonstrations of activities likely to have taken place here. Visitors to Blount Mansion also get a two-for-one deal. The **visitors center** for the mansion is the 1818 Craighead-Jackson House, an example of Federal-style architecture. Both are open all year. The hours are March–December 9:30 A.M.–4:30 P.M. Monday–Saturday, and 12:30–5 P.M. Sunday. The one-hour tours begin on the hour, with the last tour at 4 P.M. In January and February, the mansion is open Tuesday–Friday only. Visitors may arrange a weekend tour by calling 865/525-2375. Admission is $5 for adults, $4.50 for seniors, and $2.50 for children 6–12. Visit the website www.blountmansion.org.

Civil War Sites

Knoxville was the Confederate center of the most Union-sympathizing part of the state—some claim it was the most evenly divided city in the country.

West of downtown along Kingston Pike lies **Confederate Memorial Hall** (3148 Kingston Pike, 865/522-2371, www.knoxvillecmh.org, 1–4 P.M. Tues.–Fri., $5 adults, $4 seniors, $3 children 12–18, and $1.50 those under 12), otherwise known as **Bleak House.** Confederate General James Longstreet used this 15-room house as his headquarters while laying his futile siege to Knoxville, and some claim it was from the three-story tower of this house that a Confederate sniper killed Union General William Sanders, who was several hundred yards away. What is more certain is that the Union army hit the tower with an artillery shell fired from more than a mile away, killing one sniper and wounding two others. One observer called that "the prettiest single shot of the war." Owned by Chapter 89 of the United Daughters of the Confederacy, the house contains period furniture and artifacts.

Fort Dickerson sits atop a hill across the Tennessee River from downtown Knoxville. Union General Ambrose Burnside set up earthworks here, and the remnants of these still exist on the 85-acre park. The earthworks are at the top of the hill, for what is literally a commanding view of Knoxville, and a section of the park overlooks an abandoned quarry that is full of water. In recent years, Fort Dickerson has become a cruising ground for gay men, so evenings might not be the best time to visit. To get there, take Henley Street across the Tennessee River and turn right up the hill. The entrance to the fort is on the right.

Mabry-Hazen House (1711 Dandridge Ave., 865/522-8661, www.korrnet.org/mabry, 10 A.M.–4 P.M. Mon.–Fri., 1–5 P.M. Sat.–Sun., $4 adults, $2 for children 6–12) was built by Joseph A. Mabry in 1858 and is now on the National Register. In the Civil War, Mabry outfitted an entire Confederate regiment at a cost of $100,000—almost $2 million in today's dollars. This house served as headquarters for both sides during the Civil War. Mabry, along with his son, was killed in a famous gunfight on Gay Street in 1882, an incident reported by Mark Twain in *Life on the Mississippi*. All three participants died on the scene. The Hazen family lived here until 1987, and the house contains their original furnishings. To get there, go east on Hill Avenue to its intersection with Dandridge Avenue.

A two-block walk from the Mabry-Hazen House leads to **Confederate Cemetery,** where 1,600 Southern troops rest.

Knoxville National Cemetery (www.cem.va .gov/nchp/knoxville, beside Old Gray Cemetery) began receiving Union dead in 1863, many of them from the battle of Fort Sanders. Almost 9,000 people rest here, including one Confederate soldier as well as General Robert Neyland, the legendary football coach at the University of Tennessee.

Farragut Folklife Museum (11408 Municipal Center Dr., 865/966-7057, www.farraguttn.com/ museum, 10 A.M.–4:30 P.M. Mon.–Fri., free) is named for David Farragut, born west of Knoxville and famous in the Civil War for this cry of "Damn the torpedoes, full speed ahead!" He was the first admiral of the Navy. This little museum contains Farragut artifacts, papers, and photos, as well as dollhouses, antique tools, and items from the nearby Battle of Campbell's Station. Farragut is a town along Kingston Pike some 13 miles west of Knoxville.

Other Historic Spots

Old Gray Cemetery (543 N. Broadway, 865/522-1424, www.korrnet.org/oldgray) is Knoxville's contribution to the Victorian cemetery-as-garden school of thought. Its 13 acres, dedicated in 1852, were named for the English poet Thomas Gray of "Elegy Written in a Country Churchyard" fame, and it became "Old Gray" when the New Gray Cemetery was opened. This is a wonderful place for a walk. Old Gray's lanes lead through a collection of mausoleums, carved angels, all sheltered by large trees. This place seems to be the resting place of the relatives of famous writers. Tennessee Williams's father is buried here, as is the mother of the woman who wrote *Little Lord Fauntleroy,* along with a cousin of Emily Dickinson. To get there from downtown, walk north on Gay Street, go left at Emory Place, cross Broadway at the Lutheran church, and there it is.

Blount Mansion may have wowed the rubes in town, but outside of Knoxville, Francis Ramsey hired an English-born master carpenter and cabinetmaker to design and build a home appropriate for the owner of more than 2,000 acres of land. **Ramsey House** (865/546-0745, www .korrnet.org/ramhse) was the result, a stately 1795 Georgian stone house—Knox County's first such structure. Knoxville's first elected mayor was born here, and the W. B. A. Ramsey family inhabited the house until 1866. The house is filled with period furniture, including two Chippendale chairs that are original to the mansion, and the paint inside dates back to more than 200 years. The house, which sits on 100 acres

Knoxville

near the confluence of the French Broad, Holston, and Tennessee rivers, is open April–December, 10 A.M.–4 P.M. Tuesday–Saturday, 1–4 P.M. Sunday. Admission is $3.50 for adults and $1.50 for children. To get there, take Exit 394 off I-40, go east on Asheville Hwy., then right onto Hwy. 168. Cross Strawberry Plains Pike, then turn left onto Thorngrove Pike. Ramsey House is on the left.

John Sevier was the first governor of Tennessee, back in the days when Knoxville was its capital, and he lived at **Marble Springs** (865/573-5508) during this time and until his death in 1815. The house is surrounded by seven period structures and contains Sevier family artifacts. Hours are year-round 10 A.M.–5 P.M. Tuesday–Saturday, 2–5 P.M. Sunday. When a guide is present, admission is $5 for adults and $3 for children and seniors. When the guide isn't around, the admission price drops by half. To

get there, take, appropriately enough, the John Sevier Hwy., either from U.S. 129 near the airport, or from U.S. 441.

ST. JOHNS LABYRINTH

The St. Johns Labyrinth is part of a growing number of modern-day versions of ancient and medieval floor patterns outlining a path that people can follow. Some labyrinth walkers use them as a place to pray, others to meditate, or some just to collect their thoughts. This particular one is a copy of the famous labyrinth in Chartres Cathedral. It is open during business hours at the beautiful 1892 St. Johns Episcopal Cathedral, 413 W. Cumberland Avenue, at the intersection of Walnut Street. James Agee was once a choirboy here. Admission is free. To see if it is open on weekends, call 865/525-7347 or visit www.stjohnscathedral.org.

Recreation

KNOXVILLE ZOO

The Knoxville Zoo (865/637-5331, www.knoxville-zoo.com, 9:30 A.M.–4:30 P.M. daily, $10.95 adults, $6.95 children 3–12, $8.95 seniors, free for ages 2 and younger, $3 parking) shelters more than 1,000 creatures representing 225 species, most of which live in re-creations of their natural surroundings. The zoo boasts an extensive large-cat collection, and visitors can walk through habitats with names such as Gorilla Valley, Cheetah Savannah, and Tortoise Territory. The zoo has five African elephants, and local animals are featured as well. Black Bear Falls re-creates the forests of the Great Smoky Mountains and enables visitors to observe black bears amid a setting with four waterfalls. To get to the zoo, take Exit 392 off I-40 east of downtown and follow the signs.

GARDENS AND NATURE CENTERS

Crescent Bend

Crescent Bend (2728 Kingston Pike, 865/637-

3163) is a relatively easy-to-find place that consists of a lovely house, formal gardens, and a collection of 18th- and 19th-century English silver and Federal furniture. The house, also known as the Armstrong-Lockett House, was built in 1834 as the centerpiece of a 600-acre farm. The terraced Italian garden steps down from the house to the Tennessee River. Crescent Bend is open March–December, 10 A.M.–4 P.M. Tuesday–Saturday and 1–4 P.M. Sunday. The gardens are frequently rented out for weddings, so call ahead during wedding season. Admission, which includes a guided tour, costs $4.50 for adults, $2.50 for kids 12–18, and it's free for children under 12.

Ijams Nature Center

Ijams Nature Center (pronounced EYE-ams, 865/577-4717, www.ijams.org) is a 150-acre woodland and meadow area with six miles of nature trails, a city greenway, and a boardwalk. Just two miles upstream of downtown Knoxville, the center is open every day from 8 A.M. until dusk.

To get there from downtown Knoxville, take Henley Street Bridge south to Baptist Hospital. Turn left on Blount Avenue. Bear right on Sevier Avenue. Follow Sevier Avenue and turn left by railroad tracks at major bend onto Island Home Avenue. Follow Island Home Avenue and then turn right by entrance to Island Home Park (still Island Home Avenue) and follow signs to Ijams, approximately one mile on the left.

Knoxville Botanical Gardens and Arboretum

Knoxville Botanical Gardens and Arboretum (2743 Wimpole Ave., 865/637-0004, www.knoxarboretum.com, open during daylight hours) sits on a ridge that was a family nursery business for more than 200 years. The 16-acre site contains whimsical round stone buildings, stone-sided greenhouses, and secret garden paths and alleys. Mature specimens of rare and unusual trees and shrubbery remain, surrounded by thousands of feet of beautiful stone walls that define the planting areas. This site has been purchased by a nonprofit organization that is in the process of opening it to the public.

UT Gardens

UT Gardens (off Neyland Dr. at the Agriculture Campus, 865/974/7324, http://utgardens.tennessee.edu, dawn–dusk daily, free) offers a look at 2,000 annuals and perennials, formal gardens, water gardens, and almost 100 labeled trees. To get there, take Exit 386B from I-40 and go south to the exit for Neyland Drive. Go east on Neyland Drive to the second light, turn left onto the Agriculture Campus, then turn right at the light to enter parking lot number 66, which is across from the entrance to the Gardens.

Seven Islands Nature Center

Seven Islands Nature Center (2809 Kelly Ln., www.sevenislands.org) is a 400-acre wildlife area lying halfway between Douglas Dam and the confluence of the French Broad and Holston Rivers. The center contains a 4.8-mile hiking trail and a cable bridge across the river. This is an excellent place for bird-watching.

To get there, take I-40 East to Exit 402, Midway Road. Turn right on to Midway Road toward Three Rivers Golf Course, pass Curtis Road and Smith School Road intersections, follow the green Seven Islands Wildlife Refuge signs, turn left on to Maples Rd, turn right at the intersection with Kodak Rd, turn left on to Kelly Lane at the large, white Bethel Church. Kelly Lane takes you to the gate.

SPORTS

Sports are a very big deal at UT. Neyland Stadium is the third-largest stadium in the country, seating more than 104,000 people, and the Thompson-Boling basketball arena seats 24,535 for basketball games. UT is a member of the Southeastern Conference, and fans enjoy high-level performances in 17 NCAA sports. The women's basketball team has one of the more successful programs in the country, coached by Pat Head Summitt.

Tickets, at least for the football games, are hard to come by. If fans show up the day of the game, however, all manner of helpful people will emerge from parking lots and dark alleys with tickets to sell. Smart consumers wait until five minutes before kickoff before forking over the cash.

To find out who's playing what, call the **UT Sports Information Office** at 865/974-1212. To buy tickets, call 865/656-1200. Out-of-town fans can call 800/332-VOLS (332-8657) from anywhere in Tennessee. Or try www.utsports.com.

Entertainment and Events

PERFORMING ARTS

The University of Tennessee has a very strong theater department, and Knoxville enjoys excellent productions by professional thespians as well as students. The crown jewel is the **Clarence Brown Theatre** built with funds provided by the alumnus and longtime MGM director. Adjacent to the Clarence Brown is the in-the-round **Carousel Theater.** For information about plays and tickets at all UT theaters, contact 1714 Andy Holt Avenue, 865/974-5161, www.clarencebrowntheatre.com.

Jubilee Community Arts (1538 Laurel Ave., 865/522-5851, www.korrnet.org/jca) located off 16th Street in the Fort Sanders neighborhood near the University of Tennessee, is dedicated to preserving and presenting the traditional arts of the Southern Appalachians. They offer concerts of fiddle, banjo, string bands, a cappella singing, gospel, blues in the **Laurel Theater,** a former church built in the 19th century.

NIGHTLIFE

As the largest city on this end of the state, and with the biggest college in the state right here, Knoxville offers a wide array of places to go and things to do. The following were compiled by Karyn Adams, freelance writer.

Baker-Peters Jazz Club (9000 Kingston Pike, 865/690-8110, www.bakerpetersjazzclub.com, Mon.–Sat., live jazz Tue.–Thurs.; live blues Fri.–Sat.) housed in a Civil War–era home, plays to an older set with live jazz and blues, an onsite humidor and a full menu of high-end American cuisine. Buy a cigar, then sidle up to your waitress to hear the story of Abner, the club's own ghost.

Luminescent and coy, in a low-lit, tight tables kind of way, **Lucille's** (100 N. Central St., 865/637-4285, Thurs.–Sat.) feels like another time and another place. In the summertime, the room expands through a backdoor that opens onto a courtyard for live jazz. Martinis and a full

bar keep the spirits high; a full menu of upper crust creations is also available.

Visitors will get noticed at **The Spot** (6915 Kingston Pike, 865/588-8138, www.beerspot .net, open every night), because its clientele is composed of 95 percent regulars. College frat dudes and post-college hangers-on unite in a jolly beerfest every night. Music is always local, and doesn't stray far from the traditional tunes of rock and blues. You won't find any fancy drinks or foufou food at The Spot—this is a beer-only dive.

Americana and singer/songwriter nights are standard fare at **Barley's Taproom and Pizzeria.** (200 E. Jackson, 865/521-0092, www.barleystap room.com/knoxville, open every night). The two-story building has plenty of room to house a full bar and 56 taps—the largest beer selection in town. And to make a good scenario even better, the pizza at Barley's gets a definitive thumbs-up.

Like a smooth operator, **Michael's** (7049 Kingston Pike, 865/588-2455, www.michael-sontheweb.com, open daily) has been hitting on Knoxville for more than 20 years. Located in west Knoxville near West Town Mall, you can shake your boots to disco and '80s dance hits, dine in the back room, and partake a plethora of drinks. The crowd doesn't care where you've been or who you came with, only where you're going and whose on your arm as you leave.   Sporting more than 10,000 square feet of dance floor space, the **Electric Ballroom** (1213 Western Ave., 865/525-6724, www.electricballroom.net, Tue.–Sat.) attracts a wide variety of patrons and performances: gay and straight, drag shows and live local bands, DJs and raves. Located underneath a bridge of I-40 in a renovated warehouse, the Ballroom's karaoke, male revues, and dance parties await.

When you're down, when you're out, when you're almost broke, or have just been broken up with, the **Long Branch** (1848 Cumberland Ave., 865/546-9914) is the place to slum and knock 'em back. The Branch is an odd original meshed among carbon-copy, fast-food joints. This stretch of Cumberland Avenue is locally known as "The Strip," for its high concentration of average commercial establishments, and runs between the University and the student-populated neighborhood of Fort Sanders. Music acts vary from thrash to trash on an unpredictable schedule. This is the place your mother warned you about—smoking, beer, and pool tables, every dang day of the year.

Tucked inside one of the numerous restored Victorians of 4th & Gill (the intersecting streets of the neighborhood) is **Sassy Ann's House of Blues** (820 N. 4th Ave., 865/525-5839, www.sassyanns.com, Wed.–Fri.). Wednesday and Sunday nights open the floor to blues jams for all interested and willing musicians; Friday's feature some of the South's best blues and R&B artists. There are synesthetic moments to be had on a hot summer night, blues belting into the humidity, and a cold drink of choice from the full bar.

4620 Jazz Club (4620 Kingston Pike, 865/766-0994) opened without fanfare or to-do, lending an air of speak-easy mystique to its underground digs. Its name is simply its street address, yet this understated establishment is one of K-town's preferred spots for more sophisticated nightlife. The upscale atmosphere touts a martini bar and regular live performances of jazz, R&B, and funk.

Although a laid-back, neighborhood watering hole, **Preservation Pub** (28 Market Sq., 865/524-2224, www.preservationpub.com, open every day and night) takes its role in the community very seriously. In addition to being vocally dedicated to preserving downtown's historic structures and unique culture, the Pub also takes fiscal actions—proceeds from the bar's tabs go to community charities and efforts. A broad spectrum of brews on tap and a full bar keep thirsts quenched while live shows of alt-music (of all flavors) tune up several nights a week. But save some change for the jukebox—it's stocked with local music and everyman favorites.

One location, three identities. **Blue Cats** (125 E. Jackson Ave., 865/544-4300, www.bluecatslive.com, Tues.–Sat.), the premier venue for drinks, dancing, and diggin' your favorite live music, is the anchor concept. Shows cover all types of music from the about-to-make-it-big circuit (Norah Jones made her Knoxville debut at this in-timate showcase) to already established rock and bluegrass groups. **Tonic** (Thurs.–Sat.), the sister club of Blue Cats, is connected to its brother by a cool, front-facing courtyard. Catering to the college-age dance crowd, the music cranks up, the drinks flow, and the bar food keeps even the wallflowers happy. On Saturday nights, the entire property takes on its third alter ego to become **Fiction@125** (Sat. only). It's a dance party with all the DJs and VIP-ness one can stand.

An incubator for music that defies easy description and tidy pigeonholing, **The Pilot Light** (106 E. Jackson Ave., 865/524-8188, www.thepilotlight.com, Wed.–Sun.) deserves great credit for keeping the town's innovative and experimental music scene alive and kicking. A volunteer effort among a small circle of dedicated music lovers—the Pilot Light is still on and burning strong. Set your expectations for easy-to-drink beer, random and distressed fixtures, cheap covers, and a generally considerate, if not tragically hip, clientele. Sunday nights are free movie nights with showings of the simply classic to the simply bizarre.

CRUISES AND TRAINS

Passengers on cruises offered by **Tennessee Riverboat Company** (865/522-4630, www.tnriverboat.com) can choose from a sightseeing cruise or a dinner cruise. The former lasts one-and-a-half hours, while the latter takes a leisurely two hours. Seeing the sights costs $10.43 for adults, $6.95 for kids, and it's free for children under 3. Dinner cruises cost $27.95 for adults and $17.50 for kids Sunday–Wednesday. On weekend nights, the dinner cruise costs $34.90 and $17.50. The 325-passenger boat is hard to miss on the waterfront; it docks at 300 Neyland Drive. The boat runs April–New Year's Eve.

Three Rivers Rambler (865/524-9411, www.threeriversrambler.com, $16.95 adults, $9.95 children) is a train ride from the Volunteer Landing near the Gateway Regional Visitor Center up the Tennessee River to the confluence of the Holston and the French Broad Rivers—thus the name. Pulled by a 1925 locomotive, the train takes one hour and twenty minutes to go 5.5 miles and then come back the same way. Highlights include the Three Rivers Bridge and a look at several marble quarries. The train runs makes two trips on weekend afternoons from late May through mid-August and again on weekends in October and in December.

FESTIVALS AND EVENTS

The **Dogwood Arts Festival** (865/637-4561, www.dogwoodarts.org) gets its name from the many dogwood trees that grace Knoxville. Held in April, the festival offers all manner of performing arts, big-name concerts, athletic activities, and various events all over the city. Knoxville suburbanites position lights under their dogwood blossoms and show off their property at night to hordes of slow-driving admirers along "Dogwood Trails," whose intricacies are marked by pink arrows painted onto streets.

Rossini Festival (www.knoxvilleopera.com) held in April, and combines an Italian street fair with performances of opera over a period of days.

Later in spring, **Kuumba** in late June is a huge African American festival held in Chilhowee Park.

If visitors somehow miss the Fourth of July, then **Boomsday** (865/693-1020), held the night of Labor Day, will catch them up very quickly. Said to be the largest fireworks display in the Southeast, it's held on the waterfront.

The biggest fair on this end of the state is the **Tennessee Valley Fair** (865/215-1470, www .tnvalleyfair.org, $7 adults, $3 children 6–11), held every year beginning on the first Friday after Labor Day. The usual agricultural contests and exhibitions take place, along with live entertainment, usually of the country music persuasion. To get to the fairgrounds, take the Cherry Street exit off I-40 east of downtown Knoxville, go south, then turn left onto Magnolia. Or just follow the crowd.

When the weather is warm and Thursday evening rolls around, thousands of people pour onto Market Square to enjoy one of Knoxville's shining successes—**Sundown in the City** (www.sundowninthecity.com). When this free concert series began in 2001, it focused on quantity, totaling 25 shows in all. In recent years, the schedule has retooled to roughly twelve shows per season, but the acts, such as Gillian Welch and Bela Fleck and the Flecktones, just keep getting better. Beer is for sale, but coolers, chairs, and pets are not allowed.

Accommodations

BED-AND-BREAKFASTS AND INNS

Hotel St. Oliver (407 Union Ave., 888/809-7241 or 865/521-0050, $55–180) contains 24 rooms filled with antiques and reproduction antiques in a downtown structure just off Market Square. When local leading lady Patricia Neal comes to town, this is where she stays.

The **Maple Grove Inn** (8800 Westland Dr., 800/645-0713 or 865/690-9565, www.maple-groveinn.com), on 16 acres west of Knoxville, is a 1799 house whose eight rooms all offer private baths. Two master suites feature fireplaces and whirlpool baths. Guests have access to a

swimming pool and tennis court. Rates run $125–250 on weekends or $95–200 during the week for two people. Dinner is available for guests on Thursday–Saturday nights.

Maplehurst Inn (800 W. Hill Ave., 800/451-1562, www.maplehurstinn.com, $69–150) sits discreetly in a riverside neighborhood between downtown Knoxville and the University of Tennessee. More like a small European hotel than a bed-and-breakfast, this place is small enough to allow you to enjoy the interesting guests and large enough to comfortably escape the bores. Eleven rooms with private baths on four separate floors overlook the Tennessee River.

HOTELS AND MOTELS

Like most larger cities, Knoxville is blessed with national-chain hotels—Hilton, Holiday Inn, Hyatt, and Radisson—downtown and the usual motels stretched along the Interstates. Keep in mind that hotel rooms are very difficult to find when the University of Tennessee plays a home football game. For a list of weekends to avoid, go to www.govols.com/mens/football.

Options include **Days Inn Campus** (1719 W. Cumberland Ave., 800/DAYS-INN, $60 and up), **Executive Inn** (3400 Chapman Hwy., 866/496-4496, www.executive-inn.com, $40 and up), **M Hilton Knoxville** (501 W. Church Ave., 865/523-2300, www.hilton.com, $89), **Holiday Inn Select Convention Center** (525 Henley St., 800/465-4329, www.holiday-inn.com/tys-downtown, $100 and up), **M Marriott Knoxville** (500 Hill Ave., 800/228-9290, www.marriott.com/tysmc, $89), **M Radisson Summit Hill** (401 W. Summit Hill Dr., 800/333-3333, www.radisson.com/knoxvilletn, $140), **Super 8 Motel Downtown/West** (6200 Papermill Rd., 800/800-8000, www.super8.com, $40 and up).

Food

Knoxville's local cooking can be, at first blush, overshadowed by cookie-cutter, corporate, chain restaurants. But a closer look will reveal, peppered throughout the city, individually owned and operated beacons of great food that will surprise and satisfy. Whether you're after upscale dining, international flavors, or budget eats, the food scene in Knoxville can deliver. The following were compiled Karyn Adams, a great freelance writer in Knoxville.

ITALIAN

Serving gourmet pizzas, sandwiches, salads, and daily specials, the **M Tomato Head** (12 Market Sq., 865/637-4067, open every day, entrées $6–20) occupies an historic building in the heart of downtown. Its location, commitment to innovative and garlicky-good food, monthly rotating art, kid-friendliness, and eclectic staff have made it much more than a restaurant—it's a cultural hub of Knoxville. The menu is diverse and all made from scratch, from the pizza dough and bread to the salad dressings and pesto. Vegetarians, vegans, and carnivores all frequent the Head and leave happily fed. A broad collection of beers and a carefully selected wine list are additional perks. The Sunday brunch boasts all the traditional dishes plus Southwestern specialties. Grab a table outdoors if weather permits. Market Square makes for great people-watching.

These days, Italian cuisine is largely overshadowed by national chains, but **Naples** (5500 Kingston Pike, 865/584-5033, lunch Tues.–Fri., dinner nightly, entrées $6–20) is an outpost of the individually owned and operated Italian restaurant. Its red neon sign and rosy-hued interior have been luring couples and families for decades. Traditional favorites—spaghetti and meatballs, veal Marsala, eggplant Parmesan, and lasagna—are prepared every night. Try the *pane basilica* for a doughy, balsamic vinegar–spiked appetizer.

The mantra of **Puleo's Grille** (I-40 Exit 398, Strawberry Plains, 865/673-9101; or 260 N. Peters Rd., 865/691-1960, daily, entrées $6–20) is "Southern roots, Italian heritage," which aptly describes their menu's seemingly conflicted specialties. Respectable pasta primavera and chicken Parmesan are stationed next to damn good shrimp and grits and country fried steak. Odd as it may sound, it works.

NEW AMERICAN

New American, upscale American, contemporary cuisine, call it what you will, but Knoxville's got plenty of it. **By the Tracks Bistro** (5200 Kingston Pike, 865/558-9500, dinner nightly daily, entrées $12–30) sits at the top of this category with a modern, sophisticated atmosphere and refined selections such as cumin-crusted

M
Knoxville

THE ORIGIN OF MOUNTAIN DEW

Among other distinctions, Knoxville is the birthplace of Mountain Dew. Two brothers, Barney and Ally Hartman, created the drink and sold it from a bottling plant they built on Magnolia Avenue in 1932. Concocted as a mixer to go with whiskey, it got the name "mountain dew" from a Tennessee slang term for moonshine whiskey.

Capitalizing on the moonshine theme, the brother advertised the drink with images of a stereotypical bewhiskered hillbilly complete with rifle, hound dog, and outhouse. Persons of a certain age can recall the "Ya—hoo! Mountain Dew" ads from those days.

In 1954, the brothers entered into a franchise deal with Johnson City's Charles Gordo—bottler of Dr. Enuf, another East Tennessee creation—whose plant manager, Bill Bridgforth, fiddled with the formula and came up the version sold today. Barney Hartman died, his brother sold the Mountain Dew name to Gordon, who sold it again. Pepsi-Cola bought the rights to Mountain Dew in 1964, and they canned the hillbilly themes in an effort to market to the young the restless.

chicken breast with goat cheese, New Zealand lamb chops, fennel-braised salmon, or a roasted squash tamale. But the Bistro remembers the side of the tracks from which it came (its erstwhile location being a postage-stamp building beside a railroad). Black-eyed peas, chowchow, and fried green tomatoes are regular sides.

Most established and historic of this category is **Regas** (318 N. Gay St., 865/637-3427, Mon.–Sat., entrées $10–25). Older generations remember the steak and seafood restaurant as an extravagance, and it's still a special place. Although today, it's trafficked by daytime politicos more than evening couples in search of haute cuisine.

Riverside Tavern (905 Volunteer Landing, 865/637-0303, daily, entrées $7–25) occupies an enviable location on the city's riverfront. Generous salads (the baby spinach salad with granny smith apples is a favorite), and anything—from pizza to steak—put through the wood-fired rotisserie oven will complement the view of the Tennessee and the sun setting behind the Gay Street bridge.

The Bearden Hill area, connected to downtown by a well-groomed, old-money stretch of Kingston Pike, has recently become a diner's mecca, including an understated little place called **Little Star** (5003 Kingston Pike, 865/558-0210, dinner Tue.–Sat.). Playful chef's tastings intersperse each plate of Little Star's three-course prix-fixe menu. The $38 price tag is incredibly

reasonable for such pleasures as roasted quail with foie gras stuffing, grilled venison tenderloin, and chocolate panna cotta on almond shortbread, but diners should expect their palates, and wallets, to be seduced by additions from a stellar wine list and enticing small plates.

Cozied inside Bearden's Homberg shopping area is another gastronomic gem, **Bogartz** (5032 Whittaker Dr., 865/602-3583, dinner Tue.–Sat., entrées $12–30). With gusto, it delivers a wide range of inspired American cuisine: sautéed scallops sided by unforgettable cheese grits, filet "sliders" that melt in your mouth, roasted beet salads, gumbos, and duck. It's high cuisine in an environment that allows you to be as casual, or as formal, as your occasion requires. Of note, a recent annex to the location, called **Ciao,** is a culinary playground for chef/owner Bruce Bogartz. It offers an equally tempting, Italian-focused addition to the seasonal Bogartz menu.

FRENCH

Fine, French, and fantastic, **The Orangery** (5412 Kingston Pike, 865/588-2964, lunch Mon.–Fri., entrées $18–22, dinner Mon.–Sat., entrées $35–50) is a feather in Knoxville's cap of upscale dining. Opulent décor and dignified service make both lunch and dinner an event to anticipate, sit back and to fully enjoy. Lamb *loin au poivre,* rosemary-infused eggplant coulis, mustard aioli, garlic, spinach, balsamic syrup, and a wine list to match. It remains a place to see and be seen.

MEXICAN/SOUTHWESTERN

Tortilla Macs' (722 Gay St., 865/546-0620, breakfast and lunch Mon.–Fri., entrées $5) offers the Big Pig burrito, filled with chipotle barbecued pork, jalapeño coleslaw, corn salsa, and pico de gallo is a sure bet. You'll also find tasty steak, chicken, and veggie fillings. Made to order, the appealing and affordable lunch will have you rubbing elbows with folks from all walks of life— from lawyers and artists to writers and bankers.

El Charro (6502 Kingston Pike, 865/584-9807, daily, entrées $5–12), a favorite among Knoxvillians for more than 20 years, can be found westward in the Bearden area. The fare is standard Mexican American with the extra bonus of televised Spanish soap operas and soccer.

Chez Guevara is a bit further west, (8025 Kingston Pike, 865/690-5250, dinner nightly, entrées $7–14). The clever name belies a similar attitude of fun experimentation with Mexican ingredients: the salmon, goat cheese, and cucumber salsa burrito is a revolutionary experience. The bar at front is almost always packed because the margaritas are memorable, even after you've had enough to forget. Expect the green salsa, part of the free appetizers, to disappear quickly.

ASIAN

Stir Fry Café (7240 Kingston Pike, 865/588-2064, daily, entrées $8–17) delivers Thai and Asian food in an atmosphere spiked by funky blues and local artwork. Tom Yum soup, spicy noodles, a fine rendition of pad Thai, plus a laundry list of modernized entrees and traditional curries give even the nonadventurous eater a full plate. For the veg-head in your group, there are oodles of eats with some of the tastiest tofu this side of Bangkok. Weather permitting, you'll find outdoor seating available.

China Inn (6450 Kingston Pike, 865/588-7815, daily, entrées $5–24) leads the plentiful pack of Chinese restaurants in town, electing to steer from the quantity (that is, buffet) concept and aim for quality. Dim Sum is the standout among the expected entrées of lo mein, chow mein, moo shu pork, and egg foo young. The blue-toned dining room, accented by quiet aquariums, makes the meal a calm and pleasing experience.

The exterior of **Tomo** (7315 Kingston Pike, 865/688-1161, dinner Tue.–Sun., entrées $7–15), a Japanese/sushi restaurant, at is a cramped strip mall that lacks charm. But inside, the simple décor, the exquisitely fresh sushi and the subtle soba and udon noodles, miso soups, and tempura lure Tennessee good ol' boys and Japanese businessmen alike. The goyza, steamed pork and cabbage-filled dumplings, will start the night out right.

Korea House (1645 Downtown West Blvd., 865/693-3615, lunch and dinner Tue.–Sun., entrées $7–15), another diamond in the rough of west Knoxville shopping centers. Known for friendly service, a cozy and nonsmoking environment, soothing noodles, soups, and numerous vegetarian entrées. If you've never had Korean food, this is a respectable place to embark on your first experience.

MIDDLE EASTERN

Pakoras, samosas, nan, curries, dals, and kormas run from mild to extra hot at **Sitar Indian Restaurant** (6004 Kingston Pike, 865/588-1828, lunch and dinner daily, $6–30). The lunch buffet is worth the $6 price tag. The variety of dishes and plentiful servings makes this spot ideal for larger groups wanting to sample a bit of everything by dining family style. Request your meal "hot" and your server will ask "American hot or Indian hot?" Choose wisely.

King Tut's Grill (4132 Martin Mill Pike, 865/573-6021, daily $6–16), in south Knoxville, is, truth be told, more about the experience than the food. You'll dine fine—falafel and hummus, pasta and sandwiches, veggie plates and more— but this family-owned and -operated business focuses on providing a laughably good time in a pint-sized space. Owner Mo Grigis (that's short for Mohammed) interacts with every diner to ensure satisfaction and conviviality.

Knoxville

STEAKS AND BURGERS

Located at a stretch of road beside the UT campus known to locals as "The Strip" (for all the student-targeted fast food, mini-marts, gas stations, bars, and shops) the **Sunspot** (1909 Cumberland Ave., 865/637-4663, daily, entrées $7–23) is bohemian enough for faculty and students, yet straight enough for staff and business folk. The eats run a similarly wide gamut, earning awards for vegetarian fare while still being able to boast an entree named The Carnivore Special. The beer selection will not disappoint.

After a fire destroyed its landmark, south Knox location, **Ye Olde Steakhouse** (865/577-9328, dinner nightly, entrées $12–30)—renowned for its slabs—relocated to the architecturally exquisite L&N train station at the corner of Henley and Western. Plans to return to a rebuilt empire at 6838 Chapman Highway are steadfast, but to date, unrealized. Nonetheless, massive baked potatoes, iceberg salads, iced tea, port wine cheese, and crackers set a casual tone for the flavorful filet mignon, rib eye, porterhouse, and King steak burger. Satisfying chicken and fish specialties are also available.

For the burger set, the coup de grâce will be found at **Litton's** (2803 Essary Rd., Fountain City, 865/688-0429, Mon.–Sat., entrées $7–22). A hint: Don't wait on the hostess to register your party. Grab the chalk and write your name on the board. The burgers are addictive with the fish sandwich earning a close second. There's also a daily blue plate, but the trickiest decision is between the fries and the onion rings. Get 'em both.

BARBECUE

Once folks find a barbecue joint that suits their taste and style, they tend not to stray from their beloved. Knoxville presents a different choice on almost every corner. To sample them all would require a local ZIP code and great determination. Some are homegrown empires dotting the city in every direction, others are imported franchises that have hard-won the taste buds of the natives.

Diners can take solace that by embarking on a tour of town 'cue, they'll be taking on the enviable job of sampling some of the south's best.

Started in 1967 in Seymour, Tennessee, **Buddy's Bar-b-q** (daily, $5–15) serves basic 'cue and beans and full racks of ribs, fast-food style. With six locations in Knoxville alone, you'll find at least one in any direction: 4500 N. Broadway, 865/687-2959; 4401 Chapman Hwy., 865/579-1747; 3700 Magnolia Ave., 865/523-3550; or 5806 Kingston Pike, 865/588-0528.

At **Corky's,** Memphis-style barbecue—slow-cooked over hickory—has won awards and accolades from locals and Martha Stewart alike. It's located at 4525 Kingston Pike 865/588-8553; entrées $5.50–16.

If a more diverse and refined menu is necessary, in addition to the requirements of ribs and barbecue, the hometown favorite is **Calhoun's** (daily, entrées $7–20). Its signature location is near the university on the Tennessee River (400 Neyland Dr., 865/673-3355), but seats (and bibs) can be had at two other locales in town: 10020 Kingston Pike 865/673-3444; and 6515 Kingston Pike, 865/673-3377.

Sonny's (350 N. Peters Rd., 865/692-9941, daily, entrées $7–30), a franchise import from Florida, is a fast, casual establishment that offers pulled, sliced, or barbecued pork, as well as tasty ribs.

Next door there's **Famous Dave's** (208 Advantage Pl., 865/694-9990, daily, entrées $7–19), a chain from Wisconsin boasting Georgia-style BBQ and St. Louis–style ribs and an addictive Rich & Sassy sauce. The fact that both of these spots manage to hold their own in a town thick with native 'cue should be confirmation enough.

For true, shack-smoked barbecue, hometown hushpuppies, and hand-cut fries, set your compass east for **F.A.T.S.** (2701 Whittle Springs Rd., 865/524-1929, Mon.–Sat., entrées $3–11). The name, formed from the first names of owner's Fred and Tricia, is proof of the place's deep family roots. The focus is on the food, not the milieu. There's no real place to park your bum while you eat (other than a couple of lawn chairs out front) so plan on tailgating or making a picnic of the meal. If Fido is along for the ride, ask for a dog bone and the kind folks at F.A.T.S will oblige. Go Friday or Saturday night for fresh, fried catfish.

DESSERTS

Those with a sweet tooth should forego other's temptations and beeline to **Magpies** (112 South Central, 865/673-0471, Wed.–Sat.).

Owned and operated by Ms. Peggy Hambright, the shop started out as an exclusive purveyor of wedding cakes then branched into all things sugared and wonderful. Choc-o-gasm cookies, strawberry rhubarb pies, decadent cakes, pecan tarts, and real banana pudding are all made from scratch, every day, from real butter and the finest of chocolates and ingredients. Both individual servings and whole cakes/pies are available.

Information and Services

SHOPPING

Like those in most Southern cities, Knoxville's big stores have fled to shopping malls. In their place, however, have sprung up interesting communities of shops. Try the Old City area, and Homberg Place, near the corner of Kingston Pike and Homberg Place, west of the University of Tennessee.

Book Eddy (2537 Chapman Hwy., 865/573-9959, www.bookeddy.com) is a book-lover's dream come true—85,000-plus used books on every subject imaginable. Go a half-mile south of downtown on Henley Street/Chapman Hwy.

If you're looking for something old in the Old City, **Jackson Antique Marketplace** (111 E. Jackson Ave., 865/521-6704) offers 24,000 square feet of antiques.

Arts and Crafts

Jim Gray is perhaps the best-known artist in this part of the state. His oils and drawings depict seascapes, Tennessee landscapes, people, wildflowers, and birds. His bronze statues include that of Dolly Parton in Sevierville, and of Andrew Johnson in Greeneville. The **Jim Gray Gallery** (5615 Kingston Pike, 865/588-7102, www.jimgraygallery.com) offers works in a variety of media from this talented artist.

The **Victorian Houses** at the corner of 11th Street and Laurel Avenue also have shops containing original art and fine crafts. Given the changing tastes of the public and the vagaries of the

artistic existence, shops come and go, but the quality remains high. The shops are open 10 A.M.–5 P.M. Tuesday–Saturday, 1–5 P.M. Sunday.

West of downtown is **Hanson Gallery Fine Art and Craft** (5706 Kingston Pike, 865/584-6097, www.hansongallery.com), offering oils, Thomas Pradzynski's Parisian street-scenes serigraphs, lithographs, and gifts.

In Farragut, **Homespun Crafts and Antique Mall** (11523 Kingston Pike, 865/671-3444) is a large assembly of artists and dealers selling antiques, jewelry, pottery, and all manner of creations. It's near Exit 373 off I-40/75.

Yee-Haw Industries (413 S. Gay St., 865/522-1812, www.yeehawindustries.com) uses letterpress, a type of printing seldom used anymore, to crank out posters that are wonderful works of folk art. Typical is a poster of Hank Williams Secret Theory #29, which reads as follows:

Ole Hank was a drinking man. I heard stories that he had a hollow leg. They say that his woman cheated on him. I think that if Hank was around today he would probably play jazz and he would probably kick Jr. in the ass. He was a man of double vision. He saw the light, brother. Amen.

Revolution Letterpress (125 S. Gay St., 865/544-7356, www.revletterpress.com) offers limited edition prints and posters created from carved linoleum or wood blocks. Subjects include Dolly Parton, Johnny Cash, and other figures from country music. Having two letterpresses within steps of each other on one street—much less in one city—is remarkable.

Those hankering for something sweet should head to World's Fair Park, and **The South's Finest Chocolate Factory** (865/522-2049, www.chocolatelovers.com, 9:30 A.M.–6 P.M., Mon.–Sat., 1–5 P.M. Sun.). The shop sells more than 100 kinds of candy, all made on the premises.

INFORMATION

The **Downtown Visitor Center** (Gay St. and Summit Hill Dr., 800/727-8045 or 865/523-7263, www.knoxville.org) is the best place to begin a visit to Knoxville. Exit the Interstate at either the Henley Street exit, Exit 388, or the James White Parkway. Once off the Interstate, just follow the signs.

Metro Pulse is a free weekly that keeps close tabs on the entertainment scene. Find it all over town or at www.metropulse.com.

Gateways to the Smokies

On September 2, 1940, President Franklin D. Roosevelt and thousands of other people rode in a caravan up the dirt road to Newfound Gap in the new Great Smoky Mountains National Park. The people in the villages they passed through, Sevierville, Pigeon Forge, and Gatlinburg, had no way of knowing the impact that the park would have on the places they lived.

Today, the Smokies is the most visited of the national parks, and those three towns thrive on industrial-strength tourism. Millions of cars from all over the country converge here, disgorging people looking for a good time and carrying money in their pockets to pay for it.

They'll find a myriad of ways to spend it here. Outlet shopping, country music shows, amusement parks, T-shirt shops, helicopter flights, and you-name-it await the charge card. Amid the hokum, however, visitors will find high-quality crafts, wonderful inns and bed-and-breakfasts, and places where Appalachian music rings out clearly. And kids who are weary

© JEFF BRADLEY

Must-Sees

Look for M to find the sights and activities you can't miss and M for the best dining and lodging.

M **Tennessee Museum of Aviation:** The Sevierville Airport offers this stunning collection of warbirds, most of which still fly (page 353).

M **Dollywood:** Visitors come expecting an amusement park, but find a place true to Dolly's Appalachian roots (page 356).

M **Dixie Stampede:** Tourism runs amok in Pigeon Forge. Think Civil War *Ben Hur* as dinner theater (page 358).

M **Arrowmont School of Arts and Crafts:** It's a serene island of high-end crafts amid Gatlinburg's sea of T-shirt shops (page 362).

M **Great Smoky Arts & Crafts Community:** Far from the madding crowd of Gatlinburg, meet artists and see their work (page 362).

Dollywood's Smoky Mountain Rampage Ride

M **The Townsend Y:** Nature's original water park can be found just inside Great Smoky Mountains National Park (page 376).

M **Ramp Festival:** This genuine East Tennessee festival was created to celebrate the pungent, onion-like plant—not to placate tourists (page 376).

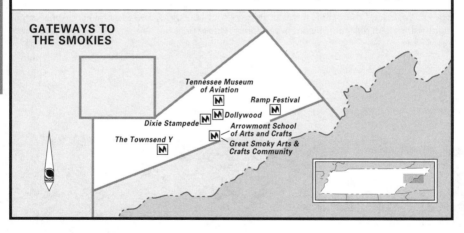

GATEWAYS TO THE SMOKIES

Tennessee Museum
of Aviation

Ramp Festival

Dixie Stampede

Dollywood

The Townsend Y

Arrowmont School
of Arts and Crafts

Great Smoky Arts &
Crafts Community

Gateways to the Smokies

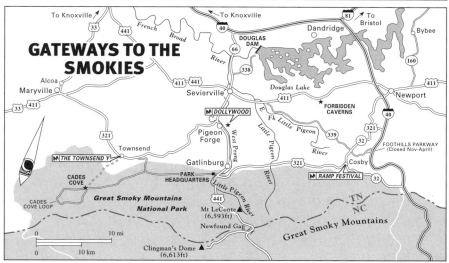

GATEWAYS TO THE SMOKIES

© AVALON TRAVEL PUBLISHING, INC.

of traveling will utterly love the Gateways area. Those parents intent on getting into the sanctity of the Smokies should stop and take in a few indulgences; they'll make the wilderness all that much sweeter.

If your destination is the national park, you will want to get through this area as quickly as possible. On holiday weekends, or every weekend during the fall color season, bumper-to-bumper traffic can extend all the way from I-40 to the Gatlinburg boundary of the park, so congestion is something not to take lightly. Other tactics include arriving early or late.

If, however, shopping in outlet stores is your idea of a good time, or individuals in your party cannot wait to get behind the wheel of a go-kart or visit museums of various oddities, welcome to the kingdom of heaven.

Despite the presence of the mountains, summers here get hot and muggy, so plan on retiring to a hotel swimming pool or water park in the afternoons.

Sevierville

The town and the county were named for John Sevier, Tennessee's first governor, who negotiated with the Cherokee to secure this area for settlers. Like many towns in those early days, Sevierville had no courthouse, so judicial proceedings were held in a local stable. According to one account, this structure was so infested with fleas that the itching attorneys finally burned it to the ground. While it stood, however, perhaps nowhere else in Tennessee did the accused receive quicker versions of the speedy trials due them.

Sevier County has produced some great music makers. Dolly Parton grew up here, as did two great dobro players, both associated with Roy Acuff. Clell Summey (Cousin Jody) joined Acuff in 1933 and became the first person to play dobro on the *Grand Ole Opry*. Pete Kirby (Bashful Brother Oswald), who became the foremost dobro player in country music, replaced him.

Sevierville provides several reasons for visitors to slow down and spend a little time. The first is its downtown, an eddy in the stream of tourism that flows close by. The **Sevier County**

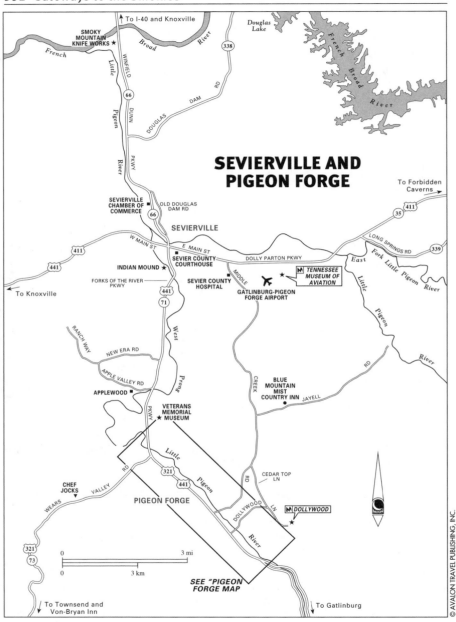

To I-40 and Knoxville

SMOKY MOUNTAIN KNIFE WORKS ★

Douglas Lake

French Broad River

French

Little

Pigeon

River

WINFIELD

DUNN

66

DOUGLAS DAM RD

338

SEVIERVILLE AND PIGEON FORGE

To Forbidden Caverns →

411

35

SEVIERVILLE CHAMBER OF COMMERCE ■

OLD DOUGLAS DAM RD

66

SEVIERVILLE

W MAIN ST

E MAIN ST

DOLLY PARTON PKWY

LONG SPRINGS RD

East Fork Little Pigeon River

339

411

441

INDIAN MOUND ★

SEVIER COUNTY COURTHOUSE ■

FORKS OF THE RIVER PKWY

441

SEVIER COUNTY HOSPITAL ■

MIDDLE

GATLINBURG-PIGEON FORGE AIRPORT ✈

TENNESSEE MUSEUM OF AVIATION

Little

Pigeon

River

To Knoxville →

71

West

Prong

RANCH WAY

NEW ERA RD

APPLE VALLEY RD

APPLEWOOD ■

PKWY

VETERANS MEMORIAL MUSEUM ★

BLUE MOUNTAIN MIST COUNTRY INN ●

CREEK

JAYELL

RD

River

Little

Pigeon

River

CEDAR TOP LN

MooN

CHEF JOCKS ▼

VALLEY

WEARS

RD

321

441

PIGEON FORGE

DOLLYWOOD LN

DOLLYWOOD ★

River

321

73

0   3 mi

0   3 km

SEE "PIGEON FORGE MAP"

To Townsend and Von-Bryan Inn ↓

To Gatlinburg →

Gateways to the Smokies

Courthouse is a Victorian structure built in 1895–96, and its four-sided Seth Thomas clock still keeps time. Beside the courthouse is the *Dolly Parton Statue,* a bronze depiction of the young Dolly by Tennessee artist Jim Gray. What's left of the small-town atmosphere is perfectly captured by Virgil's '50s Restaurant. Down the street are the Sevier Country Heritage Museum and several antique shops.

SIGHTS

Ⓜ Tennessee Museum of Aviation

The Tennessee Museum of Aviation (866/286-8738 or 865/908-0171, www.tnairmuseum.com, daily Apr. 1–Nov. 1, call about Dec. hours, $8 ages 13 and over, $4 ages 5–12, free under 5) contains a great collection of "warbirds" from World War II and subsequent conflicts. What's even more remarkable is that virtually every aircraft in this collection can fly. The collection changes as aircraft are bought and sold, but the visitor can count on seeing models such as a MIG 17, P-47 Thunderbolt, P-33, and an AT6. Jimmy Doolittle's Medal of Honor is here. Kids will appreciate a flight simulator and various "Learn to Fly" exhibits. The facility also includes the **Tennessee Aviation Hall of Fame.**

To get there from downtown Sevierville, take Hwy. 411 east a couple of miles to the airport, which will be on the right. If you like this place, don't miss the Veterans Memorial Museum in Pigeon Forge.

Sevier Country Heritage Museum

The Sevier Country Heritage Museum (167 E. Bruce St., 865/453-4058, www.korrnet.org/schm) occupies a former post office and contains the usual Native American artifacts as well as weapons from various wars. A portable camp-meeting organ is interesting, but the most unusual item has to be a robe and mask from the Sevier County Whitecaps, a vigilante organization that terrorized the area in the 1890s. Volunteers run this museum and the hours vary, so visitors should call ahead to make sure it is open.

McMahon Indian Mound

Between the Little Pigeon River and the intersection of the Forks of the River Parkway and Church Street lies the McMahon Indian Mound, all that is left of some Indians from the Mississippian period—long before the Cherokee. Excavations here revealed a village of about 75 people who lived in structures made of wood, thatch, and clay.

Bridge and Caverns

Outside of town, the **Harrisburg Covered Bridge** crosses the East Fork of the Little Pigeon River. Built in 1875, this bridge is still in use. Go east of Sevierville on Hwy. 411, turn right onto Hwy. 339, and follow the signs. Hwy. 441 East leads as well to **Forbidden Caverns** (865/453-5972 or 866/286-8738, www.forbiddencavern.com, daily Apr. 1–Nov. 1, call about Dec. hours, $8 ages 13 and over, $4 ages 5–12, free under 5), a commercial cave whose name comes from a Native American legend involving the burial of a princess in a place that is forbidden. Later the cave was used for making moonshine. The caverns contain a large wall of cave onyx as well as unusual formations.

Applewood

Halfway between Sevierville and Pigeon Forge motorists will pass Applewood, a complex that began with a family-owned apple orchard, but now offers a cider mill, cider bar, bakery, candy factory, smokehouse, winery, gift shop, and two restaurants. The winery produces eight apple wines—some of them mixed with other fruit. Cider production begins in late August and runs through February, depending on the supply of apples. The complex is open every day, with longer hours in the tourist season.

ENTERTAINMENT AND EVENTS

Sevierville, Pigeon Forge, and Gatlinburg all get together to promote **WinterFest,** a November–February celebration of the season that gives the shops and businesses a great opportunity to don thousands of lights. The events that make up WinterFest differ from year to year, but generally

© JEFF BRADLEY

the Harrisburg Covered Bridge outside of Sevierville

consist of concerts, storytelling, wine tastings, and so on. For details, contact each town's chamber of commerce or tourist bureau. In Sevierville, the number is 800/255-6411 or 865/453-6411. Or hit the Web at www.seviervillechamber.org.

RECREATION

When nearby Knoxville dithered about building a new minor league baseball stadium, the **Tennessee Smokies** (865/286-2300, www.smokiesbaseball.com, $9 adults, $6 children), an AA affiliate of the Arizona Diamondbacks, pulled up stakes and moved to a new stadium hereabouts. Just north of I-40, Smokies Park offers the best entertainment bargain in the area.

Horseback riding is offered by **Cedar Ridge Riding Stables,** (Hwy. 441, 865/428-5802, daily) and **Douglas Lake View Horse Riding** (1650 Providence Ave., 865/428-3587), which offers short rides or the overnight variety.

ACCOMMODATIONS

Sevierville, Pigeon Forge, and Gatlinburg contain one of the greatest inland concentrations of places

to stay in the South. Inns and bed-and-breakfasts are covered in some detail, but many of the rest are franchises. "Chalet" is a term often used in these parts. Originally used to mean an A-frame or building along that line, it now usually means a detached structure. Often a "cabin" and "chalet" are virtually indistinguishable. Condominiums have become a big part of the lodging scene in the Smokies, and having a kitchen can help keep costs down.

Keep in mind that, of the three cities in the Gateways area, Sevierville is the farthest from the national park. If you stay here, you will have the longest drive to get to the wilderness.

Prices for lodging hereabouts depend mightily on when you go, and in October can change dramatically from weekday to weekend. Most of the motels here are standard franchises. Visitors can contact the **Sevierville Chamber of Commerce** (800/255-6411 or 865/453-8574, www.seviervillechamber.org) for a list of lodging places that are members.

Bed-and-Breakfasts and Inns

Blue Mountain Mist Country Inn (1811 Pullen Rd., www.bluemountainmist.com,

865/428-2335, $115–160) consists of 12 guest rooms in a Victorian-style house and five guest cottages set on a 60-acre farm with views of the mountains. Each room in the inn has a private bath, and cabins come with whirlpool baths, fireplace, porch swing, kitchenette, television set, and VCR. Outside await a picnic table and grill. The Sugarlands Bridal Room—the top of the line—contains a whirlpool bath with views out of a turreted window. A large country breakfast appears every morning

The Little Greenbriar Lodge (3685 Lyon Springs Rd., 800/277-8100 or 865/429-2500, www.littlegreenbrierlodge.com, $110–135) overlooks Wears Valley and was built in the '30s as a hunting lodge. It has survived various incarnations since to become a very pleasant inn with nine rooms, all decorated with Victorian antiques. Most of the rooms have private baths. The lodge serves a full country breakfast.

The Von-Bryan Inn (2402 Hatcher Mountain Rd., 800/633-1459 or 865/453-9832, www.vonbryan.com) has one of the best views guests can get—360 degrees of mountain scenery from atop Hatcher Mountain. The inn contains seven guest rooms as well as a chalet. Each room has a private bath—some have a whirlpool or steam shower—and every guest can enjoy a large gathering room with cathedral ceiling and large fireplace. Rates run $120–200 for two people in the guest rooms, and $240–280 for four people in the chalets.

Cabins, Condos, and Chalets

Options for these kinds of accommodations include **Oak Haven Resort** (800/652-2611 www.oakhavenresort.com); **Wildflower Mountain Rentals** (800/726-0989 or 865/453-2000, www.wildflowermountain.com); and **Hidden Mountain Resorts** (800/452-5992, www.hiddenmountain.com).

Camping

It's heads or tails at the bare-bones campgrounds at Douglas Dam Headwater or Douglas Dam Tailwater, above and below TVA's **Douglas Dam** (865/587-5600). A total of 113 sites—20 with

hookups (at Tailwater)—are open early April–October. Headwater has restroom facilities.

Knoxville East KOA (241 KOA Dr., 865/933-6393, www.smokymountaincampground.com) has 200 sites, all the amenities, and is open all year. Take Exit 407 off I-40 and go north. You can't miss it.

Ripplin Waters Campground (888/747-7546, www.ripplinwatersrv.com) has 155 shady sites with full hookups—50 campsites on the Little Pigeon River. Open all year.

River Plantation RV Park (1004 Parkway, 800/758-5267, www.riverplantationrv.com) sits on the Pigeon Forge side of Sevierville and features large sites—40 by 60 feet. It offers rental cars, full hookups, outdoor pool, satellite TV, and camping cabins, and it is open all year.

FOOD

Sevierville is a dry town. There are no liquor stores; if visitors want a bottle of wine, they have to buy it at the winery or bring it with them. Restaurants do not serve alcoholic beverages, although some will allow diners to carry in their own. To be sure, call ahead.

Most of the restaurants in Sevierville and, indeed, the entire area, offer Southern cuisine. You'll see lots of biscuits and gravy, chicken-fried steak, and other artery-clogging delights. Chain restaurants and fast food abounds.

The **Applewood complex** (865/428-1222), on Apple Valley Road off the Parkway between Sevierville and Pigeon Forge, includes two restaurants. The **Applewood Farmhouse Restaurant** and the **Farmhouse Grill** offer dishes such as chicken à la Orchard and other varieties of country cooking. Both places really shine, however, when it comes to desserts: apple cider pie, apple fritters, apple butter, you name it. Both are open for all three meals every day.

Virgil's '50s Restaurant, (just off the town square on 109 Bruce St., 865/453-2782) is a fun place to go. The black-and-white tiled floor, pink neon, and colorful booths seem just right for the '50s music that's always on tap here. The cuisine is burgers, sandwiches, and country cooking.

Gateways to the Smokies

SHOPPING

Just south of I-40, an outlet store for **Lodge Manufacturing** (865/932-9047, www.lodgemfg .com, daily) offers Tennessee-made cast iron skillets, griddles, and other cookware. One of their best items is a grill press to keep bacon flat while cooking.

Sevierville has several outlet malls. **Tanger Five Oaks Outlet Center,** (645 Parkway, www.tangeroutlet.com) has over 100 stores. **Governor's Crossing Outlet Center,** also on the Parkway, contains 25 shops.

Visitors must see the **Smoky Mountain Knife Works** (3.75 miles off I-40 on Hwy. 66, 865/453-5871, www.eknifeworks.com, daily) even if they have no interest in knives. This is the largest knife store in the world as well as a museum depicting factory collections, antique knives, and antique advertisements. There is nothing like it anywhere. Tennessee's largest collection of mounted trophy heads gazes down on a waterfall that flows into a trout stream right in the store. The store carries leather jackets, jewelry, and kitchen items.

This area is not a big art center. The paintings offered for sale here—idyllic cabins with yellow light streaming from the windows and gleaming off a stream—make Norman Rockwell look like Jackson Pollock.

INFORMATION

Motorists coming south from I-40 can stop in at the **Sevierville Chamber of Commerce** (866 Parkway, 800/255-6411 or 865/453-6411, www.seviervillechamber.com, 8 A.M.–5 P.M. Mon.–Sat., 1–5 P.M. Sun.).

Pigeon Forge

Pigeon Forge got the first part of its name from enormous flocks of passenger pigeons attracted by the beech trees that lined the river. "Pigeon" became the name of the river, and in time it powered an ironworks built by Isaac Love and operated until the 1930s—thus the "Forge."

For decades, Pigeon Forge struggled as a Gatlinburg wannabe, a wide spot in the road for people bound for the mountains. As visitation to the Smokies has relentless increased, Pigeon Forge has capitalized on the one thing it has that Gatlinburg doesn't: land. Here is room for the massive outlet malls and theaters with their enormous parking lots.

Here, too, is Dollywood, the most popular tourist attraction in Tennessee. Based on the charm of the charismatic singer and songwriter and local girl—and some savvy management that introduces new features to the park every summer—Dollywood pulls some 2.2 million visitors per year.

For most visitors during the summers and fall, Pigeon Forge is a place where the only vehicles that move quickly are go-karts. Creeping along, the motorist passes outlandish miniature golf courses, bungee jump towers, and fast food along a cacophonous strip that has led some jaundiced observers to dub this town the Las Vegas for Rednecks. When it's 90°, traffic is bumper to bumper, radiators and tempers are boiling over, and tourist helicopters buzz overhead, Pigeon Forge seems like the *Apocalypse Now* of tourism.

One quick antidote to Pigeon Forge is to go southeast on Wears Valley Road, which leads to Townsend and the quiet side of the mountains. This 15-mile drive follows Hwys. 321 and 73.

SIGHTS AND RECREATION

Dollywood

This is the number-one tourist attraction in Tennessee. It combines live music—more than 40 performances daily—with more than 30 amusement park rides. Dollywood (865/428-9488, www.dollywood.com) puts an Appalachian spin on things, with 20 craftspeople working on traditional activities such as weaving, pottery, and woodcarving. The *Dollywood Express,* a steam-powered train, chugs along a

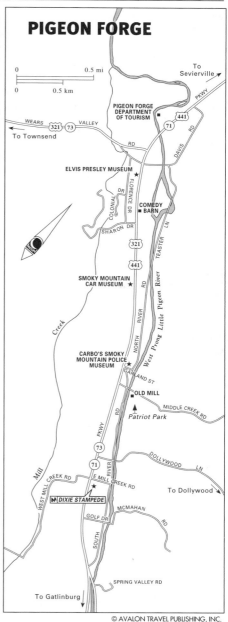

five-mile track, and **Dolly Parton's Museum** tells this extraordinary entertainer's life story. The **Eagle Mountain Sanctuary** displays bald eagles that for one reason or another cannot be released into the wild.

Dollywood opens in early April and closes at the end of December, staying open the latest during the heart of the summer. All-day admission is $42.40 for adults, $32.35 for children ages 4–11, $39 for seniors (60 and older), and for free for ages 3 and under. The prices include tax. The best deal is to enter the park after 3 P.M.; you can come back the next day free of charge.

Dollywood Splash Country

When it gets hot in the Smokies, this place will satisfy those who enjoy getting flushed through various pipes and slides. Although this 35-acre waterpark (1020 Dollywood Ln., 865/428-9488, www.dollywoodssplashcountry.com) belongs to Dollywood, it is not included in the ticket price for the main park. Admission is $32.35 for adults, $30.10 for seniors, and $26.75 for children. Multi-day, and joint Dollywood/Splash Country passes are available. All ticket prices include tax. It's open late May through the third weekend in September.

Dixie Stampede

Dixie Stampede (Mill Creek Rd. and the Parkway, 800/356-1676 or 865/453-4400, www.dixiestampede.com, $35.99 adults, $18.99 ages 4–11) has to be the most unusual dinner show in the entire state. More than 1,000 patrons sit side by side on five tiers of seats facing a U-shaped, dirt arena. The meal consists of whole rotisserie chicken, ribs, soup, and accompanying dishes, all enjoyed without silverware. The show involves 30 horses, people riding ostriches, singing, trick riding, roping, and performers dressed as Union and Confederate soldiers. Owned by Dollywood, Dixie Stampede runs full-time May–December, is closed for a few weeks in January, then opens for weekends only in February, and gradually resumes a full schedule in the spring. Call for tickets.

Museums

Carbo's Smoky Mountain Police Museum (3311 Parkway, 865/453-1358, $9.95 adults, $6.50 children over 12, $4.50 for ages 6–12), at the building with bars on the windows, takes a curatorial look at the constabulary with badges, guns—official as well as confiscated ones—uniforms, drug exhibits, etc. The centerpiece is the Buford Pusser "death car."

The late Buford Pusser was a crime-fighting west Tennessee sheriff famous for his violent encounters with rural hoodlums. Pusser died in 1974 following the wreck of his Corvette—the car in the museum. He was immortalized in three *Walking Tall* movies of the 1970s. The *Walking Tall* movie of 2004 had nothing to do with his story.

For those who can't make it to Graceland, the **Elvis Museum** (2638 Parkway, 865/428-2001, $9.75 adults, $6.50 for kids over 12, $4.50 for ages 6–12), offers the King's last personal limousine, jumpsuits, and boxer shorts, and the original $250,000 "TCB" ring.

If Elvis's limo and Buford Pusser's death car only whet your appetite, the **Smoky Mountain Car Museum** (2970 Parkway, 865/453-3433, $5 adults, $2 for ages 3–10) will prove delightful. See James Bond's cars from *Goldfinger* and *Thun-*

derball as well as vehicles once belonging to Elvis, the ubiquitous Buford Pusser, Al Capone, Stringbean, and Billy Carter. The museum is open varied hours from late spring through December. Call ahead.

Hollywood Motion Picture Museum (www.belleisland.com), new in 2005 in the Belle Island Village off Wear's Valley Road, consists of a collection of costumes, props, and memorabilia that actress Debbie Reynolds assembled over several decades. The costumes include Marilyn Monroe's white dress from *Seven Year Itch*.

Veteran's Memorial Museum (near Traffic Light 1, 865/908-6003, www.veteransmemorialpf.com, daily, $11 adults, $9.95 veterans and spouses, $6.95 ages 12–18, $4.95 ages 5–11) may not have the most professional exhibits, but they have a staggering collection of military items. Included are general's stars worn by Robert E. Lee, a Japanese sword surrendered to Douglas McArthur, Adolf Hitler's pocket watch, a D-Day jeep dropped by parachute, goggles used on the *Enola Gay* bomber, and a Nazi concentration camp inmate's uniform. Most of the items related to World War II. If you like this place, don't miss the Tennessee Aviation Museum in Sevierville.

Visitors who have never had the occasion to look at a Patriot missile should decamp to **Patriot Park,** where they'll find one of the four on display in the United States. This free public park in the Old Mill area, near Traffic Light 7, also contains flags of all the states displayed in the order in which they were admitted to the Union.

Mountain Valley Vineyards (2174 Parkway, 865/453-6334) produces 16 different kinds of wine—mostly sweet and medium sweet. Muscadine wine is the best-selling one, although berry wines run a close second. Visitors can watch wine being made in August and September. Mountain Valley is open for tastings all year seven days a week.

ENTERTAINMENT AND EVENTS

Memories Theatre (800/325-3078 or 865/428-7852, www.memoriestheatre.com) should be the

SHOWTIME IN THE TOURIST CORRIDOR

I nvestors have come to Pigeon Forge taking a cue from Branson, Missouri, a small town that has enjoyed great success with nightly shows featuring over-the-hill but still popular entertainers. Country singer Lee Greenwood performed for years, and folks such as Anita Bryant and Jim Ed Brown have tried their hand as well. The most successful shows seem to be those that feature talented and enthusiastic unknowns who can be replaced without a major change in the marquee.

Shows emphasize family entertainment. Alcoholic beverages are not served in theaters, and patrons can count on "a good, clean show." Many performances include gospel music. All this is mildly ironic, for country music's staples through the years have been drinking, honky-tonking, and broken hearts. But the roadside tradition of "fightin' and dancin' clubs" gets no homage here.

Theaters generally open in March or April for weekends only and then expand to six or seven nights a week when summer arrives. They cut back on the number of shows as the fall winds down. Since most of these places seat hundreds of people and require vast parking lots, you will see none of them in Gatlinburg. "There's No Business Like Show Business," as the song goes, and that's very true here. Acts change, theaters open, theaters close, and a new Elvis periodically comes to town.

The talent lineup changes with the season, and sometimes so do the names of the theaters. To get the most accurate information about who's playing where, check online at www.seviervillechamber.org or www.mypigeonforge.com, or stop in at the welcome centers. Tickets cost from $20 one up, with generous discounts for kids—in many places children under 11 get in free.

first East Tennessee stop for Elvis fans—the home of first-class impersonators of the King. Memories Theatre seats 900 and is open every month except January. It's on the left coming into Pigeon Forge from Sevierville before Traffic Light 1. Admission is $20 for anyone over 12; two kids get in free for each paid adult.

Comedy Barn (2775 Parkway, 800/295-2844 or 865/428-5222, www.comedybarn.com, $19.95 adults, $17.95 seniors, free children 11 and under) packs them in with corny and clean comedy. A one-man band, live country music, and juggling round out the act. It's open year-round.

Pigeon Forge joins Sevierville and Gatlinburg in **WinterFest,** November–February, a celebration of the season that gives the shops and businesses a great opportunity to don thousands of lights. WinterFest differs from year to year, but generally consists of concerts, storytelling, and so on. For details about other Pigeon Forge events, call 800/251-9100 or 865/453-8574 or visit www.mypigeonforge.com.

ACCOMMODATIONS

Most of the hotels in Pigeon Forge are lined up along the Parkway. While these places may not offer the mountain retreat that visitors have in mind, they make it possible to walk to restaurants and various attractions.

For the most up-to-date information, call 800/251-9100 and ask for a copy of the *Pigeon Forge Vacation Planner.* Another good resource is the Pigeon Forge website, www.mypigeon forge.com.

Bed-and-Breakfasts and Inns

Chilhowee Bluff (off Wears Valley Rd., 888/559-0321 or 865/908-0321, www.chilhoweebluff .com, $125–169) is secluded yet offers ready access to Pigeon Forge or the Townsend side of the Smokies. Rates include a three-course breakfast.

The **Huckleberry Inn** (1754 Sandstone Way, 865/428-2475, www.bbonline.com/tn/huckle berry, $79–89) is a log house built by hand and containing three guest rooms decorated in country style. All have private baths, and two have fireplaces and whirlpools. The inn serves a full country breakfast daily. It's 1.2 miles from Dollywood, yet just a half-mile off the busy Parkway.

Cabins, Condos, and Chalets

"Chalet," a term often used in these parts, usually means a detached structure. "Cabin" and "chalet" usually mean the same thing. The offices listed below rent cabins, condos, and chalets: **Angel's View Cabin Rentals** (800/339-3424 www.angelsviewcabinrentals.com), **County Oaks Cottages** (866/369-2942 or 865/453-7640, www.countryoaks.com), **Eagles Ridge Resort and Cabin Rentals** (866/369-2946 or 865/286-1595, www.eaglesridge.com), **Timbercreek Realty and Cabin Rentals** 800/837-7022 or 865/774-8988, www.timbercreekcabins.com), **Wildflower Mountain Rentals** (800/726-0989 or 865/453-2000, www.wildflowermountain.com).

Camping

Alpine Hideaway RV Park and Campground (251 Spring Valley Rd., 865/428-3285, www.alpinehideawayrv.com) has 90 sites. **Clabough's Campground** (half mile off the Parkway on Wears Valley Rd., 865/453-0729, www.claboughcampground.com) has 152 sites and all the amenities and is open all year.

On the Little Pigeon River, **Creekstone Outdoor Resort** (800/848-9097 or 865/453-8181, www.creekstonecamping.com) has 150 sites and full amenities. It's open year-round.

Eagles Nest Campground (111 Wears Valley Rd., 1.5 miles off the Parkway, 800/892-2714 or 865/428-5841, www.eaglesnestcampground.com) has 200 sites with the works. It's open year-round. **Fort Wear Campground** (800/452-9835 or 865/428-1951) sits a half mile off the Parkway on Wears Valley Road. Open all year, it has 150 sites and all the amenities.

KOA (2849 Middle Creek Rd., 800/367-7903 or 865/453-7903, www.koa.com) offers 200 sites. Open April 1–December. **River Bend Campground** (Henderson Rd., off the Parkway, 865/453-1224) has 101 sites between Pigeon

Forge and Sevierville. It's open April–November 15. **Riveredge RV Park** (4220 Huskey St., Pigeon Forge 800/477-1205 or 865/453-5813, www.stayriveredge.com) has 175 sites plus cabins. **Shady Oaks Campground** (210 Connor Heights Rd., 865/453-3276, www.shadyoakscampgroundpigeonforge.com) sits on the Gatlinburg side of Pigeon Forge. It offers 150 sites that are open all year.

The small **Foothills Campground** (4235 Huskey St., 865/428-3818)—only 46 sites— sits on the edge of town at. Open April–November.

FOOD

Pigeon Forge does not permit the sale of alcoholic beverages in stores or restaurants. Diners can carry in their own to some restaurants, but it's a good idea to call ahead.

Chef Jock's Tastebuds Cafe (1198 Wears Valley Rd., 865/428-9781), far from the madding crowd on the Parkway, is the best restaurant in the entire area. This very unassuming place offers a respite from country cooking in the form of sea scallops, pork tenderloin with herbs, and a great number of healthy yet tasty dishes. Open for lunch and dinner Tuesday–Saturday. Reservations are a good idea.

The Old Mill Restaurant (in the Old Mill complex, 865/429-3463, www.old-mill.com) offers dining overlooking the Little Pigeon River. Breads are made from flour and meal from the nearby mill. It offers country cooking seven days a week for all three meals.

Santo's Italian Restaurant (3270 Parkway, 865/428-5840) offers fine fettuccine with snow crab, linguine primavera, and other Italian dishes. It's open all year Monday–Saturday.

SHOPPING

One survey of visitors to the Smokies reported that the number one activity that people engaged in was shopping. Pigeon Forge has several outlet malls totaling hundreds of shops.

Pigeon River String Instruments (3337 Old Mill St., 865/453-3789, www.pigeon-river.com)

awaits folk fanciers who need dulcimers, hammered dulcimers, or psalteries; it offers a few guitars and mandolins as well.

Stages West (2765 Parkway, 865/453-8086, www.stageswest.com) offers fancy duds that are the closest thing to Nashville one will find in these parts.

When the founder of **Pigeon Forge Pottery** (across from the Old Mill on Middle Creek Rd., 865/453-3883) came to town in 1937 looking for good clay, he fired the earthen nests made by mud dauber wasps. Convinced that the clay here was of high-enough quality, Douglas Ferguson began the pottery, which now produces art objects inspired by Smoky Mountains sub-

jects. Visitors can watch the artisans at work. The biggest sellers are bears and owls.

INFORMATION AND SERVICES

For information, contact the **Pigeon Forge Department of Tourism** (2450 Parkway, 800/251-9100 or 865/453-8574, www.mypigeonforge.com, 9 A.M. to 5:30 P.M. Mon.–Sat., 1–5 P.M. Sun.).

Pigeon Forge operates the **Fun Time Trolley** (865/453-6444, www.pigeonforgetrolley.org), buses that cover some 90 percent of the town. Rides cost $0.25—$0.50 to go to Gatlinburg—and buses run March through October from 8:30 A.M. until midnight.

Gatlinburg

Gatlinburg is a town that breaks your heart. After running the gauntlet of gimcrackery that constitutes Sevierville and Pigeon Forge, motorists on Hwy. 441 enter a serpentine stretch of forest and rushing water. Seemingly at the snap of the fingers, gone are the parking lots and the blaring signs and the visual clutter of Pigeon Forge. The Parkway stays close by the Little River, and the forest closes in on either side. Newcomers to the area mistakenly believe that they are beyond All That.

Then comes Gatlinburg, and you realize that things can get worse. If this town were a haircut, it would be a mullet.

Gatlinburg was the original Smoky Mountain tourist town, a place of rocking chairs, rustic accommodations, and hearty food. All but surrounded by the Great Smoky Mountains National Park, Gatlinburg has limited space and, mercifully, cannot contain the large outlet malls and thousand-person theaters of Sevierville and Pigeon Forge. Given this situation, and its to-die-for location at the entrance to the most popular national park in the country, Gatlinburg could have been the Aspen of the Appalachians, the Nantucket of the national parks, or the Saratoga of the Smokies.

It didn't happen. Instead, Gatlinburg chose the low road, which in this case is a strip con-

sisting of a commercial carbuncle of huckster-ism and garish shops whose merchandise is so tasteless that it would shame Homer Simpson. There are no pedestrian parks here. Confined to narrow sidewalks, rotund visitors fresh from pancake breakfasts jostle one another while gangs of 12-year-olds and their mental equivalents lope from the Guinness World Records Museum to Ripley's Haunted Adventure, there to gaze in slack-jawed reverie at Tennessee's old electric chair. For the most part, the delightful creeks and the river that flows through the town are fenced off, forcing visitors to gaze down upon the splashing waters or—better yet—buy a post-card of them.

The combination of greed and a total lack of planning that characterizes Gatlinburg comes to a head at Ripley's Aquarium of the Smokies, an architectural atrocity that garishly looms up against the forested mountains. Why, one wants to ask, does a saltwater aquarium belong next to one of the great interior wilderness areas in the country? Visitors who plan to travel near Chattanooga would be better off seeing that city's Tennessee Aquarium, which is far bigger and far better and far less expensive.

Having said all that, however, Gatlinburg does offer some redeeming features for the visitor. Restaurants here are more upscale than those in

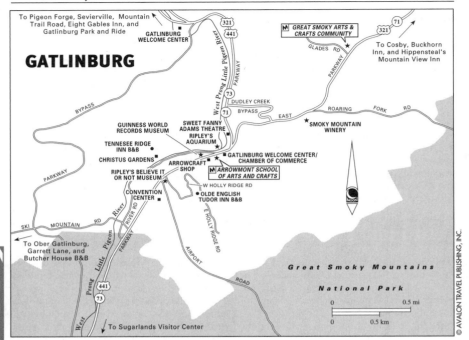

Pigeon Forge and Sevierville. The town is small enough to walk to just about everywhere, thus avoiding the often-hideous traffic that plagues the area. Gatlinburg allows its eateries to offer mixed drinks, wine, and beer, and the town has several liquor stores. And its lodges and cabins are as close to the national park as one can get.

Perhaps the best way to approach Gatlinburg is with an anthropological view, to look amusedly at your fellow pilgrims in the Land of the Yahoos. H. L. Mencken said it best: "No one ever went broke underestimating the taste of the American public." This statement belongs on the Gatlinburg town seal.

SIGHTS

During the busy season the best idea is to park the vehicle and leave it, seeing the sights on foot or taking the trolley that makes frequent stops all over town. Rides cost $.25 per person.

Arrowmont School of Arts and Crafts

The school (556 Parkway, 865/436-5860, www.arrowmont.org) brings 1,500 students and 150 instructors together each summer to a 70-acre campus to work on carving, weaving, pottery, and more than 15 other media. The school originated in 1912 when Pi Beta Phi opened a settlement school in what was then the economically depressed Appalachian town of Gatlinburg. Noting the high value people put on local crafts, the school added crafts instruction along with the other subjects. When improved public schools eliminated the need for the settlement school, the emphasis was shifted entirely to crafts.

Great Smoky Arts & Crafts Community

The Gatlinburg area has long been known for its arts and crafts. The self-sufficient mountaineers produced quilts, pottery, and other day-to-day

© JEFF BRADLEY

scenic Gatlinburg

items, and through the years the presence of tourists lured other artists to town. When rents for shop space in town became oppressive, a few artists started selling things out of their houses. Thus evolved the Gatlinburg Great Smoky Arts & Crafts Community (www .artsandcraftscommunity.com) on two roads east of town—Buckhorn and Glades—that lie off Hwy. 321.

Despite the watering down of quality, this is a good place to go. Shops offer leather goods, baskets, quilts and rugs, woodcarvings, brooms, candles, pottery, and stained glass. Others sell wooden toys and puzzles, dulcimers, photographs, and oil paintings. Here visitors can escape the crowds in town and drive from shop to shop in the woods. Many craftspeople make their items in studios beside their shops and sometimes have time to talk to visitors.

Highlights along the way include **Ogle's Broom Shop,** which produces fireplace brooms, traditional mountain brooms, and walking sticks on Glades Road. **Alewine Pottery** (www .alewinepottery.com), on the same road, sells very attractive pieces. Those who want to go home with a great photograph of the Smokies should stop at **Holloway's Country Home** (www.hollowaysquilts.com), also on Glades Road. Most of these stores are open daily, but during the winter many reduce hours or open only on weekends.

The quality of crafts here varies. Some shops are of very high quality, but others peddle items better thought of as souvenirs. The trolley comes here, but using it can be frustrating to the shopper who strolls into place and sees all that he or she wants in five minutes and is ready to move on. The next trolley might not be along for 20–30 minutes, and the shops are too spread out to easily walk from one to another.

Christus Gardens

This River Road perennial (865/436-5155, www.christusgardens.com, daily, $9.86 adults, $4.04 ages 4–13, free for under 6) is a religious wax museum. The focus here are 81 wax figures in dioramas depicting scenes from the life of Jesus, culminating in a 40-foot-long depiction of Leonardo da Vinci's *The Last Supper.* Visitors can also see collections of Bibles and other religious texts, 168 coins dating from the 6th century B.C., and oil paintings that interpret nine of the parables. This place used to sell the all-time, hands-down, best piece of kitsch in town: a jet-black shot glass featuring a gold silhouette of Jesus with the sun, also in gold, rising over his left shoulder and the mountains behind.

The most celebrated piece of art in the whole place is the "Carrara Face," a five-foot high flat piece of marble in which the face of Jesus has been carved in relief. When viewed by guests, the piece creates an optical illusion suggesting that the eyes—indeed the entire face—of Jesus is following their every movement. While no doubt comforting to the vast majority of Christus Gardens visitors, it is not recommended for those with tendencies toward paranoia.

Ripley's Aquarium of the Smokies

Easily the most visible place in town, this aquarium (888/240-1358, www.ripleysaquariumofthesmokies.com, daily, $18 adults, $10 ages 6–11, $4 ages 2–5) offers a highly sensational look at sharks and sea turtles and sharks and octopi and sharks. The highlight of the experience is stepping on a moving walkway that creeps through a large tank in a clear tunnel while bored sharks swim beside and overhead. One can step off the walkway and gaze rapturously at the sharks from what can only be called a sea urchin's perspective. All this takes place amid the sort of music that one hears in movies wherein humans encounter reasonable benevolent aliens.

And that's not all! Additional exhibits contain piranha, a "tidal pool" populated by horseshoe crabs, and a shallow tank where visitors can pet stingrays from whom the stingers have been clipped.

For Intellectuals Only

Guinness World Records Museum (631 Parkway, 865/436-9100, www.gatlinburg.com/guinness, daily, $9.95 adults, $5.95 ages 6–12)

presents a series of galleries depict such wonders as Houdini's torture chamber, personal items from Elvis and the Beatles, and the Batmobile. Other exhibits include representations of the world's tallest man, the world's heaviest man, tattooed ladies, and much more.

Devotees of shrunken heads and the like will enjoy **Ripley's Believe It or Not Museum** (at Traffic Light 7, 865/436-5096, www.ripleys.com, daily, $12.95 adults, $11.95 seniors, $7.95 ages 6–11), a collection of oddities.

Delectables

Longtime visitors to Gatlinburg remember the candy kitchens. These heavenly-smelling places have intricate machines that stretch taffy, extending it out into little finger-thick pieces, cut them off, and wrap them in paper. Fudge and other decadent delights can be had at **Aunt Mahalia's Candies, Mountaineer Kandy Kitchen,** and **Ola Kate's Candy Kitchen.** Kids love these places.

The Smoky Mountain Winery (865/436-7551, 10 A.M.–6 P.M. daily in good weather, shorter hours in the winter) is up Hwy. 321, a half mile from Parkway Traffic Light 3. Here, visitors can observe the winemaking process and sample the products. Seventy-five percent of the grapes used come from Tennessee. Among the wines offered are cabernet sauvignon and American riesling.

RECREATION

Ober Gatlinburg

This park (865/436-5423, www.obergatlinburg.com, $9.50 adults, $6.50 ages 7–11) is Gatlinburg's ski resort and summertime amusement park. Visitors can either drive up the mountain and pay to park. The best way to go is up the aerial tramway, which departs from downtown and goes two and a half miles up the mountain. The skiing, while laughable by New England or Western standards, nonetheless enthralls novices, as does the indoor ice-skating, which operates year-round. The latter is a great idea for rainy days.

Summertime activities include bungee jumping, batting cages, water slides, and an alpine slide. The chairlift that carries skiers in the wintertime carries sightseers to the top of a mountain.

There is no charge to enter Ober Gatlinburg. All activities are individually priced. Meals are available but their prices are considerably *ober* what visitors might pay at lower elevations.

Outfitters

A Walk in the Woods (865/436-8283, www .awalkinthewoods.com) offers a wide range of services for those rare souls who come to Gatlinburg to experience the wilderness of the Smokies. These guys do it all: shuttle cars and hikers, lead nature hikes, rent backpacking equipment, lead backpack trips, and do bus tours. If you think you would like to try backpacking, or would like to provide an unforgettable trip for a group or family, this should be your first stop. Rates run from $19 for two-and-a-half-hour walks to $250 for a family of five on an overnight backpacking trip.

Old Smoky Outfitters (511 Parkway in the Riverbend Mall, 865/430-1936, www.oldsmoky .com) offers fishing, hunting, and historical and nature tours. A half-day trout-fishing trip for novices begins at $135 and goes up from there. Overnight backcountry hikes, including all equipment, are available.

Smoky Mountain Angler (376 E. Parkway, 865/436-8746, www.smokymountainangler .com) offers gear, advice, and guided trips with lunch, which begin at $150 per person or $100 for a half day.

The Happy Hiker (800/HIKER-01 or 865/436-5632, www.happyhiker.com) offers gear rentals, shuttles, and lockers. It's located behind the Burning Bush Restaurant on the Parkway.

Smoky Mountain Stables (865/436-5634), four miles east of Gatlinburg on Hwy. 321, offers guided trail rides lasting one or two hours. It's open March–Thanksgiving.

ENTERTAINMENT AND EVENTS

Compared to the music halls of Pigeon Forge, the 200-seat **Sweet Fanny Adams Theatre** (461 Parkway, 865/436-4038, www.sweetfannyadams.com, $19.95 adults, $6.95 for ages 12 and under) is tiny. The entertainment consists of musical comedy, a sing-along, and a vaudeville-type revue six nights a week. A five-member cast performs one show Monday, Wednesday, and Friday, and a seven-member cast presents a completely different show Tuesday, Thursday, and Saturday. Curtain time is May–October, 8 P.M. Monday–Saturday, with shows only on the weekends in November and December. Call for reservations.

Held in July and October in the Gatlinburg Convention Center, the very popular **Craftsmen's Fairs** bring in about 150 craftspeople from all over the United States. The dates fluctuate every year—usually one week in July and one in October—so call 865/436-7479 for information.

Gatlinburg joins Sevierville and Pigeon Forge in **WinterFest,** a November–February celebration of the season for which shops and businesses decorate with thousands of lights. For details about Gatlinburg events, call 800/568-4748 or 865/430-4148.

ACCOMMODATIONS

The visitor to Gatlinburg will find a massive concentration of places to stay—some 35,000 people can sleep here on any given night. Listed below are inns and bed-and-breakfasts of note.

Long a honeymoon destination—an estimated 10,000 couples tie the knot here annually—Gatlinburg features an enormous number of establishments with whirlpool bathtubs that rival those in the Poconos of Pennsylvania. Indeed, an academic from afar studying the ads for these plumbing extravaganzas might conclude that the marital bath has replaced the marital bed for connubial pleasures.

Like most resort areas, the prices at Gatlinburg hostelries vary according to the season. As a general rule, the lowest prices are offered in the winter, and the highest during summer months and October, when the leaves turn. When inquiring about prices, keep in mind that this area has one of the highest sales taxes in Tennessee—12.5 percent when this book was written—and ask if the rate includes the tax.

Gatlinburg has fewer franchise motels than

Gateways to the Smokies

any of the other Smokies towns. Most of the motels here are older than their franchise counterparts, and have personalities of their own. The good news is that these hostelries are very often family-run operations that offer a friendliness and level of service that the visitor won't find elsewhere. Some customers return to the same places, even the same rooms, year after year, and are greeted every time as if they were kinfolks. The bad news is that many older hotels don't always have the kinds of things—workout rooms, computer connections, and the like—that many travelers have come to expect. All the more reason to get out of that room and get into the mountains. The best place to look over the offerings is www.gatlinburg.com.

Visitors who seek to avoid traffic congestion should choose cabins that are accessible from the Gatlinburg Bypass. Because they have the best views, these properties often cost more than other locations. The **Gatlinburg Chamber of Commerce** (www.gatlinburg.com) has many links to all manner of lodging.

Bed-and-Breakfasts and Inns

◊ The **Buckhorn Inn** (2140 Tudor Mountain Rd., 865/436-4668, www.buckhorninn.com, $115–300) is the grande dame of inns in the Gatlinburg area, serving guests since 1938. The inn contains six rooms and has four cottages, all situated on 32 wooded acres six miles from downtown Gatlinburg. The inn centers on a large living room with views of Mt. LeConte. The room contains a grand piano, and in the hour preceding dinner or in the evening a guest will often sit down and tickle the ivories. The Buckhorn strives to maintain an atmosphere of informal elegance; tables are set with linen, and guests should not show up for meals in jeans and T-shirts. Rooms in the inn offer neither telephones nor televisions. The cottages have TVs, as well as limited cooking facilities. Breakfast is included. Outside is Rachel's Labyrinth, a 60-foot diameter path in one of the inn's meadows.

Children must be at least 6 years old to come to the Buckhorn, and even then they must occupy the cottages. Sack lunches can be arranged, and guests must make reservations for dinner. Weekends and holidays require a two-night minimum stay.

Guests at the **Butcher House Bed & Breakfast** (1520 Garrett Ln., 865/436-9457, $79–109) rest above it all at 2,800 feet above downtown Gatlinburg. The four rooms each have a private bath. The house contains Victorian, French, Queen Anne, and American Country furniture, and outside is a deck with a wonderful view of Mt. LeConte.

◊ **Eight Gables Inn** (219 N. Mountain Trail, 800/279-5716 or 865/430-3344, www .bbonline.com/tn/eightgables, $109–165) is a large building with wraparound porches. It has 12 guest rooms, all with private baths. Two suites feature whirlpool baths, and each room has its own theme—perhaps centered on a sleigh or four-poster bed. Breakfast comes in four courses.

Vern Hippensteal is an artist who produces scenes of the Smokies in watercolors, limited-edition prints, and pen and ink sketches. His biggest creation, however, is **Hippensteal's Mountain View Inn** (800/527-8110 or 865/436-5761, www.hippensteal.com, $135), an 11-room inn in the Gatlinburg arts and crafts community. Each room has a fireplace, comfortable reading chairs, television, and private bath with whirlpool tub. A large common room enables guests to mingle, and many delight in taking in the view from rocking chairs on the wide porches that wrap around the inn.

The **Olde English Tudor Inn Bed & Breakfast** (135 W. Holly Ridge Rd., 800/541-3798 or 865/436-7760, www.oldenglishtudorinn.com, $79–150) is close enough to downtown Gatlinburg to walk to most of the attractions. The three-story building has an English garden and a waterfall out front. The eight guest rooms plus a cottage all have private baths and cable TV. The common room contains a TV and a woodstove, and a large breakfast is served.

7th Heaven Log Inn (3944 Castle Rd., 800/248-2923 or 865/430-5000, $87–137) sits beside the seventh green of the Bent Creek Golf Club outside Gatlinburg. The log structure contains five guest rooms, all with private baths. All have access to a big deck with a hot tub and a large recreation room with pool table, television, and various games. Unlike some B&Bs, in which guests feel as if they are in someone else's house, this place was built from the start as an inn. Guests have their own entrance and access to a full kitchen. Breakfast is a five-course affair with homemade bread.

Sitting a thousand feet above the town of Gatlinburg, the **Tennessee Ridge Inn Bed and Breakfast** (507 Campbell Lead, 865/436-4068, $75–135) has stunning views of the Great Smokies. The 8,500-square-foot, three-story house has a dining room with glass on three sides. Guests can choose from seven rooms, five of them with whirlpool baths. Breakfast is a full-service, sit-down affair that changes daily, from a full country meal to individual casseroles.

Cabins, Condos, and Chalets

The cabins at **M Heritage Hollow** (800/359-6117, www.heritagehollow.com, $75–160) are 100-year-old genuine cabins furnished with antiques and country collectible furniture. Equipped with modern kitchens and baths, they have an authenticity that is hard to find in these parts.

Find other places through **Alan's Mountain Rentals** (800/843-0457, www.alansmountain-rental.com), **Ski Mountain Chalets and Condominiums** (800/824-4022 or 865/436-7846, www.skimtnchalets.com), **High Chalet Condominium Rentals** (800/225-3834 or 865/430-2193, www.highchalet.com), **Masons Mountain Manors** (800/645-4911, www.masonsmountain manors.com), and **Smoky Top Rentals** (800/468-6813, www.smokytop.com).

Camping

Gatlinburg is so cramped for space that no campgrounds are downtown; the ones below are on Hwy. 321 east of town. Staying on the trolley route means you will not have to drive into town.

Camping in the **Smokes Gatlinburg RV Park** (865/430-3594, www.gatlinburg.com/campingin thesmokies) is up Hwy. 321 from town and on the trolley route. **Crazy Horse Campground** (12.5 miles up Hwy. 321 from Gatlinburg, 800/528-9003 or 865/436-4434, www.crazy-

horsecampground.com) has 228 sites. It's open April–October.

Great Smoky Jellystone Park Camp Resort (14 miles east of town on Hwy. 321, 800/210-2119 or 865/487-5534, www.campjellystone .com) offers 110 sites. Open April–November.

LeConte Vista RV Resort and Campground (865/436-5437) sits four miles east of town on Hwy. 321. Open March–December, it has all the works spread over 85 sites. This is on the trolley route, so you don't have to drive into town.

Outdoor Resort (10 miles out on Hwy. 321, 800/677-5861 or 865/436-5861, www.outdoor-resorts.com) has 150 sites. It's open all year.

Twin Creek RV Resort (800/252-8077 or 865/436-7081, www.twincreekrvresort.com) offers 75 sites within the city limits of Gatlinburg on Hwy. 321. It's open April–October. No tents. The best thing about this place is that campers can take the trolley into town.

FOOD

M The **Buckhorn Inn** (2140 Tudor Mountain Rd., 865/436-4668, www.buckhorninn.com) outside of Gatlinburg near the Great Smoky Arts and Crafts Community, offers the finest meals in the area. Typical entrees include poached fillets of salmon and red snapper with champagne dill sauce, or grilled lamb chops with rosemary butter. One of the appetizers frequently served is cappellini with prosciutto and fontina cheese in basil sauce. Bring your own bottle. Seating at the inn is limited; guests have first choice, and everyone else must make reservations no later than 10 A.M. on the day they wish to dine. Dinner is served at 7 P.M. and has a fixed price, usually $30 and worth every penny. To get to the inn, take Hwy. 321 North out of Gatlinburg. Pass Glades Road on the left. Take Buckhorn Road to the left, then go right on Tudor Mountain Road.

The **Burning Bush Restaurant** (1151 Parkway, 865/436-4669) lies about 30 feet from the park boundary and patrons can gaze out the windows and watch squirrels cavorting. The food is basic American fare, several notches up from country cooking. Breakfasts come with a glass of LeConte Sunrise, a mixture of fruit juices. It's open 365 days a year.

✖ Calhouns (1004 Parkway, 865/436-4669) is a chain offering ribs, prime rib, seafood, and chicken. It serves lunch and dinner seven days a week.

Cherokee Grill (1002 Parkway, 865/436-4287) features wood-grilled steaks, mountain trout, rotisserie chicken, and beef brisket. Open for dinner Monday–Friday and lunch and dinner on weekends.

The Greenbriar (370 Newman Rd., 865/436-6318, www.greenbrierrestaurant.com) lies east of Gatlinburg off Hwy. 321 in a log structure built by George Dempster, who was the mayor of Knoxville and of the Dempster Dumpster family. This place serves dinner only, year-round, and diners can choose from entrées such as slow-cooked prime rib or Smoky Mountains strip steak, marinated in olive oil and garlic for several days.

Maxwells Steak & Seafood (1103 Parkway, 865/436-3738, www.maxwells-inc.com) features fresh seafood and steaks, prime rib, and lamb. Begin with wine or cocktails, and finish off with a flambé dessert. It's open for dinner seven days a week.

Open Hearth, has two locations. The first is on the Parkway at the entrance to the Smokies. The other can be found at Hwy. 321 North at Traffic Light 3. Both offer fresh trout or salmon, barbecued ribs, and steak along with an extensive wine list. Open dinner every day all year, plus lunch on Saturdays. Call 800/372-2246 to place reservations for either location.

✖ The Park Grill (1110 Parkway, 865/436-2300, www.parkgrillgatlinburg.com) has a wonderful log building that pays homage to the sorts of lodges one might see in the Adirondacks or in Yellowstone National Park. The logs came from Idaho, and it took seven trucks to bring them to Gatlinburg. The food—all with Smoky-oriented names—ranges from Moonshine Chicken to Franklin Delano Rib Eye. Open for dinner only. This place takes no reservations, so get on the list and then go for a stroll.

✖ Smoky Mountain Brewery and Restaurant (behind 1004 Parkway, 865/436-4200, www.smoky-mtn-brewery.com) is a wonderful place to come back to after a long, hard hike through the mountains. Away from the Parkway, there are always at least eight microbrews on hand for the tasting. Some nights bring live music, with karaoke on other nights. The food is pizza, sandwiches, and burgers for lunch and steaks, trout, and ribs for dinner.

For those whose eyes have glazed over after seeing too much pottery and need a light lunch, this is the place. **The Wild Plum Tearoom** (555 Buckhorn Rd., 865/436-3808) is open for lunch only from March through mid-December. Try one of their combo plates of pasta salad, chicken salad, and fruit, and don't forget the wild plum tea.

SHOPPING

Unlike Pigeon Forge, Gatlinburg has no large outlet malls. Instead, dozens of small shops sell

© JEFF BRADLEY

Ogle's Broom Shop

pocketknives, t-shirts, and three Thomas Kinkade galleries. Here are some favorites.

Armour House, in the Marketplace (651 Parkway, 800/886-1862 or 865/430-2101) sells Civil War paintings, books, and artifacts.

The Happy Hiker (905 River Rd., 865/436-6000, www.happyhiker.com) caters to outdoor enthusiasts by offering all manner of outdoor clothing and camping gear. Here's the place to rent backpacks, sleeping bags, tents, and stoves. Returning hikers can take showers and do laundry.

The **Arrowcraft Shop** (576 Parkway, 865/436-4604, www.southernhighlandguild.org/arrowcraft) occupies one of the oldest and most beautiful buildings in town. Built in 1926, it features native hand-split slate. The rooms inside are paneled in chestnut, which gives the visitor a glimpse of this hardwood that once dominated nearby forests. The shop sells the work of local and regional artists—not the students at Arrowmont—and is operated by the Southern Highland Craft Guild.

The **Vern Hippensteal Gallery** (452 Parkway, 800/537-8110 or 865/436-4328, www.hippenstealgallery.com) features the work of this Gatlinburg resident—watercolors, limited-edition prints, and pen and ink sketches of the Smokies. Open seven days a week all year long.

INFORMATION AND SERVICES

The **Gatlinburg Welcome Center** (800/568-4748 or 865/436-0519, www.gatlinburg.com), on the Parkway at the Pigeon Forge side of town, is open 8 A.M.–6 P.M. Monday–Saturday, and 9 A.M.–5 P.M. Sunday.

For those who can be wrestled out of their cars, Gatlinburg has a **trolley** system that goes all over town, out to the Great Smoky Arts & Crafts Community and to Pigeon Forge. Rides begin at $0.25. For more information and a downloadable map, go to www.gatlinburg.com.

Townsend

Townsend bills itself as "the peaceful side of the Smokies," and, compared to Gatlinburg and Pigeon Forge, that's certainly the truth. Townsend lies in a cove—a flat area in mountain parlance—called Tuckaleechee Cove. Tourists have been coming to this area since 1904, when the railroad came through, but recent excavations show that this area has been popular with people for over 2,500 years.

When road crews began widening Hwy. 321 in 1999, they uncovered evidence of extensive Native American habitation, so work was halted while archeologists studied the newly exposed ground. Scientists found what was left of a big Cherokee town, as well as evidence of habitation dating back to 200 A.D. Human remains were found as well, and the Eastern Band of the Cherokee and Seminoles from Oklahoma, the presumed descendants of those who lived here, helped make the decision to leave the 70 graves intact. Each was covered with a layer of concrete before the road was paved over.

SIGHTS

Millions of people across the country have seen Townsend without realizing it. It is the site of CBS's (later the Family Channel's) *Christy,* the saga of a young teacher who comes to a remote mountain area to teach school. The story comes from the novel of the same name by Catherine Marshall.

People who want to see the greatest concentration of wildflowers in this region—400-plus species—should beat a path to **Hedgewood Gardens** (on Bethel Church Rd. off Hwy. 321, 865/984-2052). A woman named Hedy Wood designed the six acres of gardens to look as natural as possible, nurturing them for 23 years. She died in 1993 and her daughter, Hope Woodard, has opened the gardens to the public by appointment only.

Little River Railroad and Lumber Company Museum (on Hwy. 321, 865/448-2211, www.littleriverrailroad.org) gives a look into the extensive logging that took place in the Smokies. Most visitors to the verdant forests hereabouts can't imagine that virtually all of it was at one time cut down. This free museum gives a sense of what those times were like with a restored 1909 Shay locomotive, the depot used in the Walland community, and steam-powered log loader. It is open daily during the summer 10 A.M.–2 P.M. Mon.–Fri., 10 A.M.–4 P.M. Saturday, noon–4 P.M. Sunday, and by appointment only the rest of the year.

 The Townsend Y

The Townsend Y has nothing to do with the YMCA, but it is perhaps the best swimming hole in these parts. In a region full of chlorinated water parks, this is the real thing and a wonderful way to escape the heat. Just inside the park on the left—look for hordes of parked vehicles—two streams come together to provide a variety of

© JEFF BRADLEY

making a splash at the Townsend Y

fun. Families will enjoy drifting down the stream in inner tubes, with just enough white water to make it fun. On the far side of the stream and conveniently over a deep pool, cliffs provide an opportunity for brave (and exceedingly warm-blooded) souls to take the plunge. There are no lifeguards here, which is the bad news and the good news.

RECREATION

Farther downstream is **River Romp Tubes** (8203 Hwy. 73, 888/390-1190 or 865/448-1522, Memorial Day–Labor Day 10 A.M.–6 P.M.). In the Bodywear Outlet store at the junction of Hwy. 321 and Hwy. 73, this place rents high-quality inner tubes and life jackets for the float down the Little River.

Tuckaleechee Caverns (825 Caverns Dr., 865/448-2274, www.tuckaleecheecaverns.com, $8 adults, $4 ages 5–11, free for children under 5) also cools off visitors, but only to 58°. With the usual colorfully named features, this cave is a great rainy day excursion. Home to a huge room approximately 400 by 150 feet, it is open March 15 through November 15.

Horseback Riding

Cades Cove Riding Stables (4035 E. Lamar Alexander Pkwy., 865/448-6286), in the Walland area between Townsend and Maryville, offers horseback rides, carriage rides, and hayrides through Cades Cove. It's open April–October.

Davy Crockett Riding Stables (232 Stables Dr., 865/448-6411) does not require customers to wear coonskin hats on its guided rides. It's open every day except Christmas.

Double M Ranch (4033 Miser Station Rd., 865/995-9421) has horseback rides, hiking, and a paved road for bicycling.

Biking and Hiking

The **Historic Bike Trail** runs alongside both sides the main road through Townsend for four miles. A brochure available at the visitors center describes the history of the areas through which the trail passes.

Need a bike? Go to **That Scooter Place** (8270

Hwy. 73, 865/448-1949), which rents bikes and helmets.

Little River Outfitters (7807 E. Lamar Alexander Pkwy., 865/448-9459), is a guide service, fly shop, backpacking store, and clothing shop.

EVENTS

The **Townsend in the Smokies Spring Festival** takes place one week in April, and the **Autumn Leaves Arts & Crafts Fair** is held for a week in September. Contact the **Townsend Visitors Center** (7906 E. Lamar Alexander Pkwy., 800/525-6834 or 865/448-6134) for more information.

ACCOMMODATIONS

Bed-and-Breakfasts and Inns

⚊ Blackberry Farm (1471 W. Millers Cove Rd., 865/984-8166, www.blackberryfarm.com, $545–$1,045) harks back to the grand hotels of old, when guests went to one place, paid one price, and spent all their time there. This elegant inn sits on 1,100 acres and has 44 guest rooms, all furnished with English and American antiques. The price includes three gourmet meals per day and fully stocked pantries. Once guests stagger from the table, they can work off the calories at a fitness center, four tennis courts, a swimming pool, a trout pond, a three-acre bass and bream lake, and two off-site golf courses. Mountain bikes, fly-fishing gear, golf carts, binoculars, and tennis rackets are available. Special programs include cooking schools and fly-fishing expeditions.

The **Richmont Inn** (220 Winterberry Ln., 866/267-7086 or 865/448-6751, www.richmontinn.com, $135–240) was built to resemble the cantilevered Appalachian barns found in East Tennessee and western North Carolina. Inside, however, the traveler finds 18th-century English antiques, French paintings, and Swiss cooking. The 10 rooms are named for prominent Appalachian folks and contain whirlpool baths, king-size beds, fireplaces, and balconies. Pets are not welcome, but children over age 12 are. The rooms are among the best to be found in

these parts, but the food is icing on the cake—literally. Room rates include a candlelit dessert prepared by a chef who once won the grand prize in *Gourmet* magazine's dessert recipe contest. Breakfast might include french baked eggs or french toast à l'orange.

At the **Twin Valley Bed and Breakfast Horse Ranch** (2848 Old Chilhowee Rd., Walland,.865/984-0980, www.bbonline.com/tn/twinvalley, $105–120), energetic guests can pitch in with taking care of the horses, while the rest can just relax. This is not one of those B&Bs filled with antique English furniture. It is a comfortable place, housed in a hand-hewn log building decorated in country style, where guests don't have to worry about knocking into an expensive antique. The two rooms share a bath, and cabins are also available, as are backwoods wilderness shelters. The ranch serves a full country breakfast.

Cabins, Condos, and Chalets

Perhaps the most delightful place to stay hereabouts is in a cabin overlooking the Little River. Falling asleep with the window open on a cool evening, listening to the sound of flowing water, is about as good as it gets.

A word to the wise: Some property owners have had problems with guests hosting loud parties and have resorted to draconian rules, such as no visitors without written permission. If an unauthorized guest is detected (or a smuggled-in pet is found where animals aren't permitted), the rental agency has the right to throw everyone out with no refund of the rental fee.

The following is a short list of what is available, on the water and elsewhere, in Townsend. For a more complete list, call 800/525-6834 or visit www.smokymountains.org.

"Bear"ly Rustic Cabin Rentals (888/448-6036 www.townsendcabin.com) offers more than 40 completely furnished cabins and cottages. Rates begin at $99 per couple per night for two bedrooms. **Dogwood Cabins and Realty** (7016 E. Lamar Alexander Pkwy., 888/448-9054 or 865/448-1720, www.dogwoodcabins.com) offers waterside as well as mountain cabins for nightly and long-term rentals.

Carne's Log Cabins (865/448-1021, www.carneslogcabins.com) is located approximately one mile from the park entrance. **Old Smoky Mountain Cabins** (800/739-4820 or 865/448-2388, www.oldsmokymountaincabins.com) has cabins with one to eight bedrooms. **Wild Mountain Rose Log Cabin Rentals** (800/736-1938 or 865/448-6895, www.wildrosetn.com) has cabins with fireplaces, mountain views, and large porches with rockers.

Motels

Among the motel options are the **Best Western Valley View Lodge** (on Hwy. 321, 800/292-4844 or 865/448-2237), **Big Valley Motel** (7052 E. Lamar Alexander Pkwy., 865/448-6639), **Hampton Inn** (7824 E. Lamar Alexander Pkwy., 800/HAMPTON or 865/448-9000), **Highland Manor Motel** (Hwy. 321, 800/213-9462), and **Talley-Ho Inn** (8314 Hwy. 73, 800/448-2465 or 865/448-2465, www.talleyhoinn.com).

Camping

Most of the campgrounds in the Townsend area lie between Wears Valley Road and the entrance to the park along the Little River.

The 75 sites at **Lazy Daze Campground** (8429 Hwy. 73, 865/448-6061, www.lazydazecampground.com), some of them along the Little River and all with cable TV, await campers here. The campground is open year-round.

Little River Village Campground (865/448-2241, www.littlerivervillage.com) also lies along the Little River, with 136 sites and all the amenities you'll need. The campground is open March–November. Also on the Little River, **Mountaineer Campground** (865/448-6421) offers 49 sites and is open year-round.

The 144 sites at **Tremont Hills Campground** (865/448-6363, www.tremontcamp.com) are open from March 1 to the Sunday after Thanksgiving. **Ye Olde Mill Campground** (865/448-6681) offers 24 sites and fewer amenities than the larger places. It's open April–November.

FOOD

The **Carriage House** (8310 Hwy. 73, 865/448-2263) serves three daily meals of country cooking from April to November 15. The **Back Porch Restaurant** (7016 E. Lamar Alexander Pkwy., 865/448-6333) offers steaks, seafood, pasta, and other dishes, including teriyaki chicken.

Laurel Valley Country Club (865/448-6690) serves dinner on Friday and Saturday, brunch on Sunday, and lunch Monday–Friday. Meals include shrimp marinara, wild boar tenderloin, and grilled chicken. To get to the club, take Old Tuckaleechee Road off Hwy. 321, drive two miles, and follow the signs.

Mill House Restaurant (4737 Old Walland Hwy., 865/982-5726, www.blountweb.com/millhouse) occupies the former home of a Little River mill owner. The mill is no more, but the house has been transformed into perhaps the best place to eat this side of the Smokies. The Mill House is a prix fixe restaurant—all meals cost the same, in this case around $20. Seven courses make up the meal, with entrées of steak, seafood, chicken, and pork. The ambience is very relaxed; diners linger for a long time over the delicious food. Reservations are a very good idea. To get there, leave Townsend and drive toward Maryville. Watch for the sign 1.5 miles past the Walland turnoff. The restaurant is open weekends only.

SHOPPING

Nawger Knob Craft Settlement is a collection of two shops well worth a stop. If you've ever thought about taking up woodcarving, **Smoky Mountain Woodcarvers Supply** (800/541-5994, www.woodcarvers.com) has a great collection of tools, advice, and pieces of wood on which to begin.

Just next door is **Wood-N-Strings** (865/448-6647 www.clemmerdulcimer.com), a dulcimer shop featuring beautifully crafted versions of the old mountain instrument. Dulcimers are the easiest stringed instruments to play, and the ones here, crafted in woods such as walnut and cherry. On Saturday nights from May through September at 7 P.M., live mountain music is played on the front porch.

INFORMATION

The **Townsend Visitors Center** (7906 E. Lamar Alexander Pkwy., 800/525-6834 or 865/448-6134, www.smokymountains.org) is open daily 9 A.M.–6 P.M., except in January and February, when it is open only Friday to Sunday.

Maryville and Eastern Towns

The seat of Blount County, Maryville was named for the wife of Governor William Blount. This part of Tennessee saw a lot of conflict between Indians and settlers as the latter moved closer to the strongholds of the former. When the edge of the frontier was pushed west and south, Maryville lay on the route back east, and it prospered from travelers and trade.

Sam Houston, so instrumental in founding Texas, moved to this area from Virginia when he was 14 years old. When he was 19, he taught school for one term in a log schoolhouse that still stands here. In 1819, a Presbyterian minister founded a seminary that eventually became Maryville College. The college broke ground in many ways: It was the first seminary in the South, one of the first colleges to offer coeducation, and one of the few colleges open to black and Indian students.

Maryville is also the birthplace of Lamar Alexander, Republican governor of Tennessee from 1979 to 1987 and the first governor to be elected to consecutive four-year terms. He campaigned by wearing a plaid shirt and jeans and walking across the state, and was elected to the U.S. Senate in 2002.

The **Sam Houston Schoolhouse,** (865/983-1550, www.blountweb.com/samhouston, 10 A.M.–5 P.M. Mon.–Sat., 1–5 P.M. Sun., $0.50 adults, free for children) where the future president of the Republic of Texas served as a 19-year-old teacher, is a small structure built of poplar logs. It includes a visitor's center with a museum containing artifacts and pedagogical implements used by Houston and other teachers of that time. To get to the schoolhouse, drive three miles north out of Maryville on Route 33 to the intersection of Sam Houston Schoolhouse Road. Go right for two miles and look for a sign on the left.

PRACTICALITIES

Accommodations

Due to its proximity to Knoxville's McGee Tyson Airport, Maryville has an assortment of franchise motels. For something less generic try the **High Court Inn** (212 High St., 865/981-2966, $59–69), which occupies a 1911 house down the street from the Blount County Courthouse. The house, which has been completely restored, has three guest rooms, all with private baths, four-poster beds, and claw-foot bathtubs.

Food

Ⓜ Buddy's Bar-be-que (518 Foothills Plaza, 865/984-4475) is a Knoxville-based chain with good food. It's open daily for lunch and dinner.

Order in the Court Cafe (212 High St., 865/984-3861) presides Monday–Friday over lunches of soups, sandwiches, and salads. Brunch is served Sunday, 10 A.M.–1 P.M.

The Southern Skillet (1311 E. Lamar Alexander Pkwy., 865/984-9680) offers country cooking and homemade desserts. It serves all three meals seven days a week.

Shopping

Lee's World of Crafts (370 Gill St., Alcoa, 865/984-7674) sells prints, quilts, baskets, furniture, and other items. Open from 9 A.M.–6 P.M. Monday–Saturday.

Information

Visit the **Blount County Chamber of Commerce** (309 S. Washington St., Maryville, 865/983-2241, www.blountchamber.com) 8 A.M.–5 P.M. Monday–Friday.

Gateways to the Smokies

ALCOA

Several Tennessee towns were founded or controlled by industries that have extracted the natural resources of the state. Alcoa was perhaps the only company town whose raw materials did not come from Tennessee. As well as the name of the town, Alcoa is an acronym for the Aluminum Company of America. In 1910, it began buying land along the Little Tennessee River to create a series of lakes for waterpower to produce cheap electricity—a big part of the cost of making aluminum.

The company located its factory outside Maryville in 1913 and incorporated Alcoa to house workers. The town, which segregated blacks and whites, included parks, commercial areas, schools, and other facilities. Although labor strife plagued Alcoa in the 1930s, its town and its industry boomed during World War II, when the workforce hit 12,000 people. Alcoans had a high standard of living compared to the rest of the state, and that prosperity influenced Maryville and Blount County as well.

The company no longer owns the town, which is virtually indistinguishable from Maryville, but it still gets electricity from four dams on the Little Tennessee River. And the company continues to prosper, with a workforce of 2,000 that makes aluminum for beverage cans.

HARTFORD

At Exit 447 on I-40, Hartford is the first Tennessee town that the traveler from North Carolina encounters. Once a logging center, Hartford is now enjoying a revival thanks to white-water rafting on the Big Pigeon River.

Nearby is the **French Broad Outpost Ranch** (800/995-7678 or visit www.frenchbroadriver.com), a dude ranch offering horseback riding, rafting, and other activities. Eight-day

FOOTHILLS PARKWAY

To outlanders, this road makes no sense. It stops and it starts, one section dumps motorists into Wears Valley for no apparent reason, then it lurches back to life near Cosby for a short time before terminating onto I-40.

As is often with such matters, therein lies a tale. The Blue Ridge Parkway was proposed in the 1920s to link Shenandoah National Park and the Great Smokies. The proposal set off a political tug-of-war between politicians from North Carolina and Tennessee, each of whom hoped to bring the dollars and jobs to their state. North Carolina won, and today the Blue Ridge Parkway hosts around 27,000 people per day. They motor along the ridge tops, descending into valleys to fill up their gas tanks and empty their wallets.

Foothills Parkway represents an effort to replicate that golden goose, this time on the Tennessee side of the park. In 1944, Congress passed a bill creating the parkway but was slow in coming up with the money. The first mile was paved in 1960, and over the years the road has grown in fits and starts. Later, attitudes changed, and a good many people came to think that building a ridge-top road was not the best way to treat a wilderness area.

Pressure grew, however, for anything that would relieve the congestion of Hwy. 441 through the park. In 1999, money was approved for the first of 10 bridges that would complete the 1.6-mile missing link of the 16.1-mile Walland to Wears Valley segment of the parkway. The missing link consists of very rough terrain, and bridging just this 1.6-mile gap is likely to cost more than $60 million. Even after this segment is finished, the Foothills Parkway will be only half of its proposed length.

Even those who oppose completing the road have to admit that by buying the ridge-top property, the government has prevented philistines from building monstrous houses that would spoil the view for miles.

packages are available, as are three- and four-day stays.

COSBY

This small community was once considered "the Moonshine Capital of the World," a distinction that locals are only now beginning to acknowledge with pride. Cosby retains a small-town feel that long ago departed from places such as Gatlinburg and Pigeon Forge. This is a good place to stay—close enough to enjoy the national park—yet far from the hordes of people.

The Fort

Halfway between Cosby and Newport stands The Fort (423/487-2544), a singular establishment up Dark Hollow Road, an address right out of a bluegrass song. Consisting primarily of a doublewide mobile home on the side of a hill, The Fort, also known as Fort Marx, is alleged to occasionally serve the product that made Cosby famous. "Good to the last drop" takes on a whole new meaning here. Hamburgers, fried rabbit, and other delectables are available—the specialty is Moonshine Cherries. The Fort is open every day except Sunday from 4 P.M. "until everyone goes home."

To get to the Fort from Cosby, go north on Hwy. 321/32 to Wilton Springs Road. Turn right and drive one mile to Dark Hollow Road, which goes off to the right just before a bridge. Drive one mile and look up the hill on the right. And don't get in any arguments inside.

Sights

The first stop in Cosby, particularly for music lovers, should be **Musicrafts** (423/487-5543). To get there from I-40, take Exit 440 and follow Hwy. 321/73 to the intersection with Hwy. 32. Take Hwy. 32 for less than a mile and turn right into a small driveway. Founded almost 40 years ago by Lee and Gene Schilling, this very rustic center publishes books, releases folk music recordings, and distributes the music of others. It also sells dulcimers, hammered dulcimers, and other instruments. The center is open daily from 10 A.M. until "5 or so" and may close during cold winter weekends.

Cosby is also home to several apple orchards. **Carver's Orchard** (on Hwy. 321 about 3.5 miles

Gateways to the Smokies

© JEFF BRADLEY

Gene and Lee Shilling, owners of Musicrafts

beyond the Cosby post office, 423/487-2419) grows more than 100 varieties of apples—old favorites as well as exotics such as Ginger Gold, Jena Gold, and Fuji. Apple harvesting begins in June and extends well into the fall. Visitors are welcome to watch cider being pressed, taste it, and buy apples, honey, molasses, pumpkins, and Indian corn. Carver's is open seven days a week year-round.

Deerfoot Quilts (3892 Hwy. 321, 423/487-3866), located in a log building at, offers high-quality quilts—usually 80 to 100 locally made ones are in the store at any given time—plus clothing and quilting supplies.

ℕ Ramp Festival

Perhaps the best time to visit Cosby is during one of its festivals. The longest-running gathering in Cosby is the Ramp Festival, (423/625-9675, $5 adults, $3 children ages 6–12). a celebration of the ramp, a pungent, onionlike plant has been described as "the gift that keeps giving"—in one's breath and through one's pores. Ramps, now featured in tony New York City restaurants, are eaten in hereabouts in omelets, straight, or as side dishes along with barbecue and chicken. The festival, held the first Sunday in May, is a one-day affair consisting of music, crafts, the selection of the Maid of Ramps, and plenty of handpicked bluegrass music.

Accommodations

Whisperwood Farm (800/962-2246 or 423/487-4000, www.whisperwoodretreat.com), located at Middle Creek Road and Hwy. 321, offers bed-and-breakfast accommodations and a variety of one- and two-bedroom cabins.

Cosby Creek Cabins (800/508-8844, www.cosbycreekcabins.com) offers one-, two-, and three-bedroom cabins, some of which overlook Cosby Creek and have a view of the mountains. **Whisperwood Farm** (800/423-2030, www.wildwood-acres.com), features log cabins outfitted with modern appliances.

Food

Cosby Barbecue Pit (Hwy. 321 near the Cosby

post office, 423/487-5438) offers ribs, pork barbecue, hamburgers, and steaks. It's open Tuesday–Sunday except November–March, when it is open only on weekends.

ℕ The Front Porch (Hwy. 321 halfway between Cosby and Newport, 423/487-2875) is worth a visit all by itself. This restaurant features a trained culinarian—as rare in these parts as a metaphysician—and this evidences itself in portobello mushroom steaks, rib-eye steak, and dry ribs. Patrons can also enjoy live bluegrass and occasionally blues. Open only Friday through Sunday for dinner, the restaurant also serves enchiladas, chimichangas, and other Mexican dishes, as well as vegetarian versions thereof. Italian food is available, too. Brown bagging is permitted.

Get seats early for dinner on Friday and Saturday; the music takes off at 8:30 P.M. and soars until 10:30 or 11. There is no cover charge, although diners are expected to order at least $6 worth of food, and the band is very likely to pass the hat. Eating ribs while listening to bluegrass is about as down-home as you can get. But note that Sunday night's atmosphere is more akin to that of a coffeehouse. The music begins at 6:30 P.M.

Shopping

Treasures of Appalachia (4819 Cosby Hwy., 423/487-3111, www.treasuresofappalachia.com) is a collective of 40-plus local craftspeople who sell furniture, custom knives, wood art, and much more in a unassuming log cabin. Closed December–February.

Holloway's Country Home (3892 Cosby Hwy., 423/487-3866, www.hollowaysquilts.com) offers genuine Appalachian quilts, not those cheap imports from China. Cloth and quilting supplies are available as well.

Santa Cruz Woodworks (2766 Cosby Hwy., 423/623-7856) makes hutches and cabinets, pie safes, trunks and tables, maple rocking chairs, maple porch swings, and birdhouses.

Information

The best website for Cosby is www.cocke county.com. Another source of info is the **Newport Chamber Of Commerce** (423/623-7201).

NEWPORT

Anyone who has eaten canned vegetables or made pasta sauce from canned tomatoes has probably had an inadvertent brush with Newport. About the turn of the 20th century, the Stokely family, headquartered in Newport, began canning tomatoes and shipping them downstream to the growing cities of Knoxville and Chattanooga. The company grew so strong that it bought Van Camp, an Indiana food producer.

Although the Stokelys mainly produced comestibles, one branch of the family turned to food for the mind. The late James Stokely, son of the first president of the family firm, married Wilma Dykeman of Asheville, North Carolina. Together they wrote books about the causes of racism and about people who worked to overcome it. On her own, Dykeman published a series of novels, as well as a history of Tennessee. Her writings, both fiction and nonfiction, illuminate the state in a manner that few writers can match. Jim Stokely, their son, continued the literary tradition as coeditor of *An Encyclopedia of East Tennessee.*

As in Cosby, Newport and surrounding Cocke County used to be home to entrepreneurs who could transform corn into a much more portable and potable product. At one time it was said that more Mason jars were sold in Newport than anywhere else in the country.

While driving along Main Street away from I-40, look for the stone building to the right at Traffic Light 9. It's the **Rhea-Mims Hotel,** at one time one of the more famous hostelries in these parts. The round stones prominent in the walls are said to be grindstones from Cherokee Indian mills.

The **Cocke County Museum** (433-B Cosby Hwy., 423/623-7201) is located in the offices of the Newport Chamber of Commerce, where visitors can get information about the past and present. The former includes artifacts from Ben Hooper, a local boy who became governor of the state, and from Grace Moore, an East Tennessee diva. The museum is open Monday–Friday by appointment only. Admission is free.

Accommodations

Christopher Place, (800/595-9441 or 423/623-6555, www.christopherplace.com, $150–300) sits amid 200 scenic acres. Four rooms and four suites await guests, who can enjoy a pool, a tennis court, and a casual dining room. Although listed in Newport, this elegant place is located on the east side of I-40. Most of Newport's other lodging, of the franchise variety, lies along I-40.

Food

A visit to **The Grease Rack** (423/623-9279) gave one diner a sense of what it must have been like to go to a speakeasy. The parking lot of the former garage—thus the name—was full of cars and pickup trucks, yet the door was locked. After a tentative knock, someone inside peered out the peephole, then the door opened, revealing a honky-tonk bar with country music blaring away. All the patrons turned to inspect the visitor. "Is this a restaurant?" "Sure," came the reply. "Just follow me." In the back was a large, windowless room filled with all manner of folks—couples, families, and singles. Steak and seafood is the fare here, in generous portions. The knock-at-the-door business is a means of complying with Cocke County's peculiar liquor laws.

The Grease Rack is open for dinner Thursday–Saturday. To get there from the Interstate, go to Traffic Light 12, then drive right on Lincoln Avenue for 0.7 miles. At the blinking yellow light, drive 0.3 miles on Morrell Springs Road. To see a lively side of Cocke County, secure a table when a University of Tennessee football game is being televised on a Saturday night.

Newport is also home of one of the best Thai restaurants in East Tennessee. The **Thai Kitchen** (323 Village Shopping Center, 423/623-2752) serves traditional Thai food for lunch Tuesday–Friday and dinner Tuesday–Saturday.

Just outside of town, on Hwy. 160 between Morristown and Newport, Greek-American food is the order of the day. **C. J. Papadops** (551 Briar Thicket Rd., 423/623-0933) serves lamb and Greek salads as well as steak, lasagna, and spaghetti. This place is open for dinner Thursday–Sunday.

Shopping

Rhyne Clock Company (211 W. Main St., 423/623-2324) is a family-owned business that manufactures grandfather clocks using cherry, walnut, oak, and poplar wood and German clockworks.

Information

For information, contact the **Newport/Cocke County Chamber of Commerce** (803 Prospect St., 423/623-7201, 423/625-9675, www.cocke-county.com).

DEL RIO

Before the railroad arrived, farmers in East Tennessee could get the best prices for their goods in the Carolinas. And the easiest products to ship were those that could transport themselves. In *Touring the East Tennessee Backroads*, Carolyn Sakowski estimates that every year drovers herded some 150,000 to 200,000 hogs to the Carolinas along the French Broad River through what is now Del Rio. A healthy hog, it seems, could hike 8 to 10 miles per day, a porcine procession that stopped every night at designated stock stands along the way. "It was not uncommon," she writes, "for ten to twelve herds numbering from 300 to 1,000 or 2,000 animals apiece to stop overnight and feed at the stands."

The most famous person from Del Rio was opera singer Grace Moore, who was born here in 1901 and lived here until 1906. "The Tennessee Nightingale" made her debut at the New York Metropolitan Grand Opera Company in 1927. She appeared in *La Bohème, Tosca,* and *Romeo and Juliet,* to name a few. She went on to star in a series of movies; *One Night of Love* is the most famous. She died in a plane crash outside Copenhagen in 1947, at the height of her fame.

Del Rio is more famous now as the setting for *Christy,* a novel published in 1967 by Catherine Marshall and based loosely on the experiences of her mother. The book tells of a religious 19-year-old who goes to a remote corner of Tennessee—Cutters Gap in the book—to teach in a mission school in 1912. A television series based

on the novel renewed interest in the story, and for a few seasons it was performed as an outdoor drama in Townsend, Tennessee.

Christy has developed something of a cult following, as seen on any number of websites. Devotees who don't mind dirt roads can make the pilgrimage to see the community on which the novel was based.

There is not a great deal to see; only the foundations of the original buildings remain, but in warm weather this is a good place for a picnic. To get there, get off Hwy. 25/70 at Del Rio. Head south on Hwy. 107, then turn right on Old Fifteenth Road. Go 4.3 miles and turn right at the Sand Hill Church of God. Two-tenths of a mile later, go right up a hill at a fork onto Chapel Hollow Road. Continue for one mile until you see the signs. Farther up the road from the site is the home of Larry Myers, a keeper of the *Christy* flame.

Down-home music is offered every Saturday night at **Hillbilly's Music Barn** in Del Rio. No admission is charged, and no drinking is allowed. Local artists perform bluegrass and old-time music. Patrons, if they feel so inclined, are welcome to get up and do some clogging.

To hear the music, take Hwy. 107 until it becomes a dirt road. At that point, go right for about three-fourths of a mile on Blue Mill Road, which is asphalt. Look for the Hillbilly's sign and turn left. Cross a creek and drive a quarter of a mile. Hillbilly's is on the left. For more information, call 423/487-5541.

DANDRIDGE

Dandridge is a town whose historic buildings, though on the National Register, are still inhabited, where cute little shops have not invaded, and where the drugstore still has a lunch counter.

As far as anyone knows, it is the only town named for Martha Dandridge Custis Washington, wife of George. Created in 1793, Dandridge became the seat of Jefferson County. Troops moved back and forth through the town during the Civil War. One night a Union general stayed in a local house. Events the next day caused him to depart in haste, leaving a bottle of very good brandy. The following night Confederates stayed in the same house and made humorous toasts with the brandy until it was gone.

Dandridge may have been named after Martha Washington, but another president's wife once saved the town. When the Tennessee Valley Authority was planning Douglas Dam on the French Broad River, it looked like curtains for Dandridge—the town would soon be underwater. A local grande dame bombarded senators with letters of protest, to no avail. Finally, she sent her poems and pleas to Eleanor Roosevelt, who prevailed on Franklin to issue a presidential decree ordering that a dike be built to save the town. Newcomers still get a surprise when they climb what looks like a big hill behind the town and top it to see a great expanse of water.

The **Jefferson County Courthouse** contains one of those wonderfully eclectic museums that fill Tennessee. Here, in corridors that lead to offices of assorted bureaucrats, one can gaze for free on a hornet's nest, a German World War II helmet, Vietnamese sandals, the remnants of a moonshiner's still, Civil War bullets, and the marriage license issued to one David Crockett.

Across the street lies **Tinsley-Bible Drugs** (865/397-3444), a store with old furnishings and new merchandise. The action, however, takes place at the six-seat lunch counter and nearby booths, where a cheeseburger is inexpensive but the accompanying dose of small-town life is priceless. Here, one will see county officials—one dignified-looking gent addressed as "Judge"—giggling high school girls, and assorted others. It's open 8 A.M.–6 P.M. Monday–Friday and 8 A.M.–2 P.M. on Saturday.

Accommodations

The Barrington Inn (1174 McGuire Rd., New Market, 888/205-8482 or 865/397-3368, www.bbonline.com/tn/barrington, $75–125) is actually out in the country between Dandridge and New Market, but a mere 2.5 miles off I-40. The inn offers three rooms in a restored farmhouse and three more in a Dairy House. All rooms have some sort of sitting area and private baths. Perhaps the best reason to stay here is for the food, which is described

© JEFF BRADLEY

hardware store, Dandridge

Gateways to the Smokies

below. Dinner is available to guests every night by prior arrangement.

Goose Creek Farm Bed and Breakfast (865/397-6166, www.bbonline.com/tn/goose creek , $80 and up) is a restored farmhouse on 12 acres. Located next to a barn and former milking parlor, it contains three bedrooms.

Mill Dale Farm Bed and Breakfast (140 Mill Dale Rd., 800/767-3471 or 865/397-3470, $72) occupies a 19th-century farmhouse decorated with period furniture. It's one mile north of I-40.

Take Hwy. 139 west out of Dandridge for a pleasant drive to the **Mountain Harbor Inn** (1199 Hwy. 139, 866/249-1050, www.mountain harborinn.com, $65–125), a place right on Douglas Lake where one can look across the water and see the Smoky Mountains. All 12 rooms have quilts hanging on the walls and come with microwave ovens, coffeemakers, refrigerators, and private baths.

Deep Springs Settlement (865/397-1460) gives visitors a chance to experience the old ways of cabin living: woodstoves, oil lamps, and rocking chairs on the porch. This place also has a plowing festival and a molasses festival.

Camping

Douglas Lake Campground is the closest to Dandridge. It offers 100 sites with full hookups, a Laundromat, boating, fishing, and swimming. To get there, go east on Hwy. 9 out of town. Turn right on Oak Grove Road.

Fancher's Campground (865/397-3510) lies on the French Broad River (Douglas Lake) upstream from Dandridge. It has 324 sites, boating, swimming, and fishing. It also has a lot of noise from the traffic on I-40. To get there, take Hwy. 9 east out of town, cross the river, and look for the sign.

Food

The Barrington Inn (1174 McGuire Rd., New Market, 888/205-8482 or 865/397-3368) is one of the better restaurants on this end of the state; the proprietors used to run a restaurant in Key West. Dinner is offered to non-guests Thursday–Saturday. The menu includes entrées such New Zealand crown rack of lamb, beef Wellington, ground ostrich wrapped in veal, and lobster and shrimp croustade. These cost from $13 to $28 per person.

Cowboys on the Water (1435 Hwy. 139, 865/397-2529) has a name that doesn't make sense—until diners understand that "Cowboy" was the founder of this very informal and fun place. You'll find fishing and western gear on the walls and sawdust and peanut shells on the floor, but it's the food on the plates that keeps people coming back: shrimp, clams, flounder, catfish, crab legs, steak, and burgers. Open every day for dinner only.

Or try the restaurant at **Mountain Harbor Inn** (1199 Hwy. 139, 865/397-3345). It's open Friday–Sunday; reservations are a good idea. Prime rib is the specialty of the house—10 ounces for $18—while grilled chicken breast and chargrilled fish are available as well. Lunch is served Friday and Saturday and includes a wide choice of sandwiches, salads, and pastas.

If you want a burger and the **Tinsley-Bible Drugs** lunch counter doesn't satisfy, go to the Dandridge exit (Exit 417) of I-40 for a selection of franchise restaurants.

Information

For more information, contact the **Jefferson County Chamber of Commerce** (865/397-9642, www.jefferson-tn-chamber.org).

Great Smoky Mountains National Park

Always enwrapped in the illusory mists, always touching the evasive clouds, the peaks of the Great Smoky Mountains are like some barren ideal, that has bartered for the vague isolations of a higher atmosphere the material values of the warm world below. Upon those mighty and majestic domes no tree strikes root, no hearth is alight; humanity is an alien thing, and utility set at naught. Below, dense forests cover the massive, precipitous slopes of the range, and in the midst of the wilderness a clearing shows, here and there, and the roof of a humble log cabin; in the valley, far, far lower still, a red spark at dusk may suggest a home, nestling in the cove. Grain grows apace in these scanty clearings, for the soil in certain favored spots is mellow; and the weeds grow, *too, and in a wet season the ploughs are fain to be active. They are of the bull-tongue variety, and are sometimes drawn by oxen. As often as otherwise they are followed by women.*

Craddock, Charles Egbert (Mary Murfree), The Prophet of the Great Smoky Mountains, *1885*

Forget the Grand Canyon, Yellowstone, and Yosemite: Great Smoky Mountains National Park attracts more visitors than any other national park in the country—roughly 10 million guests visit every year. Consequently, if you're looking for some quality time with Mother Nature, you'll need to leave the beaten path.

Fortunately, doing this is easy for the most part: Simply get out of the car. Roughly 95 percent of all visitors to the Smokies never venture

Must-Sees

Look for **M** to find the sights and activities you can't miss and **M** for the best dining and lodging.

M Parson Branch Road: Almost everyone goes to Cades Cove, but very few take this backwoods road through the forest on the way home (page 391).

M Cataloochee Valley: Great views, historic structures, and no crowds are waiting on the North Carolina side of the park (page 393).

M Cades Cove: This wonderful combination of natural beauty and the remnants of a once-vibrant community of mountaineers is best enjoyed by wandering its hiking trails (page 394).

M Clingmans Dome: The highest point in the Park offers a 360-degree view of Appalachian splendor. A mere 1.8 miles down the trail, **Andrews Bald** presents eight acres of open space with stupendous views and few people (page 395).

Cades Cove

M Mount LeConte: Five trails lead to this summit, with its wonderful lodge and trail shelter. The shortest and steepest is the **Alum Cave Trail** (page 395).

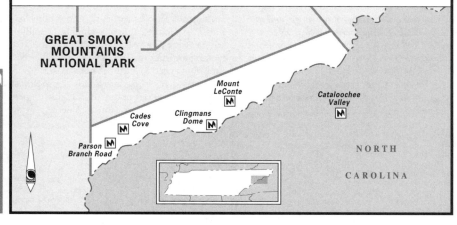

GREAT SMOKY MOUNTAINS NATIONAL PARK

Mount LeConte M

Cataloochee Valley M

Cades Cove M

Clingmans Dome M

Parson M Branch Road

NORTH

CAROLINA

Smoky Mountains

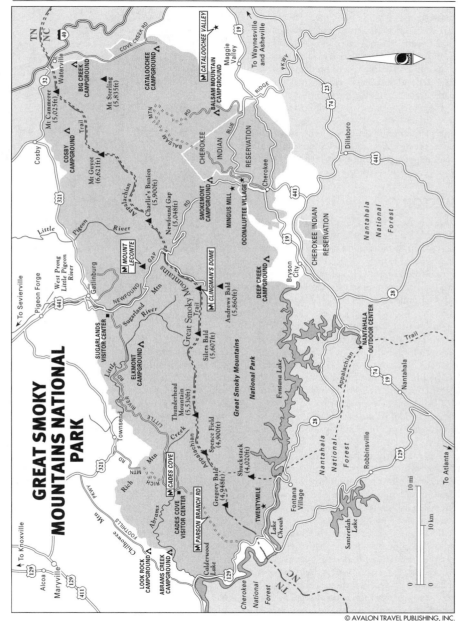

GREAT SMOKY MOUNTAINS NATIONAL PARK

Smoky Mountains

© AVALON TRAVEL PUBLISHING, INC.

more than 100 yards from their vehicles. Hike 101 yards down the nearest trail, and you have escaped nearly 9.5 million of those 10 million visitors. And the remaining half million, fortunately, don't come all at once. Even on the park's busiest summer and autumn weekends, you'll find the park's trails reasonably serene.

Certainly, you can't beat the price. Though this 520,000-acre, 800-square-mile park stands as one of the nation's most-visited tourist attractions, the original park charter forever forbid the charging of an admission fee. So even today, you won't pay a dime to enter the park.

HISTORY

The sanctuary that is Great Smoky Mountains National Park was, like most sanctuaries, born of necessity. The devastation that led to the birth of the park came at the sharp end of an axe—by way of the railroads. Once railroads gave eastern lumber interests access to long-undisturbed areas of timber, the trees began falling at a disturbing rate.

Influential Knoxville businessman Willis P. Davis and his wife returned from a trip to the western national parks in 1923 and suggested that the Park Service make a park in the Smokies before it was too late. Fortunately, as lumbermen decimated the area's forests in the 1920s, the same trains that hauled out lumber began to haul in tourists, an important (if inadvertent) step in raising public support for a park.

The early visitors to the Smokies were so impressed with what they saw—and so mortified by the encroaching devastation from logging—that they joined the Davises and their Knoxville friends in asking Washington to step in and declare the area a national park.

The Coolidge administration was willing to talk. The large national parks in the West had proved popular, but for the vast majority of Americans, these parks were a thousand or more miles away. In practice, these "parks for the people" served mainly moneyed folks like the Davises who had the leisure time and funds to travel to, say, Yellowstone or Yosemite. The Department of

This couple once lived in the area that is now the national park.

the Interior was looking to create new, more accessible parks in the East.

However, the government had run into problems. Creating parks in the out west had mostly involved setting aside lands already owned by the federal government. But the East had been settled earlier and more thoroughly than the West. Most areas of natural beauty in the East had long histories as summer or winter playgrounds for the upper classes, who held expensive deeds on their vacation properties and sway with those in power. Thus, it would not do to turn, say, the Poconos, Cape Cod, or Miami Beach into a national park. What was needed instead was an eastern area of scenic beauty, sparsely populated with people of negligible political power—people who could be bought out cheaply and forced out quietly.

Making Room

In the Smokies, the National Park Service found its prize. Some subsistence Appalachian farmers

MOST VISITED NATIONAL PARKS

In recent years, park attendance has been down. After September 11, 2001, the average American's fear of high oil prices brought visitation figures down a little from the 10 million-plus numbers of the late 1990s. The growing popularity of new Midwestern Clinton-era parks such as Ohio's Cuyahoga Valley National Park (which drew 2.9 million visitors in 2003), may have siphoned off a bit of the pressure on the Smokies' natural resources. Nonetheless, the Smokies still leads the park pack by several lengths.

1. Great Smoky Mountains National Park, 9,4 million visits annually, on 521,621 acres (18 visits per acre)

2. Grand Canyon National Park, 4.1 million visits annually, on 1,217,403 acres (3.4 visits per acre)

3. Yosemite National Park, 3.4 million visits annually, on 761,266 acres (4.4 visits per acre)

4. Olympic National Park, 3.2 million visits annually, on 922,650 acres (3.5 visits per acre)

5. Rocky Mountain National Park, 3.1 million visits annually, on 265,722 acres (11.7 visits per acre)

6. Yellowstone National Park, 3.0 million visits annually, on 2,219,790 acres (1.4 visits per acre)

would undoubtedly be happy to sell for what seemed like a good price, and those who weren't would not be well connected enough to stand up against the pro-park forces. Though many wealthy Knoxvillians owned vacation homes in the area, many were willing to allow—and even supported—the creation of a national park as a way to protect the scenic beauty around their weekend cabins and lodges. Once all the proper donations had been made and strings had been pulled, the National Park Service allowed these people to lease for as long as they, and in some cases their children, were alive.

Even still, the farmers and lumber companies who owned land in the Smokies did have to be paid *something*. Congress balked at footing the bill. However, the states of North Carolina and Tennessee, which had been working to build their economies through increased tourism and improved roads, willingly contributed. Both state governments hoped to rope the park within their borders. The present-day border-straddling location of the park serves as a nice compromise.

In 1926, President Calvin Coolidge—himself a flinty son of the Appalachians of southern Vermont—signed the bill that authorized and protected the area as a federal park, but it could not be created until the NPS had acquired 150,000 acres in the area.

Private citizens and companies gave land and money, but it would take nearly $12 million to acquire all the desired parcels. North Carolina finally gave up its quest to have the park completely within its borders and agreed to donate $2,162,283 toward a park straddling the Tennessee line—but only if Tennessee coughed up $2 million of its own. Tennessee's legislature raced into session and came out with $2,345,330, and Congress eventually came through with $2,293,265 from Washington. Then a couple of major park supporters buttonholed John D. Rockefeller Jr. and persuaded him to cut a check for $5 million. Suddenly, the fund-raising portion of the venture was over.

But having the money and owning the land were two separate things. More than 6,000 parcels had to be purchased, including some 1,200 small farms owned by mountain families, many of whom had lived on the land for generations. Eventually, the 150,000 acres—and more—would come: All the money suddenly floating around the mountains mollified most of the park's opponents quickly enough. The lumber companies, which had initially led the opposition to the park on economic grounds, could be and were bought out. Entire lumber company towns such as Smokemont were

Smoky Mountains

CANTILEVER BARNS

While log cabins in the Great Smokies were not all that different from log houses built anywhere else in a hardwood forest, the overhanging barns erected in East Tennessee were found in few other parts of the country. Writing in the *Tennessee Encyclopedia,* Marian Moffett reported that she and another researcher found "only six cantilever barns in Virginia and another three in North Carolina. By contrast, 316 cantilever barns were found in Tennessee, with 183 in Sevier County, 106 in Blount County, and the remaining 27 scattered from Johnson to Bradley counties." Professor Moffet coauthored *East Tennessee Cantilever Barns,* published by the University of Tennessee Press in 1993.

Cantilever barns imaginatively create shelter with a minimal use of material. As best seen at the **Tipton Farm** in Cades Cove, a cantilever barn begins with two boxlike log structures measuring 12 by 16 or 18 feet and placed about 15 feet apart. The logs at the top of these boxes extend out to support a second floor, which not only bridges the gap between the two structures but also stretches eight or 10 feet out in each direction to create shelter underneath. In an area where annual rainfall can be 63 inches or more, sheltering animals and farm equipment was very important.

Most cantilever barns were built during a 50-year period beginning in 1870, yet innovative architects still use the form. The main building of **Richmont Inn,** a luxurious resort in Townsend (www.richmontinn.com), takes the shape of a four-story cantilever barn. And Maya Lin, the award-winning designer of the Vietnam Veterans Memorial, restored and re-created a cantilever barn as an ultramodern sky-lit reading room for the Langston Hughes Library at the **Children's Defense Fund's conference and training center** in Norris, Tennessee.

evacuated and dissembled. The companies were compensated for their losses.

More sustained opposition came from some of the area's 7,300 farmers. Roughly half gladly took the money and moved to cities or more fertile farming lands, but the other half wanted to stay. They became the biggest obstacle to the park's founding. In the days before Social Security cards, most mountain people had experienced little if any contact with the federal government. They found it outrageous that flatlanders in business suits were suddenly going to take their land—to make, of all things, a park for flatlanders. Some gave up, bewildered, but others stood up courageously to the strange, powerful forces that had come for their land. Courage, however, doesn't buy good attorneys, and nearly all of these opponents ended up expelled from the park's boundaries within the next several years. By 1939, the *WPA Guide to North Carolina* would describe the park as "largely deserted by its inhabitants."

In a humane gesture, the government allowed a few elderly and sick mountain people lifetime leases to their own land. But they couldn't hunt

and fish, cut firewood, or farm using the old ways. Many who had permission to stay ended up leaving anyway, out of frustration. Others, over the next decades, saw their ex-neighbors making a good living providing tourist amenities in the gateway towns and moved outside the park to share in the bonanza.

One last group of park opponents consisted of local conservationists who favored national forest rather than national park status for the Smokies. They believed that a national park would attract huge crowds of visitors, compromising the mountains' peaceful atmosphere and threatening its distinct vegetation and wildlife. They lost the battle, of course, but you can't fault this group for a lack of foresight.

A Park Is Born

By 1934, the governments of Tennessee and North Carolina had purchased more than double the required acreage—more than 300,000 of the park's present-day 520,000 acres—and signed it over to the Department of the Interior. On June 15, 1934, the U.S. Congress formally bequeathed

COURTESY OF GREAT SMOKY MOUNTAINS NATIONAL PARK

The Smokies are named for the mist that usually hovers in the mountains.

national park status to the Smokies, freeing up the Park Service to develop the area for visitors. The Depression was on, but the Civilian Conservation Corps (CCC) was at full throttle. The corps went on to build the park a strong infrastructure— roads, bridges, trails, and campgrounds—and other sturdy, often inspired, amenities.

Although as late as 1939 not a single campground had yet opened for business, on September 2, 1940, President Franklin D. Roosevelt bumped along in a caravan up the dirt road to Newfound Gap for a dedication ceremony. Thousands of others arrived in hundreds of cars to attend. Thus, from the beginning, traffic and crowds have been part of the park scene.

Humans and Nature

Great Smoky Mountains National Park, as it appeared in those days, would shock us today. Under private ownership, whole sections had been clear-cut; large gullies ran down the hillsides, and many streams were filled with silt and nearly devoid of life. Bear, deer, and other game had been hunted to the edge of extinction

and were only slowly beginning to reassert themselves in the area. Left alone, however, nature quietly reclaimed the land. Now towering trees grow along roads that were once railbeds, and the vegetation is so lush that most folks drive blissfully by what they assume to be virgin forest.

Visitation has steadily increased in the Smokies over time. The interstate highway system soon put the park within a day's drive of an estimated one-third of the U.S. population, and a great portion of that one-third made the trip. While the number of visitors has doubled and doubled and doubled again, the roads in the park have largely stayed the same size, causing congestion during summer and even worse traffic during the fall foliage season. The Park Service has resisted efforts to widen the roads and ignored other schemes meant to increase accessibility at the expense of ecology, among them a suggestion to run a chairlift from Gatlinburg to Clingmans Dome. In doing so, the Park Service has preserved a wonderful wilderness area, one that continues to provide inspiration and joy to those who come to see it.

Smoky Mountains

Recent Developments

In October 2000, Mike Tollefson became the park's new superintendent. A Seattle native, the new chief came straight from the head position at Sequoia and Kings Canyon National Parks in central California, where he had overseen the removal of nearly 300 park buildings as part of an effort to protect ancient sequoias. His announced priorities at the Smokies included improving air quality and, not unrelated, reducing traffic in the Cades Cove area. By 2004, debate was still underway concerning proposals to replace private vehicular traffic in Cades Cove with a shuttle or rail system. Plans were also being discussed to destroy and remove the buildings in the Elkmont area so that the Victorian-era logging and resort community could be returned to its natural state. But before that issue could be decided, Tollefson was shuttled back to the Sierras to head up Yosemite National Park, and Yosemite's National Park Superintendent David Mihalic was assigned to take over the reins at GSMNP. But Mihalic refused the job, retiring from the National Park Service rather than being forced to complete a pair of projects that he had personally opposed since his days as GSMNP's deputy superintendent in the 1980s: the completion of a road along the north rim of Fontana Lake, and the transfer of the Ravensford tract, within park boundaries, to the Cherokee Nation for development as a site for three schools. Ron Tipton of the National Parks Conservation Association dubbed the proposed projects "two of the largest threats to any park in the national park system."

This latter project allowed the Cherokee to bridge a NPS-owned gap in the Qualla Boundary, while giving them access to some of the only suitable, available land for their schools. Nonetheless, it raised the ire of many enviromentalists, generally political liberals who nonetheless found themselves opposing a Native American tribe as it attempted to regain possession of land their ancestors had held for thousands of years. When the ironies had settled, the Ravensford Tract had been transferred to the Cherokee (in exchange for the Yellow Face tract along the Blue Ridge Parkway). At publication, Mihalic had moved to Montana and had run unsuccessfully for Lieutenant Governor as a Republican.

The Battle of the North Shore Road

The proposal for the 28-mile North Shore Road along Fontana Lake dated back to 1943, when one of Franklin Delano Roosevelt's TVA dam projects drove thousands of Appalachian residents from their homes, and flooded the road they used to access over 20 cemeteries where their family members were buried. As part of the agreement with the displaced residents, the New Dealers promised to build a road to the cemeteries, and to compensate Swain County for the loss of county lands, but other priorities kept the road from being started until the late 1950s. In 1962, after blasting a 1,200-foot tunnel through solid rock and laying nine miles of road, park officials realized that the proposed road would cut through Anakeesta rock, releasing acids and heavy metals into the park's lakes and streams.

This realization, coupled with their increasing grasp of the sheer magnitude or the project—and the budget required to fund it—kept Congress from allocating the money needed to complete the project. Then, in the 1990s, North Carolina senator asked for and received $15 million to restart the project. Most of this money was needed simply to see what the completed project would cost in terms both financial and ecological. Some estimates came in at $150 million, prompting some to encourage Swain County to accept a "mere" $50 million to settle the issue once and for all. Many in Swain County supported this compromise, pointing out that the interest on $50 million alone would pay a third of the county's annual budget . . . a much surer way of kick-starting the region's economic development in the region than building a winding two-lane road through the park. At publication, however, the road's future was still in question.

ORIENTATION

Getting In

For now at least, nearly everyone who visits the park arrives by car, usually via one of three roads. More than one-third enter via the **Gatlinburg**

© JEFF BRADLEY

the Smokies in winter: beauty with no crowds

entrance, on the Tennessee side, making this the park's de facto main entrance—a reality that has its good side and its bad side. On the good side, the Park Service has sensibly loaded up most of its best visitor amenities near this entrance, including the Sugarlands Visitor Center and Park Headquarters. From here, you can either head up the Newfound Gap Road over the mountains or turn right and head for the Cades Cove area along Little River Road.

The downsides of the "main" entrance are the crowds and the tourism gauntlet you'll have to run in Pigeon Forge and Gatlinburg just to get into the park. If you've come to the Smokies to get away from it all, accessing the park via Sevierville, Pigeon Forge, and Gatlinburg may bring to mind the old Steve Miller line about having to go through hell before you get to heaven.

At the reservation outside of North Carolina's **Cherokee entrance,** the trend seems, thankfully, to be away from the concrete tepees and Sioux headdresses of the past and toward lower-key, Cherokee-respecting attractions—and a mod-ern-day, Cherokee-enriching casino. Once inside the park, you'll find the interesting Oconaluftee Visitor Center and Pioneer Farmstead and the photogenic Mingus Mill—but then you've got to continue on up Newfound Gap Road (U.S. 441) for about 10 curvy miles before you hit the next roadside pullover at Newfound Gap.

Townsend is the least-used of the three main entrances to the park. It leads to an intersection of the Little River Road, which heads toward the Sugarlands Visitor Center and Gatlinburg, and Laurel Creek Road, which goes to Cades Cove.

Major Roads

Newfound Gap Road, also known as U.S. 441, crosses the park and the park's namesake mountains at Newfound Gap. This is the road you'll travel if you enter the park by either the Gatlinburg or Cherokee entrances.

During the push to establish Great Smoky Mountains National Park in the 1920s and 1930s, supporters cultivated public interest in

Smoky Mountains

the project by including an over-mountain road in the plan. A direct route between east Tennessee and North Carolina, the supporters argued, would stimulate trade and help both areas' economies.

The route they chose largely followed the existing dirt path over Newfound Gap, first blazed as early as the 1850s. Until its discovery, travelers over the main range of the Smokies had to use the higher Indian Gap. This "new-found gap" was lower and hence more passable later into the winter and earlier in the spring. It soon replaced Indian Gap as the primary crossing point in this region.

Newfound Gap Road was paved, and the supporters were right about the economic development—probably more right than they knew. Today, Newfound Gap Road crosses the park from one tourist town to another, climbing from 1,465 to 5,048 feet at its highest point. Motorists sense that they're seeing most of the park, since they're crossing from one side to the other and even changing states along the way. Unfortunately, on most warm-weather days, what you'll mostly see traveling Newfound Gap Road is traffic, sometimes of the bumper-to-bumper variety.

For many, the highlight of the drive lies at the gap itself, where you'll find breathtaking views, the state line sign (a popular picture spot), a crossing point for the Appalachian Trail, and a monument where Franklin D. Roosevelt formally dedicated the park in 1940.

Clingmans Dome Road

Named after its endpoint, the highest mountain in the park, this road spurs off the Newfound Gap Road at Newfound Gap. Clingmans Dome was named for the man who first measured it accurately—a little-known, part-Cherokee, Confederate brigadier general, Thomas Lanier Clingman. Before that, the Cherokee knew the dome as Ku wa' hi—"Mulberry Place." They believed that bears had great "townhouses" under this and three nearby mountains. The Great White Bear, chief and doctor to the rest, lived at Mulberry Place. The bears would come here to chat it up and

dance before heading downstairs to hibernate for the winter.

Reaching 6,300 feet in elevation, the dead-end, six-mile road (Skyland Drive), which leads to an observation tower, is the highest paved road east of the Mississippi.

Roaring Fork Motor Nature Trail

This road is a one-way, five-mile loop just outside of Gatlinburg. It'll take you into the park and uphill to the **Grotto Falls** parking area, then downhill back to town along a rushing stream. The water cavorts over rocks, cooling the air and providing moisture for luxurious ferns and mosses. A great place for photographers, the road is off-limits to RVs and closed in winter.

Little River Road

One of two main roads in the park, Little River Road leaves from the Sugarlands Visitor Center over Sugarlands Mountain, descends to the Little River, and follows it toward the Cades Cove area. Some of this 18-mile road was constructed on the remains of the Little River Railroad, which was used to bring logs out of the mountains in the early 20th century.

A turnoff to the left leads to the **Elkmont** community, a group of cabins long occupied by families who owned them when the park came into existence. Back on the road, a turnoff to the right leads to **Metcalf Bottoms,** where you'll see a log schoolhouse and several old cabins.

The Little River grows in volume the further it goes. It plunges over a small waterfall at **The Sinks,** a popular if bone-chilling swimming hole. Further downstream, you'll see people tubing on the river. The National Park Service takes a dim view of this sport, since it's hazardous, especially when the water is high. But it's allowed and people do it. Little River Road ends at an intersection with Laurel Creek Road, which leads to Cades Cove and the road out of the park to Townsend. **Laurel Creek Road** is a pleasant drive, but you won't see much but trees.

Cherokee Orchard Road

Here's a true back road, lying just outside Gatlinburg. Follow the Historic Nature Trail Road to

Gatlinburg to Cherokee Orchard Road. It runs three and a half miles through an old orchard and past the site of several log cabins. In season, it's a great drive for wildflower viewing.

Ⓜ Parson Branch Road

You can read about the Cades Cove Loop Road below, but here are a couple of good roads that lead *out* of the area. Cades Cove residents used to take **Rich Mountain Road** to do their shopping, trading, and hollering down in Maryville. Today this seven-mile road starts out one-way as it winds out of the cove, offering several views

of farmland, and crosses Rich Mountain at the park boundary. Outside the park it becomes a two-way road and descends to U.S. 321 near Townsend. The one-way, eight-mile **Parson Branch Road** is even prettier; it leaves the cove just beyond the Cable Mill parking area and wanders down to U.S. 129 between Fontana and Chilhowee. Beautiful, lush mountain laurel and fern surround the road, and it fords a creek several times. If Cades Cove is crowded—and it often is in summer—this is an excellent escape from the crowds. Both Rich Mountain Road and Parson Branch Road are closed in winter.

Sights

Consider this: Of the roughly 10 million people who visit Great Smoky Mountains National Park each year, some 2.5 million of them visit **Cades Cove,** a large, relatively flat area first settled in 1821. If Cades Cove were a national park all by itself, it would be one of the top 10 most visited national parks in the country.

Thousands of small-scale farmers once worked 1,200 farms within the boundaries of today's Great Smoky Mountains National Park. Although most of the farm buildings have fallen, the few that remain can help you get an idea of life before the park. The biggest collection of ante-park structures lies in Cades Cove. At its peak, the 5,000-acre valley supported 685 residents, who kept several churches and mills in operation. Today the park permits cattle grazing to keep the pastures from returning to forest, and it also maintains the farm buildings, churches, and a mill. A narrow, 11-mile, one-way road circles the cove, with 19 interpretive stops that explain the old ways of life here.

The restored and preserved buildings and farms of Cades Cove are well worth seeing. Bring or rent a bike, and you'll be able to pass up the motorized masses on the often RV-crammed one-lane road. Even better, on Saturdays and Wednesdays from May to September, the road is open to bicyclists and pedestrians only until 10 A.M.

Along the road you'll see **Tipton Place,** which features a cantilevered barn. This sort of structure is an example of mountain ingenuity: The building spreads out at its second story to provide shelter for outdoor chores and for animals.

The best part of the cove, however, centers on **Cable Mill,** a working mill alongside a frame house and several farm buildings. During visiting season, crafts and farming demonstrations take place. One weekend in October, re-enactors at the mill make sorghum molasses the old-fashioned way.

The Cherokee called this area Tsiyahi, meaning "Otter's Place," but the settlers renamed it, presumably after a human, though nobody is quite sure whom. To many students of the subject, the name most likely refers to a Cherokee chief named Cade, or Kade, who once held land in the cove. Another story says that the cove is named for Kate, the settlers' name for the wife of Cherokee chief Abram. Others argue that the cove was named after an early settler family named Cade, and yet another story says that the name was originally Cage Cove, referring to the "cage" created by the mountains surrounding the cove.

One popular hike out of the area leads to 20-foot-high Abrams Falls, a worthwhile trek. And the Cades Cove campground, though often crowded, offers the only camp store in the park.

Smoky Mountains

ELKMONT

Pennsylvanians Colonel W. B. Townsend, J. W. Wrigley, and F. H. McCormick acquired more than 75,000 acres of Smokies timberland in 1902 and formed the Little River Lumber Company, headquartered outside current park boundaries in the little community of Tuckaleechee (renamed Townsend). The company built the Little River Railroad to span the 18 miles between Townsend and Elkmont, from where Shays—geared locomotives designed for steeper grades—climbed even higher into the mountains to pick up the prized lumber. Before long, sportsmen were riding up from Knoxville to Townsend on the Southern Railroad Line and then switching over to the Little River Railroad to be carried deeper in the mountains than they'd ever ventured before. Making a base camp in Elkmont, they headed up further to hunt and fish. Shrewdly, Colonel Townsend, the LRLC's president, quickly added passenger and observation cars to the train and raised the passenger fare.

By 1907, many of Townsend's regular customers, men who came up on weekends from Knoxville, Maryville, and Chattanooga to hunt, fish, and rub dirty elbows with the loggers, had founded the Appalachian Club. To show its appreciation for their business, in 1910 the Little River Lumber Company deeded the club a 50-acre tract for a clubhouse. The company also agreed to lease hunting and fishing privileges on some 40,000 acres above Elkmont exclusively to the Appalachian Club for 10 years. In exchange, the club was expected to manage the fish and game and to patrol the area for poachers.

Of course, once the large, comfortable clubhouse went up, the tough logging camp went the way of Crane's Yellow Sky. A less sports-minded breed of flatlander soon wanted to join the club. Men began bringing their wives for the weekend. The whiskey and games of dice and five-card stud were replaced by teas and dances and bridge tournaments. Soon the town had a post office, boarding house, theater, and church. Men of leisure began building cottages and bringing their families not just for the weekend but for the entire summer. With ruggedness and sta-

mina no longer requirements for admission in the Appalachian Club, wealth and connections became key factors to admission. And the club denied access to its facilities and functions to all nonmembers.

Elkmont continued to grow. Though it no longer felt like a lumber town, timber was still the town's chief industry, and the trees continued to fall. As the trees were clear-cut, the lumber company had no more interest in the land and sold it for good prices. In 1912, three brothers bought 65 acres and built the two-story, white clapboard **Wonderland Park Hotel.** A couple of years later, a group of men from Knoxville who hadn't made the cut at the Appalachian Club bought the Wonderland and formed their own club. They reserved some rooms for club members, but left others open to the public.

The Little River Railroad shut down in 1926. The railroad bed became the base for today's Elkmont Road, and as the automobiles rolled into town, a greater boom seemed on the horizon. But then the government came calling. Despite the best legal maneuverings of some Appalachian Club members, the land became a national park. However, though the members lost their land, their lawyer was able to get them long-term leases to their cabins. The leases were renewed in 1972, but most of them expired in 1992, the same year the Wonderland finally closed its doors.

Nowadays, visit the fast-eroding (but not bulldozed) historic district and you'll find a ghost vacation town, abandoned and eerie as a crime scene, particularly since so many of the cabins were occupied into the 1990s. (On a recent visit, I snuck between two of the cabins and inadvertently startled a white-tailed buck lounging beneath the splintering porch of one of the houses.) As debate continues regarding the fate of the Elkmont Historic District—including the Wonderland Hotel—the Elkmont area has become home to the park's largest campground and to a very rare phenomenon—**synchronized fireflies** (lightning bugs). For some reason, at only this elevation (2,200 feet) the fireflies light up and black out in sync with one another, creating a memorable sight. Look for them in May, June, and July (and sometimes early August) in the late evening—9–10 P.M.—on the nature trail past the campground and across the stone bridge.

◪ CATALOOCHEE VALLEY

If you want to see historic structures but find Cades Cove too congested, the hard-to-get-to Cataloochee Valley may offer you the Smokies experience you were hoping for. The Cataloochee Historic District sits about 11 winding miles from I-40 and 16 twisting miles south of Big Creek. The upper Smokies were one of the last areas in the Southeast to be settled, and Cataloochee Valley was one of the last areas in the Smokies to be settled—just before the Civil War.

In the early 20th century, the Cataloochee Valley was home to two prosperous villages, Big Cataloochee and Little Cataloochee, with more than 200 buildings and more than 1,200 residents between them. It was the largest settlement in all of the Smokies, roughly twice as populous as Cades Cove.

Today, a thin, carefully preserved human residue lingers over the Cataloochee region. An old school, churches, and quite a few houses and barns still stand. While Cataloochee's restored structures can't compare to Cades Cove's, neither do its traffic and crowds. In fact, you can't even *get* to Little Cataloochee by car—that requires a two-mile hike. For some folks, the sheer quiet of the 29-square-mile area makes the entire experience superior to that found at Cades Cove. The spot is so remote that when bears run into trouble with visitors elsewhere in the park, they're hauled up here and released so that they won't be able to find their way back.

The name Cataloochee, incidentally, comes from the Cherokee term for "waves of mountains," an accurate description of the view, even now. There's camping up here, including a very popular camp for equestrians.

Back on the beaten path—Newfound Gap Road—you'll find **Oconaluftee Mountain Farm Museum** right beside the visitors center near the Cherokee entrance. It offers periodic demonstrations of old-time farming methods.

Nearby **Mingus Mill** is also worth a stop—especially if you're tired of the same old grind. That is to say, don't expect the vertical waterwheel usually found in the region's other mills. The Mingus Mill, a "tub" or "turbine" mill, features a wheel that lies on its side. And the old spattering wooden flume that scoops water out of the creek to feed the mill is worth a couple of snapshots all by itself.

The mill grinds corn and wheat. In fact, you'll find cornmeal and flour on sale inside the mill, packaged in miniature sacks. Unfortunately, these products aren't actually ground there at the mill—they're ground in a modern facility in Tennessee. Blame the newfangled health codes.

Recreation

HIKING

Whether it's a stroll in the woods or a multiday trek in the backcountry, hiking ranks high on the list of things to do in the Smokies, where more than 800 miles of trails await the walker. Below is a selection of good **day hikes** in the park. Most are on well-marked trails, but it's never a bad idea to carry a good map. An excellent guidebook for hiking is *Hiking Trails of the Smokies*. Printed on lightweight paper, it's easy for hikers to carry. It costs $16.95 and is available at visitors center gift shops.

Anyone wanting to hike for longer than a day and to camp along any trail in the park needs a permit, available from ranger stations.

Appalachian Trail Hikes

The most famous trail in America runs through the Smokies, along the 68-mile mountain crest that makes up the Tennessee–North Carolina border. Here, Maine-to-Georgia hikers tramp alongside weekend hikers, who mingle with day-trippers who want to experience the famous trail. As a result, the section of the trail near Newfound Gap can be very crowded.

Leave the Newfound Gap parking lot and head east four miles to **Charlies Bunion,** a sheer drop of 1,000 feet. A spectacular view awaits. The trail climbs 980 feet in the first three miles.

Newfound Gap to Clingmans Dome, a 7.5-mile, one-way trek along a section of the Appalachian Trail, is the highest trail in the park and the highest stretch along all of Appalachian Trail's 2,100-mile length. The trail offers superb views as the elevation rises 1,600 feet.

Cades Cove

The five-mile round-trip **Abrams Falls** hike is a good one for kids; they love to play in the water at Abrams Creek, which drains Cades Cove. Begin along the Cades Cove Loop Road and hike down to the falls, or go to the Abrams Creek Ranger Station off the Foothills Parkway on the west side of the park and hike upstream to the

looking into Cades Cove

© JEFF BRADLEY

Smoky Mountains

HIKING REMINDERS

You've heard these rules before, and you'll see them on signs throughout the park, but here are a few points to keep in mind as you hike through the Smokies:

1. Thief-proof your vehicle. Unfortunately, thieves are known to steal valuables from hikers' cars parked at trailheads. If you don't want to hike with it, leave it at your hotel, or better yet, at home.

2. Stash a windbreaker or sweater in your pack. The higher you go, the colder it gets, so a shirt that feels cool and comfortable at the bottom of a mountain trail may prove inadequate for the cold weather at the mountaintop. Getting chilled is rarely any fun, and in bad weather it can be life-threatening.

3. Never drink from streams or creeks. You may be getting "back to nature," but no one wants to carry wildlife home in their digestive tract. Tote your own drinking water or take a filtering device with you.

4. Keep kids close. Because of the park's dense foliage, kids can bolt ahead and get lost faster than you can say "Hansel and Gretel." Consider equipping young folk with a whistle, provided they use it only if necessary.

5. Bring bug repellent. Unless, of course, you want to walk along doing a Leonard Bernstein–at-the-podium impersonation.

6. Carry a poncho. "Smoky Mountain Rain" isn't just a Ronnie Milsap song; the Smokies get between 55–85 inches of rain per year.

falls. The latter is the prettier route, even if it's a bit out of the way.

Two trails lead to **Gregory Bald,** a former summer pasture. The Gregory Ridge Trail, 11 miles round-trip, begins at the turnaround at the start of Parson Branch Road and climbs 2,600 feet up Gregory Ridge. The Gregory Bald Trail, nine miles round-trip, begins farther down the Parson Branch Road and climbs 2,100 feet. Keep in mind that Parson Branch Road is a one-way road leading out of the park. Hikers camping in Cades Cove are in for a long drive to get back to their sleeping bags.

The **Rich Mountain** trail begins on another of those one-way roads out of Cades Cove. Once motorists get to the boundary of the park—Rich Mountain Gap—traffic runs in both directions. Walk east from here along a fire road until the trail takes off to the left. Follow it to the top of the mountain and the intersection with the Indian Grave Gap Road. A good view of the mountains and Cades Cove awaits.

Hikers can reach the beautiful mountain bald of **Spence Field** by two trails. The first is the **Bote Mountain Trail,** a jeep road that begins on Laurel Creek Road, which leads into Cades Cove. Spence Field lies 13 miles ahead, a climb of 2,900 feet. The shortest trail is also the steepest. Begin at the Cades Cove Picnic Area and follow the **Anthony Creek Trail** to its intersection with the Bote Mountain Trail. Prepare to walk nine miles and gain 3,200 feet in elevation.

Clingmans Dome

The highest point in the park, at 6,643 feet, Clingmans Dome has a paved path that spirals up to an overlook tower at the top, and for most visitors, this constitutes the extent of their wilderness experience. Those willing to walk less than two miles, however, are in for a treat if they take the **Forney Ridge Trail** to **Andrews Bald.** The highest bald in the park, and a mere 1.8 miles from the Clingmans Dome parking lot, this eight-acre open space is wonderful for a picnic, a nap, or both. Go there when the rhododendron are blooming or the blackberries are ripe for a special treat.

Mount LeConte

Mount LeConte is the third highest mountain in the eastern United States if you measure from sea level to each mountain's peak. But if you measure from the valley floor below each mountain to that mountain's uppermost point, LeConte ranks as the tallest mountain east of the Mississippi. Consequently, it offers some of the park's most striking views.

These views, and the lodge they inspired, have made Mount LeConte very popular with park visitors. In fact, in the late 1920s and 1930s, when the Great Smoky Mountains Conservation Association was trying to win support for a park, it used to bring influential people to a special camp on the top of the mountain to let the views work their magic.

The old Masonic argument that "all roads lead to the mountaintop" may or may not be true, but at least five trails lead to the top of Mount LeConte. If you're making the climb, you might want to spice things up by hiking up one trail and down another, though depending on which trails you choose, you may need two vehicles to pull it off.

One popular trail for the ascent is the **Boulevard Trail.** It begins at Newfound Gap, thus eliminating a good deal of the climb. To get to the trail, park at Newfound Gap and head east on the Appalachian Trail. The Boulevard Trail will turn off to the left. The total distance is eight miles one way, with an elevation gain of 1,545 feet. Since the trail follows a ridge top,

with lots of ups and downs, you'll feel like you're climbing much more.

The **Alum Cave Trail** is a steep, 2,800-foot, 5.5-mile climb that offers a lot to see. If your knees are sturdy, it's a good choice for the downward trek. Along the way, as you might guess, you'll pass Alum Cave, which incidentally was named all wrong. The spot is not a true cave, but really a large overhang. The alum—a mineral found in the overhang—is not truly an alum, but actually a pseudo-alum.

Miners came up here starting in the 1830s to remove the pseudo-cave's deposits of pseudo-alum, used for dyeing fabric and stopping external bleeding. They also mined other non-pseudo-minerals up here, including Epsom salts and saltpeter (used in gunpowder). During the Civil War, with medicine and munitions in short supply, the Confederacy mined here extensively.

In addition to the un-cave, the trail also offers Arch Rock (which, incidentally, really is both rock, and an arch) and other great scenery. Alternatively, if you're starting from the bottom, you'll find the hike to Arch Rock to be a pleasant (and thus, popular) there-and-back 2.5 mile streamside hike along shaded paths and across log bridges. The trail begins at the Alum Cave Bluffs parking lot off Newfound Gap Road. Once you pass Arch Rock, things turn highly vertical in a hurry, which is why the trail is much more popular as a descent than as an ascent.

The next three Mount LeConte trails leave from the Gatlinburg area. They'll come in handy if the park is jammed with cars that make it difficult to get to the other trails.

So named because the mountain it crosses resembles the head of a bull, **Bullhead Trail** begins in the Cherokee Orchard parking lot near Gatlinburg. The elevation gain is 4,017 feet, and the hike is 7.25 miles one-way.

Rainbow Falls Trail, another trail setting off from the Cherokee Orchard parking lot, is a 6.75-mile, one-way hike that passes an 80-foot waterfall and gains 4,017 feet. Some hikers avoid this trail because it's rocky and steep with lots of gullies.

Hikers coming from the Gatlinburg area can save 700 feet of elevation gain by taking the **Tril-**

Smoky Mountains

© JEFF BRADLEY

hikers on Alum Cave Trail

lium Gap trail, which begins along the Roaring Fork Motor Nature Trail at the Grotto Falls parking lot. The elevation gain is 3,473 feet over seven miles one-way.

More Trails on the Tennessee Side

Right outside of Gatlinburg on the Newfound Gap Road and one of the more popular trails in the park, **Chimney Tops** is only two miles one-way, with an elevation gain of 1,335 feet. By the end most people are using hands and feet, but the view is worth it.

The 1.5-mile, one-way **Grotto Falls** hike is cool on even the hottest days. Leave the Roaring Fork Motor Nature Trail at the Grotto Falls parking area and walk upstream to this waterfall.

LEARNING IN THE SMOKIES

During the peak visiting season—roughly June through August—the National Park Service provides daily walks, hikes, and talks involving various aspects of the Smokies. Some are geared for children, while others can be enjoyed by all ages. Check the visitors centers for information on what is happening when you're there.

Two groups provide educational experiences in the Smokies for teachers, children, families, or individuals who wish to immerse themselves in some aspect of this park.

The **Smoky Mountain Field School** (865/974-0150, tuition varies) offers courses ranging from two days to one week involving topics such as geology, stream life, waterfalls, hiking, birds, insects, mammals, bears, and mushrooms. Classes are run in conjunction with the University of Tennessee. Participants are responsible for arranging their own lodging and meals.

By contrast, the **Great Smoky Mountains Institute at Tremont** (9275 Tremont Rd., Townsend , 865/448-6709, fees vary) offers a package deal—program, lodging, and food all in one price. The institute, on the Middle Prong of the Little River in Walker Valley, offers days filled with geology, wildflowers, forest ecology, or cultural history. Evenings include Appalachian music, guest speakers, night hikes, and other activities. The institute has a dormitory with 125 beds, and participants sleep Shaker-style—males on one side and females on the other. It serves hearty, family-style meals. Typical programs include a three-day spring adult backpack trip, $215; and a women's backpack trip, $205. Other programs include photography workshops, grandparent-grandchild weeks, teen backpacking weeks and teacher escape weekends.

In Gatlinburg, the **Arrowmont School of Arts and Crafts** (556 Parkway, 865/436-5860, www.arrowmont.org) brings 1,500 students and 150 instructors together each summer to a 70-acre campus to work on carving, weaving, pottery, and more than 15 other media. The school originated in 1912 when Pi Beta Phi opened a settlement school in what was then the economically depressed Appalachian town of Gatlinburg. Noting the high value people put on local crafts, the school added crafts instruction along with the other subjects. When improved public schools eliminated the need for the settlement school, the emphasis was shifted entirely to crafts.

Outside the park's western perimeter, just down U.S. 129/19 from Murphy, Brasstown is home to the 380-acre **John C. Campbell Folk School** (1 Folk School Rd., 800/365-5724 or 828/837-2775, course fees vary), founded in 1925 and modeled after Danish schools to preserve the crafts, music, dances, and other traditions of the Appalachian people by teaching outlanders about them. It's a wonderful day-trip from the park; you can visit the school's History Center free and browse the craft shop, a founding member of the Southern Highland Craft Guild, which features the work of more than 300 local and regional artists. You can also take the local trails and visit artists' studios to watch work in progress. For a longer stay, the school offers three- to 12-week classes in mountain music, dance, and crafts.

Smoky Mountains

Hikers gain only 500 feet in elevation and can look for salamanders on the way. The park shelters 23 species of them.

The **Hen Wallow Falls** hike leaves from a less crowded area. Drive to the Cosby Picnic Area on the northeast end of the park for a two-mile, one-way hike. The elevation gain is 600 feet through a forest with magnificent poplars and hemlocks. The falls are two feet wide at the top and 20 feet wide at the bottom.

The **Ramsay Cascades** trail offers quite a finale. The 100-foot Ramsay Cascades, while not a straight drop, is the highest waterfall in the park. The trail begins in Greenbrier Cove, about six miles due east of Gatlinburg on Hwy. 321. Four miles one-way, the trail gains 1,600 feet in elevation. Hikers should be careful at the falls; several people have fallen to their deaths.

More Hikes on the North Carolina Side

At Cataloochee you'll find the remote but popular, 7.4-mile **Boogerman Loop Trail,** which climbs around 800 feet to a peak elevation of around 3,600 feet. As Allen R. Coggins recounts in his delightful book *Place Names of the Smokies,* the trail is named for Robert "Boogerman" Palmer, whose abandoned cabin you'll pass on the trail. Asked in school what he wanted to be when he grew up, the bashful Palmer supposedly put his head down, laughed, and answered, "the Boogerman." His friends laughed along and began using the name. The older Palmer got, the more his neighbors realized that he hadn't been kidding about his chosen vocation. He withdrew more and more from his mountain neighbors. He grew his beard long and enjoyed frightening children with his appearance. They rewarded him by creating tall tales about their encounters with "the Boogerman." When the lumber companies came around and bought up his neighbors' land, Palmer refused to sell—which is why his namesake trail threads in part through all-too-rare virgin Appalachian forest.

In addition to old-growth forest, the Boogerman Loop Trail also offers some wonderful color in autumn, remnants of settlers' cabins, and

pretty views of *cataloochee*—"waves of mountains." To get there, take Cove Creek Road to the Caldwell Fork Trail and follow the signs.

BIKING

Mountain bikes are prohibited on all Smokies trails—as are all vehicles—but a few unimproved roads make good riding. You might try the **Cataloochee Valley** on the eastern end of the park. Or try the **Parson Branch Road** out of Cades Cove—but keep in mind that even for bicycles, this is a one-way road.

In the more populated areas of the park, the roads can get quite busy with distracted drivers. So if you're going to bike the park, get out there early, The best place to ride is **Cades Cove.** A concessionaire at the campground store there rents bikes. When the Cove is jammed with cars, you'll be glad to be on your bike. Note however, that the **Loop Road** is treacherously steep at points—even without 40-foot RVs bearing down on you—so much so that at points, you'll see signs requiring you to dismount and walk your bike downhill.

FISHING

Approximately 730 miles of streams thread through the park, and **Fontana Lake** lies on the southern border. Except for Fontana, which harbors smallmouth and rock bass, trout is the name of the game here. The park is one of the last refuges of the brook trout, the only species native to these parts; anglers who catch one must release it. Efforts to restore brook trout populations have led to the closing of some streams, and rangers can tell you which ones. Rainbow trout are the interlopers whose exploding populations have made the brook trout so rare, so they are fair game.

Trout season never stops in the Smokies. A Tennessee or North Carolina fishing license enables you to fish all over the park year-round, and you'll find licenses for sale in the gateway towns. Trout stamps are not required, but you're only allowed to use one-hook artificial lures—no bait of any sort is allowed.

You can fish right beside the road or, if you're serious about it, backpack deep in to the most remote streams in the park. You can even hire a guide to take you to the best places. A good book for anglers is Don Kirk's *Smoky Mountains Trout Fishing Guide*, available at local bookshops and tackle stores.

HORSEBACK RIDING

Horse owners can ride in the park and even take overnight equestrian camping trips with Park Service permission. The park limits the number of horse camps, and you'll need to bring your own horse feed. For a complete set of guidelines for horseback riding, call 865/436-1200 or write to Superintendent, Great Smoky Mountains National Park, 107 Park Headquarters Rd., Gatlinburg, TN 37738.

Horses are available to rent from several places in the park, generally for about $20 for about an hour's ride. All rides are guided, usually at a sedate pace, and children under 6 have to ride with an adult. On the Tennessee side, visitors can rent horses near **Park Headquarters** (865/436-5354); at **Cades Cove Riding Stables** (865/448-6286); and east of Gatlinburg on Hwy. 321 (865/436-5634). On the North Carolina side, try **Smokemont** (828/497-2373). No credit cards or personal checks accepted.

May through October you can tour Cades Cove in a truck-drawn **hay wagon** in the evening. The rides costs $8 a person. No reserva-tions are required. The wagons depart from the Cades Cove Riding Stables. If you've got a group of 15 or more, you can reserve your own wagon for day trips. For group reservations, call 865/448-6286.

WATER SPORTS

Except in spring and after torrential downpours, you'll have a bear of a time trying to canoe, raft, or even kayak the park's rivers and streams. You may spot some intrepid, experienced kayakers (or some foolish, inexperienced ones) within the park, but for true white water you'll probably need to go outside, preferably to the French Broad or Nantahala River.

If you're seeking a milder experience and don't mind taking a cool dip, you can ride **inner tubes** at the Sinks area of Little River Road. Use caution, though. Rocks—both underwater and not—can make this activity hazardous. Lots of people tube this area every year, and you'll probably be fine if you keep your head about you—specifically if you keep it away from the rocks.

SKIING

The park offers no downhill skiing, but during winter cross-country skiers practice various forms of their sport on roads and trails. Clingmans Dome Road, the Cherokee Orchard Road, and the Roaring Fork Motor Nature Trail provide excellent skiing when the weather cooperates.

Smoky Mountains

Accommodations

When it comes to a place to stay inside the most visited national park in the country, **Mount LeConte Lodge** (865/429-5704, www.leconte-lodge.com) is the only game around—and it's 5.5 miles from and 2,560 feet above the nearest road. Jack Huff built LeConte Lodge in the 1920s, and when the park came into existence the lodge was allowed to remain. Various environmental hard-liners have argued for the demise of the venerable lodge, but public sentiment has overwhelmed them every time.

LeConte Lodge holds about 50 guests, either in cabins or private rooms within cabins. Rooms run $83 a night *per person,* and while this does include breakfast and dinner (and lunch if you're staying more than one night), accommodations are extremely rustic: no electricity, hot water, or telephones. You'll need to carry up your own towels. The flush toilets stop working in cold weather, so you may have to use a pit toilet. Most of dinner and breakfast comes out of cans carried up the mountain by pack llamas—used because they damage the trails less than horses. The staff serves hearty meals family-style, a great chance to mingle and swap stories with other travelers. The sunset over Clingmans Dome is the evening's sole planned entertainment, and guests retire to their toolshed-sized cabins with wool blankets and kerosene heaters to beat back the cold.

And most guests wouldn't have it any other way.

LeConte Lodge enjoys more demand for its rooms than any other hostelry in the region. Open from late March–November, the lodge accepts reservations for the following year beginning on October 1 (or the following business day if October 1 falls on a weekend). To contact by mail, write Wilderness Lodging, 250 Apple Valley Road, Sevierville, TN 37862. Reservations for the entire year are usually snatched up completely within two weeks. But folks have been known to cancel—it won't hurt to call at the last minute to see if a cabin's opened up.

An alternate way to get a bunk at the lodge is to sign up for a Smoky Mountain Field School hike. The lodge reserves three Saturdays a year for these hikes—one each in the spring, summer, and fall. Call 800/974-0150 for dates.

CAMPING

The National Park Service takes a rather stoic stance toward campers: Tent here and you're going to rough it, like it or not. You'll find no sissy pay showers here, and only when the numbers overwhelm pit toilets do the flush toilets open up. Neither will RVers find electrical or water umbilical cords.

Sites run $14–17. You can reserve one up to five months in advance at the park's three most popular campgrounds, Cades Cove, Smokemont, and Elkmont, from May 15 through October 31. Just call 800/365-2267 and type in the park code, GREA, at the prompt. All sites at the park's other campgrounds, and any unreserved campsites at the campgrounds listed above, are available on a first-come, first-served basis. No more than six people can occupy one site, either in two tents or one RV and one tent. During summer and fall campers can stay only seven days; the rest of the year they can stay 14 days. Pets are permitted in campgrounds but you'll have to restrain them.

Overall, the park offers 1,008 campsites at 10 developed campgrounds: five in Tennessee and five in North Carolina. The larger campgrounds offer campfire programs in the evenings. Call 865/436-1200 for information.

Tennessee Campgrounds

Though it's one of the first campgrounds to get crowded, if you're camping with kids, it's hard to beat Cades Cove. With 161 sites, **Cades Cove Campground** offers a lot of things to do, and since most Smokies visits of any length seem to end up here, why not start out here? Besides the historic cabins and the Cable Mill, nearby trails lead to a bald and a waterfall. The Cades Cove Loop Road is arguably the best place in the park to ride a bike, and the stables offer horseback riding and carriage rides. And perhaps most im-

© JEFF BRADLEY

looking out a cabin at Mount LeConte Lodge

River. In late May, June, and early July, you can see the amazing synchronized fireflies along the nature trail past the campground. Laurel Falls is nearby, and Elkmont is also the campground closest to the worldly pleasures of Gatlinburg. It can handle all sizes of RVs, is wheelchair-accessible, and is open year-round.

Look Rock offers 92 sites on the extreme western edge of the park. Since it's out of the way, it's a good place to look for a spot when other campgrounds are full. Look Rock offers access to Abrams Creek. It can handle 25-foot RVs and is open late March–October.

Abrams Creek, with 16 sites, is the smallest park campground in Tennessee. This gem lies in a forest of huge conifers that lend it a cathedral effect. It is the trailhead for a hike up to Abrams Falls and is also wheelchair-accessible. It can handle 16-foot RVs and is open late March–October.

North Carolina Campgrounds

Balsam Mountain, with 46 sites, is a good base for exploring the Cherokee Reservation; Mingo Falls is a good day trip from here (though you can drive very close to it along Big Cove Road out of Cherokee). The campground can handle 30-foot RVs and is open mid-May–October 18.

Deep Creek, with 108 sites, lies three miles north of Bryson City and within two miles of three waterfalls: Juneywhank Falls, Indian Creek Falls, and Toms Branch Falls. The campground can handle 25-foot RVs and is open mid-April–October.

Smokemont, with 140 sites, is the largest campground on the North Carolina side and a good place to take in the Mountain Farm Museum at Oconoluftee and Mingus Mill. It's also the park campground closest to Cherokee, North Carolina. Open year-round and wheelchair-accessible, it can take all RV sizes. It doesn't do much for me but it is functional.

Big Creek, with nine sites, is the smallest campground in the park. It lies on the far eastern end of the Smokies. It's open May 1–November 2 and can take 26-foot RVs.

Cataloochee, with 27 sites, also on the eastern end of the park, lies at the end of a rough, unpaved road that will guarantee campers freedom

portantly, this is the only campground with a store, which means that if you're staying here, a forgotten grocery item doesn't necessarily sentence you to a Gatlinburg or Cherokee visit. And while the some may spit half-chewed GORP at the idea, a short "hike" to the campstore for Popsicles can put the perfect finish to a Coleman-cooked supper. The Cove's campground can handle 35-foot RVs, is wheelchair-accessible, and is open year-round.

Cosby, with 175 sites, features smaller crowds. It's also more convenient if you're planning to see the Greenbrier area and hike to Ramsay Cascade. Tubing Cosby Creek is a favorite activity here. Cosby can handle 25-foot RVs and is open late March–October.

Elkmont, with 220 sites, is the biggest campground in the entire park. It's close to the Metcalf Bottoms Historic Area and the delightful Little

Smoky Mountains

from crowds. The Cataloochee area contains several old buildings left behind by a community of 1,200 settlers. The campground is open late March–October.

Trail Shelters

Shelters, most of them on the Appalachian Trail, offer accommodations for hikers who do not want to carry tents or sleep under the stars. Each shelter has three walls and a chain-link fence across the front. Inside you'll find 8 to 14 beds made of wire mesh strung between logs. Outside you'll find a pit toilet. The good news is that shelters are dry and bear-proof, with beds up off the ground. The bad news for some folks is that you may find yourself in close quarters with up to 13 total strangers, any of whom may be champion snorers or Amway enthusiasts.

You don't have to pay to stay in one of the shelters, but you do need to reserve your bunk in advance. Call **Park Headquarters** at 865/436-1231 up to one month before your visit.

Backcountry Camping

Despite all the talk of crowding in the park, it offers close to 100 backcountry sites where, some contend, the ultimate camping experience takes place. Park workers have established backcountry sites all over the park; they shift the locations from time to time to minimize the wear and tear on the land. A site can accommodate from 8 to 20 campers, who can stay up to three days before moving on. Reservations are required for some sites, but there is no charge. Write to Backcountry Permits, Great Smoky Mountains National Park, Gatlinburg, TN 37738 or call 865/436-1231. If you're already in the park, stop by one of the visitors centers—at Sugarlands, Cades Cove, or Oconaluftee—or one of the ranger stations.

To keep things as pristine as possible, the park requires backpackers to pack out all garbage. Don't bury it or throw it in a pit toilet. In general, practice zero-impact camping: Tents should not be trenched, and hand-dug toilets must lie well away from the campsite and any water sources. Campers can build fires in established fire rings,

BLOCKADER'S GLORY

For many years, mountain people called Sugarlands "Blockader's Glory," which, roughly translated, meant "Moonshiner's Heaven." "Blockade liquor" was another name for moonshine, and the then-isolated valley—now the site of park headquarters and the visitor's center—was a haven for moonshiners.

but park officials prefer that you use a portable stove to lessen the impact on the land.

A final note: Park rangers are very strict about camping in unauthorized places. You can't spend the night in a parking area or picnic area or on the side of the road, even if all the campgrounds are full. The same holds true for the backcountry. Be sure to reserve ahead and allow enough time to get to your destination.

INFORMATION AND SERVICES

The best place to get oriented to the park and to find out what's happening is the **Sugarlands Visitor Center,** just outside Gatlinburg. It includes a small natural history museum, a slide show, free maps, and people who can answer questions. A bookstore offers helpful volumes and films. The **Oconaluftee Visitor Center** sits on the North Carolina side of the park. Both centers are open daily 8 A.M.–7 P.M. Rangers at stations scattered throughout the park can also answer questions and deal with problems.

Emergencies

In case of trouble, call **Park Headquarters** (865/436-1230); **Gatlinburg police** (865/436-4212); or **Cherokee police** (704/497-4131). **Sevier County Hospital** on Middle Creek Road in Sevierville (865/453-7111) is 15 miles from Gatlinburg. **Blount Memorial Hospital** on Hwy. 321 in Maryville (865/983-7211) is 25 miles from Cades Cove, and **Swain County Hospital** in Bryson City, North Carolina (704/488-2155), is 16 miles from Smokemont.

The First Frontier

If there's any part of Tennessee where one can come close to seeing the same views and vistas that the Indians enjoyed, this is it. The very mountains that held back settlers from the east resisted change, encouraging people to move farther west.

This was the country's first frontier, and the brave souls who left civilization and made their way across the Appalachians clearly understood that they were on their own. They lived beyond the bounds of government, beyond protection from the Indians, and beyond the fledgling commerce of the colonies.

What they found was a land rich in game, soil, and timber. A family willing to work could have a good life on the west side of the mountains. Individually, they learned to be self-reliant. Together, they developed a fierce independence whose intensity would utterly surprise the British in the Revolutionary War.

As the more western parts of Tennessee were settled, the towns and villages of the First Frontier became routes that connected points west with the rest of the country. Presidents and other national leaders traveled through Rogersville, Kingsport,

Must-Sees

Look for **M** to find the sights and activities you can't miss and **M** for the best dining and lodging.

M Rogersville: Its main street lined with 19th-century buildings is a great stop on the old 11-W "Blue Highway" (page 422).

M Cumberland Gap National Historical Park: The natural beauty equals anything found in the Smokies—with one-twentieth of the visitors (page 427).

M Roan Mountain: When the rhododendrons are blooming, this summit high on an Appalachian ridge is the loveliest place in the state (page 433).

M Down Home: In Johnson City you'll hear bluegrass, blues, rock—it's the best place for live music on this end of the state (page 439).

M National Storytelling Festival: Three days of tall tales, ghost stories, and sacred telling are centered in Jonesborough, which also offers a delightful introduction to the First Frontier (page 446).

Andrew Johnson's home

M Andrew Johnson National Historic Site: This site celebrating Lincoln's successor makes for a history-filled visit to Greeneville (page 453).

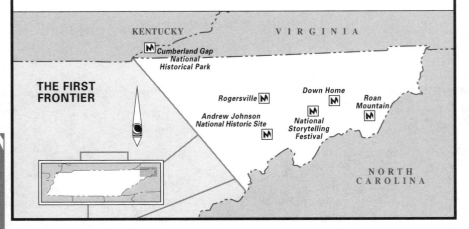

THE FIRST FRONTIER

KENTUCKY

VIRGINIA

M Cumberland Gap National Historical Park

Rogersville **M**

Down Home **M**

Roan Mountain **M**

Andrew Johnson National Historic Site **M**

National Storytelling Festival **M**

NORTH CAROLINA

The First Frontier

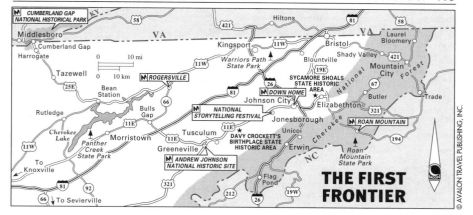

THE FIRST
FRONTIER

© AVALON TRAVEL PUBLISHING, INC.

Jonesborough, and Greeneville; several of the places in which they ate and slept are still there.

Visitors to the First Frontier will hear a twangy accent that differs from voices farther south and west. To some inhabitants, a word pronounced "flare" can mean a burning device that warns motorists of dangers ahead, the blossoming part of a plant, and the chief ingredient of bread.

When cars are backed up in the Great Smoky Mountains National Park, when the trails are clogged, and the air in Gatlinburg smells of fresh exhaust, the mountains here are seldom crowded.

HISTORY

West of the Mountains

As the American colonies grew in the 1700s, a pattern emerged: Settlers moved too far west, got into trouble with the Native Americans, and then appealed to the British army for help. Hoping to hold down expenses, King George III in 1763 ordered all settlers to come back and stay on the eastern side of the Appalachian Mountains.

Few paid any attention to this. In 1770, a young man named James Robertson crossed the mountains to investigate the territory. He came back home so enthusiastic about what he found that he convinced a group of families to move to Sycamore Shoals of the Watauga River—later the site of Elizabethton. By 1772, there were al-most 85 farms along the Watauga and Holston Rivers, and the inhabitants all thought they were living in Virginia. When surveyors proved that this was not the case, the locals realized they were literally beyond the law. Considering that the law was British, that was not so bad, but they also had no statutes to help them with practical matters such as marriages, land transactions, and wills.

They decided they needed some kind of government, so in May 1772, a call went out for all men over age 21. Those who showed up formed the Watauga Association, an organization loosely based on Virginia law. This was the first constitution west of the mountains.

Dealings with the Cherokee

The second realization from the survey was that every one of these farms was on Native American land. The British might huff and puff and express annoyance at those who defied them, but the Indians posed a very real problem, one the settlers solved using a modern-day technique. They offered to lease the land for 10 years, paying its owners several thousand dollars' worth of merchandise. The Cherokee who brokered the deal was Attakullakulla, also known as "Little Carpenter," who years earlier had traveled to London and met the king.

When North Carolinians back on the eastern side heard that the Cherokees would deal, they decided to go for a much larger transaction.

The First Frontier

Richard Henderson and a group of investors summoned the Cherokee and began negotiations for the entire Cumberland Valley and the southern half of the Kentucky Valley, a piece of real estate almost the size of South Dakota.

This was a staggering amount of land—more than 20 million acres—comprising a big part of what would become Tennessee and Kentucky. The Cherokee began gathering at Sycamore Shoals to discuss Henderson's offer of 2,000 English pounds in cash and 8,000 pounds' worth of goods. In March 1775, more than a thousand Cherokee listened as Attakullakulla, by then 80 years old, made his case for accepting the deal.

He was opposed by Dragging Canoe, his son, who insisted that this was the beginning of the end for their people. He argued that the whites would not be happy with this purchase, and that other Indian lands were now gone. Attakullakulla won the debate, however, and the deal was consummated.

When he saw that his side had lost, Dragging Canoe stalked out of the gathering and stated that the settlers might buy the land, but they would find it a "dark and bloody ground." He spent the rest of his life trying to make that prophecy come to pass.

Revolution

Then came the Revolutionary War. The Wataugans and others west of the mountains could have ignored the entire thing; surviving and making a living were challenge enough. Although they expressed support for their colleagues farther north and east in the war, it took a letter from an arrogant British commander to stir them to action. Major Patrick Ferguson threatened to march his own men over the mountains, "hang their leaders, and lay their country to waste with fire and sword."

These words so incensed the recipients that they called for volunteers to assemble at Sycamore Shoals in September 1780, prepared to fight. After a stirring prayer by Reverend Samuel Doak, roughly 1,000 men and boys set off tramping over the mountains. A month later they found Ferguson and a force numbering about the same size as their own on top of a narrow ridge named, appropriately enough, Kings Mountain.

It was not to remain the king's mountain for long. Using hunting skills they had honed all their lives, the mountain men picked off the British one by one, forcing them to surrender in a little more than an hour. Ferguson lay dead among his 353 casualties.

Things had not been going so well for the Americans in the war, and Kings Mountain proved to be the turning point of the war in the South—some claim the entire war. The Overmountain Men, as they now were called, jubilantly marched home in time for Christmas.

THE LEE HIGHWAY

One of the most famous "blue highways" on the East Coast is U.S. 11, the Lee Highway. Following the old stage routes through Virginia, the road splits in Bristol into 11 West and 11 East before rejoining in Knoxville. Those are the routes, with a few diversions, that this chapter will follow. We'll begin far up in the point of Tennessee in each case.

U.S. 11 West

This is a well-traveled path. Stagecoaches passed up and down here carrying people such as Andrew Jackson, who while president once stopped to go to church in the little town of Blountville. A tavern along the way at Bean Station was said to have the finest wine cellar between Baltimore and New Orleans.

Until I-81 was completed, this stretch of the Lee Highway rumbled day and night with trucks going from the Eastern Seaboard to points south and west. Hank Williams, whose final day is recalled in the Knoxville chapter, probably breathed his last on this stretch of road. With the Interstate traffic gone, it remains a good way to slow down and see some of the history of East Tennessee.

U.S. 11 East

The southern swing of the old Lee Highway never had as much traffic as its northern branch, but it passes through towns of greater historic significance.

Driving west on U.S. 11 East, the traveler follows the path of settlers coming into Tennessee.

First come high mountain towns, Elizabethton with its Fort Watauga, then Jonesborough and its tales of Andrew Jackson. The land gets flatter and more suited for farming as Greeneville swings into view, and the historic houses, reflecting the growing prosperity of the people, get bigger and bigger. These places cannot hold a candle to the magnificent plantations of Middle Tennessee, but a modern-day traveler can certainly see where things were headed.

Mountain City and Vicinity

Sitting at an elevation of 2,350 feet, the county seat of Johnson County is the highest town in the state. It is also the town where movies come to die.

A successful Hollywood movie might have 2,000 or more prints when first released. As the film moves from first-run theaters to second-run houses and then to video, the demand for prints decreases. When a print is ready to be recycled, it comes to Mountain City, where most of it is chopped up into flakes and sold as an ingredient for fuel pellets.

PRACTICALITIES

Accommodations

The Butler House Bed and Breakfast (309 N. Church St., 423/727-4119, www.butlerhouse .com, $65–75) has an upstairs porch just dandy for looking over the 15 acres of lawn and gardens. The 1870s house is on the National Register, and rates include breakfast. **Prospect Hill B&B Inn** (801 W. Main St., 423/727-0139, www.prospect-hill.com, $100–169) occupies an 1889 house built by a Civil War major. This place has large rooms, some with whirlpool baths, and fireplaces. There is also a wedding garden and pavilion for special engagements.

Mountain City has two motels, both south of town on U.S. 421: **Days Inn** (800/329-7466, $70) and the larger **Mountain Empire Motel** (423/727-7777, $54).

The Valley View Motel is southwest of Mountain City in the Doeville community (at the intersection of Hwy. 67 and Hwy. 167, 423/727-2500, nine rooms for $40–45).

Callalantee Campground and Stables is on U.S. 421 south in Mountain City (423/727-8156).

Food

Suba's (423/727-5657) above the Days Inn, is run by a young couple who received their culinary training in Charleston, South Carolina. They offer soups, sandwiches, and pasta for lunch, while dinnertime brings forth chicken, steak, barbecued ribs, and a wonderful smoked trout cake.

Mountain City offers a cluster of fast-food emporiums, but locals prefer the country cuisine of **Cooks Cafeteria** (beside the Mountain Empire Motel). Cooks serves three meals a day Monday–Saturday and breakfast and lunch on Sunday.

Information

The Johnson County Welcome Center (U.S. 421, 423/727-5800) offers exhibits, information, and a campground on the premises.

LAUREL BLOOMERY

This little town up in the point of Tennessee is the birthplace of Frank Proffitt (1913–65), whose singing and playing of traditional mountain ballads brought them to much wider audiences.

When song collectors first came to the mountains, Proffitt eagerly contributed the ones he knew, among them "Tom Dooley," which he said was the first song he remembered hearing his father play on a banjo. The song tells the tale of a man who kills the woman he loves and is sentenced to hang—not exactly cheerful stuff. In the late '50s, the Kingston Trio released its interpretation of the old song, a version that sold three million copies and helped launch the folk music boom of the '60s. In *An Encyclopedia of East Tennessee*, Jim Stokely tells of Proffitt's hearing the song on television, walking outside his

The First Frontier

house, and crying. Late in his life he did receive some of the attention he deserved, performing in folk festivals and recording two albums.

TRADE

This little town holds two distinctions: it's the oldest unincorporated community in Tennessee as well as the easternmost one. When the Europeans first came to these parts, this was the place where they traded—hence the name—gunpowder, furs, and whiskey with the Native Americans. Following the route of an ancient Indian trail, Daniel Boone, an early highway contractor, cut a road over the mountains and came right through Trade. Locals can point out remnants of Boone's road that exist as country lanes today.

During the last week in June the town rouses to celebrate **Trade Days** (423/727-5800, www.tradedaysfestival.com), a gathering of Indians and locals who engage in tomahawk- and knife-throwing contests—not at each other—shooting matches, period dancing, old-time games, and the more conventional demonstrations of agricultural pursuits such as milking, spinning, churning, plowing, and horse shoeing.

The **Tennessee Rose Bed and Breakfast** (843 Wallace Rd., 423/727-6574, $60–70) sits amid 50 acres of gardens, streams, and ponds. The two guest rooms have private baths, a common sitting area, and a private kitchen/dining space.

SHADY VALLEY

From Mountain City, U.S. 421 leads 10–15 miles north out of town over Iron Mountain to a great view of Shady Valley, a relatively flat farmland that got its name from the thick forest that used to cover the land. Here, scientists claim, lies the basis for the American cranberry industry. During the last ice age, glaciers 3,000 feet thick ground through Mass-

© JEFF BRADLEY

Backbone Rock

achusetts and other northern states where cranberries are now commercially grown, effectively wiping out the red berries—and virtually every other plant. The glaciers moved so slowly, however, that cranberries carried by birds grew just ahead of the ice in cool, wet climates. These traveling cranberries found a home in Shady Valley, where a Canadian-type climate enabled them to flourish. When the glaciers retreated, birds carried the berries north, there to grow and wait for the Pilgrims to eat them at Thanksgiving.

The Tennessee cranberries survived glaciers, but the U.S. Army Corps of Engineers just about killed them off by straightening a stream in Shady Valley. Fortunately, the botanical and historical value of the tart berries has been recognized. The Nature Conservancy owns **Orchard Bog and Quarry Bog,** which are open from dawn to dusk every day. To get there, go northeast on Hwy.

133 about one mile from the intersection with Hwy. 421, then turn left.

The Cranberry Festival, (intersection of U.S. 421 and Hwy. 133, 423/727-5800), a Friday and Saturday event held the second week in October, attracts 5,000–7,000 people who turn out to eat at the Cranberry Bean Dinner and enjoy bluegrass and gospel music, clogging, children's events, and a parade. Proceeds benefit the Shady Valley Elementary School.

Turning right onto Hwy. 133 leads the visitor to one of the odder geological formations in the state. **Backbone Rock** (423/735-1500, campground open mid-April–October) is a natural stone wall standing 75 feet high. The wall averages 20 feet thick and was pierced in 1901 for a railroad. Now the highway goes through what is sometimes called "the shortest tunnel in the world." The rock is surrounded by a park with a picnic area and 13 campsites.

Bristol and Vicinity

LAND AND HISTORY

Bristol is one of the few cities where the late Johnny Cash could literally walk the line. Bristol, Tennessee, and Bristol, Virginia, meet at the state line, which runs right down the middle of the street. The two Bristols are now proud of this unusual juxtaposition, but early in this century it took a Supreme Court decision to help straighten out the problems that come from having two towns too close.

Bristol lies in an area called The Great Valley, an easily traveled route that served as a pathway into Tennessee from the northeast. In 1771, an enormous fort covering 1.5 acres was built from which to conduct trade and protect settlers. More than 100,000 people came through during the 1780s.

Industry

An enterprising gent named James King calculated that all those new residents would soon need nails, so he built an ironworks and eventually supplied the frontier with the products of 29 furnaces. Seeking an easy way to ship his heavy goods, he traveled 25 miles to the Holston River, where he built King's Port—the beginning of Kingsport.

King's early industry set a pattern for Bristol, which was named for a British industrial city. Bristol was a natural place for the railroad to come through in 1853, and by the time a 35-year-old New Yorker named Ralph Peer got off the train in the summer of 1927, the city produced steel, paper, furniture, leather goods, and mine cars.

Musical Gold

Peer was interested in none of those products. He was looking for music. The wide sales of phonographs had tapped an insatiable market for music—any kind of music: classical; Tin Pan Alley; and, especially for rural customers, ballads and string music from the South. At first the record companies had brought blues and traditional musicians to New York to record, but this proved expensive, inefficient, and sometimes outright disastrous, especially when bright lights,

The First Frontier

Bristol's famous sign

© JEFF BRADLEY

the big city, and strong drink combined. Peer had the inspiration to dispatch recording crews to the places where musicians lived, and that's what he had in mind when he got off that train. Having placed an ad in the local newspapers, he waited in a makeshift studio at 408–410 State Street to see who would show up. Ernest "Pop" Stoneman was one of the first artists to record there, a man whose "Wreck of the Titanic" had sold a million copies in 1924.

On August 1 and 2, Peer hit even bigger gold. Over those two days he made music history with four people who answered his ad. The first three were the Carter Family, and the fourth was Jimmie Rodgers, a Mississippi-born singer who happened to be performing in the area when he learned of Peer's sessions.

The Carter Family was A. P. Carter, his wife, Sara, and A. P.'s sister-in-law, Maybelle. Their honest and simple tunes—songs such as "Wildwood Flower," "Will the Circle Be Unbroken?," and "Keep on the Sunny Side"—were instantly popular and have remained so for decades.

The trio broke up in 1943 after recording more than 300 songs, and Maybelle Carter went on to found a musical dynasty, recording with her daughters as Mother Maybelle and the Carter Sisters. One of those daughters, June, married Johnny Cash.

Jimmie Rodgers was the first musical superstar. Blending the black blues he had grown up with in Mississippi with the hillbilly music of Tennessee, he burst on the national scene with an outpouring of recordings that included railroad songs, "blue yodels," sweet ballads, honky-tonk numbers, and cowboy and corny songs. Stricken with tuberculosis before he ever began recording, his career came to an end after fewer than four years; he died at age 35 in 1933. He was the first person voted into the Country Music Hall of Fame, where his plaque reads "The Father of Country Music."

THE CARTER FAMILY MEMORIAL MUSIC CENTER

The Carter Center isn't in Tennessee, but it's significant enough and close enough to be mentioned in this book. The Carter family came from southwest Virginia; A. P. and Sara lived in Maces Spring and raised their family here between road trips and broadcasts on far-flung radio stations. After the couple retired from show business, A. P. operated a grocery store here until his death in 1960.

In 1974, their youngest daughter, Janette, who had appeared on stage with her parents as a buck dancer at age 6 and an autoharp player at age 12, began performing again at the Carter Family Store. The acoustic music she brought forth, true to the Carter tradition, drew such crowds that two years later she, her sister Gladys, and her brother Joe built the **Carter Family "Fold,"** a shed seating 800–1,000 people. The name comes from the biblical parable of sheep returning to the fold.

Music lovers from all over the world and just down the road gather here, some to listen and some to raise the dust with traditional dances on the floor right in front of the stage. Bluegrass and folk music, with the occasional country performer, is all one will hear at the Fold. No electrical instruments are permitted. Shows are presented every Saturday at 7:30 P.M. Admission is a wonderfully low $5 per adult, $1 for children 6–12, with impressionable children under 6 getting in for free. This is possibly the biggest entertainment bargain in this entire book. No advance tickets are sold, but the huge Fold rarely sells out.

The adjacent store now makes up the **Carter** Family Museum, where one can view the family's 78 rpm records, fancy "show clothes" worn in performances, photos, books, and other memorabilia. The museum is open every Saturday 5–7 P.M. Admission is $0.50. Children accompanied by parents get in free. The log cabin in which A. P. Carter was born has been moved to the Fold and is being restored.

On the first weekend in August, a festival commemorates the historic Carter Family 1927 recording session. Continuous live music plays daily 2–11 P.M., with a headliner such as Robin and Linda Williams. A nearby meadow becomes a small village of tents in which local artists sell crafts and local cooks sell food. For information on weekly shows or the festival, call 540/386-6054. For more details about the Fold, call 276/386-6054. or visit www.carterfamilyfold.org.

Cautionary note: Unlike some bluegrass festivals, Mama don't 'low no drinking round here. Anyone tippling or who has toppled will find that the Carter Family circle will be broken—quickly.

To get to the Carter Center from I-81 going north, take the Kingsport exit onto I-181, then follow I-181 to the U.S. 23 exit north toward Gate City. By now you will begin to see green highway road markers pointing in the direction of the Fold. Turn right at the second traffic light onto U.S. 58 west toward Bristol. Follow U.S. 58 to Hwy. 709 and turn left in Hiltons. Follow Hwy. 709 over the railroad tracks and bear right on Hwy. 614 for about three miles till you see the Fold on your left.

Other important music figures have come out of Bristol. In the days when live performances were a staple of radio stations, WCYB in Bristol featured the Stanley Brothers, second only to Bill Monroe in bluegrass annals; Mac Wiseman; Jim and Jesse McReynolds; and Earl Scruggs and Lester Flatt and the Foggy Mountain Boys. Radio station WOPI had a young announcer named Ernie Ford who, later known as "Tennessee" Ernie Ford, helped bring country music to mainstream America. His most popular song was "Six-

teen Tons," a snappy, almost jazzlike song that became a 1955 hit.

SIGHTS AND RECREATION

Visitors to Bristol usually begin on State Street, once the main shopping district. A large mural at State and 8th commemorates the birthplace of country music, as does a monument close to the site of the famed Bristol Sessions. The **Paramount Center for the Arts,** a restored art deco

The First Frontier

movie theater built in 1931, offers concerts and other events. Bristol's trademark sign, "Bristol Va Tenn A Good Place To Live," ever cheerful, presides over the street.

Roots music fans should head next for the **Birthplace of Country Music Alliance Museum** (276/645-0035, www.birthplaceofcountrymusic.org) located in a shopping mall. To get there, take Exit 1 of I-81-on the south side of the Interstate—and go to the lower level of the mall. The museum is open whenever the mall is open, and contains exhibits of Bristol's musical roots such as Sara Carter's guitar, Ralph Stanley "show clothes," and various musical instruments.

The **Birthplace of Tennessee Ernie Ford** (1223 Anderson St., 423/989-4850)is a modest house open to visitors by appointment only. The chamber of commerce handles appointments.

A year-round favorite of visitors is **Bristol Caverns** (423/878-2011, www.bristolcaverns .com, daily except Thanksgiving and Christmas, $9 ages 13 and over, $5 ages 5–12, free for ages 4 and under), a long cave with a long history. It seems that the local Native Americans used the caverns as a way of sneaking up on unsuspecting settlers and then mysteriously disappearing when chased. The section of the cave now open to visitors has walkways and stairs and the requisite named formations. This is a good place for children. Tours depart approximately every 20 minutes. They are five miles southeast of Bristol on Hwy. 435.

Most people think of dams as huge, concrete structures. Nearby **South Holston Dam,** one of the many built by the Tennessee Valley Authority, is made of earth and is one of the largest such structure in the world. The top of the dam has a visitors center, and the land around the dam offers picnicking and fishing; bring your own boat. Below the dam, visitors can cross a footbridge to Osceola Island, which contains a one-mile long nature trail. To get there, take U.S. 421 out of Bristol toward Mountain City. Turn right at the sign that says TVA South Holston Dam.

Steele Creek Park has 2,000 acres containing a children's park with a half-mile scenic train ride and paddleboats. The park offers 25

RACING FOR ACCOMMODATIONS

While NASCAR stock-car racing may not be every traveler's cup of tea, visitors to the First Frontier who want a hotel room on certain weekends should pay close attention to the activities at the Bristol Motor Speedway.

Big races in Bristol attract in excess of 160,000 people, who fill up all the lodging in the area and rent rooms as far away as Knoxville. Furthermore, local hostelries, hoping to cash in on life in the fast lane, often raise their rates precipitously. To get the exact dates, check www.bristolmotorspeedway.com.

miles of hiking trails, a nature center, and a nine-hole golf course. To get there go west from Bristol on U.S. 11 West and turn left on the Blountville Hwy. The entrance to the park will be on the left.

ENTERTAINMENT AND EVENTS
The World of Speed

For most people, NASCAR racing exists in a kind of parallel universe; they are only vaguely aware of its presence. Stock car racing grew up in the South, and though its appeal now spans the country, the South remains the hotbed of interest. The **Bristol Motor Speedway** (423/764-1161, www.bristolmotorspeedway.com, tickets $55–88), at 0.533 mile long, is the shortest major racecourse in the country. The 36-degree high-banked track poses special challenges for drivers, who must constantly fight the effects of a relentless centrifugal force. These circumstances, however, prove advantageous for fans, who can clearly see all of the competitors all of the time, a situation not possible at some of the larger racetracks.

The stands here seat 160,000 people, who happily fill up all the lodging in the area and stay as far away as Knoxville. NASCAR sets the race dates, but Bristol usually has a big race on the first or second weekend in April and the next-to-last weekend in August. Visitors to the First Frontier should keep this in mind.

The NASCAR races at Bristol Motor Speedway attract thousands of stock-car fans.

The route to the Speedway from I-81 is on U.S. 11 East. Take Virginia Exit 3 and U.S. 11 East will take you directly to the Speedway. From I-81 South, take Tennessee Exit 69 and turn south on Hwy. 394. Hwy. 394 will take you to the Bristol Dragway entrance (the Dragway is adjacent to the Speedway). Turn on U.S. 11 East north to reach the north entrance and south entrance to Bristol Motor Speedway. Or just follow the crowd. Visitors can take a tour of the track on weekdays 10 A.M.–noon September–May and 10 A.M.–4 P.M. June–mid-August. No tours are offered when major races take place.

Racing fans who prefer their competition on the straight and narrow need only go to the adjacent drag strip, the **Bristol Dragway** (423/764-3724, www.bristoldragway.com). Situated in the appropriately named Thunder Valley, the stands seat 17,000. Don't forget the earplugs.

Baseball

Baseball fans turn out to cheer for the **Bristol White Sox** (276/645-7275 or 276/669-6859, www.bristolsox.com, games usually start at 7 P.M.), a farm team for the Chicago White Sox.

The team plays at DeVault Memorial Stadium, which is off I-81 at Exit 3. Follow Commonwealth Avenue to Euclid Avenue, and then go right for a half mile. Except when there's a rare advance sellout, tickets are always available at the stadium before games.

ACCOMMODATIONS

Sitting beside I-81, Bristol has a good selection of franchise motels from which to choose. Some are in Virginia and some in Tennessee; if travelers are tired enough it doesn't really matter.

In Tennessee, try the **Days Inn** (536 Volunteer Pkwy., 423/968-2171). Right off the Interstate is the biggest cluster of lodgings: try the **Best Western I-81** (I-81 and U.S. 11 West Exit 74B, 423/968-1101). A dozen or so more options sit just across the state line in Virginia along the Lee Highway.

Observation Knob Park (553 Knob Park Rd., 423/878-5561, Apr. 1–Nov. 1) is a county park on South Holston Lake where visitors can, among other things, fish from a wheelchair-accessible fishing pier. The park has 191 campsites

The First Frontier

plus overflow. To get there from northbound I-81, take Exit 1 in Virginia and get on U.S. 421 south. Follow it through Bristol to Hwy. 44. Take a left on Hwy. 44 and go two miles. Turn right at the sign.

FOOD

Barbecue

Anyone this close to the **Ridgewood Restaurant** (423/538-7543, lunch at 11 A.M. and dinner available Mon.–Sun.) should know about it. Frequently described as the best barbecue place in East Tennessee, it is about nine miles from Bristol on U.S. 19 East, between Elizabethton and Bluff City. On Friday and Saturday night, the place is packed. Go there and taste the beef or pork barbecue and see why. Oddly enough, it doesn't serve ribs.

From Bristol, head south on U.S. 11 West. Turn left on U.S. 19 East and go about 1.2 miles and turn right onto Old Elizabethton Hwy. Ridgewood is about 1.5 miles up this road. Look for lots of cars.

Steak and Seafood

The **Athens Steak House** (105 Goodson St., 276/466-8271, three meals Mon.–Sat.), in Virginia, specializes in Greek salads and great shish kebob.

Troutdale Dining Room (412 6th St., 423/968-9099, dinner Mon.–Sat.) is one of the best restaurants at this end of the state. Although renowned for trout—it keeps a 750-gallon aquarium full of them—this place offers leading-edge American and international dishes such as veal, lamb, venison, and quail. The menu changes depending on what is fresh and seasonal. "We make everything here except the butter," comes the report from the kitchen. Reservations, especially on weekends, are a good idea.

The **Vineyard Restaurant and Lounge** (603 Gate City Hwy., 540/466-4244, three meals daily) features steaks, seafood, Italian dishes, and chicken.

Lighter Fare

Mad Greek Restaurant (2419 Volunteer Pkwy.,

423/968-4848, lunch and dinner daily) serves gyros, kabobs, and mouth-watering baklava.

Bella's Pizza (1351 Lee Hwy. in Virginia, 540/466-3281, open daily for lunch and dinner) offers beer with homemade pizzas that are as honest as Carter Family lyrics.

The Feed Room (620 State St., 423/764-0545, Mon.–Fri.), in the historic H. P. King Building, is a lunch spot offering sandwiches, soups, and salads.

Right beside the Paramount Center for the Arts, **Martin's K. P. Duty** (520 State St., 423/764-3889, lunch Mon.–Sat., dinner Fri.–Sat.) offers sandwiches, specialty salads, and a wide choice of desserts. The **Gourmet Shoppe and Cafe** inside Martin's features quiche and soup.

INFORMATION

The **Greater Bristol Area Chamber of Commerce** (423/989-4850, www.bristolchamber.org, 9 A.M.–5 P.M. Mon.–Fri.) has its office at the corner of State Street and Volunteer Parkway.

An excellent source of information for a much wider part of the state is the **Tennessee Welcome Center** (423/764-5821) on I-81 off the southbound lanes at Exit 1 in Virginia.

BLOUNTVILLE

This little town, the county seat of Sullivan County, is said to have more original log homes along its main street than any other town in Tennessee. Whether this is true or not, Blountville's historic district has 20 structures that are on the National Register. Among them are the **Deery Inn,** whose guests included the Marquis de Lafayette and Presidents James K. Polk, Andrew Johnson, and Andrew Jackson.

Jackson, while president, came through Blountville in 1836 on a Sunday morning and decided to go to church. His party stopped at the **Blountville Presbyterian Church** just as the sermon was beginning. The surprised minister halted the service, announced the new arrivals, led a hymn, and resumed his sermon. Not one Secret Service agent was present.

Sights

Blountville's Historic Society's headquarters are in the **Anderson Townhouse** (April 15–Labor Day 10 A.M.–4 P.M. daily), a two-story log cabin that is 200 years old. It sits across from the courthouse and beside the Blountville Presbyterian Church. Visitors can go there to hear a little bit about the town and obtain a map for the walking tour. Every Friday, an old-time music jam session takes place.

When one log house begins to look like another, it is time to retire to **Countryside Vineyards and Winery** (423/323-1660, www.cvwineryandsupply.com, 10 A.M.–6 P.M. Mon.–Sat., 1–6 P.M. Sun.) for sustenance. Fourteen wines are made from the grapes grown here: four reds, six whites, and four dessert wines. Tours and samples are available whenever visitors drop by.

To get there take Exit 63 off I-81 and go past Sam's Club and a water tower. Follow the signs to Henry Harr Road, the third road on the left. The winery is approximately 1.5 miles from Exit 63.

Accommodations

Smithhaven Bed and Breakfast (2357 Feathers Chapel Rd., 423/323-8554, $75–145) occupies a house built between 1848 and 1851. A large porch complete with rocking chairs wraps around the house. The three rooms have private baths.

Those who prefer to camp will find both of Blountville's campgrounds at Exit 63 of I-81. The way to each is amply marked with signs. **KOA Campground** (425 Rocky Branch Rd., 423/323-7790, open year-round) has 73 sites and six cabins. **Rocky Top Campground** (496 Pearl Ln., 423/323-2535, open year-round) a little closer to the Interstate, offers 35 sites and a handful of cabins.

Kingsport and Vicinity

LAND AND HISTORY

The Cherokee had long cherished an island in the south fork of the Holston River, for it was close to an intersection of warpaths. They used it as a sacred place on which to negotiate treaties with other tribes, and they wouldn't even kill animals there.

Settlers also used it as a gathering place. Bristol industrialist James King established a port here from which he shipped his iron products, thus giving the town its name. Daniel Boone and his company of axmen began their Wilderness Road to Cumberland Gap and into Kentucky in 1775 from here, and various Revolutionary War militias used it as a rendezvous. When the Cherokee decided to wipe out all of the interlopers, they knew where to come.

In 1776, Dragging Canoe, a Cherokee who vehemently opposed settlers, led a force of warriors toward the island. Having been warned by Nancy Ward, a Cherokee who befriended the settlers, the locals readily repelled the attackers. The Battle of Island Flats, as it came to be known, marked the end of all-out warfare on the part of the Cherokee. They would still engage in skirmishes, but upper East Tennessee was now relatively safe for settlers, and some of them began to think of moving even farther west.

If they decided to move on, King's Port gave them access to a river that flowed in the right direction, and the inhabitants helped travelers build boats and shove off downstream. In 1779, the founders of Nashville set forth from here. (Their story is recounted in the Nashville chapter.) And, as settlers made their way back for business or government reasons, they tended to travel this way and very often spent the night at the Netherland Inn.

A Model City

Over time King's Port became Kingsport. The town grew slowly through the 19th century; a couple of skirmishes took place during the Civil War, but the town escaped any real damage. It took the arrival of the railroad in 1909 to make Kingsport shift gears. The men at the throttle, New Yorker John B. Dennis and local boy J.

KINGSPORT

To Bristol

To Bristol

DR

To Bristol

81

11W

STONE

37

93

JOHN

B

To Hwy 421

KINGSPORT

GREENBELT

DENNIS

GREENBELT

KINGSPORT

CENTER

11W

To Gate City, VA

GRANBY RD

STONE

DR

NETHERLAND INN RD

KINGSPORT SPORTS COMPLEX

ALLANDALE MANSION

To Rogersville

NETHERLAND INN

HERITAGE PARK

26

To Bristol

To Bristol

To Blountville

HISTORIC EXCHANGE PLACE ★

GREENBELT

OREBANK RD

DENNIS

RD

HWY

93

COUNTRYSIDE VINEYARDS ★

FORT HENRY MALL

WARPATH DR

ST

FORT HENRY

36

KONNAROCK RD

HWY

DR

WILCOX

DR

RESERVOIR RD

PARK RD

BAYS MOUNTAIN

NATURE CENTER AND PLANETARIUM ★

BAYS MOUNTAIN NATURE PRESERVE ★

Long Island

TRI-CITY REGIONAL AIRPORT ✈

AIRPORT

PARKWAY

Boone Lake

Holston River

Warriors Path State Park

Fort Patrick Henry Lake

Fort Patrick Henry Lake

FORT PATRICK HENRY DAM

HEMLOCK RD

FORT HENRY

36

To Johnson City

DR

To Johnson City

81

To Johnson City

DENNIS

B

JOHN

26

93

To Knoxville

To Greeneville

SCALE NOT AVAILABLE

© AVALON TRAVEL PUBLISHING, INC.

THE KING PLAYED HERE

Kingsport deserves a footnote in Tennessee's musical history, for it was here in 1955 that Elvis played the last concert in which he was second on the bill. He also created a lifelong memory for a local girl.

As recounted by Kingsport author Vince Staten, Elvis appeared at a country music show between the Louvin Brothers and Cowboy Copas, sang for a half hour—collecting $37 and change for his efforts. He was still with Sun Studio and was four months away from releasing "Heartbreak Hotel," his breakout hit. The Kingsport date was the last night of the tour.

Elvis was driving a pink Cadillac, and while signing autographs after the show, he met Billie Mae Smith, who got in the car and took Elvis cruising on Broad Street. The man who would be king was hungry, so they had pizza at a local hangout and then went to her house for a cup of coffee. Her boyfriend, who had seen her on Broad Street—who could miss a pink Cadillac—followed them home and appeared at the door. Red West, one of Elvis' buddies/bodyguards, told the jealous boyfriend to hit the road, which he did, only to return with some buddies of his own, ready to get this Memphis interloper all shook up.

As recounted later by the boyfriend, Elvis said, "I'm breaking this guy's heart. Maybe I'd better leave." He did, but not before giving Billie Mae a searing goodbye kiss. "He sure could kiss," she recalls. "It was very thrilling."

Fred Johnson, set out to create a modern industrial city.

They began by drumming up business for the new railroad. They based their plan on an abundance of raw materials, plenty of hardworking people who had never heard of unions, and industries that would complement each other.

To make everything work right, they commissioned a Massachusetts planner to design America's first "model city." The plan was simple: Line the rivers with factories, put houses on the hills, and let commercial districts fill up the land between. To set up a school system, the city fathers pulled in Columbia University professors as consultants.

It worked beyond their wildest dreams, especially when representatives of George Eastman of Kodak fame bought a defunct factory and founded the Eastman Chemical Company. During World War II, the company set up and ran Holston Ordinance Works, which produced RDX, a powerful explosive. Today Eastman, although no longer a part of Kodak and no longer running the explosives plant, is one of the largest chemical manufacturing plants in the country. Some 7,500 employees out of 12,000 worldwide work in Kingsport. Among the 400

products are polyester plastics for packaging and cigarette filters.

One thing the planners never gave a thought to was pollution, which the various industries produced in spades. After reaching a low point in the '60s and '70s, Kingsport's air and water are cleaner than they used to be, but it remains a town where one doesn't need a weatherman to know which way the wind blows. Bob Dylan has a song called "Kingsport Town," but it appears to have no connection to this town.

SIGHTS AND RECREATION

Downtown

Broad Street in downtown Kingsport leads from the 1916 train station on one end to Church Circle, a graceful collection of Protestant houses of worship. Once Kingsport's principle shopping street, Broad Street is now an antique lover's delight. **Wallace News Stand** (205 Broad St.) opened in 1932 and is one of the very few places where readers can walk out with a copy of the *New York Times* and *Grit and Steel,* a magazine for cockfighters. The place also sells hot dogs and popcorn.

The First Frontier

The **DKA Gallery** (140 West Main St., 423/246-6550), a few steps off Broad Street, features juried shows of Tennessee artists. The gallery is housed in the restored Gem Theater.

A short drive or long walk leads to ◤ **Up Against the Wall Gallery** (316 E. Market St., 423/246-7210), one of the larger galleries on this end of the state. It began as a custom frame shop and now offers original works from regional and national artists: paintings, sculpture, jewelry, and pottery. The store carries a large collection of prints.

Kingsport is the home of two large statues, one a unique specimen of folk art and the other a piece of roadside Americana. The first is a 25-foot high statue of a male Indian, cleverly named **"The Big Indian."** Constructed in the 1950s and originally erected along Blue Highway 11-W coming into town from Bristol, he now presides over Pratt's Real Pit Bar-B Q at 1225 East Stone Dr. From time to time, this figure's loincloth has been known to blow off in storms, causing local hilarity and much scrambling on behalf of his keepers.

The second statue is atop Pals, a local fast food chain, at 1316 Lynn Garden Drive. This chap is one of the famed "Muffler Men" (www.roadsideamerica.com/muffler) a veritable army of fiberglass figures that all came from the same mold beginning in the early 1960s.

Bays Mountain Nature Reserve

At 3,500 acres, the reserve (423/229-9447, www.baysmountain.com, $3 per car or $12 per bus) is a jewel. Sitting above Kingsport on Bays Mountain, the city-owned park offers hiking and a museum/planetarium that interprets the local flora and fauna for visitors. Set around a 44-acre lake, the park has deer so tame that they often do not run when people pass by. A few animals such as foxes, and a raccoon, are kept in medium size habitats, while waterfowl, deer, otters, birds of prey, and wolves are kept in larger—and separate—habitats.

The park has trails varying from a few hundred feet to 4.8 miles. Mountain bikes are permitted on the gravel service roads, but riders should check in with park personnel first to get a $2 permit. Helmets are required.

The visitors center is a good place to go anytime, but it is especially good for children when the weather is bad. Inside are nature exhibits and a planetarium. The **Harry Steadman Mountain Heritage Farmstead** is a large building with antiques and old farming implements. The **herpetarium,** contains an exhibit of snakes. Nature programs varying from barge rides on the lake to wolf education are abundant; one can easily spend the day here. There are even moonlit hikes which visitors should call about in advance. Visitors should bring their own food, for there is nothing available at the top.

The **Nature Interpretive Center** itself is free, but planetarium shows, barge rides, or other programs cost $1.50 per person.

Turn off I-181 at Exit 52 at Meadowview Conference Center. Turn right at the red light onto Reservoir Road. Continue on Reservoir Road for approximately three miles. Turn right onto Bays Mountain Park Road, take the left fork and continue up the mountain.

Older Kingsport

Each of the American colonies had its own currency, so early travelers coming from Virginia were obliged to exchange one kind of money for another when they crossed boundaries. The **Exchange Place** (4812 Orebank Rd., 423/288-6071, www.exchangeplace.info, 10 A.M.–2 P.M. Thurs.–Fri, 2–4:30 P.M. Sat.–Sun.) was where they performed the transaction hereabouts. Once the center of a 2,000-acre plantation, the restored house and outbuildings provide a fascinating look at the past. Consisting of eight buildings dating 1820–50—six of them original to the site—the Exchange Place and the adjacent Preston Farm frequently offer demonstrations of crafts, farming methods, musket shooting, and household activities.

The Exchange Place/Preston Farm, offers group tours of the historic grounds and farm by a costumed guide for a small fee. Daniel Boone stayed on the farm several times during his life.

An older establishment sits on the bank of

the Holston River in a section of the city known as "Old Kingsport." Across from the western end of Long Island, the three-story **Netherland Inn** (214 Netherland Inn Rd., 423/247-3211, www.netherlandinn.com, May–Oct., 2–4 P.M. Sat.–Sun., $3 adults, $2 seniors, $1 students, and free for children under 6) was established as an inn and tavern in 1818; however, the building was built in 1805. As an inn, it sheltered and quenched the thirst of three presidents and served as a hub of commerce for the nearby boatyard.

The first-floor tavern, second-floor family quarters, and third-floor guest rooms now look like they must have 150 years ago. Visitors can easily cross the road in front of the inn and then walk over a swinging bridge to Long Island. A small part of the island has been given back to the Cherokee, who have placed a monument there.

Picnicking sites lie nearby, and visitors can take a walking tour of the neighborhood. Most of the old homes in the area are still lived in and not open to the public.

A climb from the inn to a small promontory gives a very good view of the confluence of the North and South Forks of the Holston. Sunset is the best time to see this. From this place one can also see Kingsport's most striking historic home, **Rotherwood Mansion.** It was built in 1820 as a home for Frederick Ross, a man of wealth and taste who once persuaded local farmers to go into the silkworm business. To promote his enterprise, for several summers he wore a suit made of woven silk. He lost his shirt on a cotton mill investment, however, and silk suits, which hadn't exactly caught on, disappeared from the scene. The house is privately owned and is not open to the public.

Allandale

Out-of-towners leaving Kingsport and heading west on U.S. 11 West sometimes find themselves staring twice at a large home on the right that bears more than a passing resemblance to the White House. This is Allandale (423/229-9422, www.allandalemansion.com, open first weekend in Dec. only), built in 1950 by Harvey and Ruth Brooks, who set their sights on erecting what lo-

the Tennessee White House

cals call a "showplace." Hiring prominent landscape architects to shape the 500-acre farm and filling the house with elegant furniture, they achieved their goal.

Twenty-five acres of the estate and the mansion are now owned by the city of Kingsport. The barn has a hayloft for dancing, concerts, and wedding receptions. The house is rented out for weddings, receptions, Murder Mystery Dinners, and whatever the city can think of to help maintain the place. The public can tour Allandale during the first weekend in December and can enjoy ice cream there during Fun Fest.

ENTERTAINMENT AND EVENTS

The **Carter Family Memorial Music Center,** the most significant music destination in this part of Tennessee, is close to Kingsport. To get there, take U.S. 23 north toward Gate City, turn right on U.S. 58, and go to Hiltons, Virginia.

The First Frontier

For a taste of genuine Appalachian music, this place is unsurpassed.

Baseball lovers gravitate to the **Kingsport Mets** (423/378-3744 or 423/224-2627, www.kmets.com, usual starting time for games is 7 P.M.), part of the New York Mets farm system. The Mets play at the Kingsport Sports Complex; take Exit 57 off I-81 to Hwy. 181 North, then take the West Stone Drive exit. Go left on West Stone Drive, then right on Granby Road.

Almost every town and city in Tennessee has some sort of local festival; **Kingsport's Fun Fest** (423/392-8806, www.funfest.net, third to the fourth weekend in July) is one of the best. The reason is money. The city's business community, led by Eastman Chemical, heavily subsidizes this July celebration. Typical of the more than 100 events are country, rock, gospel, and folk concerts; hot air balloon races; athletic events such as an 8K run; and puppet theater for children. Some events have admission fees, but most are free.

For more information, contact the **Kingsport Convention and Visitor's Bureau** (151 E. Main Street, 800/743-5282 or 423/392-8820, www.kcvb.org).

ACCOMMODATIONS

Kingsport has a new conference center and hotel that usually has room for passersby. **Meadowview Conference Resort and Convention Center** (1901 Meadowview Pkwy., 800/820-5055 or 423/578-6600) is operated by Marriott and has 195 guest rooms, 73 of which have various business-related amenities. The place features an 18-hole golf course, outdoor pool, hot tub, and tennis court, and lies close to Bays Mountain Nature Reserve.

Most of the other motels in Kingsport lie along Stone Drive—U.S. 11 West. Good franchise choices where one can rest are the **Days Inn Downtown** (805 Lynn Garden Dr., 423/246-7126), **Kingsport Inn** (700 Lynn Garden Dr., 423/247-3133), **Comfort Inn** (100 Indian Center Court, 423/378-4418), **Econo Lodge** (1740 E. Stone Dr., 423/245-

FAST FOOD, TENNESSEE STYLE

Amid the fierce competition for fast food dollars, one East Tennessee chain continues to gain against the likes of Wendy's and McDonald's. **Pals** (www.palsweb.com) offers takeout basics: hot dogs and burgers, toasted cheese sandwiches, and "Frenchy fries." Pals' sweet tea, a Southern staple, is legendary among regulars.

Pals began in 1952 when Fred "Pal" Barger was stationed in the Air Force in Texas and noticed a takeout-only place noted for quick service. The first Pals opened in Kingsport in 1956, and the second in 1958. Four years later, at the second location, Pals put one of the classic "Muffler Man" fiberglass statues on the roof—only this guy is holding a hamburger.

The chain continued to grow, and in 1985 began offering drive-through service. Now at 19 locations, from Bristol to Morristown, Pals is noted for striking buildings sporting an enormous hamburger, hot dog, fries, and a drink on the front.

second location of Pals

The company won the Malcolm Baldrige National Quality Award, which was presented to Pal Barger by President George W. Bush.

0286), and **Ramada Inn** (2005 La Masa Dr., 423/245-0271).

FOOD

Kingsport's restaurant scene runs heavily toward upscale chain establishments; they come and go—often in the same buildings—with great regularity. Residents seem to think that their eateries, like the leaves, should change at least once a year.

Somewhat far afield but worth the trip is the **Harmony Grocery** (423/348-8000, open at 5 P.M. Thurs.–Sun. for dinner). which features Creole and Cajun cuisine. This is the place for shrimp Creole and sausage or seafood gumbo, as well as fresh seafood and steaks. Brown-bagging is permitted.

Directions to the Harmony Grocery are complicated. From Kingsport, take I-181 south to Exit 45—Eastern Star Road. Go right at the end of the road and drive one mile to a stop sign at a T-intersection. This is Kincheloe Mill Road. Follow it one mile to the right to another T-intersection. Go left onto Harmony Road. (By this point you are probably into the brown bag, but hang in there.) Go a little less than two miles, and Harmony Grocery is on the right. Call for further directions.

Rush Street Grill (1229 East Stone Dr., 423/247-3184, www.rushstreetgrill.com) gets its name from the famous street of restaurants in Chicago. Entrees cost $10–$19 and include steaks and ribs, seafood, sandwiches, and salads. Wine and beer are available, and live music takes place on weekend nights.

Tucked under a hardware store, **Motz's Italian Restaurant** (4231 Fort Henry Dr., 423/239-9560, daily) serves unpretentious but tasty Italian

and American food for lunch and dinner every day. The fresh bread alone is worth a stop.

Sharon's Barbecue and Burgers (301 W. Center St., 423/247-5588, 11 A.M.–8 P.M. daily) has a retro '50s look that proves a perfect setting for its offerings of burgers and barbecue. If Elvis is alive and ever walks in, he'll feel right at home.

WARRIOR'S PATH STATE RECREATIONAL PARK

This 950-acre park (423/239-8531, www.state .tn.us) was carved out of land surrounding TVA's Patrick Henry Lake, and aquatic pursuits are the chief focus here. Pleasure boating and water-skiing are very popular, as is fishing. Boats (including paddleboats) are available for rent at the marina.

The water, coming as it does from the bottom of upstream Boone Lake, tends to be on the chilly side for swimming, but bathers can cavort in an outdoor pool. Both operate from early summer through Labor Day.

Nine miles of hiking trails wind through the park, and park stables offer trail rides through the woods. The park has an 18-hole golf course and driving range.

The year-round **campground,** close by the swimming pool, has 135 sites, all with tables and grill. Ninety-four come with water and electrical hookups. The park does not accept reservations; campsites are offered on a first-come, first-served basis.

To get to Warrior's Path State Park from I-81, take Exit 59 and go north on Hwy. 36 to Hemlock Road. Turn right and continue to the park entrance. From Kingsport, take Fort Henry Drive south to Hemlock Road.

To the Gap

⋈ ROGERSVILLE

U.S. 11 West used to go through downtown Rogersville, and when the two-lane road became inadequate to carry the growing traffic, some good soul decided to bypass the town and build a wider road in the fields north of town. Thus today's visitor can enjoy a town full of history—and a lot less touristy than Jonesborough—with a main street lined with 19th century buildings said to be the largest collection of Federal-style buildings in Tennessee. Many of these buildings came about because of John Augustine McKinney, a Scottish attorney who, on noticing that so many luminaries came through Rogersville, began rebuilding the town in brick buildings to as to impress them.

Rogersville came into being in 1787, only 10 years after Davy Crockett's grandparents had been killed by the original inhabitants. Local farmers plowing their fields still turn up arrowheads and other Indian relics.

In 1791, it became the site of the first newspaper in Tennessee, the *Knoxville Gazette*. This seeming mix-up of names came about because the publisher had his eyes on Knoxville, which he knew would be named the state capital. He set up his press and began publication in Rogersville a year before moving to Knoxville.

In recent years Rogersville has embraced its history and now offers visitors a good place to spend some time. The first stop should be the **Rogersville Chamber of Commerce** (107 East Main St., 423/272-2186). Park in the back.

Historic Sights

A three-story building right in the middle of downtown, the 1824 **Hale Springs Inn,** is one of Tennessee's oldest hostelries, and well worth a stop. Like similar places in Kingsport and Blountville, this one was host to Presidents Jackson, Polk, and Johnson. (These three are mentioned so often in this book that to some it must seem as if they traveled together like the Wise Men. But Jackson died the year Polk became

president, and Polk died 16 years before Johnson moved into the White House.) The Hale Springs Inn, which now serves meals, is undergoing renovation and will offer rooms to the public

The Hawkins County Courthouse, erected in 1836, is the oldest operating courthouse in Tennessee. Its main courtroom resembles Independence Hall in Philadelphia, an architectural point probably unappreciated by the miscreants who find themselves doing business there.

Rogersville has an excellent walking tour to show off its significant buildings. Free copies of a brochure that points them out are available in various locations, among them the **Tennessee Newspaper and Printing Museum** (415 S. Depot St., 423/272-1961, www.rogersville-heritage.org, 10 A.M.–4 P.M. Tues.–Fri., other days by appointment). The museum contains collections of wooden and lead type, old presses, and a Linotype machine, truly one the mechanical wonders of printing days gone by. This restored Southern Railway depot serves as a visitors center as well.

The privately owned **Sarah McKinney Heiskall House** (324 W. Main St.) was built around 1830 out of homemade brick and has an English boxwood hedge thought to be more than 200 years old. The house is not open to the public.

Ebbing and Flowing Spring

The spring, outside of town, begins with a barely discernible trickle and, two hours and 47 minutes later, reaches a flow of 500 gallons per minute. It has been doing this for more than 200 years, and no one knows exactly why. One theory holds that an underground basin is right under the spring. When the basin fills to the top, a siphon action works to empty it. Then the siphon is broken, and the spring has to wait until the basin is full again.

The second remarkable thing about this phenomenon is that it has not been commercialized. The people who own the spring charge no admission and sell no souvenirs. A lane to the side of the spring leads up the hill to Ebbing and Flowing United Methodist Church, a beautiful country church that stands beside an old school built before 1800. The cemetery contains a famous epitaph:

Remember me as you pass by
As you are now so once was I
As I am now, you soon shall be,
Prepare for death and follow me.

Some wag suggested the following lines:

To follow you I would not be content
Unless I knew which way you went.

To get to the spring, go east on Main Street 1.1 miles to Burem Road, bearing right at the Amis House historical marker. Turn left on Ebbing and Flowing Spring Road at 2.3 miles. Go 1.4 miles to the spring, which is behind a little dairy house on the left. A lane on the right leads to the school and church. This spring is on private property, and visitors should keep that in mind as they come here.

Events

Rogersville holds **Heritage Days** on the second weekend in October. This harvest festival features agricultural demonstrations, open houses, and all manner of fun. For information on this and other Rogersville activities, go to the Tennessee Newspaper and Printing Museum. Rogersville also holds a **Renaissance Fair** in mid-June.

Accommodations

Kyle House Bed and Breakfast (111 W. Main St., 423/272-0835, www.kylehousetn.com, $75 and up) is across the street from the Hale Springs Inn. Occupying an 1832 Federal-style home, it offers casual rooms with private or shared baths.

The **Cherokee Lake Campground** (423/272-3333) 10 miles west of Rogersville on U.S. 11 West, has 84 sites available year-round.

Shopping

Main Street Studio and Gallery (116 E. Main St., 423/272-3879) sells functional pottery, while **Mountain Star Antique and Craft Mall** (122 E.

Main St.) offers all manner of antiques and collectible figures made of stone—bear stones, doll stones, and folk stones.

Tennessee Books and Autographs (112 S. Church St., 423/921-9017) contains one of the largest stock of Tennessee history that visitors will find anywhere. An autograph of President James K. Polk goes for $900.

Information

The **Tennessee Newspaper and Printing Museum** (415 S. Depot St., 423/272-1961, www .rogersvilleheritage.org, 10 A.M.–4 P.M. Tues.–Fri., other days by appointment) serves as the town's visitors center. The Hale Springs Inn also has brochures of walking tours and other local sites.

SNEEDVILLE

Hancock is perhaps the most remote county in the state, yet it is an area of great beauty that is called the "Over Home Country." Sneedville is the county seat, the birthplace of country singer Jimmy Martin, and the center of Melungeon culture.

Hwy. 66 goes to Sneedville from Rogersville, but it is a long and winding road best suited for sports cars and people who do not get carsick. An easier route to Sneedville is on Hwy. 31 from Hwy. 11 West. **Elrod Falls** is a series of cascading falls just off Highway 31 south of Sneedville off to the west. Follow the signs. A small park has picnic tables and grills and a covered pavilion. The second waterfall contains an unusual flowstone formation, one seldom seen outside of caves.

In town, the **Melungeon Cultural Heritage Museum** occupies the historic Hancock County Jail, built in 1860. Exhibits include photographs, artifacts, and books. The museum is on Jail Street, one block south of the courthouse.

North of Sneedville Hwy. 63 goes over Newman's Ridge, a longtime home to Melungeons. On the north side of the ridge lies the **Vardy** community, which was first settled about 1780. The Presbyterian Church established the Vardy school in 1892, and it was in operation until 1973. The school provided educational opportunities for

THE MELUNGEON MYSTERY

East Tennessee was settled primarily by people from the British Isles, and anyone who had a darker complexion was usually of Indian or African descent. In various parts of East Tennessee and southwest Virginia, however—primarily Hancock and Hawkins Counties—there lived communities of folks who had blue eyes, darker than usual skin, and straight blond or black hair. These people became known as "Melungeons," a term whose origin is not clear. Various theories claimed that the Melungeons were the descendants of Portuguese sailors, Spanish Moors, Indians, or Turks. A wilder theory holds that these are somehow the remnants of the Lost Colony of Roanoke.

What did become clear, at any rate, was that being a Melungeon was something to hide. Like other racial minorities, they suffered all manner of abuse from their neighbors. Melungeons couldn't vote, own land, or go to public schools. Not surprisingly, this led to their distancing themselves from much of their culture, whatever it was and from wherever it came. Intermarriage with other people has almost entirely eliminated the distinctive Melungeon look.

In recent years, a growing number of Melungeon descendants have become curious about their hidden heritage and have brought what used to be a label of shame into a new and positive light. An annual Melungeon gathering (www.melungeon.org) has drawn crowds, and a Melungeon descendant named N. Brent Kennedy has written a book called *The Melungeons, The Resurrection of a Proud People: The Untold Story of Ethnic Cleansing in America.* Another book, by Mattie Ruth Johnson, is *My Melungeon Heritage,* published by the Overmountain Press.

One observer in Sneedville, however, noted that most of the people who are celebrating Melungeon power have never lived in Hancock County, where the legacy of resentment and shame still exists. If out-of-towners see someone they think might be a Melungeon, it would not be a good idea to leap out of the car and ask.

students from Vardy, Blackwater Creek, and Newman's Ridge, and from neighboring Lee County, Virginia. Vardy residents enjoyed a superb education, better health care than most of their neighbors, and encouragement to go to college. The Vardy church has been restored as a museum, and it is open by request. See contact information below. To get to the Vardy community, take Hwy. 63 from Sneedville across Newman's Ridge 3.8 miles to Vardy Road. Turn right, and the Vardy community is 3.8 miles ahead.

The Newman's Ridge area was the home of Mahala Mullins, a famous Melungeon woman who lived 1824–98. She allegedly sold moonshine openly from her home, and she grew to an estimated 600 pounds. A deputy complained that, "She's catchable, but not fetchable." When she died, her coffin was constructed around the bed in which she lay. The chimney on one end of her cabin was being replaced, and to get the enormous coffin out a section of the wall was taken down. This cabin has been restored and moved to the Vardy community, where it serves as a museum that is open by appointment.

Practicalities

At Aunt Bea's Restaurant (breakfast and lunch Mon.–Sat., lunch Sun.), just down Jail Street from the museum, country cooking is the fare.

The best source of information about Sneedville is Scott Collins, clerk and master of **Hancock County**, at 423/733-4524, or visit www.korrnet.org/overhome.

Tours of the Vardy community are available on request from the **Vardy Community Historical Society** (423/733-2305).

THE WARRIOR'S PATH

In following U.S. 11 West southwest from Rogersville, the traveler follows an ancient route. The Warrior's Path of the Cherokee came this way, and later Daniel Boone and 30 axmen cut a road from the Long Island of Kingsport to Cumberland Gap. They came through what is now Rogersville, following the Holston River, and then turned north to get to the Gap.

Mooresburg

This little community is a couple of miles south of Mooresburg Springs, which, according to the WPA guide, were "highly impregnated with iron." The discoverers deeded the spring and about two acres of land "to the sick and afflicted of the State of Tennessee." According to the terms of the gift, any sick Tennessean could build a cabin there and stay as long as he or she wanted.

Modern-day visitors to Mooresburg can relax at the **Home Place Bed and Breakfast** (132 Church Ln., 800/521-8424 or 423/921-8424, $45–100). The owner is descended from the founders of Mooresburg and Rogersville and offers four bedrooms and three baths. The first floor is wheelchair-accessible.

Bean Station

The place where Boone and his men turned north became known as Bean Station, which, as the population and commerce grew, became an important crossroads for travelers coming from as far as New Orleans and Baltimore. Travelers found an assortment of taverns and inns, the most famous of which was the Bean Station Tavern, a place that in its 1830s heyday could accommodate 200 people. Guests such as Andrew Jackson, James K. Polk, Andrew Johnson, and Henry Clay hobnobbed in parlors and had access to one of the finest wine cellars in the entire South.

Bean Station prospered even as horses and buggies gave way to railroads. In the late 1800s, Tate Springs became one of the better-known resorts in the state. Six hundred guests could take the waters, play golf, or indulge in perhaps the laziest game ever invented—fly poker. The rules were simple: each player put down one card, and the first card on which a fly landed was the winner. As the new century rolled around, Tate Springs drew wealthy families, among them the Studebakers, Firestones, and Fords, but the advent of the automobile spelled

the end for such resorts, and the Depression pushed them over the edge.

Tate Springs was bought in 1943 by a Methodist minister, Reverend A. E. Wachtel, who established the Kingswood School for neglected children. The students lived in the old hotel until 1963, when it burned down. New buildings were erected, however, and today the school continues serving children ages 5–18. Some are residents, while others are day students who are having behavioral or emotional problems in local schools. John Wachtel, son of the founder, presides over the school today. All that remains of the old resort is a gazebo that stands over the original spring. Kingswood School is not open to the public.

Rutledge

Farther down U.S. 11 West lies the town of Rutledge, the seat of the only county in Tennessee named for a woman. Mary Grainger was the wife of John Sevier, the first governor of Tennessee.

On the grounds of the Grainger County Courthouse, in the middle of Rutledge, stands a brick building so small that it looks like a playhouse. This modest structure was once the tailor shop of Andrew Johnson. Here he stayed less than a year before returning to Greeneville to the woman who became his wife. Perhaps another reason for leaving Rutledge was that he had to share this building with the local sheriff.

Fish fanciers will appreciate the **Buffalo Springs Trout Hatchery** (8 A.M.–4 P.M. daily) just south of Rutledge. This state-run hatchery has concrete raceways filled with thousands of trout. Admission is free, and someone is on hand every day to answer questions and give a brief tour. To get to the hatchery, take Hwy. 92 south of Rutledge to Owl Hole Gap Road. Turn right, and follow it to the hatchery.

Blaine

The town of Blaine was for years the home of the last widow of a Union Civil War veteran. Gertrude Janeway died in 2003 at the age of 93. She had married John Janeway when she was 18

THE TOMATO WAR

Almost every town in Tennessee has some sort of annual celebration with live music, crafts, beauty pageant, road race, and so on. **Rutledge's Grainger County Tomato Festival** has all of these, but adds one very unusual event: the Tomato War.

Here are a couple of the actual rules of this one-of-a-kind contest.

All participants will wear white T-shirts and will be provided with a fixed amount of tomato ammunition. A team member will be considered "dead" when there is evidence of a direct hit on his shirt. Hits elsewhere will only be considered "wounding." To discourage excessive "wounding," the amount of ammunition will be strictly limited.

The only possible improvement for this event would be speeches by politicians. The Tomato Festival (865/828-3433, www.graingercounty tomatofestival.com) is held every year on the last weekend in July.

and he was 81 in 1927. She received a pension every month of $70.

Farther down U.S. 11 West in Knox County is **House Mountain State Park** (www.state.tn.us), an 850-acre park with steep hikes that offer great views from the highest point in the county. Expect a 900-foot gain in elevation along trails that vary from 0.9 miles to 1.2 miles in length. This is an excellent place to see raptors and great views of the Smokies.

Visitors who are anywhere near House Mountain can also see an exceedingly tall antenna to the north of U.S. 11 West. At one time, this 1,750-foot-high antenna was the tallest structure in the world.

Harrogate

Back at Bean Station, U.S. 25 East heads northwest, climbing a series of ridges in the process. Just before coming to Cumberland Gap, the road leads through the town of Harrogate. A lot of English capital flowed into this part of Tennessee during the 1880s, and here it took the form of an enormous resort hotel, the Four Seasons, which contained 700 rooms. A mere three years later this structure was demolished to make room for the Harrow Academy, a private school.

O. O. Howard, a former general in the Union army, spoke at a Harrow graduation and decided to champion the school. Recalling that President Lincoln had so appreciated the loyalty of East Tennesseans during the Civil War, the old general suggested dedicating the school to Lincoln and changing its name. The Harrow School evolved into Lincoln Memorial University, which was chartered in 1897 and has been educating locals since.

The university's **Abraham Lincoln Museum** (423/869-6235, www.lmunet.edu/museum, open year-round, $2 adults, $1.50 seniors, $1 children 6–12, free for kids under 6) features a large collection of "Lincolniana," as some call it. The collection, which is housed in a building largely paid for by Colonel Sanders of chicken fame, contains the cane Lincoln used the night he was shot, various watches and his clothing, and a plaster model of the statue in the Lincoln Memorial in Washington, D.C. Other exhibits deal with Civil War medicine and documents from Lincoln's career. To get there, follow the signs from U.S. 25 East.

Through the Gap

CUMBERLAND GAP

The town of Cumberland Gap was never a large place, and when passenger travel on railroads declined, it seemed to go into a long sleep. As a result, it largely escaped the ravages of modernization that were inflicted on so many Tennessee towns and it has now become a very pleasant place to visit. Most of the places to stay and fast food joints are in Middlesboro, Kentucky.

The **Cumberland Gap Towne Hall,** which occupies a 1925 school building at the corner of North Cumberland Drive and Colwyn Avenue, is a good place to start. Here visitors can get a map.

Food so good you'll think we stole your mom" is the motto at **Webb's Country Kitchen** (602 Colwyn Ave., 423/869-5877), which offers country cooking such as biscuits and gravy, pinto beans, and hoecakes. Webb's has open-mic on Friday nights and live music on Saturday nights.

Perhaps the fanciest restaurant in Cumberland Gap is **Ye Olde Tea and Coffee Shoppe** (527 Colwyn Ave., 423/869-4844), where the menu is far more extensive than the name might suggest. The restaurant is in an old brick building that once housed a bank, hardware store, and general store. In 1910, the bank was robbed, netting the crooks—caught shortly afterward— the grand total of $7. The vault from the bank is still there. Prime rib, steak, mesquite-grilled chicken, and seafood are available with the espresso and cappuccino.

Cumberland Gap Inn (630 Brooklyn St., 888/408-0127, $70–90) is the place to lay your head.

The **Cumberland Gap General Store** (503 Colwyn Ave., 423/869-2282, www.cumberlandgap.com, 9 A.M.–5 P.M. Mon.–Sat., noon–5 P.M. Sun.) offers more than 6,000 giftware items—among them reproductions of antiques, Depression glass, and cast-iron toys. It also has more than 300 dolls.

CUMBERLAND GAP NATIONAL HISTORICAL PARK

Though only a small section of this park is in Tennessee, it deserves mention, both for its historical significance and natural beauty. Indeed, one can make the case that the visitor with a limited amount of time in Tennessee would get more out of this park than a trip to the much larger— and vastly more crowded—Great Smokies National Park.

While the Appalachian Mountains cannot compare in size to Western ranges, they provide formidable obstacles. Anyone not believing this should try marching up the side of one of these mountains or ridges. Now imagine crossing them in muddy or snowy conditions, and doing so with a wagon.

CUMBERLAND GAP TUNNEL

The 4,600-foot-long twin tunnels that now guide U.S. 25 East traffic under Cumberland Mountain are engineering marvels. Work was begun in 1991 with a 10- by 10-foot pilot tunnel that revealed several challenges hidden in the depths of Cumberland Mountain.

Several caves lay in the path, including one with an entrance 85 feet high and another with an underground lake 30 feet deep. In addition, pockets in the rock contained large amounts of clay. The company that insured the project estimated that four to six workers would die during the project.

Work commenced on the Tennessee and Kentucky sides, and workers met in the middle on July 9, 1992. The project was opened to traffic a little more than five years after work was begun, and no one lost his life in the effort. A sophisticated ventilation system and backup power source keeps the tunnel healthy for motorists, and the whole operation is controlled from a command center on the Kentucky side.

History

The earliest travelers through the Cumberland Gap were migrating herds of buffalo. As Indians moved into the region, they followed the buffalo and used the Gap to get to prime hunting grounds in Kentucky. The first settler to tell others of the passage was Dr. Thomas Walker, an English surveyor who came through in 1750. The French and Indian War and assorted problems with the Indians, not to mention the fact that the route over the Gap was basically a path, held down substantial migration for 25 years. Daniel Boone first came through the Gap in 1769 and encountered hostile Native Americans. In 1773, while he was attempting to lead a group of settlers toward the Gap, Native Americans attacked Boone's party and killed his son James.

After the 1775 land purchase consummated at Sycamore Shoals, however, Boone and 30 others hacked out the 208-mile-long Wilderness Road from King's Port to Boonesborough on the Kentucky River. This literally got things rolling. By the end of the Revolutionary War 12,000 people had crossed the Gap, and traffic reached its peak during the 1790s. By 1800, an estimated 300,000 people had come through heading north and west, including Abraham Lincoln's parents. As people in the territory became settled and began producing more than they needed, the Gap served as a trade route back to the east.

In the 1820s and 1830s, when the Erie Canal and railroads pierced the mountains farther north, traffic through the Gap declined. The Civil War sparked interest in the Gap once more. Andrew Johnson, afraid to ride a train through hostile Confederate territory, used the Gap as a way to travel to Washington to take his place in the Senate. Thousands of Tennesseans who were loyal to the Union came the same way to join the Union army.

Realizing that these men and boys might come back through the Gap, this time wearing uniforms, the Confederacy built seven forts, all facing north, and cut down all the trees within a mile of each fort. Sitting atop this denuded landscape, they awaited an attack that never came, finally abandoning their positions in June of 1862 to fight elsewhere. Union forces

CUSSING THE YANKEES

When the Confederates surrendered Cumberland Gap, one of their Fort Pitt officers refused to cease fire with his cannon and, in a final act of defiance, spiked and destroyed the piece. The Northern troops packed him off to a prison camp in Minnesota for the duration of the war.

After the war, he moved to Texas but never relented in his disgust with the Union. On his deathbed, he convinced his grandson to go to the site of Fort Pitt on the 100th anniversary of its fall, to face north, and to curse the federal government for a full five minutes. On September 9, 1963, the grandson stepped up to the site of the former fort and fulfilled his grandfather's wish.

numbering 20,000 then occupied the Gap and built their own set of forts, this time facing south. Their supply line was severed, forcing them to retreat, and the Gap was once more in the hands of Southerners. A Union force came and captured the main water supply, and the Confederates—among them the great-great-grandfather of the author of this book—surrendered. The North held the Gap until the end of the war.

During the 20th century a modern highway crossed the Gap, and in the 1940s and '50s another significant migration took place, this one involving black families moving north to take advantage of new economic opportunities. They drove through the Gap on a steep and curving road on which hundreds of motorists died.

Those days are over. U.S. 25 East now goes through a long tunnel, and the Park Service has restored the Gap to approximate the way it looked in the days of the Wilderness Road. With the completion of the project, the Gap has come full circle. Visitors can look at the road and ponder the words of Frederick Jackson Turner, who wrote in 1893:

Stand at Cumberland Gap and watch the procession of civilization, marching single file—the buffalo following the trail to the salt springs, the Indian, the fur-trader and hunter, the cattle-raiser, the pioneer farmer—and the frontier has passed by.

Sights and Recreation

Down in the town of Cumberland Gap, the remains of the **Iron Furnace** give a glimpse of how settlers supplied a basic need. Looking like a big, squat chimney, this furnace was heavy industry for the frontier; at its peak up to 300 men—some of them slaves—worked here. Their tasks consisted of assembling iron ore, limestone, and charcoal. The charcoal required 50 cords of wood each time the furnace was fired, resulting in a steady deforestation of the surrounding land. Oddly enough, the iron-makers never used coal, which is abundant in the area. The molten iron was cast into Dutch ovens, skillets, and plows, but most of it wound up as "pig iron," which was sold to blacksmiths or shipped via river to Chattanooga. At peak production, the furnace daily produced about 43 "pigs" weighing 150 pounds each.

The limestone surface is smooth inside from the heat. It was last used in the 1880s, when cheaper steel from the East made this more homegrown variety uneconomical.

Fort McCook and **Fort Lyon,** remnants of Civil War earthworks with cannons, are visible near the Pinnacle and along the Pinnacle Road. Surrounded as they are now by a dense forest, they do not give an accurate view of the barren, treeless landscape over which Union and Confederate soldiers kept a boring watch. Sometimes historical inaccuracy is not a bad thing.

Hensley Settlement consists of some of the buildings left by a 20th-century group of pioneers who climbed Brush Mountain and lived there for almost 50 years. Sherman Hensley and his family moved here in 1904, and at its 1925–35 peak the community had 12 scattered homesteads consisting of about 100 people. This was a largely self-sufficient place. If they didn't hunt it or grow it or make it—and that included about everything—they rode down off the mountain to get it. The last resident left in 1951, and since then the Park Service has restored about

25 buildings scattered over three farmsteads in a 70-acre area.

Getting there is not easy. Hikers can walk the 3.5-mile **Chadwell Gap Trail** up the side of Cumberland Mountain. To get there, take U.S. 58 east along the route of the Wilderness Road. Turn left onto Hwy. 690. Turn right onto Hwy. 688 and park at the trailhead. Keep in mind that it can be much cooler on the top of the mountain and dress accordingly.

During summer the Park Service runs a van to Hensley Settlement once daily Friday–Monday. There's a small charge, and the van holds just 10 people. Make reservations by calling park headquarters one week in advance.

Mountain bikers can come up the Kentucky side of the mountain to the park boundary, which is about a quarter-mile from Hensley Settlement. To do this, take Sugar Run Road, which after leaving the park becomes Hwy. 988. Turn right onto Hwy. 217 and drive to the Cubbage School, then go right on Hwy. 987. Go right on the Brownies Creek Primitive Road.

In addition to Cumberland Gap itself, the park runs northeast along the ridge top of Cumberland Mountain. That ridge alone, aside from having any historical significance, is worth a trip to the park. The **Ridge Trail** runs the length of the mountain—15.6 miles in all.

When Dr. Thomas Walker first came through the gap, he noted the presence of a large cave. During the Civil War, the cavern was used to store supplies, and it was the setting of an 1864 novel called *Cudjo's Cave*. The coming of the highway and tourists brought about the commercialization of the cave, which somehow came into the possession of Lincoln Memorial University. The Park Service bought the cave—restoring its name to Gap Cave, as Dr. Walker named it—and has opened it to the public once more. The sometimes-garish electrical lights have all been ripped out, and guides carry lanterns to show visitors the cave as Dr. Walker might have first seen it. Unlike Dr. Walker, however, modern-day cavers walk on man-made pathways.

A delightful natural feature of the park is **Sand Cave,** on the far eastern end of the park on the

The First Frontier

Kentucky side, though visitors must begin the hike in Virginia. The hike is about four miles one-way, but the cave is worth it. Sand Cave is technically a "rock house"—one enormous room almost an acre and a quarter in size. The 150-foot-wide entrance stands 40 feet high, and a waterfall streams down one side. The cave floor is a sloping surface of sand—tons and tons of it. Children of all ages love to climb to the top of the slope and run down. To get to the cave, take U.S. 58 east to Ewing, Virginia. Turn left onto Hwy. 724, and drive a short way to the Civitan Club parking lot.

Old-time travelers headed for Cumberland Gap on the Wilderness Road could look up and see white cliffs atop Cumberland Mountain. They viewed them with foreboding, as a symbol of the mountain barrier in their way. Today's travelers see **White Rocks** as a great hiking destination. Eons ago this area was under the sea, and the cliffs are made of conglomerate, a combination of light-colored quartz pebbles and sand. To get there, use the same directions for Sand Cave.

Practicalities

The park has a year-round, 160-site **camping** area on the Virginia side. Water and flush toilets are available, and 50 sites have electricity. Four primitive campsites lie along the Ridge Trail. These require permits from park headquarters.

The **park headquarters** (606/248-2817, www.nps.gov/cuga, 8 A.M.–5 P.M. daily year-round) is off U.S. 25 East in Kentucky.

Elizabethton and Vicinity

Jonesborough gets most of the attention from those seeking to explore Tennessee's colonial towns; it certainly has cornered the market on bed-and-breakfasts and cute shops. Elizabethton, however, with its Carter Mansion and the replica of Fort Watauga, offers a significant look at what was America's first frontier.

This was the place where President Andrew Johnson made his last visit to a tavern. In town on July 28, 1875, to visit his daughter, he dropped into a tavern on the banks of the Doe River. That night he had a stroke, and died the next night upon suffering a second stroke.

Elizabethton is noted for being the source of a genteel rivalry, the famous 1886 "War of the Roses" gubernatorial campaign between brothers Alf and Bob Taylor, respectively a Republican and a Democrat. In our age of attack ads and electronic mudslinging, the gentle race between these two seems as remote as high button shoes.

The Taylors supposedly pledged to their mother that they would confine their debates and speeches to the issues and would not lambaste each other. Both were accomplished humorists, and they entertained crowds with political speeches seasoned with fiddle music and jokes. A story dating from this time claims that the two spoke in a small town in which a makeshift wooden stage was erected atop a new manure spreader sitting outside a hardware store. After Republican Alf finished speaking, his Democrat brother climbed up and confessed that he "had never before stood on the Republican platform."

Elizabethton attracted industry throughout the 19th century, and in 1926, following the examples of Kingsport and other Southern towns, German firms began moving in and manufacturing rayon. Three years later Elizabethton was the site of a bitter strike by the rayon workers. The labor unrest involved 5,000 workers and led to a clash with 800 National Guardsmen. The strikes ultimately failed, but they served as the first examples of Southern workers challenging exploitative conditions by Northern or foreign industrialists.

SIGHTS

Sycamore Shoals State Historical Area (1651 W. Elk Ave., www.state.tn.us, 8 A.M.–4:30 P.M. daily, closed on holidays) is the best place to begin sightseeing in Elizabethton. The 50-acre park sits right beside the famous shoals, just west

Modern mountain men gather at Sycamore Shoals State Historical Area to commemorate the Revolutionary War victory over the British at Kings Mountain.

of town on Elk Avenue, otherwise known as Hwy. 321. The fort and visitors center have good exhibits, and kids will love the opportunity to run inside the palisaded structure and peer out of the old doors and over the top. A trail leads down to the Watauga River, where one can see the famous shoals.

Leaving the historical area, head downtown on Hwy. 321/Elk Avenue. As one crosses the Doe River, a look to the right reveals the **Doe River Covered Bridge.** Stretching 134 feet over the river, this 1882 structure can be crossed on foot or by bike. There are few windows, supposedly so that horses or cattle driven across the bridge would not be scared by seeing the water below. This situation aided early courtships as well.

Elizabethton has several significant homes, which are discussed at great length in Carolyn Sakowski's excellent *Touring the East Tennessee Backroads.* Perhaps the best is the **John and Lan-**

don Carter Mansion (423/543-5808, late May–late Aug., 9 A.M.–5 P.M. Wed.–Sat., 1–5 P.M. Sun., free). To get there from the Historical Area, come into town on Elk Avenue/Hwy. 321 to the intersection where Hwy. 321 turns left and is joined by U.S. 19. Go right on this four-lane road and proceed until the stoplight at Broad Street. Turn right, then turn right again on the Broad Street Extension. Go 0.3 miles; the house will be on the left.

The house may not look like a mansion now, but in the early 1770s this was high style. This house has been preserved, not restored, and the inside contains fancy woodwork—this in a time of rough log cabins—and oil paintings. An estimated 90 percent of what one sees is the original part of the house.

The Carter Mansion is administered by the Sycamore Shoals State Historic Area. During the off-season, visitors can see the house by appointment.

The First Frontier

RECREATION

The **Cherokee National Forest** (423/735-1500, www.southernregion.fs.fed.us/cherokee) offers picnicking, hiking, and various wilderness activities. The Appalachian Trail runs through the area as well.

Laurel Falls is a good place for a day trip. Head out of Elizabethton toward Hampton on U.S. 19 East/Hwy. 321/37. At Hampton, where the road splits, follow Hwy. 321/67. Go 1.1 miles from this intersection to the Dennis Cove Road. Turn right and follow this twisting road for 4.1 miles to Laurel Fork Fall trailhead on the left. This trail runs downhill with the Appalachian Trail along an old railroad bed for about a mile to the falls.

ENTERTAINMENT AND EVENTS

Sycamore Shoals State Historical Area is home to a two-act outdoor drama, *The Wataugans* (423/543-5808), which is performed at 7:30 P.M. for several nights every year in mid-July. The cast of local people works hard to bring to life the stories of their forebears.

Professional baseball takes the field in Elizabethton in the form of the **Elizabethton Twins** (423/547-6443, www.elizabethtontwins.com, usual game time is 7 P.M.), part of the Minnesota Twins farm system. The Twins play at Joe O'Brien Field at Riverside Park. To get there, take Hwy. 321 to Holly Lane. Call for schedules.

Festivals

The **Peter's Hollow Egg Fight** (423/547-3852) is a one-of-a-kind event. Held on Easter weekend, the "fighting" consists of tapping hard-boiled eggs against each other to see which will crack first. This has been going on since 1823, and it is free and open to anyone. It has a few rules: only chicken eggs can be used, adults fight adults, and children fight children. To get to Peter's Hollow, take Hwy. 91 10 miles north of Elizabethton. And bring plenty of eggs.

Sycamore Shoals was a gathering area for Indians when white folks still thought the world was flat. The **Sycamore Shoals Indian Festival** (423/543-5808) recognizes these native Americans on the first weekend in June with an annual celebration at the historical area involving tomahawk-throwing, Cherokee traditional dances, blowgun competitions, crafts, and storytelling.

Tennessee has lots of festivals, but this is perhaps the only one commemorating a bridge. The annual **Covered Bridge Celebration** (423/547-3851), held on the second weekend in June, lasting four days, provides an occasion to display antique cars, hear down-home music, and much more.

In mid-May marks the **Muster at Fort Watauga** (423/543-5808) at the Sycamore Shoals State Historical Area. Visitors can see actors and actresses wearing period clothing, firing muzzle-loading rifles, and bringing to life scenes from colonial days.

The **Overmountain Victory Trail March and Celebration** (423/543-5808) takes place September 25–26. Marchers in period clothing arrive at the historical area about 1:30 P.M., spend the night, and depart the next day at about 8 A.M. Usually 15–30 people walk all the way to Kings Mountain, South Carolina.

The second weekend in November features the **Christmas Craft Show** (423/543-5808) at the historical area, with 48 local craftspeople displaying and selling their wares.

Christmas at the Carter Mansion (423/543-5808, 6–9 P.M., $1, refreshments) takes place on the second or third Saturday in December, when the historic house is decorated in 17th-century style, lit by candles, and filled with period music. Visitors are sometimes surprised to see no Christmas trees here, for these did not come to this country until the 1800s.

For more information, contact **Elizabethton/Carter County Chamber of Commerce** (500 Veterans Memorial Pkwy., 423/547-3852, www.tourelizabethton.com).

ACCOMMODATIONS

Visitors can choose from the **Comfort Inn** (1515 U.S. 19 E Bypass, 423/542-4466 or 800/221-2222), or the **Days Inn** (505 W. Elk Ave.,

423/543-3344). Nearby in Hampton is the **Watauga Lakeshore Resort** (Rte. 2, Box 379, Hwy. 321, 423/725-2201).

Camping at the following Cherokee National Forest campgrounds is strictly first-come first-served; no reservations are taken. For further information, call 423/735-1500. **Dennis Cove** on Laurel Creek has 18 sites, with drinking water and restrooms. It's open year-round. **Carden's Bluff** has 43 campsites on Watauga Lake, with drinking water and restrooms. It's open mid-April–October.

FOOD

Dino's (420 Elk Ave., 423/542-5541, 11 A.M.–8 P.M. Mon.–Fri.) presents lunches and dinners of very good Italian food—sauces and pasta are made on the premises. Pictures of baseball greats adorn the walls.

People with big appetites head for the **Mayflower** (423/542-3667) in the Betsytown Shopping Center on the U.S. 19 East Bypass, where portions are so generous that almost every patron heads out with a doggie bag. This place offers seafood platters, steak, chicken, and daily specials.

The burgers and hot dogs at **Pal's** (413 W. Elk Ave., 423/542-0550) go toe-to-toe and hold their own with the franchises.

The **Southern Restaurant** (408 E. Elk Ave., 423/542-5132, 7 A.M.–7 P.M. Mon.–Fri.) is the kind of place Barney Fife and Andy Taylor would take Thelma Lou and Helen. It offers a full menu of—what else?—Southern food.

The **Ridgewood Restaurant** (423/538-7543) is often described as the best barbecue place in East Tennessee. It's on U.S. 19 East between Elizabethton and Bluff City. On Friday and Saturday night, the place is packed with people eating beef or pork barbecue. However, it doesn't serve ribs.

The town of Hampton lies south of Elizabethton on the way to Roan Mountain. Here is **The Captain's Table** (423/725-2201, www.lakeshore-resort.com, dinner Thurs.–Sun.), a top-notch restaurant offering a full menu and specializing in fresh mountain trout. Try the crayfish for an appetizer. It's on U.S. 321 in Hampton, overlooking Watauga Lake. Reservations recommended.

BUTLER

By and large the Tennessee Valley Authority did some wonderful things for the state, but the downside of the dams and lakes was the forced relocation of dozens of towns. "Old Butler" rests on the bottom of Watauga Lake. The town that visitors see dates from the late '40s.

The **Butler and Watauga Valley Heritage Association** (423/768-2432) has a museum on McQueen Street in Babe Curtis Park. Built by inmates of Tennessee's Northeast Correctional Complex, the building resembles an old train depot. Inside are artifacts dating to Native American days, photos and items from old Butler, and Civil War pieces.

Doe Mountain Inn (412 K&R Rd., 423/727-2726, $85) offers two suites, each of which has a fireplace, television, microwave, and views of the mountains.

Iron Mountain Inn (Box 30, 138 Moreland Dr., in Butler, 888/781-2399 or 423/768-2446, www.ironmountaininn.com, $135–250, includes a gourmet breakfast) has a new log chalet with four bedrooms and additional separate rooms, each of which has a whirlpool bath and very nice views of the surrounding mountains. The chalet starts at $175 for one night.

⋈ ROAN MOUNTAIN

Visitors who find themselves in East Tennessee during the last two weeks in June owe it to themselves to take in Roan Mountain's more than 600 acres of rhododendrons. These natural gardens contain Catawba rhododendrons, which blossom in reds and purples.

"Roan Mountain" refers to three things—a mountain, a state park, and a town. All are close together, and this entry will cover all three. The town is on U.S. 19 East close to the North Carolina border. Turning right onto Hwy. 143, visitors follow the Doe River and will soon see **Roan Mountain State Park** (www.state.tn.us, 8 A.M.–10 P.M. daily), a 2,200-acre delight, on the left. Continuing up Hwy. 143 for about 10 miles, motorists will eventually come to Roan Mountain proper, which sits on the Tennessee–North Carolina border at a lofty altitude of 6,286 feet above sea level. Although the peak is technically in North Carolina, no one really cares, especially when the flowers are in bloom. The Appalachian Trail comes through here, and the views are stupendous. Keep in mind that the weather here can be a lot cooler than down below. Snow sometimes lingers into April.

Roan Mountain is one of a series of Appalachian peaks called "balds" for their lack of trees. No one has come up with a definitive reason for this condition. Mountains that are higher, such as Mount Mitchell, have trees all the way to the top. A variety of Indian legends surround the balds, but these tales don't agree either.

However they came about, balds such as Roan Mountain are wonderful to climb. In the summer they are refreshingly cool. Here one can walk the famous Appalachian Trail as it wanders amid the rhododendrons toward the peak. At the top hikers can see the remnants of a turn-of-the-20th-century hotel that had about 200 rooms and now, thankfully, is no more.

Back down the hill lies the state park, one of the finest in the entire Tennessee park system. This place has hiking, trout fishing, and even cross-country skiing. Historic sights include the site of the Peg Leg iron ore mine, Native American artifacts, and, best of all, the **Dave Miller Homestead.** This old home sits in a hollow in the park, and here visitors can get a good sense of what life was like in the early part of the 20th century. The first house was built in 1870, and the second in 1910.

The Miller Homestead is open May 30–Labor Day Wednesday–Sunday 9 A.M.–5 P.M. and on weekends in October.

Recreation

Aside from hiking and trout fishing, this park is known for a sport seldom seen in the South—**cross-country skiing.** The park offers three trails totaling 8.5 miles. Skiers must provide their own equipment, or they can sometimes rent it from local outfitters. Ask the people at the park for tips on who offers skis.

Events

The first weekend in May signals the **Roan**

COURTESY OF THE TENNESSEE DEPARTMENT OF TOURISM DEVELOPMENT

The First Frontier

Roan Mountain

Mountain Wildflower Tour and Bird Walks. Experts in both areas lead novices and colleagues through the woods, pointing out specimens along the way.

Young trout anglers will like the **Junior Trout Tournament,** held on the second weekend in May. Kids 7–15 compete to catch tagged trout and win a variety of prizes.

The **Rhododendron Festival,** now a half-century old, takes place during the third week in June and features crafts, food, and entertainment.

For more than 30 years, the **Roan Mountain Naturalists Rally** (423/772-4772, www.state.tn.us) has offered guided walks and presentations amid the splendor of fall colors. This event usually takes place on the first weekend after Labor Day. There are usually guest speakers on Friday and Saturday nights. Note: In some circles, "naturalist" is a euphemism for nudist. That is not the case here. Participants in nature walks are requested to stay dressed.

The third weekend in September brings the **Roan Mountain Fall Festival,** an autumn version of the Rhododendron Festival.

Accommodations

The best place to stay is in the park, which has campgrounds and 30 **cabins** (423/772-3303, $90–110), basketball and tennis courts, a large swimming pool (heated!), and a playground for kids. The cabins rest against a hill close by the Doe River. They are furnished with linens and cooking necessities, have wood-burning stoves, and can sleep six. From the week of June 1 through the last Sunday in August cabins can be rented by the week only, but can be rented one year ahead of the desired date. Occasions such as Christmas, Thanksgiving, and the month of October are particularly in demand.

Those seeking more luxurious accommodations should go to **General Wilder's Bed and Breakfast** (200 Main St., 423/772-3102, www.generalwilder.com, $49–99) in the town of Roan Mountain. This 1880s house offers five rooms containing antiques and private baths.

The park's **campground** offers a total of 107 sites, 87 with electric and water hookups. Tent campers have 20 sites apart from the motor homes and trailers. Bathrooms have flush toilets, hot showers, and a Laundromat. A dumping station is on the premises. Camping sites cannot be reserved; first-come, first-served is the rule here. The campground is open only to self-contained RVs Nov. 15–April 1. The restrooms are closed, although electrical hookups are available.

Johnson City

Of the Tri-Cities—Kingsport, Bristol, and Johnson City—Johnson City is the youngest, getting its charter in 1869 and its name from David Johnson, a man for all seasons who was postmaster, depot agent, merchant, hotel keeper, magistrate, and first mayor of the town.

In 1911 the East Tennessee State Normal School came to Johnson City, and today East Tennessee State University (ETSU), with an enrollment of more than 12,000, is the center of education in the area. Johnson City enjoys the cultural, financial, and other aspects of being a college town. In 1972, the federal government decided to fund five medical schools to be affiliated with Department of Veterans Affairs medical centers. The late James H. Quillen, the congressman from this area, landed one of them for ETSU. That school, named in his honor, anchors a regional medical center that further benefits Johnson City. ETSU also has a bluegrass program wherein classes can be applied toward a degree in Music or Appalachian Studies.

Johnson City also enjoys the reputation among the Tri-Cities as being the fun place to go. All those students and a plethora of restaurants in which one can drink something stronger than Dr. Enuf keeps Johnson City rolling long after Kingsport and Bristol have shut down for the night.

The First Frontier

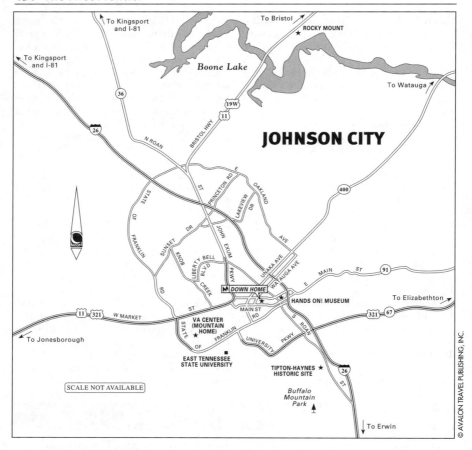

To Kingsport and I-81

To Bristol

★ ROCKY MOUNT

To Kingsport and I-81

Boone Lake

To Watauga

36

19W

11

26

N ROAN

BRISTOL HWY

JOHNSON CITY

400

STATE OF FRANKLIN

PRINCETON RD

ST

OAKLAND

LAKEVIEW DR

AVE

DR

JOHN EKUM PKWY

SUNSET

KNOB

LIBERTY BELL BLVD

CREEK

UNAKA AVE

WATAUGA AVE

E MAIN ST

91

★ DOWN HOME

★ HANDS ON! MUSEUM

To Elizabethton

MAIN ST

RD

321 67

S ROAN

11 321

W MARKET

VA CENTER (MOUNTAIN HOME)

STATE

FRANKLIN

OF

UNIVERSITY PKWY

To Jonesborough

■ EAST TENNESSEE STATE UNIVERSITY

TIPTON-HAYNES ★ HISTORIC SITE

26

ST

SCALE NOT AVAILABLE

Buffalo Mountain Park

To Erwin

© AVALON TRAVEL PUBLISHING, INC.

SIGHTS AND RECREATION

Historic Sights

Downtown Johnson City does not offer much of a historical nature, but significant places lie outside the city limits. The most significant is the site of the oldest territorial capital in the country, **Rocky Mount** (423/538-7396, www.rockymountmuseum.com). It is open March–mid-December 10 A.M.–5 P.M. Tuesday–Saturday. Winter hours are 11 A.M.–3 P.M. Monday–Saturday. It is now a living history museum on U.S. 11 East between Johnson City and Bristol. When the United States came into being, the states ceded their westernmost lands to the federal government, which pronounced them territories. William Blount was named governor of the Southwest Territory, and he set up his capital at the home of William Cobb. Here Blount held forth for two years until he moved operations to Knoxville.

Today at Rocky Mount, individuals act out the roles and do the chores of the people who lived here 1790–92. To get there from I-181, either north or south, take Exit 57A onto I-181/U.S. 23 south to Johnson City. Take Exit 3—State of Franklin Road. Turn left on I-381 north to Bristol. Rocky Mount is less than four miles on the right.

COURTESY OF THE TENNESSEE DEPARTMENT OF TOURISM DEVELOPMENT

Rocky Mount is the country's oldest territorial capitol.

On the other side of town sits the **Tipton-Haynes Historic Site** (423/926-3631, Apr.–Oct., 10 A.M.–5 P.M. Mon.–Sat., 2–5 P.M. Sun. Nov.–Mar., 10 A.M.–4 P.M. Mon.–Fri., $4 adults, $3 ages 12–3, free for 3 and under). This place got its start as a watering hole for buffalo, then as a campsite for Native Americans and white hunters who stayed in a nearby cave. The home was built in the 1780s by Colonel John Tipton, who was a member of the 1776 Constitutional Convention. In 1839, it was sold to the Haynes family and became the home of Landon Carter Haynes, a gentleman who bet on the wrong side in the Civil War. A Confederate senator, he was forced to skedaddle to Virginia at war's end.

The house has been restored to its 1860s glory and includes a museum, an herb garden, nature trails, and a gift shop. Children are intrigued by the cave.

Museums

The Carroll Reece Museum (423/439-4392, http://cass.etsu.edu/museum, 9 A.M.–4 P.M. Mon.–Wed. and Fri., 9 A.M.–7 P.M. Thurs., 1–4 P.M. Sat.–Sun., free) is ETSU's showplace for temporary exhibits, workshops, lectures, and films. Of its six galleries, three are usually de-

voted to items from the museum's collection. These include early settlement artifacts, musical instruments such as pianos and dulcimers, and antique toys. The other three galleries are filled with traveling exhibits, usually devoted to art or history.

To get to the museum, take Exit 31 off southbound I-181. Turn left at the traffic light and get on University Parkway. Proceed about one mile, where the university will appear on the left. Take the second entrance to the university—Stout Drive—and pull into the University Public Safety Building on the right to get a parking permit. The museum is straight ahead. Follow the signs.

For the visitor with children who threaten to scream if taken to another historic site, the **Hands On! Regional Museum** (315 E. Main St., 423/434-4263, www.handsonmuseum.org, 9 A.M.–5 P.M. Tues.–Fri., 10 A.M.–5 P.M. Sat., 1–5 P.M. Sun., $5 adults and kids 3–17, free for kids 2 and under) is the place to go. Following the trend of science museums nationwide, this place offers hands-on exhibits varying from an airplane cockpit to a coal mine. Best suited for children under age 12, the museum features demonstrations and exhibits. This is highly used

The First Frontier

DR. ENUF

Much like cities and towns that used to have their own breweries, Johnson City is the birthplace of a regionally celebrated soft drink. Dr. Enuf (www.drenuf.com), invented by a Chicago chemist, is a lemon-lime–flavored concoction containing 260 percent of the daily vitamin B1 requirement, 90 percent of vitamin B3, and 120 percent of potassium iodide. The drink was marketed beginning in 1949 as a tonic that contained a burst of energy, and to anyone with a vitamin deficiency, it probably did work wonders. (It was also said to be especially helpful for those with a hangover.) Whatever Dr. Enuf accomplished, it fit right in with folks who were accustomed to using Coca-Cola as a cure for an upset stomach.

Although the Food and Drug Administration prevents Dr. Enuf's makers from claiming any healthful benefits, the bottles are making their way from country-store coolers to the shelves of stores alongside bottles of ginseng tea and other modern-day nostrums, and today they can be found all over the South.

by school groups, so if going during the school year, try to go in the afternoon.

Paleontological Wonders

While widening Hwy. 75 near Gray, a hamlet between Johnson City and Kingsport, a construction crew unearthed a 600- by 700-foot layer of Ice Age fossils 140 feet thick. Scientists identified bones as coming from crocodiles, tapirs, mastodons, and a giant ground sloth. Preliminary studies indicate this site was some sort of watering hole during the Pleistocene era, some. This website contains good photos of the site: www.state.tn.us/environment/tdg/gray. Plans are underway to build a museum and visitors center on the site.

Mountain Home

Mountain Home is the old name for the **James H. Quillen Veterans Affairs Medical Center** (State of Franklin Street, 423/926-1171, www.va.gov/621quillen) in Johnson City. Seldom listed in

tourist promotions, it is both a beautiful place to visit as well as an interesting look at how medical treatment has changed over the years.

Founded in 1903 as an old soldiers' home for Union war veterans, Mountain Home was a self-contained community on 450 acres consisting of a large farm, dairy, power plant, and its own fire department. Most of the Beaux Arts buildings date from 1901-05. Andrew Carnegie gave $15,000 for a library, and a theater was built to provide entertainment. Herem the veterans lived out their lives in "companies" complete with captains and sergeants. When they died, they were buried in a landscaped cemetery that now holds 9,300 graves.

After World War I, Mountain Home changed from a soldiers' home to the National Sanitorium, a 1,000-bed hospital for disabled vets and those suffering from tuberculosis. The buildings were altered to provide "sleeping porches" in keeping with that era's treatments. When the Veterans Administration (VA) came into being in 1930, Mountain Home became a part of it, with patients filling 2,000 beds in the "doms," or domicilaries, and 605 beds in the hospital.

After World War II, the VA began putting its hospitals near medical schools in urban centers. Mountain Home languished during those years, but when ETSU landed a new medical school, Mountain Home had a renewed life.

Instead of taking veterans in and keeping them for life, the goal of the center shifted to helping them live at their own homes while providing care for those who need it. The Veterans Affairs Medical Center, as it is now called, has 202 hospital beds and 350 beds in the domicilaries.

Visitors are welcome to the grounds at Mountain Home. The turn-of-the-20th-century buildings are well-maintained, and guests should look for the chapel and the theater. To get to Mountain Home, find State of Franklin Street, where the entrance is clearly marked. The sign will say Veterans Affairs Medical Center.

The **James H. Quillen V.A. Mountain Home Museum** (423/439-8069) new in 2005, chronicles the medical care history of Appalachia including exhibits on Veteran care and radiology.

One artifact included in the 9,000-square-foot museum is an original iron lung and a doctor's office from the turn of the century. It is located in the clock tower building of the Veterans Affairs building, campus building #34.

Buffalo Mountain Park

This outdoor playground lies just outside of Johnson City. The park offers picnicking and hiking, with some of the trails reaching the ridge top of Buffalo Mountain, 3,500 feet above sea level. Mountain bikers can enjoy a 1,500-foot-plus descent on Tower Road, or, if they've had their grits that morning, they can ride up it.

To get to the park, take the University Parkway exit off I-181. Go left onto the parkway to Cherokee Road. Go left, then take an immediate left onto Buffalo Street. Follow it to Rolling Hills Road. Turn right on that road, which will merge with High Ridge Road, which leads into the park. For more information, call 423/283-5815.

ENTERTAINMENT

⊠ Down Home

Down Home (300 W. Main St., 423/929-9822, www.downhome.com, open Wed.–Sat. nights, doors open at 6 P.M. for dinner, music starts at 9 P.M.) is the First Frontier's premier place for live music. Founded as a bluegrass picking parlor, it now bills itself as "the eclectic music room," a place one can hear bluegrass, blues, rock, and the inimitable Tennessee Swampadelic of Webb Wilder. John Lee Hooker and Koko Taylor have played Down Home, which seats 175 people. Call for information on upcoming concerts. Tickets are sold in person or by mail only.

Baseball

The **Johnson City Cardinals** (423/283-5815 or 423/461-4866, www.jccardinals.com, tickets $4 for box seats, $3 adults, $2 seniors, $1 kids under 12), part of the St. Louis Cardinal farm system, belong to the Short Season Rookie League and play professional baseball every summer at Howard Johnson Field. To get to the field, take Roan Street, then turn left on Main Street. The park is visible from there.

ACCOMMODATIONS

Bed-and-Breakfasts

The **Hart House Bed and Breakfast** (207 E. Holston Ave., 423/926-3147, $60 for two people, $50 for one) occupies a 1910 Dutch colonial house. Each of the three bedrooms has a private bath and comes with telephone and cable TV. Guests can enjoy two sitting rooms, an exercise room with various machines, and a large porch.

The **Jam 'n' Jelly Inn** (1310 Indian Ridge Rd., 423/929-0039, www.jamnjellyinn.net, $75–95) is a new log structure with six rooms, all of which have reproduction antique furniture and private baths. Other amenities include a hot tub, volleyball court, and business equipment.

Hotels and Motels

With 207 units, the **Holiday Inn** (101 W. Springbrook Dr., 423/282-4611) is the big boy in Johnson City. Other good choices among the multitude of offerings include the **Red Roof Inn** (210 Broyles Dr., 423/282-3040), **Days Inn** (2312 Browns Mill Rd., 423/282-2211), **Fairfield Inn** (207 E. Mountcastle Dr., 800/228-2800), **Garden Plaza Hotel** (211 Mockingbird Ln., 423/929-2000), **Ramada Inn** (2406 N. Roan St., 423/282-2161), and **Super 8 Motel** (108 Wesley St., 423/282-8818).

FOOD

Johnson City has a large number of restaurants, particularly on the north side of town. Most of these are of the franchise persuasion. Here are a few of the many eateries.

Barbecue

The **Dixie Barbecue Company** (3301 N. Roan St., 423/283-7447, www.dixiebarbeque.com, 11 A.M.–9 P.M. Mon.–Sat.) seats 51 people, all of whom can partake of pork and beef barbecue, ribs, chicken, and other earthly delights.

In an old firehouse, the **Firehouse Restaurant** (627 W. Walnut St., 423/929-7377, 11 A.M.–10 P.M. Mon.–Sat.) offers hickory-smoked pork and beef barbecue, pork ribs, and chicken dishes.

The **House of Ribs** (3100 N. Roan St., 423/282-8077, 11 A.M.–10 P.M. Mon.–Fri., 4 P.M.–10 P.M. Sat.) is about the fanciest barbecue place one will find. It offers barbecue, steaks, and chicken lunches and dinners.

One hundred and ten barbecue fanciers can sit down every day for lunch and dinner at the **Red Pig Bar-B-Q** (2201 Ferguson Rd., 423/282-6585).

Steak and Seafood

Local bed-and-breakfast owners almost always recommend the **Peerless Steak House** (2531 N. Roan St., 423/282-2351, dinner Mon.–Sat.) one of the finer restaurants in the Tri-Cities. Steak heads the menu, but it is followed closely by fresh seafood. This place prides itself on making items such as salad dressings, desserts, and breads in-house.

Ethnic

Misaki Seafood and Steak House of Japan (3104C Bristol Hwy., 423/282-5451, 11 A.M.–2 P.M., 5–9 P.M. daily) features hibachi-fired foods.

A little farther afield but worth the trip is the **M Harmony Grocery** (423/348-8000, dinner Tues.–Sat., noon–2:30 P.M. Sun.), which features Creole and Cajun cuisine. This is the place for shrimp Creole, sausage or seafood gumbo, and fresh seafood and steaks. Brown-bagging is permitted.

INFORMATION

Visitors will find one of the best craft shops in the area between Johnson City and Kingsport. **Boones Creek Potter's Gallery** (4903 N. Roan St., 423/282-2801, www.boonescreek pottery.com) carries pottery, sculpture, and stained and blown glass as well as works in wood and iron.

For more information, contact the **Johnson City Chamber of Commerce** (603 E. Market St., 800/852-3392 or 423/461-8000, www.johnson citytn.com, 8 A.M.–5 P.M. Mon.–Fri.).

Erwin and Vicinity

Tucked between the Unaka Mountains and the Nolichucky River, the Erwin area was first known as Greasy Cove. This curious appellation came from early hunters who would bring their game to this area, dress it, render the fat, and tan the hides.

Southern Potteries used to operate up here. When it comes to pottery, the phrases "hand-decorated" and "mass-produced" don't seem to go together, but for 30 years they did in Erwin, where Southern Potteries employed up to 1,200 people who rolled out as many as 324,000 pieces of dinnerware per week—the largest such operation in the country. The most popular pottery was called Blue Ridge, which sold nationwide. Many of the workers were women, who hand-painted designs on the dishes before glazing them. The company closed in 1957, a victim of imports and plastic dishes. Today Blue Ridge pottery is prized by collectors—54 pieces of it were for sale on eBay on a random day—and

samples of it can be seen at the Unicoi County Heritage Museum.

Erwin is also home to Nuclear Fuel Services, a company that is the sole supplier of fuel rods for nuclear reactors on U.S. Navy vessels. The company is the largest employer in Unicoi County; for that reason, Erwin probably has the highest per capita collection in the entire state of residents with a "secret" or "top secret" clearance.

HISTORY

Greasy Cove was the site of one of Tennessee's greatest sports events, a horse race involving Andrew Jackson and Colonel Robert Love—two fiery men with fast horses. In 1788, Jackson sent a challenge to Love to race their mounts. Word went out all over the region, and sporting types placed bets and made plans to attend the race. Ten days before the race, Jackson's jockey got sick and the future president announced that he would ride in the man's place, further whetting interest. On the appointed day an enormous crowd (for those days) gathered and the horses were led out. The race began.

Riding his own horse was a mistake. Jackson stood six feet, one inch tall—hardly jockey size—and he and his horse were left in the dust. Never a good loser, he loudly and profanely denounced Colonel Love, his family, and the horse he rode in on. Love responded in kind, and friends intervened, no doubt preventing a duel.

In 1909, Erwin was selected as the headquarters of the Carolina, Clinchfield, and Ohio Railroad. The repair yards and offices gave the town an enormous economic shot in the arm and played a major role in perhaps the most bizarre event in Tennessee history.

Our story begins in Kingsport in 1916, where a circus was parading through the town. The author's maternal grandmother, then a teenager, was there. The headliner of the parade was Mary, billed as the largest elephant on earth. For some reason, still in dispute, she trampled her handler to death in front of a horrified crowd. The owners of the circus, in a move that would have made Colonel Tom Parker proud, announced that at that night's performance the elephant would be electrocuted. At the climax of the show, 44,000 volts were shot through Mary, who reportedly only "danced around a little bit."

That's when some bright soul thought of Erwin and the large railroad cranes available there. Mary was taken there and hanged in front of an estimated 5,000 gawkers. My grandmother was *not* one of them. The first chain placed around Mary's neck broke when she was five feet off the ground, but the second chain did the trick.

No one can remember what happened to poor Mary's body. Perhaps some future paleontologist will stumble on her bones and write academic papers for the rest of his life on the occurrence of elephants in East Tennessee.

SIGHTS
Hatcheries and Museum
Just east of town on Hwy. 107 lies **Erwin Na-**

tional Fish Hatchery (7:30 A.M.–4 P.M. Mon.–Fri., free), one of the oldest fish hatcheries in the country. Built in 1897, complete with a Victorian mansion for its superintendent, the hatchery now produces millions of fertilized fish eggs and about 50,000 fully grown trout per year.

All this takes place in 24 concrete tanks flowing with water from a large spring. Children particularly like seeing all the fish, and this is a good place to have a picnic. Visitors can see a section of it on the weekend.

An added attraction at the hatchery is in what was the hatchery superintendent's home. The **Unicoi County Heritage Museum** (423/743-9449, May–Sept., 1–5 P.M. daily; Oct., last two weeks in Nov., and first week in Dec., 1–5 P.M. Sat.–Sun.; $2 adults, $1 children) contains many railroad items as well as Erwin collections. Here visitors can see Blue Ridge Pottery—the settings are changed with the seasons—and a photograph of the infamous elephant hanging. If the listed times aren't convenient, call the curator at 423/743-4335 for a private tour. Make arrangements as far in advance as possible.

Those who haven't seen enough fish should try the **Erwin State Fish Hatchery** (423/743-4842, 8 A.M.–4 P.M. daily) not as well known as its federal counterpart, but one that welcomes visitors nonetheless. This is a rearing hatchery, a place that takes fingerlings and raises them until they are large enough to release into mountain streams. Visitors can see as many as 150,000 fish on the 12-acre hatchery. To find it, take the Jackson–Love Highway exit off I-181. Go left, over the interstate and under the railroad tracks, and pass a fire department on the left and the Erwin Motel. The hatchery is behind J. D.'s Market and Car Wash. Take a left on Banner Springs Road. The employees are sometimes out stocking fish, so it's a good idea to call ahead.

Arts and Crafts
Negatha Peterson bought some of the molds from the old Southern Pottery and carries on the tradition at **Erwin Pottery** (1219 N. Main St., 423/743-8278), where visitors can see dishes and bowls take shape. Each piece is signed and available for sale. Erwin Pottery is across from

McDonald's. The hours are uncertain—the place is open longer in the summer and has shorter hours in the winter.

Farmhouse Gallery and Gardens (800/952-6043 or 423/743-8799, www.farmhousegallery.net) is in Unicoi, a small town between Erwin and Johnson City, and there is no place in Tennessee quite like it. In essence, the story here is a couple who want to "live off the land" in a way that works with nature instead of exploits it or plows it under.

Johnny Lynch is an artist whose wildlife and wildflower prints are created in a 160-year-old cabin. His wife, Pat, grows and dries wildflowers and herbs, some of which make good teas. Visitors who make repeat visits to the gardens find something new every year—waterfalls, nature trails—and can learn through seminars, lectures, and classes. And you can get something to eat there as well, for the Farmhouse folks serve barbecue for lunch early April–early October.

To see this enviable way of living, take the Unicoi exit off I-181. Go south to the old 19/23 highway, then go left for three miles.

The **Valley Beautiful Antique Mall** (109 S. Main St., 423/743-4136) sells a variety of collectibles and antiques.

Rick Murray (423/743-6868) runs a one-man wood-turning shop on the banks of the Nolichucky River. He also has some campgrounds that are very close to the Appalachian Trail. Call to make sure he is in and to obtain directions.

Stegall's Pottery and Crafts Gallery (200 Nolichucky Ave., 423/743-3227, 10 A.M.–5 P.M. Tues.–Sat.) specializes in creative pottery that is meant to be used. This work can be microwaved, put in a dishwasher, and baked in ovens. One of the lighter-hearted works is a ceramic dog-biscuit container labeled "Bone Appétit."

RECREATION AND EVENTS

Cherokee National Forest

The following recreation areas all offer picnicking, hiking, and wilderness activities. The **Appalachian Trail** runs through Beauty Spot and the Unaka Mountain Wilderness. For further

information, go to the Cherokee National Forest's Nolichucky/Unaka Ranger District just east of Exit 23 of U.S. 19 West/23. Or call 423/735-1500. Fees of $2 per vehicle are now charged for any activity at National Forest sites. Camping fees range from $10 to $12. Visit online at www.southernregion.fs.fed.us/cherokee.

Rock Creek Park lies a few miles out of town on Rock Creek Road (Hwy. 395). Here visitors can fish, swim, and camp.

Continue past Rock Creek Park on Hwy. 395 to the top of the mountain, then go left on a rough road for about two miles. The road forks here. Take the right fork to the top of the mountain. This is **Beauty Spot,** an aptly named bald that straddles the Tennessee–North Carolina border at an elevation of 4,437 feet. The Appalachian Trail crosses the bald, and, unfortunately, this area has a bad reputation with hikers. It seems that the road enables local louts to prey on hikers. Be careful up there.

Continue northeast along the ridge to the **Unaka Mountain Wilderness.** Home of the 60-foot-high Red Fork Falls, this is an excellent place for hiking.

White-Water Rafting

The Nolichucky River offers the finest white-water rafting in upper East Tennessee. The water, even in the summertime, is chilling, so rafters should at a minimum bring a change of clothing. In spring or fall, wool clothing is the best; wet cotton fibers can quickly wick body heat away. In comparing prices, see if the quoted rate includes everything—the raft trip, wetsuits, taxes, and river fees. Ask about group and off-season rates.

Three rafting companies offer trips ranging from three hours to overnight. **Cherokee Adventures** (423/743-7733 information, 800/445-7238 reservations, www.cherokeeadventures.com), off Exit 18 of U.S. 19 West/23, runs the upper Nolichucky, the Watauga, and the Russell Rivers. From Erwin, go one mile north on Hwy. 81 along the Nolichucky River. The shortest rides cost $28 per person, depending on the day of the week.

The **Nantahala Outdoor Center** (800/232-

7238, www.noc.com, $65–72) runs the No-lichucky March–mid-July. The trips last five to seven hours, with three to five hours on the water. Its outpost is about 20 minutes outside of town at its take-out point and is not always staffed.

USA Raft (800/872-7238, www.usaraft.com, $31–68 per person) with trips ranging from two to seven hours on the Nolichucky, has another far-flung outpost.

Biking

If two-wheeled adventure is more to visitors' lik-ing, **Cherokee Adventures** (423/743-7733 for information, 800/445-7238 for reservations, $27–69 per person) will haul riders and their bikes to the crest of Rich Mountain, from where it is almost all downhill. Rental bikes are available, and a snack is included.

Festivals

The **Apple Festival** (423/743-3000) pulls to-gether Erwin and Unicoi County during the first full weekend in October for handmade crafts, a Blue Ridge Pottery show, food, music, dancing, a footrace, and other activities. More than 300 craftspeople and thousands of participants jam the town.

PRACTICALITIES

Motels

Try the **Best Southern** (1315 Asheville Hwy., 423/743-6438), or **Holiday Inn Express** (2002 Temple Hill Rd., 423/743-4100). Closer to John-son City is the **Buffalo Mountain Resort/Fam-ily Inns of America** (423/743-9181) in Unicoi.

If you want to learn about hiking, perhaps the best place in the state to stay is the **Nolichucky Hostel, Cabins, Camping, Etc.** (423/735-0548, closed Jan.–Feb.), an establishment that caters to through-hikers on the Appalachian Trail by offer-

ing rooms, showers, shuttle services, and a camp-ing store. Situated 80 feet from the trail and 80 feet from the Nolichucky River, it has a wood-fired hot tub that is enormously popular with hikers. It's 1.1 miles from Exit 15 on Hwy. 181 near the Chestoa Bridge.

Camping

Private campgrounds include **Nolichucky Campground** (423/743-8876, open year-round), right on the Nolichucky River. Take Jones Branch Road. **Cherokee Adventures** (423/743-7733 or 423/743-4502, Mar.–mid-Nov.), a rafting com-pany, has a campground farther downstream on Hwy. 81.

The U.S. Forest Service operates two camp-grounds in the Erwin area. **Limestone Cove Recreation Area** lies east of town on Hwy. 107. Closer in, **Rock Creek Park** lies east of Main Street on 10th Street. These are usually open from the first weekend in May though the first weekend in October, but sometimes open late or close early because of inclement weather. For further information, call 423/735-1500.

Nearby Unicoi offers the **North Indian Creek Campground** (Limestone Cove Road, 423/743-4502). It has 22 sites and is open year-round.

Food

Most Erwin eateries describe their fare as "coun-try cooking." Local dispensers of such include Unicoi's **Clarences Restaurant,** which is open for three meals every day.

Information

For more information, contact the **Unicoi County Chamber of Commerce** (100 S. Main Ave., 423/743-3000, www.unicoicounty.org, 8 A.M.–5 P.M. Mon.–Fri.). Outside is a kiosk with information on local attractions.

Jonesborough

HISTORY

House builders on the First Frontier seldom had to worry about zoning laws; people built whatever and wherever they wanted. This was not the case in Jonesborough, a town that seemed destined to make sure its old buildings survived. The oldest incorporated town in the state, Jonesborough was laid out in 1780, and the town officials made sure things were done right. The land was divided into lots and sold, and owners were required within three years to build a brick, stone, or frame house of a certain size. Anyone who didn't do this lost the land.

Jonesborough, as the county seat of North Carolina's Washington County, had a built-in business: government. Deeds were registered, criminals prosecuted and defended, and cases argued. In 1788, a 21-year-old lawyer rode into town and was admitted to the bar. His name was Andrew Jackson.

The Lost State of Franklin

Four years before, in 1784, North Carolina ceded its western lands to the young federal government, which didn't immediately accept them. This ambiguous situation bothered people in the area, who felt that during this interim they were without a government. Accustomed to providing for themselves, they organized into a new state, which they called Frankland. Later, thinking more politically, they called it Franklin, after the famed kite-flyer, and applied for admission to the new country.

Hearing of this, North Carolina reconsidered its offer and repealed the law that gave away the western lands. This plunged the overmountain people into chaos. Who was in charge? The Franklinites or the mother state of North Carolina? Who could make deals with the Native Americans? Would marriages and wills made during this time stand up in court?

The controversy swirled around Jonesborough, leading to fistfights and sometimes more serious conflicts. The idea of Franklin slowly faded away, and Jonesborough found itself back in North Carolina again, at least until the United States formally deemed this area part of the Southwest Territory. What would have been the 14th state is now drilled into Tennessee schoolchildren as "The Lost State of Franklin." Meanwhile, the town of Jonesborough underwent a spelling change. To show their distaste for the British after the War of 1812, a lot of American towns ending in "-ough" dropped the "ugh" from their names. Thus, Jonesborough became Jonesboro.

Abolition and Reconstruction

Jonesboro seemed to be a magnet for men bent on upsetting the status quo. In 1820 Elihu Embree began publishing the first newspaper in the country devoted entirely to antislavery. *The Emancipator* lasted for only seven issues—Embree's death ended it—but it was read all over the United States.

In the 1830s, another newspaper began running a fiery series of political articles written by a young minister. The editor persuaded the writer, William G. Brownlow, to abandon the ministry for journalism, a career switch that was to have profound implications later on for Tennessee, when Brownlow became Tennessee's Reconstruction governor, arguably the most hated elected official in the history of the state.

Jonesboro mercifully escaped the ravages of the Civil War—another plus for building preservation—and eased into the 20th century. New highways and discount stores began to erode the downtown, however, and by the late '60s Tennessee's first town began to look run-down.

Restoration

In the early 1970s, town officials decided to restore the buildings, preserve the town, and go after the many tourists who come to Tennessee. At last forgiving the British—particularly the traveling ones—Jonesboro reverted to Jonesborough. Officials got the entire downtown placed

COURTESY OF THE TENNESSEE DEPARTMENT OF TOURISM DEVELOPMENT

the lovely Chester Inn

on the National Register of Historic Places. As in many other towns, to celebrate the place and its people, they launched a festival—the usual gathering of craftspeople, food vendors, musicians, etc.

In 1973, the big idea landed: the National Storytelling Festival. Naming it the National Storytelling Festival was a stroke of brilliance. As far as anyone in Jonesborough knew, there was no other storytelling festival at all, so they declared theirs the national one, and that has made all the difference. Jonesborough is now to storytelling what Nashville is to country music. The International Storytelling Center, housed in a beautiful building, contains archives, publications, and tapes along with classrooms and performance space.

With all its success in renovation and preservation, however, Jonesborough has all but succumbed to a Disney-esque version of its colonial heritage. The shops, bed-and-breakfasts, and traffic-stopping festivals are wonderful for the droves of tourists, but the visitor has to scan faces a long time to detect a local—unless it is one who has found himself fresh out of lilac-scented oatmeal soap.

SIGHTS

Pulling in from U.S. 11 East, travelers to Jonesborough should turn on Boone Street and stop at the **Historic Jonesborough Visitor Center** (423/753-1010, www.jonesboroughtn.org). Behind the center lies Duncan's Meadow, where Andrew Jackson once fought a duel, and behind it is an 1880s schoolhouse that is slated to become a museum about education.

Boone Street intersects with Main Street, along which most of Jonesborough's offerings lie. On a slow day, one can park on Main Street, but during festivals and the like a good place to park is behind the Washington County Courthouse.

If someone could conjure Andrew Jackson back from the dead, Jonesborough's Main Street is one of the few places in Tennessee where he would recognize several buildings that were there when he was. Perhaps the most significant is the **Chester Inn.** Built in 1797 as an inn and a tavern, it was host to Tennessee's three presidents—Andrew Jackson, James K. Polk, and Andrew Johnson—as well as to other luminaries such as Charles Dickens.

The First Frontier

Beside the inn stands the **Christopher Taylor House,** a 1778 log structure that may well be the oldest log house still standing in the state. It stood for about 200 years outside of town before being moved to its present location.

Farther down the other side of the street stands the **Blair-Moore House.** Now a bed-and-breakfast, the house was built around 1832 and provides a good example of stepped gables, an architectural feature in which a stepped wall provides what might be called a false side. Jonesborough's Main Street has several buildings with this feature.

EVENTS

M National Storytelling Festival

The National Storytelling Festival (800/ 952-8392, www.storytellingcenter.com, full weekend $110 per adult, $90 per child 6–12, family rate of $365) is always held on the first full weekend in October. Lasting three days, it fills the town with tall tales, ghost stories, "sacred telling," and the "Swappin' Ground." Visitors are strongly urged to register by phone ahead of time, thus ensuring admission to popular events such as the open-air ghost storytelling—not recommended for children under 6. Call to register. This festival is not cheap. Those who buy their tickets early can get discounts, and the festival also sells tickets good for one day only.

Other Events

Other events include the **Spring Doll Show,** held in April, which offers collectors and fanciers the chance to marvel over dolls varying from Madame Alexanders to Barbies.

The Fourth of July brings forth **Historic Jonesborough Days,** an old-fashioned, family-oriented bash complete with art, food, crafts, and fireworks.

August marks the three-day **Quiltfest,** featuring 25 instructors offering 50 classes. Lectures, buffets, and oodles of quilts round out this gathering.

For more information on all of the above, call the **Historic Jonesborough Visitor Center** (423/753-1010).

RECREATION

The town of Jonesborough owns **Wetlands Water Park** (423/753-1550, $7.50 adults, $5.50 seniors and children 4–12, free for ages 3 and under) west of town on U.S. 11 East. A decidedly nonhistorical complex, it is open from Memorial Day to Labor Day. Here one can take the waters on slides, a wave pool, or a simulated lazy river.

ACCOMMODATIONS
Bed-and-Breakfasts

Not surprisingly, Jonesborough has the greatest concentration of B&Bs in upper East Tennessee. **Hawley House** (114 E. Woodrow Ave., 800/ 753-8869 or 423/753-8869, www.hawleyhouse .com, $105–150) must be considered first, for it occupies lot number one in the town, and has been featured in *National Geographic Magazine* and HGTV. The 1793 building, the oldest one in Jonesborough, is made of dovetailed chestnut logs. Hawley House is filled with museum-quality antiques, the newest of which dates from 1840. The owner is an eighth-generation Jonesborough resident. Hawley House offers three bedrooms, each with a private bath. People with children should call ahead.

Aiken-Brow House (104 3rd Ave., 423/753-9440, $75–100) is an 1850s board-and-batten house with antique furniture throughout. Two rooms have private baths—one in the room and one across the hall from the room. A third room with twin beds can be rented in conjunction with one of the others.

The **Blair Moore House Bed and Breakfast** (201 W. Main St., 888/453-0044 or 423/753-0044, www.blairmoorehouse.com, $115–125) is about as downtown as you can get in Jonesborough. This place has three guest rooms, one of them a Western Room that comes with a bearskin rug, old guns, Indian artifacts, and—best of all—a second-story porch overlooking Main Street. All of the rooms have private baths, and all come with a gourmet—not a country—breakfast. Their breakfast has placed in the top five for two years in a row in national B&B competitions.

Franklin House (116 Franklin Ave., 423/753-

3819, $45–80) has three rooms and an extended-stay apartment, all with private baths, inside a reconstructed 1840 home just a few minutes' walk from Jonesborough's historic district.

May Ledbetter House (130 W. Main St., 423/753-7568 or 423/913-2205, $80, includes a full country breakfast) is a 1904 Victorian home that has two rooms with private baths down the hall. The beds are covered with quilts and the wraparound porch has bentwood rockers.

The **Old Yellow Vic** (411 W. Main St., 423/753-9558 or 423/753-2141, $89) gets its name from the fact that the house is an 1887 yellow Victorian home. The proprietor offers one room with a private bath or two rooms with a shared bath. Smokers can smoke in the house, but not in the bedrooms. The entire house is furnished with antiques.

Farther from the crowded streets is the **Bugaboo Bed and Breakfast** (211 Semore Dr., 423/753-9345, $70–80). This is a contemporary house with an old English flair. Sitting amid 15 acres of woods and meadow, the house is very open. Guests particularly like the hot tub on the deck under the stars. Two rooms each have a private bath. One pet is permitted, if it occupies its own bed.

Camping

Davy Crockett Birthplace State Park is a popular place to camp near Jonesborough. Then there's **Home Federal Park** (1521 Persimmon Ridge Rd., 423/753-1555, open all year, sites cost $10 per night), the campground that sounds like a bank. The name comes from the fact that a bank donated the land to the town, which owns this 45-site, full-hookup campground right beside the Wetlands Water Park in Jonesborough.

FOOD

Andrew Jackson probably would snort at the news that Washington County restaurants are dry. This is bring-your-own-bottle country.

N The **Harmony Grocery** (423/348-6183, dinner Tues.–Sat., noon–2:30 P.M. Sun.) is out in the country from Jonesborough, but well worth the drive. This great eatery serves shrimp Cre-

ole, Cajun sausage or seafood gumbo, and fresh seafood and steaks. Brown-bagging is permitted. Call for directions.

The **Main Street Cafe and Catering** (117 W. Main St., 423/753-2460, lunch and early dinner Mon.–Fri., lunch Sat.) is a great place for sandwiches and homemade soups, salads, and desserts.

INFORMATION AND SERVICES

Jonesborough's shopping district is concentrated within a block of the Washington County Courthouse. The shops include the **Tennessee Quilts** (123 E. Main St., 423/753-6644), where quilting aficionados can choose from more than 1,000 bolts of cloth.

The National Storytelling Festival has a **gift shop** in the festival headquarters. Here buyers can find tapes and compact discs of more than 100 storytellers—perhaps the greatest collection of tales in the entire state.

For more information, contact the **Historic Jonesborough Visitor Center** (117 Boone St., 800/400-4221 or 423/753-1010, www.historic jonesborough.com).

WEST OF JONESBOROUGH

From Jonesborough U.S. 11 East leads southwest straight to Greeneville, or the traveler can take a more meandering route to see some sights. A few side trips offer some diversions for the traveler. Leave Jonesborough heading south on Hwy. 81, then turn right on Hwy. 353 by Little Limestone Creek. Note: Hwy. 353 and Old Hwy. 34 are the same. Go past Davy Crockett High School to the community of Telford. Here is a classic country store, a good place to go in, get a soft drink, and have a chat.

Then it's on down the road to Washington College Academy. Founded by the Reverend Samuel Doak, who is buried in the cemetery just a couple of hundred yards past the school, this place has graduated 22 college presidents, 28 members of Congress, three governors, 63 physicians, 16 missionaries, and 162 ministers. It is the eighth-oldest American school or college still in existence, but in recent years, the institution has struggled, and its

a replica of the cabin where the famed defender of the Alamo was born

future, alas, is in question. To inspect the Salem Baptist Church, which is on the campus, call the academy at 423/257-5151 a day or so ahead.

Stay on Old Highway 34. After Westview Elementary School, take the second left onto Gravel Hill Road, which leads to the community of **Broylesville.** People came here in the early 1800s to take advantage of the water power offered by Little Limestone Creek. In its heyday, Broylesville had 300 residents, who supported mills, tanneries, a shoe factory, smithies, sawmills, gristmills, a cooperage, a distillery, and a store. Nine buildings that date as far back as 1797 are all that is left, all of them in private hands and not open to the public.

All except two. The 1869 **Bashor Mill** (203 Gravel Hill Rd.) is occupied by Margaret Gregg and her **Mill 'n Creek Art Place** (generally 9 A.M.– 5 P.M., call 423/257-3875 to make sure someone is in), where visitors will find works in textiles, silkscreen prints, sculpture, printings, collectibles, and mixed media. Those who wish to spend more time in Broylesville can rent a room at the mill or make arrangements to pitch a tent in the yard.

To get from Broylesville back to U.S. 11 East, follow Old Hwy. 34 to the west. To get to the Davy Crockett Birthplace State Historical Area, also take Old Hwy. 34 west, then turn left on Davy Crockett Road.

Flintlock Inn and Stables (790 G'Fellers Rd., Chuckey, 423/257-2489, $96) offers guests a chance to take to the saddle and ride through farms or into the mountains. Riders can bring

their own horses or use the ones at the inn. Nonriding guests are also welcome at the inn, which was built by combining three log cabins. Lunch and dinner are available, and other add-ons include driving a Jeep on mountain roads, hot-air balloon rides, golf, or cruising in a 1929 Model A pickup truck.

Davy Crockett Birthplace State Historical Area

Follow the signs from U.S. 11 East to this park, which lies on the banks of the Nolichucky River. The first thing that people of a certain age notice on seeing Davy Crockett's birthplace is that it is not "on a mountaintop in Tennessee," as the theme song for the old television show used to assert every week.

The centerpiece of the park is a replica of the Crockett Cabin, where David—people in his day did not call him Davy—first saw the light of day. The cabin is a replica of a typical cabin of that time and has no items in it that belonged to the famed wearer of coonskin caps. Crockett cut quite a swath in his time, moving from east to west Tennessee and coming to a glorious end at the Alamo. In between, he was a scout, bear hunter, humorist, statesman, and even industrialist.

This 60-acre park on the banks of the Nolichucky River has picnic and camping areas—75 sites, a pool, and a visitors center (423/257-2167 or online at www.state.tn.us) with exhibits on Crockett.

Back on U.S. 11 East near Chuckey is some down-home entertainment that shouldn't be missed. Once a week the **Rheatown Food Market** (pronounced RAY-town, 423/257-5784) is transformed into a picking parlor. Local string musicians such as the Horse Creek Mountain Boys gather, pull up chairs, and play. Sometimes two or three groups will play at once throughout the store. Unpretentious, unrehearsed, and, judging by the reception, unbeatable. Coming from Jonesborough, turn right off U.S. 11 East onto Hwy. 351. Go less than a mile to Rheatown, where the music kicks into gear on Saturday between 7 and 8 P.M. Admission is free, and sometimes the picking lasts past midnight. On the way back, visitors should tune their radios to 630 AM and listen to the *Grand Ole Opry.*

Tusculum

This little town east of Greeneville is home to Tusculum College and well worth a stop. Home to approximately 1,700 students, this Presbyterian-affiliated college serves as a cultural center for Greeneville and outlying areas. The name allegedly comes from that of Cicero's home outside Rome.

Tusculum College came into being because of a merger with Greeneville College, founded in 1794, and Tusculum Academy, a private school founded in 1818 by father and son ministers, Reverend Samuel Doak and Reverend Samuel Witherspoon Doak. The latter engineered the academic merger and saw that his institution's name won out over that of Greeneville College. Tusculum has a museum studies program, and the campus contains two museums worthy of a stop.

Andrew Johnson was a trustee of the college, which served as his official presidential library.

THE REVEREND SAMUEL DOAK

The area between Jonesborough and Greeneville was once the domain of a singular Presbyterian minister, the Reverend Samuel Doak, whose legacy is one of education. A Virginian who was educated at Princeton, he rode a horse to what is now Washington County in 1777 and, following the sound of axes, found some pioneers cutting trees.

On learning that the well-spoken stranger was a minister, the woodcutters asked him if they could round up a congregation and hear a sermon. Reverend Doak agreed and, sitting on his horse, preached to those who came to hear. They convinced him to settle with them, and he bought a farm and began spreading the Gospel, most notably in a rousing send-off prayer for the Overmountain Men as they left Sycamore Shoals to go off and fight the British.

Reverend Doak founded the Salem Presbyterian Church on his farm in 1780, one of the first churches in what would become Tennessee. Four years later, he erected the first schoolhouse west of the Appalachians, naming it The Martin Academy in honor of the governor of North Carolina. In 1795, Reverend Doak rode a horse to Philadelphia and came back laden with books; some say he walked back so the horse could carry more volumes. He eventually changed the name of his school to Washington College.

During the period of the Great Revival that swept the country in the early 1800s, Reverend Doak became one of the first educated ministers who delivered sermons accompanied by "the jerks," a very physical, emotional style of preaching. Anne Kebenow, in her wonderful *200 Years through 200 Stories,* quotes a member of a congregation who saw Reverend Doak when he was feeling the Spirit:

Often it would seize him in the pulpit with so much severity that a spectator might feel it would dislocate his neck and joints. He would laugh, stand and halloo at the top of his voice, finally leap from the pulpit and run to the woods, screaming like a madman. When the exercise was over he would return to the church, calm and rational as ever.

When the Reverend Doak was 69 years old, he resigned the presidency of Washington College to join his son, also named Samuel, in founding **Tusculum Academy** just east of Greeneville. Doak's slaves built him a large house, and when the house was finished, he gave them their freedom. Reverend Doak lived out his days and, while president of the school, taught subjects as diverse as chemistry and Hebrew. In 1830, like Abraham, "he gave up the ghost and died in a good old age, an old man, and full of years." He was 81, and he lies buried today in a cemetery across the road from what is now **Washington College Academy.**

The First Frontier

The **Andrew Johnson Museum and Library** (800/729-0256 ext. 5320, http://ajmuseum .tusculum.edu, 9 A.M.–5 P.M. Mon.–Fri., free) occupies an 1841 building that contains several exhibits pertaining to the president: most of the books from his home, some carpet from the White House, the bed in which he died, and personal items such as his collar box and various items belonging to his wife. The building is wheelchair-accessible.

The elder Reverend Doak lived the last years of his life in a large house whose construction began in 1818. Academy classes were taught there until the next building, now called Old College, was erected. **Doak House Museum** (800/729-0256, ext. 251 or 423/636-8554, http://doakhouse .tusculum.edu, 9 A.M.–5 P.M. Mon.–Fri. by appointment) exhibits college-related artifacts, Doak family artifacts (1830–65), and educa-tional and religious artifacts and documents from Northeast Tennessee.

The other noteworthy building on campus is **Virginia Hall,** one of only three buildings in the South designed by Chicago architect Louis A. Sullivan. To find out what plays, concerts, or other collegiate activities are taking place at Tusculum College, call 423/636-7304 or visit www.tusculum.edu.

A pleasant place to eat is **Ye Olde Tusculum Eatery** (423/638-9210, 10:30 A.M.–2:30 P.M. Mon.–Fri.) across the road from the college. Lunch is mostly sandwiches—with specials such as portabello mushrooms.

Next door, the **Three Blind Mice** gift shop (423/639-0180) has artworks and craft pieces from local and national artists. It's closed on Sunday except in November and December.

Greeneville

If Frankin is the lost state, then Greeneville is the lost capital, for it was in this pleasant town that the Franklinites located their government for the two-year existence of that would-be state.

Greeneville is most associated with Andrew Johnson, who moved here as a teenager in 1825. He found a town that occupied the center of a rich agricultural area, one that readily grew tobacco and other crops. The farmers and merchants here were what would later be called "self-made men," and their pride was exceeded only by their independence.

Just how independent they were was evidenced in 1861, when the state of Tennessee voted to leave the Union. This action, driven by interests in Middle and West Tennessee, found little support in the eastern part of the state. Nine days later, 26 East Tennessee counties sent delegates to Greeneville to discuss seceding from the secessionists, and they asked the state legislature to let them form a separate state. Permission was denied.

This did nothing to halt the division in East Tennessee and in Greeneville, a situation best exemplified by the murder of Confederate General John Morgan. Morgan had led a band of mounted troops on an unauthorized raid deep into Kentucky, Ohio, and Indiana. Depending on how one viewed it, the raid was either a daring feat that gave the Yankees a taste of their own war, or a bunch of thugs on a spree of terror.

After one of his forays, the general came to Greeneville for some needed rest and found hospitality at the spacious Dickson-Williams House, the home of a local doctor and his wife. Someone—no one ever found out just who—slipped off and informed a Union general a few miles off that Morgan was in town. The general led Union forces into town and surrounded the house. According to one Southern account, Morgan leapt out of bed and ran into the back garden, where he was captured. As he stood there, a Union soldier ran up and shot him dead, snatched up his body, and rode off with it across his horse. After parading the late general around the Union camp, the soldier unceremoniously dumped the body in a ditch. This incident, probably magnified in the telling, further inflamed passions in this divided town.

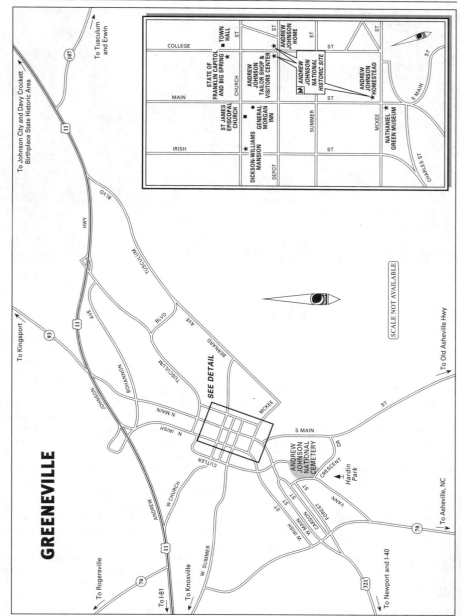

GREENEVILLE

To Rogersville

To I-81

To Knoxville

To Kingsport

To Johnson City and Davy Crockett Birthplace State Historic Area

To Tusculum and Erwin

To Newport and I-40

To Asheville, NC

To Old Asheville Hwy

SEE DETAIL

SCALE NOT AVAILABLE

The First Frontier

COLLEGE

MAIN

IRISH

TOWN HALL

STATE OF FRANKLIN CAPITOL AND BIG SPRING

ST JAMES EPISCOPAL CHURCH

DICKSON-WILLIAMS MANSION

GENERAL MORGAN INN

ANDREW JOHNSON TAILOR SHOP & VISITORS CENTER

ANDREW JOHNSON NATIONAL HISTORIC SITE

ANDREW JOHNSON HOME

ANDREW JOHNSON HOMESTEAD

NATHANIEL GREEN MUSEUM

SUMMER

MCKEE

DEPOT

CHARLES ST

S MAIN

CHURCH

ANDREW JOHNSON NATIONAL CEMETERY

Hardin Park

CRESCENT DR

VANN

FOREST ST

CARSON ST

W MAIN ST

W IRISH ST

W SUMMER

S MAIN

BERNARD AVE

TUSCULUM BLVD

TUSCULUM BLVD HWY

BOHANNON

JOHNSON AVE

N MAIN

N IRISH

CUTLER

W CHURCH

ANDREW

© AVALON TRAVEL PUBLISHING, INC.

COURTESY OF THE TENNESSEE DEPARTMENT OF TOURISM DEVELOPMENT

Andrew Johnson's home

The divisions that once split Greeneville still show in the Civil War monuments that stand in the courthouse yard. One is a rhapsodic paean to Morgan, while the other commemorates Union soldiers.

Today Greeneville is the county seat of Greene County and a center of the tobacco business. In recent years the town has acknowledged its heritage and abundance of historic buildings. Most conveniently for the visitor, most of Greeneville's historic sites lie along a route following Business Hwy. 321 coming from U.S. 11 East. Here stand the old homes, bed-and-breakfasts, the General Morgan Inn, and the Andrew Johnson National Historic Site. The best guide to the town is a brochure titled "A Walk With the President," which is available at the General Morgan Inn, the Andrew Johnson National Historic Site, and the Greeneville/ Greene County Area Chamber of Commerce at 115 Academy Street.

SIGHTS

The **Cumberland Presbyterian Church,** the Greek revival church with the tall steeple on the

right, was used as a hospital and a stable during the Civil War. The day that General Morgan was killed, the church was shelled, and you can still see a cannonball from the skirmish embedded in the front wall.

The block across from the Cumberland Presbyterian Church contains **Bicentennial Park and Big Spring,** the source of water that caused Greeneville to be located here. The same block contains what might be called **The Lost Capitol Building of the Lost State of Franklin.** The real capitol stood for years beside Greene County's present courthouse on Main Street. During Tennessee's centennial celebration in 1896, however, the old log building was shipped off to Nashville, where it was displayed, dismantled, and promptly lost. A few years ago interest in the Lost Capitol of the Lost State was rekindled, and a suitable replacement building was found.

After crossing Church Street and looking to the right, the **General Morgan Inn and Conference Center** (111 N. Main St., 800/223-2679 or 423/787-1000) is worth a look even if you have no intention of staying here. This complex came about when Greeneville, like so many towns in Tennessee, was trying to revitalize its downtown. Four buildings that had been "railroad hotels" stood close to each other. Chief among these was the Hotel Brumley, which had operated from 1920 until 1981. Using a combination of local and federal money, the General Morgan Inn came into being and opened in 1996.

Just off the lobby, Brumleys restaurant retains the name of one of the old hotels. Above the bar is an etched-glass scene depicting nymphs cavorting on wineglasses. In the old days, this was considered so naughty that on Sunday curtains were drawn so as not to give offense. This now-quaint prudishness still prevails.

General John Hunt Morgan had his sleep, and shortly thereafter, his life interrupted while he was a guest at the **Dickson-Williams Mansion** (423/639-0695, open by appointment only), which stands behind the General Morgan Inn. Begun in 1815 as "the showplace of East Tennessee," this home and its extensive gardens once occupied an entire city block. Guests in the home included the Marquis de Lafayette, Andrew Jackson, James K. Polk, and Henry Clay. The house passed out of the family and began the decline that so often overtakes such mansions. After being a school, a tobacco factory, an inn, and a hospital, it was bought by the city.

The **Old Greene County Gaol,** which stands behind the current Greene County Detention Center on Main Street, was built in 1804–05 beside a creek whose water was periodically channeled through a trough in the stone floor to flush out the contents. In 1838, it was moved to its present locale, and a half century later its brick second story was added.

Named for the man for whom the county and the town were named, the **Nathanael Greene Museum** (on West McKee off Main St., 423/636-1558, 10 A.M.–4 P.M. Tues.–Sat., free) of Greene County History, contains an eclectic mixture of town memorabilia. Visitors can see a suit made by tailor-turned-president Andrew Johnson, tickets to Johnson's impeachment trial, and other relics of Greeneville and Greenevillians.

Andrew Johnson National Historic Site

Returning to Main Street and turning right onto Depot Street brings the visitor to Johnson Square and the national historic site. The log-cabin replica of the president's birthplace is not a part of the park, which includes three separate units. Begin at the **Visitor Center Complex** (423/638-3551, www.nps.gov/anjo), which contains Johnson's original tailor shop, a museum, and park headquarters. The museum displays a coat that Johnson stitched, as well as a poster from a disgruntled employer in North Carolina offering a reward for his runaway apprentice.

Across the street sits a two-story brick home where Johnson and his family lived from 1838 to 1851. Oddly enough, Johnson bought this property on which the house stands from the heirs of Abraham Lincoln's second cousin. Two rooms here are open to the public, and they contain a genealogy of the family as well as changing exhibits.

The **Homestead** (tours every hour 9:30 A.M.–4:30 P.M., on the half hour, free) on South Main Street, the second unit, was the home of Johnson from 1851 until his death in 1875. Because of astute real-estate dealings, Johnson was at one time one of the wealthier people in Greeneville, and this house reflects his prosperity. It was vandalized by both Union and Confederate sympathizers during the Civil War. Now the house contains Johnson family furniture and items given to him while he was president.

The final unit is the **Andrew Johnson National Cemetery** (free admission), where the 17th president and his family are buried. To get there, follow the signs down West Main Street from the Homestead.

RECREATION

Kinser Park

Kinser Park (423/639-5912, March 15–Oct. 15, and possibly longer if weather permits) along the Nolichucky River has a nine-hole golf course, driving range, tennis courts, water slide, and playground. To get there, take Hwy. 70 south about

ANDREW JOHNSON

COURTESY OF THE NATIONAL PARK SERVICE, ANDREW JOHNSON HISTORIC SITE, GREENVILLE.

From the day Andrew Johnson immediately followed Abraham Lincoln into the White House, this remarkable Tennessean's life has been in eclipse. Johnson's rise from a poor, uneducated worker to the highest office in the land is an embodiment of the American dream.

Even more so than Abraham Lincoln, Andrew Johnson came from humble beginnings. He was born in Raleigh, North Carolina, in 1808, and his childhood was one of poverty; he never spent a day in school, and by age 10 was apprenticed to a tailor. The young Johnson got in a dispute with his master about how long he should serve, and he fled to Greeneville, Tennessee, riding into town on a wagon at age 16.

Keenly aware of his lack of education, Johnson strove to improve his mind. He had once worked in a shop where a man read aloud to the tailors, and in Greeneville he hired people to read to him. He entered a local debating society and honed his public speaking, eventually becoming an orator who could hold a crowd for two or three hours and, typical of hard-knuckled Tennessee politics, sarcastically belittle an opponent as well as take care of any hecklers in the process.

Johnson was a good tailor who prospered in Greeneville, and in 1829 he consented to run for alderman in an election that pitted wealthier candidates against Johnson and a more working-class slate.

President Andrew Johnson achieved a series of firsts in his remarkable political career.

Johnson's group won, and the victory launched his political climb. If anything can characterize Johnson's politics, it was a willingness to stand up for the common man and woman. His supporters, small farmers and shopkeepers typical of East Tennessee, distrusted the wealthy plantation owners who controlled politics in Middle and West Tennessee, and Johnson never forgot those who elected him. A Democrat, he served as mayor, state representative, state senator, and congressman. Always intent on educating himself, during his five terms in Congress he read for hours in the Library of Congress, possibly spending more time there than any representative before or since.

In 1853, he was elected governor of Tennessee, and for two terms he supported public education and the construction of railroads, and he brought about the purchase of Andrew Jackson's home, the Hermitage. Johnson followed his gubernatorial terms with election to the U.S. Senate in 1857. In the critical 1860 election to select his fellow senator, he and his supporters backed a Democrat who favored secession—a so-called "war Democrat." Nonetheless, when the issue of secession arose in Tennessee, Johnson argued long and loudly against it. When the state left the Union, Johnson traveled to Washington and became the only Southern senator to keep his seat.

In reward for Johnson's loyalty, in March 1862, President Lincoln appointed him military governor of Tennessee, the first Southern state to fall to Union armies. Johnson proved a stern figure in this post, jailing ministers for preaching pro-Confederate sermons and earning the contempt of many Tennesseans from the Mississippi to the mountains. His two years as military governor ended when Lincoln picked Johnson as his running mate on the 1864 ticket. Lincoln, a Republican, and Johnson, a Democrat, ran together on the Union Party ticket.

Johnson had been vice president for 42 days when John Wilkes Booth fired his pistol into the box at Ford's Theater. Lincoln had always argued that, since secession was impossible, the Southern states had never left the Union and should be treated with compassion, and Johnson was left to carry out his policies. Ulysses Grant, who followed Johnson into the White House, expressed in his autobiography an interesting assessment of his predecessor:

He would have proven the best friend the South could have had, and saved much of the wrangling and bitterness of feeling brought out by reconstruction under a president who at first wished to revenge himself on Southern men of better social standing than himself, but who still sought their recognition, and in a short time conceived the idea and advanced the proposition to become their Moses to lead them triumphantly out of all their difficulties.

This Moses might have wanted to lead, but the Congress was in no mood to follow. With the Great Emancipator gone, the radical Republicans in Congress showed no restraint in their attack on the man who was left to carry out Lincoln's reconciliatory policies. They began to look for reasons to remove him from office.

Johnson had inherited Lincoln's secretary of war, Edwin Stanton, who proved extremely disloyal to his new boss. Knowing that Johnson wished to rid himself of Stanton, Congress passed the Tenure of Office Act, which stated that a president could not remove an officeholder who had been approved by the Senate without getting that body's consent. Johnson, wanting to let the courts decide this constitutional matter, and confident that he would win, ordered Stanton to resign anyway.

The House of Representatives now had what it considered a smoking gun. Not willing to let the courts settle the issue, it impeached Johnson on several charges based on his violation of the Tenure of Office act. Put on trial before the U.S. Senate, he was saved from conviction by only one vote. He ended his term in bitterness, refusing to attend Grant's inauguration in 1869, but returned to Greeneville in triumph. The man who had been so detested as military governor was now considered a hero in Tennessee as well as in the rest of the South.

Out of office for the first time in 30 years, and in no way content to rest on his laurels, Johnson jumped right back into politics. Running for the U.S. Senate in 1869, he lost by a vote of 55–51—in those days the Tennessee Senate elected U.S. senators—and in 1872 he lost a three-way race for Congress. Still the old campaigner fought on. In 1875, the Tennessee Senate, after putting itself through 55 ballots in a period of days, elected Johnson once more to the U.S. Senate—the only ex-president to serve in that capacity. Johnson took enormous satisfaction in his election to the group that had tried him, and he rose in a special Senate session on March 20 to attack President Grant in a speech. He ended his address, as he had done so many times over the years, with a ringing appeal to support the Constitution, and he was heartily applauded by his colleagues. He has not been so lauded by historians; a 1996 poll rated him a "failure," a fate shared by his successor as well.

Back in Tennessee during a Senate recess, Johnson had a stroke while visiting his daughter and died three days later on August 1, 1875. Sixty-six years old, he was buried on Signal Hill in Greeneville after a funeral attended by thousands of people.

The First Frontier

five miles. Turn left onto Old Allen's Bridge Road, drive about three miles, and then turn right at the fork in the road near the University of Tennessee Tobacco Experiment Station. After that turn, the entrance to the park is about a mile to the right.

Cherokee National Forest

The following recreation areas are in the **Cherokee National Forest** (423/638-4109, www.southernregion.fs.fed.us/cherokee). All offer picnicking, hiking, and wilderness activities. For further information, go to the Nolichucky Ranger District Office at 120 Austin Avenue in Greeneville.

Paint Creek Recreation Area lies in a mountain cove beside a creek south of Greeneville in the Cherokee National Forest. Dudley Falls is a popular place for swimming and picnicking, and the area is fun to simply explore. To get there, take Hwy. 70 south for about 14 miles. Look for the Forest Service signs and follow them for three more miles.

Farther up the ridge lies **Horse Creek Recreation Area,** where one can swim in the creek free of charge. Nature trails are also available, including one paved for accessibility. To get to Horse Creek take Hwy. 107 north from Greeneville for six miles, then turn right and follow the signs for two miles.

The **Old Forge Recreation Area** lies at the foot of Coldspring Mountain and is very popular with horse riders. Visitors can swim in the stream or hike on the nearby Appalachian Trail. Take Hwy. 107 north of Greeneville for six miles, and then turn right and follow the signs to the Horse Creek Recreation Area. Once there, take a Forest Service road to Old Forge.

At the bottom of Meadow Creek Mountain lies the **Houston Valley Recreation Area,** where hikers can climb to the Meadow Creek fire tower. Farther down the road boaters can enjoy the French Broad River. From Greeneville take Hwy. 70 south to the intersection with Hwy. 170. Turn right, then go about eight miles. Look for the campground on the left, just before Burnett Gap.

Close by the Appalachian Trail, **Round Mountain Recreation Area** lies at an elevation of 3,400 feet and offers great views, particularly during the

fall color season. Take Hwy. 70 south from Greeneville for about nine miles. Turn right on Hwy. 107 and continue for about 13 miles to the intersection with U.S. 25/70 at the Del Rio post office. Remain on Hwy. 107 for about six miles until the pavement ends and the road becomes gravel; it will climb Round Mountain for about six miles. Look for the sign to the campground.

To get to **Round Knob Recreation Area,** take Hwy. 350, the Jones Bridge Road, south from Greeneville toward the Camp Creek community. Continue on a country road there for two miles, then turn right onto Forest Service Road 88 for five miles.

ARTS AND EVENTS

If you can visit only one art gallery in East Tennessee, **James-Ben Studio and Gallery** (129 N. Main St., 423/787-0195, www.james-ben.com, 11 A.M.– 6 P.M. Mon.–Fri., 11 A.M. – 3 P.M. Sat., by appointment Sun.) should be the one. Just down the street from the General Morgan Inn and Conference Center. the gallery specializes in the work of Tennessee artists and craftspeople, including paintings, sculptures, works in wood, pottery, glass and much more.

Every year the **Little Theatre of Greeneville** (423/638-3481) trots out musicals, dramas, and children's plays. Call for information about theatrical events.

The **Battle of Blue Springs** (423/422-4051, www.members.tripod.com/bluesprings2, $5 ages 12 and over, free for children under 12), a Civil War reenactment, takes place west of Greeneville in Mosheim (MOSS-hime) on the third weekend in October. Those who attend will get a chance to see authentic military and civilian campsites, the firing of full-scale cannons, cavalry maneuvers, a battle with about 200 participants in period dress, a battlefield hospital, and a period church service. To get there, take Exit 23 from I-81 and follow U.S. 11 East to Mosheim, where signs lead to the battlefield. For further information, call Earl Fletcher at the Mosheim Town Hall.

The **Iris Arts and Crafts Festival** (423/638-4111) takes place in May. Traditional and contemporary crafts are available, as is food. Some crafts are demonstrated. For further information, call the Greene County Partnership.

ACCOMMODATIONS

Bed-and-Breakfasts and Inns

Tanasi Hill Bed & Breakfast (315 N. Main St., 423/638-2917, www.bbonline.com/tn/tanasi, $75–150) is a bed-and-breakfast in a turn-of-the-20th-century, three-story Greek revival house surrounded by 100-year-old trees and gardens in Greeneville's historic district. The six rooms in the inn, most of which offer private baths, are named for prominent Greeneville women.

General Morgan Inn and Conference Center (111 N. Main St., 800/223-2679 or 423/787-1000, www.generalmorganinn.com) offers perhaps the most luxurious accommodations on this end of the state. The Presidential Suite, which goes for $255 a night, has a bathroom with heated floor tiles, a fireplace, and a Chippendale-style canopied bed. More modest rooms go for $84 per night. The inn has 82 rooms in all.

Hilltop House (Rte. 7, Box 180, 423/638-2660) is a spacious old bed-and-breakfast sitting on a bluff that overlooks the Nolichucky River Valley. Decorated with English antiques, the house features afternoon tea and lawn croquet.

Nolichucky Bluffs (400 Kinser Park Ln., 800/842-4690 or 423/787-7947, $95–110) offers a B&B and cabins overlooking the Nolichucky River about seven miles south of Greeneville. The B&B has three rooms, all with private baths and one with a whirlpool bath, and the cabins have stoves or fireplaces.

Motels

Try the **Charray Inn** (121 Seral Dr., 800/852-4682 or 423/638-1331), or the **Holiday Inn** (1790 E. Andrew Johnson Hwy., 800/465-4329 or 423/639-4185).

Camping

Kinser Park has 108 campsites, some with full hookups, and is open March 15–Oct. 15. **Davy Crockett Birthplace State Historical Area** offers 75 campsites open year-round along the Nolichucky River.

Camping at the following **Cherokee National Forest** (423/638-4109, open, depending on the weather, May–mid-Nov.) is strictly first-come, first-served; no reservations are taken. For further information, contact the Nolichucky/Unaka Ranger District Office, 120 Austin Ave. in Greeneville.

Paint Creek in the Cherokee National Forest offers 21 sites. **Horse Creek** has 10 campsites. **Old Forge's** nine tent sites sit near a waterfall. **Houston Valley** has 10 campsites, and **Round Mountain** has 16.

FOOD

Augustino's Restaurant (3465 E. Andrew Johnson Hwy., 423/639-1231, 11 A.M.–11 P.M. Mon.–Sat.) specializes in Italian cuisine. The **Brumleys** (111 N. Main St., 800/223-2679 or 423/787-1000) is the in-house restaurant of the General Morgan Inn and Conference Center. It offers continental and Southern cuisine.

The **Butcher's Block** (125 Serral Dr., 423/638-4485), not surprisingly, features beef—from eight-ounce to 32-ounce steaks. It also offers seafood, barbecue, and chicken. **Pal's** (1357 Tusculum Blvd., 423/638-7555) serves up burgers and hot dogs.

Stan's Bar-B-Q (2620 E. Andrew Johnson Hwy., 423/787-0017, 10 A.M.–9 P.M. Mon.–Sat.) is one of the more upscale barbecue places on this end of the state. It serves pork, ribs, chicken, and beef. Try the dry ribs with a Memphis rub.

INFORMATION

To learn more about Greeneville and Greene County, contact the **Greeneville/Greene County Area Chamber of Commerce** (115 Academy St., Suite 1, 423/638-4111, www.greeneville.com).

The First Frontier

West of Greeneville

BULLS GAP

Here U.S. 11 East rolls through a low place in Bays Mountain and emerges in the little town of Bulls Gap, which was named for John Bull, a frontier rifle maker. The town became a rail center in the 1800s and was greatly fought over during the Civil War. Union forces holding Bulls Gap were summoned to Greeneville to capture and kill Southern cavalry leader General Morgan. By 1912, as many as 14 passenger trains per day stopped here. Bulls Gap, however, is far more famous as the home of an entertainer who made a career out of claiming he was the town's mayor.

Archie Campbell is a name most familiar to the viewers of *Hee Haw*, the CBS television show for which he was a performer and writer. Among his talents was an ability to make ordinary stories funnier by interchanging the beginning consonants in words. Cinderella thus became Rindercella, and Sleeping Beauty transmogrified into Beeping Sleuty. He began his career in Knoxville as a radio performer, working with Chet Atkins, Roy Acuff, Bill Monroe, Flatt and Scruggs, and the Carter Family. In 1959 he joined the *Grand*

Ole Opry, and 10 years later he helped launch *Hee Haw.* An accomplished painter, in later years he sold limited-edition prints of his works. Campbell died in 1987 at the age of 72.

To get to the center of town, turn southwest at the traffic light and go over a hill. If anyone wanted to establish another Jonesborough-type tourist operation, or an eastern version of Middle Tennessee's Bell Buckle, Bulls Gap lies waiting. Its railroad heritage, surplus of available buildings, and proximity to I-81 would all contribute to success. For now, the local tourism industry centers around the **Bulls Gap Tourism Complex** (May–Oct. 9 A.M.–4 P.M. Mon.–Fri., or whenever the city recorder is on duty, free, donations accepted), a fancy name for a collection of historic buildings that don't seem to have much purpose in life. Archie Campbell's boyhood home has been moved into town and restored with period furniture. Downhill stands the Town Hall, which contains a museum with Archie Campbell's artwork, items from his career, and the usual odd items that town museums contain. This one has, among other things, a samurai sword and a tommy gun.

Morristown has sidewalks on the second floors of its buildings.

Bulls Gap has a big celebration every Labor Day, with food and craft booths, games for children, and live music. For information call City Hall at 423/235-5216.

Live gospel music is presented once a month April–June and August–October in a theater downtown. Call Robin Horner at 423/235-2917 for details.

MORRISTOWN

In the 1960s many towns across Tennessee attempted to spruce up their downtowns and make them "modern." Often this resulted in beautiful 19th-century storefronts being covered with hideous fabrications of aluminum and/or plastic. Preferring to take the high road, Morristown chose to launch its sidewalks into the air.

That's right. On Main Street, which runs parallel to and south of U.S. 11 East, the sidewalks have been raised 20 or so feet off the ground. New doors were cut into the facades of buildings, and crosswalks high above the pavement enable shoppers to cross the street. There is nothing in Tennessee like this.

Sights

The second stop on the David Crockett tour is the **David Crockett Tavern and Museum** (2002 E. Morningside Dr., 423/587-9900, www.korrnet.org/crockett, May–Oct. 11 A.M.–5 P.M. Tues.–Sat., $5 adults, $4.50 seniors, $1 students). The building is a replica of his parents' tavern, and the contents are period pieces, but the visitor can get a sense here of the kind of world that made up Crockett's formative years. The Loom Room contains a very good collection of devices used to make cloth from flax fibers.

Many Tennessee towns have museums, but few have them in as beautiful a building as Morristown's **Rose Center** (442 W. 2nd North St., 423/581-4330, www.rosecenter.org, 9 A.M.–5 P.M. Mon.–Fri.). The brick 1892 former high school houses a regional museum, traveling exhibits, and gift shop. Here one can see plans and original parts of Melville Murrell's ornithopter as well as other historic exhibits.

Events

Music on the Porch (1721 S. Cumberland, free), a bluegrass jam session, takes place on the second and fourth Saturday of each month during the summer. The porch belongs to the Trade Center, which is off U.S. 11 East. The pickin' and singin' takes place on the second and fourth Saturdays of the month.

Every year on the last weekend in October the **Mountain Makin's Festival** (423/586-6382, $4 adults, $1 children) takes place in the Rose Center. More than 50 juried craftspeople display their goods, and artists demonstrate their work. Live entertainment, country cooking, and an old-time medicine show round out the festivities for the estimated 12,000 who attend.

Accommodations

Visitors can rest at **Baneberry Golf and Resort** (704 Harrison Ferry Rd. in Baneberry, 800/951-GOLF [951-4653], www.baneberrygolf.com, $96), which has accommodations for people passing through. Guests stay in a hotel or "golf villa." The price includes green fees.

Franchise options include **Comfort Suites** (3660 W. Andrew Johnson Hwy., 423/585-4000), **Days Inn** (2512 E. Andrew Johnson Hwy., 423/587-2200), **Holiday Inn of Morristown** (3230 W. Andrew Johnson Hwy., 423/581-8700), **Holiday Inn** (U.S. 25 East and I-81 interchange, 423/587-2400), and **Super 8 Motel** (2430 E. Andrew Johnson Hwy., 423/586-8880).

Camping

Owned by Hamblen County and open year-round, **Cherokee Park** (423/586-5232 or 423/586-0260) is a 178-acre recreation area containing 52 campsites with water and electricity hookups. There are also eight primitive sites. Showers and bathrooms are available March–October. From I-81, take Exit 8—U.S. 25 East—nine miles north to the park entrance.

Several miles southwest of Morristown on U.S. 11 East, a sign points the way to **Panther Creek State Recreational Park** (2010 Panther Creek Rd., 423/587-7046, www.tnstateparks.com). These 1,435 acres sit on the banks of

Cherokee Lake (the Holston River). This lake, one of the many that TVA uses for flood control, appears half empty during the fall and winter. Bird-watchers like to post themselves atop a long ridge in the park and wait for migrating hawks and waterfowl. The park also shelters some rare albino white-tailed deer. Panther Creek offers nature trails, picnic sites, a playground and swimming pool, plus camping on 50 sites, each with water and electricity. The campground is open year-round, but water is not available from Thanksgiving through mid-March.

Food

Angelo's Fine Dining (3614 W. Andrew Johnson Hwy., 423/581-4882, www.angelosmorristown .com, 5–10 P.M. Mon.–Thurs., 5–11 P.M. Sat.–Sun.) is the fanciest restaurant in town. Patrons can enjoy fresh seafood, steaks, spaghetti, and Greek dishes such as moussaka. So that it can serve drinks in a dry county, Angelo's is a "private club," with membership open to those who fill out an application and fork out $5. It's worth it, say regulars.

Buddy's Barbecue (2275 W. Andrew Johnson Hwy., 423/587-5058, www.buddysbarbq.com, 10 A.M.–10 P.M. daily) is one of a chain of barbecue places operating out of Knoxville.

The **Little Dutch** (115 S. Cumberland St., 423/581-1441, 11 A.M.–9:30 P.M. daily) is a longtime Morristown favorite. Amid decor inspired by a trip to Holland, this eatery serves lunch and dinner every day consisting of steaks, seafood, spaghetti, and Greek dishes. Whatever you order for dinner, you should finish off with the baklava.

The **Mexico Lindo Restaurant** (3351 W. Andrew Johnson Hwy., 423/587-9754) has Mexican food. Try the chile rellenos.

Information

For more information, contact the **Morristown Chamber of Commerce** (825 W. 1st St., 423/ 586-6382, www.morristownchamber.com).

JEFFERSON CITY

Travelers can go straight from Morristown to Jefferson City, but a better route turns northwest at a shoe store onto the Old Andrew Johnson Hwy.

When a Farmer's Co-op appears on the right, look up the hill to the left to see **Glenmore Mansion** (423/475-5014, May–Oct., $2.50 adults, $1 kids), built in 1869 and described as "perhaps the grandest Second Empire country house remaining in Tennessee." The mansion is often rented for weddings and other frivolities.

Jefferson County is a center for zinc mining, and from 1950 through 1995 this county produced more zinc ore than anywhere else in the country.

Jefferson City is chiefly known for **Carson-Newman College,** (which came about by a 1889 marriage between the Carson College for Men, founded in 1851, with the Newman College for Women, founded in 1852 and now has just over 2,100 students). Although affiliated with the Tennessee Baptist Convention, a subset of the Southern Baptist Convention, Carson-Newman resisted the conservative forces that captured the boards of many sister Baptist colleges by quietly voting to appoint its own leaders. This courageous stance cost the College financially, but elevated its stature among those who believe in the traditional independence of Baptists.

For further info on this town, try the **Jefferson City Chamber of Commerce** (532 Patriot Dr., 865/397-9642, www.jefferson-tn-chamber.org).

NEW MARKET

This town lay on the stage route between Knoxville and Abingdon, Virginia, and in those days Tucker's Tavern provided the accommodations for those coming or going. It was not a posh place; the 1939 *WPA Guide to Tennessee* tells the tale of one guest who was thrown out of the tavern because he objected to using a towel that had already been used by 15 people.

During the Civil War, East Tennessee was a center of support for the Union, and 450 young men gathered here in 1862 to march off and join the Northern army. They had no guns, however, and were apprehended by Confederate troops and forced to spend the rest of the war in Tuscaloosa, Alabama.

In 1865, the year the Civil War ended, 15-year-old Frances Hodgson moved to New Market with her mother and three siblings from Manchester, England. Frances and her sister ran a school to which most of the students paid tuition with the products of their families' farms. In her free time, she wrote short stories and mailed them to editors, at one point picking blackberries to obtain money for postage.

Hodgson moved to Knoxville in 1869, married a surgeon, and then moved to Washington, D.C. She continued her writing, eventually writing more than 40 novels, among them the children's classics *Little Lord Fauntleroy* and *The Secret Garden*. She often came back to visit in New Market, and locals like to think that her greatest books were written in part while she was here. A roadside marker commemorates her time here. Part of the house closest to the marker—a log cabin now covered with boards—is where she lived. It is not open to the public.

New Market's **Houston Mineral Water** (1005 Old Andrew Johnson Hwy.), was discovered in 1931. As Carolyn Sakowski tells the tale in *Touring the East Tennessee Backroads,* William Avery Houston had kidney disease so bad that he thought he was going to die. One night he had a dream that instructed him to dig a well in a particular place. He did so, drilling to a depth of 252 feet until he struck water. This was odd, for most people in New Market could hit water a mere 20 or 30 feet down. At any rate, he drank the water for several days and was cured. Later he began to bottle this natural elixir, which is available free to passersby. Look for a well house (close to the Frances Hodgson house) on the highway, which runs parallel to U.S. 11 East, and go inside. You can get a taste at a fountain or fill jugs from a spigot. A small box accepts contributions to defray the costs of making the water available.

Finally, New Market is well known in some circles as a center for social activism. The **Highlander Research and Education Center,** which occupies a 104-acre site north of U.S. 11 East, began as the controversial Highlander Folk School in Middle Tennessee, where Martin Luther King Jr., Rosa Parks, and other icons

THE GREAT NEW MARKET WRECK

N ew Market briefly entered popular culture because of a dreadful train wreck. Two Southern railroad passenger trains carrying a total of 300 people crashed head-on here at 10:18 on the morning of September 4, 1904. Sixty-four passengers died and 152 were injured.

A ballad about the wreck was written two years later by one of the survivors and was widely performed by a variety of singers. The *WPA Guide to Tennessee* contains the following verses:

One autumn morning in Tennessee
An awful wreck was heard;
East of Knoxville and New Market
Was where the crash occurred.

The east and west-bound passenger trains
Were running at highest speed;
They struck each other in the curve;
'Twas a horrible sight indeed.

The engine crew on the west-bound train
Their orders had misread;
About one hundred and fifty were hurt,
And nearly seventy were dead.

of the civil rights movement forged the tactics that brought them victories.

Highlander was more or less run off from Grundy County in 1962, then existed for a decade in Knoxville, and moved to New Market in 1972. Today Highlander works with community groups, primarily from Appalachia and the Deep South. "We bring people together to learn from each other," says the group's mission statement. This takes the form of residential workshops, training sessions, and other methods that develop leadership in issues such as fighting corporate pollution, bringing U.S. and immigrant workers together, and combating the increasing use of part-time, temporary, and contract workers. The Highlander Center is not open to the public, but you can visit its site online at www.highlandercenter.org.

The First Frontier

Know Tennessee

The Land

GEOGRAPHY

Tennessee looks like a ship steaming toward the Atlantic, with Bristol up on the bow and the propeller coming out down at Memphis. Though only the 34th state in terms of total area—about 42,250 square miles—it manages to touch eight other states, a feat matched only by neighboring Missouri.

As anyone who has ever driven the length of the state can testify, it is a long haul from Bristol to Memphis—500 miles in all. Bristol is closer to Canada than it is to Memphis, and Memphis is closer to the Gulf of Mexico than to Bristol.

The Tennessee River divides the state into three parts, known as the "grand divisions of Tennessee." Indeed, until a few years ago, signs along the highways welcomed visitors to "the three states of Tennessee."

This greeting was dropped in the 1980s in an effort to promote a more unified state, but the geographic divisions—exacerbated by the length of the state—help explain the differences in accents, food, music, and points of view that have emerged over the years across the state. People in West Tennessee have a deeper Southern accent than do their East Tennessee counterparts, who speak with more of an Appalachian twang. Catfish is a staple of "country cooking" in West Tennessee, while no decent restaurant in East Tennessee would think of serving breakfast without offering country ham. When Tennessee voted to secede from the Union, some East Tennesseans wanted to secede from the secessionists. One of the reasons for this was the small size of East Tennessee farms, which had few slaves.

The great distances from the mountains to the Mississippi River account for the fact that many Tennesseans are not very well traveled in their own state. The vast majority of East Tennesseans have never been to Memphis, while, with the exception of those who are driving to points east and north, few West Ten-

nesseans get past the Great Smoky Mountains National Park.

Geography can even account for the differences in music across the state. East Tennessee, isolated from the rest of the state until modern highways cut through, preserved Elizabethan ballads that had come from England and the British Isles. West Tennessee had, and has, the highest concentration of African Americans in Tennessee, and it was from them that the blues emerged. Nashville, a center of commerce in the middle of the state, had money for advertising on radio shows and thus was a perfect place for the music industry to emerge.

CLIMATE

Tennessee is a Southern state, but it has more variety in its weather than most of its Dixie neighbors. As a general rule, West Tennessee is hotter than East Tennessee, and East Tennessee gets more snow than the rest of the state combined.

Winters in the eastern part of the state can be rough, with temperatures spiking down to 15° below zero Fahrenheit. Mountain roads, particularly in the Great Smoky Mountains National Park, are often closed by snow December to February. A far more pernicious form of bad weather is "black ice," created when rain or snow freezes on roadways. The slippery black ice is more hazardous than a foot of snow.

Springtime is a delight across the state, although it comes with a lot of rain. Travelers should keep in mind, particularly in the mountains, that rain at a lower elevation can become snow a few thousand feet up. Spring is the best time to visit Memphis and West Tennessee, and this is when the locals hold their biggest outdoor festivals.

Summertime is hot in Tennessee. Temperatures easily reach the 90s in all but the highest places. When the humidity readings come close to those of the thermometer, it can be downright miserable.

Fall brings another round of festivals to West Tennessee and beautiful foliage all over the state. This is usually a relatively dry time, with warm days and chilly evenings.

FLORA

Trees

When settlers came across the mountains from the east, they found a land almost entirely covered by hardwood forests—trees they had to chop down to make room for fields and pastures. Tennessee remains a diversely forested state, and forest products contribute mightily to the state's economy.

In the east, the Great Smoky Mountains National Park supports more species of trees than does all of Europe. As visitors climb to elevations of 6,000 feet, the changes in the trees, a gradual shift from hardwoods to a conifer forest, reflect the variations one might see while traveling north through North America. At the top, the spruce-fir forests resemble those found in Canada.

Across the state, the hardwoods produce a pleasing set of colors in the fall, and visitors flock to the scenic highways to enjoy the views. Reelfoot Lake and the river bottoms of West Tennessee contain cypress trees, a water-dwelling plant whose knobby "knees" rise out of the water.

Wildflowers

Tennessee is noted for wildflowers, not only for their beauty but the uses to which the Native Americans and early settlers put them. Yarrow is a member of the sunflower family whose leaves have a blood-clotting component. Bloodroot gets its name from the fact that Native Americans used it to make red dye, and trilliums grow along many roads and trails in the mountains.

Kudzu

Perhaps the most amazing plant in Tennessee, found the length of the state, is kudzu, a vine-like organism with enormous leaves and a prodigious growth rate—under optimal con-

ditions, a foot or more per day. Brought in from Asia with extravagant promises, this plant was loosed on the South in the 1930s in an effort to control erosion. It certainly helped do that, then promptly set about controlling trees, abandoned buildings, and anything standing still. Although the plant has some practical uses—cattle will eat it when grass is scarce—the plant is largely regarded at best as a nuisance and at worse as an enemy of forestry. Kudzu climbs trees and then kills them by blocking out the sun.

Left alone, kudzu creates fantastic landscapes of vine-draped trees, totally covering buildings and cars and sprouting tendrils that hang threateningly from wires that cross roads and highways. Kudzu has captured the imaginations of Tennesseans and other Southerners, showing up in songs and in literature, and on a website: www.alabamatv.org/kudzu.

FAUNA

Mammals

Among the largest wild animals in Tennessee are black bears, which live in the eastern part of the state. The bears of the Smokies are the most

a deer in Great Smoky Mountains National Park

COURTESY OF GREAT SMOKY MOUNTAINS NATIONAL PARK

Never feed a wild bear.

famous, for they have the most contact with people. While black bears have a gentle reputation, they can be dangerous if cornered or if a person gets between a mother bear and her cubs. A woman was killed in the Great Smoky Mountains National Park in 2000, and a camper was attacked in 2001. People should never feed bears. Doing so causes the animals to lose their innate fear of humans. When this happens, they often cause problems and have to be killed.

Elk, which roamed the state until 1865, have been successfully reintroduced in three areas: the Great Smoky Mountains National Park; in a 670,000 acre restoration zone located in Scott, Morgan, Campbell, Anderson and Claiborne counties, and at Land Between the Lakes.

Deer live all over Tennessee, as do raccoons, muskrats, red foxes, squirrels, and smaller animals. Dead possums often grace Tennessee roads, and in recent years have been joined by armadillos in their conflicts with moving vehicles.

Birds

With its many woodlands and wetlands, Tennessee is home to a wide variety of birds. Furthermore, parts of the Mississippi and the Atlantic flyways cross the state, bringing birds that are just passing through.

Bald eagles winter at Reelfoot Lake in northwestern Tennessee. Wild turkeys appear in the Smokies and across the state. Ruffed grouse and bobwhites are found throughout the state, as are barred owls and barn owls. Crows live all over, as do pileated woodpeckers—the largest members of the woodpecker family. Turkey vultures, almost always called "buzzards" hereabouts, often feast on roadkill.

Waterfowl such as Canada geese, mallards, and black ducks live beside great blue herons and belted kingfishers.

Reptiles and Amphibians

With its temperate climate and many bodies of water, Tennessee harbors a great many reptiles and amphibians. Some 32 kinds of snakes live in

Tennessee, of which four are poisonous: copperheads, timber rattlesnakes, western cottonmouths, and pigmy rattlesnakes.

The Smokies contain 30 species of salamanders, and is sometimes called "the salamander capital of the world." These sometimes brightly colored creatures are elusive forest dwellers, often living close to streams. Perhaps the most extraordinary ones, the plethodontid family, have no lungs. They get oxygen through their skin and mouth tissue.

Insects and Arachnids

Tennessee has most of the insects found in the eastern half of America, but visitors should be aware of some relatively new arrivals. Fire ants look like normal ants, but build mounds that can be 10 or more inches in height. The ants get the name "fire" from the way they swarm out of their nests in great numbers and sting any person or animal that bothers them. The stings cause burning and itching, but pose danger to small children or people who are allergic to the ants' venom.

ENVIRONMENTAL ISSUES

Historically, Southern states in general and Tennessee in particular welcomed industry and gave little thought to the pollution that accompanied jobs and an inflow of capital. Attitudes have changed, however, and Tennessee's air and water are in better shape than they were just a few decades ago. Nonetheless, paper mills and other industrial sites belch chemicals—and odors—to an extent that is noticeable by visitors.

Coal-fired power plants are another source of pollution. Since the prevailing winds blow from west to east, the Great Smoky Mountains National Park suffers a great deal from particulates borne by the wind. Visibility from the peaks has decreased something like 30 percent during the past three decades. And Chattanooga's Rock City, which for years has claimed that visitors can "see seven states," rarely has skies clear enough to do so.

Tennessee's Oak Ridge was one of the key sites of the atomic age, and at one time the Tennessee Valley Authority had the most ambitious nuclear power plant construction program in the world. Oak Ridge is now undergoing an extensive clean-up of radioactive materials, and, as in other places in the United States, fission-based power plants have not arrived at a good solution for their nuclear waste.

History

NATIVE AMERICANS

The earliest evidence of people in what is now Tennessee comes from artifacts left by Ice Age hunters. Little is known of their culture, but they left fluted points, scraping tools, and other items that suggest they were nomadic hunters.

Anthropologists call the next group to inhabit Tennessee the Archaic Indians, who came upon the scene about 6000 B.C. These people built the first Tennessee towns, usually along rivers, where they fished using hooks and nets. Excavations of burial sites have revealed that they made jewelry from shells, bones, and copper.

The next inhabitants, the Woodland Indians, who came about 3,000 to 2,500 years ago, set the pattern for groups to follow. They cultivated corn, fashioned pottery out of clay, and used bows and arrows. They were the first people to alter the Tennessee landscape with the construction of mounds. Woodland Indian burial mounds, structures that grew in height as subsequent bodies were buried in them, exist all over the state. This group is thought to have built the "Old Stone Fort" outside Manchester.

A subsequent group, the Early Mississippian Indians, built some of the highest earthen structures in the United States. Coming to Tennessee about 1,000 years ago, they erected mounds for some sort of ceremonial purposes. Pinson Mounds, south of Jackson in West Tennessee, contains one pile of soil that reaches more than seven stories tall.

For all the native people who lived in Tennessee, the land proved a most hospitable place. The forests teemed with game, the rivers and streams with fish, and the rich soil readily grew corn, beans, potatoes, pumpkins, and tobacco. The Indians here, unlike some of their Western counterparts who had to struggle with a hostile environment, had time to focus on matters of art, government, and games.

When Europeans arrived, they encountered several tribes in what is now Tennessee. Hernando de Soto reported finding large towns of Indians on the bluffs that are now Memphis. The Chickasaw lived in what is now Mississippi, but they considered large amounts of the state their territory. The Creek lived farther east, the Shawnee inhabited the Cumberland River Valley, and a small group called the Yuchi lived in the east.

The Cherokee

The most powerful tribe, the one whose word "Tanasi" for the largest river in the area became "Tennessee," was the Cherokee. In the early 18th century, they waged war on the Creek, Yuchi, and Shawnee and drove them out of the region. When the settlers arrived, the Cherokee were the Indians with whom they had to deal.

The Cherokee lived in towns collected around the junction of what is now Tennessee, Georgia, North Carolina, and South Carolina. The Tennessee towns became known to settlers as the "overhill towns," since they were across the Appalachian Mountains from the settlements in North Carolina.

In their towns, overhill or otherwise, the Cherokee lived in permanent dwellings made of logs. Each family belonged to one of seven clans, and together the clans governed the village. Each village had a council house, some of which could hold more than 500 people, and had designated places for each clan.

The Cherokee had a national chief who had various advisers and a bureaucracy that dealt with civic, religious, and wartime affairs. During times of combat, women took part in the government, most notably in the role of "Honored Woman," a person who could decide the fate of captives and who could enter into the decision of whether or not to go to war.

Game and fish were plentiful, and the Cherokee grew corn and other crops. They lived reasonably comfortable lives, but zealously defended their hunting grounds and vigorously repelled any other tribe who attempted to encroach on them. At least one path over which they traveled to wage war was known as the Warrior's Path, and they kept it worn down.

EXPLORERS AND PIONEERS
Trade and War

Hernando de Soto's expedition was the first group of Europeans to see what is now Tennessee. This group, which single-mindedly sought gold, made no effort to exploit any of the territory's riches. The English arrived in Jamestown, Virginia, in 1607 and gradually began to explore the new world before them, recording their first contact with the Cherokee in 1673. The English were eager to trade with the Cherokee, as were the French, who approached the Indians from the Mississippi River. The traders sought deerskins, which the Indians had in abundance, and in return offered them articles of clothing, metal tools such as hoes and axes, and—most desired by the Indians— guns, ammunition, and whiskey.

As France and England began to wrestle for control of the new land, each saw the advantage of having Indian tribes as allies. The British embarked on an all-out campaign to win over the Cherokee, alternately wooing them with gifts and goods and then seeking to put fear in them with mighty displays of force. Perhaps the most extraordinary gesture during this campaign was a 1730 voyage to London undertaken by six young Cherokee men. These Indians met the king and created quite a stir in England. The voyage so impressed one of them, Attakullakulla ("The Little Carpenter"), that he became a friend of the English colonists for life.

The British built Fort Loudoun along the Tennessee River in 1756 in response to Cherokee demands for protection from the French army. This cemented the partnership for a time with the Cherokee, and kept the French at bay as well. Unfortunately, relations between the English and their Indian allies deteriorated, with both sides committing massacres and British armies sacking several Cherokee towns. Finally, the war with the French was settled by the Treaty of Paris in 1763. English control of this part of North America was set, and the empire turned its attention elsewhere. In an effort to keep a lid on further troubles with the Cherokee, the British forbade any of their subjects from settling on the western side of the Appalachians. This outraged colonists who were hungry for land, particularly those who had fought for the British during the long war and thought they were due something for their efforts. And from what these land-hungry people heard, the other side of the mountains was very alluring indeed.

The "Long Hunters"

For years a number of individuals, the kind who would later be called "mountain men" in the American West, made their own fur-gathering exploits into Tennessee. Dubbed the "long hunters" because they were gone a long time, they traveled into Middle Tennessee, amassed furs, and either brought them back or built boats and floated all the way to New Orleans. Kasper Mansker, Daniel Boone, Timothy Demonbreun, and other long hunters, whenever (and in some cases, if ever) they returned, brought back tales of rich land and plentiful game. One came back telling of herds of buffalo so thick that he was afraid to get off his horse.

Self-Government

The first recorded settler in what is now Tennessee was William Bean, who built a log cabin in 1768 along the Watauga River in East Tennessee. He and his family were quickly joined by others along the Watauga and other rivers. The Cherokee were persuaded to lease these lands for 10 years, and the residents set about providing themselves with a system of government. The document they drew up, the Watauga "Written Articles of Association," was both an attempt to maintain order so far away from established authorities and a stab at self-governance.

In 1775, Richard Henderson engineered a massive land purchase from the Cherokee at Sycamore Shoals near present-day Elizabethton. The head of the Cherokee who handled their end of the negotiations was Attakullakulla, who still fondly recalled his trip to England. A dissident faction was led by Dragging Canoe, a warrior who stalked out of the negotiations threatening to make the territory "a dark and bloody ground." A year after the Henderson purchase, the land that is now Tennessee became an official part of North Carolina. The entire area was called Washington County.

Henderson's chief focus was Kentucky, and he hired Daniel Boone to head a group of axmen cutting a road from the Long Island of the Holston River through the Cumberland Gap and into Kentucky. Part of his purchase, however, included the land on which Nashville now stands, and James Robertson resolved to build a settlement there.

The Cumberland Plateau made it all but impossible to go due west, so Robertson divided his party into two groups. Leaving in 1779, 200 men and boys drove livestock and walked 400 miles to Middle Tennessee through Kentucky, while William Donelson led a flotilla of flatboats bearing women and small children on a treacherous four-month voyage down the Holston and the Tennessee Rivers and up the Ohio and Cumberland—an incredibly arduous trip.

The place they settled was called Nashborough, and here the settlers drew up the Cumberland Compact, a document of self-government. This compact outlined procedures for recalling an elected official—the first such provisions in U.S. history.

The Revolution

Settlers on the western side of the Appalachians could have sat out the Revolutionary War. They had little contact with the British, and certainly

WALKING THE TRAIL OF TEARS

The Southeastern part of Tennessee was the setting for one of the United States's most shameful actions: the forced removal of the Cherokee from their homelands to a reservation in Oklahoma. The Native Americans still refer to it as the Trail of Tears. Today, we might call it ethnic cleansing.

Unlike their counterparts in the West, the Cherokee never waged war on a large scale against the settlers. As early as 1730, some of them traveled to England and came home with the realization that they could never overcome white men in battle. And so, for the most part, they tried to accommodate the newcomers, entering into a series of treaties and sales of their land as they retreated from the growing number of settlers. On a personal basis, they intermarried with settlers and began adopting many of the new ways of living.

By the late 1820s, the Cherokee governed their nation in eight districts, each having a bicameral legislature. The nation as a whole had a constitution that outlined courts and other parts of government. They even had a bureaucracy that took care of tax collections, licenses, education, and maintaining an infrastructure of bridges and roads. All this was centered in the Georgia town of New Echota.

In 1828 gold was discovered in Dahlonega, Georgia—less than 70 miles away from New Echota. The Georgia legislature moved to strip the Cherokee of all their rights. Among other things, the Georgians prevented the Native Americans from assembling for any public purpose. To escape this ban, the Cherokee moved their capital to Red Clay, Tennessee, the site of a huge spring that gave forth a half-million gallons of water daily. Here, the Cherokee decided to fight the Georgians on legal grounds—with lawsuits and lobbying efforts in Washington. After all, that was the "civilized" thing to do.

The United States government should have protected the Cherokee from the rapacious Georgians, and, indeed, the Supreme Court ruled that the Cherokee were not subject to the laws of Georgia. But President Jackson, despite his oath to uphold the Constitution, refused to enforce the court's decision and allowed all manner of Georgian riff-raff to brazenly steal Cherokee houses and property.

The Cherokee split over what to do. One faction wanted to give up and try to get the best deal

---

enjoyed no government services from them. An arrogant British officer, however, sent word that if the people on the west of the mountains aided the warring colonials he would "lay their country to waste with fire and sword." This was all it took to get the future Tennesseans in the war. They assembled at Sycamore Shoals, marched over the mountains, and utterly thrashed the British army at the Battle of Kings Mountain.

STATEHOOD

With the creation of the United States, North Carolina offered in 1784 to cede its western lands to the federal government, but the fledgling country was occupied by other matters and didn't immediately accept the offer. This left the future Tennesseans greatly annoyed, for they felt themselves abandoned—without any say in the matter—by North Carolina. To remedy this situation they formed the state of Franklin and sought admission to the Union. Hearing of this, North Carolina rescinded the law that had given the western lands away and refused to recognize Franklin.

Finally North Carolina did give away Tennessee, though not before granting a great deal of its land to veterans of the Revolutionary War. The United States accepted the land, gave it the laborious name "The Territory of the United States South of the River Ohio," and made William Blount governor. He moved his capital to Knoxville in 1792.

possible as they moved west. Others wanted to continue the legal and political struggle. While the latter faction was traveling to Washington in 1836, a group of 20 of the former signed the infamous Treaty of New Echota, which allowed the federal government to move the Cherokee to the Oklahoma Territory.

Those who opposed this treaty, headed by John Ross, presented petitions bearing the names of 16,000 Cherokee who did not want to leave. By one vote, the Senate ratified the treaty, and the fate of the Cherokee was sealed. Jackson was succeeded by Martin Van Buren, who put the Cherokee removal into effect.

The task of evacuation fell to General Winfield Scott, whose 7,000 troops fanned out and rounded up the Cherokee. Many had little time to gather belongings, which fell into the hands of whites who followed the soldiers. The Cherokee were crammed together in various stockades—forerunners of concentration camps—until it was time to move out.

The first group of Cherokee went by boat to Oklahoma, but John Ross and other leaders secured permission to take the remainder—about 13,000 men, women, children, and old people—overland. The Cherokee paid private contractors to supply them with food and other necessities, and they set out in 1838 in September—arguably the worst possible time to go.

It took six months to walk the 1,200 miles to Oklahoma. During the cold winter, food ran short, bad weather hit, and the Cherokee suffered shortages of warm clothing and blankets. They walked through Dayton, McMinnville, Murfreesboro, and Nashville before crossing into Kentucky and out of Tennessee forever. An estimated 10–25 percent of the Cherokee died along the route and were mostly buried in unmarked graves.

As quoted in Carolyn Sakowski's Touring the East Tennessee Backroads, a Georgian colonel in the Confederate army later admitted, "I fought through the Civil War and have seen men shot to pieces and slaughtered by thousands, but the Cherokee removal was the cruelest work I ever knew."

For more information on this cruelest work, visit www.rosecity.net/tears.

Know Tennessee

Four years later Tennessee became the 16th state. Andrew Jackson was one of the people who helped write the state's constitution, a document that Thomas Jefferson pronounced "the least imperfect and most republican."

THE GROWING STATE
The Trail of Tears

The War of 1812 brought Andrew Jackson, a prominent figure in Tennessee, to national attention. He first gained victories against the Creek who had allied themselves with the British. Based on his successes there, he was put at the head of an army that defeated the British at Mobile, Pensacola, and, most fa-mously, at the Battle of New Orleans. In 1818, he invaded Spanish Florida in pursuit of the Seminoles and this further contributed to his national reputation.

When Tennessee became a state, three-fourths of the land was still owned by the Cherokee and the Chickasaw. Through treaties and purchases, the Indians slowly gave up their property. All of West Tennessee was opened up when the Chickasaw were persuaded to sell their lands in 1818. The next year Andrew Jackson and other land speculators established the town of Memphis.

The final treaty, signed in 1835, signaled the end of the Cherokee presence in Tennessee. The remaining members of the tribe moved across the state line into Georgia, which began its own efforts to move them west. These culminated in 1838 in the forced removal of the Cherokee to Oklahoma. Initiated by federal troops and Georgians, the infamous Trail of Tears marched the Cherokee one last time through Tennessee on their way to their reservation in Oklahoma.

Clearing the Land

The removal of the Native Americans led to a population surge in Tennessee. Planters with gangs of slaves cleared the hardwood forests and set up enormous plantations in Middle and West Tennessee. The invention of the steamboat made cities such as Nashville and Memphis big trading centers connected by water to New Orleans and the world. The eastern part of the state, however, plagued by rough water on the Tennessee River below Chattanooga and at Muscle Shoals, grew slowly until the coming of the railroad in the 1850s.

Andrew Jackson was elected president in 1828 and again in 1832. He so dominated national politics that he virtually handpicked Martin Van Buren, his successor. David Crockett's exploits became a part of the nation's folklore during those years. He and other Tennesseans, among them Sam Houston, left Tennessee to take part in the birth of Texas.

The Volunteer State

When the Mexican War broke out in 1848—under the administration of Tennessean and president James K. Polk—residents of his state were so eager to fight that they were insulted to learn that Tennessee was asked to send only three regiments of troops. Some decamped for other states to volunteer, others paid for the privilege, and to be fair to everyone the military had to hold a lottery. This willingness to fight led people to call Tennessee "The Volunteer State," a nickname it proudly adopted.

The 1850s marked a time of capital improvements. New roads radiated out of Nashville, railroads connected the larger cities, and the state made important strides in education and agriculture. Democrat Andrew Johnson was elected governor in 1853 and again in 1855.

A State Divided

The final half of the decade marked turbulent times in Tennessee as the clouds of war gathered. East Tennesseans were neutral on the slavery issue, but in Middle and West Tennessee the pro-slavery fires burned hot. Surprisingly enough, Tennesseans of all stripes favored loyalty to the Union—as late as February 9, 1861, they voted to stay in the Union—but this changed drastically with the March 4 inauguration of Abraham Lincoln. Southern states, one by one, began to secede from the Union. Fort Sumter fell on April 13, and Tennessee left the Union June 8.

In the same election that catapulted Lincoln into the White House, Andrew Johnson was voted in as one of Tennessee's U.S. senators on the Democratic ticket. He went to Washington and, alone among the Southern senators, kept his seat even though his state had left the Union. He was strongly supported by East Tennesseans, who sent thousands of volunteers to join Lincoln's armies.

THE CIVIL WAR

The War between the States is covered in greater detail in other places in this book. Tennessee witnessed more battles than any state except Virginia. The state was the center of the "western theater" of the war, and it was here that Ulysses S. Grant made a name for himself with battles in 1862 at Fort Donelson and Shiloh. Shiloh was the first major battle of the war, where in two days more men died than in the Revolutionary War, the War of 1812, and the Mexican War combined.

Nashville and Memphis were captured by Union troops rather quickly. The new year of 1863 brought the battle of Stones River in Murfreesboro, and Confederate troops under Braxton Bragg were driven through Chattanooga and into Georgia. There they turned on their pursuers at Chickamauga, where the

Union army was defeated. Grant came to the rescue, however, and beat the Confederates at Chattanooga. Tennessee was almost totally in Union hands by this time, and stayed so until General William T. Sherman took Atlanta. In a desperate move, Confederate General John Bell Hood tried to invade Nashville, but his army was badly beaten at the Battle of Franklin and later at Nashville.

Several Tennesseans played prominent roles during the war. Lincoln appointed Andrew Johnson the military governor of the state, while Confederate General Nathan Bedford Forrest, a former slave trader who had no military background, became the greatest cavalry commander of the entire war. Admiral David Farragut won important Union victories at New Orleans and Mobile.

RECONSTRUCTION

The assassination of Abraham Lincoln made Andrew Johnson president, and Tennessee became the first Confederate state to formally return to the Union. A radical Republican, William G. Brownlow, became the state's first postwar governor, and his hostility toward former Confederates was ill-concealed. Although Tennessee never went though the formal Reconstruction process, the actions of Brownlow were almost as punitive. The climate created by Brownlow and others led to the 1865 creation of the Ku Klux Klan in Pulaski, and the secret organization quickly spread across the state to the extent that nine counties were placed under martial law because of Klan activities.

Tennessee's experiences under the Republicans caused West and Middle Tennessee to stay Democratic for more than 100 years. East Tennessee remained a stronghold of the Republican Party, but the GOP seldom mustered enough votes to prevail in statewide elections. Andrew Johnson, who had been impeached by the Congress and who had escaped conviction in the Senate by one vote, won election to that body in 1876—the only former president to do so.

THE NEW SOUTH

One of the reasons the South lost the Civil War was a lack of industry, and this led Tennesseans to actively seek Northern capital and factories in the years after the war. The movement to reduce the dependency on agriculture and to embrace the industrialization of the North was called The New South.

Because of the ascendency of railroads over steamboats, Knoxville and Chattanooga were ideally positioned to ship goods north and south, and in the post–Civil War years both of these cities' growth rates outpaced those of Nashville and Memphis. In the 1870s, Memphis was hit with a yellow fever epidemic so severe that for a time it gave up its charter and ceased to be a city.

Other parts of Tennessee prospered. Nashville built a replica of the Parthenon in 1896 for an exposition held there. The 1890s also saw the departure of Adolph Ochs from Chattanooga to New York City, where he bought the *New York Times* and brought it up to Tennessee journalistic standards.

The state's population topped two million in 1900, and the turn of the 20th century brought some reforms that afflict travelers today. A 1904 law prohibited the sale of alcoholic beverages in towns of fewer than 5,000 souls. Tennessee voted for the 18th "Prohibition" Amendment, thus putting several fine distilleries out of business, but voted to repeal it by passing the 21st Amendment. Rural areas in the state still tend to be "dry," to the mutual satisfaction of bootleggers and Baptists.

GROWING DISTINCTION

The 1920s began with Tennessee's ratification of the 19th Amendment, which gave women the right to vote. Tennessee was the 36th state to do so, fulfilling the constitutional requirement and thus making it law.

During the rest of that decade, Tennessee took on some of the attributes that are simultaneously a source of pride and yet a tad embarrassing.

Nashville got its first radio station in 1922, and in 1925 saw the beginning of the *Grand Ole Opry,* a show featuring country music bands who were encouraged to take names such as "The Possum Hunters" or "The Fruit Jar Drinkers." This cornball image was reinforced the same year the Tennessee legislature passed a law prohibiting the teaching of evolution. The resulting Scopes "monkey" trial showed the world a state seemingly populated by backwoods yahoos. In a makeshift studio in Bristol in 1927, the voices of Jimmie Rodgers and the Carter Family began the country music recording business. Cornball or not, the musical culture of Tennessee found an accepting market that never looked back.

THE DEPRESSION AND WORLD WAR II

The TVA

All the New South speeches and factories in Tennessee cities did little to benefit the rural population, many of whom eked out their existences on poor land whose productivity was hurt by bad farming practices. Only one out of 30 farms, for instance, had electricity as late as 1935. The Great Depression hit these people hard, and their plight attracted the attention of the federal government under the administration of Franklin D. Roosevelt.

The Tennessee Valley Authority was created in 1933 to accomplish several goals: to create cheap electrical power and deliver it to rural areas, to control floods, to develop cheap fertilizers, and to build water treatment and sewage plants. In 1934, Congress established the Great Smoky Mountains National Park. The Civilian Conservation Corps simultaneously constructed trails, dams, and other infrastructure that benefited parks and small towns. All these projects needed workers, and the money they brought home improved the lives of urban and country dwellers alike.

The Atomic Age

Tennessee was judged to be safe from German bombers, and the war years brought the Man-

hattan Project to Oak Ridge, the Arnold Engineering Center outside Tullahoma, large military bases in the state, and big contracts for existing factories. The postwar education benefits enabled more Tennesseans to take advantage of the high-paying positions required to run these new operations.

MODERN TIMES

On July 5, 1954, a young man walked into Sun Studios in Memphis and recorded a song called "That's Alright." Elvis Presley revolutionized popular music, and his decision to continue living in Memphis emphasized the state's rich musical talent. The prosperity of the postwar years led more and more tourists to come to the Great Smoky Mountains National Park and other Tennessee attractions. The law that forbade teaching evolution was repealed in 1967.

COURTESY OF ELVIS PRESLEY ENTERPRISES, INC.

Elvis in concert, 1957

Tennessee, like the rest of the South, struggled through the civil rights movement, but not with the virulence witnessed in other places. National Guard troops were called in to help integrate a high school in Clinton, and in 1964, the first black man since Reconstruction was elected to the statehouse. The worst period in race relations came in 1968, when Martin Luther King Jr. was assassinated as he stood on the balcony of the Lorraine Motel in Memphis.

During the 1970s, TVA came under attack for the pollution caused by its coal-fired power plants. Activists in East Tennessee and Kentucky also criticized the agency for the strip-mining that supplied coal to the plants. TVA had to cut back on its ambitious nuclear power building program, which proved too costly for electrical consumers. In 1974, the Big South Fork National River and Recreation Area was authorized by Congress. Elvis Presley died at Graceland on August 16, 1977.

In October 1980, after intense competition among Tennessee and other states, Nissan selected Smyrna, a Middle Tennessee town south of Nashville, as the site for a truck plant. A few years later GM picked nearby Spring Hill for a Saturn car factory. Knoxville held a world's fair in 1982, the same year that Graceland opened to the public.

The Great Smoky Mountains National Park continues to be the top-drawing national park in the country, and people come from all over to enjoy Tennessee's mountains and lakes. For those with people-oriented interests—music, the Civil War, and cultural tourism in general—Tennessee tourism is a burgeoning industry.

GOVERNMENT

Tennessee's governor serves a four-year term and is allowed to serve two terms in a row before stepping down. The legislature consists of the Senate and House of Representatives. Tennessee's constitution specifies that the House have 99 members, but says only that the Senate cannot exceed one-third of the House membership. The Senate, then, has 33 members.

Tennessee is one of the few states that does not have a personal income tax, which forces the state to rely on high sales taxes. Visitors can experience sales taxes of 10 percent or higher.

The Tennessee legislature has a distinguished history; all three of the Tennesseans who became presidents of the country first served there. Present-day senators and representatives, however, have been known to have a good time while producing laws. An aged senator from Knoxville once proposed that some petrified organism be declared the official fossil of Tennessee. A colleague modified the bill so as to designate the senator the state's official fossil.

According to another legendary tale, the Tennessee Senate used to begin each day by introducing any noteworthies in the gallery, and at one time these introductions were performed by an extremely nearsighted soul. Some of his colleagues brought in a notorious Nashville stripper, one instantly recognizable to a good number of the senators. She dressed for the occasion, was assigned a fictitious name, and was duly introduced to much applause.

Tennessee is divided into nine congressional districts, and the representatives from them, many of whom have done time in the Tennessee legislature, have so far not carried their prankish traditions to Washington, D.C.

National Politics

Tennessee has not sent anyone to the White House since Andrew Johnson, but it has provided individuals who made significant contributions on the national scene, mostly in the U.S. Senate.

Cordell Hull, after service as a congressman and senator, was Franklin Roosevelt's secretary of state from 1933 to 1944, the longest tenure of anyone in that job. Displaying an international interest far beyond his upbringing in Byrdstown, Hull worked to strengthen U.S. ties with Latin America and championed an organization in which nations could come together to work out their problems. Dubbed "the father of the United Nations," he received the Nobel Peace Prize in 1945. Hull enjoyed slipping into a Tennessee vernacular in telling stories about his home state, and he was said to have thoroughly cussed out the Japanese diplomats who were in his office in 1941 when word came that Pearl Harbor had been attacked.

Estes Kefauver, a Yale-educated Chattanooga lawyer, was elected to the U.S. Senate in 1948 as a Democrat. His appearance and intelligence distinguished him from the James Eastland and Strom Thurmond models of mush-mouthed, filibustering, segregationist caricatures of Southern senators, and his televised hearings on organized crime brought him to the attention of the rest of the country. Kefauver was Adlai Stevenson's running mate in the 1956 election.

Albert Gore Sr., born and raised in Carthage, served as a senator from Tennessee for three terms beginning in 1952. Like Kefauver, he was a progressive Democrat who was not afraid to challenge party politics to do what he thought was right. In the late 1960s, he questioned the Vietnam War, and this and other issues made voters think he was too liberal to represent them. He lost his seat to a Republican in 1970.

Howard Baker Jr., who came from Huntsville, used to tell people that he went to law school at the University of Tennessee because the line was shorter than the one for engineering school. He came from a political family—his father and stepmother served in Congress—and married the daughter of Illinois senator Everett Dirksen. Baker gained his Senate seat in 1966, and came to national attention with his statesmanlike behavior as the ranking Republican on the Senate Watergate Committee. He became the minority leader and then the majority leader in the Senate, in which he served three terms. Baker ran for president in 1980 and was considered for a vice-presidential slot several times, but he never made it. He served as President Reagan's chief of staff, and then returned home to Huntsville.

Lamar Alexander, a native of Maryville, became governor in 1978 after donning a plaid shirt, boots, and jeans and walking across the state. The Republican was elected to two terms, and then became the president of the University of Tennessee, and then George H. W. Bush's secretary of education. Alexander ran for president in 1996 with the same costume that had brought him victory in Tennessee, but it didn't work outside the state. He was elected senator from Tennessee in 2002.

Albert Gore Jr., vice president during the Clinton administration, spent much of his boyhood in Washington, D.C., where his father was a senator. He spent his summers in Carthage, however, and worked for a time for the *Nashville Tennessean*. Elected to Congress in 1977, he served four terms, then became one of Tennessee's senators. Chosen by Bill Clinton as his running mate in 1992 and 1996, Gore made a name for himself as an advocate for the environment and a champion of the Internet. He won the popular vote in the presidential election of 2000, but lost to George W. Bush in the Electoral College.

William (Bill) Frist was raised in Belle Meade, the wealthiest area in Nashville. Educated at Princeton and Harvard Medical School, he is certified in general surgery and heart surgery. In 1985, he joined Vanderbilt's medical school and headed a transplant unit, and has performed more than 150 heart and lung transplants. His family built up Hospital Corporation of America, and their foundation created the Frist Center for the Arts in Nashville. He was elected to the U.S. Senate as a Republican in 1994, and became majority leader in 2002.

ECONOMY

Like other states, Tennessee has seen steady drops in manufacturing jobs. The South in general is often the last stop before going offshore for manufacturing jobs that left Northern states to get away from unions. Manufacturing accounts for less than 15 percent of jobs now. Almost one in five Tennesseans works in the trade, transportation, and utilities category. Other percentages of employment include manufacturing at 16 percent, government at 15 percent, and various services at 26 percent.

Tennessee has more than 90,000 farms, most of which are small, producing incomes of fewer than $10,000. The leading farm products are cattle, chickens, and crops such as soybeans, cotton, and corn.

The People

The introduction to Roy Blount's *Book of Southern Humor* has a wonderful couple of sentences that aptly describe Tennessee: "The South was originally settled not predominantly by Anglo-Saxons (as was the North) but by wild, oral, whiskey-loving, unfastidious, tribal, horse-racing, government-hating, WASP-scorned Irish and Welsh and pre-Presbyterian Scots. Who then brought in Africans."

Although there are wondrous things to see in Tennessee, the absolute best reason to go there is the people. As of 2004, there are now 5,841,748 of them. As a general rule, they are friendly, polite, and happy to talk to outlanders. They will generally ask where their conversationalist is from, make some favorable comment about that place, and, if possible, ask:

Do you know so-and-so's brother there—no, he doesn't live there anymore, he got to thinking he was Elvis and they had to put him in a home.

And on from there.

One of the reasons that Tennesseans do so well in the military is that they don't have to be trained to say "sir" and "ma'am." It just comes out automatically. Tennesseans often appear inordinately polite to each other and to strangers, whether they deserve it or not.

MUSIC

Tennessee is widely regarded as one of the most musical states in the country. Sometimes outlanders, upon meeting residents of the Volunteer State, seem disappointed that they can't play a fiddle or pick a banjo.

Entire books have been written about Tennessee music and each of its various genres, so this volume will concentrate on the high points. The standard explanations of Tennessee music follow the geographic boundaries of the state: bluegrass and old-time music in East Tennessee, blues and black gospel near Memphis in the west, and country music in the middle.

While there is some truth to that stereotype,

kicking up their heels at the Museum of Appalachia's fall homecoming

Tennessee's musical heritage isn't that simple. You can find blues singers in East Tennessee and bluegrass music in Memphis. Here is a look at a few of the genres associated with the state.

Old-Time

In the days before radio and record players, the only music that people heard was what they could play themselves. Violins—called fiddles in rural areas—made the music for gatherings and dances, often backed by banjos and guitar players. Songs began with ballads from the British Isles brought over by immigrants and preserved yet changed by Tennesseans.

String bands took those old songs, speeding them up in some cases, and freely accepted influences from various ethnic traditions—Scottish jigs and reels, European waltzes—but especially from African slaves. The banjo, for example, came from Africa. Songs were religious and not religious, fast and slow, comical and sad. When Ralph Peer came to Bristol in 1927 and recorded Jimmie Rodgers and the Carter Family, this was the kind of music he was looking for.

Gospel

Early Tennesseans were churchgoing folks, and church meant hymns. Much of this music first came from hymnbooks published elsewhere, and tended to be straightforward church music. Things picked up, however, when religious people got together away from church. Camp meetings, with heightened feelings brought on by revival preachers, brought on lively music, and publishers began to issue songbooks containing religious songs and later, to send around quartets to sing those songs and promote sales.

GOSPEL MUSIC ETIQUETTE

Listening to gospel music, particularly of the African American variety, is a joyful, uplifting experience for believers as well as others. Gospel music has influenced and continues to influence secular music, and every Sunday morning in churches the length of Tennessee, preachers and singers and choirs pour forth wonderful music.

The question is, should visitors attend a black church just to hear the music?

In New York City's Harlem and other places, tours take visitors into African American churches, and the Reverend Al Green in Memphis readily invites one and all to attend his three-hour services.

I believe that if visitors want to worship, they should go to any church they want. If they simply want to hear good music, however, they should go to a gospel concert, buy a ticket, and have a great time.

How does one locate gospel concerts? These are advertised on gospel radio stations, in local publications, particularly African American ones, and on gospel TV shows.

Black gospel music began with spirituals, simple songs sung by slaves. As slavery ended, black church music diverged from white gospel, the latter now known as Southern Gospel. Although white and black groups might sing the same songs, they sang them in very different ways. White groups sounded more like barbershop quartets, whereas black groups took more musical risks. It's not at all surprising that someone like Elvis Presley was influenced by black and white gospel music, and sang gospel music all of his life.

Gospel music styles today continue to evolve yet maintain the old traditions, and tend to be presented to the public in separate events. Southern Gospel is strong, black gospel is booming, and contemporary gospel is taking this music where it has never been before. Tennessee continues to supply singers, to record them, and to appreciate them.

Blues

While a good many famous bluesmen and -women came from Tennessee, the Mississippi Delta usually gets the accolade of birthplace of the blues. Wherever the blues was born, however, the minute it was able to walk, it came to Memphis. W. C. Handy, a Memphis bandleader, was the first person to write down a blues song, and what began as field hollers on plantations was transformed into music played on Beale Street, later was cut on records, and broadcast over the radio. Much of this took place in Tennessee, especially in Memphis but also in Nashville.

Country

It's hard to mark the line when old-time music became country music. Jimmie Rodgers is said to be the father of country music, but he sang a lot of blues. He and the Carter Family proved that people would pay hard-earned money for that kind of music, and what would become country was off and running. Country music grew for two reasons: the *Grand Ole Opry* on WSM, a powerful AM radio station; and World War II, which dispersed Southerners and brought others to country music.

Because of the *Opry*, Nashville came to dominate country music and continues to do so—for good and ill. "The industry," as it is known, doesn't always take well to newcomers, and is more monolithic than it ought to be.

Bluegrass

To the uninitiated ear, bluegrass sounds like old-time music-string bands with lots of banjo. Bluegrass, however, was created by Bill Monroe in the 1940s and '50s. It is characterized by high-pitched lead vocals and lightning-fast banjo runs. Earl Scruggs, a banjo player with Bill Monroe and later paired with Lester Flatt, made the three-finger banjo style popular, and that is the biggest distinguishing feature between bluegrass and old-time. Alison Krauss and her band, Union Station, are leading lights in bluegrass.

Rhythm and Blues

For a long time, "rhythm and blues," or "R&B" for short, was a curious term for black music. **Billboard** magazine maintained separate charts for black and white music. In the early '60s, however, white teenagers began to listen to black music on stations such as Nashville's WLAC, liking what they heard, and buying records. Memphis's Stax Records put out a string of hits from people such as Otis Redding, Sam & Dave, Booke T and the MGs, and Isaac Hayes, forever breaking down racial lines in music.

STORYTELLING AND COLORFUL SPEECH

Southerners are great storytellers, and many Tennesseans are no exception. Stories are woven into everything—directions, accounts of what happened the day before, and answers to the simple "How are you?"

It's entirely appropriate that the National Storytelling Festival is in Tennessee, but visitors don't have to pay money to hear tales. Just engage someone in conversation, or sit in with several natives talking among themselves, and the stories will gradually emerge. One would never ask to hear stories, no more than one would go to Manhattan and ask the inhabitants there to be surly.

Some Tennesseans are simultaneously proud of and embarrassed by the way they speak. "Southern accent equals stupid" is an equation played out daily in television, movies, and other forms of popular culture. The most politically correct people in the world will cheerfully tell redneck jokes. Because of this, natives of the Volunteer State who live in the Northern United States often exist in a kind of linguistic schizophrenia, masking their Tennessee accent at work yet cheerfully letting it emerge when in the company of other Tennesseans or fellow Southerners.

Careful listeners who travel across Tennessee can hear differences in the way the natives speak. East Tennesseans speak with an Appalachian twang. Some of their archaic words are said to date to Elizabethan times, but they actually come from proper British speech of the 1700s. Examples of this include saying "knowed" for the past tense of "know" or leaving the "g" off "-ing" and thus saying "fishin'" or "huntin'." Moving across the state, particularly entering West Tennessee, visitors will hear speech that more resembles the accent of the Deep South.

Tennesseans can be sensitive about their accents and colorful way of speaking. Perhaps the quickest way to make Southern hospitality vanish is to laugh at the way someone from Tennessee speaks.

THE BUCKLE ON THE BIBLE BELT

Tennesseans will seldom ask where a person went to college, although they may inquire where he or she goes to church. This is not done as any sort of probing, personal inquisition, but as a means of seeking connection with that person.

Religion has a powerful influence on Tennessee, one often expressed in music. Many Tennesseans who wound up shouting the blues or fronting a rock band cut their musical teeth in church. Elvis would warm up in his all-night recording sessions by singing gospel harmony, and Tina Turner had a spot in her church choir.

Sun Studio's Sam Philips was once recorded arguing theology with Jerry Lee Lewis between musical takes.

Tennessee is indeed the buckle on the Bible Belt, and travelers will notice this in several ways. The farther one gets from the big cities, the more museums and restaurants will tend to be closed on Sunday. Bed-and-breakfast owners may matter-of-factly prohibit alcohol in their establishments, and the tonier restaurants in the boondocks have to pretend they are private clubs to permit legal drinking.

From time to time, some pontificator announces that the United States is becoming a dreary, homogenous place where everyone speaks the same way and listens to the same things. Those individuals should turn on a radio in Tennessee to the AM band on Sunday morning. In almost any part of the state, a twist or two on the knob will bring forth an out-of-breath preacher pouring it on, perhaps punctuating his sentences with a periodic and rhythmic "Hah!" The truly adventurous can see this sort of thing in the flesh by stopping off on Sunday morning at small churches—anything with "Holiness" or "Pentecostal" on the sign do.

The other side of all this religion in Tennessee is what might be called the joy of sin. It's the conspiratorial pouring of bourbon into a Coke at a University of Tennessee football game, the sidelong glance as one steps from the heat of the day into the darkened coolness of a Memphis bar, or going straight from a lecture on cholesterol to a barbecue place and blissfully biting into a Pig Pile sandwich.

The conniptions and carryings-on of the faithful, whether of the televised or more local variety, are almost always entertaining. One married Tennessee preacher, unfamiliar with the new telephone system his church installed, made a covert call to his girlfriend, unaware that his sweet nothings were being broadcast over the public address system to the intense interest of the youth group meeting in the building. Southern Baptists, who for decades shielded their youth groups and college students from the wickedness of fox-trots or similar cheek-to-cheek activities, prompted the following joke, guaranteed to be appreciated all over the state.

Why don't Baptists make love standing up?

Someone might see them and think they were dancing.

Practicalities

TRANSPORTATION

Major Airports

The largest airports in Tennessee, to no surprise, are the ones in the larger cities: Chattanooga, Knoxville, Memphis, and Nashville. Smaller airports include Jackson and Blountville, which serves the Bristol/Kingsport/Johnson City area. Travelers on a budget should also consider flying to Atlanta, which is only 115 miles from Chattanooga or 243 miles from Nashville. Sometimes the reduction in airline fare can more than pay for the additional miles to drive.

Main Highways

Tennessee is a long and lean state, and the only Interstate highway that runs the length is I-40, which goes from the Great Smoky Mountains National Park past Memphis. I-81 connects to I-40 and heads northeast to exit the state at Bristol. Interstates 65 and 24 make a large "X" at Nashville, and I-75 winds down from Kentucky and then goes toward Knoxville and Chattanooga, whereupon, like Union General Sherman, it heads for Atlanta.

Buses

Greyhound Lines offers bus service to more than 20 cities and towns in Tennessee. Travelers can connect to the state from other American cities. To learn about schedules, routes, and prices, call 800/229-9424 or visit www.greyhound.com.

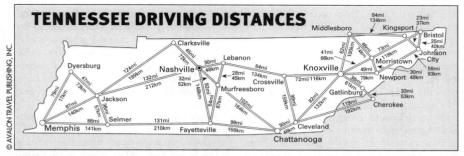

TENNESSEE DRIVING DISTANCES

TENNESSEE AREA CODES

HEALTH AND SAFETY

Poisonous Plants

Several plants that grow in Tennessee, including mushrooms, can cause problems if eaten. Visitors who go around eating unknown plants in strange places are an example of Darwinism at work, and the plants to avoid ingesting will not be listed here.

Travelers may unknowingly come in contact with Tennessee's three plants that can cause skin irritation. Poison ivy, the most prevalent, is a vine that grows on the ground and climbs up trees. Its shiny leaves grow in clusters of three, and the oil on the leaves can cause skin irritation and itching. Poison oak and poison sumac can have the same effects. It takes about 20 minutes from the time of contact for the chemicals in these plants to enter the skin. People who think they have touched one should wash the affected area with soap and water and also change clothes. If itching begins, calamine lotion may offer relief.

Animals and Insects

Probably the unhealthiest thing one can do in Tennessee is eat too much barbecue and not enough salads, but there are a few natural denizens that the traveler should keep in mind.

Rabies occurs in wild animals as well as dogs and cats. Avoid any animal acting erratically, particularly a wild one. It is not normal, for instance, for raccoons or foxes to approach humans, and such behavior should be regarded with great suspicion.

Tennessee has four kinds of poisonous snakes, but most visitors will never encounter any of them. Timber rattlesnakes and eastern diamondback rattlesnakes sometimes give a warning rattle, which sounds more like a buzzing noise. Copperheads, which live all over the state, are brown-mottled snakes that tend to live around rural outbuildings as well as the backcountry. Water moccasins, also known as cottonmouths, live in western Tennessee in water—creeks, rivers, swamps, and lakes.

The basic precaution for snakes is simple—visitors should carefully watch where they put their feet and hands. If they do see a snake, they should leave it alone. Like any wild animals, snakes will bite if pursued and cornered. Anyone who gets bitten should not attempt the old-time remedy of cutting into the afflicted area and sucking out the poison. The best thing is to stay calm and head for the nearest hospital.

Visitors are far more likely to become victims of ticks and chiggers. Ticks lurk on branches of trees or other plants and hitch a ride on passing animals or humans. Once aboard, they seek a place to attach themselves and suck their host's blood. A daily head-to-toe check can usually find any ticks, which should be removed with tweezers.

Chiggers are more nefarious. These almost invisible insect larvae burrow into the skin, raising a bump that itches profusely. For some reason, chiggers seem to always lurk in blackberry patches. Sufferers of acute chigger attacks may consider going after the little beasts with an ice pick, but a better remedy is commercial itch relievers. Prevention, as always, is the best cure, and the usual insect repellents work on chiggers as well.

Tennessee has two poisonous spiders—the brown recluse and the black widow. As with snakes, the vast majority of visitors have nothing to fear from these spiders, which inhabit basements and other dark places around buildings—including outhouses. Black widows are said to particularly like the areas around the seats of such places, so users would do well not to spend any more time than necessary there.

Suggested Reading

HISTORY

Corlew, Robert. *Tennessee, A Short History.* Knoxville: University of Tennessee Press, 1990. This condensation of a four-volume work is the definitive history book about the state.

Egerton, John. *Visions of Utopia.* Knoxville: University of Tennessee Press, 1977. Focuses on Nashoba, Rugby, Ruskin, and the "new communities" of Tennessee's past.

Johnson, Mattie Ruth. *My Melungeon Heritage.* Johnson City: Overmountain Press, 1994. A personal account of coming from a Melungeon family.

Kennedy, N. Brent. *The Melungeons, The Resurrection of a Proud People—The Untold Story of Ethnic Cleansing in America.* Macon: Mercer University Press, 1994. If there is a point book for militant Melungeons, this is it.

Klebenow, Anne. *200 Years in 200 Stories.* Knoxville: University of Tennessee Press, 1997. Prepared for Tennessee's bicentennial,

this book breaks history into enjoyable chunks.

Manning, Russ. *The Historic Cumberland Plateau.* Knoxville: University of Tennessee Press, 1993. A very good guide to this distinctive area between East and Middle Tennessee.

Neely, Jack. *Knoxville's Secret History.* Knoxville: Scruffy City Publishing, 1995. Looking at topics as various as colonial days and the death of Hank Williams, this talented writer illuminates Tennessee's oldest city.

McPherson, James. *Battle Cry of Freedom.* Oxford: Oxford University Press, 1988. A one-volume history of the Civil War.

Ward, Geoffrey. *The Civil War.* New York: Alfred A. Knopf, 1990. The companion volume to the Ken Burns Civil War documentary.

Yellin, Carol Lynn, and Janann Sherman. *The Perfect 36—Tennessee Delivers Woman Suffrage.* Memphis: Serviceberry Press, 1998. This delightful book lays out the story of how Tennessee became the state that enabled the 19th Amendment to become law. Illustrated with photos, political cartoons, and newspaper articles of the day, it weaves a fascinating story.

DESCRIPTION AND TRAVEL

Brandt, Robert. *Touring the Middle Tennessee Backroads.* Winston-Salem: John F. Blair, 1995. Written by a Nashville judge, this book interweaves historical tales with descriptions of towns, buildings, and other evidence of the past.

Sakowski, Carolyn. *Touring the East Tennessee Backroads.* Winston-Salem: John F. Blair, 1993. This book should be on the front seat of any history buff driving though East Tennessee.

Smith, Reid. *Majestic Middle Tennessee.* Gretna, LA: Pelican Publishing Company, 1982. A historic look at the mansions of Middle Tennessee.

Urquhart, Sharon Colette. *Placing Elvis: A Tour Guide to the Kingdom.* New Orleans: Paper Chase Press, 1994. A guidebook to the Memphis and Tupelo haunts of Elvis.

WPA Guide to Tennessee. Knoxville: University of Tennessee Press, 1986. A reprint of the 1939 guide written by the Federal Writers' Project of the Work Projects Administration, a Depression effort aimed at putting writers to work and supplying guidebooks for states. This book, full of the pride and prejudices of the time, gives a wonderful view of Tennessee—small towns and large.

MUSIC

Escott, Colin. *Good Rockin' Tonight.* New York: St. Martins, 1991. The story of Sun Studios, where it all began.

Gordon, Robert. *It Came from Memphis.* Boston and London: Faber and Faber, 1995. A wandering path through Memphis music since the 1950s, focusing on the great and near-great.

Guralnick, Peter. *Feel Like Going Home.* New York: Harper and Row, 1971. This book offers portraits of various blues and rock performers, among them Jerry Lee Lewis.

Guralnick, Peter. *Lost Highway: Journeys and Arrivals of American Musicians.* New York: Harper and Row, 1979. Guralnick hits a home run with tales of country performer Ernest Tubb, bluesman Big Joe Turner, and rockabilly Sleepy LaBeef.

Guralnick, Peter. *Sweet Soul Music.* New York: Harper and Row, 1986. A great look at the rise of soul music and the Memphians who made it.

Marcus, Greil. *Mystery Train.* New York: Plume, 1990. A classic on the roots of rock 'n' roll. *Rolling Stone* calls this the best book ever on rock.

McKee, Margaret, and Fred Chisenhall. *Beale Black and Blue: Life and Music on Black America's Main Street.* Baton Rouge: Louisiana State University Press, 1993. Interviews and reflections on Beale Street's heyday.

Palmer, Robert. *Deep Blues.* New York: Penguin Books, 1981. This look at Delta blues sheds light on the Memphis music scene.

Santelli, Robert. *The Big Book of Blues.* New York: Penguin Books, 1993. This book has a biographical entry on anyone who was anyone in the blues.

Tosches, Nick. *Country.* New York: Scribners, 1977. A look at the underside of country music—tales they'll never tell you at the Country Music Hall of Fame.

Wolfe, Charles K. *Tennessee Strings.* Knoxville: University of Tennessee Press, 1977. A thin but authoritative book on country music.

Zimmerman, Peter Coats. *Tennessee Music.* San Francisco: Miller Freeman Books, 1998. This combination travel book and music guide to the state is must for roots music lovers.

FICTION AND LITERATURE

Agee, James. *A Death in the Family.* New York: Grossett and Dunlap, 1967. The best Knoxville novel.

Ford, Jesse Hill. *The Liberation of Lord Byron Jones.* New York: Little, Brown, 1965. Based on events that took place in the West Tennessee town of Humboldt, this novel was eventually made into a film.

Grisham, John. *The Client.* New York: Doubleday, 1993. Another of this Mississippi writer's string of hits.

Grisham, John. *The Firm.* New York: Doubleday, 1991. This tale of a law firm with ties to the mob became a movie filled with Memphis scenes.

Haley, Alex. *Roots.* New York: Doubleday, 1976. The fascinating tale of this writer's ancestors, slaves and otherwise.

Marius, Richard. *After the War.* New York: Alfred A. Knopf, 1992. This novel takes flight from the story of Marius's father, who came from Greece to Tennessee and ran a foundry in Lenoir City.

Marius, Richard. *An Affair of Honor.* New York: Alfred A. Knopf, 2001. In his final novel, this tremendously gifted East Tennessee writer returns to Bourbonville for a multifaceted tale of a double murder.

Marius, Richard. *The Coming of Rain.* New York: Alfred A. Knopf, 1969. Set in a fictional version of Lenoir City, this book captures the turmoil of a small town.

Marshall, Catherine. *Christy.* New York: McGraw Hill, 1967. The inspiring story of a young woman who goes to teach school in a remote East Tennessee town. It later became a television show and a musical performed in the Smokies.

Taylor, Peter. *A Summons to Memphis.* New York: Ballantine Books, 1987. This account of a New York editor's summons home to help his spinster sisters prevent the remarriage of their aging father offers a look into the complex family lives of well-born Tennesseans in the middle of this century. This beautifully written story won the Pulitzer Prize and the Ritz-Paris Hemingway award.

Twain, Mark, and Charles Dudley Warner. *The Gilded Age.* New York: Nelson Doubleday, 1873. The Tennessee land owned by the Clemens family plays a role in this novel, which gave its name to the post–Civil War years.

Wells, Lawrence. *Rommel and the Rebel.* Oxford, MI: Yoknapatawpha Press, 1992. This imaginative novel, building on the legend that the "Desert Fox" of World War II fame traveled through the South in the 1930s studying the tactics of Nathan Bedford Forrest, has Rommel playing tennis at midnight with William Faulkner. A great read.

BIOGRAPHY

Escott, Colin. *Hank Williams: the Biography.* Boston: Little, Brown and Company, 1994. A very good biography of one of country music's greatest.

Guralnick, Peter. *Careless Love: The Unmaking of Elvis Presley.* Boston: Little, Brown and Company, 1999. The sad demise of the King as told by his best biographer.

Guralnick, Peter. *Last Train to Memphis.* Boston: Little, Brown and Company, 1994. This is *the* book on Elvis. The first of a two-book set, this one takes the King up to the time he left for army duty in Germany. Based on meticulous research and a keen sense of American popular music, Guralnick's opus rises above the flotsam of Elvis books on the market.

Hurst, Jack. *Nathan Bedford Forrest.* New York: Random House, 1993. The latest biography of the Confederacy's greatest cavalry leader, Ku Klux Klan leader, and source of controversy even today.

Summitt, Pat Head. *Raise the Roof: The Inspiring Inside Story of the Tennessee Lady Vols Undefeated 1997–98 Season.* New York: Broadway Books, 1999. The title says it all.

Summitt, Pat Head. *Reach for the Summit.* New York: Broadway Books, 1998. The life story of the second- (so far) winningest basketball coach in America, the coach of the University of Tennessee Lady Vols.

Trefousse, Hans L. *Andrew Johnson: a Biography.* New York: Norton, 1989. A fine recounting of an underappreciated president.

Turner, Tina, with Kurt Loder. *I, Tina.* New York: William Morrow and Company, 1986. The recollections of the most important female singer to come from West Tennessee.

ARCHITECTURE

Moffett, Marian, and Lawrence Woodhouse. *Tennessee's Cantilever Barns.* Knoxville: University of Tennessee Press, 1993. A study of the indigenous and ingenious structures found in the mountains of East Tennessee.

Neely, Jack. *The Marble City: A Photographic Tour of Knoxville's Graveyards.* Knoxville: University of Tennessee Press, 1999. Photographer Aaron Jay and East Tennessee's leading amateur historian take a fascinating look at their city's cemeteries.

West, Carroll Van. *Tennessee's Historic Landscapes.* Knoxville: University of Tennessee

Press, 1995. With photos and astute commentary, this book leads the traveler though big cities and small towns in search of architectural treasures.

West, Carroll Van. *Tennessee's New Deal Landscapes.* Knoxville: University of Tennessee Press, 2001. This master of Tennessee architecture looks at the buildings that were built during the Depression.

THE OUTDOORS

Manning, Russ. *100 Trails of the Big South Fork.* Seattle: Mountaineers Press, 2000. This handbook guides the traveler along the roads and trails in Tennessee and Kentucky.

Manning, Russ, and Sondra Jamieson. *Tennessee's South Cumberland.* Norris, TN: Mountain Laurel Press, 1994. This handy book pulls together the spread-out areas of the southern Cumberland Plateau.

Smith, Jo A. *Hiking the Big South Fork.* Knoxville: University of Tennessee Press, 1993. This book contains topographical maps and descriptions of the trails.

ODDS AND ENDS

Egerton, John et al. *Southern Food.* Chapel Hill: University of North Carolina Press, 1987. Combining recipes, fine writing, and great photos, this book takes a satisfying look at country cooking.

Kiser, Maud Gold. *Treasure Hunter's Guide.* Nashville: The Gold-Kiser Company, 1995. This thorough guide to Tennessee's antique stores also includes restaurants, bed-and-breakfasts, history, and the longest paragraphs this side of the Mississippi border.

Luther, Edward T. *Our Restless Earth.* Knoxville: University of Tennessee Press, 1977. A short and very readable guide to the geology of Tennessee.

Stokely, Jim. *An Encyclopedia of East Tennessee.* Oak Ridge: Children's Museum of Oak Ridge, 1982. An intense look at the oldest part of the state.

Verghese, Abraham. *My Own Country.* New York: Simon and Schuster, 1994. An amazing book written by a doctor from India who finds himself in Johnson City, Tennessee, treating AIDS patients. His stories about the patients are touching, and his accounts of life in East Tennessee are sometimes hilarious.

West, Carroll Van. *The Tennessee Encyclopedia of History and Culture.* Nashville: Rutledge Hill Press, 1998. If readers like the historical bits in Moon Handbooks: Tennessee, they will love this 1,193-page volume, which is filled with fascinating short articles from a great many luminaries.

Wilson, Charles Reagan, and William Ferris. *Encyclopedia of Southern Culture.* Chapel Hill: University of North Carolina Press, 1989. This stupendous book—1,634 pages long—addresses mint juleps, sacred harp singing, kudzu, and other Southern items with scholarship and wit.

Index

Civil War

Music Centers and Museums

Music Festivals and Events

National Parks, Forests, and Historical Sites

Acknowledgments

Good people in four states helped bring about the fourth edition of this book.

In Tennessee, Karyn Adams described the restaurants and nightclubs in Knoxville, Suzanne Hall took care of Chattanooga, while Fredric Koeppel handled Memphis. In Nashville, Thayer Wine wrote up the restaurants, while Paul Griffith covered nightspots. Jack Neely shared his vast knowledge of Knoxville. State folklorist Robert Cogswell was a fount of wisdom; Rich Boyd of the Tennessee Arts Commission brought me to Jonesborough to give a speech; and Greer Broemel, Linda Caldwell, and Candace Davis helped me with research.

In California, the capable crew at Avalon Travel Publishing bent deadlines to get this book out. Kevin McLain, he of great patience, improved my prose with deft editing, Ellen Cavalli copy-edited the manuscript, and Kat Smith worked up the maps. Susan Snyder selected the photos and graphics. Sarah Coglianese and Matt Kaye constantly market this and other books, and publisher Bill Newlin cheerfully writes checks to us all.

South Carolinian Mike Sigalas edited an earlier version of this book and provided much of the material that went into the chapter on the Smokies.

In Colorado, where I live, Matt Mahowald and Walker Bradley cheerfully called hundreds of phone numbers to update the book. May the few rude individuals who hung up the phone on these two have a long and intimate contact with fire ants.

Finally, thanks go to my family for the time this book has taken from them: Truman, Walker, and especially Marta.

www.moon.com

For helpful advice on planning a trip, visit www.moon.com for the **TRAVEL PLANNER** and get access to useful travel strategies and valuable information about great places to visit. When you travel with Moon, expect an experience that is uncommon and truly unique.

U.S. ~ Metric Conversion

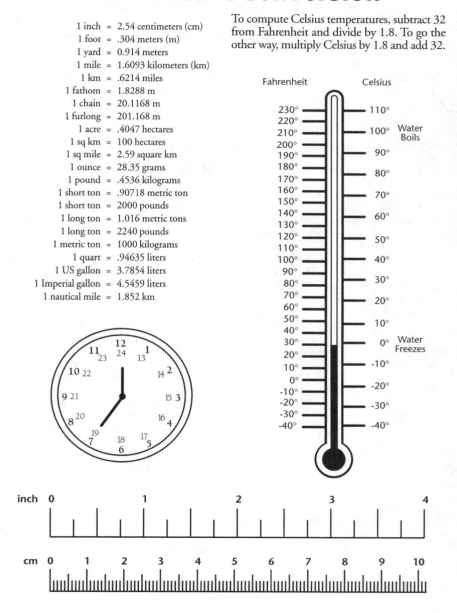

1 inch = 2.54 centimeters (cm)
1 foot = .304 meters (m)
1 yard = 0.914 meters
1 mile = 1.6093 kilometers (km)
1 km = .6214 miles
1 fathom = 1.8288 m
1 chain = 20.1168 m
1 furlong = 201.168 m
1 acre = .4047 hectares
1 sq km = 100 hectares
1 sq mile = 2.59 square km
1 ounce = 28.35 grams
1 pound = .4536 kilograms
1 short ton = .90718 metric ton
1 short ton = 2000 pounds
1 long ton = 1.016 metric tons
1 long ton = 2240 pounds
1 metric ton = 1000 kilograms
1 quart = .94635 liters
1 US gallon = 3.7854 liters
1 Imperial gallon = 4.5459 liters
1 nautical mile = 1.852 km

To compute Celsius temperatures, subtract 32 from Fahrenheit and divide by 1.8. To go the other way, multiply Celsius by 1.8 and add 32.

Fahrenheit   Celsius

230° — 110°
220°
210° — 100° Water Boils
200°
190° — 90°
180° — 80°
170°
160° — 70°
150°
140° — 60°
130°
120° — 50°
110°
100° — 40°
90°
80° — 30°
70°
60° — 20°
50°
40° — 10°
30° — 0° Water Freezes
20°
10° — -10°
0°
-10° — -20°
-20°
-30° — -30°
-40° — -40°

inch 0   1   2   3   4

cm 0 1 2 3 4 5 6 7 8 9 10

Keeping Current

Although we strive to produce the most up-to-date guidebook humanly possible, change is unavoidable. Between the time this book goes to print and the moment you read it, a handful of the businesses noted in these pages will undoubtedly change prices, move, or even close their doors forever. Other worthy attractions will open for the first time. If you have a favorite gem you'd like to see included in the next edition, or see anything that needs updating, clarification, or correction, please drop us a line. Send your comments via email to atpfeedback@avalonpub.com, or use the address below.

Moon Handbooks Tennessee
Avalon Travel Publishing
1400 65th Street, Suite 250
Emeryville, CA 94608, USA
www.moon.com

Editor and Series Manager: Kevin McLain
Acquisitions Editor: Rebecca K. Browning
Copy Editor: Ellen Cavalli
Graphics Coordinator: Susan Snyder
Production Coordinator: Jacob Goolkasian
Cover Designer: Kari Gim
Interior Designer: Amber Pirker
Map Editor: Kat Smith
Cartographers: Mike Morgenfeld,
   Kat Kalamaras, Suzanne Service
Proofreaders: Denise Silva, Sabrina Young
Indexer: Greg Jewett

ISBN-10: 1-56691-693-3
ISBN-13: 978-1-56691-693-6
ISSN: 1091-3343

Printing History
1st Edition—1997
4th Edition—February 2005
5 4 3

Some photos and illustrations are used by permission and are the property of the original copyright owners.

Front cover photo: © Getty Images

Printed in USA by Malloy